JUDAISM IN PRACTICE

PRINCETON READINGS IN RELIGIONS

Donald S. Lopez, Jr., Editor

TITLES IN THE SERIES

Religions of India in Practice edited by Donald S. Lopez, Jr.

Buddhism in Practice edited by Donald S. Lopez, Jr.

Religions of China in Practice edited by Donald S. Lopez, Jr.

Religions of Tibet in Practice edited by Donald S. Lopez, Jr.

Religions of Japan in Practice edited by George J. Tanabe, Jr.

Asian Religions in Practice; An Introduction
edited by Donald S. Lopez, Jr.

Religions of Late Antiquity in Practice edited by Richard Valantasis

Tantra in Practice edited by David Gordon White

Judaism in Practice edited by Lawrence Fine

JUDAISM

IN PRACTICE

From the Middle Ages through the Early Modern Period

Lawrence Fine, Editor

PRINCETON READINGS IN RELIGIONS
PRINCETON UNIVERSITY PRESS
PRINCETON AND OXFORD

Copyright © 2001 by Princeton University Press
Published by Princeton University Press, 41 William Street,
Princeton, New Jersey 08540
In the United Kingdom: Princeton University Press, 3 Market Place,
Woodstock, Oxfordshire OX20 1SY

All Rights Reserved

Library of Congress Cataloging-in-Publication Data
Judaism in practice : from the Middle Ages through the early modern period / Lawrence Fine, editor.
p. cm. — (Princeton readings in religions)
Includes bibliographical references and index.
ISBN 0-691-05786-9 (cloth : alk. paper) — ISBN 0-691-05787-7 (pbk. : alk. paper)
1. Judaism—History—Medieval and early modern period, 425-1789—Sources. 2. Judaism—Customs and practices—History—Sources. 3. Women in Judaism—History—Sources. 4. Jews—Biography. I. Fine, Lawrence. II. Series.
BM180 .J82 2001
296'.09'02—dc21   2001027839
British Library Cataloging-in-Publication Data is available
Publication of this book has been aided by a grant from The Lucius N. Littauer Foundation

This book has been composed in Berkeley

Printed on acid-free paper. ∞

www.pup.princeton.edu

Printed in the United States of America

1 3 5 7 9 10 8 6 4 2

1 3 5 7 9 10 8 6 4 2
(Pbk.)

IN HONOR OF MY FATHER,

JACK FINE,

AND IN LOVING MEMORY OF MY MOTHER,

MILDRED FINE

IN HONOR OF MY MOTHER-IN-LAW,

JEAN F. SEGAL,

AND IN LOVING MEMORY OF MY FATHER-IN-LAW,

RABBI JACOB E. SEGAL

PRINCETON READINGS
IN RELIGIONS

Princeton Readings in Religions is a new series of anthologies on the religions of the world, representing the significant advances that have been made in the study of religions in the last thirty years. The sourcebooks used by previous generations of students, whether for Judaism and Christianity or for the religions of Asia and the Middle East, placed a heavy emphasis on "canonical works." Princeton Readings in Religions provides a different configuration of texts in an attempt better to represent the range of religious practices, placing particular emphasis on the ways in which texts have been used in diverse contexts. The volumes in the series therefore include ritual manuals, hagiographical and autobiographical works, popular commentaries, and folktales, as well as some ethnographic material. Many works are drawn from vernacular sources. The readings in the series are new in two senses. First, very few of the works contained in the volumes have ever been made available in an anthology before; in the case of the volumes on Asia, few have even been translated into a Western language. Second, the readings are new in the sense that each volume provides new ways to read and understand the religions of the world, breaking down the sometimes misleading stereotypes inherited from the past in an effort to provide both more expansive and more focused perspectives on the richness and diversity of religious expressions. The series is designed for use by a wide range of readers, with key terms translated and technical notes omitted. Each volume also contains a substantial introduction by a distinguished scholar in which the histories of the traditions are outlined and the significance of each of the works is explored.

Judaism in Practice is the ninth volume in the series. The thirty-three contributors include many of the leading scholars of Jewish Studies from North America, Europe, and Israel. Each scholar has provided one or more translations of key works, many of which are translated here for the first time. These works include instructions for rites of birth and death, selections from the rabbinic curriculum, reflections on the role of art in Jewish practice, mystical poems, and accounts of the lives of remarkable men and women. Each chapter begins with a substantial introduction in which the translator discusses the history and influence of the work, identifying points of particular difficulty or interest. Lawrence Fine, who both edited and contributed chapters to the volume, opens the book with a general introduction to the world of Jewish practice.

Volumes on the religions of North America, Latin America, and medieval Christianity are in progress.

Donald S. Lopez, Jr.
Series Editor

NOTE ON TRANSLITERATION AND ACKNOWLEDGMENTS

The vast majority of primary texts in this volume were translated from Hebrew. Rather than seek to impose a single transliteration system, the slightly varying styles used by individual authors have been retained. Other languages from which texts are translated include Arabic, Chinese, Spanish, and Yiddish. Here too we have preserved the transliteration systems employed by the various contributors.

It is my great pleasure to express my appreciation to Professors Ivan Marcus and Kalman Bland, contributors to this book, for their helpful comments on the editor's introduction to the volume. My thanks as well to my nephew, Rabbi David Fine, for also having commented on the introduction. I alone, of course, remain responsible for the final result. My warmest appreciation goes to each of the distinguished scholars who generously agreed to contribute to this book. I believe that *Judaism in Practice* exemplifies academic collaboration at its best. I am pleased to acknowledge the generous support of the Lucius N. Littauer Foundation in connection with the illustrations that appear in the book. Finally, my deepest gratitude to my family, my sons Jacob and Aaron, and my wife Deborah, for their boundless love and support.

CONTENTS

Princeton Readings in Religions	vii
Note on Transliteration and Acknowledgments	ix
Contributors	xv
Introduction · *Lawrence Fine*	1

Rituals of Daily and Festival Practice

1. Communal Prayer and Liturgical Poetry · *Raymond P. Scheindlin*	39
2. Italian Jewish Women at Prayer · *Howard Tzvi Adelman*	52
3. Measuring Graves and Laying Wicks · *Chava Weissler*	61
4. Adorning the "Bride" on the Eve of the Feast of Weeks · *Daniel C. Matt*	74
5. New Year's Day for Fruit of the Tree · *Miles Krassen*	81

Rituals of the Life Cycle

6. The Role of Women at Rituals of Their Infant Children · *Lawrence A. Hoffman*	99
7. Honey Cakes and Torah: A Jewish Boy Learns His Letters · *Ivan G. Marcus*	115
8. Women and Ritual Immersion in Medieval Ashkenaz: The Sexual Politics of Piety · *Judith R. Baskin*	131
9. Life-Cycle Rituals of Spanish Crypto-Jewish Women · *Renée Levine Melammed*	143
10. Ritualizing Death and Dying: The Ethical Will of Naphtali Ha-Kohen Katz · *Avriel Bar-Levav*	155

Torah, Learning, and Ethics

11. Moses Maimonides' Laws of the Study of Torah · *Lawrence Kaplan*	171
12. An Egyptian Woman Seeks to Rescue Her Husband from a Sufi Monastery · *S. D. Goitein*	186

13. A Monastic-like Setting for the Study of Torah · *Ephraim Kanarfogel* 191
14. Religious Practice among Italian Jewish Women
    · *Howard Tzvi Adelman* 203
15. A Mystical Fellowship in Jerusalem · *Lawrence Fine* 210
16. The Love of Learning among Polish Jews · *Gershon David Hundert* 215

Religious Sectarianism and Communities on the Margins

17. Jewish Sectarianism in the Near East: A Muslim's Account
    · *Steven M. Wasserstrom* 229
18. Travel in the Land of Israel · *Lawrence Fine* 237
19. Karaite Ritual · *Daniel Frank* 248
20. Living Judaism in Confucian Culture: Being Jewish and Being
    Chinese · *Jonathan N. Lipman* 265

Art and Aesthetics

21. Defending, Enjoying, and Regulating the Visual · *Kalman P. Bland* 281
22. Illustrating History and Illluminating Identity in the Art of the
    Passover Haggadah · *Marc Michael Epstein* 298
23. The Arts of Calligraphy and Composition, and the Love of Books
    · *Lawrence Fine* 318
24. Jewish Preaching in Fifteenth-Century Spain · *Marc Saperstein* 325

Magic and Mysticism

25. The Book of the Great Name · *Michael D. Swartz* 341
26. Visionary Experiences among Spanish Crypto-Jewish Women
    · *Renée Levine Melammed* 348
27. Mystical Eating and Food Practices in the *Zohar* · *Joel Hecker* 353
28. Devotional Rites in a Sufi Mode · *Paul B. Fenton* 364
29. Pietistic Customs from Safed · *Lawrence Fine* 375
30. Jewish Exorcism: Early Modern Traditions and Transformations
    · *J. H. Chajes* 386
31. Rabbi Menahem Nahum of Chernobyl: Personal Practices of a
    Hasdic Master · *Arthur Green* 399

Remarkable Lives

32. The Life of Moses ben Maimon · *Joel L. Kraemer* 413
33. Dolce of Worms: The Lives and Deaths of an Exemplary Medieval
    Jewish Woman and Her Daughters · *Judith R. Baskin* 429

34. The Earliest Hebrew First-Crusade Narrative · *Robert Chazan*	438
35. Leon Modena's Autobiography · *Mark R. Cohen*	453
36. The Early Messianic Career of Shabbatai Zvi · *Matt Goldish*	470
37. The Life of Glikl of Hameln · *Paula E. Hyman*	483
38. Israel ben Eliezer, the Baal Shem Tov · *Dan Ben-Amos*	498
39. The Scholarly Life of the Gaon of Vilna · *Allan Nadler*	513
Appendix. The Jewish Holidays	521
Index	523

CONTRIBUTORS

Howard Tzvi Adelman teaches Jewish Studies at Achva Academic College, Israel.
Avriel Bar Levav teaches Jewish History at Ben Gurion University.
Judith R. Baskin is Professor of Religious Studies at the University of Oregon.
Dan Ben-Amos is Professor of Folklore at the University of Pennsylvania.
Kalman P. Bland is Professor of Religion at Duke University.
J. H. Chajes teaches Jewish History at Haifa University.
Robert Chazan is Scheuer Professor of Hebrew and Judaic Studies at New York University.
Mark R. Cohen is Professor of Near Eastern Studies at Princeton University.
Marc Michael Epstein is Associate Professor of Religion at Vassar College.
Paul Fenton is Professor of Jewish Studies at the Sorbonne.
Lawrence Fine is the Irene Kaplan Leiwant Professor of Jewish Studies, and Professor of Religion, at Mount Holyoke College.
Daniel Frank is Assistant Professor of Near Eastern Languages and Cultures at the Ohio State University.
S. D. Goitein was Professor of Near Eastern Studies at Princeton University.
Matt Goldish is Associate Professor of History at the Ohio State University.
Arthur Green is the Philip W. Lown Professor of Jewish Thought in the Department of Near Eastern and Judaic Studies at Brandeis University.
Joel Hecker is Associate Professor of Jewish Mysticism and Modern Jewish Civilization at the Reconstructionist Rabbinical College.
Gershon David Hundert is Professor of Jewish History at McGill University.
Lawrence A. Hoffman is Professor of Liturgy at Hebrew Union College-Jewish Institute of Religion.
Paula E. Hyman is the Lucy Moses Professor of Jewish History at Yale University.
Ephraim Kanarfogel is E. Billi Ivry Professor of Jewish History at Stern College for Women, Yeshiva University.
Lawrence Kaplan is Professor of Jewish Studies at McGill University.
Joel L. Kraemer is Professor of Jewish Studies in the Divinity School at the University of Chicago.
Miles Krassen is a scholar and teacher of Jewish mysticism.
Jonathan N. Lipman is Professor of History at Mount Holyoke College.
Ivan G. Marcus is the Frederick P. Rose Professor of Jewish History at Yale University.

Daniel C. Matt, formerly Professor of Jewish Studies at the Graduate Theological Union, is preparing a new English edition of the *Zohar*.

Renée Levine Melammed is Assistant Dean at the Schechter Institute of Jewish Studies in Jerusalem.

Allan Nadler is the Wallerstein Associate Professor of Judaic Studies at Drew University.

Marc Saperstein is the Charles E. Smith Professor of Jewish History at George Washington University.

Raymond P. Scheindlin is Professor of Medieval Hebrew Literature at the Jewish Theological Seminary of America.

Michael Swartz is Associate Professor of Hebrew and Religious Studies in the Department of Near Eastern Languages and Cultures at the Ohio State University.

Steven M. Wasserstrom is the Moe and Izetta Tonkon Associate Professor of Judaic Studies and the Humanities at Reed College.

Chava Weissler is the Philip and Muriel Berman Associate Professor of Jewish Civilization at Lehigh University.

JUDAISM IN PRACTICE

INTRODUCTION

Lawrence Fine

Judaism in Practice: From the Middle Ages through the Early Modern Period testifies to the great variety of religious practices that characterized Judaism in the twelve hundred years between approximately 600 C.E. and 1800 C.E. Although this vast span of time has often been regarded monochromatically, scholars have increasingly come to speak of this period's enormous complexity. The more that we learn about Judaism during this period of time, the more we recognize the dimensions of this complexity, as we will see below.

One of the many ways in which this anthology differs from earlier collections of primary Jewish source materials is in its focus on religious practice and religious experience—in keeping with the series of which it is a part. Older sourcebooks have tended overwhelmingly to be interested in either the political, social, and economic history of the Jewish people as a minority community under Islam and Christianity, or in documenting the intellectual religious achievements of medieval and early modern Jewry. There are thus a number of anthologies having to do with medieval Jewish philosophy, mystical thought, and religious poetry, but virtually nothing of scholarly consequence that seeks to encompass the broad range and variety of Jewish religious practice.

That this is the case is a matter of considerable irony, in light of the fact that Judaism has historically been regarded as essentially legal, that is, practical in nature. Yet, it is only recently that scholars have come to explore with increasing sophistication the embodied nature of Jewish religion. As the contents of this volume will demonstrate, the ways in which Judaism has been practiced can hardly be isolated from the historical and political experiences of Jews, or from their many different constructions of faith and theology. Nevertheless, a fuller appreciation of the dimensions of religious practice in Judaism requires that they be studied not merely as an appendage to treatments of Jewish history or Jewish thought but on their own terms, as well. The chapters in this book illustrate many different approaches to the analysis of ritual and practice, including literary, anthropological, phenomenological, and gender studies, as well as the methods of comparative religion.

Rather than encompass the entire history of Judaism, this sourcebook focuses on the medieval and early modern periods. There are several vantage points from which to construe the emergence of medieval Judaism. From a political point of view, the medieval period may be said to begin with the rise of Islam in the Arabian peninsula in the early seventh century, bringing with it dramatically new developments for the Jewish communities of the Near East, and eventually North Africa and the Iberian peninsula. From the point of view of religious literary creativity, the medieval period begins with the closing of the centuries-long process of the composition and editing of the Palestinian and Babylonian Talmuds (the final editing of the Talmuds took place between approximately 450 and 600 C.E.), and the gradual development of many new types of religious expression. These include, among other things, legal codes, philosophical and mystical books of diverse types, systematic treatises on ethics, and liturgical poetry. And from the perspective of religious practice, the medieval period is characterized by great variety and diversity, as we shall see below. This is the case despite the fact that the overwhelming majority of Jews during this period were united by their allegiance to what is known as rabbinic Judaism, that is, the form of Judaism that evolved during the period of the Talmuds and early midrashim (approximately 70 C.E. through 600 C.E.).

As its title indicates, this book draws a distinction between the medieval and early modern periods. The line between these is by no means crystal clear, and varies significantly from one cultural and geographical location to the next. For example, Italian Jewry participated in the cultural excitement of the Renaissance beginning as early as the fifteenth century, whereas the vast Jewish communities of Poland and Russia, as well as the Jews of the Near East, lived lives mostly undisturbed by early modernity well into the eighteenth century. Generally speaking, however, early modern Judaism is usually considered to coincide with the seventeenth and eighteenth centuries—roughly equivalent to what European historians mean when they invoke the category "early modern Europe." Early modern Judaism may be said to be distinguished by, among other things, ever-increasing interaction with the non-Jews among whom Jews lived (and related exposure to non-Jewish ways of life), a gradual breaking down of the strong hold that rabbinic authority had held for centuries, and a growth in interest on the part of many Jews in all manner of secular matters. Among the chapters in this book that exemplify aspects of these developments are "Italian Jewish Women at Prayer," "Jewish Exorcism: Early Modern Traditions and Transformations," "The Life of Glikl of Hameln," "The Early Messianic Career of Shabbatai Zvi," "Leon Modena's Autobiography," and "The Scholarly Life of the Gaon of Vilna."

Early modern Judaism may be said to have come to an end in the nineteenth century, as a result of European Jewry's political and social "emancipation," and the concomitant embrace of and integration into Western culture. This period witnessed a gradual shift in which traditional Jewish identity now found itself challenged by the cosmopolitan and secular trends of the nineteenth century. The modern period itself is distinguished by two transformational events, the devastation of two-thirds of European Jewry at the hands of Nazi Germany, and the development of Jewish nationalism in the form of the Zionist movement, eventuating in the creation of the state of Israel in 1948. In addition to these developments, the modern and contemporary Jewish experience has been dominated by the influence of a thriving Jewish community in the United States, especially since the end of the Second World War. All of these factors have contributed to dramatic changes and innovations in the entire realm of Jewish religious life and practice, not to mention the emergence of forms of Jewish identity based primarily on a secular point of view.

Medieval Jewish Law

The point of departure for any discussion of Jewish practice begins, appropriately, with the question of Jewish law. Although there is far more to Judaism than law, as we shall see, the fact is that law stands at the heart of traditional Judaism. The origins of Jewish law go back to ancient Israel (approximately the thirteenth century B.C.E. through the fifth century B.C.E.) and to the various legal sections found in the Torah, that is, the Five Books of Moses, the first part of the Hebrew Bible. The books of Exodus, Leviticus, and Deuteronomy, in particular, delineate the legal traditions that the ancient Israelites developed. These traditions address not only matters that are self-evidently "religious," such as laws governing moral conduct or devotional rites in the form of cultic sacrifice, but also matters that in our culture are considered secular, such as laws having to do with agriculture as well as property damages and torts. According to the Torah, the people of Israel were expected to devote themselves to God by becoming a "holy nation" and a "kingdom of priests." As such, it was inconceivable that any aspect of life would fall outside the purview of the sacred life. The authority of biblical law was rooted in the belief of ancient Israel that the Torah had been revealed by God, transmitted to Moses in the wilderness of Sinai.

Biblical law underwent enormous development and dramatic change during the rabbinic or talmudic period, that is, the first six centuries of the common era. This period is called "rabbinic" or "talmudic" in reference to the sages (or rabbis) whose religious scholarship became the basis for the great corpus of literature known as Talmud. Following the destruction of the sacred Temple in Jerusalem in the year 70 C.E. by the Romans—under whose authority the Jews of Palestine had lived since 66 B.C.E.—the sages who came to be known as rabbis engaged in the study of the ancient ancestral traditions preserved in the Hebrew Bible, in addition to postbiblical traditions that had circulated in oral fashion. The earliest of these rabbis, known collectively by the term *tannaim* (plural for *tanna*), transmitted these postbiblical oral traditions from master to disciple in study houses and academies. These (mostly legal) oral traditions were eventually edited around the year 200 C.E. by a leading rabbinical authority, Judah the Prince (in Hebrew, Judah ha-Nasi). The resulting corpus became known as the Mishnah, a large work divided into six main divisions or "orders," which are further subdivided into sixty-three separate treatises or books, covering a vast array of topics.

In the course of this process the rabbis determined that there were 613 basic legal obligations or precepts (sing. *mitsvah* or *mizvah,* pl. *mitsvot,* or *mizvot*) in the Torah. But from each of these 613 *mitsvot,* the rabbis derived numerous further precepts, resulting in an ever-expanding body of Jewish law, or, as it came to be known, *halakha.* The term "*halakha*" (lit., the "path" or "way") refers, then, to the entirety of Jewish law, including the Mishnah and its subsequent development.

A good example of this process may be seen in connection with the laws of the Sabbath. Whereas the Torah itself prescribes rest on the Sabbath, it provides very little specific guidance as to what such cessation from labor entails. When we turn, however, to the treatise of the Mishnah devoted to the laws of the Sabbath, we find that the sages delineated no fewer than thirty-nine types of activity that they regarded as labor. For each of these thirty-nine activities, rabbinic tradition derived still further precepts, thus exponentially expanding the laws and rituals governing celebration of the Sabbath. Another well-known example of this process has to do with the dietary laws, or *kashrut.* Whereas the Torah provides a number of general guidelines and principles with respect to which animals are fit for consumption, rabbinic law transforms these into a vast network of ritual obligations that go far beyond what the Torah itself provided.

Written in Hebrew, in a way that somewhat resembles a systematic, formal code of law, the Mishnah is organized into terse, often enigmatic, paragraphs of legal traditions. Composed with virtually no explanation of its laws, and usually without explicit reference to the scriptural basis for its traditions, the Mishnah, by its very nature, generated centuries more of discussion, explanation, and interpretation. The rabbis who participated in this process of exploring the Mishnah beginning in the third century C.E. were known as *amoraim* (sing., *amora*), and the voluminous commentaries they composed in Aramaic are known as Gemara. The development of Gemara took place simultaneously in Palestine and Babylonia, that is, in present-day Iraq, where Jews had settled centuries earlier along the fertile banks of the Tigris and Euphrates rivers.

Thus, there were two communities of amoraic scholars, each of which more or less independently pursued the study of the Mishnah, although there were continuous and intimate relations between Palestinian and Babylonian scholars. The activities of the Palestinian *amoraim* came to a close in about 450 C.E., resulting in the Palestinian Gemara. The Mishnah, along with the Palestinian Gemara, is known as the Jerusalem Talmud (even though it was produced primarily in academies in the Galilee), or sometimes as the Palestinian Talmud. The composition and editing of the Babylonian Gemara went on for approximately 150 years longer than the Palestinian, and was completed about 600 C.E. It is thus a considerably larger document than its Palestinian counterpart, and is distinguished by its greater clarity and literary sophistication. The reasons for this have to do with the fact that the center of gravity for Jewish life had shifted from Palestine to Babylonia by the fourth to fifth centuries C.E., and the community there flourished in comparison to that of the Jews of Palestine. Thus, it was the Babylonian Talmud (Mishnah plus Babylonian Gemara) that ultimately became more authoritative, and exerted far greater historical influence. Even today, rabbinical students learn Talmud primarily on the basis of the Babylonian version, whereas the Palestinian tends to be reserved for especially advanced scholars.

The importance of the Talmuds has to do with the fact that the enormous bodies of tradition found in this literature gradually became the basis for Jewish religious practice down through the centuries that followed. That is to say, although the rabbis of Palestine and Babylonia constituted an elite class of religious intellectuals and scholars, and even though there were often very considerable differences between what these individuals taught and the way people actually practiced, their teachings ultimately came to be regarded as authoritative by the Jewish community at large—at least in principle. This was true not only in Palestine and Babylonia but also in most places where Jews lived. The rabbis themselves had contended that their teachings were nothing less than the legitimate interpretation of Hebrew scripture as intended by God when He revealed Himself to Moses at Mount Sinai. They claimed only to be determining through their study what was implied in scripture from the very beginning. This view came to be regarded as axiomatic by the vast majority of Jews up until traditional rabbinic authority came under challenge, beginning in the eighteenth century in western Europe. In the centuries immediately following the editing of the Talmuds, the rabbis succeeded in so consolidating their authority that the vast majority of Jews looked upon themselves as "rabbinic" Jews. The expression "rabbinic Judaism" can thus be understood in a narrow sense, referring to the rabbinic or talmudic period per se, or it can be understood in a far broader way, referring to the whole of rabbinic culture that characterized traditional Judaism down through the medieval and early modern periods. It is for this reason that we can say that although all of the texts found in this anthology are chronologically post-talmudic, that is, from the seventh century and later, the great majority of them fall under the category of rabbinic Judaism in the larger sense.

The development of *halakha,* however, did not come to an end with the Talmuds. If the terseness of the Mishnah had served as an invitation to the rabbis to interpret it, paradoxically, the verbose, complex, and indeterminate nature of the Gemara made further clarification of that text's legal discussions necessary. The Gemara consists, in significant part, of a vast legal dialectic in which competing views on matters of *halakha* are set forth without necessarily being clearly decided; the rabbis appear to have been at least as interested in preserving their own debates as they were in arriving at definitive, practical conclusions. As a result, post-talmudic generations of rabbinic authorities devised still newer methods by which to determine how the *halakha* should be practiced. (It should be pointed out that the literature of the Talmuds contains a good deal besides legal materials. It also includes folk traditions, anecdotes about sages, ethical traditions, even prayers, all of which are known under the category of *aggadah,* or narrative, in contrast to *halakha.*)

The early medieval period, between the seventh and eleventh centuries, is sometimes called the geonic period, due to the prominence of leading rabbinic teachers during this time in Babylonia who were known as ge'onim (sing., ga'on). The ge'onim were the heads of the famous rabbinical academies at Sura and Pumbedita (near Baghdad, where these academies were eventually transferred), and played a critical role in the post-talmudic consolidation of rabbinic authority to which I have already referred. For a period of time, they served as the central spiritual and legal authorities for much of worldwide Jewry.

It was during the period of the Babylonian ge'onim that several new forms of halakhic literature evolved, two of which are of particular interest for our purposes. The first of these was the legal codes, the goal of which was to present the law in a way that was systematically organized and definitive. Two somewhat different forms of code developed during the geonic period—books of *halakhot* (laws) and books of *pesakim* (decisions). In the case of books of *halakhot,* the final conclusion as to what constitutes binding law comes after some brief discussion that identifies and explains the earlier rabbinic sources upon which the conclusion is based. The effect of this procedure was to preserve the intimate relationship between the legal conclusion and the web of prior sources from which it is derived. By contrast, codes of *pesakim* articulate the final conclusion without citing the earlier sources on which they are based, and without any discussion. These have the advantage of being unencumbered by anything "extraneous," but they also run the risk of severing legal conclusions from the rich network of sources upon which they are based. Moses Maimonides (1138–1204), without doubt the most famous of all medieval Jewish scholars, composed what became one of the preeminent codes of Jewish law, the *Mishneh Torah,* doing so in the simpler form of the *pesakim.* The *Mishneh Torah* is well-illustrated in our anthology by the chapters "Moses Maimonides' Laws of the Study of Torah," and "Defending, Enjoying, and Regulating the Visual." The latter chapter also includes passages from the influential sixteenth-century code of Jewish law, the *Shulkhan Arukh,* composed by Joseph Karo (or Caro). Maimonides himself is the subject of the chapter "The Life of Moses ben Maimon." Through letters and other documents by and about Maimonides, we gain a glimpse into the life of one of the most remarkable Jews of the medieval age.

Another principal form of post-talmudic Jewish law is known as responsa literature. In Hebrew the expression used is *she'elot u-teshuvot,* literally, "questions and answers." The Hebrew expression more accurately conveys the nature of this literature. Individuals, or sometimes communities, would submit halakhic queries to rabbinic authorities, who would respond in writing to the question. The collected questions and answers of individual rabbis would eventually assume their place as part of the larger body of legal precedent. During the geonic period it was the ge'onim themselves to whom such inquiries would be submitted. Often these inquiries would come from a considerable distance—Spain or North Africa, for example. Eventually, as authoritative rabbis were to be found throughout the Jewish world, responsa were produced in numerous places. As Menahem Elon wrote in his important study of Jewish law, the responsa literature occupies a central role in the development of Jewish law, and Jewish religious history more generally:

> Questions submitted to a respondent arose in the factual context of the time, and the responsum had to resolve the issues in a manner consonant with the contemporaneous circumstances. The subjects of the questions generally related to social, economic, technological, and moral conditions, which differed from period to period and from place to place. The social and economic circumstances of Babylonian Jewry in the eighth and ninth centuries C.E., for example, differed from those of Polish Jews in the sixteenth century; and the condition of Spanish Jewry in the thirteenth century bore no resemblance to that of the Jews of Salonika in the sixteenth and seventeenth centuries. The halakhic authorities in each generation were called upon to determine the position of Jewish law with regard to the questions that arose in their time; and if they could find no explicit solution in existing law or if, in their opinion, the existing legal rules did not satisfy the needs of the time, they sought and found a solution by means of one or more of the legal sources of Jewish law—interpretation, legislation, custom, *ma 'aseh* [a set of facts having legal significance], and legal reasoning (*sevarah*). The responsa literature thus reveals innumerable new problems that arose in the course of centuries and exemplifies how the methods for the development of Jewish law were utilized to find solutions.[1]

It is hard to overstate the importance of the responsa literature for the history of Jewish ritual and practice, as it is responsible for the vast majority of Jewish law in the medieval and early modern periods. The responsa are immensely significant as well for the study of Jewish history as a whole, insofar as they richly reflect the political, social, and economic circumstances under which Jews lived. There are approximately 300,000 extant responsa, contained in over 3,000 books of responsa by different authors. Chapters in our volume containing examples of this legal genre—from the responsa of Rabbi Meir ben Baruch of Rothenberg (c. 1215–1293)—are "Women and Ritual Immersion in Medieval Ashkenaz: The Sexual Politics of Piety" and "Defending, Enjoying, and Regulating the Visual."

In the case of both the legal codes and the responsa literature, the goal was essentially the same, even though they employed considerably different forms. Their purpose was to interpret and adapt earlier legal tradition and to arrive at binding, practical decisions so that individuals and communities might know how to practice rabbinic Judaism, that is, the form of Judaism that had come into being with the formation of the Talmuds.

If the geonic period saw the successful consolidation of rabbinic authority, principally around nearly universal allegiance to Jewish law as construed by the rabbis, how do we understand the fact that medieval and early modern Judaism were characterized by great diversity and variation when it came to religious practice? In order to answer this question, most of the remainder of this introduction will address significant factors that contributed to patterns of diversity.

Midrash and Aggadah

Before turning to a discussion of this diversity, however, we want to say a few words about *midrash,* another central genre of Jewish literature that flourished between about 400 and 1200 C.E. Originating in oral sermons given in the synagogues of late antiquity, *midrash,* which literally means to "search out," is a verse-centered literature that always seeks to interpret scripture. A midrashic text is one that uses scripture as a point of departure in order to establish a new teaching, although the authors of these texts did not claim to be innovative. Although such interpretations could be for the purpose of elaborating upon matters of *halakha,* most of the midrashic collections are known as *midrash aggadah,* referring to interpretations of a nonlegal or narrative type. Such *midrashim* (pl. of *midrash*) incorporate highly imaginative discussions of the behavior and motivations of biblical women and men, as well as ethical and theological matters, among other things. *Midrash aggadah* contributed in its own way to the development of Jewish practice, especially in the realm of ethical virtues and certain customs. More generally, it helped legitimate the highly creative processes of wide-ranging and multi-textured interpretation of Jewish tradition.

Local and Regional Variation

Although the origins of the Jewish people were in the Near East, by the twelfth and thirteenth centuries Jewish communities could be found in most parts of Europe, as well as more distant regions such as India and China (see Maps 1 and 2). This development helps account for the richly varied ways in which different Jewries evolved ways of practicing Judaism. This phenomenon goes back to at least the talmudic and geonic periods, as a result of the somewhat different, and competing, practices of Palestinian and Babylonian sages, particularly in the areas of liturgical prayer and the setting of the religious calendar. Whereas the Palestinian rabbis had historically exerted cultural influence over Syria and Egypt, Babylonian authorities had held sway over the communities in Iraq and Iran, and eventually North Africa.

From the tenth century forward, the Jews of North Africa and Spain—who for several centuries shared similar political and cultural features under the influence of Islam—became increasingly independent of Babylonian authority. As they gained their own competence in rabbinic law and tradition, they relied on their own rabbis for guidance in the sphere of religious practice. Local scholars began to answer halakhic inquiries rather then send them off to the Babylonian academies, and thus they accumulated a body of responsa literature of their own. In fact, among the very earliest medieval commentaries on the Babylonian Talmud were those by a Tunisian rabbi from Kairouan, Hananel ben Hushiel, and his student Nissim ben Jacob ibn Shahun. Their work influenced the greatest North

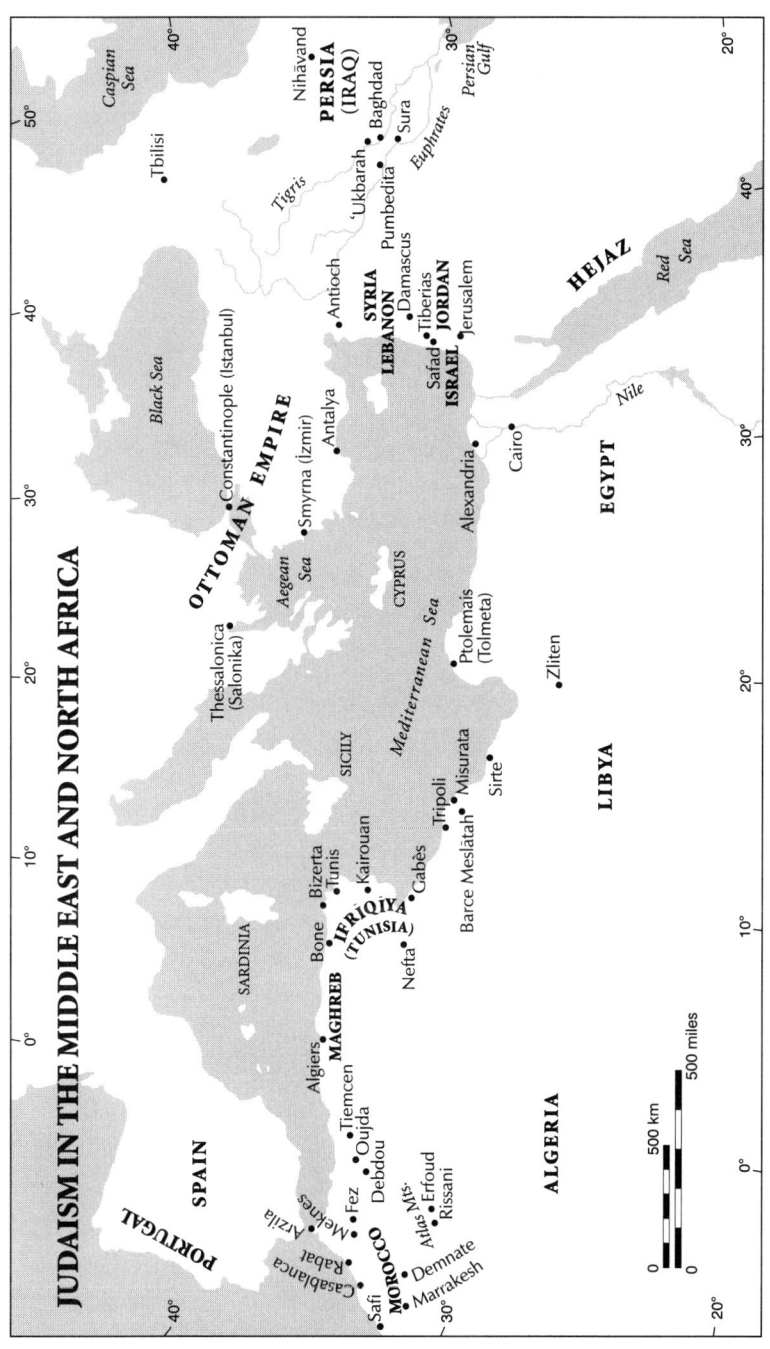

Map 1

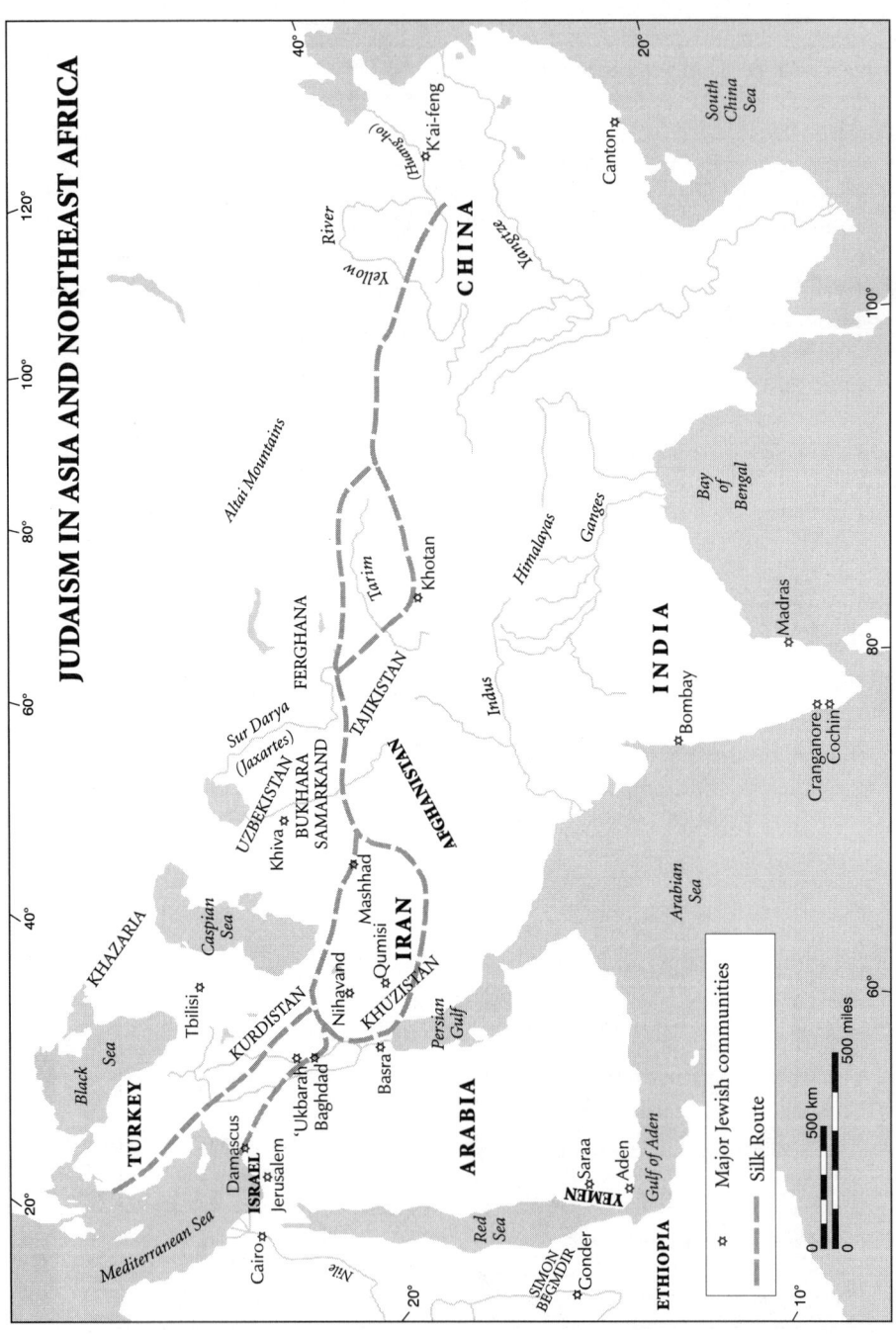

Map 2

African scholar of this period, Isaac Alfasi (1013–1103), author of the most important halakhic code prior to that of Maimonides. Alfasi's influence, in turn, was passed on to rabbinic scholars in Spain.

Although the experience of the Jewish community of Islamic Spain has frequently been called a "Golden Age," the fact is that there were strong anti-Jewish sentiment and outbreaks of terrible violence against Jews during this period. In 1066, the Jews of Granada were massacred in the wake of the assassination of the prominent Jewish courtier Joseph ha-Nagid. The Jews of Andalusia suffered further at the hands of the zealously religious Almoravids in the latter half of the eleventh century, and of the Almohads in the middle of the twelfth century, both fanatic Muslim Berber groups that had come to Spain from North Africa. Despite this, it is true that on the whole Jewish life flourished under what was generally benevolent Muslim rule. The *Sefardim* (or *Sephardim*), as the Jews of Spain (*Sefarad*) were called in Hebrew, produced immense achievements in virtually all areas of Jewish culture: art, music, and architecture, poetry and linguistics, philosophy and mysticism, law and biblical interpretation. These cultural achievements attest to the rich, complex symbiosis that took place between Jewish and Islamic culture during this period. This exemplifies a fundamental fact about Jewish culture in the Middle Ages, namely, that it was influenced and shaped in profound ways by the surrounding cultures, especially those of Islam and Christianity.

When the Jews of Spain and Portugal were forcibly exiled from their homelands in the late fifteenth century by Christian rulers, they migrated primarily to North Africa, Italy, and the Ottoman Empire (see Map 3). As they did so, they took with them their highly sophisticated and distinctive patterns of religious observance. This is a dramatic example of the way in which what began as regional variation spread widely as a result of migration, forced or otherwise. Thus, rabbinic culture as practiced by the *Sefardim* wherever they settled became one of the dominant variations of Judaism down to the present day. Sefardic culture is well represented in this anthology. Chapters that, all or in part, illustrate numerous aspects of Sefardic ritual and practice include "Life-Cycle Rituals of Spanish Crypto-Jewish Women," "Moses Maimonides' Laws of the Study of Torah," "Defending, Enjoying, and Regulating the Visual," "Illustrating History and Illuminating Identity in the Art of the Passover Haggadah," "Jewish Preaching in Fifteenth-Century Spain," "Visionary Experiences among Spanish Crypto-Jewish Women," and "Mystical Eating and Food Practices in the *Zohar*."

It is important to distinguish between those Jews who traced their ancestry back to Spain and Portugal, the *Sefardim,* and those who lived in the Islamic East without having had any direct connection to the Iberian Peninsula. The latter included Jews living in the land of Israel, the Arabian Peninsula (especially Yemen), North Africa and Egypt, Syria, and Iraq (formerly Babylonia). Traditionally, such Jews were known as *Musta'rabim,* that is, native Arabic-speaking individuals. Sometimes called today (somewhat misleadingly) "Eastern" or "Oriental" Jews, these various communities preserved highly distinctive identities and

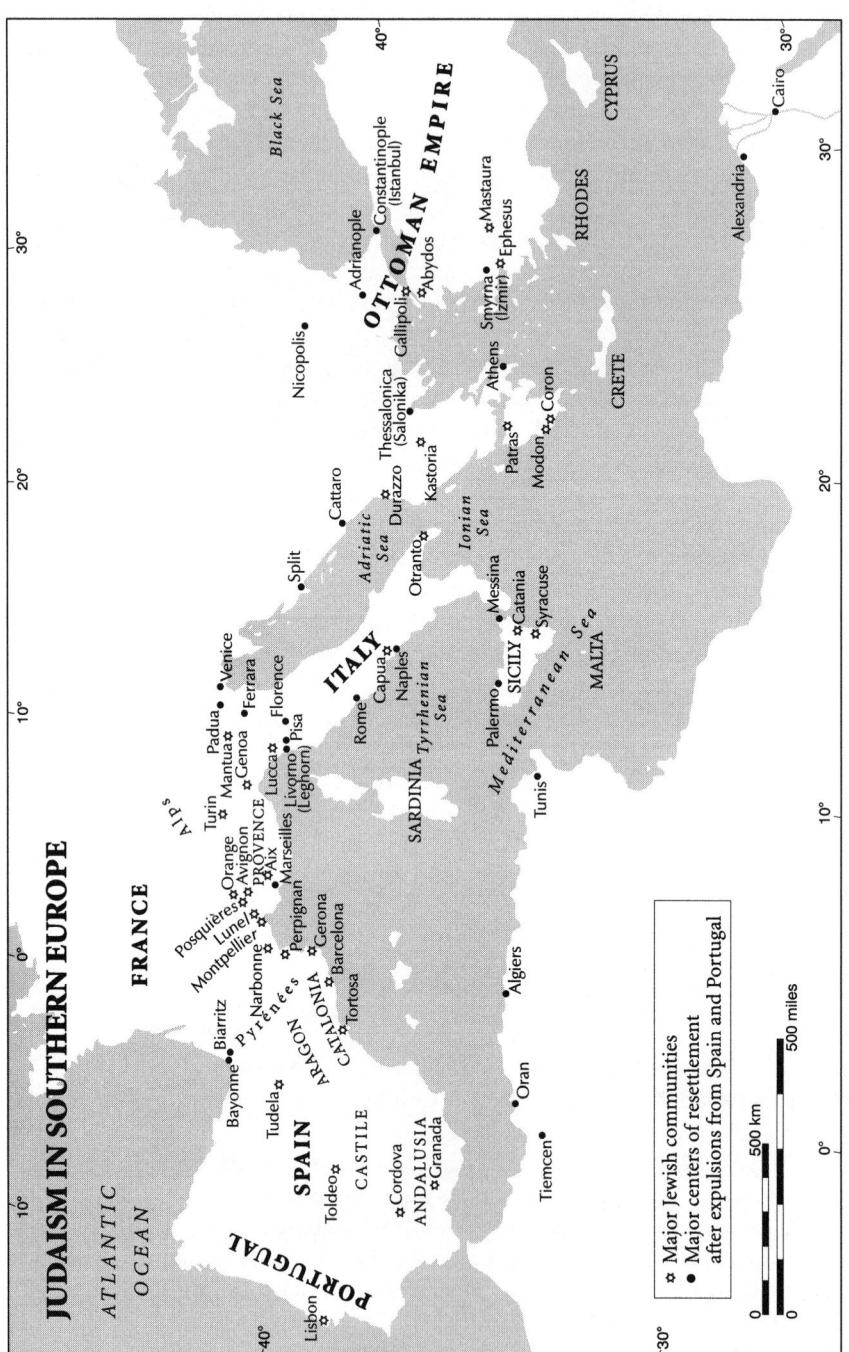

Map 3

INTRODUCTION   13

cultures of their own down through the centuries, as they do to some extent even now in contemporary Israel. The blurring of identity between the *Sefardim* and the native Jews of Arab lands is due to the fact that many of the *Sefardim,* as we know, eventually settled in the Muslim countries of the Near East and North Africa.

Besides these two distinctive cultures, the other dominant form of Jewish religious culture goes by the name Ashkenazic, referring, at least originally, to the Jewish communities of the Germanic lands, or *Ashkenaz* in Hebrew, as well as France. Ashkenazic Jewry traces its origins back to the eighth to ninth centuries, when the Frankish kings, Charlemagne in particular, sought to encourage Jews living in Italy to migrate to southern France and to the Rhineland. These rulers were motivated by the desire to attract Jewish merchants and traders who could develop the commercial life of a region whose economy was almost exclusively agricultural in nature. As a result, very significant Jewish settlements were established in the towns and cities along the Rhine River Valley, including Mainz, Worms, Speyer, and Cologne (see Map 4). These settlements would, in turn, become the basis for the great Jewish communities of western, central, and eventually even eastern Europe, including Poland and Russia.

Ashkenazic Jews originally prospered as traders and businessmen and had relatively stable relations with their Christian neighbors for a considerable period of time, at least until near the end of the eleventh century. As recent research has demonstrated, Jews and Christians lived in close enough proximity to both adapt and repudiate aspects of one another's culture. Circumstances took a catastrophic turn for the worse, however, toward the end of the eleventh century. In the spring of 1096, zealous Christian crusaders forcibly baptized Jews and assaulted Jewish communities along the Rhineland on their way to liberating the "Holy Land" from the Muslim "infidels." The chapter in this book entitled "The Earliest Hebrew First-Crusade Narrative" provides a detailed account of the religiously motivated martyrdom of Ashkenazic Jews who are depicted as having willingly given up their lives rather than convert to Christianity. Although the historical questions having to do with relations between Jews and Christians in medieval *Ashkenaz* are exceedingly complex, it is fair to say that beginning with the twelfth century, the social and political situation of Ashkenazic Jewry gradually worsened, and led to widespread expulsion and persecution during the fourteenth and fifteenth centuries. Nevertheless, Jewish religious culture in all of its dimensions was influenced by the Christian culture in which it found itself.

As was the case with the *Sefardim,* Ashkenazic Jewry constructed a rich, multitextured religious life, with its own distinctive character. Rabbinical academies developed around the beginning of the eleventh century in Mainz, inaugurating an illustrious tradition of talmudic and rabbinic scholarship. In contrast to the Arabic-speaking Jews of the Near East, North Africa, and Spain, whose interaction with Muslim culture resulted in spectacular religious creativity in many different spheres, Ashkenazic scholarship tended to focus especially on the study of the Talmud and cognate literature. The French rabbi Solomon ben Isaac, better

Map 4

known by his acronym, Rashi (1040–1105), stands out as the greatest commentator on both the Hebrew Bible and the Talmud. Influenced by his scholarship, the rabbinical academies of Champagne and northern France eventually came to supplant in significance those of the Rhineland. As was also the case in Spain, the study of Jewish law in *Ashkenaz* served practical purposes as well as academic ones. As far as possible, Jews preferred to have legal transactions and business disputes among themselves adjudicated by Jewish courts. Needless to say, when it came to matters of religious life and practice, the Jewish community looked to its rabbis to guide them. In general, religious life among Ashkenazi Jews tended to be characterized by a greater degree of austerity than that of the Jews of *Sefarad*. As we will see below, this austerity manifested itself as a full-blown ascetic lifestyle in the most important specialized religious movement to come out of medieval *Ashkenaz,* namely, the German Pietists, or *Hasidei Ashkenaz* of the twelfth and thirteenth centuries.

In addition to these especially well-known regional variations on rabbinic Judaism, numerous other Jewish communities all over the world also developed distinctive identities, including customs and practices of their own, such as in the case of Italian Jewry and Greek-speaking Byzantine Jewry. That this would take place is not hard to understand. Although Jews always preserved their identity as a minority community in the lands in which they lived, they were inevitably influenced by the larger culture, even when that culture was fundamentally hostile to them. Ways of dress, language, folk customs, popular superstition, art and aesthetics, even theological conceptions, were all colored by local and regional culture. In addition, social, economic, and political factors also contributed to distinctive ways of doing things. An excellent example of this may be seen in one of the most famous regional enactments of the medieval period, by the prominent early Ashkenazic authority Rabbenu Gershom (c. 960–1028). Rabbenu Gershom issued a *takkanah,* a legal "enactment" or "decree" that banned the practice of polygamy for the Jewish inhabitants of German and nearby lands. The adoption of this enactment was influenced by the fact that Christian law prohibited a man from marrying more than one wife, as well as by the economic and social conditions that prevailed in Europe during Rabbenu Gershom's time. There is evidence, for example, that Jewish merchants from Christian lands would travel abroad for years at a time to Muslim countries, where they would frequently marry again. On the other hand, this legislation was not enacted or accepted by Jews of Islamic countries, where economic conditions and social attitudes were substantially different, and where polygamy was widely practiced. Finally, the absence of a single central authority for all of Jewry, at least following the decline in prestige of the Babylonian ge'onim in the tenth century, contributed significantly to the growth and importance of local legislation.

How did medieval authorities look upon local or regional customs in regard to religious practice? Were these seen as a challenge to the unifying nature of rabbinic tradition? The answer to these questions is bound up with the important notion of *minhag* (custom) in Jewish law. Rabbinic law itself recognized and validated such variation, a phenomenon that goes back to late antiquity. As far as the Talmud is concerned, when there are two valid opinions about a law, proper practice can be determined either by way of following the majority view of the sages, or by following the popular practice of the people themselves (Jerusalem Talmud, *Yevamot* 12.1, 12c). In the words of the Babylonian Talmud (*Berakhot* 45a; *Pesahim* 54a), one must "go and see what the people do." The popular acceptance of one form of practice over another is regarded as valid because "if the people of Israel are not prophets, they are the children of prophets" (Jerusalem Talmud, *Pesahim* 6.1, 33a). Popular practice itself, then, came to be viewed as part of an unbroken chain of tradition. Although some customs became universally accepted, others were considered as binding only for those residing in a particular locality or region, as we saw in connection with Rabbenu Gershom's decree. The impact of this notion can be seen especially clearly, even to this day, in the considerable variation in the sphere of liturgical rites amongst traditional Jews.

Two further things should be pointed out about *minhag*. First, the diversity and variation embodied in *minhag* did not undermine the unity of rabbinic Jews or their overall practice. The vast majority of ritual practice was essentially the same from one place to the next, and Jews traveling to new locales could generally feel comfortable in a different setting. Second, what we have said about the legitimization of variant practices pertains only to the premodern period. More "radical" innovation espoused by the nineteenth-century modernizing movements of Reform and Conservative Judaism were regarded by traditionalists as falling outside the boundaries of legitimate variation.

Beyond the question of localized *minhag*, it is important to note that Jewish communities in the Middle Ages were, for the most part, self-governing, autonomous entities (albeit significantly constrained by the ruling authorities to which they were subject). As such, their basic law was predicated on *halakha* and their judges were rabbinic authorities. There was no one centralized authority for all of Jewry, and thus individual communities were in a position to adapt and accommodate Jewish practice to local or regional needs and cultural sensibilities. Beside these considerations, it is important to point out that variation in local practice also resulted from the nature of the Talmud itself. The Talmud often accepted conflicting religious practices based on the notion that different views were all "words of the living God."

Mystical Movements and Ritual Variation

A great deal of variation in practice may be attributed to the numerous esoteric movements that Jewish culture has produced. Although generally less well known than normative rabbinic Judaism, there is a rich and diverse history of Jewish mysticism. The first such movement is known as *Merkavah* or *Hekhalot* mysticism, which originated in Palestine in the early centuries of the common era alongside talmudic and midrashic literature, but which continued to develop into the early medieval period. This literature is characterized by highly imaginative descriptions of visionary ascents through the seven heavenly "palaces" (*hekhalot*), which culminate in numinous visions of the divine throne (the *merkavah*). The chapter in this volume entitled "The Book of the Great Name" includes a magical text from this literature. This particular text, probably written between the sixth and ninth centuries, provides instructions for an adept to prepare himself ritually so as to engage successfully in the recitation of esoteric names of God. It also includes fragments of poetic hymns that exalt God and His name, and describes the power of the magical book that contains this information.

German Pietism (*Hasidut Ashkenaz*), referred to earlier, was an important mystical movement of the late twelfth and thirteenth centuries. Three individuals, in particular, were the leading figures of this movement, all members of the Qalonimos family: Samuel, son of Qalonimos (mid-twelfth century); his son, Judah the Pietist (d. 1217); and the latter's disciple and cousin, Eleazar of Worms (died c. 1230). In their writings these men developed the idea that the will of God is only partially apparent in the Torah when it is read in literal ways; thus a *hasid*, or Pietist, must search the Torah for the inner, esoteric meanings that scripture encodes. The central theological conception of the Pietists was that all of life is composed of suffering and trial, tribulations imposed by God so as continuously to test an individual's faithfulness. In particular, God subjects an individual to diverse temptations so that he might strive to prevail over his passions, the "evil impulse" about which the ancient rabbis had spoken so much. Constant self-examination of one's motives and behavior served as the basis for a wide range of innovative practices, a key feature of which was asceticism. Beyond the simple avoidance of illicit pleasures, the Pietist was to pursue actively severe rites of self-affliction, both as trial and as a form of penitence.

In a way that is strikingly reminiscent of the vast medieval ecclesiastical literature of Christian penitentials, pietistic literature includes systematic catalogues of sins and their corresponding penances. Thus, they call for extensive regimens of fasting, immersion in icy water, periods of sexual abstinence, and flagellation. For example, according to *Sefer Hasidim* (The Book of the Pietists), a man who had engaged in sexual intercourse with a Gentile woman had to fast three consecutive days and nights for a period of three years, or practice three-day fasts in the course of a single year. According to Eleazar of Worms, if a man has sexual relations with another's wife, he is required to sit in icy water in the winter, and among insects in the summer. These ascetic rites are an excellent example of how a particular religious ideology led to the development of special and highly unusual ritual practices among certain medieval Jews. The German Pietists strictly adhered to all of the regular halakhic requirements of Jewish tradition, but they added to these through supererogatory rites such as described here. This movement may have provided the context for the unusual setting for religious study described in "A Monastic-like Setting for the Study of Torah." In addition, the Pietist Eleazar of Worms's depiction of his wife Dolce is found in the chapter entitled "Dolce of Worms: The Lives and Deaths of an Exemplary Jewish Woman and Her Daughters."

In the Islamic world, at approximately the same time that the German Pietists flourished, another Jewish group who also called themselves *hasidim* (pietists) appeared, this time in Egypt. Islamic mysticism, Sufism, flourished in thirteenth-century Egypt, and exerted strong influence upon various Jewish circles. One of the leading figures in this Jewish-Egyptian pietistic movement was none other than the son of Moses Maimonides, Abraham Maimuni (1186–1237). As one of the chapters in this book, "Devotional Rites in a Sufi Mode," makes clear, the adaptation of Sufi concepts and rituals was a creative process in which Jewish teachers synthesized Islamic and Jewish rituals in innovative ways. We find that Jews who were attracted to this form of spirituality took up various Sufi contemplative practices, including solitary retreats and the ritual repetition of Divine names. As with the *Hasidei Ashkenaz*, those who practiced in this way did not ignore traditional Jewish law but adapted Jewish practice so as to incorporate these novel rites into their devotional lives. At the same time, we know that some individuals became so intrigued with the Sufi way of life that they turned wholeheartedly to Islam. This phenomenon is poignantly illustrated in the chapter in this volume, "An Egyptian Woman Seeks to Rescue Her Husband from a Sufi Monastery."

"Prophetic" or "ecstatic" Kabbalah is a mystical movement associated with a Spanish Jew by the name of Abraham Abulafia (1240–1291). Abulafia was born in Saragossa, in the Spanish province of Aragon, but spent much of his life traveling, including journeys to Palestine, Greece, and Italy. Abulafia developed a highly distinctive contemplative system based upon an eclectic array of practical techniques. These included the reciting and combining of names of God and a variety of body postures and breathing exercises, some of which bear a strong resemblance to yogic practices. Abulafia spurned traditional Kabbalah (described below) in favor of his own system, the goal of which was ecstatic union with God, described primarily in terms borrowed from the philosophical system of Moses Maimonides.

The term Kabbalah is used, as well, to describe a rather different and far broader mystical movement that emerged in the south of France in the latter decades of the twelfth century. Southern France was the provenance for the appearance of the first kabbalistic work of a theosophical type, the *Sefer Bahir*. By theosophical we refer to a complex conception of divinity according to which God manifests ten aspects or qualities of personality, known as *sefirot*. The *sefirot* are the many "lights" or "faces" of divinity, which, through study, prayer, and contemplation, human beings are able to imagine and experience. These ten *sefirot* emanate or pour forth from within the hidden recesses of an otherwise concealed dimension of divine being, known by the expression *Ein Sof* (the Infinite). *Ein Sof* is the root of all being, the source of all that exists, which in and of itself remains beyond the capacity of the human intellect or imagination to fathom. In distinctive and colorful mythic symbolism, the *Bahir* describes these ten attributes that derive from *Ein Sof* and that compose the dynamic, inner life of God.

Owing to the *Bahir* and a small but prominent circle of kabbalists, Kabbalah spread to Spain by the beginning of the thirteenth century. A number of important centers came into being, beginning in the city of Gerona and eventually spreading to central Spain, Castile. This classical phase of Kabbalah, which produced a significant number of kabbalistic treatises, reached its highest development in the composition of the *Zohar* (Book of Splendor), the seminal work of Spanish Jewish mysticism. A remarkable work of the imagination, the *Zohar* was written largely if not exclusively by Moses de Leon, who began to circulate manuscripts of *Zohar* in the 1280s and 1290s. The *Zohar* was the culmination and crystallization of a century of kabbalistic literary creativity and, in turn, served as the primary inspiration for centuries more of Jewish mystical literature and life. Much of the appeal exerted by the *Zohar* was the result of the fact that de Leon wrote in a pseudepigraphic manner, attributing its teachings not to himself but to a second century rabbi, Shimon bar Yohai. De Leon claimed that he was merely distributing manuscripts that he had copied of a previously unknown work of midrash originating in the land of Israel. The influence of the *Zohar* upon halakhic practice among many Jews had to do in part with the traditional belief in the *Zohar*'s antiquity.

Beginning in the fourteenth and fifteenth centuries, the traditions of Spanish Kabbalah were carried to many parts of the Jewish world, including the Franco-Ashkenazi provinces. It was in the sixteenth century, however, in the wake of the expulsion of Jewry from Spain and the forced mass conversion of the Jews of Portugal, that Kabbalah experienced its most powerful renaissance. Exiled Jews from the Iberian Peninsula brought with them to Italy, North Africa, and the Ottoman Empire the literature of Kabbalah and knowledge of its practice. In Italy, even prior to the Spanish Expulsion, a distinctive orientation emerged in which Kabbalah was interpreted in philosophical ways and was suffused with magical techniques.

The most consequential resurgence of post-Expulsion Kabbalah occurred, however, in the land of Israel, especially after it became part of the Ottoman Empire in 1517. The small Galilean village of Safed emerged as the scene of an intense messianically oriented mystical community, the foundations of which were built upon earlier Kabbalah. The most important figures associated with Safed were Moses Cordovero (1522–1570) and Isaac Luria (1534–1572).

These several different phases of theosophical Kabbalah contributed in innumerable ways to the realm of Jewish practice. In the first place, the kabbalists taught that the traditional precepts, the 613 *mitsvot,* were to be performed accompanied by specific contemplative intentions, called *kavvanot*. These *kavvanot* enabled the practicing kabbalist to focus in a meditative way upon the *sefirot* while performing the *mitsvot*. This was also true when it came to the liturgy. For a kabbalist, the words of the prayerbook were understood as an elaborate structure by which they could contemplatively ascend the ladder of the ten *sefirot*.

But in addition to investing existing rituals with kabbalistic significance, kabbalists also created altogether new rituals of many types. This phenomenon reached its highest stage of development in sixteenth-century Safed, where a vast array of kabbalistic rites evolved, many of which are still practiced. The most well-known (and still widely practiced) of these is the preliminary service that precedes the evening service on Sabbath eve. Known as *Kabbalat Shabbat* (Welcoming the Sabbath), the chanting of this collection of psalms and songs is intended to be a way of ushering in the Sabbath by welcoming the Sabbath Bride, understood in kabbalistic terms as a feminine dimension of divinity, the *Shekhinah* (divine presence). Examples of just a few of the ways in which Kabbalah influenced and elaborated upon Jewish ritual may be found in the chapters entitled "Adorning the 'Bride' on the Eve of the Feast of Weeks," "New Year's Day for Fruit of the Tree," "Mystical Eating and Food Practices in the *Zohar*," "Pietistic Customs from Safed," and "Jewish Exorcism: Early Modern Traditions and Transformations."

In the seventeenth century, the most significant expression of kabbalistic life was the turbulent messianic movement known as Sabbatianism, which galvanized around the charismatic but troubled personality of the Turkish Jew Shabbatai Zvi (1626–1676). Zvi (also called Sabbatai Zevi or Sevi) became infamous for his claims to messiahship, his dramatic mood swings, his practice of violating Jewish law, and his eventual apostasy when he converted to Islam under duress. For much of the seventeenth century, the Jewish world was thrown into turmoil as communities became caught up in Shabbatai Zvi's activities and the intense controversies they generated. The chapter "The Early Messianic Career of Shabbatai Zvi" provides a description of Shabbatai's life by one of his followers.

Kabbalah survived the turmoil of the Sabbatian movement, but by the eighteenth century it had lost much of its potency as a living force. This was partly a consequence of the vast challenges to all types of traditional Judaism posed by the assimilationist and secularizing trajectory of modernity. At the same time, an altogether different development coopted the creative energies of Kabbalah, namely, eastern European Hasidism. Hasidism was a mass pietistic movement that originated in the rural villages of southeast Poland in the middle of the eighteenth century. Israel ben Eliezer (1700–1760), better known by his title, the Baal Shem Tov (Master of the Good Name), was a charismatic figure around whom the earliest Hasidim coalesced. As a popular movement, the Hasidic rebbes (or *tsaddiqim,* lit., righteous ones) taught that God could be served through the practice of contemplative prayer and ecstatic song and dance. One did not need to be a master of talmudic tradition in order to serve God properly. Rather, Hasidism placed a premium upon the emotional and spontaneous expression of the love of God. In contrast to the more complex mythic symbolism of the older Kabbalah, Hasidism had a simpler teaching. Sparks of divine light from above are present in every single dimension of reality. The more material the phenomenon, the more concealed the sparks seem to be. The spiritual task is to make oneself aware of the divine life force that lies at the heart of all things, and by doing so to "raise up" these sparks to the source on high from which they derive. Drawing in part upon kabbalistic ritual, the Hasidim developed a vast array of distinctive customs and practices of their own, especially in the sphere of prayer. The spiritual vitality that Hasidism manifested is illustrated in "Menahem Nahum of Chernobyl: Personal Practices of a Hasidic Master," and some of the legendary traditions concerning the life of Hasidism's central early figure are the subject of "Israel ben Eliezer, the Baal Shem Tov."

Sectarian Judaism

Religious diversity of a different type was a result of certain sectarian forms of Jewish religious practice. Sectarianism had been a prominent feature of Judaism in the several centuries immediately preceding the destruction of the second Temple. During the Hellenistic, or intertestamental period, that is, from about 300 B.C.E. through 70 C.E., a variety of sectarian groups lived alongside one another, and to a significant degree competed with one another. This was the period during which the Pharisees, Sadducees, Dead Sea Sect, Zealots, Jewish-Christians, and certain other lesser-known groups flourished. In the wake of the Roman destruction of the Temple, only the Pharisees and the Jewish-Christians survived as groups. The former served as the nucleus for what would become the rabbinic movement, whereas the latter gradually evolved into a full-fledged Christian community, now with an identity completely separate from the Judaism from which it had originally come. The success of the rabbinic movement within the Jewish community was such that in the course of the Middle Ages few sectarian groups emerged to compete with it. And when they did, they met with relatively limited success. It was not until the nineteenth century that rabbinic Judaism would find its authority significantly undermined by competing sectarian forms, namely, Reform and Conservative Judaism.

Nevertheless, there were some sectarian groups during the Middle Ages that contributed in substantial ways to religious diversity. The best-known and important of these from an historical point of view was the Karaites (from the word *mikra,* scripture), a group that emerged in Iraq in the eighth century. Karaism represented the only serious attempt to challenge the dominance of the rabbinic movement. The origins of the Karaites lies partly in political opposition to the expanding authority of the Babylonian ge'onim, whom we discussed earlier. At the center of this opposition was the figure of Anan ben David, a learned and aristocratic individual. According to some accounts, Anan had been a member of the powerful family of the Babylonian exilarch, the title held by the political head of the Jewish community in Iraq. A tendentious rabbanite account of Anan's sectarianism contended that Anan had been motivated by having been passed over for appointment to the office of the exilarch.

In any event, Anan helped to forge a schismatic movement the central principle of which was that the interpretation and practice of the Torah which the rabbinic movement had produced was, in fact, illegitimate. Instead, Anan argued that Jews must return to the practice of the Torah as it was originally intended, shorn of the elaborate misreading of it perpetrated by rabbinic sages. He believed, further, that individuals should have some freedom to interpret scripture on their own, although such independence was to be limited by the Karaites' own traditions. Anan composed a legal code of his own, *Sefer ha-Mitsvot* (Book of Commandments), in which he gathered together elements of a sectarian *halakhah*, intended to compete with rabbinic law. Despite the fact that he had repudiated the exegesis of Scripture as practiced by rabbinic authorities, ironically Anan employed similar techniques in arguing for his own version of "pure" Jewish teaching. One of the important results of Karaism was that it led to vigorous study of the Bible, even by rabbinic Jews, and inspired a new interest in the Hebrew language, its grammar, and lexicography.

Anan's approach to Scripture was particularly attractive to certain communities that were not yet firmly under the influence of the Babylonian authorities, including those in Persia. Subsequent Karaite leaders, including Benjamin al-Nahawendi and Daniel al-Qumisi, modified Anan's original teachings and developed their own traditions of scriptural interpretation and ritual practice. The Karaite rejection of rabbinic tradition was not motivated by a desire to make religious life simpler or easier. On the contrary, it was characterized by a pronounced ascetic quality—teaching, for example, that not only could lights not be kindled once the Sabbath had begun, but that even light kindled before the onset of the Sabbath was prohibited. This question eventually became the subject of controversy among the Karaites themselves. Besides a more literalist understanding of the laws of the Sabbath, other Karaite customs included not blowing the ram's horn (*shofar*) on Rosh Hashanah (the New Year festival), not waving the "four species" of plants on the festival of Sukkot, and ignoring the holiday of Hanukkah, since it is not mentioned in the Bible. The Karaites were also known for especially stringent taboos with respect to the laws of marriage between relatives.

Although the Karaites never came close to usurping rabbinical hegemony, they did succeed in attracting many followers, including distinguished scholars. By the end of the eleventh century, the Karaites had adherents in almost all of the Jewish communities of the Islamic world and the Byzantine Empire, in Palestine and Egypt, North Africa, Spain, and Asia Minor. The Karaites themselves, however, regarded the Jewish diaspora as a tragic reality. For they emphasized the obligation to live in the land of Israel, and especially believed in the messianic significance of residing in Jerusalem and practicing ascetic rites of purification. The Karaite movement began to decline in the Islamic East in the twelfth century, but continued to survive in Egypt until recently. The Karaite community in the Byzantine Empire, the center of which was in Constantinople, eventually spread as far as the Crimea and Lithuania, where it too existed until modern times. Remarkably, there are still minor Karaite communities in Israel, Turkey, and a few other places.

Although Karaism was the most significant heterodox movement in medieval Judaism, it was not the only one. The same ferment engendered by the spread of Islam that helped give rise to the Karaites also provided the conditions for a number of other smaller Near Eastern sectarian groups, all of which appear to have died out before too long. Some of these groups are described in the chapter "Jewish Sectarianism in the Near East: A Muslim's Account," and the distinctive rites of the Karaites are depicted in "Karaite Ritual."

Communities on the Margins

In addition to these sectarian phenomena, some of the most interesting forms of religious practice developed among communities living at the cultural and geographical margins of the rest of Jewry. Certain communities that were far removed from the vast bulk of Jews living in the Near East and Europe, and living under altogether different cultural conditions, adapted Judaism in unusual ways. In contrast to a sectarian group such as the Karaites, which self-consciously distinguished itself from mainstream rabbinic Judaism, these communities at the margins did not possess such antagonistic motives. Indeed, typically, they had little or no knowledge of rabbinic practice. Instead, they fashioned syncretistic Jewish identities that reflected the distinctive cultures in which they found themselves, and that enabled them to assimilate to those cultures without losing their Jewish identity.

The most prominent examples of such syncretism are the Jewish communities of China, India, and Ethiopia. In the case of China, individual Jewish merchants arrived there along with other western traders, perhaps as early as the second or first century B.C.E., in the view of some scholars. The earliest extant evidence of their presence there, however, dates only from the beginning of the eighth century. Little is known about these early Jewish settlers, and it is difficult to estimate how many there were. We have more information about the Jewish community in Kaifeng. This community traces its origins back to the eleventh century, when approximately a thousand Jews, bringing cotton from either Persia or India, were given permission to settle in this town in central China. A synagogue was built in Kaifeng, and was rebuilt several times over the years. Three monuments, or steles, were erected in the courtyard of the synagogue in 1489, 1512, and 1663. The chapter in our anthology, entitled "Living Judaism in Confucian Culture: Being Jewish and Being Chinese," contains a translation from Chinese of the stele of 1489. As Jonathan Lipman points out, we learn from the inscription on this stele that its author, a certain Jin Zhong, "put Chinese prose into the mind of Abraham, Chinese virtues into the character of Moses, Chinese ritual rectitude into the behavior of Ezra." Although they thoroughly appropriated Confucian ways, as did other foreign religions transplanted into China, Kaifeng's Jews nevertheless "survived as Jews for almost a thousand years with a synagogue, Hebrew texts and leaders who could read them, and ritual observances at odds with the overwhelmingly large populations around them."

Prior to the period of British colonialism, there existed two distinct Jewish communities in India, the Bene Israel (Children of Israel) in the Konkan region in the present-day state of Maharashtra, and the Jews of Cochin, in the region of Kerala. The larger of these two separate groups, the Bene Israel, regard themselves as descendants of Jews who fled the persecutions of the Syrian ruler Antiochus Epiphanes in the second century B.C.E., but they are not mentioned in any sources other than their own prior to their first contact with Cochin Jews in the eighteenth century. The Bene Israel assimilated to the surrounding culture by adopting the Marathi language, along with local customs and dress, and by employing the names of their Hindu neighbors. Living in a Hindu culture, where they did not experience hostility or persecution, the Bene Israel developed an appreciative understanding and positive attitude toward aspects of Hindu beliefs and values. This included Hindu teachings concerning nonviolence and the sanctity of all life. Until recently, for example, the Bene Israel believed that the eating of beef was prohibited by the Torah—a practice, of course, that conforms to Hinduism. On the other hand, they adhered with great devotion to significant elements of Jewish practice, including circumcision, the dietary laws, the Sabbath, certain Hebrew prayers, and some traditional festivals. In the eighteenth century, Ezekial David Rahabi (1694–1771) of Syria became acquainted with the Bene Israel as a result of his travels in the service of the Dutch East India Company. Struck by their ignorance of Jewish traditions, Rahabi set out to teach the community Hebrew and prayers, and arranged for their instruction throughout the many villages in which the Bene Israel were dispersed. By the middle of the eighteenth century, the Bene Israel began to settle in Bombay, where they built a synagogue in 1796. Beginning in the 1920s, many Bene Israel became Zionists and eventually settled in Israel.

Evidence concerning the Jews of Cochin goes back to about the year 1000. According to inscriptions on copper tablets, long in the possession of the Jews of Cochin, the Hindu ruler of Malabar granted privileges to settle to a certain Yosef Rabban. The famous Jewish traveler Benjamin of Tudela wrote of the presence of a thousand Black Jews on the Malabar Coast in about 1170. This community presumably resulted from the marriage of early Jewish male immigrants to local Indian women, along with others who may have converted to Judaism. According to Benjamin, they "are good men, observe the Law, possess the Torah of Moses, the Prophets, and have some knowledge of the Talmud and the *halakhah*."

A good deal more information about Cochin Jewry derives from the fifteenth century. The Portuguese destroyed the Jewish settlement of Cranganore, north of Cochin, in 1524. Refugees from this community, along with Jewish exiles from Spain, Portugal, and elsewhere, were granted land by the raja of Cochin in order to resettle. Known even to this day as "Jew Town," the community established the Paradesi (foreigners') synagogue there in 1568. When the Portuguese were defeated militarily by the Dutch in the seventeenth century, the Cochin community began a period in which they flourished. Dutch Jews became interested in the far-away community and provided it with support, including gifts of Hebrew books. According to one important historical report from this period, there were nine synagogues with a membership of 465 households of "White" Jews who had come to Cochin from Cranganore, Castile, Algiers, Jerusalem, Safed, Syria, Baghdad, and Germany. Two rather separate communities thus evolved among the Cochin Jews, Black and White, each maintaining a distinctive identity and their own communal institutions.

Over the course of the last three centuries, the religious practice of the Cochin Jews was significantly influenced by contact with Jews who continued to arrive in India. In particular, the aforementioned Rahabi family played a central role in this connection. Ezekial Rahabi's father, David Rahabi (d. 1726), instructed the Jews of Cochin in the beliefs and practices of the ancient community of Aleppo, from which he had emigrated in 1664. Rahabi's descendants continued this activity, so that by the eighteenth century the religious life of the Cochin community essentially conformed to the pattern of Syrian Jewry, including the study of the Talmud. There were approximately 2,500 Black and a mere 100 White Cochin Jews remaining in India in 1948. Shortly after the establishment of the state of Israel all the Black Jews settled there, whereas most of the White Jews remained. By 1968, there were some 4,000 Cochin Jews in Israel.

The Black Jews of Ethiopia refer to themselves as Beta Israel (House of Israel), although they are better known as Falashas, meaning "foreigners" or "wanderers," a name given to them by other Ethiopians. Although the Beta Israel have their own traditions concerning their ancestry, most scholars believe that the origins of Ethiopian Jewry go back to Jewish cultural influences from the Arabian Peninsula that made an impact upon Ethiopia. It is possible, however, to reconstruct the history of this community only from the thirteenth century forward. The religious practices of the Beta Israel are based on the Torah and other books of the Hebrew Bible, as well as certain ancient noncanonical Jewish books.

Like many other communities on the margins, the Beta Israel were unfamiliar with the literature of rabbinic tradition, Mishnah and Gemara, and the midrashim. This unfamiliarity is readily apparent, for example, in their Sabbath rites, which closely parallel the noncanonical Book of Jubilees. Thus, for instance, according to both Jubilees and Falasha legal tradition, marital relations are forbidden on the Sabbath, in direct contrast with rabbinic tradition, which teaches that sexual relations between a husband and wife on the Sabbath are highly desirable. As with the early Karaites, but unlike rabbinic law, the Beta Israel believed that the Torah (Exod. 35:3) proscribed not only kindling fire on the Sabbath itself but before the Sabbath as well. Thus it seems that Falashas did not kindle lights on Sabbath eve, or employ methods to keep food warm during the Sabbath.

Strong evidence for the rootedness of Falasha practice in biblical law may be seen in their highly elaborate purity rites. Falashas believed that any contact with individuals outside of their community could generate a state of ritual impurity, and necessitated purification by way of ritual bathing, a rite that constituted one of their most important practices. The Falashas used ritual purity as a means of preserving their separateness from people beyond their own community. As Michael Corinaldi points out in his study of Falasha identity, "Falasha villages were built near rivers, so as to make immersion easier, and the Ethiopian Jews, both male and female, regularly bathed before the Sabbath, the women after each menstrual cycle as well. Ritual immersion was [also] essential for purification after contact with strangers, and it had to be performed in the running waters of a river—'live waters.' "[2] With the settlement of most of the remaining Jews of Ethiopia in Israel, the Falashas have increasingly taken on the ritual practices of rabbinic Judaism.

Finally, it should be pointed out that there have been many other Jewish communities on the margins that developed distinctive religious identities and practices, especially in Inner Asia, such as the Jews of Georgia in the Caucasian Mountains, and the Jews of Bukhara, Kurdistan, Uzbekistan, and Afghanistan.

Women and Judaism

There is a whole other group of Jews whose religious lives and practices have not received the attention they deserve in accounts of Jewish religious life, for reasons having nothing to do with geographical isolation. Until recently, the modern study of Judaism virtually ignored the history of women. This is especially apparent when it comes to premodern Judaism. Jewish scholarship is only now beginning to turn its attention in a serious way to the question of women and Judaism. The most frustrating difficulty in the study of the history of Jewish women has to do with the fact that we have only the scantiest evidence from women themselves. We are almost entirely dependent upon sources of various types written by men, and thus must use these sources in creative ways to learn as much as possible about the actual religious lives of women. Beyond the idealized expectations men had with respect to how women should behave, and beyond the halakhic parameters that prescribed what women were and were not supposed to do, what do we know about the actual religious lives of Jewish women in the Middle Ages and the early modern period? Although the study of what was expected of women by men is a significant question, it is hardly the whole story. We are learning increasingly not only about how *halakha* limited opportunities for women, particularly in the realm of public, communal ritual, but also about how women found diverse ways to cultivate and express religious life.

As several chapters in this book indicate, rabbinic law significantly circumscribed women's religious activities. According to traditional Jewish law, women are obligated to practice all those *mitsvot* that are formulated in negative terms, that is, prohibitions, of which there are 365. Thus, for example, women, like men, must refrain from practicing idolatry, from blaspheming God's name, from eating unpermitted foods, from stealing, perpetrating injustice, or from committing murder. As for the 248 positively formulated *mitsvot,* women are obligated, in general, to practice all except whose enactment are time-bound, that is, limited to a specific time. Examples of positive precepts that women are obligated to practice include resting on the Sabbath and other festivals (although they are not obligated to observe every ritual of these celebrations), returning lost property to its owner, giving charity to the poor, loving one's neighbor, and honoring one's parents.

Positive commandments that are considered bound by a specific time, and that women were thus exempt from performing, included the obligation of formal, public prayer, insofar as the three daily prayer services must be performed within specific hours of the day. Rabbinic tradition does not provide clear or elaborate rationales for this important exemption, but there is every reason to infer that the primary motive was that women were expected to attend to their domestic responsibilities without being distracted by the requirement of making a public appearance three times a day for communal prayer.

Insofar as women were exempt from the religious obligation of participating in public prayer, rabbinic tradition taught that they were prohibited from being counted as part of a quorum (*minyan*) of ten adults required for communal worship, as well as from leading the congregation in prayer. Nor were they permitted to come up to the Torah for an *aliyah,* an honor involving the recitation of a blessing during the reading of the Torah in the synagogue. On the other hand, women certainly could go to the synagogue, as they tended to on Sabbaths and important festivals. When they did attend synagogue, women sat in a separate section or gallery, although it is clear that such separation of the sexes was not a fully established practice until the late twelfth and early thirteenth centuries. Girls who came from wealthier or more highly educated families, especially rabbinic families, tended to have higher levels of literacy and education themselves, and could thus more fully participate in synagogue services. In fact, we know that beginning in the twelfth and thirteenth centuries in Germany and France, such learned women often served as prayer leaders within the women's galleries. Women also participated in the life of the synagogue in other ways. Sometimes poor women would serve as beadles or caretakers, whereas wealthier women contributed financially to the support of the synagogue by donating not only money but also such items as Torah scrolls, oil for lamps, and prayer books.

Although these are the general principles set forth by rabbinic tradition, there are important exceptions to them. The most significant exception has to do with the study of Torah, that is, the study of sacred texts as a whole. Even though this is a precept that is not bound by a specific time (one can study at any time of the day), women are nevertheless not obligated to such study. Exemption in this case, as in many other cases, often translated into de facto exclusion. According to one well-known passage in the Mishnah (*Sotah* 3:4) pertaining to this question, a sage by the name of Ben Azzai teaches that "a man is obligated to teach his daughter the law" (*torah*), but Rabbi Eliezer opposes this by arguing that "if anyone teaches his daughter the law, it as though he taught her lasciviousness." Even though this rabbinic discussion appears to concern whether daughters should be taught about a certain matter of Jewish law in particular, many medieval authorities cited Eliezer's view to justify the exclusion of women from studying altogether.

Not all rabbinic authorities, however, shared this view. In her chapter "Women and Ritual Immersion in Medieval Ashkenaz: The Sexual Politics of Piety," Judith

Baskin provides the view of the German Pietistic text, *Sefer Hasidim,* a work not normally known for liberal attitudes. It promotes education for girls in the practical areas that pertain to them: "A father is obligated to teach his daughters the commandments, including halakhic rules. This may appear to contradict the talmudic ruling. . . . However, the rabbis were referring to deep immersion in Talmudic study, discussion of the reasons behind the commandments, and mystical understandings of the Torah. These should never be taught to a woman or to a minor. But one must teach her practical laws because if she does not know the rules for the Sabbath, how will she observe the Sabbath? The same goes for all the other commandments she must perform."

Despite this view, and others like it, the exemption from all but rudimentary study had incalculable consequences for women. Religious study, nearly universally practiced by Jewish males, was considered the most essential ritual of Judaism, as the most desirable activity, and as the crucial ingredient in religious life. It was also the primary means of achieving power and prestige within the religious community. With very few exceptions, only men possessed advanced knowledge of Jewish law and tradition, and certainly only men became rabbis. And only rabbis had responsibility for the further evolution of that tradition, even when it directly affected the lives of women, for example in matters of marriage and divorce. Thus, even though study of Torah is but one precept out of 613, its significance was extraordinary. The exemption from participating in communal prayer, together with the exemption from formally studying sacred texts, served to limit dramatically women's involvement in the two spiritual activities most prized by traditional male Jews.

On the other hand, there are three precepts that are considered specifically to be "women's *mitsvot,*" including the practice of ritual immersion (*tevilah*) following the menstrual period (see Baskin, "Women and Ritual Immersion"), the lighting of Sabbath candles to usher in the Sabbath on Friday evening, and the baking of *challah* bread for the celebration of the Sabbath. More generally, women's religious lives revolved primarily around the home and family, which in premodern Judaism occupied an especially crucial role in Jewish practice. Women were responsible, for example, for maintaining the dietary laws, the laws of *kashrut.* In fact, women were sometimes consulted about fine points of these complex laws by rabbinic authorities. Women also instructed their young children, especially their daughters, in aspects of the tradition.

But women managed to devise various other ways, as well, to engage in religious practice, as evidenced by many of the chapters in this volume. Our sourcebook includes a wide variety of materials that attest to the fact that despite the restrictions imposed by tradition upon women's practice, women nevertheless were involved in many different activities, including prayer. In one of the texts in the chapter "Karaite Ritual," for example, we learn that Karaite women were expressly included in instructions concerning proper prayer: "The Congregation, both men and women, should concentrate their attention behind the leader. Both men and women should pray in soberness and purity. . . . Neither men nor women in the

INTRODUCTION 29

congregation should occupy their minds with news or gossip, lest their worship be spoiled." According to the testimony of an ordinary Jew by the name of Eleazar of Mainz (d. 1357): "They [my sons and daughters] should attend synagogue in the morning and in the evening where they should be particularly attentive to the recitation of the standing prayer and the *Shema*" (see Baskin, "Women and Ritual Immersion").

For centuries, Ashkenazic women, during the period of Rosh Hashanah and Yom Kippur (New Year and Day of Atonement), made special candles and engaged in special prayers of supplication in Yiddish. These were for the purpose of memorializing deceased ancestors as well as for praying for the living. More generally, Yiddish petitionary prayers, *tekhinnes*, were part of a rich devotional literature written expressly for and often by Ashkenazic women, and described in the chapter "Measuring Graves and Laying Wicks." The *tekhinnes* are important historical evidence inasmuch as they constitute the only premodern corpus of religious literature that was composed, at least in significant part, by women themselves. These prayers and rituals provide unusual and invaluable insight into the nature of religious experience among Ashkenazic women, connected especially but not exclusively to affairs of the household, preparation of food, family and children, and home celebrations associated with the Sabbath and other festivals, as well as pregnancy and childbirth. The business, domestic, and religious life of women in early modern *Ashkenaz* is also vividly described by Glikl of Hameln (seventeenth to eighteenth centuries). Glikl left us a fascinating lengthy autobiographical account of her life, with detailed descriptions of weddings and marriages, relationships between children and parents, her moral values, and, perhaps most interesting of all, her ruminations on matters of faith and God. This exceptionally important document is among the first full-fledged Jewish autobiographies, and certainly the first authored by a woman. Selections from it are found in the chapter "The Life of Glikl of Hameln."

We find that in early modern Italy, women took a special interest in prayer, as well. There is evidence that some women practiced the donning of *tephillin* (phylacteries), the leather boxes and straps worn by men during the daily morning services, although authorities apparently sought to prohibit such behavior. We learn about quarrels by women over the seating arrangements in the women's section of the synagogue in sixteenth-century Verona, and that in Modena women practiced the custom of interrupting the service in order to announce publicly their grievances against particular men in connection with various kinds of domestic matters.

From early modern Italy we also learn that some women chose to adopt certain special pietistic practices, including voluntary regimens of fasting, whereas others became expert ritual slaughterers, and that a number of private rituals were practiced by women, including the custom that a woman in labor would hold a scroll of the Torah as a protective means of easing her delivery. Our knowledge of many of these phenomena derives from evidence preserved in halakhic literature in which rabbinic authorities either question such behavior or seek to prohibit it altogether.

An especially interesting form of women's piety occurred among Spanish crypto-Jewish women, or *conversas,* beginning in the fourteenth century. These were individuals who, along with Jewish men, converted to Catholicism either as a consequence of forced conversion or under the pressure of the Spanish Inquisition, but who continued to practice Judaism surreptitiously. That is, in public they behaved as Christians, but in private they placed themselves at risk by maintaining as much Jewish ritual as possible. In the chapter entitled "Life-Cycle Rituals of Spanish Crypto-Jewish Women," we discover a wide variety of ways in which *conversas* preserved their faith by adapting Jewish rituals to the dangerous circumstances in which they found themselves. In a related chapter, "Visionary Experiences among Spanish Crypto-Jewish Women," we find that around the beginning of the sixteenth century messianic ferment emerged among the *converso* communities of the region of Extremadura, and that certain young *conversa* girls experienced prophetic visions that they proclaimed publicly.

Although they are not represented in this volume, it is worth noting that we have other examples of visionary women in premodern Judaism. We know that in the kabbalistic community of sixteenth-century Safed there was a small number of women who were known as mystical visionaries, although they were not participants in the formal, organized activities of kabbalistic men. In the seventeenth century, there were women associated with the Sabbatian movement who cultivated visionary experiences of a prophetic type. It is significant that in the case of both *conversas* and Sabbatian women this behavior manifested itself in circumstances where traditional Jewish law had been subverted, although for very different reasons. These were both communities where the normal rules of Jewish behavior did not apply, and in which some individuals expressed themselves in ways that were highly unusual for Jewish women. This is consistent with historical patterns in other religious traditions, where often under anomalous conditions women find ways of going beyond the boundaries normally placed upon them. The case of sixteenth-century Safed is especially interesting in this connection, for this was not a culture in which traditional rules had been broken. On the other hand, it was a period in which revelatory and visionary experiences were highly prized and quite common among male kabbalists.

Along somewhat different lines, we have evidence that there were certain rituals in which women once played a significant part but from which they were eventually excluded, or at least marginalized. In "The Role of Women at Rituals of Their Infant Children," we discover that mothers were at one time more actively involved in the rituals of circumcision of sons (*brit milah*) and "redemption of the firstborn son" (*pidyon ha-ben*). According to the ninth-century prayer book of Rav Amram Gaon, the first known comprehensive prayer book, the mother of an infant about to be ritually circumcised was integrally involved in the ceremony. Prayers were made on behalf of her healing, and she was given a cup of wine to drink. In connection with redemption of the firstborn son, we learn that not only was the mother expected to be present but also that she testified personally to the standing of the firstborn in question. Even more, despite the fact that only the father is obligated to redeem the son, the geonic ritual has the mother saying "*We* are obliged to redeem him." On the other hand, there is evidence that the involvement of mothers in such ways in these two rituals was deliberately curtailed by subsequent European rabbinic authorities.

Finally, evidence concerning the faithfulness of Jewish women to God in the face of the most extreme duress derives from the Crusade chronicles, referred to earlier. As Robert Chazan points out in his introduction to the *Mainz Anonymous*, a narrative account of the Crusade of 1096, women are depicted as having played a central role in choosing martyrdom for themselves and their children rather than submit to baptism. The most compelling episode in this account concerns a women by the name of Rachel, whose anguish over her unbearable situation is described in the most poignant terms. Taken together, the kinds of evidence presented in this volume make it clear that the realities of medieval and early modern Jewish women's religious lives were far more complex than once realized. It also suggests that the study of the history of women in premodern Judaism is still in its infancy and that there is much more to be discovered.

The Religious Lives of Ordinary People

In the recent past, historians of religion have given increased attention to the lives of ordinary people, a type of inquiry often referred to as "popular religion." Such inquiry is especially significant in the study of Judaism in light of the fact that Jewish scholarship has historically focused on "normative" religious activities prescribed by elite authorities. Judaism tends to be viewed through the lenses of the texts written by rabbinic authorities and the intelligentsia, the systems of beliefs espoused by philosophers, mystics, and ethicists, and the expectations for religious practice prescribed in halakhic literature. Although there is, of course, a significant correlation between these and the experiences of ordinary individuals, the realities are more complex. Just as we have seen that women's religious lives cannot be measured simply in terms of normative rabbinic expectations, the same is true with respect to the lives of ordinary people as a whole (which included most women). The actual religious experience of most people was informed by an endless and variegated array of folk customs, popular superstitions, and magical practices, sometimes sanctioned by rabbinic authorities, and sometimes discouraged or even repudiated by them.

We have already seen examples of such phenomena in connection with women's rituals. Women's practice of making special candles on certain occasions, of holding a Torah scroll while giving birth, and innumerable other customs associated with women's life experiences attest to the great significance of rituals generated from among the folk themselves. But the lives of both men and women were equally shaped by such forces "on the ground," as illustrated in a number of the chapters in this book. In the chapter "Honey Cakes and Torah: A Jewish Boy Learns His Letters," for example, we learn about a folk ritual practiced by medieval Ashkenazic Jews in connection with the initiation of very young boys into formal schooling. On the morning of the festival of Shavuot a young boy would be brought to a teacher and seated upon his lap, shown a tablet on which the letters of the Hebrew alphabet had been written, have the letters read to him, and eventually invited to lick off honey that had been smeared upon the writing on the tablet. He would similarly be given to eat various other foods upon which Hebrew letters and words had been written; this was intended to inaugurate the experience of Torah study as one of sweetness. Moreover, he would be asked to recite a magical incantation adjuring the "prince of forgetfulness" so that his learning would forever remain with him. As Ivan Marcus makes clear, these folk practices were influenced by the Christian environment, as Jews creatively adapted or responded to non-Jewish cultural phenomena, a process quite common in connection with popular rituals.

As the chapter in this volume entitled "The Book of the Great Name" suggests, the practice of magic in Judaism is well documented as far back as the Greco-Roman world. An interest in magic was widespread in the Middle Ages, as evidenced by the extensive number of Hebrew manuscripts and printed books devoted to this subject, along with huge numbers of amulets containing magical inscriptions. Jewish magic entailed such features as invoking the names of angels and demons, and employing various types of unusual, often esoteric, names of God in a formulaic, ritualistic manner. As the case with other religious traditions, magic among premodern Jews was typically used for purposes of satisfying some personal need on the part of a practitioner, such as acquiring esoteric knowledge, divining the future, healing illness, and most frequently, appeasing and warding off evil powers. Magic could be practiced by individuals equipped with complex and sophisticated specialized knowledge, as well as by the simplest individuals armed with little more than common, well-known formulaic incantations.

Another chapter in this volume that illustrates well the religion of the folk is "Jewish Exorcism: Early Modern Traditions and Transformations." Here we learn about a range of ritual techniques designed to extirpate evil spirits from those believed to be demonically possessed. Such undesirable spirit possession is well documented in Judaism, although cases of ritual exorcism proliferated in the sixteenth and seventeenth centuries, especially in communities influenced by Kabbalah. Even though rabbinic authorities sometimes regarded certain expressions of popular religion with wariness, rabbis themselves were hardly immune from the appeal of these practices. An excellent example of this is offered in "Leon Modena's Autobiography," where we find that this prominent seventeenth-century Venetian rabbi was fascinated with astrology, various forms of divination, and alchemy, as were many other members of the rabbinic elite in the medieval and early modern periods.

Ethical Practice

Beginning with the Hebrew Bible itself, one of the central foundations of Judaism has been the practice of ethical behavior and proper interpersonal relations. The Torah is replete with ethical instruction: honoring one's parents; valuing human life; protection and compassion for the vulnerable in society: the poor, the widow, the orphan, and the stranger; dealing justly and honestly in business and in judicial matters; not bearing a grudge; and loving one's neighbor as oneself. The sages of the rabbinic period took up all of these issues and more, concentrating great intellectual energy on the complex questions of virtuous human conduct. Their teachings on these matters are found scattered across the vast sea of rabbinic literature, the Talmuds, and midrashim.

For the most part, it was not until the medieval period that we see attempts to organize ethical theory and ethical practices in a systematic manner. A significant genre of ethical literature appeared beginning in the tenth century, often written by religious philosophers. This includes such classics as the last chapter of Saadia Gaon's *Book of Doctrines and Beliefs,* Moses Maimonides' *Eight Chapters,* Jonah Gerondi's *The Gates of Repentance,* and Bahya ibn Pakuda's *Duties of the Heart.* Beginning with the sixteenth century, kabbalists also produced influential ethical treatises based upon their own particular brand of esoteric metaphysics. Many of the most popular ethical works among Jewry in the late medieval and early modern periods derived from this synthesis of Kabbalah and ethics. Among the most important of these are Moses Cordovero's *Palm Tree of Deborah,* Elijah de Vidas's *The Beginning of Wisdom*, Eleazar Azikri's *Book of the Devout,* Isaiah Horowitz's *Two Tablets of the Covenant,* and Zvi Hirsch Kaidanover's *The Straight Path.*

A number of the chapters in *Judaism in Practice* exemplify medieval and early modern Jewish ethics, although the texts presented here were chosen precisely because they are not part of the above-mentioned classical literatures. In lieu of these better-known treatises, we have selected materials that are slightly off the beaten track. From the mystical community of sixteenth-century Safed we have a number of texts known as *hanhagot* (lit., customs or behaviors). These are in the form of lists that enumerate ritual and ethical practices in a concise manner, either by way of describing how kabbalists of Safed behaved or prescribing how they ought to behave. The two sets of *hanhagot* presented in "Pietistic Customs from Safed" were authored by Abraham Galante and Abraham Berukhim, and provide a valuable window onto the distinctive ethical and spiritual life of this community. The interpersonal aspirations of another kabbalistic community are presented in the chapter entitled "A Mystical Fellowship in Jerusalem." Here we find a "contract" agreed to by the members of a small, intentional kabbalistic fellowship of the seventeenth century that called itself *Ahavat Shalom* (The Love of Peace). Among other things, the participants in this brotherhood "agree to love one another with great love of soul and body," and agree that "each one of us will think of his associate as if the latter were part of his very limbs." The *tsaddiqim,* that is, the charismatic masters of the Hasidic movement in Eastern Europe, adapted the earlier kabbalistic habit of writing *hanhagot,* but they did so in a highly personal way by addressing their own disciples and encouraging them to cultivate a spiritual practice. This widespread Hasidic genre is illustrated in our volume by "Rabbi Menahem Nahum of Chernobyl: Personal Practices of a Hasidic Master."

In "The Love of Learning among Polish Jews," we are informed about the responsibility that the vast Polish Jewish community at large assumed for education of its younger male members, about the obligations of hospitality to strangers and the requirements of charity, as well as about the structure of the judicial system intended to ensure communal justice. The ethical practices of women, in particular, are illustrated to some extent in the texts describing the lives of two German-Jewish woman, the twelfth-century Dolce of Worms, and the seventeenth-century Glikl of Hameln. With respect to Dolce, for example, we are told that "she adorned brides and brought them [to their wedding] in appropriate [garments]," and that she "bathed the dead and sewed their garments."

Art and Aesthetics

Finally, we turn our attention to an area of inquiry that has been neglected until recently, namely, the realm of the aesthetic in Jewish history and tradition. Despite the image of Jewish religious culture as more interested in matters of law and intellect than in the sensual and the beautiful, or in the natural world, the fact is that art and aesthetics have played a significant role in Judaism nearly from its beginnings. Artistic sensibilities were central to the building of the portable sanctuary (*mishkan*) in the wilderness by the ancient Israelites as described in the Torah, as well as in connection with the construction of a permanent Temple in Jerusalem, as artisans of all kinds were involved in the building and decoration of the first and second Temples. In the period following the destruction of the second Temple, we have numerous examples of exquisite mosaics on the floors of synagogues throughout the Mediterranean world, along with the famous pictorial murals that adorn the walls of an ancient synagogue at Dura-Europos in Syria. Ancient Israelites, as well as Jews during the Greco-Roman period, also cultivated rich musical traditions that became the basis for the musical cantillation chanted in the synagogue when Scripture is recited. And the literary artistry of so much of the Hebrew Bible, along with the highly imaginative qualities of rabbinic narrative (*midrashim*), represent a sophisticated literary sensibility. Each of these aesthetic impulses—architectural and decorative, pictorial, musical, and literary—found significant expression in medieval and early modern Jewish culture.

In his chapter "Defending, Enjoying, and Regulating the Visual," Kalman Bland demonstrates that despite the biblical prohibition against idolatry and the graphic representation of an incorporeal divinity, Jews were nevertheless artistic. As Bland writes: "If observant Jews are forbidden to worship idols, and they are, it does not follow that they are also forbidden to illuminate manuscripts, engrave burial markers, design jewelry, decorate synagogues with sculptured lions, weave tapestries picturing biblical heroes, hang portraits and paintings on the walls of their homes, or embellish marriage contracts with intricate designs and patterns. Premodern Jews performed all of these visually creative acts."

"Illustrating History and Illuminating Identity in the Art of the Passover Haggadah" presents examples of the often beautiful hand-painted illuminations that accompanied Hebrew manuscripts. Here we see that the pictures which accompanied the text of the Haggadah—the book used at the *seder* meal on the festival of Passover—served as a "countertext and commentary" on the primary liturgical text of the Haggadah. The visual thus played a crucial role in the *seder* celebration. It is worth mentioning in this connection the attention paid to the design of ritual objects so that they might be as beautiful as possible: candlesticks and wine cups for use on Sabbaths and other festivals, *etrog* boxes (to contain the lemonlike fruit used on Sukkot), spice boxes used for *havdalah* (the ritual that accompanies the end of the Sabbath), and so on. This was in keeping with the rabbinic conception of beautifying the performance of a ritual act, in Hebrew, *hiddur mitsvah*.

The preaching of sermons in the synagogue, a practice rooted in late antiquity, provided the opportunity for rabbis to cultivate the rhetorical arts of inspiration, admonition, instruction, and persuasion. As the author of "Jewish Preaching in Fifteenth-Century Spain" suggests, fine preaching was not simply a matter of devising an intelligent, learned, or clever text, but was a performative art that involved "the appearance of the preacher, the sound of his voice, his gestures, the level of his animation, his pace and pitch, his emphases and silences. In the best preachers, the quality of the sermon was dependent not merely upon the power of an intellect, or the quality of writing, but on a highly sophisticated performance art." This chapter includes the only two known examples of guidance in the art of Jewish preaching prior to the modern period, as well as a text that critically assesses the contemporary state of Jewish preaching in fifteenth-century Spain.

The centrality of textual learning in Jewish culture—well represented in this volume—transformed the book into an aesthetic object, above and beyond the illumination of manuscripts already mentioned. Not only were books, handwritten or printed, valued for their fine physical production but they were also to be treated with great care, attention, and even affection. In "The Arts of Calligraphy and Composition, and the Love of Books," we see that fine calligraphy and skill at composition were prized, especially among Jews influenced by Islamic culture. And we learn that books were to be handled and cared for with the utmost respect as physical repositories of sacred tradition.

We hope that taken together, the multifaceted texts in this volume will provide a window onto the diverse worlds of medieval and premodern Jewish religious experience. Although the texts presented here represent, of course, only a tiny fraction of what could have been included in this volume, we believe that they exemplify those diverse worlds in rich, interesting, and significant ways. In lieu of providing a single bibliography, we invite readers to follow the endless paths to study found in the suggestions for further reading included in each chapter.

Notes

1. Menachem Elon, *Jewish Law-History, Sources, Principles* (Philadelphia: Jewish Publication Society, 1994), vol. 3, p. 1,461.

2. Michael Corinaldi, *Jewish Identity: The Case of Ethiopian Jewry* (Jerusalem: Magnes Press, 1998), pp. 74–75.

Rituals of Daily and Festival Practice

1

Communal Prayer and Liturgical Poetry

Raymond P. Scheindlin

The patterns of public prayer, one of the most characteristic rituals of the traditional Jewish religion, are generally held to have been established even before the destruction of the Second Temple (70 C.E.). The texts used in the prayer services were developed in Roman and Byzantine Palestine as well as in Sassanian Babylonia between that date and the early seventh century. They reached their final forms in Abbasid Iraq, especially in the eighth and ninth centuries, thanks to the efforts of the *geonim,* the heads of the rabbinic academies of the time, whose ecumenical authority enabled them to establish the Babylonian Talmud and the rites customary in the rabbinic academies of Iraq as normative for Jews worldwide. The process by which the prayer texts emerged is still unclear in its detail, though its stages are broadly intelligible.

In the earliest stage, the chief public observance seems to have been the public reading of Scripture on Sabbaths and festivals. By 200 C.E., two daily public prayers, one at dawn and one in the late afternoon, were well established. By the time the Babylonian Talmud was completed (c. 500 C.E.), an evening service had also become established. This routine of three daily public services remains the framework of synagogue life. But the central role played by the reading of Scripture in public worship from its beginnings has also left its mark on the development of the synagogue service.

The most obvious ritual involving Scripture, and the central event of the morning service of Sabbaths and festivals, is the formal reading from the Torah, followed by the formal reading of a passage from the Prophets. The Torah is read in consecutive segments beginning after the autumn holiday season and completed in the course of a year. (Throughout the Middle Ages, a few communities followed the alternative practice of completing the reading over a period of three and a half years.) But in a less dramatic way, the reading of Scripture determines the form of the ordinary morning and evening services, as well, for at the heart of these services is a recitation called the Shema ("Hear, O Israel!"), after its first word; this recitation consists of three passages from the Torah (Deut. 6:4–10,

Deut. 11:13–22, and Num. 15:37–41) that are believed to embody the central principles of rabbinic Judaism.

Both the formal reading from Scripture and the recitation of the Shema were accompanied by prayers of a type called *berakha* (pl. *berakhot*), or benedictions. These benedictions, ubiquitous in rabbinic Judaism, both in public and private rituals, were originally—and in some cases remain—short statements of praise in the form "Blessed are you, Lord, our God, King of the world, who. . . ." The relative clause can be a short one describing one of God's activities, as in the familiar blessing recited before eating bread: "Blessed are you, Lord our God, King of the world, who brings bread out of the earth." Sometimes the relative clause is longer, in which case part of the opening formula is repeated to form a conclusion. An example of this form may be found in the first text below. Sometimes the benediction begins with a sentence or two praising God for some act or attribute of his and concludes with the brief formula "Blessed are you, Lord, . . ." An example of this form may be found in the second text.

Like the reading of the Torah, the Shema was given a framework of benedictions, but these were developed more elaborately. In the morning service, the Shema is preceded by two benedictions. The first, or "Creator" benediction, acknowledges God as creator of the luminaries, shaper of night and day, and creator of the world. The second benediction, called "Love," acknowledges God's bestowal of the revelation to Israel in the form of the Torah; it is immediately followed by the three passages from the Torah that make up the Shema. After the Shema, the third benediction, called "Redeemer," formally affirms the truth of the revelation just recited, and goes on to acknowledge God's intervention in Jewish history when He saved the Israelites from Egypt.

The actual wording of these prayers was, in the beginning, somewhat fluid, though the opening and closing phrases as well as some of the wording between these were fairly stable. The prayers tended to expand throughout the long period up until the geonic canonization of the prayer book in the eighth and ninth centuries, as individual worshipers improvised on the familiar texts. Texts 1 through 3 below are early versions of the three benedictions accompanying the Shema. No present-day community uses exactly the wording reproduced here in translation, but the much longer versions that have been recited since geonic times incorporate the wording of these short early versions almost verbatim.

The Shema and its benedictions are followed, in the morning and evening services, by a series of benedictions commonly known as the Amida, or "Standing Prayer." The number and content of its benedictions varies depending on whether the service at which they are recited is a weekday, Sabbath, or festival service. It was designed to be recited by the leader on behalf of the congregation, though early in the history of the liturgy the practice arose of having the congregation first recite the benedictions silently. The benedictions consist of statements of gratitude and petitions for God's favors. This prayer follows the recitation of the Shema in the morning and evening services, and, originally, it made up the entire content of the afternoon service.

Jewish public worship, thus, consists fundamentally of two sets of prayers (the Shema together with its benedictions, and the Amida). But it is also controlled by two cyclical elements: the annual cycle of Torah readings already described, and the annual procession of festivals, beginning with Rosh Hashanah, Yom Kippur, and Sukkot in the fall; Hanukkah in early winter, and Purim in late winter; Pesah and Shavuot in the spring; and the fasts of Tammuz and Av in the summer, with many minor holidays and fast days interspersed among these. Early on, methods were found to coordinate the fixed prayers with these two liturgical cycles, creating a liturgy that was much more dynamic than could be afforded by the daily repetition of nearly identical texts.

This variation was achieved by the introduction of liturgical poetry. The process and chronology by which this development occurred is still unclear, but it is certain that by the end of the Byzantine period (early seventh century) it was normal in at least some congregations to use, instead of the prose texts, versified versions of the prayers that were devised by the prayer leaders. Such prayers in verse form are known in Hebrew as *piyyut* (pl. *piyyutim*), derived from the ordinary Greek word for poet (*poietes*). After the geonic canonization of the prayer book, the poetic versions of the prayers were no longer used in lieu of the simpler prose versions but were recited in addition to them. Thus, for most of the Middle Ages, the prayer service consisted of two kinds of prayers alternating throughout the service: fixed prayers in prose, which were repeated with minor and predictable variations throughout the year, with which the congregation was perfectly familiar, and which were fairly uniform throughout the Jewish world; and prayers in verse form added to each of the benedictions and changed on each Sabbath and festival. In the course of the Middle Ages, the various communities each developed a regular repertoire of such poems, which resulted in fixed cycles of liturgical poetry known as *mahzor* (plural, *mahzorim*), which are the core of the local rites.

The subject matter of *piyyut* derives from the intersecting of the fixed element (the benediction to which the poem is attached) and the varying occasion on which the benediction is recited. This varying element might be supplied by a festival within the annual cycle of festivals, or by the cycle of readings from Scripture. In the early part of the Middle Ages, mahzorim were composed based on the scriptural reading, such that each week of the year (or, for congregations that read the Torah in a triennial cycle, each week of a three-year period) had its own set of liturgical poems recited in lieu of or in addition to the prose prayers. The liturgical poetry became more and more elaborate. In some communities, the familiar short, simple prose texts came to be buried inside a huge and constantly changing architecture of poetic prayers; in such communities, the poetry was the real point of interest in the liturgy, whereas the fixed prayers got little attention.

The result was a very intellectualized type of liturgy, a liturgy resembling *midrash* (pl. *midrashim;* scriptural interpretation) in the sense that its most characteristic technique was the drawing together of ideas from different realms. Just as midrash created an imaginative link between the verse of Scripture chosen as the subject of the homily and an apparently unrelated verse from somewhere else in the Bible, so piyyut created an imaginative link between the fixed benediction and the varying occasion, whether a festival or a scriptural reading. Much of the contents of the piyyut can be traced to the classic midrashim, to the point that piyyut is sometimes characterized as poeticized midrash. But in some periods, the poet had freedom to range far from traditional materials.

Selections 4 through 6 below are piyyutim designed to elaborate on the three benedictions that accompany the Shema. The anonymous Text 4, which was probably composed in Palestine before 600 C.E., belongs to the benediction on light ("Creator," Text 1), and was meant to be recited in the morning service of Yom Kippur, the Day of Atonement. Its overall theme is the congregation's petition to God for forgiveness of sins accumulated during the course of the past year, but because its liturgical function is to elaborate the first benediction, nearly every verse in the poem refers to the word "light," sometimes meant literally as the light of morning and sometimes figuratively as the light of God's forgiveness, guidance, or presence. The references to light are sometimes concrete enough to remind us that the words were meant to be uttered at the first glimmering of dawn, when the Shema was actually recited. The poem is composed in couplets, and is preceded and followed by a three-clause refrain. Such refrains gave the ordinary worshipers the opportunity to participate in the poeticized liturgy, which they could not be expected to know, especially in congregations where new poetry was provided for each service.

Similarly, Texts 5 and 6 are elaborations on the second and third benedictions, which deal with God's love of Israel and redemption. But Texts 5 and 6 come from a very different cultural sphere, for they are by one of the great poets of the Hebrew Golden Age, the period of cultural efflorescence among the Jews of Muslim Spain between the tenth and the twelfth centuries, when poetry became one of the Jews' chief literary activities. Text 5 resembles an Arabic secular love poem; in fact, the first four of its five verses (represented by the first eight lines of the translation) are a close translation from a well-known Arabic poem, which was adapted by Judah Halevi (c. 1075–1141) to introduce the benediction on God's love for Israel. Both poems are written in metrical patterns derived from Arabic and employ a simple, unaffected diction much closer to that of biblical Hebrew than the diction of Text 4.

A more elaborate kind of linkage between benediction and occasion is illustrated by Text 7. The third benediction of the Amida, in its simplest form, celebrates God's attribute of holiness in the words "Holy are you, awesome is your name, and there is no god but you. Blessed are you, Lord, the holy God." Under the influence of the mystical movement known as Merkava mysticism, this passage was expanded in Byzantine Palestine into a ritual called Sanctification: the congregation, normally silent during the precentor's recitation of the benedictions, breaks in by reciting aloud several biblical verses, including "Holy, holy, holy, the Lord of Hosts! The whole earth is full of his glory!" (Isa. 6:3) and "Blessed is the glory of God from his place" (Ezek. 3:12), thereby imitating the praise of God by the angels, as described by the prophets. Liturgical poets were particularly drawn to this moment in the morning service. Besides greatly expanding the Sanctification itself, they composed introductions to it, often in the form of long and complex series of poems in varying styles, lengths, and poetic patterns. The final poem of such a series always ends with the verse from Isaiah, introduced by the statement that the congregation is about to recite this verse in imitation of the angels.

The fixed theme of the Sanctification is this parallel between the praise of God by angels and by men. The challenge for the poet is to link this fixed theme with the transient occasions of the year. Text 7, an anonymous poem probably composed in Byzantine Palestine, and today one of the highlights of the New Year service in Ashkenazic synagogues, is just such an introductory poem for the Sanctification on Rosh Hashanah, the day when God is said to judge all creatures and determine their fate for the coming year. The festival is interpreted as a kind of foreshadowing of the Last Judgment. The poem begins in heaven, as the poet describes the terror experienced even among the hosts of heaven as the Day of Judgment is proclaimed and the book in which all creatures' deeds are recorded is opened. In this way, the vision of the angels—the object of the Merkava mystics' contemplation and the basic theme of the Sanctification—is given a turn specific to the theme of the New Year. From the eschatological judgment in heaven, the poem descends to the annual judgment of mankind on the New Year. The poem lists the various fates to which mankind can be condemned, and broods on the frailty and evanescence of human life. From this low point, the poem reascends to the divine world. Its language becomes less pictorial and more sonorous, as it speaks of God's transcendence and of the eternal praise with which He is surrounded in His heavenly abode. As required by the rules of the genre, the poem concludes with the sound of angels and men together proclaiming, "Holy, holy, holy, the Lord of Hosts, the whole earth is full of his glory."

Another benediction that, like the Sanctification, attracted much poetry was the benediction praising God for forgiving sins: "Blessed are you, Lord, clement and freely forgiving One." This benediction was given special attention on fast days. Public fasting was a statutory obligation on days that commemorated some of the disasters of Jewish history, such as the day when the Temple was destroyed. Fasts could also be declared by local authorities in case of famine, warfare, or other community disasters. In both cases, the purpose was to induce God to forgive the sins that were thought to have brought about the disasters, whether past or present. For such fast days, poems were composed to introduce the benediction that dealt specifically with forgiveness. Such poems often concluded with biblical verses in which God promises to forgive Israel's sins, such as Exodus 34:6–7; sometimes the biblical verses serve as refrains or are otherwise worked into the poem, as if to remind God of His promise. Poems of this type are called *selihot,* meaning poems of forgiveness. They were also recited as part of the Amida on Yom Kippur, the annual Day of Atonement, the one statutory fast not originally connected with a historical event. (On Yom Kippur, the selihot are attached to the benediction "Blessed are you, God, King of the world, who sanctifies Israel and the Day of Atonement.") Eventually, selihot became separated from the Amida and came to be recited independently in a nonstatutory predawn service, also called Selihot, particularly on weekdays preceding and following Rosh Hashanah. Text 8 is a seliha by the late-ninth-century Amittai ben Shefatia, a rabbi and mystic of southern Italy. It is notable for its personification of God's attribute of mercy; the attribute, addressed in the second-person feminine, is begged to turn to Israel's favor and to intercede with God on Israel's behalf. The poet also refers, in stanza 3, to the biblical verse Exodus 34:6–7, which ancient rabbis understood to contain thirteen words that signify God's attributes of mercy and forgiveness; this verse also serves the poem as a refrain. The poem is recited to this day in Ashkenazic synagogues near the end of the Yom Kippur service.

The final selection represents a new and important genre of liturgical poetry introduced in the Golden Age. Unlike their predecessors, the Golden Age poets were educated not only in traditional rabbinic lore but also in Arabic literature, including the Greek philosophical tradition, which was accessible to them through Arabic. One of the consequences of their engagement in Greek philosophy was a far greater concern with the fate of the individual soul than was usual in earlier Jewish liturgical writing, which is mostly concerned with the fate of the worshiping community as a whole. In order to express this more personal kind of religious thinking, they sought new locations in the service that had never before received the attention of poets, and found their domain in the prayers immediately preceding the benedictions of the Shema. This part of the service, traditionally considered private, preparatory prayer, gave the poets the foothold to introduce poetic meditations of a rare intimacy and individuality. Many of these poems, like Text 9, were composed as introductions to an ancient prayer that begins with the words "The soul of every living thing blesses your name." This prayer, like all the ancient Jewish prayers, speaks in the name of the community of worshipers; the opening line, just quoted, actually extends that community of worshipers beyond the walls of the synagogue to embrace all living creatures. To a Neoplatonist like Ibn Gabirol, the author of this poem, the word soul suggests not just the animating force in living creatures but, on the one hand, the World-Soul, from which individual souls derive and to which they return; and, on the other hand, the highest faculty of the individual soul of man, the intellect. The poem is a meditation on the paradox that this infinite divine force can be contained in a finite and imperfect creature like man.

All translations are by the author of the chapter. The sources of the Hebrew texts are as follows: Texts 1 through 3 are translated from fragments of medieval liturgical manuscripts discovered in Egypt, and published by Solomon Schechter in his article "Genizah Specimens" in *Jewish Quarterly Review* o.s. 10 (1898), reprinted in Jakob J. Petuchowski, ed., *Contributions to the Scientific Study of Jewish Liturgy* (New York: Ktav Publishing House, 1970), pp. 374–75. Texts 4, 7, and

8 are translated from Daniel Goldschmidt, ed., *Mahzor layamim hanoraim* (Jerusalem: Koren, 1970), vol. 2, pp. 99–101; vol. 1, pp. 169–72; and vol. 2, pp. 663–64, respectively. (The translation of Text 7 first appeared in *Conservative Judaism*, Spring 1998, pp. 48–50.) Texts 5, 6, and 9 are taken from Raymond P. Scheindlin, *The Gazelle: Medieval Hebrew Poems on God, Israel, and the Soul* (New York: Oxford University Press, 1999), pp. 77, 115, and 177, respectively.

Further Reading

Liturgical texts: A serviceable introduction to the Jewish liturgy, containing good translations of the most important liturgical texts and cogent explanations of their function and meaning, is Joseph Heinemann and Jakob J. Petuchowski, *Literature of the Synagogue* (New York: Behrman House, 1975). The most complete and accurate editions of the Ashkenazic prayer book that include complete English translation are the two volumes by Philip Birnbaum, *Daily Prayer Book* (New York: Hebrew Publishing Co., 1949) and *High Holiday Prayer Book* (New York: Hebrew Publishing Co., 1951).

History of liturgy: The standard scholarly work on the history of the liturgy is Ismar Elbogen's *Jewish Liturgy: A Comprehensive History*, translated by Raymond P. Scheindlin (Philadelphia: Jewish Publication Society, 1993). The book was originally published in 1913, but the English translation reflects more recent scholarship, since it includes all the material from the revised edition, which appeared in Hebrew in 1972. More recent research is reflected in Joseph Heinemann, *Prayer in the Talmud: Forms and Patterns*, translated by Richard S. Sarason (Berlin and New York: de Gruyter, 1977); Lawrence A. Hoffman, *The Canonization of the Synagogue Service* (Notre Dame: University of Notre Dame Press, 1979), and other works; and Stefan Reif, *Judaism and Hebrew Prayer: New Perspectives on Jewish Liturgical Poetry* (Cambridge: Cambridge University Press, 1993).

Liturgical poetry: Except for Ezra Fleischer's *Sacred Poetry in Hebrew in the Middle Ages* [Hebrew] (Jerusalem: Keter, 1979), which deals nearly exclusively with the verse forms of liturgical poetry and barely touches on their actual contents, no up-to-date account exists in any language. Elbogen's discussions of piyyut are adequate. Jakob J. Petuchowski's *Theology and Poetry: Studies in the Medieval Piyyut* (London: Routledge and Kegan Paul, 1978) gives a useful but random sample of piyyutim with theological discussions. Old-fashioned translations of liturgical poems by three medieval Hebrew poets can be found in a series of volumes published by the Jewish Publication Society of America: *Selected Liturgical Poetry of Solomon Ibn Gabirol*, translated by Israel Zangwill (Philadelphia, 1923); *Selected Poems of Moses Ibn Ezra*, translated by Solomon Solis-Cohen (Philadelphia, 1945); and *Selected Poems by Judah Halevi*, translated by Nina Salaman (Philadelphia, 1928). My book, *The Gazelle*, contains thirty liturgical poems from the Golden Age in translation, with cultural and literary analysis.

BENEDICTIONS ACCOMPANYING THE SHEMA

1. "CREATOR" BENEDICTION

Blessed are you, Lord our God, King of the world, who creates the light and calls the darkness into being, makes peace and creates everything, who in great mercy lights up the world and those who live upon it, whose goodness renews the creation daily and eternally. Blessed are you, Lord, who creates the heavenly lights.

2. "LOVE" BENEDICTION

You have ever loved us, Lord our God; you cared for us greatly on account of our ancestors. They trusted in you, and you taught them the laws of life; so may you care for us. Our Father, merciful Father, O you who are merciful to us, permit us to observe, perform, study, and teach all the words of your instruction in love. Enlighten our eyes with your instruction, and make our hearts adhere truly to your service, so that we may proclaim your unity in fear and awe. Blessed are you, Lord, who chooses his people Israel in love.

3. "REDEEMER" BENEDICTION

True, valid, right, eternal, just, faithful, and good is this, and binding on us, our ancestors, and our descendants; on our generation and all generations descended from Israel, your servant; on the early-born and late-born, forever and ever, fixed and unbreachable. Truly, you are the Lord, our God and God of our fathers forever; you are our King and the King of our fathers. Save us for your name's sake, as you saved our fathers. Truly, your name is eternal, and by it we are called; there is no God but you.

Who is like you, mighty King, who split apart the mighty sea? In joy and song and great delight, all said:

> Who is like you among the mighty, Lord?
> Who is like you: revered in your Sanctuary,
> praised for your awesome deeds, working miracles?

Your children beheld your royal presence when you split the sea before Moses. Open-mouthed, all said,

> This is our King, our salvation!

O Lord, our King, eternal King, by your name we are called. The Lord is King, the Lord was King, the Lord will be King forever and ever. The Lord our King will rescue us and save us in a final, perfect act of redemption. Blessed are you, Lord, Israel's Rock and Redeemer.

PIYYUTIM FOR THE BENEDICTIONS OF THE SHEMA

4. A PIYYUT FOR "CREATOR" OF YOM KIPPUR

Forgive a people holy
  on this day holy,
    O Lofty One, and Holy!

Of old, you taught pardon on Yom Kippur,
light and forgiveness to the people you made,
the day when you pardon the sins of the people,
gathered on the Tenth in their houses of prayer.
Sins gathered force while I was asleep.
Then came that day in the course of the year
for speaking, for pleading with him who pardons,
to knock at the door of the Maker of light and forgiveness.
Sweeten the light on this day of our pardon,
by answering, saying, "I have forgiven."
Make our eyes shine, pass over our sins.
Do not punish unwitting sinners with death.
We have done wrong with our wicked deeds.
You are righteous, whatever our fate.
We sinned against you, King of the world.
Guide us with light, do not send us from you in shame.
O Good One, and Clement!—Justice is yours.
Cleanse us in your spring, God clad in justice!
By day and by night we pour out our hearts:
shine pardoning light on this day of our fasting.
Search out our secrets, but do it with pity,
forgive the sins of the people you bear,
that we may leap joyously forth from your presence,
and not trudge away from you empty-handed.
O you who whiten sins like snow,
O Master of the fountain of life and of mercy,
we come to you now: By Israel's covenant,
sustain us with light, as once you sustained
the prophet Elijah, hiding in Kerit.
Master, who forgives the flock of his pasture,
shelter us with light, as once you sheltered
our master Moses, beholding your face.
Answer us, Father, in our deep need;
rouse the Lily of the Valley with light.
Open the gate, so our prayer can ascend,

when we petition you, Dweller on high.
Cleanse us of refuse, record not our sin,
refine us like silver seven times smelted.
Bring near your salvation by the light of the fawns,
Moses and Aaron, who called this day sacred.
Pasture us as before, make our faces shine,
Merciful One, hear us, do not delay.
We pour out like water our stony hearts;
let the dawn gleam with light, Searcher of hearts!
Purify us as with hyssop on this day of forgiveness;
Hear us crying, "Forgive!" and answer, "Forgiven."

  Forgive your people holy
    on this day holy,
      O Lofty One, and Holy!

Anonymous

5. PIYYUT FOR "LOVE" BENEDICTION

  From time's beginning, you were love's abode:
    My love encamped wherever it was you tented.
  The taunts of foes for your name's sake are sweet,
    So let them torture one whom you tormented.

  I love my foes, for they learned wrath from you,
    For they pursue a body you have slain.
  The day you hated me, I loathed myself,
    For I will honor none whom you disdain.
  Until your anger pass, and you restore
    This people whom you rescued once before.

Judah Halevi

6. PIYYUT FOR "REDEEMER" BENEDICTION

  Pour over me your pleasure
  As once you poured your rage.
  Must my sin between us
  Stand from age to age?
  How long until you join me?
  Must I wait in vain?

  You who dwelt on cherubs'
  Wings, in Temple spread,
  Made me slave to strangers,
  Who was your garden bed,

Savior, look from heaven,
To save my throngs again.

Judah Halevi

7. INTRODUCTION TO THE SANCTIFICATION FOR ROSH HASHANAH

And now may the Sanctification rise to you, for you are our God and King:

Let us speak of this day's sanctity,
For it is terrifying, fearsome;
the day your kingdom is established,
your throne set firmly in mercy
and you sit on it in truth.

Truly: you are the judge, the accuser, the omniscient witness.
You write and seal, count and enumerate,
call to mind all things forgotten.
You open the book of records,
order it read:
Every man has signed his name therein.

The great horn sounds;
A thin, dim echo rebounds.
Angels, panicking,
seized by terror and shaking, say:
"The Day of Judgment!"—
For you bring the hosts of heaven to judgment,
and even they cannot count on being cleared in your judgment,
when all who dwell in the world pass before you
like those who dwell in the heavens.

Just as a shepherd examines his flock,
passing his sheep beneath his staff,
so you make pass, count and enumerate,
consider every living thing,
fix the fate of each creature,
write down his decree.

On the New Year it written, and on the Day of Atonement sealed
how many will come into being and how many will pass away;
who will live and who will die;
who in his time and who too soon;
who by fire and who by flood,
who by sword and who by beast,
who by hunger and who by thirst,
who by earthquake and who by plague,
who by the rope and who by the stone;

who will be still and who will go wandering,
who will be calm and who will be anxious,
who will be tranquil and who will suffer,
who will find poverty, who will have riches,
who will sink and who will rise.
But repentance, prayer, and charity cancel the harsh decree.

For you are praised for what you are:
Hard to make angry, easy to appease.
You do not want a man to die,
but to turn back from sin and live.
Until his life has run its course, you wait;
if he repents, you accept him right away.
Truly, you made them,
and know that they are made
of flesh and blood.

Man is made of earth and returns to earth.
He spends his life to get his daily bread.
What is he like? A broken shard,
a heap of dried-out grass,
a withered blossom;
a passing shadow,
a wisp of cloud,
a blowing breeze,
a puff of dust,
a fleeting dream—
but you are the King, the God who lives forever.

Your years have no end, your days have no measure,
your chariots cannot be numbered,
your Name's mystery cannot be known.
You are your Name,
and by your Name you have called us.
Act now for the sake of your Name;
Sanctify your Name for those who sanctify your Name,
for the sake of your glorious Name, fearful and holy,
in the words of the seraphim, holy,
who sanctify your Name in the place holy,
who dwell in the heavens
together with those who dwell in the world,
all repeating the words of your prophet:
"Holy, holy, holy, the Lord of hosts!
The whole earth is full of his glory!"

Anonymous

COMMUNAL PRAYER, LITURGICAL POETRY

8. SELIHA

"The Lord, the Lord: merciful, clement, and slow to anger, full of kindness and truth . . . forgive our misdeeds and sins and make us yours."

> I call on God's Name out of my great pain,
> for I see every city stands proud on its hill,
> but the city of God is reduced to the ground.
> Yet, still we are God's and to God we gaze.
> "The Lord, the Lord: merciful and clement."
>
> O Name-that-means-mercy!—turn in our favor
> and pour out our prayer before Him-whose-you-are.
> Beg mercy of him on behalf of your people,
> For every heart aches, and every head bleeds.
> "The Lord, the Lord: merciful and clement."
>
> I pegged my tent with Thirteen Words,
> at the Gates of Tears, which never are shut,
> and I pour my prayer before Him-who-tests-hearts,
> certain of these and patriarchs' intercession.
> "The Lord, the Lord: merciful and clement."
>
> May it be your will, O You-who-hear-weeping,
> to collect our tears in your vessel of tears,
> and save us from every evil decree,
> For only to you are our eyes upraised.
> "The Lord, the Lord: merciful and clement."

Amittai ben Shefatia

9. RESHUT

> With lowly spirit, lowered knee and head,
> In fear I come; I offer thee my dread.
> But once with thee, I seem to have no worth
> More than a little worm upon the earth.
>
> O fullness of the world, Infinity—
> What praise can come, if any can, from me?
> Thy splendor is not contained by the hosts on high,
> And how much less capacity have I!
> Infinite thou, and infinite thy ways;
> Therefore the soul expands to sing thy praise.

Solomon ibn Gabirol

— 2 —

Italian Jewish Women at Prayer

Howard Tzvi Adelman

Although very few sources were written by Jewish women about their spiritual life in early modern times, material by men, often from a reactive perspective, contains some information about the religious life of women. Male writers generally tried to silence women who initiated rituals of their own, studied traditional texts, spoke in public, and wrote; women, nevertheless, did pray, study, speak, and write.

The early modern period, which often was associated, especially in Italy, with a growing involvement on the part of Jews with the Renaissance, has been presented as a period of positive change in attitudes toward women in society in general and in the Jewish community in particular. In fact, however, the incorporation of humanistic study into traditional Jewish scholarship produced new grounds to support denigrations of the spiritual capabilities of women. For example, Ovadia Sforno (1470–1550), a leading rabbi whose Bible commentary is considered a milestone in Jewish humanism, was not able to get past conventional philosophical terminology and traditional rabbinic teachings when commenting about women (Gen. 3:15): "The woman would be despised in the eyes of the imaginative power, even her own, as it is said, 'A woman is a bag filled with excrement, and her mouth is filled with blood.' "

Women at Prayer

For many Italian Jewish women, prayer, in Hebrew or Italian, constituted an important part of their daily activity. Others attended synagogue at least on the Sabbath and holidays. *Tephilin* (phylacteries), the traditional ritual leather straps worn on the arm and head, constituted an essential component of prayer for Jewish men. According to some rabbis, this practice applied to women, too. Most, however, exempted women from this practice on the grounds that it was a time-bound positive commandment—although there was much discussion about whether it indeed was time-bound or not, and to what extent women were exempt from time-bound commandments. Rabbinnic literature never resolved completely whether women who wanted to wear *tephilin* were allowed to do so. According to a source preserved in the Talmud and midrash, Michal, the daughter of King Saul and the wife of King David, wore *tephilin* and the rabbis did not protest. From the ancient period to the Middle Ages through the sixteenth century, some rabbis ruled against women wearing *tephilin,* whereas others reported instances of the practice. Two traces of this discussion are found in early modern Italy. One document, a letter, mentions women in Italy wearing *tephilin* (see Text 1). The other, a seventeenth-century ritual manual on mourning by Rabbi Aaron Berekhiah Modena, rules against such a practice; it bases its attempt to limit the practice on an analogy with a man in mourning who is exempt from fulfilling all positive commandments of Jewish law. In his word play, he rearranged the letters of Michal's name to form the Hebrew "he will rule," connecting *tephilin* with masculine authority (see Text 2).

Based on material in the Tosefta (an early compendium of Jewish law) and the Talmud, during the daily morning service the Jewish man gives thanks to God, for among other things, that he was not created a woman, *shelo asani ishah.* Rabbinic tradition developed several explanations for the recitation of this blessing by men. According to the Tosefta, men acknowledged that they had to fulfill all of the commandments, "that women are not bound by the commandments" (to which some later rabbis amended to "all commandments"), and that women were not capable of fulfilling the commandments properly. According to Rashi, the eleventh-century French interpreter of Jewish tradition, the man was glad because "a woman is also a servant (*shifha*) to her husband as a servant (*eved*) is to his master." And according to the fourteenth-century commentary on the prayerbook by David ben Joseph Abudraham of Seville, the man was like a worker who planted in the field of his neighbor with his permission, whereas the woman, who was not commanded to perform the time-bound positive commandments, was like a worker who entered another's field without permission. Moreover, because the fear of her husband was upon her, she was not able to fulfill even what she had been commanded—an explanation for the woman's exemption from time-bound commandments echoed in the contemporaneous *Kol bo,* which citing the anonymous author of the *Sefer Hamelammed,* which expressed concern that if a woman were performing commandments at a time when her husband needed her help, he would be without her help, his authority over her—for good and bad—would be challenged, and they would quarrel. Instead, Abudraham noted—following his contemporary, Jacob ben Asher—women recited an alternative blessing thanking God "who made me according to his will," a blessing that Abudraham explained as being said, "as one justifies the rightness of the evil which has befallen him."

There is evidence, however, that not everyone accepted the traditional morning blessings for men and women. A fourteenth- or fifteenth-century Judeo-Provençal translation of the prayerbook contains an alternative blessing: ". . . who has made me a woman" (see George Jochnowitz, ". . . Who Made Me a Woman," *Commentary* [April 1981], pp. 63–64). A fifteenth-century Hebrew prayerbook in manuscript from Mantua includes a revised morning blessing (see Text 3).

Both of these prayerbooks were written for women, but copied by men—the first one cited was given as a wedding gift by a man to his sister, and the second was copied by Rabbi Abraham Farisol in 1480. It is clear that, despite wider evidence, these revised morning blessings were a liturgical change supported by some but not all. In the seventeenth century, Rabbi Aaron Berekhiah Modena felt the need to justify the traditional morning blessing (see Text 4).

Women in the Synagogue

Women had to sit in their own section of the synagogue—if indeed, as the text indicates, the place where they sat, usually the balcony, was actually considered by the community to be the synagogue—and often had a very different worship experience than the men. In Rome, Anna d'Arpino had the masculine job title of *shaliah tzibbur,* "representative of the community," and functioned for the women, as did men who led the male service, in this capacity on Sabbaths and holidays for at least two and a half years. She received indirect payment in the form of a loan, since Jewish law did not allow accepting actual payment for this work.

In sixteenth-century Verona, the women quarreled among themselves for many years over their seating arrangement in the synagogue until permanent seats were assigned. The seating plan described in the communal record book contains a curious mixture of masculine and feminine names and titles in Hebrew, Italian, and German. It seems to represent a hierarchical structure whereby the older, more educated women would lead the others. Women who sat at the head of the first several benches were designated as Rabbanit, a title of distinction found in classical rabbinic literature for a woman who participated in rabbinic discussions, with their husbands' name or only their own name. Next came women with the title of Marat, "Ms.," referring to both married women (*Frau*) and single women (*Fraulein*)—clearly the congregation had strong German roots—then those with the designation Almanat, "the widow of." Finally, the women who often sat at the far end of the bench had the title Kalat, "the bride of" or "the fiancée"; these were probably the younger women. The back rows were headed by women who had the title Marat but not Rabbanit. One woman has the title of Shamashit, the female sextant (see Text 5).

The segregation of women in the balcony did not mean that they silently accepted their position in the synagogue. In Verona, edicts passed by the communal leaders against excessive talking in synagogue during prayers and Torah reading included the women. Sitting together, without men, not only did they have their own leaders and texts but they also participated in the Sabbath and holiday worship services by disrupting them. According to a long-standing Jewish custom, authorized by some of the leading rabbis of the Middle Ages although opposed by others, if a Jew had a grievance against another member of the community, he could—usually only if all other channels had failed—interrupt the service (*bittul hatamid*) or stop the reading of the Torah (*ikkuv hakeriah*). This public protest, also found in Italy, was allowed to women and orphans, as well.

In Modena these customs were taken to an extreme when women regularly cursed men during the Torah service, a practice that illustrated to some rabbis the connection between women's learning and religiosity and their disobedience to their husbands. The sins of the men are not mentioned, but they appear in other sources, and include broken engagements, unfavorable divorce settlements, abandonment, nonsupport, physical and verbal abuse, the taking of a mistress or a second wife, impotence, the seduction or impregnation of servants, the blackmail of an abandoned wife or of a dead brother's widow, or the refusal to acknowledge or support children born out of wedlock. In the last instances there are cases of women who threatened to bring the child to the synagogue as part of their protest against the men involved, or to pressure the lay leaders reluctant to come to their aid.

Men also could use the service as an arena to air marital grievances, particularly in cases where their wives refused to have sexual intercourse. Before a woman could be ruled a rebellious wife and subjected to the loss of the rights stipulated in her marriage contract, she had to be warned publicly in the presence of the congregation four Sabbaths in a row. In 1534, Rabbi Azriel Diena (d. 1536), then of Sabbionneta, wrote a responsum to the Jewish community of Modena asking the leaders of the community to put a stop to the women's cursing during the service. It is illustrative of the separation of the worship services that some men did not hear the cursing of the women in their segregated balcony. Thus, women in their own section were involved in a service that paralleled that of the men but included features of which some men might not have been aware, especially when women were publicly demanding restitution of wrongs done to them. In expressing the view that husbands should rule over their wives, Diena made it clear that this was not always the case (see Text 6).

Sources translated: Text 1: *Iggerot beit rieti*, edited by Yacov Boksenboim (Tel Aviv: Tel Aviv University, 1988); Text 2: Aaron Berekhian Modena, *Ma'aver yabbok, Sefat emet* (Vilna: Joseph Reuben, 1860; reprint Jerusalem 1989), chapter 32, p. 242; Text 3: A Prayerbook for Women, Jerusalem MS 8° 5492, fol. 7a; Text 4: Aaron Berekhian Modena, *Ma'aver yabbok, Siftei tzedek* (Vilna: Joseph Reuben, 1860; reprint Jerusalem 1989), chapter 1, p. 95a; Text 5: *Pinkas Kahal Verona*, edited by Yacov Boksenboim (Tel Aviv: Tel Aviv University, 1989), no. 459, pp. 403–6; Text 6: Azriel Diena, *Sheelot uteshuvot*, edited by Yacov Boksenboim (Tel Aviv: Tel Aviv University, 1977), no. 6.

Further Reading

See the following works by Howard Adelman. "The Literacy of Jewish Women in Early Modern Italy," in *Women and Education in Early Modern Europe*, edited by Barbara Whitehead (New York: Garland, 1999), pp. 133–158; "Family and Gender in Jewish Venice," in *The Jews of Venice*, edited by Robert Davis and Benjamin Ravid (Baltimore: Johns Hopkins University Press, 2001, pp. 143–165); "Servants and Sexuality: Seduction Surrogacy, and Rape: Some Observations Concerning Class, Gender, and Race in Early Modern Italian Jewish Families," in *Gender and Judaism*, edited by T. Rudavsky (New York: New York University Press, 1995), pp. 81–97; "Custom, Law, and Gender: Levirate Union among Ashkenazim and Sephardim in Italy after the Expulsion from Spain," in *The Expulsion of the Jews: 1492 and After*, edited by Raymond Waddington and Arthur Williamson (New York: Garland, 1994), pp. 107–26; "Wife-Beating among Early Modern Italian Jews, 1400–1700," *Proceedings of the Eleventh World Congress of Jewish Studies*, B, vol. 1 (Jerusalem: 1994), pp. 135–42; "Finding Women's Voices in Italian Jewish Literature," in *Women of the Word: Jewish Women and Jewish Writing*, edited by Judith Baskin (Detroit: Wayne State University Press, 1994), pp. 50–69; "The Educational and Literary Activities of Jewish Women in Italy during the Renaissance and the Counter Reformation," in *Sefer yovel lishlomo simonsohn* (Tel Aviv: Tel Aviv University Press, 1993), pp. 9–24; "Rabbis and Reality: The Public Roles of Jewish Women in the Renaissance and Catholic Restoration," *Jewish History*, 5.1 (1991): 27–40; "Italian Jewish Women," in *Jewish Women in Historical Perspective*, edited by Judith Baskin (Detroit: Wayne State University Press, 1991), pp. 135–58; revised for second edition 1998; "Images of Women in Italian Jewish Literature in the Late Middle Ages," *Proceedings of the Tenth World Congress of Jewish Studies* B, vol. 2 (Jerusalem, 1990), pp. 99–106.

TEXT 1

Listen to me, I will provide my witnesses and they will vindicate [me] before you. Two women who wear tephilin-like Michal, they are so-and-so and so-and-so.

TEXT 2

. . . because he [the mourner] is still garbed in the fabric of the world of women. For this reason they protest against the authority of a woman who wants to wear tephilin, which is not the case with the other positive commandments from which she is exempt, and Michal the daughter of Saul is different because she was the daughter of the king and she was totally sincere and a hint of this is that the interpreters of the Torah showed that in reverse alphabetical code [*atbash aleph* = *tav, bet* = *shin, mem* = *yod, kaf* = *lamed*] Michal becomes *yimlokh,* "he will rule."

TEXT 3

Blessed are you Lord, King of the universe who made me a woman and not a man.

TEXT 4

How many people, either men or women, disguise their basic character by means of their deeds? There are many who for most of their lives serve others as servants and this shows the lowliness of their souls because the internal reflects itself externally. Therefore [the rabbis] established the recitation "who has not made me a woman" and "has not made me a slave" every day. . . . [H]e intends with the three above-mentioned blessings to remove from himself and from upon himself every type of servitude, frivolity of women, and servile capacity and impure thought.

TEXT 5

No. 459: Sunday, 27 Tishrei, 1586, the members of the holy congregation [Verona], may its Rock guard it and may it flourish, convened. . . . The rumor had circulated among the tranquil women. They rose up and quarreled concerning their seats in the synagogue. All this was because since the small sanctuary had been built seats had not been assigned to the women. Rather each one said, "Here I will sit because I so desire it," and that did not necessarily mean that it became her seat. From this developed several quarrels, and as is the way of quarrels and strife; contentiousness is like a burst of water that becomes wider and wider. In order to quiet all these matters of quarreling, a resolution was proposed by the honorable lay leaders of the community to elect now in the holy congregation by means of a vote three people who will assign the seating places for the women by a majority vote. After they finalize the arrangements they will place plaques on the seat of each woman. No woman can in any way refuse her assigned seat and she can only sit in her assigned seat where her name has been placed. And if she dares to sit in the seat of another against the latter's wishes she will surely be fined three golden *scudi*, which will be collected and distributed according to the wishes of the sage Rabbi Menahem, may his Rock guard him and may he flourish, to support the fulfillment of a religious commandment as he sees fit. And from henceforth now and forevermore their husbands will enter as guarantors for complaints against them according to this vote, even if there will be any votes against this motion, as long as it remains accepted by the majority, all are bound by it, husbands being responsible for their wives. Even if their husbands pay the above-mentioned fine, in any case the rest of the women shall remove themselves from speaking or doing business with her, because she will be treated as one who has been "rebuked," until she returns to sit in the place that she had been assigned by the process described here. The three who had been appointed as mentioned above are not able to refuse, or they will be assessed a fine of three gold *scudi* to be paid to the sanctuary, which will be collected by the assessors of the community, and they will be separated from every matter of holiness until they pay the required fine. And they will finish their task within eight days so that every woman will peaceably be able to take her own seat. The motion passed by a vote of 25 yeses, 2 noes, and 1 abstention.

This is the order to the location of the seats of the women according to the division of the three chosen leaders:

Bench 1:
The Rabbanit of our Teacher, our rabbi, Rabbi Yoetz; the Rabbanit of the rabbi, Rabbi Mordecai; Marat Gotlein Sangueni; Marat Stella; Marat Bella the wife of Rabbi Moshe; Marat Pesslein Shabbetai; Marat Rosa the wife of the honorable Nahum; the Kalah of our Teacher the honorable Teacher, Rabbi Barukh;
And the second, western section:
Marat Tuelzlein the wife of Rabbi Aaron; Marat Pesslein the wife of the honorable Teacher Jedediah; Marat Limnat Margalit; Marat Gotlein Benjamin;
Tally: 12
On the window side:
The Rabbanit of the rabbi, our Rabbi, our Teacher, Bat Sheva family [hereafter, B.S.]; Marat Fraulein Sarval; Marat Gotlein the widow of B.S.; Marat Yentlein the wife of Asher B.S.;
Tally: 4

The second bench, near the first:
The Rabbanit Gotlein; Marat Frau Pesslein Basan; Marat Pesquin . . . B.S.; Marat Ricca Samson Grigo; Kalah of the honorable Shemarya B.S.;
The second section—
Marat Esther, the widow; Marat Camilla; Marat Suesslein Moses Grigo; Marat Richlein B.S.;
Tally: 9
And those near the synagogue:—
The Rabbanit of the rabbi, Rabbi Feibes; Marat Frau Limnat; Marat Sheinlein Prinz; Marat Brendlein the wife of Joseph Leib; Kalah of the honorable teacher Rabbi Hosea of Mantua; Kalah of the honorable teacher Rabbi Isaiah Ashkenazi;

Marat Hanah Lazar Lieberman; Marat Pesslein the wife of Joshua; Marat Hanah Sangueni; Marat Yutlein Zalman;
Tally: 10

The third bench:
The Rabbanit Tamar; Marat Rachel the widow of Leib; Marat Kelein the wife of the cantor; Marat Shevia B.S.;
And the second section—
Marat Rebecca the wife of Falcon; Marat Bella the widow; Marat Naomi; Marat Rachel Abraham B.S.; Marat Rosa the wife of Samuel;
Tally: 9

The fourth bench:
Marat Scheinlein the widow of the rabbi, Rabbi Y. of blessed memory; Marat Judita; Marat Frumit Sangueni; Marat Sarah;
And the second section—
Marat Rachel Isaac Levi; Marat Tuelzlein the shamashit; Marat Ventorina; Marat Hanah Lazar B.S.;
Tally: 9

At the western wall:
Marat Pessslein the widow of B.S.; Marat Lifheit the wife of Moses; Marat Ricca [the wife of] Joseph Shemarya; the Kalah of the honorable Rabbi Mordecai B.S.;
And the second section—
Marat Bat Sheva the wife of Moses; Marat Sprinza; Marat Mita the wife of Leib;
Tally: 7

TEXT 6

Over his woman, every man shall be ruler in his house and rebuke his wife at the gate. Let this be his consolation—you, the nobility of the holy congregation of Modena, may it see its seed extend its days, Amen. The Lord will bestow upon it his blessing, and peace from Sabionetta. To remove a stumbling block from the way of your people I went out to the well and to your gates to proclaim and to advise concerning a matter of sin and guilt that is found among all of you. When at the time of the taking out of the Torah scrolls on your Sabbaths, your festivals, and your new moons, instead of standing and honoring and praying to him who gave us the Torah of truth and who blesses you, bad-tempered women among you rise and denounce God. Their mouths are full to curse and to avenge everyone who, when their hearts were deluded, led them astray and did not give them according to their requests. The sin is great, and these women move like the blind people in your streets.

Thus I will proclaim and announce my words of truth to you, that no longer shall anybody terrify your land with their curses, because it is a sin of rebellious magic, too great to bear according to the teachings of the Torah and the scribes as I will demonstrate to you. Until now all were in error because they did not consider this astonishing thing to be a sin which had been committed in your midst. Now you will surely advise them that it is time for a change, that they must leave with their staffs, because I will send among them the curse and the rebuke so that they might repent their sin. Woe unto them because of their curse and they will be devastated in your city. Go rouse the princes, anoint a protector and speak to your women. They will give honor to the Lord, and when they take out his Torah, the mothers and the servants shall draw close and bow down, and these groups of women will stand and bless the people, because by virtue of our Torah, the Lord is with you, because he commanded the blessing they will live forever and the sword will not pass through your land.

From the words of the Torah we have found that it is forbidden to curse one's neighbor, as is said: "Do not curse the deaf and before the blind do not place a stumbling block [Lev. 19:14]." What does it mean not to place a stumbling block before the blind? It is not the intention to speak actually of the blind, but rather anybody who is blind in a certain matter should not be given advice that is not suitable for him. Similarly, not cursing the deaf does not mean those who are actually deaf but anybody who cannot hear the curse. And even though one was not ashamed because the curse was not heard, is it true that it is an obstacle and a stumbling block to him? As the sages of truth said, "Because great is the strength of the word to act for the good and for the opposite, that the letters in coming out of the mouth make an impression on the air and what goes on above." . . . Therefore the gentle women who are in your midst should hearken to my voice, trusting women must listen to my word, and they must not curse any man for sinning against them and any young man for wounding them, a woman to her neighbor a dirge, lest wickedness will go forth like fire and she will be quickly subdued and excommunicated. And because there is no whipping, although it is allowed, I am accordingly attempting to enlighten you that these women should no longer persist in their sin.

3

Measuring Graves and Laying Wicks

Chava Weissler

The three eighteenth-century texts translated below are rooted in a centuries-old Ashkenazic women's ritual known as *kvorim mesn* (measuring graves) and *kneytlakh legn* (laying wicks). During the High Holiday season (and also in times of illness or trouble), women walked in a circle around the circumference of the cemetery and measured the cemetery or individual graves with candlewick, all the while reciting supplications in Yiddish, the vernacular language of central and eastern European Jews. Between Rosh Hashanah and Yom Kippur, and often on the eve of Yom Kippur, they made the wicks into candles "for the living" and "for the dead" members of their families, again reciting supplications as they did so. The candlewick would be cut into lengths, one piece for each family member, living or dead, and the wicks would be rubbed with wax, while petitions concerning that family member were recited. The litany of dead family members often went back to Adam and Eve, or Abraham and Sarah, and continued on to recently departed relatives only after a listing of important patriarchs and matriarchs of Israel. The wicks were then twisted into two heavy candles. According to some customs, the candles were burned at home on Yom Kippur, and according to others, one or both of them burned in the synagogue. Often the candle "for the living" was regarded as a kind of oracle: If it burned out or was extinguished before the end of Yom Kippur, it portended a death in the family. There are hints of this ritual complex going back nearly a thousand years, and it is well attested in literary and ethnographic material over the last three centuries.

The supplications women recited during this ritual are part of the genre of prayers known by the Yiddish term *tkhines*, derived from a Hebrew root meaning to plead or to supplicate. Beginning in the late sixteenth century, short booklets of these Yiddish supplications began to appear in print; this devotional genre flourished especially in the seventeenth and eighteenth centuries. Tkhines were voluntary prayers, recited primarily by women for a variety of occasions: lighting Sabbath candles, pregnancy and childbirth, visiting the cemetery, coming into the synagogue for worship, as well as "every day," on Sabbaths, and on Jewish holidays. One of the most popular topics was the penitential season from the beginning of the month of Elul in late August through Rosh Hashanah (the New Year) a month later, the Ten Days of Penitence, and Yom Kippur (the Day of Atonement).

Unlike the prayers of the regular liturgy, which were in Hebrew, the sacred and scholarly language, tkhines were in Yiddish, the spoken language, and thus readily comprehensible by women, who were rarely taught more than the bare fundamentals of Hebrew and were sometimes completely illiterate. The recitation of the liturgy was regulated by clock and calendar: morning, afternoon, and evening prayers, weekday prayers, Sabbath prayers, and festival prayers. Essentially a communal form of worship, the Hebrew liturgy is phrased in the plural and requires, for its complete performance, the presence of at least ten adult men. Tkhines, by contrast, are voluntary and private, phrased in the individual voice, and recited when and if the woman wishes.

Although some tkhines were composed by men, and others were anonymous, tkhines published in eastern Europe were often composed by women. The most renowned of these women was Sarah daughter of Mordecai (or sometimes daughter of Isaac or Jacob) of Satanov, great-granddaughter of Mordecai, rabbi of Brisk, known as Sarah bas Tovim, Sarah "daughter of good people." (The *tovim* were a type of Jewish communal official.) She became the emblematic tkhine author, and one of her two works, *The Tkhine of Three Gates* (*Tkhine shloyshe sheorim*) was perhaps the most beloved of all tkhines. Unlike many other tkhine authors, who are easy to document, Sarah is an elusive figure who, in the course of time, took on legendary proportions. She even became the subject of "The Match; or, Sarah bas Tovim," a short story by the Yiddish writer I. L. Peretz, in which she appears as a sort of fairy godmother. The fact that the name of her father (although not of her great-grandfather) changes from edition to edition of her work, and the unusual circumstance that no edition mentions a husband, makes documenting her life difficult. Indeed, some earlier scholars insisted that she never existed at all.

Yet so many women authors of tkhines have been historically authenticated that there now seems no real reason to doubt that there was a woman, probably known as Sarah bas Tovim, who composed most or all of the two eighteenth-century texts attributed to her: *Tkhine shaar ha-yikhed al oylemes* (Tkhine of the Gate of Unification Concerning the Aeons, a title with mystical overtones) and *Tkhine shloyshe sheorim* (Tkhine of Three Gates). By analyzing the sources the author uses, it is possible to determine that the texts themselves were composed in the 1740s or 1750s. The author repeatedly refers to herself as "Sarah" within her texts; in *The Three Gates* she even works her name into an acrostic, a common method of claiming authorship in Hebrew works. All the information we have about her comes from her own texts, which are unusual in that they contain extensive autobiographical sections, thus enabling us to grasp something of her personality and history. She seems to have begun life in a wealthy family; as a young woman, she says, she liked to show off her clothing and jewelry in the women's section of the synagogue. Later, having become impoverished, she also seems to have become homeless, and describes her forced wandering as a punishment by God for her youthful sins. Both texts say that she hailed from Satanov, in Podolia, now in Ukraine.

Both *The Gate of Unification* and *The Three Gates* contain tkhines connected to the penitential season, and in fact, for different stages of the custom of laying wicks to make candles for Yom Kippur. Each collection also contains several additional tkhines on other topics. And both these tkhines are grounded in a certain set of assumptions about the significance of the Days of Awe, the relations between the living and the dead, and the fate of the people of Israel.

The penitential season in general, and the Days of Awe in particular, are the time when God judges the world and determines the fate of individuals and of nations for the coming year. In the background of these two tkhines is the image of the heavenly court, drawn from the liturgy for the Days of Awe. On Rosh Hashanah, each person comes before the divine throne. The accuser (Satan) reminds God of sins committed, the heavenly advocates defend the soul and remind God of its righteous deeds. God decrees each person's fate: who shall live and who shall die, who shall prosper and who shall be in want, who shall be healthy and who shall be ill. Repentance, prayer, and righteous deeds can help the individual "earn" a better fate. On Yom Kippur, after the Ten Days of Penitence, God seals, or finalizes, the decree. Similarly, God determines the fate of the entire people of Israel. Do their sins warrant bitter suffering in exile, or an amelioration of their conditions? Or will they finally merit the advent of the Messiah, the end of exile, and the final return to their land, redemption, and resurrection of the dead?

Who is it that can serve as a heavenly advocate, either for the entire people, or for individual Jews? Although some texts picture angels as advocates, these tkhines—and the ritual of laying wicks and making candles—put the dead in this important role. In some ethnographic and literary descriptions of laying wicks and making the candles, the women call upon the dead members of their family, parents, grandparents, and others, to aid them in the heavenly court. In other descriptions, and in the texts translated below, women appeal to the ancestors of Israel—Adam and Eve, Noah, Abraham and Sarah, Isaac and Rebecca, Jacob and Rachel, Moses, Aaron, and David and Solomon—to assist them. Not only do these prayers remind God of the merit of these forebears, they ask the forebears themselves to act as advocates, both in ensuring health and prosperity for the individual worshiper, and in bringing about an end to Israel's exile. Indeed, the very act of measuring the graves and laying the wicks for each of the ancestors establishes a relationship of reciprocity between the living and the dead. The living include the dead in the meritorious act of donating lights to the synagogue, and in return, the dead are obligated to help the living. Thus, this ritual portrays women as having the power to wake the dead and help bring about the end of Israel's exile.

Although most prayers and tkhines for the penitential season have repentance for sin as their major theme, Sarah's two tkhines give this theme only second place. Most important in these texts is the plea for the messianic redemption, the end of the sufferings of exile, and the resurrection of the dead. Sarah has clearly been influenced by mystical conceptions of the redemption. She prays that God's attributes of justice and mercy be unified, a common kabbalistic trope for the messianic era, and stresses repeatedly that this era will bring the end of death. Further, she uses material that derives from the *Zohar,* the great classic of medieval Jewish mysticism, although she gets it from an intermediate source, a Yiddish paraphrase of portions of the *Zohar* called *Nakhalas Tsevi* (Inheritance of Tsevi), by Tsevi Hirsh Khotsh, first published in Amsterdam in 1711. This was one of several popular works that made kabbalistic ideas available to women and to men who could not read the mystical texts in the original Aramaic and Hebrew.

The final text included below is a prayer for measuring graves by Simeon ben Israel Judah Frankfurt, who was born in Schwerin, in the Duchy of Mecklenburg, in the first half of the seventeenth century, and was active in Amsterdam after 1656. It is found in his guide for dealing with the sick, the dying, and the dead, entitled *Sefer ha-ḥayyim* (The Book of Life), first published in Amsterdam in 1703. The primary audience for this book is the ḥevra qadisha, the "holy society" that concerns itself with aid to the sick and dying, preparation of the dead for burial, and funeral arrangements. Male members of the ḥevra qadisha prepared men for burial, and female members prepared women. Thus, *Sefer ha-ḥayyim* is bilingual: the first section of the book, in Hebrew, is intended for male readers, and the second section, in Yiddish, is addressed to women. The tkhine for measuring graves is found only in the second section of the book, thus providing further evidence that this was exclusively a women's ritual.

Although Frankfurt's tkhine provides a liturgy for the measuring of the graves and, incidentally, instructions for the correct way to measure, his underlying assumptions differ sharply from Sarah's. Far from seeing the dead as powerful advocates for the living, Frankfurt is careful to stress that prayers should be addressed only to God. The relationship between the living and the dead portrayed in Frankfurt's text is simple and one-sided: the acts of the living, such as making the candles, can bring benefit to the dead. Further, this text stresses atonement for sin as the purpose of bringing the candles into the synagogue.

The contrast between Frankfurt's tkhine on the one hand and those by Sarah bas Tovim on the other give evidence of two sharply differing attitudes about the relations of the living and the dead, and the efficacy of women's ritual performance. It should come as no surprise that a ritual existing over many centuries could be subject to different interpretations, even within the same era.

Eastern European tkhines were published in little booklets on bad paper with poor type and little proofreading. Because they were in Yiddish, a language with less prestige than Hebrew, and for women, only a bare minimum of resources was invested in their production. Most eighteenth-century eastern European tkhines made no reference to date or place of publication. For the two tkhines by Sarah bas Tovim, I have used undated editions found in the library of the Jewish Theological Seminary of America, New York. Western European Yiddish books were published with greater care. For the tkhine for measuring graves by Simeon Frankfurt, I have used the edition of *Sefer ha-hayyim* published in Kötten in 1717, found in the Jewish National and University Library, Jerusalem. The tkhine is found on pages 128b–129a of the Yiddish section of the book.

Three technical notes about the translation: First, the term "gate" is often used in Hebrew and Yiddish books to mean "chapter." Second, although the tkhines are in Yiddish, they make use of many Hebrew phrases, biblical verses, and proverbial expressions. These Hebrew phrases are often followed by a translation or explanation in Yiddish. I have therefore used boldface type for the Hebrew words that occur in these texts; this will explain what might otherwise seem to be extraneous repetition. Third, some works that are entirely in Yiddish have Hebrew titles. In these cases, I have romanized the titles in accordance with the rules for Yiddish rather than Hebrew.

Further Reading

To learn more about the women's prayers known as tkhines, see Chava Weissler, *Voices of the Matriarchs* (Boston: Beacon, 1998); and Devra Kay, "An Alternative Prayer Canon for Women: The *Seyder Tkhines*," in *Zur Geschichte der jüdischen Frau in Deutschland,* edited by Julius Carlebach (Berlin: Metropol, 1993). For a more extended discussion of all of the texts translated below, see Chava Weissler, " 'For the Human Soul Is the Lamp of the Lord: The *Tkhine* for 'Laying Wicks' by Sarah bas Tovim,' " *Polin* 10 (1997): 49–65; I have used some language from that article in the present essay. Several anthologies of tkhine translations have recently been published; see Tracy Guren Klirs, ed., *The Merit of Our Mothers: A Bilingual Anthology of Jewish Women's Prayers* (Cincinnati: Hebrew Union College Press, 1992); Norman Tarnor, ed. and trans., *A Book of Jewish Women's Prayers: Translations from the Yiddish* (Northvale, N.J.: Jason Aronson, 1995); and Rivka Zakutinsky, *Techinas: A Voice from the Heart* (Brooklyn, N.Y.: Aura, 1992). The anthologies by Klirs and Zakutinsky both include the Yiddish text on pages facing the English translation.

Three brief descriptions of the candlemaking ritual are available in English. The earliest is found in the autobiographical novel *Of Bygone Days* by Mendele Mokher Seforim (pseudonym of Sholom Jacob Abramovitch, 1835–1917), set in Kapulie, Lithuania, in the 1840s. This short novel, translated by Raymond Scheindlin, is included in *A Shtetl and Other Yiddish Novellas,* edited by Ruth R. Wisse (New York: Behrman House, 1973), pp. 249–358. Chapter 5 describes a group of women, led by the character who represents the author's mother, reciting a text quite similar to the tkhine for laying wicks in *The Three Gates* by Sarah bas Tovim. In *Burning Lights* (New York: Schocken, 1946), a memoir of growing up in early twentieth-century Vitebsk, Bella Chagall recalls helping her mother to make the candles by holding the ends of the wicks as her mother rubbed each wick with wax. Her mother improvises prayers for each of the living and departed family members as she waxes each wick; see pages 84–88. Finally, Shmuel Yosef Agnon briefly describes the making of the candles by women and the accompanying recitation of supplications in *Days of Awe* (New York: Schocken, 1965), pp. 142–43.

For a comprehensive study of illness and death in Ashkenazic Judaism, including discussions of the relations between the living and the dead, see Sylvie-Anne Goldberg, *Crossing the Jabbok* (Berkeley and Los Angeles: University of California Press, 1996). A modern ethnographic study records both the texts and the chant melodies of cemetery tkhines still recited by women in Rumania in the 1960s; see Gisela Suliteanu, "The Traditional System of Melopeic Prose of the Funeral Songs Recited by the Jewish Women of the Socialist Republic of Rumania," in *Folklore Research Center Studies,* vol. 3, edited by Issachar Ben-Ami (Jerusalem: Magnes, 1972), pp. 291–349.

Tkhine of the Gate of Unification Concerning the Aeons

This tkhine was made by the important woman, Mistress Sarah bas Tovim, daughter of the rabbinical scholar, very learned in Torah, the renowned Rabbi Mordecai, son of the rabbi, the great luminary, Rabbi Isaac of blessed memory, of the holy community of Satanov.

O dear women and maids, if you read this tkhine your hearts will rejoice. They are taken out of holy books. By their merit will you be worthy to enter the land of Israel. I have set down a beautiful new tkhine to be said on Mondays and Thursdays and fast days and on the Days of Awe. **Grace is deceitful and beauty is vain** [Prov. 31:30]. Beauty is nothing, only righteous deeds are good. **The wisest of women builds her house** [Prov. 14:1]. The main thing is that the woman should run the house so that one can study Torah therein, and that she should guide her children **in the straight path** to God's service.

I, poor woman, I have been **scattered and dispersed** [Esther 3:8], I have had no rest, my heart has moaned within me. I have recalled from whence I come and whither I shall go, and where I will be taken. A great fear has come over me, and I have begged the living God, blessed be he, **with copious tears**, that the tkhine may come out of me.

I, the well-known woman Sarah bas Tovim, of distinguished lineage, who has no **strange thought**, but has made this tkhine only for the sake of the dear God, be blessed, so that it may be a memorial for me after my death. Whoever reads this tkhine, her prayer will certainly be acceptable before God, may his Name be blessed. I, the woman Sarah bas Tovim daughter of the rabbinical scholar, learned in Torah, the renowned Rabbi Mordecai, son of the great luminary, Rabbi Isaac, of blessed memory, of the holy community of Satanov, may God protect it. . . .

This prayer is to be said for the candles that one makes in honor of the Day of Atonement.

May it be your will may it be your will, God our God, and the God of our forebears Abraham, Isaac, and Jacob, that our **thought** and our **deed** may be acceptable to you, as we make the candles to honor the holy Day of Atonement, which is an awesome day. By the merit of the lights that we make today in the synagogue so that we may pray by their light, may we have atonement this Yom Kippur for our sins. And may you draw us out to **the great supernal light**, and may you enlighten my eyes, and my husband's eyes and my children's eyes, and my children's children's eyes in the Torah. May you give us abundance, and livelihood, and life, and peace, and heart's ease, so that we may be able to serve you. And make my light, and my husband's light, and my children's and grandchildren's lights and all of my dear relatives' lights continue to burn, so that their lights are not extinguished before their time. And raise my luck, and the luck of my husband and children and grandchildren, for everything good.

Enlighten our darkness, so that the **light of the Torah** may shine for us, as it says in the verse, **The commandment is a lamp, and the teaching is light** [Prov. 6:23], which means in Yiddish: A commandment is compared to a light, as King David, peace be upon him, said: **Your word is a lamp to my feet, a light for my path** [Ps. 119:105], which means in Yiddish: Your speech is like a light for the course of my feet, and a light for my path. May you enlighten the darkness of your people Israel, who are in such great trouble, **whether in captivity or in plague or in illness or in prison or in famine or in the desert,** in all the places where your people Israel are found, **whether on land or sea.**

And may it be your will, God, my God, that all those who can give no lights in the synagogues may have a portion in these lights we make. And by this means, may our prayers be accepted, so that we may be helped out of all the troubles of this bitter exile. May we have a good year, a year in which all the terrible troubles will be removed from your people Israel, here and in all corners of the world. May there come before you the merit of Abraham, Isaac, and Jacob, so that their good deeds may make our darkness light. Lead us on the straight path, as you made the **pillar of fire** and the **pillar of cloud** shine for us when you drew our forebears out of Egypt. So may you deliver us also from the exile, and lead us to our land with great joy and with great shining fiery pillars. May we be worthy to have our **pure candelabrum** and our Temple **in our days, Amen.**

May it be your will may it be your will, God, my God, the God of my forebears, Abraham, Isaac, and Jacob, and of Sarah, Rebecca, Rachel, and Leah, the God of righteous men and women, of male and female martyrs, that for the souls that have already been forgotten, and for the souls who died before their time in their youth, and for the souls who have no one to make lights for them in the synagogue; may it be your will, God, my God, that they may have a portion in these lights, so that our lights will not be extinguished, heaven forbid, before the proper time. As we have not forgotten the souls who sleep in their graves—we go to pray to them and measure them—so may we be measured for good in the heavenly court, so that our sentence may be with great mercy, not with anger. For whomever God, blessed be he, inscribes for life on Rosh Hashanah, this festival is a good festival, and for whomever, God forbid, is not inscribed for life, this festival is no festival, but a dark festival. Therefore we beg the dear God, blessed be he, that our sentence may be pronounced with great mercy, not, heaven forbid, with anger, so that we may not, heaven forbid, leave any little orphans. May the souls announce to the souls that sleep in the Cave of Machpelah [in Hebron, the resting place of the Patriarchs and Matriarchs] that they should pray for us, that we may have a good year, that we may be worthy to see the red thread turn white [*Mishnah Yoma* 6:9], that we may be delivered, and that we may have **a year of mercy for good, Amen.** . . .

Our sages write [*Nakhalas Tsevi,* beginning of *Vayikra,* a paraphrase of *Zohar* 3:6a–b] that the **final redemption** will not be the same as it was in the first [Babylonian] exile, for which God set a length of time for them to be in exile, and when the time was up, they returned from exile by themselves. But God alone will raise the Congregation of Israel out of the **latter exile**, and will lead them out of exile.

There is a parable of a king who was angry at his wife. He banished her from his palace for a set time during which she should not come to him. When the time came, she went of her own accord before the king and came before him. Thus it happened again. Two or three times the king banished her **for a time**, and when the time came she returned home **before the king** of her own accord. But **at the final time**, at the moment of redemption, after the king had banished her **for a long time**, thus spoke the king: this time is not like the other times, that she should come of her own accord, rather, I myself will go after her with all the **courtiers** and will lead her back to me. When the king comes to her, he has been holding her **in lowliness on the ground in the dust**: in her house she lies on the earth **in lowliness**. When he sees the queen **at that time**, he conciliates her and puts his arms around her and restores her and brings her **to his palace**, and swears an oath to her that he will never separate himself from her again, and will never distance himself from her to eternity.

Thus, too, the Holy One, blessed be he. Whenever the Congregation of Israel were in exile, each time, when the moment came, they came **before the King** of their own accord. But in the **final exile**, it will not be that way, but rather the Holy One, blessed be he, will clasp them by the hand, and will restore them and cause them to return **to the palace**, into his Temple, **speedily in our days, Amen.**

The Tkhine of **Three Gates**

This tkhine was made by the virtuous woman, Mistress Sarah, may she live long, daughter of our teacher the rabbi Jacob, of blessed memory, grandchild of the rabbi, our teacher Mordecai, of blessed memory, who was head of the rabbinical court in the holy community of Brisk, may God protect it.

I, Sarah bas Tovim, I do this for the sake of the dear God, blessed be he, and blessed be his name, and arrange, this second time, yet another beautiful new tkhine **concerning three gates**. **The first gate** is founded upon the three commandments that we women were commanded: **Hannah is their name**; their name [acronym] is Hanna"h, that is to say, **ḥallah** [separating a piece of dough in memory of priestly tithes], **niddah** [menstrual taboos and purification], and **hadlaqat ha-nerot** [kindling Sabbath lights]. **The second gate** is a tkhine to pray when one blesses the New Moon. **The third gate** concerns the Days of Awe.

I take for my help the living God, blessed be he, who lives forever and to eternity, and I set out this second beautiful new tkhine in Yiddish with great love, with great awe, with trembling and terror, with broken limbs, with great petition. . . . May God have mercy upon me and upon all Israel. May I not long be forced to be a wanderer, by the merit of our Mothers Sarah, Rebecca, Rachel, and Leah, and may my own dear mother Leah pray to God, blessed be he, for me, that my being a wanderer may be an atonement for me for my sins. May God, blessed be he, forgive me for having talked in synagogue in my youth, while they were reading the dear Torah.

Lord of the whole world, I lay my prayer before you. As I begin to arrange my second beautiful new tkhine, with entire devotion and with the entire foundation of my heart, may you protect us from suffering and pain. I pray the dear God, blessed be he, that he may soon have great mercy on all Israel, and also on the years of my old age, that I not be forced to wander, as he heard the prayer of our Fathers and Mothers. Remember when our Father Abraham grasped the neck of Isaac with his left hand, and took the slaughtering knife in his right hand, to slaughter his son Isaac, and he did this for love of you, and did not delay in performing your mission upon which you sent him. So does it become you also to have mercy upon us. And I beg heaven and earth and all the holy angels to pray for me, that both of my tkhines may be accepted; may they become a crown for his holy name upon his head, Amen. . . .

This tkhine one should say before making candles on the eve of the Day of Atonement.

Lord of the world, I pray you, most merciful God, may you accept my observance of the commandment of the lights that we make for the sake of your holy Name, and for the sake of the holy souls.

May it be your will; May it be your will that today, on the eve of the Day of Atonement, we be remembered before you by performance of the commandment of the lights that we will make in the synagogue. May we be remembered for good, and may we be worthy to give lights to the Temple, as it was of old. And may the prayers that are said by the light of these candles be said with great devotion and **fear and awe**, so that Satan may not hinder our prayer. And may the lights that will be made for the sake of the holy souls . . . [words missing]. May they awaken and each announce to the next all the way back to the holy Fathers and Mothers, who should further announce to each other back to Adam and Eve, so they may rectify the sin by which they brought death to the world. May they arise out of their graves and pray for us. For they caused death to enter the world, so it is fitting for them to plead for us that we may be free of the Angel of Death.

As I lay the next wick for the sake of our father Noah, it is fitting for him, too, to pray for us, for he was in great need; of him it is written: **"For the waters have come up to my neck"** [Ps. 69:2]; the water came up all the way to his neck. May the God who helped him save us from fire and water and from all evil that we fear; may it not, God forbid, come to us.

As I lay the third thread of the wicks for our Father Abraham, whom you saved from the fiery furnace, may you purify us of our **sins and trespasses**. May our souls become pure, just as they were given to us, without guilt, **without any fear or terror**, as they came into our bodies.

By the merit of my laying the thread for our Mother Sarah, may God, blessed be he, remember for us the merit of her pain when her dear son Isaac was led away to be bound on the altar [cf. Gen. 22]. May she be an advocate for us before God, may he be blessed, that this year we not, God forbid, become widows, and that our little children may not, God forbid, be taken away from the world during our lives.

By the merit of our laying a thread for our Father Isaac's sake, may you have compassion for us. You have commanded us to blow the shofar on the New Year: **The horn of a ram, in memory of the binding of Isaac** [Babylonian Talmud, *Rosh Hashanah* 16a]. May you remember this merit for us, that we may be able to tend to our children's needs, that we may be able to keep them in school, so that they accustom themselves to God's service, to repeat **Amen, may his great Name be blessed forever and ever** [congregational response to the Kaddish prayer]. May the merit of my performance of the commandment of the lights be accepted as was the light that the high priest kindled in the Temple; may it enlighten our children's eyes in the holy Torah. I also entreat the dear God, while I perform the commandment of blessing the lights, that my prayer and my performance of the commandment of the lights be accepted by the dear God, blessed be he.

As I lay the thread for the sake of our Mother Rebecca, who caused the blessings to come to our Father Jacob, may these blessings be fulfilled for us [cf. Gen. 27]. May we be redeemed out of exile.

Because of our laying the thread for the sake of our Father Jacob—as you rescued him from Esau and Laban, so may you save us from all demons and accusers, that they may not be able to accuse us before this Day of Judgment. May our sentence come forth from you for good, with great mercy. May we have a good judgment, with our husbands and children, **for a good life**—may we not, God forbid, become widows, nor our children orphans.

By the merit of my laying a thread for our mother Rachel's sake, may you cause to be fulfilled, by her merit, "**And your children shall come back to their own country**" [cf. Jer. 31:15–17]; that means, by Rachel's merit, God, blessed be he, will bring us back to our land, Amen. May her merit defend us, that she did not let herself be comforted until the coming of the righteous redeemer, may he come speedily and soon, in our days, Amen.

By the merit of our laying a thread for our Father Moses our Teacher, peace be upon him, may his merit defend us: he went into heaven and prayed for us and brought us the dear Torah from God, blessed be he. May his merit stand by us, that we may be delivered speedily and soon. When he went into heaven for forty days, you let him know that the holy days are days of favor. God said: "**I have forgiven according to your words**" [Num. 14:20]; this means: I have forgiven the Israelites for the sin of the Golden Calf. I pray you, dear God, that you may forgive us in these days for the sins that we have committed during the whole year, and that you may inscribe us for a good year.

And by the merit of our laying a thread for our Father Aaron the Priest, and by his merit, may we be worthy to give candles to the Temple. May we live to see how he performs the priestly service. May his merit defend us, and enlighten the eyes of our children and our children's children in the dear Torah, like a light.

By the merit of David and Solomon, who built the Temple: They asked that when a non-Jew comes into the Temple and prays, that his prayer be accepted for their sake [1 Kings 8:41–43]. May God, blessed be he, pronounce our judgment with great mercy and compassion.

By the merit of all the righteous and pious people who have ever lived, from the time of Adam until our own day—may their merit defend us on the Day of Judgment so that we will be sealed for good. May our lights, and our husbands' lights, and our children's lights, not be extinguished before their time, God forbid. By the merit of the holy Fathers and Mothers, by the merit of the little children who say, "**Amen, may his great Name be blessed forever and ever**"—may their merit defend us so that the Resurrection of the Dead will come speedily and soon, that they may rejoice **in the time to come.**

May it be your will May it be your will that today, on the eve of Yom Kippur, we may be remembered for good as we bring the candles into the synagogue, for this commandment that we perform. May we be worthy to bring candles to the Temple as it was of old. And may the prayers said by these lights be with great devotion and great awe, so that Satan will be unable to hinder our prayer. May these lights, which were made for the holy and pure souls, awaken them so that they arise and announce to one another back to the holy Fathers and Mothers, and further back to Adam and Eve, that they repair the sin by which they brought death to the whole world. May they arise from their graves and pray for us, that this year, may it come for good, there may finally be the Resurrection of the Dead. May the Attribute of Justice become the Attribute of

Mercy; may they be unified. May they pray for us that the Resurrection of the Dead may be fulfilled. And may all the holy and pure angels pray that the dry bones live again speedily and soon [cf. Ezek. 37:1–14].

Lord of the world, you have commanded us to make candles for the holy day. I beg you, kind Father, accept today my fulfillment of the commandment of laying the threads. May you increase life and peace. And may you accept the prayers that are said by these lights just as if we had prayed with great devotion and with whole hearts. May you forgive the sins we have committed during the whole year, **whether knowingly or unknowingly**. May you not remember our sins, but rather the good deeds we have done. On the Day of Judgment, may you search out and decree for us that we have a healthy year, a year of vigor, and that we may be finally delivered from the hard, bitter Exile. I entreat you, most dear God, may nothing of mine or of all Israel be diminished, and may you lay up for us an easy livelihood, without troubles. May I and my husband be privileged to marry off our children in great honor, without troubles. And may you favor us with a good seal, amen and amen.

Lord of the world, I pray you, merciful God, that you may accept the lights that we make for the holy pure souls. For each thread that we lay, may you increase life for us. May the holy souls awake out of their graves and pray for us that we may be healthy. It is appropriate for us to pray for the dead, for those who died in our own generations, and for those who have died from the time of Adam and Eve on. Today we make candles for the sake of all of the souls—for the sake of the souls that lie in the fields and the forests, and for all the martyrs, and for all those who have no children, and for all the little children. May they awake, may the dry bones live, speedily and soon. May we be worthy to see the Resurrection of the Dead this year, Amen, Selah.

From *Sefer ha-Ḥayyim* [The Book of Life]
Compiled by Simeon ben Israel Judah Frankfurt

The women who measure the graves should say this prayer. However, first she should say [some Hebrew prayers]. Then she should say this:

I pray you, O Lord my God I pray you, my dear God, accept my prayer that I pray before you in this holy place [that is, the cemetery] where lie the pious who sleep in the earth. We are come here for the sake of your glory, and for the sake of the pious souls who are in the light of paradise, and whose bodies rest in the earth, to measure the cemetery and all the graves, so that all may have a part in the candles that we shall bring into the holy synagogue, to honor you with, and that the lamp may bring atonement for the souls, who are called **"the human soul is the lamp of the Lord"** [Prov. 20:27]. And when we say our prayers in synagogue by the light of these candles, may you accept and receive our plea to forgive all our sins. And may you enlighten us with the light of your Shekhinah [divine presence]. And may the light be an atonement for the sin of Eve, who extinguished Adam's light, and brought death to the world. O dear God, may you deliver us and enlighten us with the light from your holy candelabrum in the Temple, and make all the dead live, and do away with death unto eternity, just as you have spoken. Amen, Selah.

And they should begin to measure from the right side, and should measure all the graves with the wick, except for the grave of some one who did not do right during his life. And they should make wax candles from it in the synagogue. And when they have measured, they should say [some additional Hebrew prayers].

4

Adorning the "Bride" on the Eve of the Feast of Weeks

Daniel C. Matt

The festival of *Shavu'ot* (Weeks) is celebrated on the sixth day of the Hebrew month of Sivan. Its name derives from the fact that it falls seven weeks after the second night of Passover. When the Temple stood in Jerusalem, barley from the late spring harvest was brought on *Shavu'ot* as an offering, along with first fruits. Beginning in rabbinic times, however, *Shavu'ot* also was associated with the giving of the Torah on Mt. Sinai, and the festival became known as *zeman mattan torateinu*, "the time of the giving of our Torah." The biblical account of the giving of the Torah (Exod. 19–20) is therefore chanted in the synagogue on the first day of *Shavu'ot*.

A custom arose to stay awake all night on the eve of *Shavu'ot* and study Torah. This vigil, known as *Tikkun leil Shavu'ot*, "the *tikkun* [adornment; to be explained below] of the eve of *Shavu'ot*," is first mentioned in the thirteenth century in the *Zohar*, the major work of Kabbalah, the Jewish mystical tradition. One later commentator, Abraham Gombiner (*Magen Avraham*, on *Orah Hayyim* 494; Jerusalem: Mif'al Shulhan Arukh, 1998, 6:474) connects the custom with the ancient midrash (*Shir ha-Shirim Rabbah* on 1:12; *Pirqei de-Rabbi Eli'ezer*, 41) that on the morning Israel was to receive the Torah at Mt. Sinai, they overslept! God and Moses had to wake them up. In order to make sure that this never happens again, on each anniversary of the revelation at Sinai Jews stay awake all night and study Torah.

The origins of *Tikkun leil Shavu'ot* are unclear. Yehuda Liebes has suggested (*Studies in the Zohar*, pp. 74–82) that something similar may already have been practiced in rabbinic times in the circles of the Merkavah mysticism. The *Zohar* (3:98a) claims that "the ancient *hasidim* [pietists] did not sleep on this night; they would engage in Torah." Similarly, Moses de Leon writes (*Sod Hag ha-Shavu'ot*, in *Qovets Sifrei Qabbalah*, 87a–b, Schocken MS 14, Schocken Library, Jerusalem) that "the ancient ones" used to study Torah the entire night: Torah, Prophets,

Writings, Talmud, midrash, and secrets of Torah. "They maintained the tradition (*qabbalah*) of their ancestors."

How ancient these "ancient ones" were is open to question. Even in the centuries following the *Zohar* we hear next to nothing about the *Tikkun* until the sixteenth century, when an all-night study session is described by the kabbalist and mystical poet Solomon Alkabez, composer of the Sabbath hymn *Lekhah Dodi*. In 1529, Alkabez decided to settle in the land of Israel. On his journey there, he stayed briefly in Adrianople and visited Nikopolis (in what is today Bulgaria), home of the famous halakhist and mystic Joseph Caro. (Alkabez's description first appeared in Caro's mystical diary, *Maggid Meisharim,* and later in Isaiah Horowitz, *Shenei Luhot ha-Berit, massekhet shavu'ot* [Jerusalem; n.p., 1975], 29d–30b.) Together Alkabez and Caro celebrated *Shavu'ot.* Although it is likely that Alkabez had already practiced the *Tikkun* in his native Salonika, in the presence of Caro something new transpired.

Alkabez outlines the passages they studied, beginning with the opening section of Genesis (1:1–2:3). The two mystics chanted the text "in a melody out loud." They continued with various passages relating to revelation: Exodus 19–20, 24 (the revelation at Mt. Sinai); Deuteronomy 5:1–6:9 (a second account of the revelation at Sinai and the *Shema* prayer); 34 (the last chapter of the Torah); Ezekiel 1 (the prophet's vision of the divine throne whirling through heaven, which serves as the *haftarah* (prophetic portion for the first day of *Shavuot*); Habakuk 3 (the prophet's vision, which serves as the *haftarah* for the second day); Psalms 19 (praising the Torah) and 68 (a psalm about the revelation at Sinai); Song of Songs (interpreted as a love song between God and Israel, who were married at Sinai); Ruth (traditionally read on *Shavu'ot*); and the conclusion of Chronicles, the final book of the Bible, "all of this in awe, in melody, in intonation that cannot be believed if it were told." The two kabbalists continued with *Zera'im,* the opening tractate of the Mishnah (rabbinic legal treatise) and then began studying the Mishnah again *al derekh ha-emet,* "according to the path of truth," that is, from a mystical perspective. At this point, at midnight, after studying two tractates from the Mishnah, they heard a "voice speaking through the mouth of the *hasid* [Caro], a powerful voice, enunciating clearly. All the neighbors heard and did not understand. The melody was powerful, the voice increasing in power. We fell on our faces."

The voice speaking through the mouth of Joseph Caro was the voice of his personal *maggid* ("preacher," mentor, heavenly voice). This phenomenon of automatic speech was experienced frequently by Caro, who recorded the pronouncements in his mystical diary. On this occasion, the *maggid* identifies itself as *Shekhinah,* the feminine divine presence.

> Listen my beloved ones, finest of the fine! *Shalom* to you! Happy are you! Happy are those who gave birth to you! Happy are you in this world, happy are you in the world that is coming! For you have devoted yourselves to crown me on this night. For many years the crown has [lain] fallen from my head.

She goes on to say that it would have been better if there were ten of them assembled together: "I would have ascended even higher." She also urges them to journey to the land of Israel.

All night Alkabez and Caro continued studying, and early the next morning they immersed themselves in a *mikveh* (a ritual bath, as suggested in *Zohar* 3:98b). They did not sleep during the daytime, either; rather, Alkabez attended a sermon delivered by Caro. The next night, the second night of *Shavu'ot,* they followed the advice of Shekhinah and assembled a quorum of ten to engage in the *Tikkun.* This time the voice spoke through Caro sooner: as soon as they finished reading the account of the revelation in Deuteronomy and were reading the *Shema,* "the voice of our beloved knocked," conveying words of wisdom and praising them "for about half an hour." Afterward they continued studying. At midnight, the voice returned and spoke through Caro for more than an hour.

The festival passed. Alkabez journeyed on and eventually arrived in the land of Israel, settling in Safed in the hills of Galilee. Safed was already a center of mystical Judaism, attracting scholars and devotees from both Sephardic and Ashkenazic centers. Soon Caro arrived, too. In Safed, *Tikkun leil Shavu'ot* was practiced widely, and from here it spread throughout the Jewish world.

Abraham Galante, one of the Safed kabbalists, offers this description of the custom:

> On the eve of *Shavu'ot* it is customary to sleep for an hour or two after preparing for the festival, because that night, after eating, people gather in the synagogues, each congregation in its own synagogue. They do not sleep the entire night, and they read Torah, Prophets and Writings, Mishnah, *Zohar,* and interpretations of biblical verses until the light of dawn. Then all the people immerse themselves in water before the morning prayer.
>
> Y. D. Wilhelm, "Sidrein Tikkunim," p. 125

The well-known kabbalist Hayyim Vital was apparently born in Safed in 1542, several years after Alkabez and Caro arrived. In his description of *Tikkun leil Shavu'ot* (in *Sha'ar ha-Kavvanot* [Jerusalem: n.p., 1988], 2:202a–203b), he assures his readers that anyone who manages to stay awake the entire night studying Torah will not be harmed for the entire coming year. He outlines the course of study for the night, which, as we can see, has expanded somewhat since Alkabez and Caro's *tikkun* in Nikopolis. Vital's menu consists of: Genesis 1:1–2:4, 6:6–8 (the concluding verses of the first weekly portion of the Torah), then the first three and last three verses of each of the remaining weekly portions of the Torah. Vital includes the sections on revelation from the Torah and the Prophets mentioned by Alkabez, along with several other passages—for example, the Counting of the Omer (the period between Passover and *Shavu'ot*) and the offering of the first fruits. The devotee is instructed to read as well the first and last three verses of each book of the Prophets and of the Writings, twenty-four books in all. The verses of Lamentations, which graphically describe the destruction of Jerusalem, are read quietly, in honor of the festival. The entire book of Ruth is read, as well.

The rest of the night one should spend on "secrets of the Torah and the Book of *Zohar*, as far as your mind can apprehend." Shortly before dawn, one should immerse in the *mikveh*.

Vital's older contemporary, Moses Cordovero, who also lived in Safed, offers a somewhat different list (in his commentary on the *Zohar, Or Yaqar* [Jerusalem: Ahuzat Yisrael, 1962], 1:76b), emphasizing the Bible less and the Mishnah more. By the time of Isaiah Horowitz (c. 1565–1630), who also spent time in Safed, the *Tikkun* has expanded to include more biblical material than that in Vital's list, as well as the first and last mishnah of each tractate, the first and last mishnah (section) of *Sefer Yetsirah*, a selection from the *Zohar* (3:97b–98b) and a list of the 613 commandments (*Shenei Luhot ha-Berit, massekhet shavu'ot*, 29d). Horowitz adds that it is customary to speak only Hebrew the entire night.

Today, *Tikkun leil Shavu'ot* is practiced widely. In many congregations rabbis, scholars, and lay people alternate in presenting their own gems of Torah throughout the night. The various forms the ritual has assumed all derive from the description in the *Zohar* (1:8a), to which we now turn.

As the passage opens, we find Rabbi Shim'on, the hero of the *Zohar*, deeply engaged in study on the eve of *Shavu'ot*. He is preparing for the next morning, the reliving of the revelation at Mt. Sinai. According to Kabbalah, the moment of revelation is the moment of union: the marriage of *Shekhinah*, the feminine aspect of God, with Her husband, *Tif'eret*, the Holy One, blessed be He. He is symbolized by the written Torah, the Five Books of Moses; She, by the oral Torah, the expansive interpretation of the written Torah contained in rabbinic literature. *Shavu'ot* is their wedding celebration.

Rabbi Shim'on is accompanied by the *havrayya*, the "companions," who together with him are adorning the bride, *Shekhinah*, in preparation for Her union with *Tif'eret*. The adornments they offer Her consist of gems of Torah. The connection between ornaments and books of the Bible is already made in the Midrash (*Shir ha-Shirim Rabbah* on 4:11, in the name of Shim'on ben Lakish): "Just as a bride is adorned with twenty-four ornaments [cf. Isa. 3:18–24] and if she is lacking one of them, she is considered worthless, so a disciple must be fluent in twenty-four books [of the Bible], and if he is lacking one of them, he is worthless."

The Hebrew root *tkn* ("adorn, prepare, array") appears frequently in this passage, which explains why the all-night study session became known as *Tikkun leil Shavu'ot*, "the adornment of the eve of *Shavu'ot*."

Rabbi Shim'on and the companions proceed from Torah to the Prophets, from there to the Writings, then on to midrash and mystical interpretations. The first stages in their itinerary recall those of the second-century mystic Shim'on ben Azzai, as recounted in the midrashic collection *Vayikra Rabbah* 16:4:

> Ben Azzai was sitting and expounding, and fire was blazing around him. They [his disciples] came and told Rabbi Akiva. . . . He went to him and said, "Perhaps you are engaged in the chambers of the Chariot [the secrets of Ezekiel's vision of the Chariot]."
> He replied, "No, I am joining words of Torah to the Prophets, and words of the

Prophets to the Writings, and the words of Torah are as joyous as on the day they were given from Sinai."

Rabbi Shim'on assures the companions that their devotion to *Shekhinah* will be rewarded, for they will participate in the wedding ceremony the next day and be blessed there. He concludes by interpreting a verse from Psalm 19: "Heaven declares the glory of God, and the sky proclaims the work of His hands." According to Rabbi Shim'on's mystical interpretation, this verse refers to the ritual of *Tikkun*. Accompanied by camps of angels, *Shekhinah,* known as Glory, awaits those who adorned Her. The divine groom, *Tif'eret,* who is called Heaven, shines upon Her, and all those who adorned Her are proclaimed as "the work of His hands." These mystical companions of *Shekhinah* are described, too, as "masters of the sign of the covenant with the Bride, Her partners." The covenant is the covenant of circumcision, and the masters of this covenant are those who have mastered the sexual urge and lead holy sexual lives. They embody the divine quality of *Yesod,* the divine phallus, and so their virtue is proclaimed by *Yesod,* symbolized by the sky. Thus the companions are invited to participate in the union with *Shekhinah.*

The passage below is from *Zohar* 1:8a. My translation will appear in *Sefer ha-Zohar: The Book of Radiance,* a new translation with commentary sponsored by the Pritzker Family Philanthropic Foundation.

Further Reading

Yehuda Liebes discusses *Tikkun leil Shavu'ot* in *Studies in the Zohar* (Albany: State University of New York Press, 1993), pp. 55–63, 74–82. He presents evidence for an early origin of the ritual and argues that *Tikkun leil Shavu'ot* is the setting of the *Idra Rabba,* one of the most dramatic and profound sections of the *Zohar.* Isaiah Tishby translates and interprets the passage I have presented here in *The Wisdom of the Zohar,* translated by David Goldstein (London: Littman Library of Jewish Civilization, 1989), vol. 3, pp. 1,318–19). Hebrew readers can consult the study by Y. D. Wilhelm, "Sidrei Tikkunim," in *Alei Ayin: Minhat Devarim li-Shlomo Zalman Schocken* (Jerusalem: n.p., 1948–1952), pp. 125–30; and Moshe Hallamish, *Kabbalah in Liturgy, Halakhah and Customs* (Hebrew) (Ramat-Gan, Israel: Bar-Ilan University Press, 2000), pp. 595–612. The development of various kabbalistic rituals in Safed is discussed by Gershom Scholem, "Tradition and New Creation in the Ritual of the Kabbalists," in *On the Kabbalah and Its Symbolism* (New York: Schocken, 1965), pp. 118–57. On the kabbalistic center of Safed, see Lawrence Fine, *Safed Spirituality* (Ramsey, N.J.: Paulist Press, 1984). Joseph Caro and his mystical *maggid* are explored by R. J. Zwi Werblowsky, *Joseph Karo:*

Lawyer and Mystic (Philadelphia: Jewish Publication Society of America, 1977). For an introduction to the Kabbalah, see Daniel C. Matt, *The Essential Kabbalah* (San Francisco: HarperSanFrancisco, 1995).

Adorning the "Bride" on the Eve of the Feast of Weeks

Rabbi Shim'on was sitting and plying Torah on the night when the Bride is joined with Her Husband. For we have learned: All those companions who are initiates of the bridal palace need—on that night when the Bride is destined to be the next day under the canopy with Her Husband—to be with Her that whole night and to rejoice with Her, in Her adornments in which She is arrayed, plying Torah, from Torah to the Prophets, and from Prophets to the Writings, and midrashic renderings of verses and mysteries of wisdom, for these are Her adornments and her finery.

She, with Her maidens, enters and stands above their heads. She is adorned by them and rejoices with them that whole night. The next day She does not enter the canopy without them, and they are called "sons of the canopy." As soon as She enters the canopy, the blessed holy One inquires about them and blesses them and crowns them with bridal crowns. Happy is their portion!

Rabbi Shim'on along with all the companions were singing the song of Torah and innovating words of Torah, each one of them. Rabbi Shim'on rejoiced along with all the other companions.

Rabbi Shim'on said, "My children, happy is your portion, for tomorrow the Bride will not enter the canopy without you. For all those who arrange Her adornments tonight and rejoice with Her will be recorded and inscribed in the Memorial Book, and the blessed Holy One blesses them with seventy blessings and crowns of the supernal world."

Rabbi Shim'on opened and said, "Heaven declares the glory of God [and the sky proclaims the work of His hands]" [Ps. 19:2]. We have already established this verse, but at this time, when the Bride is aroused to enter the canopy the next day, She is arrayed and illumined with Her adornments, together with the companions who rejoice with Her that whole night, while She rejoices with them. The following day, many troops, soldiers, and camps assemble with Her, and She waits with all of them for each and every one who adorned Her on this night. As soon as they join together, and she sees Her Husband, what is written? "Heaven declares the glory of God." Heaven—this is the Groom entering the canopy. Declares (*mesapperim*)—sparkles with the radiance of "sapphire" (*sappir*), sparkling and radiating from one end of the world to the other. "The glory of God"—this is the glory of the Bride, who is called God, as it is written: "God rages every day" [Ps. 7:12]. Every day of the year, She is called God, but now that She has entered the canopy, She is called Glory as well as

God, glory upon glory, radiance upon radiance, dominion upon dominion. Then, at the moment when Heaven enters the canopy, coming to illumine her, all those companions who adorned Her are designated there by name, as it is written: "The sky proclaims the work of His hands" [Ps. 19:2]. "The work of His hands"—these are the masters of the sign of the covenant with the Bride, Her partners.

5

New Year's Day for Fruit of the Tree

Miles Krassen

The *Tu bi-Shevat seder,* a ritual meal involving the eating of specific fruit, drinking wine, and studying or reciting specific selections from the sacred literature of Judaism, does not seem to have been known before the late seventeenth century. Although the fifteenth of the Hebrew month of *Shevat* was recognized as the New Year's Day for Trees by the school of Hillel in the Mishnah, its significance lay mainly in fixing the date from which fruit-bearing trees must be tithed. No specific laws or customs governed its observance, however. This may account for the fact that the thirteenth-century Spanish kabbalistic classic, the *Zohar,* fails to deal with the day. Kabbalists of this period were more concerned with providing mystical bases that would strengthen the motivation for observing the laws and traditions of classical Judaism than with creating new rituals. The kabbalists of sixteenth-century Safed did, however, create some new rituals, most notably the kabbalat Shabbat service. The kabbalistic *Tu bi-Shevat seder* was probably created sometime later, in the wake of kabbalistic creativity in sixteenth-century Safed.

The text of the seder, which has come to be known as *Peri 'Ez Hadar,* is essentially the same as the section on *Tu bi-Shevat* that appears in the Sabbatian-influenced anthology of kabbalistic customs, *Hemdat Yamim* (Izmir, 1731–1732). It is not yet possible to determine, however, when the text was actually composed or who its author may have been. The *Hemdat Yamim* was itself primarily a reworking of materials copied from various kabbalistic sources, some of which, at least, date back to the final decades of the seventeenth century. From internal references in the text, it is clear that the chapter on *Tu bi-Shevat* did not originally follow the chapter that precedes it in *Hemdat Yamim.* It seems probable, therefore, that the compiler of *Hemdat Yamim* copied the *Tu bi-Shevat* seder from one of these earlier sources. At any rate, the text has been printed separately many times as a pamphlet entitled *Peri 'Ez Hadar* since its first edition in Venice, 1728.

Both the text of *Peri 'Ez Hadar* and the *seder* that it contains seem to have been popular only among various Sefardic communities. No mention of the text or its customs is to be found in the classic Hasidic literature of eastern Europe. This may be due to the fact that *Hemdat Yamim* was condemned as a heretical Sabbatian text by Jacob Emden, who attributed it to the Sabbatian theologian Nathan of Gaza. Emden's influence, it seems, did not extend beyond the Ashkenazic community. In the Sefardic communities, the *Peri 'Ez Hadar* continued to be reprinted until the present day. It now appears that as a result of the unique historical conditions that have resulted from the establishment of the state of Israel, the *Tu bi-Shevat seder, Peri 'Ez Hadar,* is finally gaining acceptance among certain elements in the contemporary Askenazic communities as well. This is due, in part, to the unprecedented proximity of diverse Jewish communities in Jerusalem, which results in a period of mutual influence. Sefardic Torah scholars study in Ashkenazic *yeshivot* (rabbinic academies), and sages of Baghdad and Morocco have become experts in the writings of Hasidic masters. At the same time, Ashkenazic kabbalists have increasingly come under the influence of works composed or popularized among the Sefardic communities. It may be added that under these favorable conditions, kabbalistic works of all types and periods are appearing in print with ever greater frequency.

A recent Baghdadi edition of *Peri 'Ez Hadar* contains four basic sections. After an introduction that explains the basis for the *Tu bi-Shevat seder,* there is a prayer to be said before the actual seder begins. This is followed by a description of the order of the fruit to be eaten and the way wine should be blended in each of the four cups. The bulk of the seder consists of selections from the Bible, early rabbinic texts, and the zoharic literature. In fact, the greatest portion of this material is taken from the *Zohar*.

As a result, the *Peri 'Ez Hadar* is essentially a kabbalistic work, meant to be read and applied by a reader thoroughly schooled in the outlook of the Kabbalah, particularly as it developed in the school of Isaac Luria. This fact renders the text, even in translation, difficult for a modern reader to comprehend. In fact, many of those in the Sefardic community who participate in this ritual do not understand the *Zohar* texts. This is due to several factors. First, the text does not explain the rather complex basic principles of Kabbalah as they developed since the late twelfth century. In particular, comprehension of the text would require familiarity with the kabbalistic classic *Sefer ha-Zohar,* an esoteric work characterized by obscure allusions and highly symbolic language. In addition, the outlook of the *Peri Ez Hadar*'s author involves certain fundamental notions about nature, the cosmos, and the spiritual role that human beings are meant to play. These may be unfamiliar and even strange to a contemporary reader. Such notions, moreover, are not defended or justified but are implicit in the author's and the intended reader's worldview.

The *Tu bi-Shevat seder* celebrates an important moment in the yearly cycle of nature, the appearance of fruit on trees. In the land of Israel, this stage occurs during midwinter. In order to understand how the *Peri 'Ez Hadar* approaches this celebration, it is necessary to gain some understanding of how the kabbalists viewed nature. In general, the kabbalistic view shared many traits that were typical of other premodern cosmological systems, which tended to regard nature as in some sense sacred. This approach to nature is in marked contrast to those that have become typical of the modern period. For the kabbalist, nature is neither a source to be exploited for utilitarian benefits nor a sentimental vestige of the past to be romanticized by poets and naturalists. It is rather an ultimate link in a chain of divine manifestation that directly emerges from the divine source of life. Implicit here is a notion of sacred cosmology, which is not limited to material existence. The kabbalists' faith involves a hierarchy of worlds that are ontologically higher than the material world. These worlds are populated by angels and spiritual forces that span the ontological regions that separate humanity and the material world from God. Moreover, the forces in these worlds serve as conduits and sources for the divine energy that becomes manifest in nature and in Creation in general.

Although each world is characterized by an increasing degree of opacity that veils its divine root, all worlds share a common underlying structure. Thus contemplation of any world can lead to knowledge of the structure of the ultimate theosophical realm, the "world of emanation." This realm is the world of the ten *sefirot* (sing. *sefirah*) or ten divine qualities and aspects that constitute the inner life of God, insofar as it is accessible to human imagining. This principle is no less true of nature. Indeed, nature (along with the human body) is, in a sense, the most available arena of divine revelation, since the higher worlds are not apparent to the senses. As such, nature may serve as a mirror in which all of the mysteries of the concealed Godhead are reflected.

For example, the cosmology assumed in the text consists of four worlds that are hierarchically arranged between the divine source and the forces of evil. The ritual involves contemplating, blessing, and eating thirty types of fruit, ten for each of the second, third, and fourth worlds, called "Creation," "Formation," and "Making," respectively. The fruits are classified according to the nature of their shells and rind, which symbolize the type of protection required due to the way that each world may be threatened by evil. For example, the fruits that correspond to the "World of Creation" have no shells, because their roots are so far beyond evil's reach as to require no protection.

This fundamentally sacred view of nature renders it comparable to the Torah itself. For the kabbalist, the Torah is not merely an account of the sacred history of Israel and its divinely mandated laws. It is a primary manifestation of divine revelation. All of the secrets and mysteries of the cosmos and the inner workings of the Godhead are somehow contained within it. It is a cipher, however, that only yields its concealed meanings to those who hold the keys of divine gnosis. These mystics, the kabbalists, through contemplation and mystical experience have gained access to the symbol system that opens the Torah's deeper levels of meaning. For the kabbalist, nature parallels the Torah. The very same secrets that are concealed within the quintessential sacred text may be learned through directly contemplating aspects of nature. The structure of different kinds of fruit, the growing patterns of trees, the habits of birds, indeed all natural phenomena are, in essence, aspects of a divine epiphany that proclaims the truth of God's existence.

Here it should be added, however, that the kabbalist's position is not identical to that of medieval religious philosophers, like Maimonides, who also viewed nature as a source for knowledge of God. In their view, the knowledge of the wondrous construction of nature and its laws led to an appreciation for its Creator. Here, however, knowledge of God is theosophical. It regards nature as a symbolic representation of the hidden divine realm and not merely as an immaculately designed product of divine engineering.

We have thus far been considering nature as source for divine knowledge. There is another aspect of the kabbalist's view of nature that is equally fundamental. This is the question of humanity's relation to nature.

The kabbalistic cosmos in its present state, especially according to the school of Isaac Luria, is dualistic. Evil as well as good is present in some sense and to some degree in each of the worlds that exist below the world of divine emanation itself. Indeed, the way in which evil is present in each world is symbolized in the seder by the classification of fruits, according to the location of their shells, skin, or rind. Thus the presence of evil in our material world is also a reflection of conditions in the higher worlds, which themselves reflect the state of things in the theosophical realm. There, however, evil by definition cannot exist, although its roots, or potential for existence, are located in the highest ontological levels of divinity. Nevertheless, although evil is external to the divine realm of holiness itself, it is located in proximity to its tenth *sefirah, Malkhut*. Thus, as long as evil has not been entirely vanquished, it has the capacity to threaten the tenth *sefirah* and to separate her from the higher *sefirot*. The ascendancy of evil above is reflected by various conditions in the material world that are characterized by injustice. In terms of the sacred history of Judaism, the disruption of the divine realm is represented by Israel's exile among the nations, which symbolizes the absence of God's kingdom on earth.

The duality of good and evil is also symbolically present within nature. Sources of life, such as food, represent the powers of holiness. That which may not be eaten symbolizes the external evil forces. The edible portion of wheat, for example, symbolizes the tenth sefirah, whereas chaff represents the external forces. The edible portion of fruit is associated with forces of holiness, whereas its shell represents the forces of evil. Here we should note that the symbolism compels us to recognize that the "external forces" have an important role to play. They are not evil in an absolute sense. Indeed, the examples from nature teach us that when the cosmos is in a harmonious state, the "external forces" perform the positive function of acting as guardians that protect the more vulnerable manifestations of holiness.

It is obvious that nature alone is not sufficient for maintaining a harmonious state, however. Just as evil may assail the tenth sefirah above, those aspects of nature that should protect its life-giving elements can, under certain conditions, overrun them. As a result, the forces of holiness in nature can be cut off from the sources of life that sustain them, just as *Malkhut* can be separated from the higher sefirot.

If, then, neither the divine realm nor nature can be counted on to maintain a state of cosmic harmony, what factor remains that might act to fulfill this function? For the kabbalist, the answer is humanity. Indeed, according to kabbalistic exegesis, the separation of the tenth sefirah was first caused by the sin of Adam. Symbolically, through eating the fruit in direct violation of the divine command, Adam and Eve separated the forces of holiness in nature from their divine source, thus empowering the external forces. As a result, the edenic state of harmony was broken and humanity and nature became adversaries. Thus, from the kabbalistic point of view, the sin of Adam and Eve testifies to the awesome power that humanity possesses. It is humanity that is primarily responsible for the state of nature and the cosmos.

Although the first humans misused their power to disrupt the edenic state of harmony, the kabbalists believe that same power may still be used positively to reestablish and maintain the fragile cosmic balance. It is important to understand how, from the kabbalistic point of view, this power may be exercised. First, we should recall that Adam and Eve's sin consisted in separating an aspect of nature from its divine source. From this we may infer that a positive exercise of the human power to affect the cosmos involves connecting it, or more correctly, maintaining its connection, to the forces above. To a certain extent, this is directly accomplished by observing those laws concerning nature that are explicitly mandated by the Torah and interpreted and elaborated upon by the rabbinic authorities. Although the kabbalist believes implicitly in the cosmic efficacy of such divine commandments, however, he also believes that their effectiveness depends fundamentally on a deeper, essentially human quality: intentionality.

The kabbalist not only fulfills the external obligations of Jewish law but also transforms them into theurgic acts by having their specific cosmic effects in mind at the time that he performs them. Thus in fulfilling a specific commandment, he has in mind a precise effect, which he believes will occur in the upper worlds as a result of his action and intention. This intention is called the *kavvanah* (pl. *kavvanot*) of the commandment. Typically, this intentionality is practically expressed through a magical, contemplative technique, that involves visualization of the letters of divine names and their combination. Knowledge of these *kavvanot* constitutes one of the most important areas of kabbalistic concern.

Knowledge and practice of the *kavvanot* have important ramifications in the realm of nature. Indeed, nature's well-being, from the kabbalistic point of view, is largely dependent on the *kavvanot* of commandments that pertain to nature, such as blessings said over food. The *kavvanot* that accompany the fulfillment of these commandments are meant to insure that divine energy, or *shefaʿ*, will be drawn down from its ultimate source of life in the divine realm through the intermediate channels that deliver it to the realm of nature. Failure to perform this sacred role of guardianship impairs the functioning of this concealed process and threatens the ability of the guardian angels to replenish nature.

The school of Isaac Luria places emphasis on two additional concepts that are relevant to our text. According to this school, kabbalists are not only concerned with taking responsibility for the ongoing process of maintaining cosmic harmony. The cosmos has suffered serious structural damage in a catastrophic process of creation. Thus a long historical process of rectification, or *tiqqun,* is required in order to restore the cosmos to its proper state. As a result of the catastrophe, sparks of divine light fell from their allotted places in the upper worlds and became embedded and concealed in the lower orders. A primary responsibility, according to kabbalists of the Lurianic school, is the retrieval of these sparks, which must be elevated through performing the commandments and studying Torah with *kavvanah.*

The catastrophic effect was not limited to the lights of the world of emanation, however. As a result of Adam and Eve's sin, a parallel shattering occurred within the unity of the human soul. Sparks from the collective soul became separated and fell. Consequently, the sacred history of Israel was interpreted by Lurianic kabbalists as a complex process of transmigration. In order to return to a state of perfection, the various elements of Adam's original soul had to restore themselves gradually through penitential acts, performed over the course of a series of lives. This process was further impeded by human sin. As a result, some of the soul-sparks fell to lower levels of existence and became sources of vitality for nonhuman aspects of creation, such as plants and animals. Thus the sacred act of eating food took on an additional kabbalistic significance, since it was believed that fallen soul-sparks, awaiting redemption, were present in food. This belief added an additional significance to the *Tu bi-Shevat seder,* with its emphasis on eating and blessing fruit. Although the Lurianic theory of transmigration may strike modern sensibilities as strange, it may be well to observe that this theory serves to connect humanity to nature in a fundamentally spiritual way. Every aspect of nature, whether animal, vegetable, or mineral, may potentially contain sparks of holiness that are essential for the completion and redemption of a person's soul and those of his or her relatives.

Because of the kabbalistic perspective, *Tu bi-Shevat* takes on a significance that goes beyond a simple celebration of an important stage in the cycle of nature. For one thing, the symbol of the cosmic tree is so central to kabbalistic thinking that any dramatic change affecting trees in the material world must be seen as a reflection of a cosmic event of the greatest importance. Thus *Tu bi-Shevat* represents not only the New Year's Day for trees in this world, but even more importantly, for the kabbalist, the time when the cosmic tree becomes fecund. Since nature and all of creation are directly dependent on the spiritual bounty that is received from the cosmic tree, the kabbalistic perspective of the *Peri 'Ez Hadar* considerably magnifies the importance of *Tu bi-Shevat.* Indeed, one may say that the day becomes associated with a cosmic myth of divine potency and fertility. Thus the introduction to the *Peri 'Ez Hadar* indicates that the central focus of the *tiqqun* is the ninth *sefirah, Yesod,* which represents the divine phallus, or male generative principle within God. An emphasis is placed on contemplating the relationship between *Yesod* and *Malkhut,* the female principle, which "bears fruit" as a result of being impregnated by *Yesod.*

The mythological perspective is complemented by a theurgic practice. As is often the case, kabbalistic practice involves numerical correspondences between words, or *gematria.* In this case, the letters of the Hebrew word for tree, *'ilan,* have the same value as the sum of the letters that spell two divine Names, *YHVH* and *'ADoNaY.* This indicates that the New Year's Day for the *'ilan* involves the union of the two Names. Moreover, in kabbalistic tradition, these two Names represent the male and female divine principles. When the letters of these two Names are combined to form Y'AHDVNHY, they become an object on which a kabbalist can meditate in order to bring about the actual union of the corresponding *sefirot.* This meditation is appropriate for *Tu bi-Shevat.*

As a result of the association of the *tiqqun* of *Tu bi-Shevat* with divine potency, an additional motive is discussed in the introduction to the *Peri 'Ez Hadar.* It is assumed that the harmony of the relationship between *Yesod* and *Malkhut* is adversely affected by human sexual improprieties. Thus *Tu bi-Shevat,* with its emphasis on rectifying the *sefirah Yesod,* becomes an occasion for correcting, or atoning for, the damage that was done to *Yesod* by improper sexual behavior. This introduces another mythic and magical element, the tendency to view nature's bounty as related to, and even dependent upon, human sexuality. This motive is addressed through the theurgic, contemplative focus on *Yesod* as well as devotionally through adopting an attitude of atonement. The pietistic element, which seems to conflict to a certain extent with the otherwise celebrational character of the *seder,* may be a compensation for the fact that *Tu bi-Shevat* occurs during a penitential period. This period, called *Shovavim,* occurs during the first six weekly readings in the book of Exodus. The period is characterized by fasting and penitential acts. The weeks of *Shovavim* are explicitly connected in *Hemdat Yamim* with correction of "damage to the [sign of the] covenant," that is, ejaculation in halakhically unacceptable circumstances.

It is important to note the chain of associated symbols here that must be connected. *Tu bi-Shevat* is associated with trees. The cosmic tree is nourished by the *sefirah Yesod. Yesod* is identified with the divine phallus. The functioning of the divine phallus that impregnates *Malkhut* (the Tree of the Knowledge of Good and Evil) is affected by male sexuality. The time of year during which *Tu bi-Shevat* occurs is appropriate for atoning for male sexual misdeeds.

To sum up, the *Tu bi-Shevat* seder, which is presented in *Peri 'Ez Hadar,* essentially views *Tu bi-Shevat* as part of a penitential season when atonement can be made for male sexual impropriety. As such, the *seder* is a kabbalistic *tiqqun* for the *sefirah Yesod.* As a result of this *tiqqun,* the fertility of the cosmic tree is enhanced. This ultimately results in nature's receiving the vitality required for bringing forth its bounty. The *tiqqun* involves three types of activity: blessing fruit, eating fruit, and meditating on the kabbalistic symbolism of the fruit. This latter activity primarily involves the contemplative study of selections from the zoharic literature.

The translation was made from the text of *Peri 'Ez Hadar* printed in *Sefarim Qedoshim: Seder Hamishah Asar Bi-Shevat ve-Hamishah Asar Be-Av* (Brooklyn, N.Y.: Beyt Hillel, 1990).

Further Reading

Arthur Waskow and Ari Elon, eds., *Tu Be'Shvat Anthology* (Philadelphia: Jewish Publication Society, 1999). David Abraham Mandelbaum, *Tehillah Le-David: Tu Bi-Shevat Be-Halakhah u-Ve-Aggadah* (Jerusalem: Makhon Imrey David, 1993). Tidhar Elon, *Siddur Kavvanot Ez Hadar: Seder Tu Bi-Shevat im Sefer Peri Ez Hadar* (Jerusalem: Shemen Sasson, n.d.).

New Year's Day for Fruit of the Tree

Although the fifteenth of *Shevat* occurs during the "days of the *Shovavim*," the six weeks during which the first six portions of the book of Exodus are read, it is not a fast day, since it is the New Year's Day for the fruit of the tree. Through the *tiqqun* [mending] that is performed on this day with fruit, the *sefirah Zaddiq* ["Righteous One," *sefirah Yesod*], Life of the Worlds, is aroused. This mystery is mentioned in the *Zohar,* Genesis, 33a, "on the third day, the earth made fruit from the potency of that [supernal] *Zaddiq*." As it is written, "And God said, let the earth bring forth ... fruit trees that produce fruit ..."[Gen. 1:12]. "Fruit trees" refers to "the tree of the knowledge of good and evil" that bears fruit [the tenth *sefirah, Malkhut*]. "That produce fruit" alludes to *Zaddiq* [*sefirah Yesod*], the foundation of the world. ...

It is a good custom for the faithful to eat many fruits on this day and to celebrate them with words of praise, just as I have instructed my companions. Even though this custom is not mentioned in the Lurianic writings, it is nevertheless a wondrous *tiqqun* on both exoteric and esoteric levels.

For in the Palestinian Talmud, *'Asarah Yuhasin,* ch. 10 [Yerushalmi, *Kiddushin,* 48b], the following appears. " 'Listen, humble ones, and rejoice' [Ps. 34:3]. R. Hezkia [and] R. Kohen said in the name of Rav, 'In the future a person will have to account for everything that his eyes saw and he did not eat. R. Eleazar was concerned about this teaching and used to save [a] poor man's gleanings. He would eat them, each one at its time.' " The reason is that whoever enjoys produce in this world without pronouncing a blessing is called a robber [Babylonian Talmud, *Berakhot,* 35b]. For by means of the blessing, one draws down *shefa'* [divine vitality]. The angel who is assigned to that fruit [which was eaten] is filled by the *shefa'* so that a second fruit can replace the first. Thus one who enjoys the fruit without blessing it is a robber. For through eating an aspect of creation [without blessing it], he eliminated the spiritual element that it contained. [Thus he] prevented that divine power from being manifest in the world, when he should have drawn down a blessing from above. As a result, the angel's power is annulled, since it no longer possesses the shefa' [that it needs in order to replenish the fruit]. That is why the person is called a robber.

[Rabbi Hanina bar Papa] also said [there] that it is as if he robbed from his father and mother. For through the *kavvanah* [mystical intention] of the blessing recited when eating fruit, a person who eats rectifies the sparks of his own soul as well as the sparks that pertain to the souls of his parents. This is the esoteric meaning of "I will make him disgorge what he has swallowed" [Jer. 51:44], which is related to [the secret of the verse], "the riches he swallowed, he vomits, [God empties it out of his stomach]" [Job 20:15]. So if one enjoys the fruit without a blessing, it is as if he robbed his parents of the divine sparks that pertain to their souls. "He is a comrade of the Destroyer" [Prov. 28:24]. For the Destroyer's only intention is to rob the divine sparks and to absorb them [in the realm of evil] and to [prevent them from] returning to [their source] in holiness. That is the esoteric meaning of "for a person does not live on bread alone, but on all that goes forth from the mouth of the Lord" [Deut. 8:3]. This alludes to the secret of the blessing, which retrieves [the sparks] from impurity to holiness. It is brought about through the "mouth of the Lord," that is, by means of the chewing of the thirty-two teeth that correspond to the thirty-two times that 'Elohim is mentioned in the Story of Creation [Gen. 1], as we have explained at length in the previous section concerning the *tiqqun* of the meal.

The punishments [for these transgressions] also apply to someone who sees species of fine fruit and allows them to dry up and go bad without eating them. [By not eating them], he prevented the angels of the fruit from receiving [their share of] divine goodness. Since he did not say a blessing over the fruit, the angel's power is annulled and it is bereft of the *shefa'* that depends on the blessing. He also robs his parents. For since he did not eat the fruit, he also neglected to eat the sparks that pertain to their souls, as has been explained. Accordingly, R. Eleazar used to save [a] poor man's gleanings for all kinds of new fruit to eat. [For he wanted] to increase blessings and perform the tiqqun immediately, so as not to miss the [opportunity for fulfilling] the *mizvot* (sing. *mizvah;* Jewish legal obligations).

In order to effect this *tiqqun,* it is fitting for us to eat all kinds of fruit on this very day and to bless them with this intention. For a *mizvah* is best when performed at the proper time.

According to the *Zohar,* "R. Yehudah said, why is it written, 'even this God made corresponding to that' [Eccles. 7:14]? God made the earth to correspond to the firmament. Everything [below] alludes to what is above. For when R. Abba would see a certain tree whose fruit would change into a bird that flew from it, he would weep and say, 'if human beings only knew to what this alludes. . . .' As R. Yose said, these trees from which wisdom can be learned, such as the carob, palm, pistachio, and the like were all borne in one chariot.

All those [trees] that bear fruit, except the apple tree, allude to one supernal mystery. . . . And all the small ones, except for the hyssop, are the offspring of one mother. In heaven, powerful intermediaries are placed over each of the earth's plants, and each has its own mystery, just as above" [*Zohar*, Exod., 15b].

From this you can understand that although the blessed Creator rules over the earth and everything has an angel assigned to it, nevertheless of greatest importance is the fact that everything is connected to the supernal attributes. As they said there in the *Zohar:* "why is it written, 'I went down to my walnut garden' [Song of Songs 6:11]? He said to him, come and see. This is the garden that went forth from Eden and it is the *Shekhinah* [the *sefirah Malkhut*]. 'Walnut' refers to the Holy Chariot, the four tributaries that spread out from the garden like a nut. . . ." From this we can infer that herbs can be distinguished by the preeminence of their divine roots above.

R. Hayyim Vital explained that there are thirty kinds of fruit trees. Ten [have their divine roots] in the World of Creation, corresponding to the ten *sefirot* of that world. Since their roots are far removed from impurity and close to the purely divine World of Emanation, they have no shell, either within or without. They may be eaten as they are [in their entirety]. They include the following: grapes, figs, apples, citrons, lemons, pears, quince, strawberries, sorbs (fruit of *sorbus* trees, in the rose family), and carob.

There are ten types of fruit [whose roots are] in the World of Formation. Esoterically, they correspond to the ten *sefirot* of Formation, which are intermediate, between the World of Creation and the World of Making. They are neither as close to the forces of evil as [the sefirot] of the World of Making nor as distant as the [*sefirot*] of the World of Creation. Consequently, the seed kernels within the fruit are not eaten, since they are not soft like the seeds within the fruit that correspond to the World of Creation. They include: olives, dates, cherries, jujubes, persimmons, plums, apricots, hackberries, lotus fruit, 'uzerar [a crab apple].

There are ten other kinds of fruit [whose roots are] in the World of Making, corresponding to the ten *sefirot* [of that world]. Consequently, we eat what is within and discard what is without. For the fruit's shell is a barrier between it and the World of Delights, so that it will not take on the impurity [of the evil forces]. This is the esoteric meaning of "the evil urge and 'the *qelippah*' [shell] that cleave to the *nefesh* [lowest grade of the soul]." The following correspond to *sefirot* of the World of Making: pomegranates, walnuts, almonds, pistachio, chestnuts, hazelnuts, acorns, coconut, pine nuts, peanuts.

Now the ten kinds of fruit [that represent the World] of Creation have been purified of everything that relates to the forces of evil (*pesolet*) and are left completely good. But a barren tree [represents] the opposite. It corresponds to pure evil, containing nothing but the *qelippah*. Just as the ten kinds of fruit [that correspond to the World] of Formation have an edible exterior and a hard interior, the kernel within, so it is with the *qelippah*. When a fallen holy spark is great, the *qelippah* is not able to contain all of that light within itself. So [the *qelippah*] enters within the holiness and surrounds it.

The ten kinds of fruit [that correspond to] the World of Making have a soft interior surrounded by a hard shell. This is like the *qelippah*, when it takes a holy spark within itself, in order to be enlivened by it. It surrounds the spark just as a shell encompasses the fruit. Consequently, we learn that there is no physical thing here below that does not correspond to something above. "For one is protected by another on a higher level, and both of these by still higher ones" [Eccles. 5:7]. As things are below, so they are above. For there would be no shadow if there were no one to cast it.

My father perceived the esoteric wisdom [alluded to by the] wording of the Mishnah, which says, "New Year's Day for fruit of the tree," rather than "for fruit of the trees." The [sages of the Mishnah] were alluding to the Holy Tree, the Tree of Life [the *sefirah Tif'eret*], as Isaac Luria's disciples explained. For tree (*'ilan*) has the same numerical value [91] as the holy name, YAHDVNHY, as they wrote in their explanation of the following passage from the *Zohar*, '*Aharey Mot*. "That great and mighty tree [which contains nourishment for all is called the Tree of Life], the tree that planted its roots in these living ones" [*Zohar*, Lev., 58a]. Also, the Lurianic writings state that when the word tree (*'ilan*) is spelled out fully, its numerical value [311 + 1] is the same as twelve permutations of the name YHVH [26 × 12 = 312]. Thus [tree] alludes to *Tif'eret*, the Tree of Life, which contains twelve permutations of YHVH, as stated in *Zohar, Beshalah*, "twelve [supernal, engraved] regions ascended [in the scale], in the great and powerful holy Tree" [*Zohar*, Exod. 66b]. Also see the passage, " 'And they came to Elim and there were twelve springs of water there and seventy date palms . . .' [Exod. 15:27] and the Holy Tree grew strong in twelve regions . . ." [*Zohar*, Exod. 62b].

The meaning is that the fifteenth of *Shevat* is the New Year's Day for tithing the fruit of trees. For most of the year's rain has already fallen. The sap has begun to ascend through the trees and fruit begin to take form on the trees from this time. Similarly, in the divine realm, it is the New Year's Day for the fruit of the supernal tree that bestows its holy abundance on its fruit, the [upper worlds]. From them the *shefa'* descends until it reaches the trees in our world below and the powers that oversee them.

"And establish for us, the work of our hands" [Ps. 90:17]. Through the special power of this *tiqqun*, performed on this very day, through the power of the blessings and contemplation of the mystery of the fruit's divine roots, an effect will be produced in their structure and character above. Moreover, the person performing the *tiqqun* can also be affected. For through the beauty of this *tiqqun*, he can correct what he distorted [after Eccles. 1:15] in damaging the [sign of the] covenant through unchastity. By virtue of performing this *tiqqun* for the fruit tree, he will heal his part in the flawing of *Zaddiq* [the *sefirah Yesod*] who makes fruit. There is the added benefit of the penitential period [*Shovavim*], mentioned above. Thus a *tiqqun* for the flaw of the covenant is performed, as explained in the first chapter.

My teacher used to say that one should intend through eating the fruit to correct the sin that Adam committed with the fruit of the tree. Even though our intention is directed toward this end all the days of the year, a *mizvah* is best when observed at its proper time, and this day is the beginning for fruit of the tree. Moreover, as we have frequently stated, speech has the power to arouse the *sefirot* and to cause them to shine more wondrously with a very great light that sheds abundance, favor, blessing, and benefit throughout all the worlds. Consequently, before eating each fruit, it is proper to meditate on the mystery of its divine root, as found in the *Zohar* and, in some cases, in the *Tiqqunim*, in order to arouse their roots above. But, first of all, read the following selections.

> Torah: Genesis 1:9–13; Deuteronomy 8:1–10; Leviticus 26:3–13
> Prophets: Ezekiel 17:22–24; 34:22–31; 36:27–36; 47:1–12; Joel 2:18–27
> Writings: Psalms 72, 147, 148, 65, 126
> *Zohar,* vol. 1, 33a; vol. 3, 86a, 270b

After this say the following prayer:

Please, God, who makes, forms, creates, and emanates supernal worlds and created their likeness on the earth below, according to their supernal form and character. "All of them you made with wisdom" [Ps. 104:24], supernal [forms] above and lower [forms] below, to join together the tent so as to be one. You caused trees and grass to grow from the earth, according to the structure and character of [the forms] above, so that human beings might gain wisdom and understanding through them, and thus grasp the hidden [forms]. You appointed your holy angels over them as agents to oversee their growing. And you caused *shefa'* [divine blessing] and the power of your supernal qualities to flow upon them.

"The fruit yielded a harvest" [after Ps. 107:37], every "fruit tree producing fruit after its kind" [Gen. 1:11].

"The earth is sated from the fruit of Your work" [Ps. 104:13] so one may "eat of its fruit and be sated by its bounty" [after Jer. 2:7]. From [the fruit], every living soul is enlivened through the spiritual power that is in them, [which is] the fruit of the mouth of your holy angels who guard its fruit.

"From me your fruit is found" [Hos. 14:9] the reward of children.

"Its fruit is food and its leaves a source of healing" [Ezek. 47:12]. So on this day, the beginning of Your deeds concerning [the trees'] budding and renewal, "a person will earn with its fruit . . ." [Song of Songs 8:11], "producing fruit after its kind" [Gen. 1:11]. For so the days of budding will be full for the fruit of the supernal tree, "the tree of life which is in the midst of the garden" [Gen. 2:9] and it makes fruit above.

May it be your will O Lord our God and God of our ancestors, that through the sacred power of our eating fruit, which we are now eating and blessing, while reflecting on the secret of their supernal roots upon which they depend, that *shefa'*, favor, blessing, and bounty be bestowed upon them. May the angels appointed over them also be filled by the powerful *shefa'* of their glory, may it return and cause them to grow a second time, from the beginning of the year and until its end, for bounty and blessing, for good life and peace.

And fulfill for us the word that you promised us through Malachi, your seer, "And I will banish the devourer from among you and he will not destroy the fruit of your earth and the vine of your field will not miscarry, says the Lord of hosts" [Mal. 3:11]. Look down from your sacred dwelling place in heaven and bless us this year with bounty and blessing. "You will make him a source of blessings forever, you will cause him to rejoice in the joy of your countenance" [Ps. 21:7]. "And the earth will bestow its harvest and the tree of the field will yield its fruit" [Lev. 26:4]. The blessing of goodness will come upon them, that its fruits will be blessed within us. Whether one eats a lot or a little, the health of his body will also be blessed. "There YHVH commanded blessing, eternal life" [Ps. 133:3].

And may the splendid power of the blessings [said] while eating the fruit illuminate the source of blessings, *Zaddiq,* the Life of the worlds, and let the rainbow appear, proudly rejoicing in its colors. From there, may *shefa'*, favor, and compassion be bestowed upon us, to pardon and forgive the iniquities and misdeeds that we committed and sinned. We violated the covenant and damaged the fruit of *Zaddiq,* the Life of the worlds, and caused the rains of its beneficence to be withheld, so that all the sources [of *shefa'*] were harmed. Now let everything return to its original might "and let his bow remain taut" [Gen. 49:24]. "For you, YHVH, bless the *Zaddiq,* favor crowns him like a shield" [Ps. 5:13].

And may all the holy sparks which were dispersed by us or by our ancestors and [also] through the sin that Adam committed with the fruit of the tree now return to be included in the splendid power of the Tree of Life. May all evil be removed from them through the power of your great Name which emerges from the verse, "the power that he swallows, he vomits out" [Job 20:15].

And may everything return to its original might and not be rejected. For only you, YHVH, restore the dispersed of Israel. Therefore, swiftly cause the offshoot of your servant David to flower and raise up its might through your salvation. And the hand of YHVH is upon the whole world in its entirety.

"Instead of a brier, a cyprus will arise, instead of the nettle, a myrtle will arise. And it will be a testimony for YHVH and an everlasting sign which will never be effaced" [Isa. 55:13].

"Let abundant grain be in the land to the mountain top, let its fruit tremble like [the cedars of] Lebanon and may the inhabitants of cities sprout like the land's grass" [Ps. 72:16].

"Then the trees of the forest will rejoice" [Ps. 96:12] and the tree of the field lift its branch and bear fruit daily.

"And you shall take from the first of the fruit of the earth" [Deut. 26:2] to bring first fruits before the altar of YHVH in praise and thanksgiving to YHVH, our God, and [it shall result in] great good for the house of Israel. "The arid desert will be glad and the wilderness will rejoice and blossom like a rose, it shall greatly flower and also rejoice and be glad. The glory of Lebanon will be given to it, the splendor of Carmel and Sharon. They will see the Glory of YHVH, the splendor of our God" [Isa. 35:1–3].

May it occur swiftly, in our days, amen.

Act for the sake of your Name. Act for the sake of your loving-kindness. Act for the sake of your right hand. Act for the sake of your Torah.

"May the words of my mouth and the meditations of my heart find favor before you, YHVH, my Rock and my Redeemer" [Ps. 19:15].

"May the favor of the Lord, our God, be upon us . . ." [Ps. 90:17].

Now, after offering this prayer, one's word can prosper through the ritual *tiqqun* of fruit according to the following *seder* ["order"].

Wheat: Make some kind of pastry or dessert and reflect on *Zohar*, vol. 3, 188b. Then everyone should say the blessing, "Creator of various kinds of food."

Olive: Reflect on *Zohar*, vol. 3, 247a and also on the *Ra'aya Mehemna* there. Then one of those present should say the blessing, "Creator of the fruit of the tree." The *kavvanah* is simply YHVH.

Dates: Reflect on *Zohar*, vol. 3, 17a. Afterward, one of those present who did not already eat from the previously blessed fruit says the blessing with the *kavvanah*, YHHV. Similarly, one person who has yet to partake says the blessing for each of the remaining fruits.

Grapes: Reflect on *Zohar*, vol. 1, 192a and vol. 3, 127a. Then one says the blessing for the grapes, "Creator of the fruit of the vine," with the *kavvanah*, YVHH. Then everyone drinks a cup of entirely white wine with the *kavvanah* of the Name of 72. [YVD HY VYV HY, which equals 72. This Name is associated with the World of Emanation.]

Figs: Reflect on Mishnah, *Ma'asarot,* chapter 2. The *kavvanah* is HVHY.

Pomegranate: Reflect on *Tiqquney Zohar,* beginning of tiqqun 24. The *kavvanah* is HVYH.

Citron: Reflect on *Zohar*, vol. 2, 120b. The *kavvanah* is HHYV.

Apple: Reflect on *Zohar*, vol. 3, 74a and 286b. The *kavvanah* is VHYH. Here everyone should drink a cup of wine that is mostly white with a little red in it. Their *kavvanah* is the Name of 63. [YHVH spelled YVD HY VAV HY. This Name is associated with the World of Creation.]

Walnut: Reflect on *Zohar*, vol. 2, 15b. The *kavvanah* is VHHY.

Chestnuts, Almonds, or Hazelnuts: Reflect on *Zohar*, vol. 1, 161b, "Secrets of the Torah." The *kavvanah* is VYHH.

Carobs: Reflect on *Zohar*, vol. 3, 216b, *Ra'aya Mehemna*. The *kavvanah* is HHVY.

Pears: Reflect on the first mishnah of *Berakhot,* chapter 6. Also reflect on the fourth mishnah in *Kela'im.*, chapter 1. The *kavvanah* is HYHV. Everyone should now drink a cup of wine that is half white and half red. The *kavvanah* is the Name of 45. [YHVH spelled YVD HA VAV HA. This Name is associated with the World of Formation.]

Medlar: Reflect on the second mishnah of *Berakhot*, chapter 6 and the first mishnah of *Demai*, chapter 1. The *kavvanah* is HYHV.

Quince: Reflect on the third mishnah of *Berakhot*, chapter 6 and the third mishnah of *Ma'aserot*, chapter 1. The *kavvanah* is AHVH.

Hackberry: Reflect on the fourth and fifth mishnayot of *Berakhot*, chapter 6. The *kavvanah* is the name of 72.

Jujube: Reflect on the sixth mishnah of *Berakhot*, chapter 6. The *kavanah* is YAHDVNHY.

Pistachio: Reflect on the seventh mishnah of *Berakhot*, chapter 6. The *kavvanah* is AHVH.

Cherry: Reflect on the eighth mishnah of *Berakhot*, chapter 6. The *kavvanah* is the Name of 52. [YHVH spelled YVD HH VV HH. This Name is associated with the World of Making.]

Nishpolas: Reflect on the first mishnah of *Berakhot*, chapter 7. The *kavvanah* is 'EL.

Lupine: Finish all of chapter 7 in *Mishnah Berakhot*.

Afterward, everyone should drink a cup of red wine with a little bit of white wine in it. The *kavvanah* is the Name of 52 [YVD HH VV HH].

Wherever all thirty of the fruits mentioned above, whose roots are in the worlds of Creation, Formation, and Making, can be found, it is a *mizvah* to obtain them. For whoever does much is surely worthy of praise. However, wherever they are not all available, there should be no less than twelve types of fruit, corresponding to the fruit of the supernal tree, the Tree of Life. It is established as a Holy Tree in twelve directions, the secret of the twelve permutations of the Name, YHVH. For each of these the kavvanah should be one of the twelve permutations, according to the order mentioned above.

Rituals of the Life Cycle

6

The Role of Women at Rituals of Their Infant Children

Lawrence A. Hoffman

Communal Jewish ritual in the Middle Ages was distinctly a male domain. The rules delimiting participation of women in public places generally, and the synagogue service in particular, had come into being by the end of the second century, and had then been further delineated in great detail during the several centuries following. Authorities in the Middle Ages thus inherited a legal tradition that denied women formal roles in the various events that constituted public religious ritual.

In part, the logic was purely a matter of legal entailment. Rabbinic literature is legal literature, after all, so that the standards for Jewish worship are couched in a rhetoric of requirement and prohibition. Certain basic axioms governed the system, including what we can call "The axiom of limited obligation for women." Jewish law is divided into positive (Thou shalt . . .) and negative (Thou shalt not . . .) precepts. The positive precepts are further broken down into those that must be performed within a certain window of time (time-bound) and those that are always in force. "The axiom of limited obligation for women" arises from the allotment of each of these types of precept to the specific instance of women's lives.

In general, the rabbinic system holds men responsible for all classes of precept. Women, by contrast, though liable for all negative precepts, are answerable only for those positive precepts that are not dependent on time. Women, that is, are asked to lead lives free of sin (they may not contravene any negative commands), and also to observe general demands that obtain without regard to the flow of time, like honoring parents and loving their neighbors. But only men are assigned the task of fulfilling those duties that depend on the hour of the day or the day of the year. Since public ritual is very largely composed of just such time-bound rules, medieval women found themselves legally exempted from it.

Another way of approaching our subject is to divide Jewish prayer into the usual two categories of private and public. Private prayer may be spontaneous, the free expression of the human soul, prompted by the desire at any time to commune with God; or it may be fixed, a set of demanded responses to the ordinary phenomena of daily life, like eating food or observing a blossoming tree. Judaism sees such moments as demonstrations of God's reality, which call forth the private recitation of a benediction praising God for the moment in question. All of this is private, personal, potentially moving, and equally demanded of men and of women, both of whom may discover the divine presence in moments that range from the perfectly ordinary to the extraordinarily sublime.

Public prayer is similar, in that it too presupposes the entry of God into human life and the consequent necessity to acknowledge God's presence. But in this case, the occasion for God's entry is the change of times and seasons. Jewish worship is therefore not content to assign prayer to individuals at private moments like seeing trees in blossom, or satisfying thirst and hunger. Jewish spirituality is corporate. It demands a representative community of worshipers who take note of a new day, the dawn of the Sabbath, or the onset of a festival, and who gather to affirm the divine hand in the occasion.

This public ritual is best likened to a sacred drama in which worshipers are sacred actors. The ritual is very largely determined in advance by a fixed liturgical script and a standardized set of requirements that govern how the script is to be recited: who says what, when, and how. Since this public ritual is dependent on time—indeed, meeting the natural flow of time is its whole purpose—it follows from "the axiom of limited obligation for women" that there is never any reason for women even to be present for public prayer, and should they happen to be there anyway, there is no reason to assign important ritual roles to them. Indeed, a further legal stipulation actually forbids the assignment of such roles to women, so that theoretically, anyway, we should picture public prayer throughout late antiquity and the Middle Ages as solely a male enterprise. If women were present, they were not officially so.

We shall turn shortly to the question of how much that official position actually mirrors historical reality. But first, it is necessary to see that issues of legal entailment went hand in hand with extralegal concerns that the rabbis had regarding women. Their legal logic reflected a deeper gender bias. Meeting successfully for prayer, day in and day out, precisely as the times and seasons warranted it, required a high degree of personal control: one had to show up at just the right moment, and do just the right thing in just the right way, or the opportunity for successful encounter with the divine would be lost. But it was precisely this degree of self-control that the rabbis imputed to men and denied women.

The limited involvement of women in public ritual followed logically from "the axiom of limited obligation for women," therefore, but the axiom was itself rooted in a deeper consideration, which was not legal at all but was part of the religious anthropology wherein the rabbis categorized women as uncontrolled and apt to act inappropriately in public places generally. Excluding women from public ritual was symptomatic of their deeper concern: banning them from public displays in general.

We get a good sense of rabbinic worries on this score from their discussions on divorce. The rabbis in antiquity had endeavored to protect the rights of women by denying a husband free rein in how he treated his wife. As part of the wedding ritual, a husband had to give his wife a wedding contract called a k'tubah, which served as a conditional promissory note from him to her. It obliged him to grant his wife a divorce and a monetary payment (equivalent to "damages") if he maltreated her. The monetary settlement would be hers also, if he chose to divorce her without cause. The wife, however, was expected to behave according the norms considered appropriate to married women. Should she choose to disregard such norms, her husband had the right to divorce her without paying her the amount of money designated. The word k'tubah came to mean the document as well as the amount of money stipulated within it.

Texts 1 and 2 below delineate some of the conditions that husband and wife were expected to meet, and the situations that permitted either to divorce the other, with or without payment of k'tubah. They differentiate "Law of Moses" (dat moshe) from "Law of Israel" (yisra'el) or "Law of the Jews" (y'hudit). The latter two terms are probably identical, different names for the same thing. "Law of Moses" is actual law. "Law of Israel" (or "of the Jews") is not; its breaches are matters of propriety, and, as far as women are concerned, they are mostly instances in which they do not "properly" refrain from "going public." Women are expected to retain a sense of seclusion about their hair, their clothes, and their voice—none of which may extend into the public domain; that is, hair may not be left to fly free in the wind; clothes may not flail in the air; voices may not be raised. In keeping with the rabbis' view of women as uncontrolled, women are portrayed as suspect of spreading sexual allure beyond their home. They act without shame; they tempt men; so are best restrained from "loose" hair, clothing, speech, and so forth. Even when no particular law forbids such behavior (that is, "Law of Moses" has nothing to say on the subject), general propriety (that is, "Law of Israel") comes into play, and is supported by the sanction of the k'tubah, which a woman risks losing if she acts "inappropriately" in public.

These two texts come from the Mishnah and the Tosefta, rabbinic compendia of Jewish law, which are generally dated around 200 C.E. and shortly thereafter. They therefore predate the medieval period as defined by this book. But they demonstrate the legal and moral strictures under which women lived according to the official definition of their role in society; and even though women, in practice, may have been quite a bit freer than the texts would allow, the texts were eventually canonized as normative and held out as the ideal situation to which later generations of rabbis should aspire. As of the tenth century, marriages were contracted by promising a marriage "according to the law of Moses and of Israel"—a phrase taken today to imply the proper legal actions that establish a marriage, but obviously intended originally as a statement of the legal and extra-legal relationship that a proper marriage ought to have. It was an understanding of the way the marriage should operate, not the way it should be brought into being.

We would like to know the extent to which women actually were held accountable for all of these laws of Moses and of Israel. My topic here, however, is more limited. A very significant consequence of the closeting of women from public performance was the evolution of the prayer service with no women necessarily present. To a very great extent, medieval rabbis were able to define a system in which women were simply absent from synagogue life. But even here, there are intimations of exceptions. One especially interesting case study is the role women played in life-cycle events of their baby sons: their circumcision, and what is known as the Redemption of the Firstborn.

Both rituals go back to biblical times, but their accompanying liturgical rites are rabbinic. Circumcision (*b'rit milah*) features the surgical removal of the foreskin from a boy's penis when the boy is eight days old. Accompanying benedictions are recited by the father and by the man doing the operation (the *mohel*), who also prays for the boy's welfare, and bestows upon him his Hebrew name. The event is public: when the father affirms his desire to "admit him [his son] into the covenant of Abraham our father," those gathered say, "As he has been admitted into the covenant, so may he enter [study of] Torah, marriage, and [the performance of] good deeds." Originally, the rite was somewhat simpler. The respondents addressed the father, rather than referring obliquely (in the third person) to the son, and said, "As you admitted him to the covenant, so may you [do the other things that fathers must do for their male children:] introduce him to Torah and to marriage." Circumcision can best be described as the beginning of a boy's lifeline as a man, the means by which he enters the covenant that God made with Abraham and with every male thereafter. The lifeline begins with circumcision, then takes root with the study of Torah, and entails (if possible) marriage for the purpose of having one's own children and continuing the covenant for another generation.

Circumcision is required of all male children. Redemption of the Firstborn (*pidyon haben*) is less widespread. It is a ritual that occurs on the first-month birthday of firstborn males only. Moreover, some firstborns are exempt, namely, those descended from fathers who trace their lineage back to biblical priestly stock (they are *kohanim*; sing. *kohen*) or to the biblical tribe of Levi (they are Levites, *l'vi'im*; sing. a *Levi*), which enjoyed semipriestly status. The rationale behind all of this is the biblical view that, technically, all firstborn males belong to God (see, for example, Exod. 13:15, Num 3:13). Boys who are priests or Levites are born to do God's work, and are assigned certain ritual obligations that are reminiscent of the responsibilities of their priestly and Levite progenitors during biblical days. Nonpriestly fathers, however, must buy their firstborn sons back from divine service, in order to allow them to lead ordinary lives as nonpriestly and non-Levitical Israelite men. In the ritual, the father attests that the boy is his firstborn, a priest (*kohen*) asks him if he wishes to redeem his son for a token monetary payment, and the exchange is made: the kohen takes the money from the father, and the father takes his son from the arms of the kohen.

What makes these life-cycle events particularly interesting is that they are both personal and public. Personally speaking, mothers as well as fathers have some emotional stake in what occurs. Moreover, mothers (who, in most eras, would normally have been breast-feeding) are likely to have been present. But by and large, Jewish law assigns the ritual care of boys to their father, not their mother, and as personal as the life-cycle events may seem to us, they would have been defined more publicly by medieval Jews, who would have seen both circumcision and redemption as public displays of proper Jewish duty by the father, not the mother. That public duty interfaced with gender roles that were not necessarily consistent with the private nature of family ritual moments.

The case of circumcision is easy to define. Circumcision normally occurred in the middle of public worship, and in the synagogue sanctuary, where women attended as mothers even though they were officially excluded as worshipers.

Redemption was more complicated. To begin with, it was private: it did not occur within the worship setting. It was also less frequent, as it involved only firstborn males, not all of them. But "firstborn" was defined as "firstborn" through the mother, "the firstborn of the womb," as the Bible puts it (for example, Num. 3:11). A man who had a firstborn with a wife who had previously given birth to another child (in a prior marriage, perhaps) did not count his own child as firstborn, because he was firstborn only to him, not to his wife. Similarly, stillbirths and even late miscarriages counted as a birth for purposes of canceling out the need for a child born thereafter from counting as "firstborn." Redemption, then, invited the mother to be present not only as caregiver but also as official ritual witness, the only person present who knew for sure that the boy was, in fact, a firstborn altogether.

How did medieval Judaism deal with the anomalies involved in public yet personal life-cycle ceremonies for baby boys?

Today, the mother has no ritual role in either of these events. To be sure, liberal Jewish circles may have admitted her to the ritual script, but the official ritual that Jewish tradition has handed down prescribes nothing for her to say or do, and semiofficial norms often proscribe her from even attending. It is not unusual, in some traditional Jewish circles, to observe a circumcision where she hovers at a distance, in the background, or even in another room, while the proper rite is performed on her son by, first, the father (who says his prescribed blessing); second, another man who is the *mohel* (the circumciser); and third, a man called the *sandek* who holds the child during the operation. As for the Redemption of the Firstborn, to the extent that one sees that at all, it is equally likely that the mother will be altogether absent, in the next room perhaps, or at most somewhere in the background, a silent witness to a ritual that features not her but the father, who testifies that the boy is a firstborn from her.

There is reason to believe, however, that despite the clear implications of Jewish law, women used to be more actively involved in the public ritual of their infant sons. The rest of the texts that are presented below demonstrate the extent of such involvement, and then the slow but steady growth away from it.

Text 3 is taken from *Seder Rav Amram,* a ninth-century document and our first known comprehensive written prayer book. Amram was a *gaon,* that is, a leader of Babylonian Jewry, who was attempting to exercise leadership of Jews the world over. His prayer book sums up the state of ritual practice in his day and place, and mandates it for Jews everywhere. In its time, Amram's practice was contested by Jews still living in the Land of Israel, for whom ancient Palestinian custom was normative, and who, in any event, resented the Babylonian gaon's claim to represent established Jewish law. The two Jewish communities differed on the documentation that was to be considered probative. The Babylonian master, Amram, claimed the dictates of the Babylonian Talmud as the only thing that counted, whereas Palestinians pointed with equal insistence to their own talmudic corpus, the Palestinian Talmud, as their source of authority. In addition, established custom was important. Babylonians had begun attempts to displace Palestinian practice in the middle of the eighth century, when the first gaon of any importance, a man named Yehudai, had written to the Palestinians admonishing them to follow Babylonian rulings. The Palestinians had written back, with the claim, "Custom annuls legal rulings." Now Amram continued the campaign for Babylonian cultural hegemony, and even though he too was not immediately accepted as authoritative, his prayer book eventually became the norm for all subsequent Jewish worship. Posthumously, Amram and the Babylonians proved successful.

Given this background animus that Amram has to all things Palestinian, we are surprised to find that Amram includes two prayers that we no longer have, both of them in ancient Palestinian Aramaic. They are clearly so old that they have become part even of Babylonian custom, so that Amram cannot exclude them.

The second of the two prayers is especially interesting, because it provides clear evidence that the mother was not yet relegated to another room or even to the sidelines—not completely, anyway. She is given a cup of wine to drink, and the people pray for her health, no doubt with the understanding that she needs healing so soon after childbirth. On the other hand, a final section in Amram's ritual provides the meaning of circumcision for what was becoming an all-male bonding rite. The text comes as a complete surprise, since no Jews today or in recent memory follow its instructions. In fact, even other medieval sources do not echo its contents. But Amram is clear on what he did in his time—ninth-century Babylonia.

We see three generations of "men" gathered for the ritual: the infant, his father (and the father's friends, others, that is, of his generation), and an unidentified third party, given incorrectly in the printed version of Amram as *no'adim,* meaning "those invited." Alternative texts, however, make it clear that the third party is not *no'adim,* but *n'arim,* meaning "adolescent boys." The circumcision is performed so that the blood from the operation drips into a bowl of water, and the three generations of men wash their hands in the blood-water mixture, as if to say, "This is the blood of circumcision that mediates between God and Abraham our father."

We turn next to the ritual for Redemption. Text 4 also comes from the geonic era. It was first published in 1931 by an assiduous collector of geonic material, Benjamin Manasseh Lewin, but has since been found in a variety of sources copied from an original that is generally said to be by Hai Gaon, not Amram's immediate successor, but an illustrious authority who functioned as gaon at the beginning of the eleventh century. It is of interest for many reasons.

First, it contains a prayer that we no longer say, but that provides a glimpse of medieval embryology. People knew the fetus developed in the womb, and turned to the Bible for some sense of how it occurred. This prayer lays down the stages of presumed fetal development.

Of greater immediate interest, however (given the topic of women's involvement in the life-cycle rituals of their children), is the fact that as late as the eleventh century, we find both mother and father present for the ritual. Not only that: the mother, not the father, testifies as to the standing of the firstborn in question. And finally, most surprising of all, despite the clear ruling that only the father, and distinctly not the mother, is obliged to redeem the son, the geonic ritual features the mother saying "*We* are obliged to redeem him."

Text 5, however, shows us what later European authorities thought of the precedent. Though it is not clear exactly when and where it happened, it seems that the mother's involvement was curtailed. A variant form of the same geonic communication is passed on by an anonymous European rabbi, who introduces it with the observation that earlier generations introduced novelties into the ritual, and then omits the mother's role, even though he mentions that she had one. At the end, however, he describes the custom of redeeming grown men, who, for whatever reason, were not properly redeemed as children. It was his practice to bless the man with a litany of biblical phrases—an innovation that has also dropped out of current practice.

From all that we have said so far, it becomes clear that Babylonian and Palestinian custom up to roughly the year 1000 engaged women in these two life-cycle celebrations for their male children. On the other hand, the message of the male orientation of these rituals was by no means ambiguous, especially in the case of circumcision, which was an operation for boys and which featured three generations of men who celebrated "the blood of circumcision that mediates between God and Abraham our father." We should like to know how the theory of male ritual eventually won the day to the extent that it squeezed the mothers out of the ceremony. Fortunately, we have a document (Text 6) that tells us that. It has been preserved for us from the thirteenth century.

Perhaps the most important authority in that strain of European Jewish tradition in the area that we call Ashkenaz (northern Europe, mostly German and eastern Europe, as opposed to custom in Spain, which is called Sefarad) was Meir of Rothenberg (1215–1293), known also as the Maharam, an acronym formed out of the initials of his name and title. The Maharam spent the last seven years of his life imprisoned by the emperor Rudolph I, who had arrested him in the hope that the Jewish community would pay a royal ransom for him. For reasons that are not entirely clear, but probably because he feared setting a precedent for wholesale arrests of rabbinic authorities, Maharam refused to be ransomed, and remained imprisoned until his death, the martyrlike nature of which only underscored his authority at the time. His students turned out to be enormously influential, because they spread out far and wide, bringing their master's views with them. Among these views was the opinion that women should have no involvement whatever in the circumcision ritual.

We know about it because of one student, Samson ben Tzadok, also known by an acronym, the Tashbetz, who dedicated his life to seeing to it that his teacher's views on matters of ritual were carried out. His colorful description of the events associated with his zealous championing of the Maharam's opinions gives us the rationale behind the ultimate exclusion of women, and even some idea of how long it took for the deed to be done. Using other texts of the time, we can summarize the final stages of women's exclusion in some detail.

When the Tashbetz launched his campaign (which cannot be later than the closing decades of the thirteenth century), the prevailing custom was to have mothers bring their infant sons to the synagogue during morning prayers, where they sat holding them, awaiting the moment for the circumcision ritual to begin. The operation occurred on the mother's lap. The Maharam objected to all of this, on a variety of grounds given in the text, most of them puritanical in nature. When the Tashbetz tried to enforce them, people objected, thinking it cruel to remove a newborn from his mother. In the end, however, the Tashbetz prevailed, as we see from Text 7, which recalls testimony by Rabbi Jacob Moellin (1365–1427), the Maharil (as he is known), and another candidate for the most influential Ashkenazi rabbi of all time. It is clear from his statement that women had by then been successfully removed from the ritual proceedings. They stayed home altogether now, handing their baby to another woman at the door. This second woman (who is given a technical title only then coming into being, the *ba'alat brit,* literally, Mistress of the Covenant), carried the boy to the synagogue, but being a woman herself, was not allowed to enter. She therefore handed the boy to a man, who presented him for circumcision. Instead of the mother, it was a man now who held the boy for the operation. He too was given a new ritual title, either *ba'al brit* (Master of the Covenant) or (the name that proved lasting) *sandek,* a designation that was borrowed from a mistaken Hebraized version of a title bestowed on the godfather in the Christian rite of baptism. Simultaneously, Jewish interpreters emphasize the circumcision ritual as a kind of sacrifice, so that the man who held the boy was considered to have served as the sacred altar, akin to the altar that had functioned in the temple in Jerusalem. In keeping with the movement toward demanding that a man hold the baby, the act of holding him took on theological significance that explained why a woman could not do so.

Our final two texts (8 and 9) bring the story of women's exclusion to its close. The first comes from Maharil's students, who allude to the developing theology of sacrifice and tell us how the master himself used to prepare for the holy task of holding a baby for his circumcision; the latter is by Moses Isserles, a distinguished Polish rabbi from the sixteenth century. He summarizes the long course of events with a short but clear statement forbidding women from holding their babies, and allowing them, at best, to carry them to the synagogue, where a man would take over.

Text 1 is from the first authoritative rabbinic compendium of Jewish law, known as the Mishnah (promulgated c. 200 C.E.). The second text comes from a similar compilation made shortly after the Mishnah (but at an uncertain date) and known as the Tosefta. Text 3 is from our first-known prayer book, a Babylonian work of the ninth century known as *Seder Rav Amram Gaon*. The fourth text is from a responsum (an answer to a legal query) by an authority known as Hai Gaon, probably written in the early eleventh century. The fifth text is anonymous so cannot be dated with any certainty. It is from western Europe, perhaps in the twelfth or thirteenth century. The sixth text is German, an extract from the work of Samson ben Tzadok, somewhere near the end of the thirteenth century. Text 7 is by R. Jacob Moellin, text 8 by his students, and text 9 is by R. Moses Isserles.

Further Reading

On the role of women in Jewish law and society, see especially, Judith Romney Wegner, *Chattel or Person: The Status of Women in the Mishnah* (New York and Oxford: Oxford University Press, 1988). Chapter 3 is devoted to the status of a wife in rabbinic legislation, and chapter 6 explores the exclusion of women from the public domain. The background for the role of women in rabbinic ritual is discussed here and there by Wegner, but is put into context relative to women generally in late antiquity by Ross Shepard Kraemer, *Her Share of the Blessings: Women's Religions among Pagans, Jews, and Christians in the Greco-Roman World* (New York and Oxford: Oxford University Press, 1992), chapters 8 and 9. A fuller summary of what rabbinic sources reveal regarding ritual and women (but without the crosscultural comparisons with women's ritual in general) is found within Lawrence A. Hoffman, *Covenant of Blood: Circumcision and Gender in Rabbinic Judaism* (Chicago: University of Chicago Press, 1996), chapter 10. The same book explains in much greater detail all the material presented here. A larger analysis of the ritual of Redeeming the First-Born is found in Lawrence A. Hoffman, "Life Cycle Liturgy as Status Transformation," in E. Carr, S. Parenti, A. A. Thiermeyer, and E. Velkovska, eds., *Studia Anselmiana, Eulogema: Studies in Honor of Robert Taft, S.J.* (Rome: Centro Studi, Sant Anselmo, 1993), pp. 161–77.

1. M. K'tubot 7:6. "According to the Law of Moses and Israel"

These women go forth from their marriage without the payment of the *k'tubah* obligations at all. She who transgresses the Law of Moses, or Jewish Law (*dat moshe vi'y'hudit*).

What is the Law of Moses? If she feeds him untithed food, has sexual relations with him while she is menstruating, does not remove the dough offering, or vows but fails to keep her vow.

All of these are actual legal stipulations that devolve on women. Food from which a tithe has not been removed is forbidden, as are sexual relations during menstruation. The dough offering is a kind of tithe, involving the removal of part of the dough prior to its being baked into bread. The reference to vows reflects the fact that in rabbinic law, husbands are legally liable for their wives' vows. All four examples are alike: Since women cooked and baked, only they would know if tithes had been removed; only they know if they are menstruating; and only they know if they have made a vow somewhere. The Law of Moses holds women liable for things that are their responsibility, of necessity.

What is Jewish law? If she goes outside with her hair flying loose, spins [wool] in the marketplace, or talks with just anyone at all. Abba Saul says, also if she curses his parents in his presence. R. Tarfon says, also if she is a loudmouth. What is a loudmouth? When she talks in her house but the neighbors can hear her. [These are all instances of stepping outside the bounds of propriety: having "loose" hair; working in public, not at home; and having a "loose" tongue.]

2. Tosefta K'tubot 7:6/7. "More on the Law of Moses and Israel"

If he [the husband] required her [his wife] by vow to give a taste of what she was cooking to everyone who came by [possibly a sexual allusion], or that she "fill and pour out on the rubbish heap" [again, possibly a sexual allusion] or that she tell everybody about things that are between him and her [again, alluding to their private, and therefore sexual, life together], he must grant her a divorce and pay off her marriage contract, because he has not behaved with her in accord with the Law of Moses and Israel. [Above, we saw that women may not act loosely; now we see that men may not make their wives engage in loose behavior.]

Likewise, if she goes out with her hair flying loose or her clothes in a mess; or if she acts without shame in the presence of her male or female servants or her neighbors; or if she goes out and spins wool in the market place; or if she washes or bathes in the public bath with just anyone; then she is divorced without payment of her marriage contract, for she has not behaved with her husband in accordance with the law of Moses and Israel.

What is a loudmouth? Someone whom the neighbors can hear when she is talking in her own house.

All these women who have transgressed the law must have fair warning, but [if they persist after fair warning], then they are divorced without receiving payment of their marriage contract.

3. Seder Rav Amram. The Order of the Circumcision Ritual

The blessing over circumcision which you requested is this:

[First the *mohel*—the ritual circumciser—says], "Blessed are you, Lord, our God, King of the universe who has sanctified us with your commandments and commanded us regarding circumcision."

Then the father of the boy says, "Blessed are you, Lord our God, King of the universe who has sanctified us with your commandments and commanded us to admit him [the boy] to the covenant of Abraham our father."

Those in attendance say, "As you admitted him into the covenant, so may you admit him to Torah, marriage, and good deeds."

Then they mix a cup of wine and say, "Blessed are you, Lord our God, King of the universe, who creates the fruit of the vine. Blessed are you, Lord our God, King of the universe, who sanctified the beloved one [probably a reference to Abraham, who is the first male to initiate circumcision] in his mother's womb, and set a statute in his [Abraham's] flesh, and stamped his descendants with the sign of the holy covenant. Therefore, as a reward for this [the continuation of circumcision throughout the generations] the living God, our portion and our rock, commanded that the beloved of our flesh be delivered from the pit, for the sake of his covenant which he placed in our flesh. Blessed are you, Lord, who makes a covenant."

The wording of the blessing has changed through time, incorporating enough additions and alterations as to make its meaning difficult to fathom at times. "Therefore, as a reward for this" and "for the sake of his covenant which he placed in our flesh" seem redundant, for instance. At various times, the pronoun "he" may refer to Abraham or to another patriarch, or even to God. The idea is reasonably clear, however: God commanded Abraham to circumcise himself and his male progeny; he and every male after him obeyed the command. Circumcision is an act that guarantees salvation—being "saved from the pit." What medieval Jews meant by "salvation" is unclear, however. The blessing had been framed by the second century as part of a debate between Jews and Christians as to whether we are saved by works or by faith. Christians asserted the latter: only faith in Jesus Christ will save. Jews argued the former: Jewish law generally, and (in this case) obeying the commandment of circumcision, in particular, saves. Someone unnamed continues the ritual by reciting the next two prayers for healing.

"May healing of life and mercy be sent from heaven, to heal this child, and let his name in Israel be _____. May he be healed as the waters of Marah were healed by Moses and as the waters of Jericho by Elisha. So may he be healed, speedily in a time not far off, to which, say: 'Amen.' "

"May healing of life and mercy be sent from heaven, to heal the mother of this child, for she requires healing. May she be healed as the waters of Marah were healed by Moses and as the waters of Jericho by Elisha. So may he be healed, speedily in a time not far off, to which, say: 'Amen.'"

These are references to the Bible, Exodus 16:22–25 and 2 Kings 2:19–22. In the former, Moses throws a tree into the waters of Marah, a place of Israelite encampment, to render the water there drinkable. In the latter, the prophet Elisha does the same—using salt, not a tree—for a city along the banks of the Jordan.

They pass the cup to the mother of the infant. Why pass it to the mother? . . . The mother is sick and requires healing. Thus the mother of the infant drinks the wine.

Tzadok Gaon [a geonic predecessor of Amram's, but the name has been garbled in transmission, so we do not know precisely who is intended] said the following. They bring water containing myrtle and various very sweet-smelling spices, and they circumcise the child so that the blood of the circumcision falls into the water. Then all the adolescent boys wash their hands in it, as if to say, "This is the blood of circumcision that mediates between God and Abraham our father."

4. Hai Gaon. The Order of the Redemption of the Firstborn

He [the father] brings his son before the priest and says to the priest that he is the firstborn of the womb [that is, he is the firstborn of the mother, not necessarily the father].

The priest takes him, and says to the father, "Do you want your firstborn son? Then give me the five selahs that you need to redeem him."

The Bible—Numbers 18:16—calls for five shekels of silver, a shekel being a kind of coinage common in biblical times. Although new shekels were minted from time to time as late as the second century, it was much more convenient to use the Roman system of coinage, including a coin that Jews called a selah, which replaced the shekel in the ceremony of redemption. By medieval times, Jews used whatever coins they had, preferring silver if they could find it. One custom called for the father to give five silver coins to the priest and then to ransom back the coins by handing over some other form of possession, such as clothing or household goods.

The father replies, "I want my firstborn son. Here are your five selahs. Blessed are you, Lord our God, King of the universe, who has sanctified us by your commandments and commanded us concerning the redemption of the firstborn. Blessed are you, Lord our God, King of the universe who has given us life, sustained us and brought us to this season."

They mix a cup of wine for the priest and hand him some spices, and he says, "Blessed are you, Lord our God, King of the universe who has created the fruit of the vine. Blessed are you, Lord our God, King of the universe who has created sweet smelling trees."

He [the priest] also says, "Blessed are you, Lord our God, King of the universe who sanctified the fetus in its mother's womb. From the tenth day on, He [God] apportions 248 bodily parts, and after that breathes a soul into him, as it says [Gen. 2:7]: 'He breathed a living soul into his nostrils and the man became a living being.' You have clothed me with skin, and intertwined me with bones and sinews, as it is written [Job 10:1]: 'You have clothed me with skin, and intertwined me with bones and sinews.' Through the miracle of his [God's] wonders, He feeds him with food and drink, honey and milk, to make him rejoice, and summons his angels to watch over him in his mother's womb, as it is written [Job 10:12]: 'You granted me life and favor, and your command sustained my soul.'"

The boy's father says, "This is my firstborn son," and his mother says, "This is my firstborn son, for God opened the doors of my womb with him. We are obligated (*nitchayavnu*) to give the priest five selahs as his redemption, as it is written [Num. 18:16]: 'Take as their redemption price from the age of one month and up, the money equivalent to five shekels by the sanctuary weight, which is twenty *gerahs*.' Also it says [Num. 18:15]: 'You shall have the firstborn of man redeemed.' Just as this firstborn has merited redemption, so may he merit Torah, marriage, and good deeds. Blessed are you, Lord our God, King of the universe who sanctifies the firstborn of Israel in their redemptions."

5. Anonymous European Source. Evaluating the Novelty of Earlier Generations

The early geonim established innovative practices and blessings in the order of the Redemption ritual, the burden of which is as follows.

The father brings his son before the priest, with money in hand. If the child has a [surviving] mother [who can come] she comes with him. The priest asks him [the father] if this is the firstborn, which is to say, the firstborn of his mother, via the birth canal leading from the mother's womb. [Since the biblical term is "firstborn of the womb," Jewish law ruled that "firstborns" who require redemption had to be born vaginally, not in caesarean section.] The father says, "I know this boy is the first born of his mother, via the birth canal leading from the mother's womb, and I have to redeem him from a priest."

The ritual follows, as in 4, above, but without any involvement by the mother. At the end, however, we get the following novelty that was not mentioned in the earlier geonic text.

The priest takes the money in hand, and passes it over the head of the boy, saying, "This money in exchange of this [boy]; this instead of that; this as a redemption for that. Let the money go forth to the priest, and the boy go forth [in exchange] to life, Torah, marriage and the fear of heaven."

Then the priest blesses the father of the boy, saying, "May it be the will of our God in heaven that as you admitted this boy into redemption, so may you admit him to Torah, marriage, and good deeds.

If the child is already an adult [who comes to be redeemed because he somehow never was redeemed as a child], the priest blesses him with whatever words seem appropriate. He puts his hand on his head, and says, for example, "May God keep you and give you life, 'for length of days and years of life and peace will be added to you' [Prov. 3:2]; 'He will not allow your foot to slip; He who keeps you will not slumber' [Ps. 121:3]; 'The sun will not strike you by day nor the moon by night. The Lord will keep you from all evil. He will keep your soul. He will guard your going out and your coming in from this time forth and forevermore' " [Ps. 121:6–8].

Expanding upon the blessing is meritorious.

6. The Tashbetz (Samson ben Tzadok). On Removing Women from the Synagogue

I am not at all in favor of the technically permissible custom that one finds in most places: namely, that a woman sits in the synagogue among the men, and they circumcise the baby in her lap. Even if the *mohel* is her husband, or her father or her son, it is not appropriate to allow a beautifully dressed-up woman to be among the men and right there in the presence of God.

We know from other texts that the event occurred in the synagogue sanctuary, in which case, the mother would have been sitting with the men during the worship service, as well. Though women and men probably sat together when the prayer service was first established in late antiquity, by the Middle Ages mixed seating had ceased and was technically forbidden. Nonetheless, we see here a case where women customarily sat among the men anyway, in order to have their sons circumcised appropriately.

This is exactly what they object to in the Talmud, when they ask "Could it be that women were allowed in the Temple courtyard?" The reason [for excluding women from the courtyard] is that they were afraid that the young priests would compete for her. Besides, with respect to the principle of circumcision, *she* [the mother] is not commanded to circumcise even her own son. Scripture says, ". . . which [God] commanded *him*"—that means *him* [the father], not *her* [the mother]. If so, how could it possibly be that they circumcise children on mothers' laps, thus snatching away the commandment from the men. Anyone who gets the opportunity to prevent such goings-on should do so. May people who act stringently in this case find blessing and peace. [This is a communication of] Meir ben Rabbi Barukh [of Rothenberg, that is, the Maharam], may he rest in peace.

When my teacher wrote this, I cried out for many days, but no one paid any attention to me, since it seemed very cruel to them. I grant that [during the act of circumcision], the people pay strict attention to their work, and do not let their thoughts wander along sinful paths. But still, people who see them will be suspicious, even if it is a case of a husband [who is the *mohel* performing the operation on his own son] and wife.

His objection is based on the fear that sexual thoughts will cross the mind of a man who is leaning over a women's lap to circumcise the baby whom she is holding. Moreover, even it be imagined that no such thoughts are likely here, since the *mohel* is probably concentrating on the operation that he performing, nonetheless, people may imagine that he is thinking lustful thoughts, and even the suggestion that he might be doing so is sufficient grounds for objection.

Moreover, not everyone knows that she is his wife. Is it for nothing that the Temple had a separate courtyard just for the women? Without it, [the sacrifices of the Temple] would have appeared like commandments that are carried out only at the cost of sin, a circumstance that scripture warns against when it says [1 Sam. 15:22], "To obey is better than to sacrifice." Every man who fears the word of God is obliged to walk out of the synagogue [if they try to circumcise babies on their mothers' laps], lest he give the false impression of aiding and abetting sinners. My teacher, Rabbenu Tuviah Yekutiel bar Moses, may he rest in peace, warned us about this, and I agree with him, adding only this [advice of Rabbi Yochanan, from the Talmud], "It is better to walk behind a lion than behind a woman."

7. The Maharil (Rabbi Jacob Moellin). The *Sandek* Replaces the Mother

Regarding a woman who is the *ba'alat brit* [the woman charged with transporting the boy to the synagogue], the Maharam wrote that she should take the child from its mother in order to bring him to the synagogue for his circumcision. She should bring him as far as the synagogue door, but should not go inside to be his *sandek* [the person who holds the child on his lap], since the child should not be circumcised in her lap. A woman should not walk among the men, on account of the need to maintain modesty.

8. The Maharil. The Theological Significance of Being a *Sandek*

When Maharil was appointed a *sandek* he used to bathe himself in order to bring the child to his circumcision while he himself was in a state of purity.

He said that the commandment [of being the *sandek*] is greater than the commandment performed by the *mohel* [doing the actual circumcision], since his knees are likened to an altar as if he were offering incense to heaven.

9. Rabbi Moses Isserles. On the Final Elimination of Women from the Ritual

The *sandek* takes precedence over the *mohel* in being called to the Torah, since a *sandek* is likened to someone who offers incense at the altar.

When the Torah scroll is unrolled and read liturgically, individual worshipers are honored by being summoned to recite a blessing that accompanies the reading, and to stand at the side of the reader; the inference is that the *sandek* is especially worthy of honor.

A woman may not serve as a *sandek,* because that would constitute brazenness, although she may help her husband take the boy to the synagogue where the man takes him from her and becomes the *sandek.* However a man may do the whole thing without a woman, and that is what the Maharil would do.

7

Honey Cakes and Torah: A Jewish Boy Learns His Letters

Ivan G. Marcus

At age five or six—perhaps even as young as three—a Jewish boy living in medieval Germany or France might begin his formal schooling by participating in a special ritual initiation ceremony. Early on the morning of the spring festival of Shavuot (Pentecost), someone wraps him in a coat or *talit* (prayer shawl) and carries him from his house to the teacher, who is either in the synagogue or the teacher's house. The boy is seated on the teacher's lap, and he shows him a tablet on which the Hebrew alphabet has been written. The teacher reads the letters first forward, then backward, and finally in symmetrically paired combinations, and he encourages the boy to repeat each sequence aloud. The teacher smears honey over the letters on the tablet and tells the child to lick it off.

Cakes on which biblical verses have been written are then brought in. They must be baked by virgins from flour, honey, oil, and milk. Next come shelled hard-boiled eggs on which more verses have been inscribed. The teacher reads the words written on the cakes and eggs, and the boy imitates what he hears and then eats them both.

The teacher next asks the child to recite an incantation adjuring POTAH, the prince of forgetfulness, (*sar ha-shikhehah*), to go far away and not block the boy's heart (*lev,* that is, *mind*). The teacher also instructs the boy to sway back and forth when studying and to sing his lessons out loud.

As a reward, the child gets to eat fruit, nuts, and other delicacies. At the conclusion of the rite, the teacher leads the boy down to the river and tells him that his future study of Torah, like the rushing water in the river, will never end. Doing all of these acts, we are told, will "expand the [child's] heart."

The four Hebrew texts presented here in complete, annotated translations for the first time describe different variations of this ceremony. They all are preserved in twelfth- through fourteenth-century compilations of Jewish law and custom that were set down in northern and southern France and in the Rhineland towns of the German Empire. Although each text has its unique features, all share common themes and may be interpreted as a set of related sources. For example, Texts 1 and 2 from Germany indicate that the ceremony took place in the late spring festival of Shavuot; the French ones, in contrast, do not mention a time of the year and imply from the location of the ceremony in parts of books that deal with a boy's maturation that it was held at whatever age the boy was ready to begin learning, not on Shavuot.

Although the authors of Texts 1 and 2 claim that the ceremony is an ancestral custom, no evidence of it survives earlier than these medieval texts. On the other hand, several of the elements that are found in the ceremony can be traced to earlier sources, including the Bible, the Talmud, early medieval authors, and anonymous magical practices connected with early Jewish mystical circles known as *heikhalot* (palace) or *merqavah* (chariot) mystics. They practiced a special mnemonic magic on the festival of Shavuot, the traditional anniversary of the giving of the Torah on Mt. Sinai.

By weaving together elements from earlier Jewish traditions, Jews developed a ceremony in the late twelfth- or early thirteenth-century Germany and northern France that in many ways parodied and subverted aspects of Christian rituals and symbols. By doing so, the Jewish rite of passage transformed its constituent parts into an identity-affirming Jewish initiation rite for young boys whom parents or other elders introduced to a life of Torah literacy. Eating special cakes baked with foods that symbolize Torah (flour, honey, milk, and oil), and shelled hard-boiled eggs on which words of Torah were written served as a Jewish antidote to the increasingly more prominent central Christian rite of the eucharist that bound Christians to one another and to the living sacrificed Christ.

By protectively wrapping the small Jewish boy in a coat or prayer shawl when he was carried from home to the teacher, Jews acted out the message that Jewish boys, not Jesus, were to be sacrificed—to a life of Torah study. This rite developed just when Christian iconography and narratives describe the Jesus in the Host as a sacrificed Christ Child. Similarly, the illumination of the ceremony that survives in the fourteenth-century *Leipzig Mahzor* (see Figure 7.1) portrays the Jewish boy caressing his father's cheek as he is brought to the schoolteacher and as seated on the teacher's lap. These are Jewish adaptations of two well-known Madonna and Child types: the *mater amabilis* (lovable mother) and the Throne of Wisdom, respectively.

By combining ancient and early medieval Jewish Torah symbols and memory enhancements with contemporary medieval rites and symbols of Christian ritual, the Jewish initiation ceremony illustrates the powerful dynamic process that I call "inward acculturation." Characteristic of how Jewish culture adapted creatively over centuries as a minority culture living intimately with a vibrantly attractive and potentially hostile majority culture, Jewish inward acculturation enabled Jews to remain firmly planted inside a single identity as Jews by combining early and contemporary Jewish symbols with contemporary non-Jewish symbols and rites to support their own cultural identity as Jews. They often did this through rituals

Figure 7.1. The school initiation scene. *Leipzig Mahzor,* Universitätsbibliothek, Leipzig, Hebrew MS Vollers 1102, vol. 1, fol. 131a. Reproduced with permission. Photo: Suzanne Kaufman.

or narratives that denied and even mocked the competing stronger ideology of Christianity in medieval Europe.

Jewish inward acculturation contrasts with "outward acculturation," which can become total assimilation, such as the extreme Jewish Hellenizers during the time of the Maccabees (second century B.C.E.) and modern Western acculturation and assimilation, in which a Jewish identity is shared with or replaced by an explicit second cultural self-awareness (I am Greek, German, Socialist, Communist, American, and so on), as a central or even definitive part of a Jew's identity. For most of Jewish history, inward acculturation served well to enable Jews who did not convert to adapt to living in overwhelmingly different and often hostile cultural environments without having to compromise their identity as Jews much of the time.

They did this not by ignoring their non-Jewish neighbors either in northern Europe (Ashkenaz) or Spain (Sefarad). Rather, they got to know them so well they were able to manipulate and transform elements in both religious cultures into positive expressions of a Jewish one that they regarded as trumping the culture of the majority. Inward acculturation worked for most of Jewish history until Jews came to live in modern secular societies that permitted, encouraged, or demanded that they embrace varying degrees of mixed identities in outward acculturation or assimilation and with it a blurring or obliteration of their Jewish identity.

The ceremony for small boys was not accompanied by a similar rite for little girls. In traditional Jewish communities, in fact, other than giving a name to a little girl soon after her birth, no special rites existed before her betrothal (which could be very early, even in childhood) and later actual marriage, sometimes to a very young "man." On the other hand, girls learned from their mothers and fathers how to follow the ways of Judaism by imitating their parents at home and sometimes in the synagogue, as well. The pietistic collection *Sefer Hasidim* (Book of the Pietists), from the late twelfth and early thirteenth centuries in Germany, insists that a father should teach his daughters the laws of Jewish practice that involve them, for, as the author puts it: "If they do not know the laws of the Sabbath, how will they be able to observe the Sabbath?" (Judah ben Samuel, *Sefer Hasidim,* edited by Jehuda Wistinetzki [Frankfurt am Main: Wahrmann, 1924], par. 835).

Elementary schooling, usually in the form of private tutors, was reserved for boys in medieval Europe, because Jewish literacy was thought of as a tool for male synagogue participation. For most, Jewish education remained minimal, a functional skill such as the ability to read the prayerbook and sometimes from the Torah scroll when called up to do so. Girls did not lead the prayers or read from the Torah scroll, and so did not receive what would have been considered a dysfunctional formal education. In some learned families there were literate women, even some who served as Hebrew scribes, but they were exceptions. Consequently, no special ceremony marks the beginning of a young girl's continuous apprenticeship, in effect, for becoming an informed Jewish woman prior to marriage.

The school initiation rite was practiced especially in the twelfth through fourteenth centuries. The entire elaborate ceremony was gradually forgotten, and only a few elements survived. Occasionally one hears about the abbreviated custom of teaching a boy his Hebrew alphabet and throwing candies on the letters as the teacher says in Yiddish, "Look what an angel has thrown down from Heaven." One finds this scene portrayed in seventeenth- and eighteenth-century Italian Jewish alphabet wall charts, and it is also depicted in the American film *Hester Street,* about the Lower East Side of New York in the early twentieth century.

Recently, however, part of the honeyed alphabet custom has been revived in Ultra-Orthodox Jewish circles (*haredim*) in Israel and America, but with the unprecedented twist of combining it with another custom, the first cutting of a boy's hair at age three. That practice never had any historic connection with the alphabet initiation ceremony. It originated as the Arab custom that parents cut a newborn boy's hair and burned it in a fire as a sacrifice. Jews in Palestine learned this custom from Arabs and adapted it to a special Jewish context. In the sixteenth century, Jewish mystics in the circle of Isaac Luria in Safed, in northern Palestine, started cutting the hair of small boys for the first time on the spring holiday of Lag Ba-Omer, a day celebrating the temporary cessation of the Hadrianic persecution of Torah scholars in second-century Palestine. They did this in the northern town of Meron, near Safed, at the grave site of Rabbi Shimon bar Yohai, the traditional author of the mystical classic, the *Zohar*. The custom of lighting bonfires on Lag Ba-Omer in Palestine and today in Israel derives from the Arab practice of burning the child's cut hair.

Sometime in the late eighteenth or nineteenth century, the practice of cutting a small child's hair spread to eastern Europe among the growing communities of the new Hasidim or Jewish Pietists who were powerfully influenced by the liturgical practices of the mystical circles of Safed in northern Palestine. They adapted the haircutting rite, but observed it in eastern Europe on a boy's third birthday, on the basis of an early midrashic passage that compares small boys to new fruit trees whose yield may be harvested and eaten only after the third year. Although Hasidic Jews refer to the haircutting rite as the *upsheerin,* which is Yiddish for haircut, Israeli Hasidim today refer to it as the *halaka,* which is Arabic for haircut, thereby preserving its Arab origins even in Yiddish. The haircutting practice continued in both places for centuries without any connection to the nearly forgotten honeyed alphabet initiation rite until just a few years ago.

Today, how-to-do-it books are available in Hebrew and English for parents of three-year-old boys. They explain that on the child's third birthday, he receives his first pair of long pants, his first little ritually fringed undergarment, a kind of mini prayer shawl worn under the shirt, and he also gets his first haircut. Following the haircutting, the boy is taught his Hebrew alphabet on a special chart that is smeared with honey, and he licks it up. He also may eat special eggs and cake, other parts of the medieval initiation ceremony that still survive.

In combination, these two formerly independent ceremonies represent an innovation, a new compound rite that Ultra-Orthodox Jews have invented in the late twentieth century. Other Jews have already picked up the idea, and it has begun being diffused into other sectors of the Jewish world. Just as the medieval ceremony itself was an adaptation of earlier elements from Jewish antiquity, so the combined haircutting and honey ceremony is an innovation made up of earlier older elements.

Text 1 is from the *Sefer ha-Roqeah* (Book of the Perfumer), which appears to describe the earliest version of the rite. R. Eleazar b. Judah of Worms's *Sefer ha-Roqeah* was written down before 1230 in the Rhineland. The author was a legal scholar and also a significant member of the circle of medieval German Jewish Pietists known as *hasidei ashkenaz* (the Jewish Pietists of Germany). He was the primary disciple of Rabbi Judah b. Samuel the Pietist (d. 1217) and claims to have written down exegetical keys to his teacher's secret interpretation of Scripture and the Prayerbook.

In other ways, R. Eleazar departed from his mentor by advocating earlier customs, despite his teacher's opposition to doing so. One of these customs is the Jewish boy's schooling initiation ritual. No earlier text probably exists than that found in R. Eleazar's *Sefer ha-Roqeah* or the nearly contemporary northern French version in the *Mahzor Vitry* (Text 3). The text is based on R. Eleazar b. Judah of Worms, *Sefer ha-Roqeah,* Fano, 1505, par. 296, corrected according to Paris Bibliothèque Nationale, Heb. MS 363, fol. 96a.

Text 2 is from *Sefer ha-Asufot* (Book of Collections), an anonymous compilation of German-Jewish customs and ritual laws produced in Germany probably in the middle of the thirteenth century, a generation after R. Eleazar of Worms' *Sefer ha-Roqeah,* and based in part on it. It resembles Text 1 but departs from it in the verses stipulated in the ceremony, especially the inclusion of several verses of Psalm 119, which Jews used for magical mnemonic purposes in earlier times. Text 2 also mentions several other details that are variations from or additions to the ceremony. One ancient magical element mentioned for the first time was associated until recently with the *havdalah* (separation) ceremony recited at the end of the Sabbath. This is an incantation that POTAH, the prince of forgetfulness, vanish and not impair the boy's memory and mental capacities. Other new elements appear toward the end of the text: bringing the child to the riverside and the recipe for making the special cakes that he eats. River water, honey, oil, and milk all have biblical and rabbinic associations with Torah. The foods are associated with God's sweet word, based on the powerful imagined gesture in Ezekiel's vision of eating the sweet scroll of God's words (3:3). Text 2 is based on *Sefer ha-Asufot,* London, MS Jews College 134 (Montefiore 115), fol. 67a; published in Simha Assaf, *Meqorot le-Toledot ha-Hinukh be-Yisrael* (Tel Aviv: Dvir, 1925–1948), vol. 4, pp. 11–12 and elsewhere.

Text 3 is from the *Mahzor Vitry,* a collection that in its earliest form is attributed to R. Simha of Vitry (twelfth century) a younger contemporary of Rashi of Troyes (d. 1105). The earliest manuscript versions of the liturgical compilation of the *Mahzor Vitry* do not quote the ceremony. The earliest manuscript that does is MS New York, Jewish Theological Seminary of America (JTS) Microfilm no. 8092, dated 1204, fols. 164b–165a, which concludes with a large alphabet chart at the end of the ceremony not found in other witnesses. The text in the printed edition of Shim'on Halevi Horowitz (Berlin: n.p., 1889–1897), pp. 628–30, is based on London British Library Heb. MS Add. 27200/01 (Margalioth Catalogue, no. 655), from the mid-thirteenth century.

The passage on the rite in the *Mahzor Vitry* consists of two parts: part 1 describes the details of the ceremony; part 2 offers explanations for each element. The JTS manuscript and the Horowitz edition are nearly identical in part 1. In part 2, however, the list of explanations in the JTS manuscript does not correspond completely to the sequence in part 1. Although this manuscript version is earlier than the Horowitz edition, it seems more corrupt than the later British Library base text that Horowitz used. For this reason, the Horowitz text has been selected for this translation.

This version of the ceremony, like the other French ones, does not mention that the initiation rite is to take place on the festival of Shavuot, an ancient Palestinian tradition transmitted only to the German-Jewish versions. It alone contains the memorable pedagogic Hebrew motto: "first we entice him and then the strap is applied to his back." The *Mahzor Vitry* version is the earliest French one and may be nearly contemporary with, or even earlier than, Text 1 from the Rhineland. It seems to have influenced the southern French ones, as the end of Texts 3 and 4 indicates.

Text 4 is from *Orhot Hayyim* (Paths of Life), a compilation of Jewish law and custom made by Rabbi Aaron b. Jacob ha-Kohen of Lunel in southern France in the fourteenth century. The description of the initiation rite follows the *Mahzor Vitry* but omits certain items such as eating eggs. For the first time we see the possibility that the alphabet may be written "on parchment or on a tablet." The most significant addition is the mention of an additional custom at the end, attributed to Palestinian Jews, according to which Jews would train their young children to fast. As is the case of the French versions, in general the custom of early fasting emphasizes that it is the age of the child, not a time of the year, that is important.

The translation is based on *Sefer Orhot Hayyim,* Part 2, edited by M. Schlesinger (Berlin: Z. H. Itzqawicki, 1902), vol. 2, p. 24.

In addition to the four texts presented here, two other full texts survive, as well as two other fragments and a single manuscript illumination. In addition to Texts 1 and 2, which are derived from the Rhineland, there is a long, anonymous text, also from Germany, found in a commentary on liturgical poems (*piyyutim*) in the prayerbook, probably from the end of the thirteenth century: Hamburg, Staats- und Universitätsbibliothek, Heb. MS 17 (Steinschneider Catalogue, no. 152), fols. 81a–82b. It was published in a facsimile edition by Ernst Roth, *Cod. heb. 17 und 61 Hamburg* (Jerusalem, n.p., 1960). Like Text 3 from the *Mahzor Vitry*, it consists of two parts: a description of the ritual and a set of explanations of its elements. In it the father is said to bring the child to school wrapped in a prayer shawl instead of a coat; it also has variations as to which verse are to be written on each of the physical symbols.

In addition to Text 4, a second fourteenth-century southern French text is the anonymous compilation *Kol Bo* (Miscellany) (Naples, 1490), sec. 74, which closely resembles it. I am grateful to Dr. Elisheva Baumgarten for calling to my attention two previously unknown fragmentary texts: Vatican Library, Heb. MS 318 f. 284b, and Parma, Bibliteca Palatina, Heb. MS 2342 (de Rossi 541), f. 286a. Finally, there is a manuscript illumination of the ritual from the fourteenth-century *Mahzor Leipzig,* Leipzig Universitätsbibliothek, Heb. MS Vollers 1102, vol. 1, fol. 131a. It was published in a facsimile edition: *Machsor Lipsiae,* edited by Elias Katz, with an introduction by Bezalel Narkiss (Hanau an Main: W. Dausien, 1964).

The following works are referred to in bracketed editorial notes in the texts: Midrash *Bereishit Rabbah,* edited by J. Theodor and H. Albeck, 1903–1936 (reprint 3 vols., Jerusalem: Wahrmann, 1965); *'Aggadat Shir ha-Shirim,* edited by Solomon Schechter (Cambridge, Eng.: D. Bell, 1896); and *Masekhet Soferim,* edited by Michael Higger (New York: "De-Vei Rabanan," 1937).

Further Reading

The illumination and a discussion of the rite's anthropological historical meanings may be found in my *Rituals of Childhood: Jewish Acculturation in Medieval Europe*

(New Haven: Yale University Press, 1996). An example of the new initiation books for small children is Beverly Geller, *The Upsheerin: Ephraim's First Haircut* (New York: CIS Publishers, 1991).

1. *Sefer ha-Roqeah* (Book of the Perfumer)

It is the custom of our ancestors to sit the children down to study [the Torah for the first time] on Shavuot because that is when the Torah was given. A [scriptural] indication that the boy should be covered so that he will not see a Gentile or a dog on the day he is instructed in the holy letters is "[No one else shall come up with you, and no one else shall be seen anywhere on the mountain;] neither shall the flocks and the herds graze at the foot of this mountain" [Exod. 34:3].

The boys are brought on Shavuot morning at sunrise, according to [the verse], "[On the third day,] as morning dawned, there was thunder, and lightening" [Exod. 19:16].

He is covered with a cloak on the way from [his] house to the synagogue or the teacher's house, according to [the verse], "and they took their places at the foot [or: nether part] of the mountain" [Exod. 19:17].

The child is placed on the lap/bosom (*heiqo*) of the teacher who sits them down to study, according to [the verse, "and Moses said to the Lord, . . . 'Did I conceive this people, did I bear them, that You should say to me, "Carry them in your bosom] as a nurse carries an infant" ' " [Num. 11:12]; [and according to the verse,] "I have pampered Ephraim, taking them in My arms" [Hos. 11:3].

They bring over the tablet (*lu'ah*) on which is written [the alphabet forward, beginning] *alef, bet, gimel, dalet;* [the alphabet written backward, beginning] *tav, shin, resh, qof;* [and the verse, "When Moses] charged us with the Torah as the heritage of the congregation of Jacob" [Deut. 33:4]; [the phrase] "May the Torah be my occupation" [see Babylonian Talmud, *Berakhot* 16b]; and the first verse of Leviticus, beginning], "The Lord called to Moses . . ." [Lev. 1:1].

The teacher recites aloud each letter of the *alef bet* [forward], and the child [recites them] after him; [then the teacher recites] each word of *tav, shin, resh, qof* and the child does so too; similarly, [they both recite the verse beginning, "When Moses] charged [us] with the Torah . . ." [Deut. 33:4]; and [the phrase beginning], "May the Torah be . . ."; and likewise [the verse beginning], "The Lord called [to Moses . . .]" [Lev. 1:1].

And [the teacher] puts a little honey on the tablet, and with his tongue, the child licks the honey which is on the letters.

After this, they bring over the cake kneaded with honey on which is written, "The Lord God gave me a skilled tongue, to know how to speak timely words to the weary. Morning by morning, He rouses, He rouses my ear to give heed like disciples. The Lord God opened my ears, and I did not disobey, I did not run away" [Isa. 50:4–5]. The teacher recites aloud each word of these verses, and the boy [does so] after him.

After this, they bring over a cooked egg that has been peeled and on which is written, "as He said to me, 'Mortal, feed your stomach and fill your belly with this scroll that I give you.' I ate it, and it tasted as sweet as honey to me" [Ezek. 3:3]. The teacher recites aloud each word and the boy [does so] after him.

They feed the boy the cake and the egg because it is good for the opening of the heart (*li-petihat ha-lev*).

Let no one deviate from [following] this custom, as we say in [tractate] *Pesahim,* in [the] ch[apter beginning] *Maqom she-nahagu* ["Where they were accustomed"] [Babylonian Talmud, *Pesahim* 50b]; and [we read] in Midrash *Bereishit Rabbah,* section *Va-yeira eilav* ["And He appeared to him"] [Gen. 18:1 ff.] [ed. Theodor-Albeck, 2:491]: "When you come to a [new] place, follow its custom"; and [we read] in Ch[apter] 1 of Jerusalem [Talmud, tractate] *Ta'anit* [1:6, 64c] and in the ch[apter beginning] *Maqom she-nahagu* [Jerusalem Talmud, *Pesahim* 1:1, 30c] and in *'Aggadat Shir ha-Shirim'* [ed. Solomon Schechter]: "Custom is valid."

2. *Sefer ha-Asufot* (Book of Collections)

It is the custom of our ancestors to sit the children down to study [Torah for the first time] on Shavuot because that is when the Torah was given. The boys are brought at sunrise [of Shavuot morning] to the synagogue to the teacher [according to the verse, "And it came to pass on the third day,] as morning dawned, there was thunder, and lightening" [Exod. 19:16].

They bring over the tablet on which is written [the alphabet forward, beginning] *alef, bet, gimel, dalet;* and [the alphabet written backward, beginning] *tav, shin, resh, qof;* [and the verse, "When Moses] charged us with the Torah [as a heritage of the congregation of Jacob]" [Deut. 33:4]; [the phrase] "May the Torah be my occupation"; and the first verse of Leviticus.

And the teacher recites aloud each letter, and the child recites [them] after him.

And he puts a little honey on the tablet, and with his tongue, the child licks the honey that is on the letters.

These verses are written on a cake kneaded with honey: "as He said to me, 'Mortal, feed your stomach and fill your belly with this scroll that I give you.' I ate it, and it tasted as sweet as honey to me" [Ezek. 3:3]; "The Lord God gave me a skilled tongue, to know how to speak timely words to the weary. Morning by morning, He rouses, He rouses my ear to give heed like disciples. The Lord God opened my ears, and I did not disobey, I did not run away [Isa. 50:4–5]; "How can a young man keep his way pure?—by holding to Your word" [Ps. 119:9]; "In my heart I treasure Your promise; therefore I do not sin against You" [v. 11]; "Blessed are You, O Lord; train me in Your laws" [v. 12]; "Open my eyes, that I may perceive the wonders of Your teaching" [v. 18]; "Give me understanding, that I may observe Your teaching and keep it wholeheartedly" [v. 34]; "O how I love Your teaching! It is my study all day long" [v. 97]; "The words You inscribed give light, and grant understanding to the simple" [v. 130]; "Your word is exceedingly pure, and Your servant loves it" [v. 140].

And he should write on the egg: "I have gained more insight than all my teachers, for Your decrees are my study" [v. 99]; "I have gained more understanding than my elders, for I observe Your precepts" [v. 100]; "How sweet is Your word to my palate, sweeter than honey to my mouth" [v. 103]; "Your word is a lamp to my feet, and a light for my path" [v. 105].

Ten times he should say these three words: NGF, SGF, AGF. I adjure you, POTAH, the prince of forgetfulness, that you extract and remove from me a fool's heart, I so-and-so, son of so-and-so, and throw it on a high mountain, in the name of [line blank].

And the teacher recites aloud with the boy everything [written] on the tablet, and on the cake, and on the egg. And the egg will be peeled and cooked.

After the boys have completed their study, they feed the boy the cake and the egg because it is good for the opening of the heart.

The boys are covered under a cloak when they are taken from their house to the teacher's house or to the synagogue. And the reason is according to [the verse], "and they took their places at the foot of the mountain" [Exod. 19:17].

And he is placed on the arm of the teacher, who sits him down to study, according to [the verse, "carry them in your bosom] as a nurse carries an infant" [Num. 11:12]; and according to "I have pampered Ephraim, taking them in my arms" [Hos. 11:3].

After the study session, the boy is brought to the riverside, according to the Torah's being compared to water and [the verse], "Your springs will gush forth [in streams in the public squares]" [Prov. 5:16], so that the boy should have an expanded heart.

And the cake is prepared from three measures of fine flour corresponding to the manna, the well and the quail [in the desert]. And one mixes into it honey, oil, and milk, symbolic of [the verse], "He fed him honey etc. [from the crag, and oil from the flinty rock]" [Deut. 32:13], and it is written, "honey and milk are under your tongue" [Song of Songs 4:11].

3. *Mahzor Vitry*

Part 1, which explains the details of the ritual, is as follows.

[1] When a man brings his son to study the Torah [for the first time], the letters [of the Hebrew alphabet] are written out on a tablet for him. [2] He is washed and dressed in clean clothes. [3] Three loaves made of fine flour and honey are kneaded for him. [4] A virgin kneads the dough. [5] Three eggs are cooked for him. [6] And apples and various [other] fruit are brought to him. [7] One looks for an important learned man to bring him to the school. [8]

He covers him under the folds of his [cloak] [9] and brings him into the synagogue. [10] He is fed the loaves [made] with honey, [11] the eggs and the fruit. [12] The letters are read out to him. [13] Afterward, [the letters] are covered with honey and [14] he is told: "Lick!" [15] He is covered up and taken back to his mother.

[16] And when he begins to study Torah, at first he is enticed and afterward the strap is on his back. [17] One opens first for him Torat Kohanim [i.e., Leviticus]. [18] He is trained to shake his body when he studies. [19] When he gets to "[All fat is the Lord's.] It is a law for all time [throughout the ages, in all your settlements: you must not eat any fat or any blood]" [Lev. 3:17], he reads it [the first time] as [it is read in] public, and a festive meal is made to honor him for doing so.

You should know that [when a father does] this ceremony it is as though he brings him near Mt. Sinai, as it is written, "on *this* day, they entered the wilderness of Sinai" [Exod. 19:1]. It is not written, "on that day." The Torah said: Let each and every day be to you as though it were the very day on which the Torah was given, to teach you that when you initiate him in the study of the Torah, follow this custom of bringing him covered [to the school]. For we have found that Moses followed this procedure with Israel, as it is written, "Moses led the people out of the camp *toward* God, and they took their places *under* the mountain" [Exod. 19:17], [meaning]: It appeared as though they were covered under the mountain when he brought them in to receive the Torah [for the first time]. And He warned them that there should be no barrier between them and their Maker, as it is written, "[And Moses led the people . . .] toward God" [Exod. 19:17]; [it does] not [say], "toward man and beast." For the same reason, He warned them, "neither shall the flocks and the herds graze at the foot of this mountain" [Exod. 34:3]. It is written, "And Moses sent his father-in-law away" [Exod. 18:27] so that nothing should be a barrier between any Israelite [and their Maker]—for he was a Gentile—as it is written, "And Moses sent his father-in-law away" [Exod. 18:27], and immediately afterward it says, "On the third new moon [. . . they entered the wilderness of Sinai]" [Exod. 19:1].

Part 2 gives explanations for most of the elements in Part 1.

[1] Why are the letters written out for him on a tablet and not on something else? There is a tablet in one's mind, as it is written, "Write them on the tablet of your mind" [Prov. 3:3; 7:3]. In other words, [the Torah] should be permanently [written] on your mind's tablet.

[2] Why is he washed and dressed in clean clothes? This is as it was when the Torah was given, [where it says] "stay pure today and tomorrow. Let them wash their clothes" [Exod. 19:10].

[3] Why are three loaves [baked] especially for him and then fed to him? It is a reminder of the three [kinds of] good food that Israel received [in the

desert]: the well [water], manna, and quail [see Exod. 16:14–16, 35—manna; Num. 21:16—well; Exod. 16:13, Num. 11:31–32—quail]. Why are the loaves kneaded with milk and honey? Because it is said, "He fed him honey from the crag" [Deut. 32:13] and because it is like a verse that is good for opening the mind (*petihat ha-lev*), as it is said, "honey and milk are under your tongue" [Song of Songs 4:11].

[4] Why is only a virgin permitted to knead the dough? We have found that the Torah stipulated that no one discharging semen [see Lev. 15:18–19; *Mishnah Berakhot* 3:6] could be present when the Torah was given, as it is written, ["And he said to the people,] 'Be ready for the third day: [do not go near a woman]' " [Exod. 19:15]. For this reason, they said: Let a pure virgin knead [it] for a pure boy.

[5] Why is he brought three hard-boiled eggs? It is not an obligatory part of the religious ceremony. Rather it is just something useful for carrying it out [see Deut. 4:9 in Babylonian Talmud, *Qiddushin* 29b and *Megillah* 26b], since one is supposed to eat them with relish. For if he just wolfs it down, his mind might be distracted, and so just as one trains him to follow the whole Torah, so all the details [of the rite] must be followed. Why eggs? A small child is fond of eggs.

[6] He is also brought apples and other fruit when available for dessert. This is so because someone said, "wine and spices made me wise" [Babylonian Talmud, *Yoma* 76b].

[7] Why is a sage or an important man sought after to bring him to the school? It was so when the Torah was given. The H[oly one, blessed be he], looked for an important man and found none like our rabbi Moses through whom to give the Torah. Why was so great [a man needed]? So that they would last forever, as it is said, "[the words which I have placed in your mouth] shall not be absent from your mouth, etc. [nor from the mouth of your children, nor from the mouth of your children's children—said the Lord—from now on, for all time]" [Isa. 59:21]. For the actions of the righteous last forever, and the Holy one, blessed be he, supports their behavior, as it is said, "He will fulfill the prediction of His messengers" [Isa. 44:26].

[8] Why does a sage cover him under the folds [of his cloak]? In this way we teach him modesty and humility, which was also true when the Torah was given, [as it says], "in order that the fear of Him may be ever with you, so that you do not sin" [Exod. 20:17].

Another interpretation: [We do it so as] not to make him visible in public to passersby, so the evil eye or anything else will not harm him. It was so when the Torah was given [to Israel]. The first tablets were given in the open amidst thunder and lightening and the sounding of the shofar. The angels were jealous and Satan came and subverted the world by bringing about the sin [of the Golden Calf] so that the first tablets were smashed. The second tablets were given in private and they lasted forever.

[15] For this reason [the boy] is also brought back to his mother covered.

[9] Why [is he taken] to a synagogue? It is just as when Israel came close to Mt. Sinai when the Torah was given.

[12] The learned man reads the letters [of the alphabet] out loud to him as a reminder of [God's saying out loud], "And God spoke [all these words . . .]" [Exod. 20:1].

[13–14] Why after the letters are read out loud to him do we cover [the tablet] with honey and tell him, "Lick!"? This is like what is described in Ezekiel, "I ate it, and it tasted as sweet as honey to me" [Ezek. 3:3]. This means that [just as] it is pleasant for him to lick the letters, so will it be pleasant for him to learn Torah regularly and teach it [to his children]. To ingest [the Torah] is like a honeycomb which is like, "Mortal, feed your stomach and fill your belly [with this scroll that I give you]" [Ezek. 3:3].

[16] Why "at first he is enticed and afterwards the strap is on his back"? It is like the beginning of the Torah, as [the prophet Jeremiah hints], "You [first] enticed me, O Lord; I was enticed; [and then] You overpowered me and You prevailed" [Jer. 20:7]. For in the beginning [of the Exodus law code], is written, "but you shall be to Me a kingdom of priests and a holy nation" [Exod. 19:6]. In other words, you will receive only rewards. But afterwards it says, "Whoever sacrifices to a god other than the Lord alone will be proscribed" [Exod. 22:19]; "he who profanes it shall be put to death" [Exod. 31:14], and "one who strikes his father [or his mother shall be put to death]" [Exod. 21:15]; "He who fatally strikes a man shall be put to death" [Exod. 21:12]; "the adulterer and the adulteress shall be put to death" [Lev. 20:10].

[17] Why does one begin with Torat Kohanim, the Book of Leviticus? As it is taught [Midrash Vayyiqra Rabba 7:3]: Rabbi Yossi taught: We start off the small children with the order [of sacrifices] in Leviticus. The Holy One, blessed be he, said: Let the pure ones come and study purities. I consider it equivalent to their offering a sacrifice to me.

[18] Why do we train him to shake his body when he studies? We found something similar at the giving of the Torah: "When the people saw it they were shaken" [Exod. 20:15]. Not only the men trembled but even the mountains and the trees. Concerning mountains it is written, "and the whole mountain trembled" [Exod. 19:18]; and it is written in Psalms, "Why so shaken up, O jagged mountains?" [Ps. 68:16]. Concerning trees it is written, "All the trees of the field shall clap their hands" [Isa. 55:12]. This is what David said: "Serve the Lord in awe; tremble in joy" [Ps. 2:11]; and Solomon also expounded, "His lips are like lilies; they drip flowing myrrh" [Song of Songs 5:13]. Do not read "lilies" (*shoshanim*), but rather [as though written] "those who study" (*she-shonim*); do not read "flowing myrrh" (*mor over*), but rather [as though written] "drop bitterness" (*mar over*). This means, then, that a student must always be in great fear of the Place [= God; see Babylonian Talmud, *Shabbat* 30b].

How do we know that all of the details [of the ceremony] derive from the [narrative about the] giving of [the Torah]? It is written, "And make them known to your children and to your children's children" [Deut. 4:9], and right after, it says, "The day you stood [before the Lord your God at Horeb (= Sinai)"] [Deut. 4:10]. [The juxtaposition of the verses] teaches that the Place [God] considers [the day a man brings his child to study the Torah for the first time] to be like the day Israel stood at Mt. Sinai.

[19] What is the reason [the boy] concludes [by reading] the verse, "[it is law for all time throughout the ages, in all your settlements:] you must not eat any fat or blood" [Lev. 3:17]? The H[oly One, blessed be he] said: Let him recite before me [the law about] fat and blood [derived] from a domestic animal which is sacrificed on the altar before me. [It is] for the sake of small boys who lose fat and blood from [the strenuous effort of] Torah [study], [and] I credit them as though they were sacrificed before me. The proof text is [from the case of] the [prohibited] sciatic nerve [*gid ha-nasheh,* derived from Gen. 32:32]. The [rabbis] said: Should we enjoy [eating] something that caused pain to that righteous man [Jacob]? That is why it was prohibited.

But if you ask, Why did the Torah prohibit the blood of wild [permitted] animals and fowl? [Answer,] because of the commandment to cover [the blood], as it is written, ["And if any Israelite . . . hunts down an animal or bird that may be eaten,] he shall pour out its blood and cover it with earth" [Lev. 17:13]. Infer from this that the fat of such animals is permitted, since no one offers it as a sacrifice. And that is why [the child] reads that verse as a kind of song. He sings praises to the Place that he has fulfilled such a commandment.

[It is though God says,] "And I count it as though they sacrificed his blood and fat on the altar." Therefore, one must make a feast for him like the one made on the day [he was] circumcised when he [also] lost blood. One who participates in this feast must bless him by saying: "May the Place enlighten your eyes with his Torah," which is analogous to the way one blessed him [as an infant boy] when he was circumcised, when those present say, "As he entered the convenant [of circumcision], so may he enter the Torah, [the wedding chamber, and many good deeds"; Babylonian Talmud, *Shabbat* 137b]. The end. [Compare the end of Text 4].

4. *Orhot Hayyim* (Paths of Life)

The custom that the s[ages], [may their] m[emory be] b[lessed], followed when they had their children sit down to study Torah. It was customary when a person sat his son down to study Torah that the letters be written on parchment or on a tablet. He is washed and dressed in clean clothes. Loaves are kneaded with honey and milk for him. Fruit and various other delicacies are brought to him. He is delivered to a scholar who brings him to the school. [He covers him under his outer garment (*kenafav*) and takes him to the school] [So *Kol Bo* sec. 74; a line fell out because of similar endings "school . . . school"]. He eats of the loaves [made with] honey and milk, of the fruit and of the various delicacies and the letters are read out loud to him. Afterward [they are] covered with honey and he is told to lick the honey on the letters. He is then taken back to his mother.

And when he begins to study Torah, he begins with Torat Kohanim [that is,] the Book of Leviticus. A festive meal is made for him because to his father it is as though he brings him close (*maqrivo*) to Mt. Sinai.

The Torah said: Every day let the words of the Torah be to you as though they were given today, as it is written, "on this day" [Exod. 19:1]; it is not written, "on *that* day."

He is fed fruit and various delicacies as a reminder of the good foods which Israel was given in the desert, such as the manna, well [water], and quail.

The loaves are kneaded with honey and milk as a reminder of "He fed him honey from the crag" [Deut. 32:13] and it is written, "honey and milk are under your tongue" [Song of Songs 4:11].

They begin with the book of Leviticus because the sages, may their memory be blessed, said: The children begin with the Book of Leviticus because the Holy One, blessed be he, said: Let the pure ones come and study purities. I then consider it as though you offered a sacrifice (*hiqravtem*) before me.

One looks for a scholar to bring him to school because when the Torah was given, the Holy One, blessed be he, went to get Moses, a great yet very humble man [see Num. 12:3].

He covers him under the folds [of his cloak] in order to make him love the Torah in humility and modesty. For it is written, ["for God has come] . . . in order that the fear of Him may be ever with you, so that you do not sin" [Exod. 20:17]. Why so much? In order that the Torah continue forever: the deeds of the righteous last forever.

After he reads the letters, they are covered with honey and he is made to lick it so that the words of the Torah should be as sweet in his mouth as honey, as it is said, "and it tasted as sweet as honey to me" [Ezek. 3:3].

Some hold that only virgins are permitted to knead the loaves because we find the Holy One, blessed be he, warning against anyone discharging semen when the Torah was given, as it is said, "Do not go near a woman" [Exod. 19:15].

The reason that "at first he is enticed and afterward the strap is on his back" is because when the Torah was given, it is first written, "but you shall be to Me a kingdom of priests and a holy nation" [Exod. 19:6]. In other words, you will receive only rewards. But afterwards it says, "Whoever sacrifices to a god other than the Lord alone will be proscribed" [Exod. 22:19]; "he who profanes it shall be put to death" [Exod. 31:14], and [mentions] the other punishments.

The children are taught to shake their bodies when they study, as it is written about the giving of the Torah, "and when the people saw it, they were shaken" [Exod. 20:15]. This is what King David, may he rest in peace, meant by "Serve the Lord in awe" [Ps. 2:11]; and Solomon also says, "His lips are like lilies; they drip flowing myrrh" [Song of Songs 5:13]. Do not read "lilies" (*shoshanim*), but rather [as though written] "those who study" (*she-shonim*); do not read "flowing myrrh" (*mor over*), but rather [as though written] "drop bitterness" (*mar over*). This means, then, that a student must be in great fear of his teacher.

How do we know that all of these details [in the ceremony] derive from the [narrative about the] giving of [the Torah]? It is written, "And make them known to your children and to your children's children" [Deut. 4:9] and right after, it says, "The day you stood [before the Lord your God at Horeb (Sinai)"] [Deut. 4:10]. The [juxtaposition of the verses] teaches that on the day a man brings his child to study the Torah [for the first time], he stands before God, like the day Israel stood at Horeb.

This custom was the custom of the ancients (*qadmonim*). The people of Jerusalem did it and even today it is done in some places.

There was another good and proper custom [practiced] in Jerusalem. From the ages of three and four, people would train their sons and daughters to fast until noon on a fast day. From four or five, they taught them to fast all day [see *Mishnah Yoma* 8:4 and the even stricter ancient Palestinian custom of making one- and two-year-olds fast, mentioned in the variant readings of Masekhet Soferim, 18:7 edited by Michael Higger, pp. 318–19].

Afterward, the father would hold him up and bring him to each elder to bless him, "that he merit [studying] Torah, [entering the] wedding chamber and [doing] good deeds." He would rise in the presence of anyone in town who was more important than himself, stand before him, bow before him, [entreating him] to pray for him. This teaches you that they were proper and acted properly—all their desires were pious. They took their small children to the synagogue to teach them and encourage them to do the commandments at an early age.

8

Women and Ritual Immersion in Medieval Ashkenaz: The Sexual Politics of Piety

Judith R. Baskin

Rabbinic Judaism, which established the normative patterns of Jewish life from late antiquity through the modern period, is an androcentric system designed by men, intended to guide and direct every aspect of human conduct and religious practice according to what are perceived as divine mandates. This detailed and complex system of evolving legislation (*halakhah*), codified in the Mishnah (third century C.E.) and the Babylonian Talmud (sixth century C.E.), has traditionally considered women primarily as they pertain to men and as they can best support and advance male needs, aspirations, and religious obligations. Since there is a strong recognition that women can disturb the ordered structure of men's lives, impeding fulfilment of their primary goal of obedience to divine ordinances, Jewish legal rulings have always been anxious to limit the female potential for disruption by relegating women, whenever possible, to domestic roles under the authority of a father or a husband.

Female physical and biological differences from men are fundamental to this separation of women from rabbinic Judaism's central spiritual endeavors of public worship, study of sacred texts, and communal leadership according to the dictates of talmudic law. Anthropologists have pointed out that cultural notions of women often center around female characteristics such as fertility, maternity, and menstrual blood. Certainly, significant voices within rabbinic Judaism are anxious to circumscribe, defuse, and control the sexual and biological attributes of the female as both sexual temptress and potential source of ritual pollution.

Since ritual uncleanness implies a separation from God, biblical and postbiblical Judaism have valued ritual purity as a religious ideal. Among a number of sources of ritual pollution, biblical strictures (particularly Lev. 12, 15, and 18) identify contact with a *niddah*. This term, derived from the Hebrew root *n-d-h*, "banned, shunned, ostracized," denotes a woman suffering a flow of vaginal blood from whatever cause. Rabbinic *halakhah,* particularly in the talmudic tractate

Niddah, which deals with the practical consequences of women's menstrual and nonmenstrual discharges, developed these biblical ordinances into a complicated system of rules for avoiding not only sexual intercourse but any physical contact between husband and wife during the wife's menses and an additional seven days following the cessation of flow. On the eighth "white" day, the wife, after a thorough cleansing, must immerse in the *mikveh* [pl. *mikva'ot*], or ritual bath, before marital relations may resume.

Rabbinic interest in menstruation stems entirely from halakhic concern with the ritual purity of men; one might say that men inscribe their own piety on the bodies of their wives. The possibility that being in a state of ritual uncleanness could have any spiritual impact on women is never considered. Indeed, only married women are required to immerse following their periods of ritual impurity and this is purely in order to preserve their husbands from the risk of pollution. However, procedures for calculating the interval of time when spousal contact is forbidden relies heavily on the menstruant's knowledge of the stages of her cycle. As Judith Romney Wegner has noted, this creates a curious paradox: woman is constructed both as an object that generates pollution and as a responsible person who must actively avoid transmitting her impurity to vulnerable men. Thus, women were considered trustworthy to report accurately as to whether or not they were sexually available to their husbands, and were expected to visit the *mikveh* as soon as they were legally able to do so. But this also meant that a woman could delay her immersion or report inaccurately on her state of ritual purity as a strategy for exerting power in her marriage. Thus, a significant theme in the education of medieval Jewish girls was to stress the need for strict and prompt compliance with *hilkhot niddah*, laws connected with the *niddah*.

Although women's ritual immersion (*tevilah*) at the appropriate time was of central importance in the married lives of medieval Jews in Ashkenaz (the medieval Hebrew term for France and Germany), the *mikveh* was not only for the *niddah*; it was also used for immersion by those converting to Judaism as part of the conversion ceremony, by particularly pious men prior to the Sabbath and other Jewish holidays, and for the purification of new metal and glass utensils before they were used in food preparation. Medieval *mikva'ot*, constructed according to halakhic specifications, survive from as early as the twelfth century in several German Rhineland cities that were sites of medieval Jewish settlements, including Worms, Speyer, and Cologne. These were usually excavated underground buildings, built as close as possible to a source of water. At Worms, nineteen steps descend to the *mikveh*'s entrance hall and then another eleven steps lead to the *mikveh* itself.

The medieval Jewish documents that follow illuminate issues directly and indirectly connected with women's observance of *hilkhot niddah*. However, no surviving medieval documents provide insight into how women themselves viewed their obligations in this most intimate aspect of their lives, since virtually no documents written by medieval Jewish women are extant; their feelings about the expectations imposed upon them and the limitations for their sex inherent in rabbinic social policy are therefore all but unrecoverable. Nor are there are any medieval accounts of how exactly medieval Jewish women went about their ritual immersions. *Halakhah* demanded that immersion, which took place only after the body had been thoroughly cleaned (perhaps at a public bath), had to be complete; although one total immersion was sufficient according to *halakhah,* three became customary. From a halakhic point of view, the immersion of the *niddah* had to be accompanied by the proper spiritual intention and required the recitation of the prayer mandating ritual purification for those in states of ritual impurity. Our documents imply that women could recite this benediction in the vernacular language. Postmenstrual and postpartum women usually went to the *mikveh* at night, often accompanied by other women.

The sources relevant to medieval Jewish women and their observance of *hilkhot niddah* reveal male projections of what women's understandings of their obligations in this area should be. The rabbinic stance concerning the *niddah* and her ritual obligations is essentially negative. A rabbinic commentary on Genesis, *Genesis Rabbah,* states that menstruation was imposed on women as a punishment for the first woman's failure to obey God: " 'And why was the precept of menstruation given to her?' 'Because she shed the blood of Adam [by causing death], therefore was the precept of menstruation given to her' " (17:8). Similarly, according to the Mishnah, a woman who disregards regulations applying to the *niddah* can be punished by death in childbirth (*Mishnah Shabbat* 2:6). Such a dire pronouncement may have been part of a rabbinic polemic against widespread noncompliance with these precepts; certainly the anxiety one can discern in rabbinic literature in regard to controlling women's activities may reflect the dissonance between what many women actually did and what the rabbinic sages preferred that they would do. However, the underlying themes of the female as deservedly disadvantaged, at fault in human mortality, and, indeed, as in some ways threatening to men, which are invoked to explain why women are subject to menstruation and its attendant rituals, are unmistakable.

Male lack of compliance with *hilkhot niddah* was also a concern to rabbinic authorities, and men were frequently warned of the dire consequences of contact with a *niddah*; a cautionary anecdote in the Babylonian Talmud (*Shabbat* 13a–13b) about a scholar who died young because he slept in the same bed with his wife when she was in a state of *niddah,* even though sexual relations did not take place, is often repeated and expanded upon in medieval texts.

Some of the themes of niddah as a deserved female chastisement appear in early modern supplicatory prayers (*tekhines*) written for women to say in their everyday language while performing rituals. In a mid-eighteenth century *tekhines* documented by Chava Weissler, a woman, inspecting herself following the end of her period, describes menstruation as a punishment willingly accepted:

> God and my King, you are merciful. . . . You punished Eve, our old Mother, because she persuaded her husband to trespass against your commandment. . . . So we women must suffer each time, and have our regular periods, with heavy hearts. Thus, I have had my period with a heavy heart, and with sadness, and I thank your holy

Name and your judgment, and I have received it with great love from my great Friend as a punishment.

Although such prayers were recited by women, they were almost certainly written by men, and their content reflects the ways in which women's religious roles and attitudes were shaped by an androcentric Jewish culture.

Women's internalization of rabbinic attitudes can also be found in the adoption of extreme strictures by the medieval *niddah* herself. Shaye J. D. Cohen has demonstrated that during the Middle Ages customary law (*minhag*) concerning the menstruating woman became more exclusionary than the *halakhah* itself, particularly in the Christian sphere. According to the sixth- or seventh-century text *Baraita de-Niddah,* the menstruant was forbidden to enter a synagogue, to come into contact with sacred books, to pray, or to recite God's name. Although rabbinic authorities stated that these exclusions were not demanded by *halakhah,* since being in a state of ritual impurity does not bar any person from holding a Torah scroll or engaging in prayer and study, many religious leaders praised these demonstrations of personal piety. Cohen cites a document from twelfth-century France that describes women who refrained from entering the synagogue or from touching Hebrew books during their periods, even though they were certainly not required to act in this way by rabbinic law. The text opines, however, that since the synagogue is a place of purity the women are acting properly and "may they be blessed" for going beyond what the law requires. Although it is impossible to know the extent to which women adopted these isolating practices willingly and the degree to which they were imposed on women by male piety, by the sixteenth century it was customary practice in many central and eastern European communities that a woman in a state of *niddah* would not attend synagogue. R. Moses Isserles (1520–1572), the principal Ashkenazic halakhic authority of this era, notes this practice but adds that on the "white days" it is the custom to permit women to attend synagogue even in the strictest places, and he writes that "On the High Holidays and Yom Kippur, she can enter the synagogue like other women for otherwise it would cause her great sorrow to remain outside while everyone congregates in the synagogue" (*Shulhan Arukh, Orah Hayim* §88:1).

The texts presented below bear both indirectly and directly on women's observance of *hilkhot niddah*. The first group of examples, from *Sefer Hasidim* (The Book of the Pious), originate in the twelfth- and thirteenth-century milieu of the *Hasidei Ashkenaz,* German-Jewish Pietists known for their extreme devotion to punctilious halakhic observance and for their frank assessment of the multiple moral dangers of the busy urban world in which they lived. *Sefer Hasidim,* which consists of independent paragraphs arranged in groups, is an immensely rich, if idiosyncratic, source for Jewish life in medieval Germany. Primarily concerned with ethical issues, it is traditionally attributed to R. Judah the Pious (1140–1217). Judah's father, R. Samuel b. Kalonymous he-Hasid, may have written parts of the work, and R. Eleazar of Worms (1165–1230), Judah's most prominent disciple, might also have written some passages and could have been the book's editor.

An excerpt from a second document from the same milieu, the *Sefer HaRoqeah HaGadol* of Eleazar of Worms, indicates the extent to which the *niddah* came to be invested with dangerous qualities in certain circles in medieval Europe. These dire warnings about the consequences of failure to observe *hilkhot niddah,* and, conversely, the rewards for doing so, may also reflect a widespread lack of popular compliance with these regulations in all their details.

The third text, also from Germany, is an excerpt from the beginning of the ethical will of the fourteenth-century Eleazar of Mainz (d. 1357), an "ordinary Jew" of whom little more is known. Eleazar's personal testament to his children is remarkable in its detailed account of the potential pitfalls of everyday life, and in its author's concern with his daughters' education, religious practices, and private behavior, as well as those of his sons. The last text selections, taken from the responsa of Rabbi Meir ben Baruch of Rothenburg (c. 1215–1293), the most important scholar and legal authority of thirteenth-century Ashkenazic Jewry, indicate the role *hilkhot niddah* could play in the sexual politics of marital disputes. Responsa literature records the binding rabbinic decisions of recognized authorities that were written in response to halakhic queries. Although responsa literature often addresses extraordinary situations that could not be resolved by regular communal means, its illumination of specific moments of everyday Jewish life makes it a significant source for Jewish social history.

A final source on this topic is a manuscript illustration from the Hamburg Miscellany, a collection of documents including synagogue prayers for the liturgical year, a Passover Haggadah, religious poetry and dirges for specific holidays and historical events, and prayers for various rituals, including circumcision and marriage (Figure 8.1). It was completed around 1427 in Mainz, Germany, and was decorated and illustrated by several different artists. The illustration reproduced here, which was placed on the bottom right of a page containing a poem for the festival of Hanukkah, depicts a woman immersing in a *mikveh* while her husband awaits her in bed. The apparent connection with the text is the legend that during the persecutions commemorated by Hanukkah, the Syrian king forbade women to use *mikva'ot*. However, God miraculously provided women with secluded ritual baths to keep them and their husbands from sin.

These texts demonstrate that male ritual purity was taken extremely seriously in Ashkenazic Judaism and that sources of potential pollution were to be avoided. The *niddah,* with her potential to spread her impurity, was often viewed as a dangerous object whose contacts both with her husband and with the public domain of the synagogue had to be controlled. These documents also reveal concerns about educating women to fulfil *hilkhot niddah*; several of these sources stress that women must be taught the laws and liturgy essential to their domestic lives and religious obligations. Another focus is the need for husbands and wives to foster a positive sexual relationship while at the same time maintaining physical separation during the wife's periods of menstrual impurity. Thus, several texts insist that women should be not only assiduous but also as expeditious as possible in observing *hilkhot niddah* so that their husbands will not be deprived of marital

Figure 8.1. A woman immersing in a mikveh while her husband awaits her in bed. *Hamburg Miscellany,* Staats-und-Universitätsbibliothek, Hamburg, Cod. Heb. 37, fol. 79v. Reproduced with permission.

relations any longer than necessary. It is evident in several examples, as well, that refusing to immerse in the *mikveh* could play a central role in domestic quarrels, often providing wives with a strategem for the assertion of power or husbands with an apparent route out of an unhappy marriage. Underlying all of these issues, moreover, is an appreciation of the urgent nature of male sexual needs and an anxiety regarding women's potential for sexual misconduct in contacts with men outside the family circle. This preoccupation with an imagined female propensity for promiscuous behavior in the absence of strictly enforced social safeguards, together with the conviction that any education for girls beyond the required minimum could lead to sin, is typical of both Jewish and Christian writings of the medieval period.

Excerpts from *Sefer Hasidim* are my translations from the Bologna edition, edited by Reuven Margolit (Jerusalem: Mosad ha-Rav Kook, 1964); translation of Eleazar of Worms is from *Sefer HaRoqeah HaGadol* (Jerusalem: Otsar ha-Poskim, 1966), *Hilkhot Niddah* §318, pp. 205–206. My translation of excerpts from the ethical will of Eleazar of Mainz is based on the Hebrew text in Israel Abrahams, ed., *Hebrew Ethical Wills* (Philadelphia: Jewish Publication Society, 1926) and informed by Abraham's English translation. The translations of the responsa of Rabbi Meir of Rothenburg are from Irving A. Agus, *Rabbi Meir of Rothenburg: His Life and His Works as Sources for the Religious, Legal and Social History of the Jews of Germany in the Thirteenth Century* (New York: KTAV, 1947). The Hamburg Miscellany is in the Staats- und Universitätsbibliothek, Hamburg, Germany, Cod. Heb. 37; this particular illustration is on fol. 79v. Among scholars who have discussed this illustration are Bezalel Narkiss, *Hebrew Illuminated Manuscripts* (Jerusalem: Keter, 1969), pp. 118–19; and Thérèse and Mendel Metzger, *Jewish Life in the Middle Ages* (New York: Alpine Fine Arts Collection, 1982), pp. 75–76. Works on surviving medieval mikva'ot include Georg Heuberger, ed., *Mikwe: Geschichte und Architecktur jüdischer Ritualbäder in Deutschland* (Frankfurt: Jüdisches Museum, 1992).

I refer to the work of several scholars in my essay. The full citations are: Shaye J. D. Cohen, "Purity and Piety: The Separation of Menstruants from the Sancta," in *Daughters of the King: Women and the Synagogue,* edited by Susan Grossman and Rivka Haut (Philadelphia: Jewish Publication Society, 1992), pp. 103–15; Judith Romney Wegner, *Chattel or Person? The Status of Women in the Mishnah* (New York: Oxford University Press, 1988); and Chava Weissler, "Prayers in Yiddish and the Religious World of Ashkenazic Women," in *Jewish Women in Historical Perspective, Second Edition,* edited by Judith R. Baskin (Detroit: Wayne State University Press, 1998), pp. 169–92.

Further Reading

Some of the issues raised by this material are discussed more fully in essays I have published elsewhere: "From Separation to Displacement: Perceptions of Women in *Sefer Hasidim*," *Association for Jewish Studies Review* 19.1 (1994): 1–10; "Jewish Women in the Middle Ages," in *Jewish Women in Historical Perspective,* edited by Baskin, 2nd ed. (Detroit: Wayne State University Press, 1998); and "Some Parallels in the Education of Medieval Jewish and Christian Women," *Jewish History* 5:(Spring 1991): 41–51. *Women and Water: Menstruation in Jewish Life and Law,* edited by Rahel Wasserfall (Hanover, NH: Brandeis University Press, 1999) is an important anthology of essays on niddah and mikveh in Jewish tradition.

1. Excerpts from *Sefer Hasidim*

Paragraph 313. A father is obligated to teach his daughters the commandments, including halakhic rules. This may appear to contradict the talmudic ruling, "Whoever teaches a woman Torah it is as if he teaches her obscenity" [Babylonian Talmud, *Sotah* 20a]. However, the rabbis were referring to deep immersion in Talmudic study, discussion of the reasons behind the commandments, and mystical understandings of the Torah. These should never be taught to a woman or to a minor. But one must teach her practical laws because if she does not know the rules for the Sabbath, how will she observe the Sabbath? The same goes for all the other commandments she must perform. This is how it was in the days of the biblical king, Hezekiah of Judah, when men and women, old and young, were all knowledgeable about the laws, even the laws of ritual purity and Temple sacrifices [Babylonian Talmud, *Sanhedrin* 94b].

It is not appropriate for an unmarried man to teach unmarried girls, however, even if the father stands there and keeps watch so the teacher won't be alone with them. For even this will not avail if the teacher's sexual desire overcomes him or her desire is too much for her. Moreover, according to the Talmud, "A woman's voice is a sexual incitement" [Babylonian Talmud, *Hullin* 11b]. Rather, the father himself should teach his daughter and his wife.

Paragraph 588. If someone comes to you who does not understand Hebrew and he is a righteous person who wishes to intensify his connection to God, or if a woman comes before you in a similar situation, tell them that they should study the prayers in a language they understand. For prayers are a declaration of the heart and if the heart doesn't understand what comes forth from the mouth what use is it? It is better that a person prays in a language that he or she understands.

Paragraph 506. A man who is about to give his daughter in marriage must instruct her never to delay the time of her immersion in the *mikveh*. She must never say to her husband, "I will not immerse unless you give me such and such a sum of money, or a certain object." If the two of them devote their thoughts to heaven when they are intimate, their sons will be good and righteous.

Paragraph 873. A devout woman had a miserly husband who would not give to charity or buy religious books. When the time came for her to immerse in the *mikveh,* she would not immerse. He asked her, "Why haven't you immersed?" She responded, "I will not immerse until you resolve to buy holy books and donate money to charity." However, he would not acquiesce and she continued her refusal to immerse unless he would agree to her demands. He complained about her to a wise rabbi. The rabbi said, "For this may she be blessed for she is trying to compel you to fulfill a commandment and she doesn't know any other way to do it."

But the rabbi said to the wife, "If you can manage to convince him by words to act properly, that's good, but concerning your marital relations don't delay in fulfilling his desire. Otherwise, he will fantasize about illicit sexual activities, you will not become pregnant, and you will only increase his wrath."

Paragraph 874. A husband who was on a journey notified his wife which day he would return home. His wife, knowing this, went to immerse in the *mikveh* prior to his arrival. Her husband said to her, "Since you made an effort to immerse before I came home, I will give you a gold coin to purchase a coat." She replied, "Give me the gold coin with your permission to purchase a book or to pay a scribe to write a book for me. I will lend it to scholars who will study it." She become pregnant and gave birth to a son. All of his brothers were ignorant except for this son, who became a scholar.

Paragraph 1,117. A certain man had a wife who acted immodestly and he strongly suspected her of adultery. The husband was also aware that she was not strict in examining herself during her period of menstrual impurity. He said to the rabbi he consulted, "What should I do? I suspect her of adultery and I know she's not careful about observing her *hilkhot niddah* obligations. Thus it happens that I am intimate with her both when she is in a state of *niddah* and in a state of ritual purity because I am not able to live without a woman. I want to divorce her [without returning her dowry (*ketubbah*), as penalty for her conduct] but her relatives won't allow it. I have complained to the communal leadership but they don't believe my accusations and refuse to investigate the matter."

The rabbi advised him to move to a distant land and send his wife a divorce document from there. He should remarry only after informing the leaders of the community of the whole story so that they will not say it is forbidden for him to remarry since he already has another wife. . . . And if she accepts the divorce document, that is good, but if she does not, he has not committed a sin in remarrying since he knows that she has been wicked, whether through adultery or through flouting *hilkhot niddah.* However, if she accepts the divorce document, he must send her the amount of her dowry specified in the marriage contract.

The return of the dowry appears to be the central issue in this broken marriage, and it is resolved in the wife's favor, since there appears to be some question here as to the trustworthiness of the husband's accusations. Ordinarily a wife whose adultery or whose failure to observe "family purity" laws was proven would be divorced without receiving her dowry payment.

2. Excerpt from *Sefer HaRoqeah HaGadol* of R. Eleazar of Worms *Hilkhot Niddah* §318.

Directly prior to these remarks R. Eleazar has emphasized that among the dire consequences for both husband and wife of not obeying *hilkhot niddah* are having defective children and losing the world to come.

Therefore, a woman in a state of *niddah* may not wear eye makeup or jewelry. A woman who observes her state of *niddah* properly will not cook for her husband, she will not bake, she will not dance, she will not prepare the bed, and she will not pour water from one vessel to another, because she is in a state of impurity and she can transmit impurity. And she is forbidden to enter a synagogue until she has immersed in water. The saliva of a *niddah* transmits impurity. A *niddah* who has sexual relations with her husband causes her sons to be stricken with leprosy, even for twenty generations. . . . R. Halafta said, she is happy and happy are her children and happy is her husband and happy is the family of every woman who observes her *niddah* appropriately, since she preserves herself and her husband from the judgement of Gehenna [the place of eternal punishment] and brings them to the life of the world to come.

There is a story about a scholar who died and not even ten men followed his coffin. His friend began to weep and and said: So much was his Torah and this is his reward! The Holy One Blessed Be He opened the friend's eyes in a dream and said to him, "Your colleague never sinned in his life except that one time his wife passed him while in a state of *niddah* and he touched her garment. This is why a punishment was exacted from him." In the dream that night the friend saw the scholar walking about in the grove in the midst of the fountain of water in the Garden of Eden.

3. Excerpts from the *Ethical Will of Eleazar of Mainz*

These are the practices that my sons and daughters should follow at my request. They should attend synagogue in the morning and in the evening, where they should be particularly attentive to the recitation of the standing prayer [the central part of the worship service] and the *Sh'ma* [the statement of divine unity]. Immediately following worship, they should spend a little time studying Torah or Psalms, or in charitable activities. Their business transactions are to be conducted in good faith and in honesty with everyone, Jews and Gentiles alike. They should be pleasant to everybody, and acquiescent to every worthy request. And they should not say more than necessary in any circumstance. Such discretion will preserve them from slander, defamation, and derision. They shall donate exactly a tenth of their wealth, and they must never turn away a poor man empty-handed. They must give him something, whether a great deal or a small sum. And if someone they don't know seeks lodging they should give him enough money to pay an innkeeper. In this way, they will meet the many needs of the poor.

The women of my family must be exceedingly careful to examine themselves throughout their monthly cycles and to stay apart from their husbands during their unclean days. They should have sexual relations with their husbands in modesty and sanctity, not with passion and not with frivolity but in reverence and silence. They must be as scrupulous as possible to undertake their ritual immersions with care, accompanied by trustworthy women lest anyone encounter them. They should cover their eyes while returning home so that they won't see anything unclean. They must honor their husbands as much as possible, and they should be agreeable to them night and day. The men of my family, too, must honor their wives more than themselves; they must not have sexual relations with them in a state of anger but are to wait until they consent willingly and disputes are resolved.

My sons and my daughters should make every effort to live in Jewish communities, both for their own spiritual advantage and so that their sons and daughters will learn Jewish traditions. Even if, Heaven forbid, they are forced to beg school fees from others, they must not allow their offspring to remain uneducated. Arrange marriages for your sons and daughters, as soon as they have reached puberty, with distinguished families. And my offspring must not pursue wealth by contracting a marriage with a family of questionable origins. However, if my children find that the father's connections are praiseworthy, they shouldn't be concerned if they are undistinguished on the side of the mother since the Jewish community ranks lineage according to the father's family background.

Beginning early Friday mornings, my children are to be especially active in preparing to honor Sabbath observance; they should be ready to light candles before the day wanes and to stoke the fire in the furnace of the winter quarters before the Sabbath begins at sunset. For they must not desecrate the Sabbath. The women of my family should craft beautiful candles to honor the Sabbath.

I appeal to my children not to gamble, beyond wagering for the price of a meal or a drink during the intermediate days of Jewish festivals. And the women may play games for trinkets or eggs when they celebrate the New Moon.

My sons should be as circumspect as possible in their contacts with women, avoiding bathing, dancing, physical contact, and flirtatious conversation with them. My daughters, too, must not speak, banter, or dance with men outside the family. They are not to engage in casual chatter with any men except their husbands. My daughters should always be inside their homes and not roaming about; nor may they stand at the doorway watching everything that goes by. I absolutely insist that the women of my household should never sit unoccupied with no work to do, for idleness leads to boredom and then to unchastity. They should keep busy with spinning, cooking, and sewing.

4. Responsa of Rabbi Meir of Rothenburg

Yoreh De'ah 162. A woman is permitted to cohabit with her husband immediately after her immersion in the ritual bath, even if such immersion took place in the daytime [of the eighth day]. However, R. Tam holds that a woman is not permitted to immerse herself in a ritual bath during the daylight time of Sabbath even if it be her eighth day.

Yoreh De'ah 170. Question: A certain man swore by the Ten Commandments that he would never live with his wife again and that he would divorce her if she would not take a ritual bath on that particular night. Can such an oath be dissolved by a scholar?
Answer: During the period of the Geonim [rabbinic leaders from the sixth to tenth centuries] the strict law was adopted that no oath could be dissolved by a scholar if such oath was taken by the pronouncing of the name of God, by the Torah, or by the Ten Commandments.

Even ha-Ezer 311. This is in answer to your query regarding a certain man who demands that his father-in-law permit his wife to join him. Even if she is sick, she must immerse herself in a ritual bath. If she refuses to do so, she is considered a rebellious wife.

A husband is entitled to sexual relations with his wife; similarly she is entitled to sexual relations with her husband. A *moredet,* or "rebellious wife," who refuses to live with her husband, is subject to a daily monetary fine; her husband may ultimately divorce her and she forfeits any claim to her dowry. If the rabbinic authorities determined, however, that she had fled because her husband was repulsive to her, or to escape blatant physical or emotional abuse, or economic lack of support, her husband could be compelled to give her a divorce and return her dowry.

9

Life-Cycle Rituals of Spanish Crypto-Jewish Women

Renée Levine Melammed

As the result of the forced mass conversions of tens of thousands of Jews in 1391, all of Spanish society had to deal with a new phenomenon, namely, the *converso*—the convert to Catholicism or descendant of converted Jews. Those Jews who converted to Catholicism had to decide if they would accept their fate and attempt to integrate into the Catholic world, or if they would remain faithful to Judaism, albeit surreptitiously, while maintaining a façade of loyalty to their new faith. Those who chose the latter path were called crypto-Jews or judaizers, whose covert practice of Judaism became extremely dangerous once the Spanish Inquisition was established. This institution, based on the papal precedent whose aim was to extirpate heresy, considered the crypto-Jews to be heretics because they were essentially baptized Catholics whose judaizing beliefs and actions were acts of apostasy in the eyes of the Church.

The rituals and observances presented below reflect the life of Spanish crypto-Jewish women in fifteenth- and sixteenth-century Castile. These women had either converted themselves or were the descendants of Jews who had converted by force or even by choice. Life for these *conversas* (female *conversos*) was difficult enough in the early portion of the fifteenth century, for they did not fit comfortably into either Jewish or Christian society, but by the mid-fifteenth century, they were rejected outright by the latter. This rejection was reflected in the discriminatory laws (purity of blood) which, although anathema to the teachings of the Catholic Church, were eventually instituted anyway. In the long run, once the Inquisition was established in 1478 and began to function in the 1480s, life for these *conversas*, whether they had opted to judaize or not, would never be the same.

The information presented here is culled from Inquisition documents. The Spanish Inquisition kept precise records of the trial proceedings, and a large number of these trial records are still extant. As will be seen, information regarding the lives of these secret or crypto-Jews can be found in the accusations, the witness testimonies, and the confessions of the defendants themselves.

Childbirth and Purity Rites

In medieval Spain, the birth of the child (male or female) was celebrated on the eve of *hadas* (lit., fates) which took place on the eighth night of birth. The origin of this custom is unclear; the Latin root of the term implies prognostication and prediction, determination of fate. Whether the *hadas* originated in classical Rome or in pre-Expulsion Spain, the celebration became associated with judaizing. Participation in this rite is recorded in the Inquisition files of various *conversas,* who almost invariably celebrated in the company of others, usually relatives. There was always a collation and sometimes singing and dancing.

At the same time, some *conversos* developed their own custom of washing off the water from the baptismal font, to *descristianizar* or debaptize their children and restore them to a state of purity as they perceived it, and preserve their Jewishness. Needless to say, this was not a Jewish custom but rather an original development within the crypto-Jewish society.

Ritual immersion is required for Jewish women prior to the wedding ceremony, after menstruation, and following childbirth. Each of these types of ritual immersion can be found to have been performed by crypto-Jewish women, although the ritual bathhouse gradually disappeared by the end of the fifteenth century. Nevertheless, bathing would occur at the appropriate times, and women would refrain from intercourse with their husbands until after bathing.

A custom often associated with bathing and cleaning is the paring of nails. Fingernails were to be treated with care, trimmed, and burned or buried. Some of the conversas, as we will see below, even specify how they dealt with the trimmings.

Death and Mourning Rituals

Death and mourning rituals observed by crypto-Jewish women were a combination of traditional halakhic (legal) requirements and special Jewish customs indigenous to the Iberian Peninsula. There are, for instance, variations on the tradition of pouring out water in the home where a death has occurred. This might be viewed as a method of announcing a death, or considered a symbol of the extinction of life or the pouring out of the soul. At the same time, superstitious explanations for this custom appear as well, such as preventing the angel of death from cleaning his knife in the water.

Once the death has been determined, the body has to be ritually bathed and purified. Burial societies often take on this responsibility, particularly in order to ensure that only Jews will have contact with and prepare the corpse. In Spain, washing of the dead was considered to be women's work, and the *conversas* did not neglect their duty. Some of them managed to prepare a traditional shroud, and women would donate cloth as well as sew the shrouds themselves. There are examples in which they put a pillow of earth under the head of the deceased in the hope that God would forgive the dead for his sins.

The postfuneral meal in Spain is the *cohuerzo,* and the Spanish tradition was to refrain from eating meat at this meal; preferred foods were eggs, fish, lentils, olives, and other vegetables and fruit. These meals were usually eaten at low tables, frequently while seated on the ground. This meal usually marks the beginning of the seven-day mourning period, and the Inquisition files contain descriptions of the fulfillment of these laws, as well. Often the term "behind the door" was used to signify the seven days of mourning following burial, that is, sitting *shiva* (seven in Hebrew). Some *conversos* covered up their wells during this week or placed a glass of water in the room where the death had occurred. There was also a custom of keeping water and a towel in the room to provide for the souls of the dead.

Mourners would don the *barbillera,* literally, a bandage placed under the chin of a dead person in order to keep the mouth closed or, in this case, a covering such as a scarf or bandage placed under the chin of the mourner. This custom has precedents from the Bible and the Talmud, and seems to complement the fact that the mourner, whose door is open, cannot rise and greet those who come to visit.

As is customary, friends, neighbors, and relatives would come to the house of the mourners to comfort them during the *shiva* period. Different ways of expressing grief and affliction can be discerned; and professional Jewish female mourners seem to have continued the medieval tradition. These women would sing dirges and lamentations and clap their hands in grief at the time of the funeral, or, in these cases, when such behavior would be out of the question, during visits to the mourner's homes.

The original files or portions thereof analyzed here are housed in the Archivo Histórico Nacional in Madrid. The trials from the community of Ciudad Real have been transcribed by Haim Beinart of the Hebrew University; information taken and translated (by me) from this four-volume work is duly noted. Transcription entails paleographical knowledge of the notarial scripts of the period, which enables the scholar to convert the originals into texts in modern Romance letters; the transcribed trials from Ciudad Real are only available in Spanish. The remainder of the trial information has been transcribed and translated from the original handwritten records. Each proceeding is registered by file (*legajo*) and a subordinate number (*número*).

Further Reading

For general reading on the Jews of Spain, see Yitzhak Baer, *A History of the Jews in Christian Spain,* 2 vols. (Philadelphia: Jewish Publication Society, 1992). For details of converso life in Ciudad Real, see Haim Beinart, *Conversos on Trial by the Inquisition* (Jerusalem: Magnes, 1981). A detailed analysis of the mourning rites discussed here appears in Renée Levine Melammed, "Some Death and Mourning Customs of Castilian Conversas," in *Exile and Diaspora,* edited by A. Mirsky, A. Grossman, and Y. Kaplan (Jerusalem: Ben Zvi Institute, 1991), pp. 157–67. Analyses of observances of birth and purity rites as well as the Sabbath, holidays, fasts, and so on appear in Renée C. Levine, "Women in Spanish Crypto-Judaism 1492–1520," Ph.D. dissertation, Brandeis University, 1982.

CHILDBIRTH AND PURITY RITES

The wife of Pedro González of Agudo confessed in Legajo 178, número 15 (1501):

When I gave birth, after seven nights, relatives of mine came and ate fruit and sang and danced and they say that these were *hadas*.

A witness named Clara stated in Leg. 144, no. 3 (1491–92) that:

It could have been five years [ago], more or less, when the wife of Alonso López, cloth-shearer, resident of the said locale, gave birth and within six or seven days after she gave birth, the said Alonso López invited this witness and her husband and some other Jews and gave them a collation and fruit in the fashion practiced by the Jews for their sons and daughters that is called *hadas,* [all of] which was seen twice when the said wife of Alonso López gave birth.

A Jewish witness also told the court about this family's celebration:

Twice when his wife gave birth, the said Alonso López invited this witness and his wife, both times the night before baptism and said, "Tomorrow I have to baptize and you must celebrate with me tonight," and he went there and rejoiced and they were given fruit and it was as when the Jews make *hadas* for their children.

In Leg. 137, no. 4 (1484–85), as transcribed by Haim Beinart in *Records of the Trials of the Spanish Inquisition in Ciudad Real* 1 (Jerusalem: Israel Academy of Science and Humanities, 1974), p. 456, Miguel Díaz, a tailor, said:

At the time of a birth, when the child lived, I saw that they made *hadas,* and all the young women came as did other relatives and they played their tambourines there and ate many fruits and there they had the *hadas*.

A second report in this trial (p. 458) contains a refrain from a *hadas* song. Marina González narrated:

As this witness was a young woman at the time, [when] at the birth of a son of Rodrigo de Olivos, this witness was invited to go to the hadas, and she went to their house and they sang that night: "*Hadas, hadas,* good fortune should come." And there were many *conversos* there, among whom she knew Rodrigo the mayor, because the woman who had delivered was his sister, and his first wife was present too, for at the time they were married.

This unusual observance was reported in the home of Catalina Gómez and Juan de Fez, following the baptism of their twin son and daughter. A servant named Elvira described the following in Leg. 148, no. 6 (1493–1494), *Records* 1, pp. 198–99:

Since the wife of the said Juan de Fez had given birth, this witness entered the home of her said mother-in-law by the small gate, in order to see the new mother, the wife of the said Juan de Fez, who had given birth to a son and a daughter. And when this witness entered, it was shortly after having brought them back from baptism. This witness said to the new mother: "What's with the Madame, your mother?" And she said to this witness: "She's by the fire." This witness went into the kitchen and saw the said mother and saw a cauldron of water that had been removed from the fire. She ordered her daughter Beatriz, sister of the nursing mother, to bring the baby and she took him and unwrapped him and ordered her to remove the swaddling clothes and [said] that she should bring a change of clothes and they washed the entire male child with warm water and then did likewise with the girl child.

In Leg. 153, no. 13 (1500–1501), the confession by Beatriz González, wife of Fernando González de la Barrera includes the statement:

When I menstruated, I would clean myself by bathing my entire body as per Jewish ceremony.

In 1486, María González, wife of Diego de Córdova, admitted in Leg. 155, no. 6 (1500–1501):

When I gave birth and when I menstruated, I separated my bed from my husband until I had bathed according to ceremony.

Isabel Rodríguez, wife of Pedro González, made the simple admission in Leg. 178, no. 15 (1501):

Sometimes I bathed and afterwards there was *tibila* [immersion] as per Jewish ceremony.

Leg. 163, no. 7 (1512–1522) contains María's confession of 1486, which includes:

When I would have my period, I removed my bed from my husband and then I bathed ceremonially.

An accusation in Leg. 144, no. 3 (1491–1492) as presented to the wife of Alonso López was:

And when her menstrual cycle would begin, and after childbirth, she would perform immersion as the Jewesses do in order to sleep with her husband. . . . Each time that her menstruation would begin or she would give birth, she would wash herself in a large metal vessel of water in order to sleep with her husband.

The wife of Fernando, *herrero* (smith), confessed in 1486 as recorded in Leg. 150, no. 11 (1500–1501):

When I was after childbirth or when my period came, I would separate myself from my husband's bed and would not return to the bed until I had bathed and was clean.

The confession in Leg. 132, no. 8 (1500–1501) includes the following:

The night prior to Yom Kippur I bathed and cut my nails ceremonially and threw them in the fire. . . . When I was menstruating or after childbirth, I separated my bed from my husband's and I did not approach him until I was clean and had bathed and cut my nails.

Catalina de Zamora testified about prenuptial ceremonies in the trial of María Díaz, *la cerera* of Ciudad Real, Leg. 143, no. 11 (1483–1484), *Records* 1, p. 53:

They had to bathe her in cold water, and in this way, the wax maker, María Díaz, and her daughter Constanza, took her and covered her with a sheet and bathed her in a stream or river that passed by the entrance in the town of Palma, where they were located at that time.

Inés de Mérida of Ciudad Real stated in Leg. 167, no. 4 (1513, 1522) as transcribed in *Records* 3, (1981), p. 361:

This confessant saw her mother cut her nails a few times and collect them and make a hole in the ground and place them there and cover them with earth and at other times she threw them into the fire.

DEATH AND MOURNING RITUALS

A servant of Guiomar Fernández of Guadalajara testified in Leg. 156, no. 2 (1520–1523):

In the said time two of the sons of Luis Alvarez passed away and they, [including] the mother of the said Luis Alvarez, ordered this witness to pour out all the water in the said house and she poured it out; and when a nephew died in the home of the said Luis Alvarez, his mother and wife [Guiomar] of the said Luis Alvarez ordered this servant to pour out all the water in the house.

The accusation presented to Elvira, the wife of Juan de Sigüenza of Guadalajara, Leg. 153, no. 16 (1493–1494) stated:

When someone died in her neighborhood, she ordered the water she had in her home to be poured out and said that [she did so] because the enemy killed that [dead] person and came to clean his sword in that water.

Leg. 181, no. 3 (1492–1493) of Mencia Rodríguez de Medina, widow of Pedro de Madrid, contains this accusation:

And when her father died, she had all the water in the pitchers in the house poured out [twice], for they said that the soul of the dead would come to bathe in that water.

María Alfonso of Herrera in Leg. 132, no. 8 (1500–1501) confessed that:

When some relative or person of her lineage died [when her father died], she bathed him and consented to have him bathed.

Constanza Díaz, the wife of Alfonso de Villarreal, resident of Ciudad Real, confessed in Leg. 141, no. 14 (1511–1512) that:

Sometimes she had gone to where there were some who had passed on from this life [that is, homes of the deceased] and had seen water placed [there] and she believed it was in order to cleanse them.

Inés López, the wife of Alonso de Aguilera, included in the addition to her confession in Leg. 162, no. 3 (1495–1496) as published in *Records* 2 (1977), p. 67:

Likewise, sirs, I say that when my father died, I saw placed [by two women] inside the room where he was ... a cauldron of water, but did not know [for] what, except that I heard it said that it was to wash my said father who was dirty, and I placed a bowl of water in the said room with a cloth and I do not remember who it was who directed me to do so except that I understand that it was Mayor Alvarez, my sister, who was present.

The arraignment of Isabel García of Hita as appears in Leg. 158, no. 9 (1520–1523) states:

Also the said Isabel and other persons bathed a certain corpse in the [Jewish] manner and according to Jewish ceremony.

Elvira López of Toledo, the widow of Juan de Torres, confessed in Leg. 160, no. 15 (1510–1511):

I gave orders and aided in bathing my father when he died and bathed Gonzalo of Olmo and similarly my mother as well when they died, and I made preparations in the Jewish way that was required to prepare them in order that they could be buried.

In this same trial, a witness named Beatriz Lorenzo:

Saw in the house of Isabel, wife of Rodrigo García who is a widow, a certain deceased person whom she wanted to shroud and who was covered up as if recently washed, and this witness marveled to see the corpse but recently washed, and I believed that it was washed in the Jewish way and that when this witness entered the said house there was no one present except for the said Isabel and a certain other person, [both] Jewish renegades.

In Leg. 178, no. 15 (1501), the wife of Pedro González from Agudo, Isabel Rodríguez said:

I ate fish and eggs at funerals in accordance with Jewish ceremony.

Constanza Díaz confessed in Leg. 141, no. 14 (1511–1512):

Sometimes I was seen at mourners' homes and I sent food there and I ate fish dishes while seated on the floor.

Beatriz González of Toledo confessed in Leg. 153, no. 10 (1487–1494):

I ate fish, eggs and olives and other similar things at some funeral meals at low tables.

The accusation in Leg. 134, no. 5 (1492–1493) refers to María Alvarez:

And she ate fish and eggs at funeral meals and at low tables, [sitting] on the floor as observed by the Jews at the death of their relatives.

Teresa Acre, the widow of Diego Alonso of Toledo, confessed in Leg. 131, no. 5 (1493–1494):

Sometimes I ate dishes of fish and other things at funeral meals of some relatives. . . . I also remember that my husband and I ate at a funeral meal of his brother-in-law and we ate at low tables.

In Leg. 153, no. 13 (1500–1501), Beatriz González explained:

When some relative of mine would die, we ate at a low table and did not eat meat but rather fish as in accordance with Jewish ceremony.

Mayor González of Herrera, made a similar statement in Leg. 155, no. 6 (1500–1501):

When some of my relatives died, we ate on the floor at low tables and we ate fish and eggs and we did not eat meat.

María Alfonso related in Leg. 132, no. 8 (1500–1501) that:

When my father passed away and [then] my mother and we, my brothers and I and other relatives, ate [the *cohuerzo*] and when my father-in-law passed away, we, my in-laws and husband and other relatives, ate [this meal].

Leonor Alvarez, the wife of Juan de Haro, in Leg. 133, no. 20 (1495–1496) in *Records* 2, pp. 53–54, confessed:

In addition, Sirs, I saw my sister[s], Mayor Alvarez and Violante that when my father died; and we, they and I, ate [sitting] on the floor; and I do not recall if my mother ate [there] with us, for she was in a poor state at the time.

Elvira López of Guadalajara confessed in Leg. 160, no. 14 (1493–1494):

We ate, I and my husband, [seated] on the floor at the funeral meal of a brother-in-law of mine whose name was Ruy López de Buen Día, and we ate fish and eggs and olives, and Luis de Salmento, his son-in-law, and María his wife ate with us.

Leg. 181, no. 12 (1498–1499) contains this confession given in 1499 by Elvira Ruíz of Escalona:

I ate twice at low tables while seated on the ground, after the death of an uncle, the brother of my mother, and with a neighbor from the village named Alonso Martínez's wife, who had come in to console.

The accusation presented in Leg. 154, no. 33 (1500) to María González of Casarrubios del Monte claimed that the defendant:

Kept silent and hid how she had been indoors for seven days upon the death of her kinsmen and had pillows with earth in them placed [by the head] for the said deceased in order to fulfill the Jewish rites and ceremonies and how

Jews came to the house of the said deceased to pray and prayed for them and she also prayed [in] the said ceremonies.

In Catalina López's trial, Leg. 160, no. 5 (1503–1504), the prosecutor claimed that:

When someone died, she covered up the well saying that the souls of the dead should not come there to bathe in observance and fulfillment of the ceremony and custom that the Jews observed in their burials.

In the addendum to her confession in Leg. 141, no. 14 (1511–1512), Constanza Díaz related:

From the time that my father passed away, I saw a glass of water placed in the room where he died and a lit candle, all of which was ordered to be put there by a wife of Juan de Toledo.

A charge presented to Inés López of Ciudad Real in Leg. 162, no. 3 (1495–1496), *Records* 2, p. 65, was:

Likewise she remained silent as to how she bathed some of the dead and helped to bathe them and put a cup of water in the spot where they had died and some towels and a saddler's needle with lit candles, believing as a Jewess that the souls of those very deceased would come there to bathe their souls.

In Leg. 134, no. 8 (1516–1518), Juana, the wife of Juan de Pedrosa, related:

It would have been more or less three years ago when this witness came to the house of Alonso de Baena who had died when this witness entered his house [after] about five days and found the wife of the said Alonso de Baena behind the door of their house, and she is called Mencía, and found her in this way. She began to say to this witness, "Juana, what will I do without Baena? Grief has come upon me! Grief has befallen me!" while raising and lowering her head and she said and did the aforementioned many times until this witness consoled her.

One charge presented to Isabel of Hita, Leg. 158, no. 9 (1520–1523) was:

Also that the said Isabel went to console and consoled certain persons who were [behind the door] mourning the death of a certain deceased individual and there, together with them, she was behind the door and lamented in the Jewish way.

A witness, a maidservant, in this trial declared:

She saw the wife of Rodrigo García, whom she believes is named Isabel, a New Christian of Jew[ish origin], resident of Hita, and certain other persons who went to the home of a certain deceased person, climbed on top of the bed of the said deceased and sang and cried and wailed, praying, raising and lowering their heads, clapping their hands, and a certain person called out the songs and then the said Isabel and the others continued the singing and cried and prayed and walked around the deceased.

According to another witness in the same trial:

It might have been twelve or thirteen years more or less since Rodrigo García, a resident of Hita, died, and that for the duration of a year after he died, I always saw his wife reclining in bed with a bandage on her, sometimes singing and sometimes crying.

Yet another witness said:

And I know that she was "behind the door" due to the death of the said deceased person, [with] one door closed and the other open, and she was seated behind the closed door with a headdress roomy enough at the head; and the end of the headdress was placed as a "bandage" beneath the chin [in a place] where certain other persons came and all of them were there together in grief crying and lamenting and consoling themselves . . . and also they went to the home of the said deceased and were "behind the door" and that on the day of the interment of the said person, when they came from burying, they, all the said persons, closed the doors of the house and threw down their cloaks and began to cry and lament and sing and clap their hands, crying for a while and singing for a while, saying, "I, the unhappily married woman, went to the countryside, and gathered the grass."

This same file contains more witness accounts, including that of a twenty-three-year-old servant named Francisca:

This witness saw that a certain person died in Hita and after the interment during the seven days after the death, she saw a certain person in the house where the said person died, who was seated every day behind a door of a room on the floor, undergoing grief, with a covering beneath the chin, one door of the said room being open and the other being closed, and that she was seated without engaging in any labor, and that in the said time that the aforementioned was behind the door in the aforementioned manner, the wife of Rodrigo García, who is currently a widow, and certain other persons went to visit the said person every day, and they remained there consoling her and observing with her one and two and three hours after eating and that all of those who gathered there were New Christians.

The observances of María Alvarez of Buitrago are described in Leg. 134, no. 8 (1516–1518) by a clergyman:

> Her son had died while out in the fields and [when] the shepherds brought the news of his death; two or three days later this witness was passing by the door of the said wife of Sosa and saw that the door facing the street was closed and the other was open and behind the said door that was closed this witness saw the said Sosa who at the time was alive located behind the said door that was closed, seated on a stone seat, wearing an old sheepskin jacket and a muffler or "bandage" of dirty linen and that the said wife was seated on another stone seat just a bit further inside and that he does not recall if she had a chin-covering.

The same conversa faced widowhood, as related by a witness:

> It might have been three or four years ago, more or less, when Diego de Sosa, newly converted Jew, died . . . and when the *novenas* (prayers) of the said deceased were made, this witness saw María Alvarez, wife of the said Diego de Sosa, behind [closed] door [for] some days and that one door was closed and the other open, behind the door that was closed he saw her seated without doing any labor . . . and in the mornings the said María Alvarez went to the said church and that likewise after attending novenas some days he saw her in the said state and that this seemed wrong to this witness and that he had heard his father say that the Jews used to be "behind the door" like this when a Jew would die.

10

Ritualizing Death and Dying: The Ethical Will of Naphtali Ha-Kohen Katz

Avriel Bar-Levav

The publication of *Ma'avar Yabbok* of Rabbi Aaron Berechia of Modena, in Mantua in 1626, marks the beginning of a new literary genre: books for the sick and the dying, a subgenre of Jewish "conduct" literature (*hanhagot*). The new genre, which flourished during the following two centuries, is the carrier of new death rituals—part of the ritual creativity typical of that period. Although this creativity has generally been regarded as an outcome of the spread of Lurianic Kabbalah, modern scholars such as Zeev Gries and Moshe Idel have shown that Lurianic Kabbalah was not as widespread as previously thought, and that conduct literature, the main vehicle for its diffusion, became well established only in the eighteenth century. These new rituals should be viewed as part of a socioreligious process undergone by Jewish society in that period. This process, which might be called "Ritualization of Life," saw the creation, collection, and formulation of new rituals that reshaped the religious existence of Jewry. Whole domains of Jewish life became more ritualized: new prayers were added to the prayerbook, and new practices were added to the Jewish ritual cycle, such as the midnight vigil (*tikkun hazzot*), welcoming the Sabbath (*kabbalat shabbat*), and the celebration of the new moon (*tikkun erev rosh hodesh*), to mention just a few. Among those newly reinforced ritualized domains, the place of the new death rituals was central.

Rituals were created and collected mostly by a literary elite, but their significance was important for a wider public that was not necessarily highly educated. Many of the new rituals provided a meaningful religious role for that very public, sometimes through the organization of "societies" (*hevrot*) that participated in and shaped specific aspects of religious life. The most important of these was the burial society, and soon the term *hevra kadisha* (lit., "holy society") became a synonym for this group. Often the rabbi of the community served as the formal head of this society, as was the case with Rabbi Naphtali Ha-Kohen Katz. The new death rituals provided a significant role for society members, who would gather around the deathbed to recite psalms and prayers, before and after death, as well as during purification of the body and burial. This ritualizing process can also be viewed in the context of the developing print culture, which produced a widening circle of readers who wanted to enhance the religious meaning of their life. Although Judaism in general is a religion of observance, the new rituals and customs soon became the most important means of participation for a new audience of readers, because the practical aspects of rituals and customs were quite appropriate for nonscholars who wished to amplify their religious life.

The content of some of the new rituals having to do with death and dying will be briefly explained below. It is important first to say a few words about its author, however. Rabbi Naphtali Ha-Kohen Katz was born around the middle of the seventeenth century in Stepan in Polish Volhynia, and died in 1719, in Orta Kiya, then a village near Constantinople (and now a suburb of the city), while on his way to the land of Israel. A central halakhic figure in his time, rabbi of important communities in Poland and Germany, participant in the Councils of the Four Lands (Polish Jewry's central organization), he was also a famous kabbalist, in both the theoretical and practical fields. Moreover, Rabbi Naphtali had a genuine interest in both the theoretical and ritual aspects of death. He discussed issues regarding the origin and nature of death in his book, *Birkat ha-Shem* (Blessing of the Lord), published in Frankfort on the Oder in 1704, during his time as a chief rabbi of Frankfort on the Main. He also formulated detailed death rituals in two smaller compositions: *Sha'ar ha-Hakhana* (Gate of Preparation), and in part of his ethical will. These were published posthumously in Turkey (1734) and in Germany. His ethical will became quite popular, and was printed more than twenty times in the following two centuries. Although the death rituals that Rabbi Naphtali proposed in his ethical will were personal, in the sense that they were meant for himself, they had a wide appeal, in part because of his fame. Thus, though it is an example of an elite text, its popularity indicates that the kind of ritualism it proposed appealed to a wide public.

The text is written in the framework of the genre of ethical wills. This subgenre of Jewish ethical literature, which originated in the medieval period and became popular in the early modern period, contains statements made by the author to relatives, either as preparation for death or before a dangerous journey, by means of which the author expresses his views about the important things in life. Some of the ethical wills, like the one partly translated here, contain material regarding death. Rabbi Naphtali wrote his will mainly for his family, but he was aware of the general interest that the document might engender and of its moral value. He therefore gave permission for the will to be copied by people outside the family, and demanded from his family that they have the will bound, both as a practical matter and a sign of respect, and read it regularly.

The text starts with a rhetorical justification of the preparation for death. The idea that it is necessary to be aware of the possibility of death was, of course, not new—it is found in the literature of the Sages, and then repeatedly in ethical literature. Obviously, though, as the death rituals became more complex, the preparation acquired a different kind of meaning and significance. Another important idea that actually supplied the foundation to most of the rituals was the belief that living people are able to assist and improve the situation of the soul of the deceased by performing certain rituals for his or her sake. The process of *tikkun,* literally correction or repair of one's soul, which in some kabbalistic circles of the early modern period was considered to be the central function of human beings during their life, is therefore prolonged, since it can be done by the living for the sake of the dead. One of the implications of this is a sense of continuity and support between the domains of the dead and the living. In Jewish culture this idea can be found in different degrees, and although this document is a rather extreme example, nevertheless it is important to emphasize that there are also other cases in which it is much attenuated.

Following the literary convention of the genre, the text is addressed to the author's family, and especially to his children. But it makes a sharp distinction between his "real" children, from his actual wife, and his "improper" children, the children of a she-devil. The idea that men are responsible for the existence of semihuman devils, "human afflictions," may be found in the Midrash (e.g., *Bereshit Rabbah* 20:11, 31,10) and in the *Zohar* (e.g., 1:54b), but only became widely popular in the early modern period. The danger of these devils is twofold: frustrated by their bodilessness, they try to capture the body of their human father and to penetrate it when his soul leaves, causing him great pain. Moreover, the whole family, human and semihuman, gathers together during the period of mourning, and the devils might, out of jealously, severely harm their human semisiblings in their fragile state. In order to avoid this danger, the text warns the devils to go away and not bother the human family; but for the sake of their safety, the human children are told not to approach the room where the body is kept, and not to escort it.

At crucial moments during the process of dying and the rituals that followed, Rabbi Naphtali requested that charity be given according to specific numerical denominations. Since the value of the coins was of less importance to him than their number, his demand did not necessarily determine the sum that was to be given. Like those of certain other languages, each Hebrew letter has a numerical value, as do their combination in words—the result of the arithmetic combination of the sum of the letters, a process known as *gematria.* The numbers mentioned by Rabbi Naphtali are connected to certain numerical values of the divine name, and giving charity in those very amounts is supposed to have positive results for the fate of the soul of the deceased. The biblical verse "righteousness delivers from death" (Prov. 10:2, 11:4) is used to establish the connection between charity and death, and the author goes on to transform and develop this idea. Charity is to help the deceased in his heavenly journey, and it is the proper numbers that make the difference. The importance of the numerical value is probably derived from magical traditions related to practical Kabbalah, and from aspects of Polish Kabbalah, which took a great interest in such matters. It should be mentioned that Rabbi Naphtali is apparently one of the first sources of a specific version of a numerically based healing ritual, namely, the *pidyon* or the ransoming of the soul, in which charity is given according to a specific complicated sequence in order to help the sick. These rituals therefore have not only magical implications but also a positive social effect insofar as the charity is given to the poor.

Rabbi Naphtali speaks out against the saboteur, that is, the devil, who is accused of tempting the dying to deny their faith and reject the heavenly yoke. The idea of deathbed temptation is well known in Christian *ars moriendi*, and is also prevalent in some early modern Jewish sources. The solution to the danger of temptation is often a legal one. The basis for his statement is legal, and is used here for spiritual protection against blasphemy. This dangerous temptation is part of a struggle between the powers of good and evil that takes place during the deathbed scene. Many of the deathbed rituals are intended to empower the positive forces in this situation, for example by requesting the presence of a *minyan*, a quorum of ten (in which, according to talmudic sources, dwells the divine presence, the *Shekhinah*); these ten should be ritually purified, and recite psalms and prayers, and so on. The expulsion of the semihuman devils, mentioned before, should also be viewed in this context.

The first ritual that he requests take place after death is the ritual of "The Four Kinds of Death Penalty." According to the Sages (*Mishnah Sanhedrin* 7:1), these are stoning, burning, beheading, and strangling. According to a talmudic explanation, these punishments, although no longer carried out because of the loss of political power by Jewry, have been transformed into heavenly punishments. Rabbi Naphtali's will provides evidence of another stage, in which a form of the death penalties is executed on the soul after it leaves the body, as part of the punishments that come after the Final Judgment. The ritual requested by Rabbi Naphtali is designated to be a substitute for the "real" forms of capital punishment, that is, for the punishments that might be inflicted on his soul. It is therefore a ritual of protection. Rabbi Naphtali is the first known author to use it, and after his time it was developed in other versions, although it remained obscure and did not gain much popularity. On the other hand, some of the other rituals that are mentioned here became quite popular, such as reading the Mishnah during memorial celebrations—a ritual that apparently makes one of its first appearances here.

The personal expressions from the will that are translated here supply the human context of the rituals. Rabbi Naphtali's concern for ritual certainly did not contradict his deep emotions toward his family, and especially his wife. Although he regretted the mutual promise they made to attempt to die soon after each other, he still tries to build a permanent sense of connection between the living and the dead, perhaps seeing it as a form of victory over death.

The text is taken from the first edition of *Sha'ar ha-Hakhana* (Constantinople, 1734). It is very rich in idiomatic Hebrew and in references and allusions to many sources, only part of which could be conveyed in the translation.

Further Reading

Alfred Philip Bender, "Beliefs, Rites and Customs of the Jews Connected with Death," *Jewish Quarterly Review* 6 (1894): 317–47, 664–71; 7 (1895): 101–18, 259–69. Michael Fishbane, *The Kiss of God: Spiritual and Mystical Death in Judaism* (Seattle: University of Washington Press, 1994). Simcha Paul Raphael, *Jewish Views of the Afterlife* (Nortyhvale, N. J.: Jason Aronson, 1994). Elliot S. Horowitz, "The Jews of Europe and the Moment of Death in Medieval and Modern Times," *Judaism* 44 (1995): 271–81. Elliot R. Wolfson, "Weeping, Death, and Spiritual Ascent in Sixteenth Century Jewish Mysticism," in *Death, Ecstasy and Other Worldly Journeys,* edited by John J. Collins and Michael Fishbane (Albany: State University of New York Press, 1995), pp. 209–47. Sylvie Ann Goldberg, *Crossing the Jabbok: Illness and Death in Ashkenazi Judaism in Sixteenth through Nineteenth Century Prague,* translated by C. Cossman (Berkeley and Los Angeles: University of California Press, 1996). Meir Benayahu, *Ma'amadot u-Moshavot* (Jerusalem: Yad ha-Rav Nissim, 1985) (Hebrew). Zeev Gries, *Conduct Literature: Its History and Place in the Life of Beshtian Hasidism* (Jerusalem: Mosad Bialik, 1989) (Hebrew). Avriel Bar-Levav, "Rabbi Aaron Berechia of Modena and Rabbi Naphtali Ha-Kohen Katz, Founding Writers of the Jewish Literature for the Sick and the Dying," *Asufot* 9 (1995): 189–233 (Hebrew). Bar-Levav, "The Concept of Death in Sefer ha-Hayyim by Rabbi Shimon Frankfurt," Ph.D. dissertation, Hebrew University, 1997 (Hebrew). Bar-Levav, "Games of Death in Jewish Books for the Sick and the Dying," *Kabbalah: Journal for the Study of Jewish Mystical Texts* 5 (2000).

From the Ethical Will of Rabbi Naphtali Ha-Kohen Katz

"The Lord has given and the Lord has taken away, blessed be the name of the Lord from this time forth and for evermore" [Job 1:21]. It is written: "Man knows not his time" [Eccles. 9:12], and it is [also] written: "That he will command his children and his household after him," etc. [Gen. 18:19]. These seem like two contradictory verses, because the time might come suddenly, God forbid, "for the days of man are like a shadow that passes away" [Ps. 144:4]. And you should fear a sudden death, God forbid, or dying without being able to speak. . . . You must reproach yourself and mend your ways before death, as was the case with Jacob, Moses, and David, who reproached themselves near their death. But where is all this if one dies suddenly, God forbid? A third verse can decide between the two, in saying: "And the living will lay it to his heart" [Eccles. 7:2], referring to matters of death. You should prepare a will while you are still in good health, and have your strength. So it occurred to me to do, and so indeed I did.

You, my sons, may the Lord preserve you, you that God has graciously given to me are my proper children, a right seed, excluding wastrel sons, tormented souls, with whom I will have nothing to do; not one of them shall remain, none of their multitude, nor of their splendor, neither will they be mourned. For they are the children of harlotry, whom I have cast out and sent to a barren land, where no man has passed, and no man has dwelt. There they will die and be buried, for they will not be heirs with my sons, and they have no portion or inheritance among us. I will make my will solely in favor of my proper sons, born to my proper wife, who is modest in her deeds, and rightly called Esther Shendel, daughter of the great *gaon* [head of a rabbinical academy], our teacher Rabbi Shmuel of blessed memory. These are their names: The first is Rabbi Yitshak Isaac Katz, and the second Rabbi Mordekhai Katz, and the third, Rabbi Betsalel Katz, and the fourth, Rabbi Shmelke Katz, and the fifth, Rabbi Shealtiel Isaac Katz. Together with their wives, their sons, and their daughters—their proper offspring—and my sons in-law Rabbi Saadya Yeshaya and our teacher Rabbi Wolf, with their wives, my modest daughters from my aforementioned goodly wife. With their proper sons and daughters, these are all good people. Hear me and your soul shall live. I will go the way of all the earth, but you must be strong and act like men, doing the will of the Lord your God, to walk in His ways, to keep His statutes and commandments, judgments and testimonies, as it is written in the Law of Moses, that you may prosper in all that you do, wherever you turn.

Now these are the words with which King David, of blessed memory, charged his son Solomon [1 Kings 2:3], although I have changed it from the singular to the plural, because he charged his son only in the singular. In truth, in its plain meaning this verse incorporates all the Torah, all the rest of which is just explanation. You should be quite sure that this verse is holy in the extreme, because it has twenty-six words—the numerical value (*gematria*) of the name of God, blessed be he. Nahmanides has written in his book *Rose of Secrets,* that in every place where there is a verse possessing twenty-six words, it is holy in the extreme, since it entails the name of God, blessed be he, and there is no limit to its holiness. King David, of blessed memory, did not compose it in vain, since he meant to engage his son in the holiness of the name, and to cause him to cleave to the Lord, as in the verse "you that did cleave to the Lord your God," etc. [Deut. 4:4], and as in "the Lord was with him," etc. [1 Sam. 18:14]. Each word alludes to a great and awesome matter. I will not now go into the secret of holy matters, since I am not dealing with [esoteric] secrets but with revealed matters. Even in its revealed sense each word of the verse points to a postulate and one of the principles of our holy Torah. As is the case with the Talmud's explanation [Babylonian Talmud, *Sanhedrin* 56b] of the seven commandments bestowed upon Adam. These are inferred from the verse "And the Lord commanded the man," etc. [Gen. 2:16], and explained thus: "Commanded—this refers to idolatry," and so on with the rest of them. Many verses have been interpreted in such a way, and so it is with this verse, that every word demonstrates a question and one of the principles of our holy Torah, because this verse has to do with the divine Name, blessed be he, and the whole basis of our Torah is interwoven with the secret of the divine Name, as is explained in *Raya Mehemna* in the *Zohar,* "this commandment," etc. And now I shall explain them in detail, every word individually. . . .

Now I will give instructions concerning how to look after me from the beginning of my final illness—when the day of judgment comes, during all the period of my illness, and the time of my death, when my soul leaves my body, and when my body is taken from its bed and buried; also during purification, making the coffin, and the matters regarding shrouds, during the funeral, burial, closure of the grave; and regarding the conduct of mourning during the *shiva* [first seven days], the thirty days, and the twelve months, as well as my perpetual honor after my death, and the ritual of the annual memorial day. I have composed twenty-six paragraphs, corresponding to the numerical equivalent (*gematria*) of his great and awesome name, YHWH [that is, 26], blessed be he, to unite his name in love. So may it be that my soul will depart while saying "one." "Love" and "one" [in Hebrew] combined have the numerical value of YHWH. Each is like half of the name, that is, thirteen, corresponding to his thirteen attributes of mercy. May it be his will to be merciful with me in the hour of judgment, the time of the seven judgments that pass over the human being. He will remember me with mercy.

And these are the twenty-six paragraphs:

1. During the time of my [final] sickness, at the very beginning, when it is decreed that I must go the way of all the earth, the Holy Society [i.e., burial society] and the members of my household should look after me, following the instructions given in my book, *Bet Rachel,* in the chapter dealing with preparation, which is also called the "Gate of the Living Soul." And they should not omit anything. I ask the leaders of the burial and charitable society to do for me this true mercy, and not to move from the room where I am lying, so that together with the members of my household who are not otherwise busy, there will always be a quorum of ten men there—ten not counting me. They should take turns, so that there will never be less, day and night, during the whole period of my illness, from its beginning. They should study and pray and recite psalms, and continue doing so until the grave is closed, according to everything that is written in my aforementioned book, which is still in manuscript.

2. During the whole period of my illness, my small prayer shawl with the proper tassels and girdle should not be taken off me. Even if I should lose my sanity, God forbid, they will be kept pure. I am mentioning this separately, although it is written in my book, because of my love for this commandment.

3. As the process of dying begins, they should immediately immerse themselves ritually in water. All those who wish to take care of my body after my

death should immerse themselves that very day, and if, God forbid, my death is prolonged a day or two longer, then their first immersion is not enough, and they should immerse themselves once again after my soul has departed. No one should touch my bed, no less my body, unless he has immersed himself that very day.

4. Even though everyone makes his declaration against the saboteur, that is, the agitator who comes up to accuse throughout the year, and sometimes even every day, a word in due season is always a good thing, particularly if it is actually near one's death, when a man accepts lovingly the yoke of heaven and rejects idolatry. This is tantamount to accepting the whole Torah and fulfilling all its precepts. Because I worry that my mind will be confused and my words heavy, I hereby empower and authorize those who stand beside me at that time to do all this for me, to make a declaration and to accept the yoke of heaven in my name. Their action is for good and not for evil, because I have authorized them to do so for my benefit. And I renounced any power to abolish or even to change this authorization, God forbid, for all my earthly life. It must remain strong and valid, and any thoughts or temptations, God forbid, not to mention any words or actions to change it, are canceled and annulled, invalid and nonexistent. The authorization is valid forever.

5. During the period of my dying they should give charity as my beloved wife wishes. However, she should not give too much, so she will not be beholden to people, God forbid. But it should amount to the number fifteen, so as to "repair" the divine Name YH [fifteen, in *gematria*] which is between a man and woman, and also to practice the verse "the dead shall not praise the Lord [YaH]" [Ps. 115:17]; that is why it is appropriate to "repair" it while living. They might be small coins, since God wants the heart, and even of the offering of the poor it is said, "a sweet savor to the Lord."

6. At the time of my death the Holy Society should order that a declaration be made in the quorum of ten, under [the fear of] a great ban and with the blowing of a ram's horn, that after my death, none of my descendants should weep in the room where I lie, and that only distant relatives should accompany me.

7. When my soul departs they should take care that I do not move my legs or any other part of my body out of the bed; they should cover me, even using force, if, God forbid, I am acting like a madman.

8. Once my soul has departed from my body, this is what the Holy Society should do to me before putting me in the ground. The leaders of the burial society should take my body and lay me naked on the ground without a sheet under my body. Covering me only a span in front and two spans behind, they should say: "If this deceased was sentenced to be stoned, this should be con-

sidered as stoning, as if he had been stoned in the High Court in Jerusalem." They should do so four times, one after the other. The second time they should say: "If this deceased is sentenced to be burnt, this should be considered as stoning, which is severer than burning, because we accept what the rabbis said against Rabbi Shimon, when he claimed that burning is more severe, and a man who has received two death sentences should be punished with the severer of the two, as Maimonides ruled as well." The third time they should say: "If this deceased is sentenced to decapitation, this stoning should be instead of decapitation because stoning is severer than decapitation according to all opinions." The fourth time they should say: "If this deceased is sentenced to strangulation, this stoning should be instead of strangulation, because according to all opinions stoning is more severe than strangling."

After all this they should lift me up a little into the air to about my standing height, with my head up as if they were executing the sentence of hanging, because all those who are stoned are also hanged. After that, they should put me in the ground as is the way of all the earth. I ask the Holy Society not to deny me this, God forbid, under the pretext that this does not honor the dead. On the contrary, it does me honor and it does me merit. I do not pardon them if they change my command and fail to treat me in this way; it is a positive commandment to do what the dead request, and this is a mercy, a true mercy they can show me.

9. When my body is lying on the ground before the purification, ten or more people should encircle it, one close to the other, touching so that no space is left between them. They should study chapters from the Mishnah that begin with the letters of my name Naphtali Ha-Kohen. For example, for the "N" of Naphtali they should study the tractate *Shabbat,* chapter "Notel," etc.; and the chapter "Parat Hatat," etc. for the "P" of Naphtali; "Tefilat Ha-Shahar" from tractate *Berachot* for the "T" of my name; "Lo Yachpor" in tractate *Baba Batra* for the "L" in my name: "Yetzi'ot Ha-Shabbat" for the "Y" in my name. They should do the same for the word "Ha-Kohen," etc., and collect chapters from the whole Talmud, each in its place. They should also recite chapters from Psalms that start with the letters of my name. The "N" of my name is from Psalm 76, "Nodah Yehudah"; since there is no psalm starting with "P," they should recite the verses starting with the letter "P" from Psalm 119; Psalm 22 for the "T" in my name; Psalm 24 for the "L"; Psalm 91 for the "Y," and so on from all the psalms, and the same for the word "Ha-Kohen." In reciting these psalms and verses of the letters of my name, they should concentrate on asking for mercy on my behalf, so that when I am asked my name in the World of Truth, I will not forget it. My name will be ready on my tongue, so I will suffer no shame or disgrace and say it immediately, and also to "repair" my name.

10. While washing my body with the purification water, they will pour nine *kab* measures of water over it. This should be done four times, to "repair" the

four letters of the divine Name [YHWH] that I have blemished.... They should also concentrate on correcting the blemish that I brought about in the Four Worlds [of the cosmos in the kabbalistic system]: Emanation, Creation, Making, Action, and then my flesh will be like that of a young person who has not tasted sin. The vessel of the nine *kab* measures should be measured in the equivalent of eggs, in the same way as the amount of bread for Passover is measured, that is, approximately.

11. While washing my body they should recite Psalm 29 with the seven verses that [King] David said over water, with the intention that their prayer should ease for me the judgments of the seven eras that pass over man.

12. While washing and dressing my body they should recite all the verses that are explained in the book *Ma'avar Yabbok,* and do the same while lowering me into the grave. They should also recite all the verses that are set forth in my aforementioned *Sha'ar Ha-Hakhana,* neither hiding nor omitting anything.

13. While clothing me in the shrouds, they should recite all the verses in Exodus 28, Leviticus 8, and Numbers 20, dealing with the priestly garments. Their intention should be as if to clothe me in the priestly garments in order to stand to serve [God]. This will atone for certain transgressions, remove my iniquity, and purge my sins.

14. All this should be done specifically by people who have ritually immersed themselves in water. Before their immersion they should confess and think of repentance, as it is said "Gather yourselves together and assemble together" [Zeph. 2:1], and as it is said, "The innocent shall come and atone for the guilty."

15. During my funeral no one who has hated me or mocked my learning should be allowed to escort me. This will be declared when I am taken out of the house. Their hatred and envy is now long gone.

16. My [burial] shrouds, together with a prayer shawl, a gown (*kittel*), and everything that is needed, are ready. It is all sewn in a garment of black linen, so it will not get wet, and on the sack is written "shrouds for a man." They are kept in the box that I have always taken on journeys, and always kept with me, so that I should not be wrapped in a prayer shawl that is not mine, and so that I should always remember the day of my [impending] death. It also contains soil from the land of Israel, wrapped in paper. Most of this should be scattered over my body and all my limbs, and especially on the phallus, while the verse "and His land will atone His people" [Deut. 32:43] is recited.

17. Since I am a *kohen* (priest) and a firstborn, who, according to the custom, is buried in a full coffin, in which the flesh does not disintegrate easily, I ask

the burial society to use thin planks and to drill holes in the planks so the earth will get in and the flesh will disintegrate quickly.

18. During my funeral, a copy of my book *Birkat Ha-Shem* should be put on my bier until it reaches the grave, but not in the grave itself. Charity should be given both during the funeral and when my body is placed in to the grave, as in the verse "Righteousness shall go before him" [Ps. 85:14], even if only a little can be given. It is written "For he put on righteousness as a breastplate" [Isa. 59:17].

19. If the Lord should favor me so that I might buy a burial site during my lifetime, how good it would be. But if not, I ask my modest and pious wife, may she live, even though everything is left for her, that she donate from the money she has in order to provide a vessel for the synagogue in my eternal memory. This will be instead of purchasing a burial place, and so I will not rest on plundered land.

20. It is my order, on penalty of the ban of my fathers, that I shall not be eulogized anywhere. Letters should be sent to every place where the couriers reach, that I have ordered, on penalty of a ban, that I should not be eulogized, neither in the cemetery nor in the synagogue. Even without a eulogy, I should not be praised by any title, as righteous or pious, and so on. This is the only way I wish to be praised: That he was accustomed to study page by page, and was well versed even in homilies, and was close to the truth in everything. This will I speak in the world of Truth, even against kings, and I will not be ashamed. What was done to me in this world of Falsehood was due to pride and jealousy. No praise is to be carved on the whole tombstone, only these words and no other: "Here lies the rabbi, our teacher, Naphtali Ha-Kohen, son of the great rabbi who was prominent in his generation, our teacher, Rabbi Isaac Ha-Kohen, descended from a high succession of several generations of the greatest of the land, who were the heads of his family from all sides, and he enjoyed priestly descent from Aaron, priest to the Lord of heavens." And the details of the year should also be written.

21. During the entire seven days of mourning, and during the thirty days after the grave is closed, there should be a quorum of ten in my house—specifically scholars—who should pray evening and morning, as well as on Sabbaths and festivals. They should recite one set of psalms every week so that it will be completed in a week, with [the prayer] "may it be His will" that belongs to each book, at the beginning and end. Also, the *Song of Unity* is to be said every day, together with Kaddish prayers. After the prayers they should study two chapters of Mishnah in the morning and two in the evening, following the order of the six books of the Mishnah, starting from [tractate] *Berakhot*.

22. For the whole year round, the group should study two chapters of Mishnah daily, one in the morning and one in the evening, starting from the place at which those who studied during the thirty days stopped, until all the six books of the Mishnah are completed. They should concentrate on the fact that the word *Mishnah* is made up of the same letters as *Neshamah* [soul]. The *Zohar* should also be studied every day, a page from the Lublin edition, which is 264 pages, and then from *Zohar Hadash,* which is about 86 pages, making altogether 350 pages. Since each year consists of 365 days, ten of which are the ten days of repentance, when *Tikkunei Zohar* has to be read completely, because it represents the "seventy faces" [of the Torah], as explained in the writings of Rabbi Isaac Luria, 345 days remain in each simple year. The group will have to complete the five remaining pages in these days, in order to finish all of the *Zohar, Zohar Hadash,* and *Tikkunei Zohar* of "seventy faces" during the year. They can study these remaining pages on the Yahrzeit instead, the annual memorial day, because this is another day in this year. I prefer this idea.

They should also study the tractate *Berakhot* every day, even if only a little, adding one *novellum* [new teaching] from my composition, so there should be at least one novellum every day. They should learn one novellum each day from my book *Semihat Hakhamim,* so that my lips will be moving [even] in the grave. They should study well and not be in a hurry to reject the ideas. . . . They should study it slowly and with great attention. They should publicize all my novellae in order to bring merit to the many, and if, indeed, I have erred, it is my fault, and I apologize.

23. Ten people should spend the year in study; five of them should study Mishnah as mentioned, two should study the *Zohar* as mentioned, and three should study tractate *Berakhot* with my novellae. It would be good if the same ten people who prayed and studied during the first thirty days [of mourning] would be able to continue to study all year round, as set out above. But if not, ten others should be hired after the thirty days, to study the whole year.

24. Candles should be lit in the synagogue in the place where I used to sit. If the place in question is no longer mine, then they should hire it for a full year in order to light them there. And if this is not possible, God forbid, then they should light the candle at the place where the eternal light is lit [in the synagogue]. During the first thirty days they should also light candles in my home, continuing to light them in the synagogue until after the Yahrzeit.

25. During each daily lesson of Mishnah, *Zohar,* and *Berakhot,* there should always be a quorum of ten, and the rabbis should not come in in groups. They should also say Kaddish in a quorum of ten after each lesson separately.

26. In order to cover the payment for those who would study on my behalf during the thirty days and throughout the whole year, as well as the expenses

for the candles, I have put aside one hundred copies of my book. Each of those who studies should take some books as payment. My in-laws and my relatives will also help to fulfill such a religious obligation in order to benefit my soul and those of others. Everyone should buy some of the books. "Those who are for the Lord will come to me," in order to be among those who achieve this merit. This will be called upon their name. Wealth and riches shall be in their house, and their righteousness shall endure forever.

This is the end of the twenty-six paragraphs having to do with the dignity of the Lord, for the unification of the Lord and his *Shekhinah*, and for the merit of my soul.

Torah, Learning, and Ethics

11

Moses Maimonides' Laws of the Study of Torah

Lawrence Kaplan

Moses Maimonides (1138–1204 C.E.), one of the truly heroic figures of all of Jewish history, was both a towering rabbinic scholar and a towering philosopher. His monumental code of Jewish law, written in Hebrew, the *Mishneh Torah* (completed c. 1178), is an all-encompassing summa of the totality of rabbinic law, comprising both laws governing practice and laws governing belief, both laws applicable in his own day and laws dependent upon the Temple or the land of Israel. It bids fair to be the most important work of Jewish law written by a single individual. (The Mishnah and Babylonian Talmud, the most fundamental and authoritative works of Jewish law, are collective enterprises.) At the same time, his philosophical masterpiece, the *Guide of the Perplexed,* written in Arabic and completed before 1191, is certainly the greatest and most influential work of medieval Jewish philosophy, perhaps of all Jewish philosophy. Moreover, his philosophy informs his legal scholarship, and the *Mishneh Torah* thus allows us to take the measure of Maimonides the philosopher, while his legal scholarship, though perhaps to a lesser extent, informs his philosophy, and the *Guide* thus allows us to take the measure of Maimonides the jurist.

Maimonides chooses to formulate the law in the *Mishneh Torah* in normative, apodictic form. He does not identify and rarely cites any of his sources directly. Yet, as he states in the introduction to that work, his presentation of the law is based upon the Mishnah of R. Judah the Prince and the five classical rabbinic works that, in his view, are devoted to its elucidation: the Babylonian and Jerusalem Talmuds and the *Sifra, Sifrei,* and Tosefta. In theory, then, all the material found in the *Mishneh Torah,* with the exception of those statements prefaced by "It appears to me," and the like, despite their anonymity, are not original with him, but derive from those six works. Indeed, for over eight hundred years, ever since the completion of the *Mishneh Torah,* scholars have devoted themselves to identifying Maimonides' sources. Yet, as those same scholars have realized, Maimonides' choice and arrangement of those sources, his careful reformulation and reshaping of his underlying texts, and the distinctive nuances, emphases, and original interpretations that he subtly—and sometimes not so subtly—insinuates into them all serve to endow the work with a clear Maimonidean stamp and coloration.

The *Mishneh Torah* is divided into fourteen books; each book is divided into sections (laws of a particular commandment or group of commandments), which are, in turn, subdivided into chapters and paragraphs. The selection below is taken from the *Laws of the Study of Torah* of the *Book of Knowledge*.

The *Book of Knowledge*, as Maimonides states, consists of "commandments that are the fundamental principles of the religion of Moses, our master, and that a person must know at the very outset." Included in it, alongside the *Laws of the Study of Torah,* are the *Laws of the Foundations of the Torah,* the *Laws of Moral Dispositions,* the *Laws of Idolatry,* and the *Laws of Repentance.* The book thus encompasses laws governing beliefs, moral qualities, and actions.

The *Laws of the Study of Torah,* as Maimonides states, includes two positive commandments: to study Torah (and to teach it); and to honor those who teach it and know it. The first four chapters of the section, translated below, deal with the first of the two commandments. In one sense, this commandment requires of one an action—the action of study—as opposed to either a belief or moral quality. At the same time, the commandment of study, for Maimonides the most important mode of service of God, is contrasted with and, as he states twice, "in all circumstances takes precedence over practice" (1:4 and 3:4).

The first chapter sets forth the basic commandment of both study and teaching, who is obligated to study and who to teach, what is he obligated to study and what to teach, and finally, "until when is [he] obligated to study" (1:13). The second chapter deals with elementary education. The third chapter, a passionate and poetic paean to the value and preciousness of Torah study, is a veritable mosaic of reworked quotations skillfully assembled from the far ranges of rabbinic literature. Finally, the fourth chapter deals with advanced education. We may say that the advanced students of chapter 4 are those who have taken Maimonides' encomium in chapter 3 to heart. Note also how in chapter 2 Maimonides refers to children or minors and teachers, whereas in chapter 4 he refers to students and masters.

Although the most concentrated praise of Torah study is to be found in chapter 3, its importance and seriousness emerge in the most unexpected of places. The remarkable reference to the "artisan . . . who occupies himself with his trade for three hours daily and with the Torah for nine [!] hours daily" (1:3), the requirement that a city whose inhabitants persistently refuse to appoint teachers for the young is to be laid waste (2:1), the demand that an elementary teacher should teach his charges "the entire day and part of the night" (2:3), the laws governing behavior in the house of study (4:14)—all serve to underscore the truth "that there is no commandment among all the commandments as weighty as the study of Torah" (3:4).

In accordance with Maimonides' philosophical orientation, wisdom, in these chapters, takes its place alongside Torah. Thus in 3:14, Maimonides paraphrases his talmudic source, "The Torah abides only with one who mortifies himself on its behalf" (*Berakhot* 63b), to read "The Torah abides only with one who mortifies himself in the tents of wisdom"; in 3:16 he exhorts the reader to spend his nights in the "the study of Torah and words of wisdom." Beyond such paraphrase and exhortation, this orientation finds its sharpest and clearest expression in Maimonides' inclusion of the study of Pardes, that is, the natural and divine sciences, as an integral part of the Talmud component of Torah study (1:15). We are confronted here with the bold and controversial claim that those who possess the requisite ability and background are religiously and legally obligated to pursue the study of philosophy.

The cluster of laws, 1:14–16, raises the question of Maimonides' curriculum. Although this is not the place for a full discussion, a few remarks are in order. Once again we see Maimonides' original paraphrase of his underlying source. The Talmud states, "One should always divide his years into three: a third to Miqra, a third to Mishnah, a third to Talmud" (*Kiddushin* 30a). Generally these three categories were understood in the post-talmudic halakhic literature preceding Maimonides as referring to three texts: the Bible, the Mishnah of R. Judah the Prince, and the Babylonian Talmud. Maimonides keeps the first category unchanged, but radically transforms the other two. For Mishnah he substitutes the oral Law, that is, the laws of the Torah presented in normative, apodictic form. Since, as we saw earlier, this is precisely the way that the Law is presented in the *Mishneh Torah,* one could, in Maimonides's view, fulfill the oral Law component of Torah study through mastery of his own code. Maimonides understands Talmud as referring not to a text but to a mode of study of the laws of the Torah involving inference, argumentation, and interpretation. It is not surprising, then, that the study of the natural and divine sciences, which involves "speculation concerning the fundamental principles of religion" (*Guide* 3:51), that is, speculation concerning the laws governing belief, is, for Maimonides, part of Talmud. We have here a move to, as it has recently been termed, a notion of "textless Torah."

A disconcerting note is introduced by Maimonides' exclusion of women from both studying and teaching Torah (1:1, 17–18; 2:4). Particularly troubling is the fact that Maimonides (1:18) rules in accordance with the view of the talmudic sage R. Eliezer that "One who teaches his daughter Torah, it is as if he taught her frivolity," as opposed to the view of Ben Azzai that a person is obligated to teach his daughter Torah (*Sotah* 21b). Maimonides' ruling has been the subject of much discussion, and, again, a few remarks must suffice. First, since I decided to translate the Hebrew root *zvh* consistently as "command," I translated Maimonides in 1:17 as saying, "The sages have commanded (*zivu hakhamim*) that a person should not teach his daughter Torah." However, as scholars have recently shown, Maimonidean statements preceded by the phrase "the Sages have commanded" should not be viewed as full-fledged legal rulings but rather as religious and moral exhortations (cf. 3:9, 12). Moreover, the reason Maimonides offers for this exhortation is that "the minds of most women are not directed to being taught." Presumably, even in his view there are a minority of women to whom this stricture does not apply, and such women could study the oral Law as mature individuals. Indeed, such women also ought to study the Pardes, so as to fulfill properly the commandment of the love of God (*Laws of the Foundations of the Torah* 2:2; 4:12). Finally, Maimonides believes that such exceptional women actually exist, as emerges from other passages in his writings (*Laws of Repentance* 10:1; *Guide* 3:51).

Maimonides' categorical statement that "A woman should not teach children on account of their fathers who visit their sons" (2:4) raises the issue of the relationship between theoretical codification and actual practice. Since Maimonides bases his rulings on talmudic sources, they often have a classical air to them, and do not always reflect contemporary halakhic procedure. Indeed, we know of several instances where in the *Mishneh Torah* Maimonides makes a blanket ruling concerning a certain matter, but when confronting in a responsum a real-life case that involves that same matter, offers a more nuanced decision. The above appears to apply to the question of women teaching. Thus we have two Maimonidean responsa dealing with a bitter matrimonial dispute, where the husband sought to prevent his wife, who was a teacher of children, from continuing in her profession, "for fear [of] their fathers, who will come to visit their children." Maimonides, who sympathizes with the wife—the husband, it seems, was a loafer and deadbeat—offers her a stratagem by means of which the rabbinic court would compel her husband to divorce her. She would then, Maimonides concludes, "be her own woman, [free] to teach whomever she pleases and do whatever she likes." The problem of fathers visiting their children was no issue, for the woman was assisted in her teaching by her eldest son, who could serve as a chaperone if the woman had to meet one of the fathers.

In sum, a close examination reveals that Maimonides' exclusion of women from the study and teaching of Torah is less absolute than would appear at first glance. The crown of Torah was available to at least some exceptional women, who, if they so wished, could come and take it.

This translation is based on the Oxford manuscript of the *Book of Knowledge,* which contains a colophon by Maimonides himself that attests to the fact the manuscript was copied from his own autograph. Paragraphing follows that of the Oxford manuscript and not that of the printed editions. A translation by Bernard Septimus of the complete *Book of Knowledge,* to be published by Yale University Press as part of its Judaica Series, is scheduled to appear in the near future.

Further Reading

For an authoritative study of the *Mishneh Torah,* see Isadore Twersky, *Introduction to the Code of Maimonides (Mishneh Torah)* (New Haven: Yale University Press,

1980). See, as well, Twersky's seminal article, "Some Non-Halakhic Aspects of the *Mishneh Torah*," *Jewish Medieval and Renaissance Studies*, edited by A. Altmann (Cambridge: Harvard University Press, 1967), pp. 95–118. For some representative studies focusing on selected aspects of the *Book of Knowledge* in general and *Laws of the Study of Torah* in particular, see Moshe Greenberg, "Bible Interpretation as Exhibited in the First Book of Maimonides' Code," *Studies in the Bible and Jewish Thought* (Philadelphia: Jewish Publication Society, 1995), pp. 421–45; Warren Harvey, "The Obligation of Talmud on Women According to Maimonides," *Tradition* 19.2 (1981): 122–30; and Leo Strauss, "Notes on Maimonides' Book of Knowledge," *Studies in Mysticism and Religion presented to Gershom Scholem*, edited by E. Urbach, et al. (Jerusalem: Magnes, 1967), pp. 269–83. The two Maimonidean responsa referred to at the end of the introduction are translated, annotated, and discussed in Renée Levine Melammed, "He Said, She Said: A Woman Teacher in Twelfth-Century Cairo," *AJS Review* 22.1 (1997): 19–35.

Moses Maimonides' *Laws of the Study of Torah*

comprising two positive commandments: 1. to study Torah; 2. to honor those who teach it and those who know it; and the explanation of these commandments [follows] in these chapters.

CHAPTER 1

1. Women and slaves are exempt from [the obligation] of the study of Torah. Concerning a minor, however, his father is obligated to teach him Torah, as it is said, "And you shall teach them to your children to speak of them" [Deut. 11:19]. A woman is not obligated to teach her son, for [only] one who is obligated to study is obligated to teach.

2. Just as a man is obligated to teach his son, so is he obligated to teach the son of his son, as it is said, "Make them known to your sons and to the sons of your sons" [Deut. 4:9]. And [this obligation applies] not only to one's son and the son of one's son, but a commandment [devolves] upon each and every Israelite sage to teach all the students even if they are not his sons, as it is said, "And you shall teach them diligently to your sons" [Deut. 6:7]. On the basis of the tradition we have learned, "Your sons": this refers to your students, for students are called sons, as it is said, "And the sons of the prophets went forth" [2 Kings 2:3].

3. If this is so, why does the commandment refer to one's son and to the son of one's son [Deut. 4:9]? [To teach] that one's [own] son takes precedence over the son of one's son, and that the son of one's son takes precedence over the son of one's neighbor. Moreover, one is obligated to hire a teacher to teach

one's son, but one is obligated to teach his neighbor's son only if it involves no expense.

4. One who was not taught by his father is obligated to teach himself when he reaches the age of discernment, as it is said, "And you shall study them and you shall observe them to perform them" [Deut. 5:1]. And so you will find that in all circumstances study takes precedence over practice. For study leads to practice, but practice does not lead to study.

5. If a person needs to study Torah and he has a son [whom he is obligated] to teach Torah, he takes precedence over his son. But if his son understands and grasps what he studies better than he, his son takes precedence. However, even though [in the above circumstance] his son takes precedence, he should not desist [from study]. For just as a commandment devolves upon him to teach his son, so is he commanded to teach himself.

6. A person should always [first] study Torah and [only] afterward marry. For if he will marry first, his mind will not be free for study. But if his inclination overpowers him to such an extent that his heart is not free, let him marry first and then study Torah.

7. When should a father begin to teach his son Torah? When the son begins to speak his father teaches him "Moses commanded us the Torah, an inheritance, etc." [Deut. 33:4], and the first verse of the section of Shema [Deut. 6:4]. Afterward he teaches him bit by bit several verses [at a time], until he is six or seven, depending on his development, at which point he takes him to a teacher of children.

8. If it is the customary practice of the province [that people] hire teachers of children for pay, then he [the father] must pay his wages. And it is his duty to pay [a teacher's] wages to have him [his child] taught until he has read through the entire written Torah.

9. In a place where people customarily teach the written Torah for pay—it is permissible [for a teacher] to teach for pay. But it is forbidden to teach the oral Torah for pay, as it is said, "Behold I [Moses] have taught you statutes and ordinances as [that is, in the same manner as] the Lord my God commanded me" [Deut. 4:5]. [This means that] "Just as I [Moses] studied [from God] for free, so you have studied from me for free. And similarly, when you will teach throughout the generations do so for free, just as you studied from me."

10. If a person cannot find anyone to teach him [the oral Torah] for free, he should study it [with someone] for pay, as it is said, "And buy the truth" [Prov. 23:23]. Might one assume then that [in such circumstances] he can teach [the oral Torah] to others for pay? The verse continues, "and do not sell"—from this you may learn that it is forbidden for a person to teach [the oral Torah] for pay even if his master taught him [the oral Torah] for pay.

11. Every Israelite male is obligated to study Torah, whether poor or rich, whether in a state of bodily perfection or afflictions, whether a youth or a very old enfeebled man. Even a poor man who goes begging from door to door or even a married man with children is obligated to set aside for himself a fixed time for the study of Torah both in the day and in the night, as it is said, "And you shall meditate therein day and night" [Joshua 1:8].

12. Some of the great sages of Israel were hewers of wood, some were drawers of water, some were blind; and even so they occupied themselves with the Torah during the day and the night. And they are included among the transmitters of the tradition from Moses our master.

13. Until when is a person obligated to study Torah? Until the day of his death, as it is said, "And lest they [the precepts] depart from your heart all the days of your life" [Deut. 4:9]. And whenever one does not occupy himself with study, one forgets.

14. A person is obligated to divide the time allotted to study into three parts: One-third to the written Torah, one-third to the oral Torah, and one-third he should intelligently infer conclusions from premises and derive one matter from another, and he should compare one matter to another matter, and he should issue rulings through use of the [thirteen] hermeneutical principles until he understands the essence of these principles and how he may derive the forbidden and the permitted and the like from those matters which he learned on the basis of tradition. And this [third] subject is termed Talmud.

15. How so? If a person is an artisan and occupies himself with his trade for three hours daily and with the Torah for nine hours daily, he should spend three hours in reading the written Torah, three hours in [reading] the oral Torah, and three hours in reflecting on how to infer one matter from another. And the words of the prophets are included in the written Torah, and their interpretation in the oral Torah. And those subjects termed Pardes [the account of the chariot and the account of creation, which Maimonides elsewhere identifies with the divine science and natural science, respectively] are included in the Talmud.

16. The above applies only to the period when a person begins his study. But once a person grows in wisdom and no longer needs to study the written Torah nor to occupy himself with the oral Torah, he should read the written Torah and the traditional teachings for fixed periods, so that he not should forget any matter of the laws of the Torah, and should devote all his days solely to Talmud in accordance with the breadth of his heart and the composure of his mind.

17. A woman who studies Torah will receive a reward, but it will not be like the reward received by a man. For she is not commanded [to study Torah]; and whoever performs an act that he is not commanded to do will not receive the same reward as one who performs an act and is so commanded, but will

receive a lesser reward. Even though she will receive a reward, the sages have commanded that a person should not teach his daughter Torah. For the minds of most women are not directed to being taught, and they will turn words of Torah into words of folly, in accordance with the weakness of their understanding.

18. The sages have said: "One who teaches his daughter Torah, it is as if he teaches her frivolity." This [statement] applies only to [teaching her] the oral Torah, but concerning the written Torah, a man should not teach it to his daughter to begin with, but if he did teach it to her it is not as if he taught her frivolity.

CHAPTER 2

1. Teachers of the young are to be appointed in each province and district. And concerning any city in which there are not to be found young school children, the inhabitants of the city are to be excommunicated until they appoint teachers for the young. If they [still] do not appoint them, the city is to be laid waste, for the world is maintained only by the breath of school children.

2. Children are to be sent to study at about the age of six or seven, all in accordance with the strength of the son and his physical build. But a child younger than six is not to be sent. And the teacher may strike them [his pupils] to instill awe in them. But he may not strike them in a cruel or vindictive manner. Therefore he may not strike them with whips or sticks, but only with a small strap.

3. And the teacher should teach them the entire day and part of the night, in order to train them to study by day and by night. And the children should not desist from study at all, except on of the eves of the Sabbaths and the eves of holidays, toward the end of the day, and on holidays. But on the Sabbath they are not to study new material, but should review what they have studied. And one is not to cause children to desist [from their studies] even for the building of the Temple.

4. A teacher of children who leaves the children and goes outside, or who does other work while he is with them, or who is remiss in teaching them is included in the category of "Cursed be he who does the work of the Lord negligently" [Jer. 48:10]. Therefore one should appoint as a teacher only a God-fearing individual who is both able to cover ground and be precise. An unmarried man should not teach children on account of their mothers who visit their sons. And, similarly, a woman should not teach children on account of their fathers who visit their sons.

5. Twenty-five children are to study with one teacher. If there were more than twenty-five children, if there are fewer than forty children a person is appointed

alongside him to assist him in teaching them. If there are more than forty, one must appoint two teachers.

6. One may transfer a minor from one teacher to another teacher who is more able, whether in covering ground or in precision. When does the above apply? When both teachers are in the same city and there is no river separating them. But one is not to transfer a minor from one city to another, nor [even] from one side of the river to another, unless there is a sturdy bridge spanning the river, a bridge that is not likely to collapse quickly.

7. If one of the residents of an alley or even one of the residents of a courtyard wishes to set himself up as a teacher, his neighbors cannot prevent him. Similarly, [if there is] a teacher of children [who is already established], and his fellow comes along and opens up a school for children nearby him, so that other [new] children shall come to him or [even] so that children from the former should transfer to the latter, the former cannot prevent him, as it is said, "The Lord was pleased for His righteousness' sake to make the Torah great and glorious" [Isa. 42:21].

CHAPTER 3

1. With three crowns was Israel crowned—with the crown of Torah, with the crown of priesthood, and with the crown of kingship. The crown of priesthood was acquired by Aaron, as it is said, "And it shall be unto him and unto his seed after him the covenant of an everlasting priesthood" [Num. 25:13]. The crown of kingship was acquired by David, as it is said, "His seed shall endure everlastingly, and his throne as the sun before Me" [Ps. 89:37]. The crown of Torah [by contrast] is set before and available to all, as it is said, "Moses commanded us the Torah, an inheritance of the congregation of Jacob" [Deut. 33:4]. Whoever so wishes may come and take it.

2. Lest you may say that the other crowns are greater than the crown of Torah, behold it is said, "By me [the Torah] kings reign and nobles decree justice. By me princes rule" [Prov. 8:15–16].

3. From this you may understand that the crown of Torah is greater than the crown of priesthood and the crown of kingship. The sages have said: "An illegitimate who is a disciple of the sages is to take preference over a high priest who is an ignoramus," as it is said, "and it [the Torah] is more precious than rubies" (*peninim*) [Prov. 3:15], [that is], it is more precious than the high priest who enters within the innermost part of the sanctuary (*lipnai ve-lipnim*).

4. There is no commandment among all the commandments as weighty as the study of Torah. Rather, the study of Torah is equal to them all. For study leads to practice. Therefore study in all circumstances takes precedence over practice.

5. If a person is studying Torah and the opportunity to perform a commandment presents itself to him—if the commandment can be performed by others, let him not interrupt his study; but if not, let him perform the commandment and return to his study.

6. A person at the first stage of his judgment will be judged concerning his study and afterward concerning his other deeds. Therefore the sages have said: "Let a person occupy himself with the Torah even not for its own sake; for as a result of [occupying himself with it] not for its own sake he will arrive at [occupying himself with it] for its own sake."

7. He whose heart lifts him up to perform this commandment fittingly and to be crowned with the crown of Torah should not turn his mind aside to other things and should not let it enter his heart that he will acquire Torah together with riches and honor at the same time. This is the way of Torah. A morsel of bread with salt you will eat, and on the ground you will sleep, and a life of pain you will lead, and [the while] you will toil in the Torah. It is not incumbent upon you to complete the work nor are you free to desist from it, but if you have piled up for yourself much Torah, you have piled up for yourself much reward. And the reward is in accordance with the pain.

8. Lest you will say, once I have gathered much wealth then I will return and study; once I have acquired sufficient for my needs then I will turn aside from my occupations and return and study—if this thought enters your heart, you will never acquire the crown of Torah. Rather make your Torah your fixed activity and your trade your casual activity; and do not say when I shall have leisure I will study, lest you never have leisure.

9. It is written in the Torah: "It is not in heaven . . . and neither is it beyond the sea" [Deut. 30:12–13]. "It is not in heaven"—it [the Torah] is not to be found among those of arrogant spirit; "and neither is it beyond the sea"—nor is it to be found among those who cross the sea. Therefore the sages have said: "One who engages much in trade cannot become wise." And they have commanded and said: "Engage little in your occupation and occupy yourself with Torah."

10. Words of Torah are likened unto water, as it is said, "O, everyone who is thirsty, come for water" [Isa. 55:1]. This teaches you that just as water does not accumulate on a slope, but flows away and gathers only in a depression, so words of Torah are not to be found among those possessed of an arrogant spirit or a proud heart, but among one who is contrite and lowly in spirit, who sits in the dust at the feet of the sages, who removes temporal desires and pleasures from his heart, and who does a little work every day, just enough for his livelihood, if he otherwise would have nothing to eat, and occupies himself the rest of his day and his night with Torah.

11. One whose heart prompts him to occupy himself with Torah and not to do any work, but to be supported by charity—such a person has desecrated the [divine] Name, and has cast shame on the Torah, and has extinguished the light of religion, and has brought evil upon himself, and has removed his life from the world to come, for it is forbidden to derive benefit through words of Torah in this world.

12. The sages have said: "Whoever derives benefit from words of Torah removes his life from the world." They further commanded and said: "Do not make of them [the words of Torah] a crown wherewith to make yourself great, nor a spade wherewith to dig." And they further commanded and said: "Love work, but hate lordship." And any Torah unaccompanied by work will in the end cease to be; and in the end this person will rob his fellow men.

13. It is an exalted rank for one to support himself by the work of his hands. And this was the manner of behavior of the early pietists. By this means a person will acquire all honor and good in this world and in the world to come, as it is said, "When you eat of the toil of your hands, happy you shall be and it shall be good with you" [Ps. 128:2]: "happy"—in this world; "and it shall be good with you"—in the world to come which is wholly good.

14. Words of Torah will not abide with one who treats them slackly nor with those who study amidst luxury and amidst eating and drinking, but only with one who mortifies himself for their sake, who constantly subjects his body to pain, and deprives his eyes of sleep and his eyelids of slumber. The sages have said by way of metaphor: " 'This is the Torah, if a person dies in a tent' [Num. 19:14], [this is as if to say that] the Torah abides only with one who mortifies himself in the tents of wisdom." And similarly Solomon said in his wisdom: "If you are slack in the day of adversity, your strength is small indeed" [Prov. 24:10]. He further said: "But my wisdom alone ('af) stayed with me" [Eccles. 2:9], [this is as if to say], "the wisdom that I learned in wrath ('af) has stayed with me."

15. The sages have said: "A covenant is established for whoever toils away at his study in the synagogue that he will not forget it soon." And whoever modestly toils away at his study in private will become wise, as it is said, "And wisdom is with the modest" [Prov. 11:2]. And whoever raises his voice while studying, his study will abide with him; but one who reads silently will soon forget.

16. Even though it is a commandment to study both in the day and in the night, a person learns most of his wisdom only at night. Therefore, he who wishes to acquire the crown of Torah should take heed of all his nights and not fritter away even one of them in sleeping and eating and drinking and conversation, and the like, but [should spend them] in study of Torah and words of wisdom. The sages have said: "The full measure of Torah is [acquired]

only at night, as it is said, 'Arise, sing out in the night' (Lam. 2:19)." And whoever occupies himself with the Torah at night, a thread of [divine] loving kindness is spun out for him during the day, as it is said, "By day the Lord shall command His loving kindness, and by night His song shall be with me, a prayer unto the Lord of my life" [Ps. 42:9]. And any house where words of Torah are not to be heard at night will be consumed by fire.

17. "Because he has despised the word of the Lord" [Num. 15:31]: this refers to one who has paid no attention at all to words of Torah. Similarly, whoever is able to occupy himself with Torah and does not so occupy himself, or whoever has read [the written Torah] and recited [the oral Torah] and has then turned aside to the vanities of this world and has set his study to the side and has abandoned it, is included among those who have despised the word of the Lord. The sages have said: "Whoever desists from the Torah on account of wealth will in the end desist from it on account of poverty. And whoever fulfills the Torah in a condition of poverty will in the end fulfill it in a condition of wealth."

18. And this matter is clearly set forth in the Torah, for it is said, "Because you did not serve the Lord your God in [a condition] of joy and gladness of heart, having abundance of all things, therefore you will serve your enemy which the Lord will send against you in [a condition] of hunger and thirst and nakedness and lacking all things, and he will place an iron yoke, etc." [Deut. 28:47–48]. And it is said, "That He might afflict you and try you to do good to you at your latter end" [Deut. 8:15].

CHAPTER 4

1. Torah should be taught only to a worthy student, whose deeds are fine, or to one of undetermined character. But if the student is walking in a path that is not good, he is to be brought back and guided in a straight path and examined, and afterward he is to be brought into the study house (*bet midrash*) and taught. The sages have said: "Whoever teaches a student who is not worthy, it is as if he cast a stone to Mercury, as it is said 'As one puts a stone into a sling, so is he that gives honor to a fool' [Prov. 26:8]; and there is no honor but the Torah, as it is said, 'The sages shall inherit honor' [Prov. 3:35]."

2. Similarly, a master (*rav*) who does not walk in a path that is good, even if he is a great sage and all the people are in need of him, he is not to be studied from until he returns to the good, as it is said, "For the priest's lips shall guard knowledge, and they shall seek Torah from his mouth, for he is [as] an angel of the Lord of Hosts" [Mal. 2:7]. The sages have said: "If the master resembles an angel of the Lord of Hosts, then they shall seek Torah from his mouth. But if not, then they shall not seek Torah from his mouth."

3. How is teaching to be conducted? The master sits in front and the students face him, surrounding him like a crown, so that they may all see the master and hear his words. And the master should not sit on a chair while the students sit on the ground, but let them all sit on the ground or all sit in chairs. Formerly, the teacher used to sit and the students would stand. But before the destruction of the Temple it became the practice of everyone to teach the students while they were sitting.

4. If the master teaches the students directly, let him do so. But if he teaches via an intermediary (*metargem*), the intermediary should stand between him and the students, and the master should address the intermediary, and the intermediary then declaim [what he heard] to all the students. And when [the students] pose a question to the intermediary, he [in turn] should pose it to the master; the master [thereupon] should reply to the intermediary, and the intermediary [in turn] reply to the questioner. The master should not raise his voice above the voice of the intermediary, nor should the intermediary raise his voice above the voice of the master when he poses a question to the master.

5. The intermediary is not permitted to detract from or add to or change [what the master said], unless the intermediary is the father or master of the sage. If the master tells the intermediary, "Thus did my master tell me" or "Thus did my revered father tell me," when the intermediary addresses these words to the people, he is to cite them in the name of the sage [quoted], and should mention the name of the master's father or master, and should say, "Thus did Rabbi so-and-so say." Even though the sage [when addressing the intermediary] did not mention the name [of his father or teacher, the reason he did not mention the name is] because one is forbidden to call one's master or father by his name.

6. If the master is teaching and the students do not understand, he should not get angry at them or chastise them, but should review and repeat the matter even one hundred times until they understand the depths of the law. Similarly, a student should not say "I understand" if he does not understand, but should ask again and again, even many times. And if the master gets angry at him or chastises him, he [the student] should say to him [the master]: "My master, it is Torah and I need to comprehend it, and my grasp is limited."

7. A student should not be embarrassed because of his fellow students who have comprehended the material after the first or second time [it was taught], while he does not comprehend until after [it has been taught] many times. For if he will be embarrassed on account of this matter, he will, as a result, enter and leave the study house without his having comprehended anything. Therefore the early sages have said: "The one who is embarrassed cannot learn, and the one who is irascible cannot teach."

8. When does the above apply: when the students have not understood the matter because of its profundity, or because their grasp is limited. But if it is

clear to the master that the students are negligent and slack in [their study] of words of Torah, and it for that reason that they do not understand, he is obliged to chastise them and shame them with words [of reproach] in order to sharpen their wits. Concerning this matter, the sages have said: "Cast fear into the students."

9. Therefore, it is not fitting for a master to act in a light-hearted manner before his students, nor may he jest in their presence, nor may he eat or drink with them, in order that his awe rest upon them thereby, and that they speedily comprehend him.

10. One does not ask a question to a master who has just entered the house of study until his mind has become composed. Nor should a student ask a question upon his entry [to the house of study], until he sits down and rests. Nor may two students ask questions at the same time. Nor may the master be questioned about a subject other [than the one they are studying], but only about the subject with which they are currently occupied, so he will not be embarrassed. And a master may try to mislead the students, both by his questions and the deeds he performs in their presence, in order to sharpen their wits and in order to know whether they remember what what he has taught them or not. And it need not be said that he has permission to ask them questions even concerning a subject with which they have not occupied themselves in order to spur them on.

11. One may not ask a question while standing, nor answer a question while standing. Nor [may questions be asked or answered] from a height or from a distance or while behind the elders. One may question the master only concerning the subject [with which they are currently occupied]; and one may ask a question only in a spirit of awe; and one may not ask about more than three laws in a particular subject.

12. Two [students] asked a question. One asked a question that is directly pertinent to the subject, while the other asked a question that is not directly pertinent to the subject, one responds to the question that is directly pertinent to the subject. [A question] about an actual case and [a question] about a legal ruling, one responds to [the question about] the actual case; [a question] about a legal ruling and [a question] about a [legal] midrash [interpretation of a scriptural verse], one responds to [the question about] the legal ruling; [a question] about a [legal] midrash and [a question] about a nonlegal matter, one responds to [the question about] the [legal] midrash; [a question] about a nonlegal matter and [a question] about an a fortiori inference, one responds to [the question about] the a fortiori inference; [a question] about an a fortiori inference and [a question] about a *gezerah shavah* [legal inference deriving from Scripture's use of the same phraseology in two different passages], one responds to [the question about] the a fortiori inference.

13. If there are two questioners—one is a sage and the other is a student, one responds to the sage; if one of the questioners is a student and the other is an ignorant person, one responds to the student. If both questioners were sages or both students or both ignorant men, and if they both asked questions about legal rulings or about judicial questions or about judicial decisions or about cases, the discretion now rests in the hands of the intermediary.

14. No one is permitted to sleep in the house of study. And whoever dozes in the house of study, his wisdom will be torn into tatters. As Solomon stated in his wisdom, "And drowsiness shall clothe one in tatters" [Prov. 23:21]. And one should converse in the house of study only about words of Torah. Even if one sneezes, one does not say "be of good health" to him in the house of study; and it need not be said [that one does not speak there] about other matters. And the sanctity of the house of study is greater than the sanctity of synagogues.

— 12 —

An Egyptian Woman Seeks to Rescue Her Husband from a Sufi Monastery

S. D. Goitein

Throughout the centuries we read about women described as Nazirites [individuals who commit themselves to certain ascetic practices], abstaining from wine and other alcoholic beverages, or as pious, devout, or saintly. In the following, the letter of a pious woman belonging to a humble class, finding herself in a very special situation, is translated. She is fighting not only for her faith and her children but also for the soul of her husband. This was the time [fourteenth century] when the influence of Sufism, Islamic mysticism, was at its highest, not only among the Muslim masses but also among the decimated remnants of the minority religions. Biographies of Sufi masters state occasionally that their mystical sessions were attended by non-Muslims, often with the result that the visitors were converted to Islam. This is reported, for instance, with regard to the classical Sufi author al-Qushayri (d. 1074); the eminent representative of Sufism, al-Sharani (d. 1565), boasts that many Jews were induced by him to embrace Islam.

Thus far, the participation of Jews in the mystical sessions of Sufi masters had been attested to only by Muslim sources. It is now corroborated by the missive translated in what follows. The Sufi master mentioned in the letter, al-Kurani, is no doubt Yusuf al-Aljami al-Kurani, who died in Cairo in January 1367. Consequently, the Nagid David [head of the Jewish community in Egypt], to whom the letter is addressed, can only be David II Maimonides, who followed his father Joshua ben [son of] Abraham II ben David I ben Abraham I ben Moses Maimonides in 1355 as head of the Jewish community in Egypt. The letter was therefore written during the years 1355–1367.

According to his biographers, Jamal ad-Din Yusuf ben Ali al-Kurani at-Tamliji al-Kurdi specialized in *taslik,* the education of fellow mystics, which is why Ibn Taghribirdi calls him Imam al-musallikin, the Master of the Trainers. He had a large following and supervised various *zawiyas* (convents of dervishes); his own zawiya was on the Qarafa al-sughra, the Muslim cemetery east of Cairo, between the town and the Muqattam mountain, the time-honored refuge of monks and mystics, referred to repeatedly in our letter as "the mountain." Al-Kurani renewed the *tariqa* (mystic way) of al-Junayd (d. 910), an early Sufi, who was of Persian origin and taught his followers to adhere to the principle of strict poverty. They were therefore called, as in our letter, *fuqara,* the poor ones, one of the synonyms designating Muslim mystics in general. When the sultan offered him a pension for himself and his followers, he refused to accept it as inconsistent with his teachings.

Al-Sharani reports many strange stories about him, some of which may be given here in illustration of the general atmosphere in which these Sufi masters lived. When he went out of his cell, his eyes were like burning coals and everyone upon whom his gaze fell was immediately transformed into a superior creature. Once, when he emerged from a seclusion of forty days, his gaze fell on a dog, who instantly became a sort of dog saint, to whom all other dogs flocked as followers; even men visited this creature in order to have their wishes fulfilled through the blessing by its holiness. After its death it was buried by some God-inspired people and its tomb was visited by fellow dogs, just as people did the tombs of human saints. Al-Kurani never allowed the convent to be opened to visitors, except when they brought presents for the fakirs. Asked about this seemingly materialistic attitude, he explained it thus: the dearest thing the fakirs have is their time, whereas money is the dearest thing to worldly people; we can spend our time for them, only if they spend their money for us. Once some of the sultan's attendants, who had fallen into disgrace, fled to his zawiya; the sultan came in person to the saint asking him to attend to his own affairs and not to meddle in matters of the state. In order to prove that the refugees had become converted, al-Kurani asked one of them to change a stone column into gold by his mere word. This was effected in the presence of the sultan, who became convinced that the influence of such a saint could only be beneficial. Al-Kurani also wrote a book on the initiation of new followers.

It was under the guidance of this sort of person that Basir, the bell maker, a Jew from Cairo, became infatuated by the Sufic way of life on the mountain in the desert near the town, amid a crown of mendicants. He forsook his wife and three small children, and intended even to sell his house, which was, of course, in the Jewish quarter, and to take up permanent residence in the Sufi convent. The Sufis lived in their convents with their families and it obviously was also Basir's intention to do the same. At this juncture, Basir's wife sent an urgent appeal to the Nagid David, the head of the Jewish community, "to go after" her husband and to bring him back to the fulfillment of his duties as a Jew and a parent. The reasons for urging his return are not without interest. To devote oneself to *tatawwu,* supererogatory divine worship, was, of course, highly meritorious from the Jewish point of view, but she argued, the Muslim mendicants had only the *zahir,* the outward appearance of piety, not the *batin,* the inner, the true, essence of religion. In any case, supererogatory works were useless, so long as a Jew did not fulfill his basic duties of attending the three daily services and of studying the divine Law. The proper place for voluntary devotion was the synagogue; furthermore, if the family was to move to the mountain, the children would be unable to visit the Jewish school, to study the Torah, and finally, there would be the danger that Basir, together with his three children, would be converted to Islam.

It may seem strange that Basir's wife, in her petition to the head of the Jewish community, dwells mainly on the religious aspects of the matter, while she puts her complaints about her solitude and her care for her hungry children in second place. In integrated Jewish society, however, as may be observed even today, it is precisely the mother of the house who, though participating only indirectly in the religious life, watches most eagerly over its proper functioning; it is she who sees to it that the boys study under good teachers, and it is she who sends the sometimes lax husband to synagogue early in the morning or in the late afternoon after he comes home tired from work. Moreover, Basir's wife evidently had discussed these religious questions, which were the source of all her trouble, with her husband, whom she clearly matched, if not surpassed, in judgment.

It can hardly be assumed that she wrote the letter herself, for she would scarcely have had an opportunity to develop the fluent handwriting of the letter; it is problematic that she knew how to write at all. But there are far too many mistakes in it to assume that a learned person, such as the scribe of a rabbinic court, had written it for her. Thus, we have to surmise that a clerk in a business house or some other person of moderate education wrote it for her, reproducing her own words, for the letter bears a very personal character. Although abounding in the usual deferential phrases, it is rather outspoken. The petitioner no doubt had direct access to the Nagid, for she reminds him that he had promised her some medicine for her boy, who suffered from an earache; we learn here, by the way, that R. David ben Joshua, just as most of his forefathers, was also a doctor. Clearly she realized that the Nagid was averse to becoming involved in a dispute with the militant Sufis, and hence she reminded him that since he was in charge of a whole region, he could not fail to succeed in this matter, if he really tried. She uses many Hebrew words and phrases, just as an illiterate Yemenite woman would do, when talking about religious matters, and she repeats herself frequently, as a person in grief is wont to do. The letter is a last attempt to save a desperate situation; all in all, it is a very human document, not without historical value.

Editor's Note

The previous introductory remarks, and the translation that follows, are from the late S. D. Goitein's *A Mediterranean Society,* his classic study of Jewish life under Islam in the Middle Ages. Goitein's five-volume study was based upon the documents of the Cairo Geniza, a treasure-trove of historical materials that was discovered in a Cairo synagogue in the late nineteenth century. The editor has added, in brackets, several explanatory comments in the introduction, edited it in minor ways for the purposes of this volume, and supplied the bibliography at the end of the introduction. The translation is found in S. D. Goitein, *A Mediterranean Society* (Berkeley and Los Angeles: University of California Press, 1988), vol. 5, pp. 473–474. By permission of the University of California Press.

Further Reading

The Islamic cultural world in which this text is situated is studied in S. D. Goitein, *A Mediterranean Society*. Concerning Jewish life under Islam more generally, see Bernard Lewis, *The Jews of Islam* (Princeton: Princeton University Press, 1984). With respect to the lives of Jewish women in the medieval period, see the essays by Judith R. Baskin, Renée Levine Melammed, Howard Adelman, and Chava Weissler, in Judith R. Baskin, ed., *Jewish Women in Historical Perspective* (Detroit: Wayne State University Press, 1991).

A Wife's Petition

In your name, You, Merciful.
To the high Seat of our lord, the Nagid, may his splendor be exalted and his honor be great.

The maidservant, the wife of Basir, the bell maker, kisses the ground and submits that she has on her neck three children because her husband has become completely infatuated with [life on] the mountain with al-Kurani, in vain and to no purpose, a place where there is no Torah, no prayer, and no mention of God's name in truth. He goes up the mountain and mingles with the mendicants, although these have only the semblance, but not the essence, of religion.

The maidservant is afraid there may be there some bad man who may induce her husband to forsake the Jewish faith, taking with him the three children.

The maidservant almost perishes because of her solitude and her search for food for the little ones. It is her wish that our Master go after her husband and take the matter up with him according to his unfailing wisdom. What the maidservant entreats him to do is not beyond his power, nor the high degree of his influence.

The only thing that the maidservant wants is that her husband cease to go up the mountain and that he may show mercy toward the little ones. If he wishes to devote himself to God, he may do so in the synagogue, regularly attending morning, afternoon, and evening prayers, and listening to the words of the Torah, but he should not occupy himself with worthless things.

Furthermore, he presses the maidservant to sell their house, to leave the Jewish community, and to stay on the mountain, [which would mean that] the little ones would cease to study the Torah. [It would be helpful] if our Lord gave orders to the maidservant in that matter and instructed her concerning it, for his wisdom is unfailing. And Peace.

Our lord—may God prolong his life—is in charge of a vast region; thus his high aspiration could not fail to hinder the above mentioned from going up the mountain and to induce him to attend the synagogue and to occupy himself with the upkeep of the family.

P.S. Our lord has promised the little one a medicine for the ear, for he suffers from it. There is no harm in trying it out, seeing that even the barber is playing with it without experience and mercy.

13

A Monastic-like Setting for the Study of Torah

Ephraim Kanarfogel

Sefer Ḥuqqei ha-Torah (The Book of the Statutes of the Torah; hereafter referred to as *SHH*) is a detailed treatise describing a bilevel educational system. Problems in education on both the elementary and advanced levels are identified and addressed. The most novel provision of this document calls for the establishment of quasi-monastic study halls for *perushim* (lit., those who are separate), dedicated students who would remain totally immersed in their Torah studies for a period of seven years. Elementary-level students would be taught in separate structures for a period of up to seven years, in preparation for their initiation into the ranks of the *perushim*. The formal initiation took place when the student was thirteen, although it could be postponed (or perhaps renounced) until age sixteen.

SHH is extant in only one version, which consists of three sections. There is some overlap between the sections, even as a number of discrepancies of varying significance can be detected. *SHH* is never cited in subsequent medieval or modern rabbinic literature, although there are two later texts that display limited similarities.

Since the publication of *SHH* by Moritz Guedemann in 1880, more than twenty-five scholars have discussed and debated the date, provenance, and purpose of the work. The attempts to identify the place and time in which *SHH* originated have essentially employed two methods. The first was to focus on terms or phrases in the text that either ruled out or suggested a particular locale. For example, the text notes that a particular custom of Torah study on the Sabbath was in vogue in northern France (*minhag Zarefatim*), which suggests that *SHH* itself was probably not composed there. On the other hand, since *SHH* refers to unnamed *geonim* (ancient rabbinic teachers in Babylonia) as the originators of certain practices, and refers also to practices of R. Sa'adyah Gaon and the Babylonian exilarch, it is possible that the text stems from a geonic milieu.

Another method employed by scholars has been to identify institutions within the text. The *midrash ha-gadol* (great study hall), which was to be maintained by a network of surrounding communities, is akin to the *yeshivot* (study academies) of southern France as described by Benjamin of Tudela in his travelogue *Mas'at Binyamin*. Norman Golb has tried to show that the *midrash ha-gadol* existed in northern France, with one such school located in Rouen. Gershom Scholem and Isadore Twersky have identified the text as Provençal, based on the claim that the *perushim* who studied in the *midrash ha-gadol* were a prototype of Provençal talmudic scholars (and mystics) in the twelfth century.

Complicating the effort to ascertain the provenance of SHH is the question first raised by Y. Loeb in 1881 (in his review of Guedemann), as to whether SHH was actually put into effect in any community, or whether it was simply a utopian suggestion. Reflecting the general consensus of modern scholarship, Salo Baron wrote that "[SHH] doubtless originated in one of the northern communities under the impact of Provençal mysticism or of German-Jewish Pietism of the school of Yehudah the Pious and Eleazar of Worms." Baron also concluded that statutes such as the consecration of the sons of *kohanim* (priests) and *leviyyim* (Levites) for Torah study, and the mandate for the establishment of a permanent group of scholars through which the community could fulfill its obligations to study "were the expression of pious wishes formulated in one or another pietistic conventicle, but [were] never formally enacted by any communal authority."

If the document is in fact of Provençal origin, it is likely that it was actually in effect or at least representative of active institutions and practices. The educational organization outlined in SHH on both the elementary and advanced levels is quite similar to that of Provence in the twelfth and thirteenth centuries. If, however, SHH is of Ashkenazic origin, the document was probably more of a theoretical blueprint. There is nothing in medieval Ashkenaz comparable to the highly organized and communally funded educational institutions described here.

Although all attempts to identify the origins of SHH with certainty may prove fruitless, the connection between SHH and the German Pietists merits further investigation. Isadore Twersky has succinctly summarized the essential provisions of SHH as follows:

> It strives, by a variety of stipulations and suggestions, to achieve maximum learning on the part of the student and maximum dedication on the part of the teacher. It operates with such progressive notions as determining the occupational aptitude of students, arranging small groups in order to enable individual attention, grading the classes in order not to stifle individual progress. The teacher is urged to encourage free debate and discussion among students, arrange periodic review . . . utilize the vernacular in order to facilitate comprehension. Above all, he is warned against insincerity and is exhorted to be totally committed to his noble profession. (Twersky, p. 25)

Several of these measures are suggested by the thirteenth-century *Sefer Hasidim*, as well. For example, a strong concern of the German Pietists was that students of different abilities were typically not separated within the Ashkenazic educational process. Such insensitivity could keep the brighter student from developing fully, and would certainly cause the weaker student to become frustrated. SHH also insists in six distinct passages that teachers not allow their own affairs to lead to distractions while they are teaching. Thus, the *melammed* (teacher) could not assume any additional employment, nor could the academy head engage in conversation when it was time for him to teach. Five sections in *Sefer Hasidim* express the same concerns, in similar terms.

SHH advises that academy heads should not conduct their classes in their own home but rather in the dormitory of the *perushim*, lest they remain constantly in the presence of their wives. The academy heads should remain with the *perushim* for the entire week and return to their homes on Friday. After the Sabbath, they should again return to the abode of the *perushim*. This procedure was to be adopted so that the academy heads could avoid sexual thoughts while they were teaching. In *Sefer Hasidim*, the *rav* (rabbi) is advised to set up a *beit midrash* (study hall) on the far side of his home. This arrangement is suggested to prevent the students from gazing at the female members of the household as they enter and leave the home. If this precaution is not taken, "their Torah study will be accomplished through sinning." Although the section in *Sefer Hasidim* is designed to shield the student from sexual thoughts, and the section in SHH seeks to protect the teacher, the problem addressed and the solution offered are essentially the same. Indeed, the arrangement in *Sefer Hasidim* would also prevent the academy head from being in his wife's presence, just as the separate dormitory for the students described in SHH would prevent them from gazing at women.

Sefer Hasidim advocates that the children of *kohanim* and *leviyyim* in particular be sent away to study Torah for a lengthy period of time, until they have learned enough to answer all questions and to resolve all doubts. These notions are based on *Sefer Hasidim*'s interpretation of Deuteronomy 33:9–10, "[The Levite] . . . will not recognize his parents or his brothers or his sons, since for so many years he has remained with his teacher. . . . They will remain [with their teachers] until 'They shall teach Your statutes to Jacob and Your Torah to Israel.' " SHH is, to my knowledge, the only other medieval text that interprets these verses in this fashion, and advocates a similar ideal. The beginning passages of SHH direct that the sons of *kohanim* and *leviyyim* are to be consecrated as youngsters to study Torah and to become *perushim*. They are to remain separated from everyone including their families for seven years, while they study. One of the two *gematria* (numerical exegesis) derivations in SHH is also found in *Sefer Hasidim*.

Another possible key to the origin of SHH that has not been probed sufficiently lies in the practices and phrases that appear to be similar to Christian monastic ideals. The *perushim*, who are chosen originally through some form of parental consecration, ensconce themselves in their fortresses of study away from all worldly temptations. The devote all of their time to the holy work of God (*melekhet shamayim*), and serve as representatives of the rest of the community in this endeavor. It is possible that SHH represents an attempt to recast the discipline and devotion of Christian monastic education, which was certainly known to, and perhaps admired by, Jews, in a form compatible with Jewish practices and values.

SHH is found in Oxford Bodleian Opp. 342, fols. 196–199 (Neubauer 873). The manuscript was copied in 1309, in a German hand, and our translation has been made from the manuscript. The Hebrew text of SHH was published by M. Guedemann, *Geschichte des Erziehungswesens und der Cultur der abendlandischen Juden wahrend des Mittelalters* (Vienna: A. Hoelder, 1880), vol. 1, pp. 91–106; Meir Ish-Shalom in *Beit ha-Talmud* 1 (1881): 61–62, 91–95; Simcha Assaf, *Meqorot le-Toledot ha-Hinnukh be-Yisra'el* (Tel Aviv: Dvir, 1954), vol. 1, pp. 9–16; Nathan Morris, *Le-Toledot ha-Hinnukh shel Am Yisra'el* (1960; reprint Jerusalem: Rubin Mass, 1977), vol. 2, pp. 417–23 (with punctuation, and a photo-offset of the manuscript); Norman Golb, *Le-Toledot ha-Yehudim be-Ir Rouen Bimei ha-Benayim* (Jerusalem: Dvir, 1976), pp. 181–84; and in my *Jewish Education and Society in the High Middle Ages* (Detroit: Wayne State University Press, 1992), pp. 106–115.

Further Reading

For a brief assessment of the main provisions of SHH and the problems inherent in identifying its origins, see Yosef Dan, "Sefer Hukkei ha-Torah," *Encyclopedia Judaica*, vol. 14, pp. 1099–1100, and Simcha Assaf, *Meqorot le-Toledot ha-Hinnukh be-Yisra'el*, vol. 1, pp. 6–9. Assaf also notes the possible reflections of SHH in subsequent rabbinic literature. The suggestion that SHH originates in the geonic period is made by David Kaufmann in his *Gesammelte Schriften*, vol. 2 (Frankfurt: J. Kaufmann, 1910), pp. 208–15.

Isadore Loeb's discussion of whether SHH is a theoretical blueprint or a description of a series of actual practices is found in *Revue des études juives* 2 (1881): 159–60. For further consideration of this issue, and for an analysis of the affinities between SHH and Provençal institutions, see Isadore Twersky, *Rabad of Posquières*, 2nd ed. (Philadelphia: Jewish Publication Society 1980), pp. 25–29. The ascetic nature of SHH and the parallels to Provençal mystical circles was also noted by Gershom Scholem, *Reshit ha-Qabbalah bi-Provence* (Tel Aviv: 1948), pp. 84–91, and see also Salo Baron, *A Social and Religious History of the Jews* (Philadelphia: Jewish Publication Society, 1958), vol. 6, pp. 140–41, 395.

For the possible northern French and German dimensions of SHH, see M. Guedemann, *Geschichte des Erziehungswesens*, vol. 1, pp. 264–72; Norman Golb, *Toledot ha-Yehudim be-Ir Rouen*, pp. 36–40. My *Jewish Education and Society in the High Middle Ages*, pp. 40, 55–56, 101–5, 128–29 n. 46, 151 n. 68, focuses on the affinities to German Pietism in particular, as well as the monastic aspects. Regarding Christian influence on SHH, see also Ivan Marcus, *Rituals of Childhood* (New Haven: Yale University Press, 1996), p. 154 n. 84; David Berger, *The Jewish-Christian Debate in the High Middle Ages* (Philadelphia: Jewish Publication Society,

1979), 27 n. 71; and Lynn Thorndike, "Elementary and Secondary Education in the Middle Ages," *Speculum* 15 (October 1940): 400–8.

The Book of the Statutes of the Torah

[Rhymed Preamble.] This is the Book of the Statutes of the Torah by the ancients, dedicated to the students and to the rabbinic teachers, as delineated by the early scholars. These are the statutes and the laws and the teachings, to understand and to instruct, since "the words of the Lord are pure words" [Ps. 12:7]. They were instituted by the wise men of yore, fearers of the Lord, with the approbation of the geonim, in regard to the Torah, to prepare it and to support it, and to increase it in Israel and Judah. And they shall be received by the children of Jacob the unblemished as an eternal law, for all their generations.

The first statute. It is incumbent on the priests and the Levites to separate one of their sons and consecrate him to Torah study, even while he is still in his mother's womb. For they were commanded this at Mount Sinai as it is written, "they are given to Me" [Num. 8:16], that is, from their mothers' wombs. And it is written, "they shall teach your statutes to Jacob" [Deut. 33:10], and it is said "they will teach my people knowledge" [Ezek. 44:23], and it is said "for the priest's lips should keep knowledge" [Mal. 2:7]. Similarly, all the children of Israel shall separate [one] from among their sons, because Jacob made such a separation, as it is written, "all that You shall give to me I will surely give the tenth [double verb] to You" [Gen. 28:22]. The verse speaks of two tithings, a tithe of money and a tithe of sons. And so said Ezekiel [23:37], "also they have caused their sons, whom they bore to me, to pass to them to be devoured." This teaches that they would consecrate from among their sons, when they were in their mother's womb. "Whom they bore to me" means to my Name.

Statute Two. To establish a study hall for the separated students (*perushim*) who accept upon themselves the yoke of Torah near the synagogue. This house would be called the great study hall. For just as cantors are appointed to discharge for the many their obligation in prayer, full-time students are appointed to study Torah without end, to discharge for the many their obligation in Torah study, and the work of heaven will thereby not fall behind. *Perushim* are those students who have been consecrated to Torah study. They are called *perushim* in the language of the Mishnah, and nazirites (*nezirim*) in the language of the Bible, as it is said "and I raised up of your sons for prophets, and of your young men for nazirites" [Amos 2:11]. And separation leads to purity as it is said, "Sanctify yourselves, therefore, and be holy" [Lev. 20:7], and it says "he cleansed it and he hallowed it" [Lev. 19:19].

Statute Three. The *perushim* may not leave the house for seven years. There they will eat and drink, and there they will sleep, and they should not speak in the study hall. Wisdom will not reside in the student who comes and goes, but only in one who exerts himself in the tent of Torah, as it is said, "This is the Torah, when a man dies in a tent" [Num. 19:14]. And one who speaks of idle things in the synagogue and study hall transgresses a precept, as it is written, "you must revere my sanctuary" [Lev. 19:30]. Just as a person consecrates one of his assets to heaven, so too he should consecrate one of his sons to Torah study. If the *perushim* leave the study hall before seven years, they must pay a set fine. A support for this policy is "and they that handle [lit., restrain themselves in] the Torah knew me not" [Jer. 2:8], which teaches that they imprison themselves in order to know the statutes of the Almighty and his teachings.

Statute Four. To collect from all Israel twelve deniers a year for the service of the study hall, in place of the half-shekel that our forefathers brought for the service of the Temple and for the purpose of the sacrifices. So too, we are obligated to bring a donation to support the study hall each year, to support the students and to pay the rabbinic teachers and assistants (*meturgemanim*) and to purchase books. Just as the sacrifices brought peace to the world, so do Torah scholars, as it is said, "And all your children shall be taught of the Lord, and great shall be the peace of your children" [Isa. 54:13], and it is said, "Those who love your Torah have great peace, and nothing can make them stumble" [Ps. 119:165].

Statute Five. To appoint a supervisor over the students who will evaluate their studies, and assess their intelligence and indolence. For the [elementary-level] teachers (*melammedim*) are comparable to workers who yearn constantly for the falling of the shadows of the evening. And this is a proper custom, to fulfill "and you shall be guiltless before the Lord and before Israel" [Num. 32:22]. Therefore, the *melammedim* should not teach in their homes, but only in the study hall for the [purpose of fulfilling the] precept. This house is called the small study hall. This supervisor is called to [assist] the *melammedim*. And if the supervisor sees amongst the youths a young man who is difficult and dense, he should bring him to his father and say to him: "The Lord should privilege your son to [do] good deeds, because he is too difficult for Torah study," lest the brighter students fall behind because of him. And his money should not be taken gratuitously, lest he [the *melammed*] be considered like a thief, and perhaps the young man might go to a different *melammed* and succeed there with him.

Statute Six. The *melammedim* should not accept more than ten students in one class. Even though the rabbis said [*Bava Batra* 21a] that a teacher of children teaches twenty-five, that was only in the land of Israel, whose atmosphere makes people wise, and at a time when Israel was securely in its land and they had the upper hand. For a free intellect is high and strong and clear, and can receive intelligence and wisdom since it is not subjugated to another. But an intellect that is subjugated is low and weak and dry, and cannot receive intelligence and wisdom. Since it is subjugated to hard and stubborn masters, all its efforts go to a person "who does not take care of it" [Jon. 4:10], and it is constantly burdened by difficult tasks. They cast fear and dread on it, and anger drives out wisdom. Therefore, the *melammedim* are warned not to accept more than ten children. Support for this policy [comes from] "The Almighty stands in the congregation of God" [Ps. 82:1]. A congregation is ten, as we learn from "in all places where I cause My Name to be pronounced, I will come to you" [Exod. 20:21]. The *gematria* equivalent of [the Hebrew word] "I will come" is ten. Just as the rabbis made boundaries and reinforcements for the words of the Torah, so too the geonim made boundaries for all the words of the rabbis.

Statute Seven. It is incumbent upon the *melammedim* not to teach the children by heart, but from the written text [of the Pentateuch], so that they can translate for them the Aramaic translation of the Pentateuch into the vernacular, just as they translate the Hebrew [text of the Pentateuch itself] into the vernacular, in order to facilitate the reading of the Talmud and to enter them into [a discussion of] the *halakhah* [law]. Onkelos translated the Torah into Aramaic because the residents of Babylonia spoke it, and he wished to impart the Torah to them in their language. So too, R. Sa'adyah Gaon explained the Torah in Arabic in order that they might understand, because they did not understand the holy tongue. The scholars who were students of the Exilarch were accustomed to reading the [weekly Torah] portion on the Sabbath, the biblical text two times, and the [Aramaic] translation once. The biblical text was read twice because of the belovedness of the Torah, since every beloved thing is read twice. The Aramaic translation was read once in order to cause the Torah to by heard by women and the unlearned, so that perhaps awe [of the Divine] would enter their hearts. Similarly, the custom of northern France was to read the portion on the Sabbath two times, and to translate once in the language of the land.

Statute Eight. To teach the young men the text of the Aramaic translation of the Pentateuch in the vernacular, in order that they will be able to read the text of the Talmud easily and be prepared to engage in [discussion of the] *halakhah*, so that the *melammedim* will be able to work with the children on the [interpretation of the talmudic] *sugya* [legal passage], and not on the meaning [of the Aramaic words themselves], since the children will be used to the meaning of the Aramaic translation of the Pentateuch.

Statute Nine. The *melammedim* should accustom the young men to ask questions of each other every day toward evening, to sharpen them and make them intellectually agile, and to increase their knowledge, as it is said, "Iron sharpens iron, so one man sharpens another" [Prov. 27:17]. And therefore, those young men who do not know how respond to each other properly should feel embarrassed, owing to their fear of the *melammed*.

Statute Ten. The *melammedim* should review with the young men on Friday what they learned during the week, and what they learned the prior week. On Rosh Ḥodesh [the New Moon], they should review what was learned in this [past] month, and in the prior month. In Tishrei, they should review what was learned during the summer months, and in Nisan they should review what was learned during the winter months, lest they forget anything, and they should remember as much as possible. As we have been taught [Menaḥot 99b], one who forgets one chapter or one law violates two negative precepts, namely, "take heed of yourself and keep your soul diligently, lest you forget the things which your eyes have seen, and lest they depart from your heart all the days of your lives, but teach them to your children" [Deut. 4:9].

Statute Eleven. The *melammedim* should teach the young men during the winter nights, from the beginning of Ḥeshvan until the beginning of Nisan, for one-quarter of the evening, since the days during the winter are short. And each and every young man should contribute his share of the oil used for lighting.

Statute Twelve. The *melammedim* should not do any [outside] work or any scribal activities during the period of their studies, lest they be distracted from their studies, and they will not be able to fulfill their commitment. They should be free, because they are obligated to do the work of heaven faithfully. The procedure for dealing with students is according to their wisdom, and according to the officers who are appointed [as supervisors] over their work.

End

The ancients ordained that a study hall should be purchased near the synagogue, and the two should be attached, a place to pray and a place for study, based on a midrash [of the verse] "They go from strength to strength, they appear before the Almighty in Zion" [Ps. 84:8]. The places of the *perushim* shall be rented, and each student (*parush*) shall contribute his share to the rental of the house, just as they contribute to the salary of the rabbinic teacher and his assistant. The house itself should be purchased [using monies] from the charity fund of the community. But it is made available to the perushim and to wealthy people [who wish to contribute] for a rental fee. The rental fee will go to the academy head or to pay the teaching assistant.

They also ordained that the study hall for the *perushim* should be established in the major city of a jurisdiction. All the surrounding communities should send yearly contributions for the benefit of the study hall, to support the students, and to pay the teachers and the assistants. This study hall is called the great study hall, from whence statutes and laws emanate in Israel.

They also ordained that the heads of the academies should not establish study halls in their own homes, but only in the houses of the *perushim*, lest they be found too frequently in proximity to their wives. They should remain there for all the weekdays, returning to their homes on Friday in order to celebrate [the Sabbath] with their wives and families. When the Sabbath ends, they should return to the houses of the *perushim*. And they should have changes of clothing, one to be worn in their own homes, and one to be worn while serving in holiness in the houses of study. All of this [was ordained] lest they become involved in sexual activity and have an emission. Their intention was to speak words of Torah in purity. The academy heads should not receive homeowners [as students], because their learning was not of paramount importance to them since they also had to think about their [business] affairs, but only students with no household responsibilities, who could be involved [solely] with study. Assistants should be appointed to recite the *halakhah* two or three times, so that it should flow freely in their mouths.

And they also ordained that the academy heads not be officers, that is, if the academy head has forty students, they should appoint for him four assistants, one for ten students. When the academy head leaves the synagogue in the morning, he should come immediately to the study hall, that is, he should not speak [to anyone] in between, and he should explain the *halakhah* according to its meaning.

The ancients ordained that [a father] should consecrate his firstborn son while he is still in his mother's womb. Support for this practice [comes] from the verse, "Before I formed you in the belly I knew you, and before you emerged from the womb I sanctified you" [Jer. 1:5]. And this is the meaning of [the liturgical phrase] "He who sanctified the friend from the womb." This was Abraham, for we interpret "knowing" [in this manner]. Regarding Jeremiah it is written "before I formed you in the womb I knew you" and regarding Abraham it is written "For I know him" [Gen. 18:19], namely, [that I knew him] already. Just as later on [regarding Jeremiah,] he was sanctified from the womb, so too here he [Abraham] was sanctified from the womb. [The father] accepts upon himself and says: "If my wife gives birth to a male, he shall be consecrated to the Lord, and he will study His Torah day and night." On the eighth day, after the child has entered the covenant of circumcision, the child is placed on a spread, a copy of the Pentateuch is placed near his head, and he is blessed by the elders of the community or the academy heads. And this is how they bless him, from "And the Almighty shall grant you" until "and those who bless you shall be blessed" [Gen. 27:28–29]. The academy head shall place his hands on him and on the Pentateuch and say, "this one shall learn what is written in this," three times, and "this one shall observe what is written in this," three times, "in order that the Lord's Torah shall be in your mouth" [Exod. 13:9], "this book of the Torah shall never depart out of your mouth" [Josh. 1:8]. The father should make a festive meal, celebrating both the circumcision and the separation (*perishut*), as it is written regarding Hannah, "and he will dwell there forever" [1 Sam. 1:22].

And it was ordained regarding the *melammedim,* that a head *melammed* can gather up to one hundred young men to teach them Torah, and take in for this one hundred *litrin*. He then hires for them ten *melammedim* for eighty *litrin,* and the remaining *litrin* will be his share. He does not teach any child but is the officer and supervisor over the [other] *melammedim,* to evaluate their teaching. He rents a large house for them, so that they can teach in the rooms and attics. Each and every young man will pay his share of the rental of the house. This house is called the small study hall. They remain there studying for seven years, [two years] the Pentateuch, two years the Prophets and Hagiographa, and three years the smaller tractates. They then go to the great study hall, which stands near the synagogue, to study the larger tractates in front of the head of the academy, and they remain there for seven years, in accordance with the statute of the *perushim*.

And they also ordained that the academy heads should not be officers. This means that if there are forty students before the academy head, four assistants must be appointed, one for every ten students. When the academy head leaves the synagogue, he should proceed immediately to the study hall, that is, he should not speak in the interim. He should explain the basic meaning of the *halakhah* and the assistants will follow his presentation, without changing the order. When the teacher concludes his interpretation, the assistants and the students will leave his presence and go to the [smaller] rooms and garrets. Each and every assistant will have the ten students for whom he is responsible, and he will repeat the *halakhah* twice for his students, after which they will go to eat. When they leave the dining table, they will review the *halakhah* a third time, and they will then return and sit before the teacher. The teacher will explain another *halakhah* to them, and they will leave his presence and, according to the procedure followed in the morning, review this *halakhah* twice. If they have the time, they will review the *halakhah* of the morning and of the evening together. This statute shall be in effect from Nisan through Tishrei. In the winter, the teacher will explain [the *halakhah*] in the morning as we have described, and once more when he leaves the synagogue at night. They will leave his presence and review twice before eating [dinner]. After they finish eating, they will review the *halakhah* a third time and they will review the *halakhah* of the morning and the *halakhah* of the evening together, and they will go to sleep. If the students wish to review their studies all night, they may do so. The rabbis said [*Avodah Zarah* 3b]: There is no joyous expression of Torah study except at night, as it is said, "The Lord commands his kindness in the daytime, and in night his song shall be with me" [Ps. 42:9], and it says "He gives songs in the night" [Job 35:10].

And the rabbis further ordained that the elders of the community should undertake the holy work on the Sabbath, to explicate the Torah of the Lord, to remove obstacles and eliminate pitfalls, in order to remind others of the words of the living God. And this is how the rabbis explained [the verse] "six days shall you labor and do all your work, but the seventh day is a Sabbath to your Lord" [Exod. 20:9–10], meaning in the Name of your Lord. For the expression of resting is applicable to man, who becomes tired and weary from his activities but this condition does not exist regarding the Creator, as it written, "He does not become tired or weary, there is no searching of his understanding" [Isa. 40:28]. Therefore the explanation of "to your Lord" is "in the Name of the Lord," to be involved in the holy work, to explicate the Torah of the Almighty, to remove obstacles from the community, to increase merits and righteousness in their midst, and to lead them along the correct path. This is the regimen of the great ones who are close to the royal court, to be involved in the work of the king for the six days of productivity and on the seventh day to be involved in Torah. They should remember the words of the living God and fulfill them, as it is said, "in order that the Lord's Torah shall be in your mouth" for at least one day of the week. And it is said, "The book of this Torah shall not depart out of your mouth, and you should meditate in it day and night."

How are young men taught, and how are the *melammedim* informed about their teaching program?

The rabbis said, "A five-year-old [should learn] Scripture" [*Avot* 5:21]. A person gives his son to Torah study under the direction of the melammed when he is five years old, on Rosh Ḥodesh Nisan, which is a propitious time for all things as the rabbis said [Midrash *Tanḥuma, parashat Noaḥ*], "He brings out the prisoners into prosperity" [Ps. 68:7], this is Nisan which is propitious for all things, neither too cold nor too warm. He informs the *melammed* of the extent of his teaching in explicit terms: "I am telling you that you will teach my son during this month the structure of the letters, during the second month their vocalization, during the third month the combining of letters into words, and from then on, 'let the pure one come and be involved in the study of purities, in the book of Leviticus.' If not, you will be paid as a furloughed worker. Each and every month you will add to my son['s knowledge]. If my son learns half of one [Torah] portion this month, he should complete it the next month. From Tammuz to Tishrei, he should learn the portion completely, in Hebrew, each week. From Tishrei to Nisan, he should [also] learn the translation into the vernacular. This is during the child's sixth year. In the second year [of study], which is the child's seventh year, he should learn the Aramaic translation [of the Torah] from the written text and not by heart, and the Aramaic translation should be translated into the vernacular as [is done for] the Hebrew. In years eight and nine, the Prophets and Hagiographa [should be taught]."

The rabbis said, "A ten-year old [should learn] Mishnah." At that age, they should expose the young man to *Gemara*, tractate *Berakhot* and the small tractates that are listed in *Seder Mo'ed*, for three years, and "in the fourth year, it shall be holy for the Lord" [Lev. 19:24], which is the child's thirteenth year.

The rabbis said, "A thirteen-year-old for [the performance of] precepts." Their words are supported by [the verse], "I have formed this people for myself, they shall relate my praise" [Isa. 43:21]. The *gematria* equivalent of the word "this" (*zu*) is thirteen. They are worthy of being counted in a quorum of the community and to pray, and they can be counted among the numbers of the perushim. The father shall take his son the *parush* and encourage him with good words, "You are fortunate that you have merited to do the holy work," and he shall be entered into the house that is designated for the *perushim*. The obligation of separation (*perishut*) does not begin until he reaches the age of sixteen. [The father] brings him before the head of the academy and he lays his hands upon him saying, "This is consecrated to the Lord." And he says to his son, "I am directing to here that which you would have consumed in my house, for I have consecrated you to Torah study." And he will remain there for seven years, to learn the larger tractates.

The rabbis also said [*Avot* 1:17], "the main thing is not study but deeds" and also "one who does more and one who does less [are both meritorious], as long as his intention is for the sake of heaven" [*Berakhot* 5b]. The explanation is that the rabbis taught these things to the masses, as a means of drawing them nearer to faith and awe. Support for their words [comes from the verse] "And now Israel what does the Lord your God require of you but to fear the Lord your God" [Deut. 10:12]. Since the people are pursuing their livelihoods, it is sufficient for them to embrace faith. But the *perushim* can wed themselves to both, to study and to deeds. The academy heads should also adhere to a teaching program. The order of *Mo'ed* [should be studied] for two years, the order of *Neziqin* for two years, and the order of *Qodashim* for two years. All of the instruction should be in Gemara, whether they are dedicated to study of the simple meaning of the text (*peshat*), or whether they are dedicated to the study of Tosafot. The heads of the academies should not linger in the synagogue for morning prayer until the prayer [service] ends, but only until the Great Sanctification (*qedushah rabbah*), so that the students will have time to review what they have learned.

The end of the Book of the Statutes of the Torah.
Blessed be the Merciful One who has aided us.

14

Religious Practice among Italian Jewish Women

Howard Tzvi Adelman

Fasting

Like several rabbis before him, Abraham Yagel (1553–c.1623) was greatly concerned for the consequences of a woman's neglecting any of her duties to her husband, home, and family. In a fascinating record of early-modern Italian Jewish women's spirituality, he explicitly singled out for rebuke women who adopted certain special religious practices, such as regimens of fasting. He did not use precedents to explain the rabbinic legal basis for demanding such devotion to domestic duties—for example, in the Talmud a maiden who gives herself up to prayer or fasting is considered to bring destruction upon the world. Moreover, he said nothing about an obvious aspect of this behavior: some Jewish women behaved very much like Catholic penitents who fasted and participated in other ascetic practices. Even though the voice of the rabbi preserves a valuable record about a little-known aspect of Jewish women's spirituality, the voice of the woman herself is not heard (see Text 1).

Although information about women's fasting is limited, a discussion is available of the role that fasting played in the life of Benvenida Abravanel, a prominent new Christian refugee from Lisbon, where she was born in 1473. She settled in Italy, where she enjoyed an illustrious career during the early sixteenth century. There she was the private tutor of Leonora, the daughter of the Spanish viceroy, who became the duchess of Tuscany and wife of Cosimo De'Medici. As a widow, like many other powerful women, she ran a major loan-banking business—which included service to the Medicis—ransomed captives, contributed extensively to charity, and supported the messianic pretender David Hareuveni. In his diaries, David Hareuveni described the religious life of Benvenida Abravanel (see Text 2).

Women as Ritual Slaughterers

The fact that there is documentary and pictorial evidence that women served as ritual slaughterers of animals is often taken as a sign of the change in the public religious status and the high level of Hebrew education attained by the Jewish women of Italy during the Renaissance. From the rabbinic literature on this subject, it appears that some women in Italy certainly had acquired knowledge, usually from male teachers, sufficient for them to serve as slaughterers, but this was a situation neither unique to Italy nor widespread in Italy. Prior to the Italian Renaissance, the question of women's slaughtering had been regularly debated in rabbinic literature, and affirmative as well as negative responses had been routinely offered by rabbinic authorities, although no examples were given of such a practice having been performed. Even during the Renaissance, it is clear that the circumstances under which women could slaughter were extremely limited. The wording of the extant licenses granted to women shows that, like men, to whom they were likened, they were subjected to the customary examinations of knowledge about the ritual involved and tests of endurance and stamina. A license from 1614 allowed a young single woman, in Mantua, to slaughter only fowl (see Text 3). Ten years later, after her marriage, she was issued another license that allowed her to slaughter cattle and to porge them—*nikkur* or *treibern,* an extensive process of removing the fat, veins, nerves, and sinews after the animal has been ritually slaughtered (see Text 4). This was so complex a process that after the seventeenth century most communities in Europe did not allow it to be done to the lower extremities of an animal, but rather required this part to be sold to non-Jews, depriving observant Jews of sirloin.

Childbirth

The existence of many manuscript collections of private Hebrew prayers, some specifically designed for Jewish women in Italy, constitutes evidence of the widespread use of Hebrew in private rituals, by women as well as men. The instructions before each prayer are in Italian, indicating that the women may have been able to read but not to understand Hebrew. These prayers treat the rituals associated with women, especially baking *hallah* (Sabbath loaves), lighting Sabbath candles, immersing in the ritual bath after menstruation, and marking transitions through the critical stages of pregnancy, from conception to returning to synagogue after the child is born. Rituals and incantations specifically associated with women were also discussed extensively in special religious, medicinal, and magic tractates circulated in Judeo-Italian, Hebrew, or Italian manuscripts and printed books. These served to meet women's needs in matters such as conception, birth control, abortion, birth, and lactation (see Text 5).

In some communities, despite rabbinic protest, the woman in labor held a Torah scroll to ease her delivery, a practice similar to reciting the legend of St. Margherita or placing a copy of it on the belly of Christian women during difficult deliveries. The excerpts here from rabbinic responsa describe the use of such scrolls and rabbinic opposition to this practice. The rabbinic discussion will ultimately turn on the issue of whether impure women—borrowing an expression from the Talmud, "a bag filled with excrement and her mouth filled with blood" [Babylonian Talmud, *Shabbat* 152a]—can serve as reliable witnesses with respect to which measures relieve their distress during childbirth. It was feared that women would desecrate the honor of the Torah scroll by using it during labor. "You do not have impurity and pollution greater than a woman crouching to give birth while the grave is open." The rabbis' concern was to return the birthing procedure to the authority of male experts who should determine the authoritative remedies for relief during childbirth or, as a group of ten men, bring a Torah scroll to the delivery room where, separated from the woman by sheets forming a partition, *mehitzah,* they will pray for her (see Text 6).

Sources of translations are as follows. Text 1: Abraham Yagel, *Eshet hayyil* (Venice: Daniel Zante, 1605–1606), pp. 18b–19a; Text 2: *Sippur David Hareuveni,* edited by A. Z. Aescoly (Jerusalem: Israel Historical and Ethnographic Society, 1940), pp. 57–58; Texts 3 and 4: Jewish Theological Society of America Microfilm 8501; C. Duschinsky, "May a Woman Act as Shoheteth?" in *Occident and Orient . . . Gaster Anniversary Volume* (London: Taylor's Foreign Press, 1936), p. 105; Text 5: Hebrew Union College-Jewish Institute of Religion, Cincinnati, MS 248; Text 6: Azriel Diena, *Sheelot uteshuvot,* edited by Yacov Boksenboim (Tel Aviv: Tel Aviv University, 1977), nos. 8–9

Further Reading

On Yagel, see David Ruderman, *Kabbalah, Magic, and Science* (Cambridge: Harvard University Press, 1988), especially p. 16, and Ruderman, *A Valley of Vision: The Heavenly Journey of Abraham ben Hananiah Yagel* (Philadelphia: Jewish Publication Society, 1990), especially pp. 64 and 197; cf. pp. 33, 185–89, and 193–99. Cf. Isaac ben Immanuel mi-Lattes, *Sheelot uteshuvot* (Vienna: I. Knöpflmacher und Söhn, 1860), pp. 139–40). See Nina Beth Cardin, *Out of the Depths I Call to You: A Book of Prayers for the Married Jewish Woman* (Northvale, N. J.: Jason Aaronson, 1992). On the genre of eastern European women's private prayer in Yiddish, *tkhines,* see the extensive work of Chava Weissler, including her chapter in this collection; and Devra Kay, "An Alternative Prayer Canon for Women: The Yiddish Seyder Tkhines," in *Zur Geschichte der juedischen Frau in Deutschland,* edited by Julius Carlebach (Berlin: Carl Winter Universitäts Verlag, 1993), pp. 49–96.

TEXT 1

Surely, if she pays heed only to the virtue of fear of God and she forgets the remainder of the other virtues and other matters incumbent upon her, such as the work which God granted her, and in order to attain the happiness of her soul, she neglects her husband and his work, and all day long she afflicts her soul with fasts (*tzom*), prayers, and fasts (*taanit*), places stove ashes on her head, wears sackcloth, and denies herself the enjoyment of worldly matters, even in the most trivial matters, and she separates herself from all pleasure and the like. So the deeds intended for good and directed toward heaven will not in this way meet the needs of God, who placed before her the ordering of the house and the work that a woman does for her husband and his house. And thus, she must balance in the scales of justice her love for her husband and her fear of him in order to keep all of the conditions of his ways as long as she follows after him in his lying down and rising up. His every step she must guard as if she were lovesick and unable to find rest except in the presence of her beloved. What will be done between this, her house, and her children who scream and ask for their daily bread each day and thus the conduct of her house. . . .

TEXT 2

And from Naples the Señora sent to me in Pisa a nice silk flag, with the ten commandments written on it in columns. . . . [A]nd I heard about how she fasts every day, and I also heard when I was in Alexandria and in Jerusalem how she would redeem captives . . . and she gave charity to all who asked her, may she be blessed before the Lord. . . . [A]nd the Señora who was in Naples had one daughter in Lisbon who had a son and a daughter, and she fasted every day, and her children fasted on Mondays and Thursdays; and how important she is, it is impossible to say. And she, like her mother, gives much charity and does many deeds of loving kindness, may she be blessed before the Lord.

TEXT 3

An authorization to slaughter ritually fowl issued to the virgin Ms. Isota, the daughter of the honorable Elhanan Yael mi-Fano, from the ritual slaughterer of the holy congregation of Mantua, the honorable Elia ben Joseph mi-Forli.

With God's Help

Many daughters have done valiantly in knowledge of the ways and laws of ritual slaughter, but this the honorable Ms. Isota, the daughter of the distinguished Elhanan Yael mi-Fano, among the daughters may she be blessed, may his Rock and Redeemer guard him, rose above all of them, because she girded her loins with strength to understand and comprehend all its rules and regulations. Thus as you taught me the undersigned in the long and short of it, I reviewed, investigated, and examined her concerning them orally and she replied to me correctly in every instance. She also slaughtered fowl in my presence on many occasions and her hands were steady in examining the knife and in executing the slaughtering. Therefore I give her absolute permission to slaughter for herself as the other women experts among our people. Any Jew is able to eat from that which she has slaughtered without feeling that she may have committed a transgression without realizing it. Indeed, the good Lord will save her from errors and lengthen her days with goodness. And all this I wrote and I signed today, Thursday, 25 Kislev—November 27, 1614, here in Mantua. I am Elia the son of the late Joseph mi-Forli.

TEXT 4

An authorization for the above-mentioned after her marriage to be a porger of hindquarters and loins. In order that the land will not be forsaken and somebody will take another's place, I was moved to testify concerning a matter of truth and justice about the honorable Ms. Isota, may she be blessed among all the daughters, the wife of the honorable Menahem Matzliah Puah, may his Rock and his Redeemer guard him, that she is an expert in the work of porging meat in all of the details of the hindquarters and the knife because I, and not another person, saw her with my own eyes many times porge according to the law and statutes. She did not change the system which I taught her even a hairsbreadth. Therefore I completely authorize her to porge for herself as her heart desires whether loins, hips, hindquarters, or kidneys. No person shall dispute her authority, because she is an expert, and the Guardian of fools [God] will protect her and save her from errors. The Lord desires that she in her authority will succeed. Amen. Today is Wednesday, of the week in which the portion "a man will prosper" is read (*Vayeshev*), 27 Kislev—December 20, 1623. Joseph, May his Rock and Redeemer guard him, the son of the honorable Raphael Voghera, porger for the holy congregation of Mantua.

With our eyes we the undersigned have seen the testimony of the elder R. Joseph Voghera, who has been accepted by us as learned and expert in the work of porging, and he witnesses that which he has undertaken to do in order to teach the enlightened young woman, the above-mentioned Ms. Isota, may she be blessed among the daughters, in porging. And also in order that there be sufficient evidence from the proof that was brought before us, we examined R. Joseph accordingly. He reported that she was a valiant woman, prompt and observant in the commandment and the above-mentioned work. Therefore we bless her from the house of the Lord, and we agree that every member of our people can rely upon her distinguished porging as described above. This was executed at Mantua, Parashat Tzav, March 31–April 3, 1624. So speaks the youngster Hananiel ben Elia Finzi, of blessed memory, and so speaks the worm who is not a man, the youngster, Barukh Gallico.

TEXT 5

May the child born from this immersion be a perpetual sage and fearer of heaven in private and fulfill your commandments, your statutes, and your ordinances for their own sake . . . that you may provide for me holy and pure seed for your service and your worship . . . that I may merit to raise him to serve you . . . enable me to give birth to male sons who engage in the Torah for its own sake . . . that I may merit to marry my daughters to worthy, righteous men, and that their husbands will not die young . . . and my daughters will be attractive, nice, graceful, modest, and pious crowned with good qualities—all the honor of the daughter of the king is domestic [Ps. 45:14] . . . may they be healthy without any defects. Bless the work of their hands so that I can merit to amass for them dowries and gifts as is appropriate for their ages. . . . Please Lord remember me with males, sages and scholars, and remember me and do not forget your servant among the righteous women. . . . And for me, your servant, prepare the milk of my flesh so that it may be sufficient to nurse it as it needs . . . so that the offspring in my womb will be a male son and will be righteous, pious, and holy for a blessing. . . . Save me from the sentence of Eve . . . that we the women will give birth to our children in pain as is written in your Torah "In pain you will give birth to children," and all is in your power. . . . That she will not give birth on the Sabbath in order so that it will not be necessary to desecrate the Sabbath, God forbid. . . . The key of pregnancy is in your right hand. Open for me without pain and distress my pregnancy and without deficiency and protect whether it is a boy or a girl that will issue forth from my womb from the evil inclination and strengthen in him the good inclination and watch him. And the child be what it will be, whether male or female, and guard it from all evil spirits and wicked ideas.

TEXT 6

A major event and a difficult image were presented to me concerning a pregnant woman about to give birth in Viadana [near Mantua]. During the most difficult pangs of delivery, "when children came to the birthing stool but there was no strength to give birth" [2 Kings 19:3 and Isaiah 37:3], because the pain was too great and she was about to die. One woman among the teachers instructed her—either from a book of cures that Hezekiah had hidden away [Babylonian Talmud, *Berakhot* 10b] [He who found a wife found something good [Prov. 18:22]. I find the woman more bitter than death [Eccles. 7:26]; *Yevamot* 63b; Midrash *Tehillim* 59:3]—or from formulas of seamen and captains and the nations he made a discovery, or they found a verse and explained it [*Avodah Zarah* 52b] as any child would know: it is a tree of life to those who hold on to it and its supporters are happy [Prov. 3:18]. Or [perhaps] none of these three possibilities happened, but only women prevailed upon her and allowed her to bring a Torah to her breast to relieve her from her distress of the grave of a closed womb, so it will widen and turn around under her, and the afterbirth will go out from between her legs, and life and peace will be granted to her. So they did this for her, and the Torah of the Lord went out to become a book of remedies. And from this day forth they made it a law, for every sick and wounded, every deathly ill, and every one taken to bed, they take out a Torah and he places it between his shoulders. So all day he covers every one infected, afflicted, and smitten by God, and every woman during her menstruation and every man with a runny discharge. The Torah of the Lord has become a girdle of sackcloth, a harp, or as a book of remedies to cure them of broken hearts and to bandage their grief. But the portion of Jacob is not like this because the creator of all gave it to us to save the affection of our souls from the pit and to bring us to the rest and to the inheritance in the light of the face of the king of life, and not to make with it amulets, chits, and remedies for cures for this ephemeral life and the vanity in which fools have engaged, or for women to rule us. Woe for great is the hatred of the house of the Lord.

15

A Mystical Fellowship in Jerusalem

Lawrence Fine

Although in the history of Jewish mysticism the eighteenth century is best known for the emergence in eastern Europe of the popular pietistic movement known as Hasidism, Kabbalah in its more traditional form still found adherents in different parts of the Jewish world. One of the great centers of kabbalistic life was in Poland itself, the so-called *klaus* in Brody where Lurianic Kabbalah in its classical form still held sway. Worlds away, in the city of Jerusalem, another community also organized its life around the intensive study and practice of Lurianic mysticism. The "Pietist's Study House of Bet El" (*Midrash Hasidim Bet El*) was established in the year 1737 under the leadership of Rabbi Gedaliah Hayon. Hayon was born in Constantinople, where he studied with the kabbalist Hayyim Alfandari. In contrast to the burgeoning Hasidic movement, which placed a premium on appealing to the masses, both the Brody klaus and Bet El preserved an older kabbalistic impulse, namely, an elitism based upon reverence for the esoteric nature of mystical study and practice. Speaking of this phenomenon, Gershom Scholem characterized it in these words in his book *Major Trends in Jewish Mysticism*: "Kabbalism becomes at the end of its way what it was at the beginning; a genuine esoterism, a kind of mystery-religion which tries to keep the *profanum vulgus* at arm's length. Among the writings of the Sephardic Kabbalists of this school, which has exercised considerable influence on Oriental Jewry, it would be difficult to find a single one capable of being understood by the laity" (329).

When Gedaliah Hayon died in 1751, the mantle of leadership of Bet El was passed to Israel Jacob ben Yom Tov Algazi (1680–1756), an important scholar of Jewish law and Kabbalah. Upon Algazi's death in 1756, Shalom Mizrachi Sharabi (1720–1777), known also by his acronym ha-Reshash, became the head of Bet El, with the title *Rav he-Hasid* (lit., Saintly Rabbi). Although Sharabi served as the spiritual leader of the community, it appears that Israel Jacob Algazi's son, Yom Tov Algazi, became the chief administrator. Shalom Sharabi was born in the city of Sana in Yemen, where the study of Kabbalah was exceedingly popular. While still a youth, Sharabi emigrated to Jerusalem by way of Damascus. He developed a reputation not only as one of the most important rabbis of Jerusalem but also as the greatest kabbalist of Near Eastern and North African Jewry during his lifetime. As was the case with Isaac Luria, legends about Sharabi's contemplative life and extraordinary piety proliferated.

Sharabi was the author of a number of works of a Lurianic nature that over time exerted enormous influence, the most well-known of which is his esoteric prayerbook *Nehar Shalom* (River of Peace), used even today by Jews with roots in the Near East and North Africa. He also composed various highly esoteric commentaries to Luria's teachings, some of which were actually incorporated into certain editions of Lurianic texts themselves. All of these writings were distinguished by a special focus on the devotional and contemplative dimensions of Lurianic mysticism. Lurianic teaching itself was based significantly on detailed and abstruse contemplative intentions, known in Hebrew as *kavvanot*. Sharabi's prayerbook and Lurianic commentaries added a yet greater degree of complexity to these contemplative guidelines and instructions. The participants in the community of Bet El employed these *kavvanot* in their own rigorous practice of Lurianic prayer. Calling themselves *mekhavvenim* (contemplatives), the Bet El kabbalists cultivated the art of meditative prayer in more elaborate ways than had ever been done before. Mastery of the *kavvanot* over the course of many years of training, accompanied by an ascetic pietistic lifestyle, were the essential ingredients in their spiritual path. This community preserved and practiced the most recondite contemplative traditions of Lurianic Kabbalah well into the twentieth century—until Bet El was destroyed in an earthquake in 1927.

We are fortunate to possess fascinating documentary evidence concerning a particular circle of these individuals from a series of several "contracts" or "bills of association" that certain individuals from within Bet El signed. The main document presented below appears to have been the second of these agreements, signed by twelve men in 1754. Subsequently, additional names were added to the original pact. In addition to those of Sharabi and Yom Tov Algazi, the signatures include that of Hayyim Yosef David Azulai, among the most important scholars of this period. The pact obligated these individuals, led by Shalom Sharabi, to pledge uncompromising loyalty, love, and brotherhood toward one another. Aptly, they referred to their fellowship by the name *Ahavat Shalom* (Love of Peace). This community is illustrative of a number of other intentional kabbalistic fellowships of which we know, beginning in the sixteenth century in Turkey and Safed (see, for example, Chapter 29, "Pietistic Customs from Safed," in this book).

In fact, the central premise of the pact is strongly reminiscent of a Lurianic tradition according to which Luria enjoined his disciples to regard one another as a single organism, so much so that "each and every person must bind himself to the others as if he were one limb within the body of this fellowship.... [I]n all one's prayers and petitions one should be mindful of his fellows." There is, in fact, good reason to believe that the Jerusalem circle and its preoccupation with unity of concern and purpose drew its inspiration from the Lurianic model. In the words of the agreement signed by the members of *Ahavat Shalom*: "Each man's soul will be bound to that of his associate so that the twelve of us will be as one man greatly to be admired. Each one of us will think of his associate as if the latter were part of his very limbs." The implications of such a commitment were highly significant. Members were to be utterly dedicated to one another's spiritual welfare, to share in each other's troubles, and to regard one another as equals. The intensity of purpose and the rigorous ethical commitment captured in this document—all within the context of a contemplative community—illustrate the ways in which Kabbalah at times led to an extraordinary degree of fellowship and communal solidarity, reminiscent of true monastic brotherhood known to us from religious traditions such as Roman Catholicism and Buddhism.

The text is found in M. Y. Weinstock, *Siddur ha-Geonim ve-ha-Mekubbalim,* vol. 1 (1970), pp. 24–39. The translation is based upon Louis Jacobs, *Jewish Mystical Testimonies* (New York: Schocken, 1976), pp. 199–202.

Further Reading

In addition to the work by Louis Jacobs noted above, see Gershom Scholem, *Kabbalah* (Jerusalem: Keter Publishing House, 1974), pp. 82–83, as well as his *Major Trends in Jewish Mysticism* (New York: Schocken, 1946), pp. 328–29; and Meir Benayahu, *Rabbi Hayyim Yosef David Azulai* (Hebrew) (Jerusalem: Mossad Harav Kook, 1959), pp. 14–18, 340–42, 351–54. Concerning Shalom Sharabi, see the *Encyclopedia Judaica* (Jerusalem: Keter Publishsing House, 1972), vol. 14, pp. 1307–8; and Shraga Weiss, *Hokhmei ha-Sephardim be-Erets Yisrael* (Jerusalem: Rubin Mass, 1981), pp. 117–47.

A Mystical Fellowship in Jerusalem

By the help of God.

Since the Lord desires the return of those who repent, the spirit took hold of us, the young ones of the flock, the undersigned, to become as one man, companions, all for the sake of the unification of the Holy One, blessed be he, and his *Shekhinah* [divine presence], in order to give satisfaction to our Creator. For this purpose we have made a pact and the following conditions are completely binding upon us.

First, we the undersigned, twelve of us, corresponding to the number of the tribes of Judah, agree to love one another with great love of soul and body, all for the purpose of giving satisfaction to our Creator through our single-minded association, although we are separated. Each man's soul will be bound to that of his associate so that the twelve of us will be as one man greatly to be admired. Each one of us will think of his associate as if the latter were part of his very limbs, with all his soul and all his might, so that if, God forbid, any one of us will suffer tribulation all of us together and each one of us separately will help him in every possible way. The main principle is that each of us will rebuke his associate when, God forbid, he hears of any sin the latter has committed. This embraces the obligation of the undersigned to bind ourselves together in the mighty bond of love. We take it upon ourselves from now onward, even after we have departed this life and gone to the world to come, that each one of us will endeavor, both in this world and the next, to save, perfect and elevate the soul of each one of our circle to the best of his ability, and with every kind of effort to do everything possible for the others' eternal bliss.

Each of us agrees to save his associate in the event it has been decreed in heaven, God forbid, that one of us should receive the goodness that belongs to his neighbor, on the basis of the idea that there are occasions when a man receives both his own portion in Paradise and that of his neighbor who has sinned. In return for the advantage each of us has received from the others, we hereby resolve to participate in that associate's tribulations, may they never come. With firm resolve, we take upon ourselves the obligation, with all the formulae required to make it binding both according to the laws of men and according to the laws of heaven, to relinquish that goodness that is to come to us for the benefit of that associate for whom it has been decreed that it be taken from him. We shall have no benefit from it "and every man's hallowed things shall be his" [Num. 5:10], as our master the Ari [i.e., Isaac Luria] of blessed memory said when commenting on the passage in the liturgy: "and let our portion be with them." Following this idea we have taken the above-mentioned obligation upon ourselves.

To sum up, from now and for ever after we are met together, we are associates, we are joined, we are bound to the others as if we were one man, we are companions in all matters of every kind. Each of us resolves to help, encourage and give support to his associate, helping him to repent, rebuking him and participating in his tribulations, whether in this world or in the next, and all in the ways of faithfulness and even more so.

We further take upon ourselves the obligation to follow every enactment, rule, or good custom agreed upon by the majority of our circle, both as a group and as individuals, unless we are prevented by forces beyond our control.

We take upon ourselves the obligation never to praise one another, even if it is clear to everyone that one associate is superior to another both in age and in wisdom. None of us will rise fully to his feet before any other associate, but we shall merely rise a little as a token of respect and we shall not say much about it. We shall conduct ourselves as if we were one man, no part of whom is superior to any other part. Though we have eyes of flesh, our heart knows our own worth and the worth of our associates, and there is no need to give expression to it in words.

We further take upon ourselves the obligation never to reveal to any creature that we have resolved to do these things.

We further take upon ourselves never to be annoyed with one another in any way, whether because of his rebuke to us or because of anything else, and if one of us offends his associate the latter will forgive him at once with all his heart and with all his soul.

All this have we taken upon ourselves under the penalty of the ban and by an irrevocable resolve in accordance with the laws of our sages of blessed memory. We are resolved to keep all these things, and we give them the full force of all the regulations that have been issued from the days of Moses our teacher, on whom be peace. And let the pleasantness of the Lord our God be upon us, and establish thou the work of our hands upon us: yea, the work of our hands establish thou it. Help us, O God of our salvation, for the sake of the glory of thy Name. As an indication of our sincerity we hereby sign this in the holy city of Jerusalem, may it be speedily rebuilt and established, on the week of the *sidrah* [Torah portion of the week]: "Behold, I give unto him my covenant of peace." [Num. 25:12] May the Lord bless His people with peace. All this is lasting and firm, the thing is right, true and established.

Shalom Mizrachi di-Ydi'a Sharabi, pure Sephardi
Yom Tov Algazi
Samuel Alhadif, pure Sephardi
Abraham Belul, pure Sephardi
Aaron Bacher Elijah ha-Levi, pure Sephardi
Menachem ben Rabbi Joseph
The Young Hayyim Joseph David Azulai, pure Sephardi
Joseph Samanon, pure Sephardi
Solomon son of my master and father Bejoash
Jacob Biton
Raphael Eliezer Parhi, pure Sephardi
Hayyim De La Roza

ADDENDA TO THE PACT

Now we have met together and the majority of the members of our circle have agreed to add to our circle the undersigned, as well as the two golden flutes who add their signatures and bind themselves with every kind of formula so that it is all irrevocable.
Abraham Ishmael Hayyim Sanguinetti

And afterwards we met at the request of Rabbi Jacob Algazi, who wished to join our holy circle. Since I agree to keep all these matters with a firm resolve and with full acceptance of the terms, I append my humble signature, lowly as a worm.
Israel Jacob Algazi
Raphael Moses Gallico, pure Sephardi

I, too, accept all these terms and conditions willingly,
The Young Abraham ben Asher, pure Sephardi

I, too, accept all these terms with the utmost willingness, behold I am a young man.
Saul, son of our master Rabbi Abraham, our master of blessed memory

— 16 —

The Love of Learning among Polish Jews

Gershon David Hundert

The Ukrainian town of Ostrih (Ostróg) was a burgeoning urban center and the seat of both an important Protestant academy and a Jewish *yeshiva* (plural, yeshivot; postelementary school for the study of rabbinic literature) when Nathan Hanover (d. 1683) was born there in the early 1620s. Some claim that his youthful studies included not only the standard rabbinic texts but also kabbalistic literature. When the uprising of local peasants and Ukrainian Cossacks began in 1648, Hanover, whose father had been murdered, fled westward together with other Jewish refugees. He wandered through Germany to Amsterdam and thence to Venice. It was there that he published the chronicle from which our text is taken. The book, *Abyss of Despair (Yeven metsulah)* consists mainly of a history of the terrible fate of Jewish communities that lay in the path of the Zaporozhian Cossack leader Bohdan Khmel'nyts'kyi (Bogdan Chmielnicki, 1595–1657) and his general, Maxim Krzywonos. It is based on written and oral accounts and Hanover's own recollections. In terms of loss of life, this was the worst catastrophe in European Jewish history to that time. Jews referred to it as *gezerot tah vetat* (the evil decrees of 1649–1649). *Abyss of Despair* is the most comprehensive and historical of the Jewish chronicles of those events.

In Venice and later Livorno (Leghorn), Hanover formed close ties with local kabbalists. After a period in Wallachia, he ended in the Moravian city of Brod, where he became preacher and judge. He published two other books: a four-language dictionary (Latin-Italian-Hebrew-Yiddish) and an anthology of prayers substantially informed by Kabbalah called *Sha'arei Tsiyon.*

The passage below is from the last chapter of *Abyss of Despair,* which, unlike the preceding chapters, does not describe the Cossack attacks on Jews but is a portrait of the Polish Jewish community before the catastrophe that began in 1648. The chapter is set off with the title: "And now I shall begin to describe the practices of the land of Poland which entirely followed the path of justice and righteousness, preparedness and steadfastness." The idyllic image of Polish Jewry that Hanover constructed serves, in the context of his book, to deepen the reader's sense of the tragedy of the losses inflicted by the Ukrainian attackers. There is virtually no hint of criticism or that there was any failing among Polish Jews. They are presented as reflecting in their behavior and values the loftiest principles of rabbinic teaching.

The dominant motif of the chapter is not hard to identify. The centrality of Torah study and its place at the apogee of rabbinic values in sixteenth- and early seventeenth-century Polish Jewish society emerges with striking clarity from the text. Hanover organized his elegy around the six "pillars of the world" (Torah, Divine Service, Charity, Truth, Judgment, and Peace). Of the six, by far the most attention is devoted to the first, which describes the system of Torah study and the yeshivot and their heads. In the section on Divine Service the emphasis is on the fact that a man would not depart from the synagogue "until he had heard some words of the Law expounded by a scholar or a passage from the commentary of Rashi on the Torah . . . for in all synagogues there were many groups of scholars who taught others immediately after evening and morning prayers." The section on Charity also devotes substantial attention to the support offered to scholars and to students. And the last section, on Peace, insists that "there was in Poland so much interest in learning that no three people sat down to a meal without discussing the words of Torah." The centrality of the study of Torah among the ideals of Polish Jewry is thus abundantly clear.

During much of the sixteenth and the early decades of the seventeenth century, Poland was one of the largest and most powerful states in Europe. Economic growth, based on the export of grain, was complemented with a vigorous cultural life stimulated by lively ties with Italian centers. The Reformation enjoyed strong, if temporary, victories in Poland—Lutheranism among the city-dwellers and Calvinism among the nobility. Indeed, Poland was known as a land of toleration.

Jews in this period also benefited from the relative prosperity, toleration, and cultural creativity. Beginning before the middle of the sixteenth century and persisting into about the second decade of the seventeenth century, there was a remarkable efflorescence of scholarship and literary activity among Polish Jews. A veritable galaxy of rabbis produced volume after volume of work devoted chiefly to the elaboration and the codification of *halakha* (Jewish law), and to Biblical commentary and homiletics. There was much less attention to systematic expositions of theology, to history, or to science or poetry. Major academies or *yeshivot* were established in Cracow, Lublin, Poznan, L'viv (Lwów), Brzesc Litewski (Brisk), and Ostrih. There were others in Krzemieniec, Luboml, Busk, Ludomir, Kowel, Chelm, Pinsk, Horodno, and Gniezno.

Young boys and, very rarely, girls were sent to elementary schools funded in part by the community, although the wealthy often hired private tutors for their children. Communal institutions for education were often supervised by a voluntary society (*hevrat talmud torah*) formed for that purpose, which acted on behalf of the *kahal* (Jewish communal government). The regulations of such a society in Cracow convey a description of the elementary school curriculum:

> The teacher ... will teach the children ... the alphabet with the vowels, the prayer-book and the Pentateuch with the commentary, *Be'er Moshe* [a Yiddish rendering of the commentary of Rashi, eleventh-century French scholar] in particular. He will also teach them Rashi's commentary and the regulations of prayer as well as manners and proper conduct. He will teach each one according to his abilities. He will teach them to read the script in which Yiddish books are published so that they can read them and learn morality, manners, and how to keep to the straight and narrow path. He will teach them how to write our spoken language [Yiddish]. He will teach the table of verbs to the most able students so that they will understand the essence of the holy language.... And he will teach them arithmetic: adding, subtracting, multiplying, and dividing. If one of the pupils is particularly able he can begin to teach him Gemara [Talmud], with the commentary of Rashi and Tosafot.... When a young man approaches the age of fourteen and is not among those capable of studying Gemara, he should be directed to learning a trade, or to domestic service with a householder.
>
> Majer Balaban, "Die Krakauer Judengemeinde–Ordnung von 1595 und ihre Nachträge," *Tahrbuch der jüdisch-literarischen Gesellschaft* 10 (1912): 296–360; 11 (1916): 88–114.

Only a small proportion continued their studies in the *yeshivot*.

The financial support for these academies came from either private or public sources. In the early seventeenth century, Rabbi Joshua Falk explained how his yeshiva in L'viv came to be funded:

> I was privileged to lead the community and to head a *yeshiva* there.... My students and I plumbed the depths of the sea of the Talmud. Our way was cleared [in the following manner]: When I saw the hardships that were imposed [on me] as rabbi and head of the community ... I asked and requested of the Lord, my Shepherd, that he fulfill my prayer to privilege me with a house of study so that I would not be alone, and that he provide me with a way to train important rabbis before whom I could teach regularly, morning and evening. And before I could call out to him, God heard my prayer. He caused my father-in-law, the noble philanthropist, elder and leader of the holy community of L'viv and its region known as R. Yisra'el ben Yosef ... to speak to me and to say: "It is fallen to me to perform a great commandment and I shall do it. I shall stand by you and support the students of your choice." He ordered, he spoke and he fulfilled his word.... He provided a large stone house of several stories and rooms in which to gather.... Because of this I was delighted and vowed to remain in this place even if I were invited to lead a large[r] community.
>
> Yehoshu'a Falk, *Sefer me'irat einayim: Hoshen mishpat* (Prague, 1614), Introduction

In Ostrih itself, where Nathan Hanover was born, the *yeshiva* was supported from public funds, as Rabbi David ben Shmu'el Halevi reported:

> It has now been three years since I was accepted by the holy community of Ostrih to teach Torah among them. They provided me with a large house of study in which

to assemble the students. Goodness and grace to the community which provides gold from its own resources to meet my needs and those of this important and large yeshiva. Praise God, many wise students have come to me from near and far—from the ends of the land. In all my days I have never seen such a great and important group of students.

David ben Shmu'el Halevi, *Turei zahav: Yoreh de'ah*
(Lublin, 1646), Introduction

The most common arrangement was the one in Ostrih. Students were housed in the homes of community residents, where they also ate. They paid no tuition and no taxes. The minimum size of a *yeshiva* was twelve students: six neophytes (*na'arim*) and six at the upper level (*bahurim*). The main determinants of the size of a yeshiva were the level of support the community was prepared to allocate, on the one hand, and the prestige and personality of the *yeshiva* head (*resh metivta*), on the other. The position of *resh metivta* was both prestigious and well rewarded. Joseph Solomon Delmedigo of Crete visited Poland-Lithuania in 1620–1625 and portrayed the position of *yeshiva* head as both a spiritual and a material ideal.

As in the medieval period, students of this era too wandered from place to place. In an autobiographical book of the early seventeenth century, Me'ir of Brod in Moravia told of leaving home at the age of fifteen to go to study in Cracow. He wrote that he left home "after the fashion of all the itinerant young men who wander from place to place and from one country to another to study there." The great prestige of the Polish *yeshivot* attracted students from all over Europe. The son of Menasseh ben Israel studied in Lublin, the brothers-in-law of Glikl of Hameln studied in Poznan; and L'viv. Some of those who came to study remained to make their homes in eastern Europe, like Saul Wahl of Padua, who settled in Brzesc Litewski (Brisk). Still, it should be emphasized that the vast majority of Polish Jewish men did not continue their studies in *yeshivot* for very long, if at all. These academies of learning were elite institutions limited for the most part to students from relatively prosperous homes. The proverbial very promising but poor student who rose in the social hierarchy by dint of his intellect was a rare phenomenon.

The course of study included mainly Talmud, with restricted amounts of time devoted to the various codes and digests such as those of Isaac Alfassi (1013–1103), Jacob ben Asher (1270–1340), and Moses of Coucy (thirteenth century). During the long breaks between terms, students could earn money, study non-curricular texts, or travel to other places of study. These breaks also provided financial relief to the host communities that were supporting the students who had come from elsewhere to study.

The involvement of the community in the supervision of education is noted in the passage. Jewish communal governments were oligarchic institutions dominated by small groups of wealthy merchants. The highest office was held usually by three or four "heads" (*roshim*), and each month one of these would act as chair of the communal council. This position was called *parnas hahodesh* or warden of the month. In addition to the lay council, there were two prestigious rabbinical positions in a community, though often both were held by the same man. The communal rabbi who was the chief judge (*av beit din*) and the head of the *yeshiva* often developed considerable influence on the basis of the loyalties of his students. In addition to his juridical function, the rabbi also signed the enactments of the communal council, hurled the ban of excommunication, and could bestow the honorific titles of "our teacher" (*moreinu*) and "the fellow" (*hehaver*). These titles recognized status achieved through learning.

In many communities, the *kahal* or Jewish communal government fulfilled virtually all of the functions of a municipal administration. It collected national and local taxes, appointed judges, supervised education, and administered matters related to health, welfare, public utilities, public morality, and commerce. The community impinged on virtually every area of life from sumptuary legislation—limiting the amount of jewelry that could be worn by women on the Sabbath and holidays, and regulating how many guests could be invited to a circumcision or a wedding—to the close supervision of business dealings between Jews and Gentiles. The communal government controlled the right of residence and could remove it as a sanction against those who broke the law. Even permission to marry had to be obtained by the children of members of the community, and it was granted only on the basis of a kind of means test. All groups in the community, be they burial or study societies, or artisan guilds, were closely supervised lest they become centers of opposition to the *kahal*.

Despite the communal government's authority, certain individuals achieved considerable independence. They could defy the *kahal* because of their ties to powerful noblemen who protected them from its jurisdiction. For example, in Przemysl in 1604, a certain apparently aptly named Jacob Bogaty ("the wealthy") refused to appear before the communal court. He had been summoned but defied the court, saying he was a servant of the Crown sheriff and "therefore I am not obliged to appear before this Jewish court in any matter."

In addition to local governments, there were Jewish regional councils and, by the second half of the sixteenth century, a national Jewish council usually known as the Council of the Four Lands. The Polish Council of the Four Lands was the most ramified and durable of the autonomous institutions developed by Ashkenazic Jews. Although similar bodies arose in Lithuania and Bohemia, the Polish council enjoyed the greatest influence and the most prestige. It consisted of representatives of larger communities and of regions made up of smaller communities. Under normal circumstances, it met twice annually to consider matters of interest to Jews in Poland and, mainly, to apportion the national Jewish capitation tax among the various communities. It was, as it were, a bicameral institution with a lay parliament and a rabbinical tribunal. The two houses worked closely together, with the parliament suggesting issues that were framed into legislation in accordance with rabbinic law by the tribunal and then executed by the parliament. Both "chambers" performed judicial functions, acting as appellate courts for Polish Jewry. The meetings of the council took place at the great fairs, particularly in Lublin and in Jaroslaw.

The fairs were fixed periods when all restrictions on commerce were suspended, but people were attracted to the fairs for more than merely mercantile purposes. Young noblemen came to gamble and to party; those who follow crowds and provide distractions for them came as well: jugglers and actors, prostitutes and thieves. There were funambulists and marionette players, sellers of medicine and exhibitors of the grotesque and the miraculous. For Jews, the fairs facilitated communication about all manner of things. Marriages were arranged, learned rabbis consulted on matters of *halakha,* and gave their approbations to monographs and commentaries, while their students took the opportunity to study in the local *yeshivot.* The best known of contemporary Jewish preachers, Ephraim of Leczyca (1550–1619), condemned the vain and frenzied pursuit of wealth by Jewish merchants at the fairs, contrasting their behavior with the gaiety of the noblemen in their pursuit of pleasure.

The translation generally follows that of Abraham J. Mesch: *Abyss of Despair (Yeven metzulah): The famous 17th-century chronicle depicting Jewish life in Russia and Poland during the Chmielnicki Massacres of 1648–49 by Nathan Hanover* (New York: Bloch, 1950), pp. 110–20.

Further Reading

The scholarly literature in English related to the subjects arising in this section is not extensive. For a historical overview of the period, see Salo Baron, *A Social and Religious History of the Jews,* vol. 16 (New York: Columbia University Press, 1976). The literary works of the period are presented in Israel Zinberg, *A History of Jewish Literature,* vol. 7, translated by Bernard Martin (Cleveland: Case Western Reserve University Press, 1975). Edward Fram has published an analysis of how the rabbis adjusted law to economic necessity: *Ideals Face Reality: Jewish Law and Life in Poland, 1550–1655* (Cincinnati: Hebrew Union College Press, 1997). And there is a not entirely satisfactory survey of *Jewish Culture in Eastern Europe* by Moses Shulvass (New York: Ktav, 1975).

Abyss of Despair

And now I shall begin to describe the practices of the land of Poland which entirely followed the path of justice and righteousness, preparedness and steadfastness.

As it is said in tractate *Avot,* "Simon the Just was among the last of the men of the Great Assembly. He used to say: 'The world is based on three things: on

Torah, on Divine Service, and on the practice of charity' " [*Mishnah Avot* 1:2]. "Rabban Shimon son of Gamliel said, 'By three things the world is preserved: by Judgment, by Truth, and by Peace' " [*Mishnah Avot* 1:18]. All of these six pillars on which the world depends were upheld in the land of Poland.

The Pillar of Torah

Matters that are well known need no proof. Throughout the dispersions of Israel there was nowhere so much learning as in the land of Poland. Each community maintained *yeshivot*. And they provided a generous wage for their *yeshiva* head so that he could maintain his school without worry, and that the study of Torah might be his sole occupation. The *yeshiva* head did not leave his house except to travel from the house of study to the house of prayer; he studied Torah day and night. Each community maintained young men (*bahurim*) and provided them with a fixed weekly allowance of money that they might study with the *yeshiva* head. And for each young man they also maintained at least two (*na'arim*) to study with him. He would recite what he had learned of Talmud with the commentaries of Rashi and Tosafot (*GeFaT*) and thus he would gain experience in the subtlety of talmudic argumentation. The boys were provided with food from the community welfare fund or the communal kitchen. If the community consisted of fifty householders it supported not less than thirty young men and boys. One young man and two boys would be assigned to a householder. And at least the young man would eat at his table as one of his sons. And although the young man received a sufficient stipend from the community, the householder provided him with all the food and drink that he needed. Some of the more charitable householders also allowed the boys to eat regularly at their table. Thus three persons would be provided with food and drink for the entire year.

There was scarcely a house in all of Poland where Torah was not studied. Either the householder himself was a scholar, or his son or his son-in-law studied, or one of the young men eating at his table. At times, all of these were to be found in one house. Thus they fulfilled all three of the circumstances of which Raba spoke in the Talmud, tractate *Sabbath*, Chapter 1:

> Raba said: "He who loves the rabbis will have sons who are rabbis; he who honors the rabbis will have rabbis for sons-in-law; he who stands in awe of the rabbis will himself be a rabbinical scholar."

Thus, there were many scholars in every community. A community of fifty householders had twenty scholars who achieved the title of "our teacher" (*moreinu*) or the title, "the fellow" (*hehaver*). The *yeshiva* head was above all these. All the scholars were submissive to him and they would go to his *yeshiva* to attend him.

This was the program of study in Poland.

The term (*zeman*) was when the young men and the boys were required to study in the *yeshiva* with the head of the *yeshiva*. In the summer it extended from the first day of the month of Iyyar [roughly April–May] until the fifteenth day of the month of Ab [roughly July–August], and in the winter from the first day of the month of Heshvan [roughly October–November] until the fifteenth day of the month of Shevat [roughly December–January]. After the fifteenth of Shevat or the fifteenth of Ab, the young men and the boys were permitted to study wherever they wished. From the first day of Iyyar until Shavu'ot [Feast of Weeks], and from the first day of Heshvan until Hanukkah, all the *yeshiva* students studied Gemara [Talmud] together with the commentaries of Rashi and Tosafot with great diligence. Each day they studied a *halakhah*, that is, one page of Gemara together with the commentaries of Rashi and Tosafot.

All the scholars and the young men (*bahurim*) of the community together with all those who showed an inclination to study Torah assembled in the *yeshiva*. The head of the *yeshiva* alone occupied a chair and the scholars and the other students stood around him. Before the head of the *yeshiva* appeared they would engage in discussion among themselves of the *halakhah*, and when he arrived each one would ask him about that which he found difficult in the *halakhah*, and he would offer his explanation to each of them.

They were all silent as the head of the *yeshiva* delivered his lecture and presented the new results of his study. After discussing his new interpretations, the head of the *yeshiva* would discuss a *hiluk* [the resolution of an apparent contradiction]. He would proceed in the following manner: he would cite a contradiction from the Gemara, or Rashi, or Tosafot, he would question deletions and pose contradictory statements and provide solutions that would also prove perplexing; and then he would propose solutions until the *halakhah* was completely clarified.

In the summer they would not leave the *yeshiva* at least until after noon. From Shavu'ot until Rosh Hashanah [the New Year], and from Hanukkah until Passover, the head of the *yeshiva* would not engage in so much *hiluk*. With the scholars he would study the Codes such as the *Arba'ah Turim* [by Jacob ben Asher, 1270–1340] with the commentaries, and with the young men he would study Isaac Alfassi [1013–1103] and other books. They studied Gemara, Rashi, and Tosafot until the fifteenth of Ab or the fifteenth of Shevat. From then on until Passover or Rosh Hashanah they studied the Codes or other books exclusively. Some weeks prior to the fifteenth of Ab or the fifteenth of Shevat, the head of the *yeshiva* would honor each of his students, the scholars as well as the young men, and they would lecture in his stead. They would present their *hilukim*, and the head of the *yeshiva* would respond with challenges in order to "sharpen" the *yeshiva* students. The same tractate was studied throughout Poland in the proper sequence of the Six Orders [of the Mishnah: Seeds, Holidays, Women, Damages, Sanctities, Purities].

Each *yeshiva* head had one inspector who daily went from school to school (*heder*) to ensure that the boys, rich and poor, studied. He would admonish them every day of the week to study and not loiter in the streets. On Thursdays, all the boys would go as a group to the supervisor of *Talmud Torah* to be examined on what they had learned that week. He who knew nothing of what he had studied or erred in one thing was flogged by the inspector at the command of the supervisor and was greatly chastised in front of the boys, so that the memory of it would lead him to study more diligently in the following week. Likewise, on the eve of the Sabbath, the boys would go in a group to the head of the *yeshiva* to be questioned on what they had learned during the week as in the aforementioned procedure. The dread and the great fear thus instilled in the boys led them to study with regularity. During the three days preceding Shavu'ot and during Hanukkah, the young men and the boys were required to review what they had studied during that term. For this, the communal elders provided them fixed gifts of money. Such was the practice until the fifteenth of Ab or the fifteenth of Shevat.

After that, the head of the *yeshiva,* together with all of his students, the young men and the boys, journeyed to the trade fair. In the summer they traveled to the fair in Zaslaw and to the fair in Jaroslaw; in the winter to the fairs of L'viv and Lublin. There the young men and boys were free to study in any *yeshiva* they preferred. At each fair there were hundreds of *yeshiva* heads, thousands of young men and tens of thousands of boys. Jewish and (one must distinguish) Gentile merchants were as [numerous as] the sand on the shore of the sea, for they would come to the fair from the ends of the world. Whoever had a marriageable son or daughter would come to the fair and arrange a match there. Everyone could find his like and his mate. At each and every fair hundreds, and sometimes thousands, of matches were made. Jews, men and women, walked about the fair dressed in royal garments for they were held in esteem by the rulers and by the Gentiles. The children of Israel were many like the sand of the sea, but now, because of our sins, they are few. May God have mercy on them.

In every community great honor was accorded to the head of the *yeshiva.* His word was obeyed by rich and poor alike. None questioned his authority. Without him no one raised his hand or his foot, and as he commanded, so it came to be. In his hand he carried a stick and a lash to smite and to flog, to punish and to chastise transgressors, to institute ordinances, to establish safeguards and to declare the forbidden. Nevertheless, the head of the *yeshiva* was beloved. Whoever had a good portion such as fatted fowl or capons, or good fish, would honor the head of the *yeshiva* with half or all, and with other gifts of money or silver and gold without measure. In the synagogue, too, most of those who bought honors would accord them to the head of the *yeshiva.* It was obligatory to call him third to the reading of the Torah on the Sabbath and on at least the first days of the festivals. And if the head of the *yeshiva* was a Cohen or Levi, he was entitled to be called up for those portions of the reading or for the concluding portion of the reading of the Torah (*aharon*) even if there were many others in the synagogue who were Cohen or Levi. Not one person left the synagogue on the Sabbath or the festivals until the head of the *yeshiva* walked out first, followed by his students. Then the whole community would accompany him until his house. On the festivals the community visited his home to greet him on the holiday. All this made the scholars covetous so that they studied diligently that they too might achieve this high status and become a *yeshiva* head in some community. And out of acting with an ulterior motive comes action without such a motive. And the land was filled with knowledge.

The Pillar of Divine Service

In this era there is prayer instead of sacrificial service, as it is written [Hos. 14:3], "So we will render for bullocks the offering of our lips." And prayer has been set in sockets of fine gold [cf. Song of Songs 5:15]. At the forefront was the fellowship of those who rose before dawn called *Shomerim laboker* ["They that watch before dawn" Ps. 130:6] to pray and to mourn the destruction of the Temple. With the dawn the members of the psalms fellowship would arise to recite psalms for about an hour before the prayer service. Each week they would complete the recitation of the Book of Psalms. And far be it that a person miss the time of the morning prayer in sleep and fail to go to the synagogue, except for unavoidable circumstances. And when he went to the synagogue, no one would depart to attend to his business until he had heard some words of Torah expounded by a scholar or a passage from the commentary of Rashi on the Torah, the Prophets or the Writings, or some Mishnah, or some laws, whatever he wished to study. For in all synagogues there were many groups of scholars who taught others immediately after evening and morning prayers. They would fulfill [the passage]: "They go from strength to strength appearing before God in Zion" [Ps. 84:8].

The Pillar of Charity

There was no limit to the practice of charity in Poland, and particularly hospitality. If a scholar or a preacher visited a community, even communities where there were "tickets" for visitors [entitling them to hospitality with a particular householder], he would not be obliged to demean himself to obtain a ticket. Rather, he would go to a communal elder and stay wherever he pleased. The communal beadle would then come to get his credentials [*kibbuts*: certification of entitlement to collect funds] and show them to the superintendent or to the head of the community for that month (*parnas hahodesh*). An appropriate gift would be decided upon and sent to the visitor with the beadle, who delivered it in a dignified manner. He was then the guest of a householder for as many days as he desired. Similarly, other visitors who received tickets would be the guest of a householder, whose turn it was by lot, for as many days as they wished. A ticket was good for at least three days. The guest was given food and drink morning, noon, and evening. When they wished to depart they would be given provisions for the road, and they would be conveyed by horse and wagon from one community to another. If young men or boys, or householders or unmarried women came from distant or other places, they would be furnished with garments immediately. Those who wished to work at a craft would be apprenticed to an artisan, and those who wanted to be domestic servants would be assigned to serve in a house. Those who wanted to study would be provided with a teacher. Afterward, when he became an important young man, a rich man would take him to his house and give him his daughter in marriage as well as several thousand ducats as a dowry. He would clothe him in royal garments "for who are kings? The scholars" [Babylonian Talmud, *Gittin* 62a]. After the wedding he would send him away from his home to study in the great *yeshivot*. When he returned home after two or three years, his own father-in-law would maintain a *yeshiva* for him in his home and he would spend much money among the householders who were prominent scholars that they should attend his *yeshiva* for a number of years, until he also became the head of a *yeshiva* in some community. Even if he was not yet an important young man at that time, but had a desire to study and showed promise that with study he would become a scholar, at times a rich man who had a young daughter would provide him with food and drink and clothing, and all his needs as he would to his own son. He would hire a teacher for him until he was prepared, then he would give him his daughter in marriage. There is no greater benevolence than this.

Similarly, there were very laudable regulations for poor unmarried girls in every region. No poor girl reached the age of eighteen without being married, and many pious women devoted themselves to this worthy deed. May the Lord reward them and have compassion on the remnant of Israel.

The Pillar of Justice

The system of justice in Poland was as it was before the destruction of the Temple in Jerusalem, when courts were established in every city. If one refused to be judged by the court of his city he went to the nearest court, and if he refused to be judged in the nearest court, he went before the superior court. In every region, there was a superior court. Thus, in the leading community of Ostrih, there was the superior court for Volhynia and Ukraine, and in the leading community of L'viv there was the superior court for Ruthenia. There were many leading communities and in each was the superior court for its region.

If there was litigation between two leading communities, the matter would be judged by the elders of [the Council of] the Four Lands [Great Poland, Little Poland, Ruthenia, and Volhynia-Ukraine], may their Rock and Redeemer preserve them, who assembled twice a year. Each leading community would choose one elder, and they added six great scholars from the land of Poland, and these were known as [the Council of] the Four Lands. They would convene at the Lublin fair between Purim and Passover and at the fair in Jaroslaw in Ab or Ellul. The leaders of the Four Lands were like the Sanhedrin in the Chamber of Hewn Stones [in the Temple]. They had the authority to judge all of Israel in the kingdom of Poland, to establish safeguards, to institute ordinances, and to punish each man as they saw fit. Each difficult matter was brought before them and they judged it. The leaders of the Four Lands chose judges from the provinces to relieve their burden, and these were called judges of the provinces (*dayyanei medinah*). They attended to cases involving money matters (*dinei mamonot*). Fines, titles, and other difficult legal matters were brought before the elders of the Four Lands, may their Rock and Redeemer preserve them. Never was a dispute among Jews brought before a Gentile judge, or before any nobleman or before his majesty, the king. If a Jew did bring his case to a Gentile court he was severely punished and chastised to fulfill: "Even our enemies are judges" [Deut. 32:31 (traditional reading)].

The Pillar of Truth

Every community appointed supervisors of weights and measures and of other business dealings so that everything would be truthful and trustworthy.

The Pillar of Peace

As it is said: "May the Lord give strength to His people; may the Lord bless His people with peace" [Ps. 29:11]. In Poland there was so much learning that no three people sat down to eat without words of Torah among them. Throughout the meal they would discuss *halakha* or remarkable exegeses of Scripture (*midrashim temohim*) to fulfill the verse: "Your teaching is in my inmost parts" [Ps. 40:9].

Religious Sectarianism and Communities on the Margins

17

Jewish Sectarianism in the Near East: A Muslim's Account

Steven M. Wasserstrom

No Jewish sect appears to have survived the Roman destruction of Jerusalem and the holy Temple. Nor has a Jewish sect been proven to have existed during the long talmudic period, roughly 200–600 C.E. With the coming of Islam, however, Jewish sectarianism dramatically reemerged. Only the most significant of these groups, the Karaites, survives to this day; the rest apparently disappeared by the thirteenth century. Almost no contemporaneous rabbinic sources specify the identities of these smaller, non-Karaite Jewish groups. The leading rabbis of this period, the geonim, were disciplined in giving the silent treatment to their opposition and rivals. Thus, aside from a few responsa (rabbinic epistolary dicta) and indirect statements, as well as some allusions in *piyyutim* (synagogue hymns) and other poems, no Jewish sectarians are specified by name by the geonim. Some rabbis do refer to contemporaneous *minim* (heretics); Saadia Gaon (882–942) cryptically criticized a group of *anashim she-nikraim Yehudim* (people who are called Jews); and, occasionally, a polemicist referred to *apikorsim* (Epicureans, an epithet used by rabbinic Jews) or in Arabic, *Khawarij* (the earliest Islamic sect). These derogations often simply referred to Karaites, or to dissident Rabbanites. Rarely can any other firm sectarian identity be teased from these oblique clues. The Cairo Genizah, a gigantic repository of texts dating roughly from the ninth through the thirteenth centuries, seems nearly as silent as do the geonim with reference to Jewish sectarians.

Nevertheless, we know that the first Islamic centuries stimulated an efflorescence of Jewish sects. The bulk of our information on Jewish sectarianism was written by Karaite Jews, that is, Jews who opposed rabbinic authority in favor of their own literalist reading of Hebrew scriptures, and by Muslims, both Shi'i and Sunni. Of the Karaite sources, by far the most outstanding was Abu Yusuf Ya'qub al-Qirqisani (first half of the tenth century) whose *Kitab al-Anwar w'al-Maraqib* (Book of Lights and Watchtowers) provides a great deal of rare and unusual detail on the varieties of sectarian Judaism in his day. Although many Muslim heresiographers, that is, chroniclers of sectarian groups, wrote on Jews and Judaism, the report by al-Shahrastani is unquestionably the most important for the history of Jewish sectarianism.

Kitab al-Milal wa 'l-Nihal (The Book of Religions and Sects (Milal), by the Muslim scholar Abu al-Fath Muhammad al-Karim al-Shahrastani (d. 1153), is generally considered to be the most learned, reliable, and comprehensive premodern history of religions written in any language. *Kitab al-Milal wa 'l-Nihal* is divided into two sections. The first, on the Muslim sects, is considerably shorter than the second, on the non-Muslim sects. In this latter section, sects are set forth in accordance with their respective (ostensible and/or assumed) divergence from the principles and practices of Islam. The first non-Muslim sects addressed are therefore those of the *Ahl al-Kitab* (People of the Book). These are, in order of Shahrastani's presentation, Jews, Christians, Zoroastrians, Manicheans, and Hindus, several dozen groups and subgroups in all. The section of *Milal* on non-Muslim groups begins with revealed religions. In this category Shahrastani discusses four groups of Jews and three groups of Christians. He then continues his magisterial survey with revealed religions that do not possess an authentic holy book, but only scriptures they themselves (and not Islamic theologians) consider sacred.

Before he presents the Jewish sects, Shahrastani devotes several pages to an analysis of "Judaism," with particular concentration on the Torah. After several more pages, he abruptly remarks that the Jews broke up into seventy-one sects, of which he declares his intention to recount "the best-known and most prominent of them and will forgo the rest."

The first of these, and thus the very first non-Muslim sect—by the implication of his system, the sect of all religious groups closest to Islam—are the ʿAnaniyya. He does not explicitly say that they are the Karaites (al-Qarraʾun, which he uses elsewhere), nor does he say that they are not. Shahrastani seems less concerned with the sect itself than with the heretical leader ʿAnan, the so-called "founder" of Karaism, and particularly with his attitude toward Jesus as prophet. Indeed, there is nothing distinctively "Jewish" in Shahrastani's description of ʿAnan's doctrine, which the scholar alleges to have comprised an ascetic ritual praxis. It is rather ʿAnan's attitude toward Christianity that is the point of this entire section. Shahrastani claims that ʿAnan, "called ʿAnan ibn Dawud, Raʾs Jalut" (Exilarch, Prince of the Exile) recognized Jesus as a righteous man, not as a prophet, but that other subsections of the ʿAnaniyya hold other opinions about Jesus. Thus, according to his interpretation of this passage, Shahrastani says that "some held that [Jesus] was one of the friends (*auliyaʾ*) of God." A second group is said to have held that the Gospel is not divinely inspired but rather was merely the biography of Jesus. Another group, according to this view, is said to have rejected Jesus and even to have murdered him.

Shahrastani follows the ʿAnaniyya with a Jewish sect known as the ʿIsawiyya. A Jew by the name of Abu ʿIsa al-Isfahani (mid-eighth century) became notorious in Muslim religious literature for his relativization of revelations—the threatening doctrine that Muhammad and Jesus were genuine prophets, but only to their own communities and not to the Jews. The militancy and the tenacity of his following caused further concern. His sect, the ʿIsawiyya, which emerged in the eighth century, led armed battles against the nascent Sunni authorities, in a turbulent milieu of numerous connections between the ʿIsawiyya and neighboring proto-Shiʿi revolutionaries. Abu ʿIsa forbad divorce; required seven or ten prayers a day; retained the rabbinic forms of the central Jewish prayers, the Shemoneh Esreh and the Shema; exalted the rabbis almost as high as the prophets; and forbad the consumption of meat, fowl, and wine. He allowed intermarriage with Rabbanites, because they celebrated the same holidays. And he used the same Torah text as did the Rabbanites. Finally, the earliest Persian-language heresiography adds these details: "[Abu ʿIsa] imposed ten ritual prayers in every twenty-four-hour period. He said, 'one to whom a nocturnal emission occurs and does not perform ablutions will not be pure for seven days.' He established a tax of two-fifths: one-fifth for the community and another one-fifth for the treasury of the Messiah (in such a manner that it remains in the treasury until the manifestation of the Messiah)." This last detail—which evokes the Shiʿi system of *khums* (one-fifth) tax for the Imam—supports the consensus that the ʿIsawiyya originated as a product of the mid-eighth-century milieu that simultaneously spawned Islamic Shiʿism.

The apparent insider quality of Shahrastani's report on the Jewish sects suggests that it may have been derived from an informant among the Jews, perhaps among the ʿIsawiyya themselves. The section of Shahrastani on the ʿIsawiyya discloses the voice (or text) of this informant, where Shahrastani quotes Hebrew terms. He says, for example, that "Abu ʿIsa Ishaq ibn Yaʿqub al-Isfahani was called ʿUfid Alluhim, that is, ʿAbid Allah." That Shahrastani quotes this name "Servant [lit., worshiper] of God" in a Hebrew form suggests that Shahrastani's informant explained to Shahrastani what it meant, which one or the other of them transliterated and then transposed, more or less, into its Arabic equivalent. Similarly, when Shahrastani gives the (Persianate) name of the ʿIsawite continuator "Yudhghan," he also adds that "it is said that his name [in Hebrew] was Yehuda." Shahrastani seems to have subordinated his "secondary sources" to the "primary source" that was his informant. He makes suspiciously similar observations regarding ʿAnan, Abu ʿIsa, and Yudghan: all three are said to have proscribed alcohol and meat, and enjoined austerity and supererogatory prayers. He says the same of the Samaritans, for which information he probably relied on Christian sources.

Shahrastani's report is the richest surviving source on the minor sects, ʿIsawiyya and the Maghariyya. These groups, he claims, were marked by ascetic practices, as were the Samaritans. In the case of the mysterious Maghariyya, he is concerned only with their hermeneutics and prophetology. Internal evidence from the *Milal* may be read to suggest that Shahrastani himself approved of the doctrines he ascribed to the Maghariyya, which may account for his disproportionate elaboration of their alleged doctrines.

Shahrastani's apparent preference for the Maghariyya may be discerned in his treatment of the doctrine of anthropomorphism. The Yudhdaniyya and the Maghariyya were the only non-anthropomorphizing Jews presented in *Milal*. That Shahrastani approves of their solution to the problem of anthropomorphism might be perceived in the fact that he cited the Maghariyya's verbatim assertion "God wrote the Torah with his Hand" in his general introduction to the Jews—in the form of a *hadith* (a canonical Muslim tradition concerning what Muhammad did, said, or approved). Since Shahrastani also concludes his report on the Maghariyya with further Qur'anic parallels, the careful reader is left with the impression that the Maghariyya's angel-centered anti-anthropomorphism therefore must be consonant with his own preferred Islamic orthodoxy. Moreover, he ascribes the hermeneutics of *ta'wil* (allegorical interpretation) to Yudghan, a form of hermeneutics that he, as an Isma'ili sympathizer, would apparently have endorsed. By contrast, he concludes his detailed report on the major Jewish sects with the Samaritans, in whom he seemed comparatively uninterested. His report on the Samaritans was derived from existing sources. Its few significant additions to the heresiographic literature on the Jews, especially his discussion of the Samaritan prophet Alfan, remain provocative but largely uncorroborated.

Given that the Rabbanite majority was disinclined to record details of heterodox Jewish practice, it fell to heresiographers such as Shahrastani to speak to this lacuna. It is striking, to say the least, that Shahrastani does not discuss the Rabbanites, the majority of rabbinical Jews.

The edition of *Kitab al-Milal wa'l-Nihal* translated here is that of Cairo 1328/1910, reedited by Muhammed Badran in two vols. (Cairo: 1947–1955).

Further Reading

Sections of *Kitab al-Milal wa'-Nihal* were translated by A. K. Kazi and J. C. Flynn, *Muslim Sects and Divisions: The Section on Muslim Sects in Kitab al-Milal wa'l-Nihal by Muhammad b. 'Abd al-Karim Shahrastani* (London: Kegan Paul, 1984). In the same year, J. C. Vadet translated the same sections into French as *Les Dissidences de l'Islam* (Paris: Librairie Orientaliste Paul Guenther, 1994). An annotated French translation of the entire work is now available as *Livre des religions et des sectes*, vol. 1, translated by G. Monnot and D. Gimaret (Paris: Peeters, UNESCO, 1986), and vol. 2, translated by G. Monnot and J. Jolivet (Paris: Peeters, UNESCO, 1993). These volumes include exhaustive discussions of all aspects of the work. Shahrastani's heresiography of the Jews has been studied in the context of contemporaneous Jewish-Muslim intellectual relations in Steven M. Wasserstrom, *Between Muslim and Jew: The Problem of Symbiosis under Early Islam* (Princeton: Princeton University Press, 1995). For more sustained studies of the section of Shahrastani on Jewish sects, see Wasserstrom, "The 'Isawiyya Revisited," *Studia Islamica* 75 (1992): 57–80, and "Shahrastani on the Maghariyya," *Israel Oriental*

Studies 17 (1998) 127–55. See also Yoram Erder, "The Doctrine of Abu 'Isa al-Isfahani and Its Sources," *Jerusalem Studies in Arabic and Islam* 20 (1996) 162–99. Another extensive treatment of Jewish sectarianism, one with which Shahrastani may have been familiar, was the *Kitab al-Anwar w'al-Maraqib* of Abu Yusuf Ya'qub al-Qirqisani. See Bruno Chiesa and Wilfrid Lockwood, *Ya'qub al-Qirqisani on Jewish Sects and Christianity* Frankfurt-am-Main: Peter Lang: (1984).

Kitab al-Milal wa'l-Nihal

We will recount the best known and most prominent of them, and will forego the rest in disregard.

The 'Ananiyya were named after a man called 'Anan b. Dawud, Ra's Jalut [Rosh Golah, Exilarch]. They differed with [respect to the practice of] the Jews' rest on the Sabbath and festivals, and forbad eating the flesh of the dove, deer, fish, and locusts. They slaughter animals by the back of the neck. They deemed credible Jesus in his rousing sermons and commandments. They say that [Jesus] absolutely did not contradict the Torah, rather he fulfilled it, and summoned men to it. Among the Children of Israel, [Jesus] belonged to the devotees of the Torah, and to the followers of Moses; but they do not believe in his prophethood and apostlehood.

Some of them say that Jesus did not claim that he was a prophet sent by God, nor that he was of the Children of Israel, nor that he was the author of a law abrogating the Law of Moses. Rather, [they claim that] he was one of the Friends of God, sincere to and recognizing the ordinances of the Torah. The Gospel is not a book revealed to him by inspiration by God, but rather it is a collection, his various biographical circumstances, from his beginning to his end, and only four of his Apostles gathered it together: So [they assert,] how can it be a revealed book?

They [also] say: The Jews wronged since they disbelieved him at first, and did not acknowledge him after his calling, and finally murdered him, and they still do not recognize his status and his importance. The Torah mentions accounts of the "Mashiha" in many places, and this is the Messiah. However, they do not mention his prophethood nor [do they mention] the abrogating of [divinely revealed] Laws. "Paraclete" is also mentioned, who is a "Man Who Knows," whose account is similarly mentioned in the Gospel. If this is found in the book, then this must be so, and is also incumbent on anyone who claims otherwise to prove it.

The 'Isawiyya were named after Abu 'Isa Ishaq b. Ya'qub al-Isfahani. It is said that his name was "'Ufid Alluhim" [Heb. *Eved Elohim*], that is, "The Servant of God." He lived in the time of al-Mansur and began his mission during the time of the last Umayyad king, Marwan b. Muhammad al-Himmar.

Many Jewish people followed him, and claimed signs and miracles for him: they claimed that when he was embattled he made a line around his followers with a myrtle stick, saying "Stay behind this line and no enemy will reach you with weapons." And the enemy would turn back upon reaching that line, fearing that he might have placed a talisman or *azima* there. Then Abu 'Isa went beyond that line, alone and on horseback, and fought and killed many Muslims. He went out to the Banu Musa b. 'Imran, who lived beyond the sand, to preach to them the Word of God. It is said that when he fought against the followers of Mansur at Rayy many of his companions were killed.

He claimed that he was a prophet and messenger of the awaited Messiah; that the Messiah has five forerunners who precede him one after the other; that God spoke to him and charged him with the mission to save the Children of Israel from the rebellious Gentiles and the tyrannical kings; that the Messiah is the best of the children of Adam; that he is of a higher status than the ancient prophets; that he is His apostle, for he is the most excellent of them all.

He enjoined faith in the Messiah, exalting the mission of the Forerunner; he believed that the Forerunner is also the Messiah; he made unlawful in his book all slaughter of animals, bird or beast, without exception; he enjoined them at times which he specified; he opposed the Jews in many of the precepts of the Great Law mentioned in the Torah.

The popular Torah is the one that one of the Roman kings had compiled by thirty rabbis so that any ignoramus can not arbitrarily use it in place of its ordinances.

The Yudhghaniyya were named for Yudhghan of Hamadan; it is said that his name was Yehuda. He used to urge austerity and many prayers. He forbad the consumption of flesh and alcoholic liquors. Among the things said about him was that he exalted the *Da'i* ["The missionary"]. He used to claim that the Torah had an extrinsic (*zahir*) and an intrinsic (*batin*) meaning, and a revealed textual form (*tanzil*) and an interpretation of that form (*ta'wil*), but he opposed the Jews in the interpretations they commonly held regarding anthropomorphism, and he inclined toward the doctrine of *qadar* [predestination], asserting that the actions of man appear real to him, but that reward and punishment are predestined for him; and he went to extremes to emphasize this.

Among them were the Mushkaniyya, followers of Mushkan. He was of the sect of Yudhghan except that he used to insist on their going out to fight their opponents. Indeed, he ordained that they should be fought. So they went out, nineteen strong, and were killed on the outskirts of Qum. It is recounted about a group of the Mushkaniyya that they affirmed the prophethood of Muhammad for the Arabs and for all the rest of mankind except for the Jews, for they are [already] the people of a recognized religious community and a Book.

One sect of the Maghariyya [text has Maqariba] claims that God spoke to the prophets through the agency of an angel whom he had chosen and whom He had placed in precedence over all created beings, and had made vicegerent (*khalifa*) over them. They say: "Everything in the Torah and the rest of the books describing God refers to this angel, for otherwise it would not be possible to describe God." They say: "The one who spoke to Moses is that angel, and the Tree (*shajara*) mentioned in the Torah is that angel. The Lord is too exalted to speak to mankind in speech. Everything mentioned in the Torah is referred to in such terms as "seeking to see [God] (*ru'ya*)," "I spoke to God," "God came," "he wrote the Torah with his own hand," "God ascended into the clouds," "he settled down on the throne firmly," "he has the form of Adam," "curly hair and black curls [below the ears]," "he wept over the Flood of Noah, until his eyes were sore," "The Mighty One (*al-Jabbar*) laughed until he showed his teeth," and so on, is attributed [according to the doctrine of this sectarian] to that angel.

[The Maghariyya say that] it is possible, in the normal course of events, that God should send an angel in his place, and should confer his Name upon him, saying, "This is my messenger (*rasul*), and his position (*makan*) is as mine among you, and his utterance (*qawl*) is my utterance, his command (*amr*) is my command, and his manifestation (*zuhur*) before you is my manifestation. Thus is the condition of that angel."

It is said that inasmuch as Arius said that the Messiah is God, and that he is the choicest [being] in the world (*safwat al-'alam*), he [Arius] took his doctrine from them [the Maghariyya], who preceded Arius by four hundred years. They were men of abstinence and [even] mortification.

It is said that an author (*sahib*) of this doctrine (*maqala*) was Benjamin al-Nehawandi, who established this school (*madhhab*) among them and taught them that the ambiguous verses (*mutashabiha*) in the Torah were interpretable; and that God cannot be described by the descriptions applicable to man; and that he does not resemble anything created; nor does anything in them resemble him; and that the referent of the aforementioned passages occurring in the Torah was that angel honored [by God].

This is as in the Qur'an, where the coming of God is reported as being that of one of the angels. Thus, again, as the Word of God on the subject of Mary: "We have breathed our Spirit into her" [21:91]. And, in another passage: "We have breathed into her with our Spirit" [66:12]. The one who does the breathing here is Gabriel (peace be upon him) when he appeared to [Mary] "in the form of a man in all respects" [19:17] to give her "a holy son" [19:19].

The Samira [Samaritans] are a community living on the mountain of Jerusalem and villages in the districts of Egypt. They lead ascetic lives of ritual purity more so than do the rest of the Jews.

They acknowledge the prophethood of Moses, Aaron, Joshua, and reject the prophethood of all subsequent prophets except for a single prophet. They say "The Torah only announces a single prophet to come after Moses who will confirm the Torah he possessed and who will legislate with his wisdom, and will not diverge from it in any respect whatsoever."

There appeared among the Samira a man called "al-Alfan" who claimed prophethood for himself and claimed that he was the one announced by Moses and that he was the "brilliant (*durrin*) star" mentioned in the Torah; and that he would shine as moonlight, and that his appearance would precede that of the Messiah by about a century.

The Samira are divided into Dustaniyya, who are the Alfaniyya, and the Kustaniyya. The "Dustaniyya" means "various lying sects." The "Kustaniyya" means the "righteous community." They believe in the hereafter, and in rewards and punishments therein. The Dustaniyya falsely believe in rewards and punishments in this world. These two sects disagree on individual religious ordinances as well as religious laws.

The *qibla* [direction of prayer] of the Samira is a mountain called Gharizim between Jerusalem and Nablus. They say that God commanded David to build the Temple on the mountain in Nablus—which is the mountain upon which God spoke to Moses—but David switched to Aelia and built the Temple there, transgressing the commandment, and so sinned. The Samira pray toward that direction, unlike the rest of the Jews. Their language is not the language of the Jews. They claim that the Torah was originally in their language—which is close to Hebrew—and was translated into Aramaic.

These four sects are the major ones, from which a total of seventy-one sects branch off.

18

Travel in the Land of Israel

Lawrence Fine

Jewish travel to Palestine in the premodern period was rooted primarily in religious tradition and religious sentiment. Until the sacred Temple in Jerusalem was destroyed by the Romans in the year 70 C.E., it was considered an obligation of Jewish law to go to Jerusalem whenever possible for the seasonal pilgrimage festivals (*shalosh regalim*) of Sukkot, Passover, and Shavuot. There pilgrims—welcomed by the Jewish residents of Jerusalem—would participate in the elaborate Temple rituals associated with these festivals. This was the case both for Jews living outside of Jerusalem but within the land of Israel, as well as for those living in the diaspora. In the wake of the destruction of the Temple this obligation no longer obtained. Nevertheless, the deeply rooted memory of the Temple and Jerusalem, preserved in numerous rites and liturgies, great love for the land as a whole, and the dream of returning to the land in the future under the auspices of the messianic age all combined to lead many individuals to either visit Palestine sometime during their lives or, even more, to reside there permanently.

Yehuda Halevi (before 1075–1141), perhaps the greatest of the Hebrew poets of Muslim Spain, is famed for his "songs of Zion," which exemplify and poignantly capture the feelings which many medieval Jews held toward the land of Israel (*Erets Yisrael*, the traditional Jewish designation for Palestine). Halevi, who himself unsuccessfully tried to reach Palestine in the year 1140, wrote the following well-known poetic homage to Zion:

> My heart is in the East and I am at the edge of the West. Then how can I taste what I eat, how can I enjoy it? How can I fulfill my vows and pledges while Zion is in the domain of Edom [i.e., Christianity], and I am in the bonds of Arabia [i.e., Islam]? It would be easy for me to leave behind all the good things of Spain; it would be glorious to see the dust of the ruined Shrine.

Although for most of the Middle Ages and early modern period, the Jewish community in Palestine (known by the Hebrew term *yishuv*, lit., settlement) was relatively small in number, travel there was continuous and frequent from the twelfth century forward, despite the extreme dangers and hardships that it entailed. Besides the religious motivations already mentioned, individuals traveled to Palestine (as well as other places) for various other reasons. Some were especially intrigued by reports of fellow Jewish communities in distant lands and sought to make contact with them. Many people traveled, of course, because they were involved in international trade and commerce, whereas others were simply adventurous. The most famous medieval Jewish traveler was the twelfth-century Spanish Jew Benjamin of Tudela, whose *Book of Travels* provides an account of his lengthy journeys through Spain, Provence, Italy, Greece, Turkey, Cyprus, and other places throughout the Mediterranean world, and eventually to Palestine. His rather impersonal, factually oriented observations about the country, including its sacred sites and various communities, is considered an historical document of considerable importance. Around the same time, a certain Petahiah of Regensburg also undertook an elaborate journey that took him eventually to Palestine, as well. Petahiah appears to have been a wealthy individual whose primary motivation was religious pilgrimage to the Jewish holy sites in Palestine, especially the tombs of famous rabbis and scholars. His visit to Palestine took place at a time when the Jewish community was in severe decline, a result of the Crusades of the late eleventh century.

Although Benjamin's and Petahiah's extremely popular travelogues were read primarily for enjoyment as belles lettres, as the historian Salo Baron pointed out, "they doubtless helped to kindle the imagination of Western Jews, maintain their morale in the midst of successive calamities, and keep alive their perennial yearning toward the Holy Land, which, a generation after Petahiah, was to erupt in the dramatic journey of three hundred Western rabbis to Palestine" (225–26). Important travel accounts to the land of Israel in the next two centuries were written by Judah al-Harizi, Moses ben Nachman, and Estori ha-Parhi, who took an unusually scholarly approach to his observations about the country. His travelogue of 1322 provides exceptionally detailed information about the topography of the land and its ancient holy sites, as well as the various Jewish communities that he encountered.

Accounts of travel to Palestine proliferated, however, in the fifteenth and sixteenth centuries as a result of a great surge in visits on the part of a number of important Italian Jews, some of whom settled there permanently. The letters of Meshullam of Volterra, Elijah of Ferrara, Ovadiah of Bertinoro, Moses Basola, Elijah of Pesaro, and David di Rossi contain some of the most interesting and beautiful descriptions of the Jewish community during a period leading up to its renaissance in the sixteenth century. The letter below is part of this literature. It was composed not by a well-known scholar but rather by a young anonymous student of the above-mentioned Ovadiah of Bertinoro, and sent, it seems, to friends or acquaintances. The author appears to have followed Ovadiah to Palestine about ten years after the latter's departure from Italy for Jerusalem.

Writing in the year 1495, our author tells of his departure from Venice and his travels through Corfu, Rhodes, Famagusta (on Cyprus), Beirut, and Damascus, which led eventually to his arrival in Safed and Jerusalem. He describes briefly each of the cities in which he stayed en route, and pays special attention to its physical nature and its inhabitants, its commercial aspects, availability and quality of foods, and often tells where he stayed and describes those who provided him with hospitality. We get a good sense from this letter of some of the perils and vicissitudes of medieval travel. He reports, for instance, of the dangerous pirates in Rhodes, the poor quality of the air and water in Famagusta, the absence of inns in the region of Damascus, and the dishonesty and thievery of toll-road collectors in various places, including Palestine: "from the village of Kana to Jerusalem the holy the way is exceedingly dangerous because of the robbers and the toll collectors, for the collectors may take a man's life and none dare protest." Relatively speaking, however, the letter describes a rather carefree journey compared to what we often find in such accounts.

The author gives a detailed and vivid description of the city of Safed in the northern Galilee, where he arrived in October 1495. Although he is impressed with the city, this is several decades prior to the flowering of Safed as a great center of kabbalistic and pietistic activity. The contemporary reader who has visited Safed will immediately appreciate the physical description of the city: "Safed is built on the slopes of a mountain and is a great city . . . when the rain falls it is impossible to walk about town on account of the dirt, and also because it is on the hillside. It is also difficult to go out in the markets and the streets even during the summer, for you must always be climbing up and down." This section of the letter is particularly interesting on account of its detailed portrayal of the numerous graves of important rabbis and scholars buried in the environs of Safed, including that of Shimon bar Yochai in Meron, to whom tradition attributes authorship of the *Zohar*. In this way it provides background for the great importance that such gravesites had as sites of pilgrimage and veneration for the kabbalists of Safed several decades later, in the middle of the sixteenth century. The author himself mentions that as soon as he arrived in Safed he went to recite prayers at the tomb of the prophet Hosea ben Beeri.

Our letter writer, however, was primarily interested in Jerusalem, his ultimate destination. Once there, he immediately sought out Ovadiah of Bertinoro (c. 1450–before 1516), from whom he sought spiritual instruction and with whom he wished to study Torah. We know about Ovadiah's life primarily from three of his own letters—written between 1488 and 1490—that describe *his* journey from Italy to the land of Israel. Ovadiah had arrived in Jerusalem just before Passover in 1488. He immediately became the spiritual leader of the Jewish community there, organized community study and prayer, and successfully enhanced its financial and material condition. Bertinoro is best known, however, for his commentary on the Mishnah, which was completed in Jerusalem and published in Venice between 1548 and 1549. This text became the standard Mishnah commentary, its great importance attested by the fact that it is traditionally published alongside the Mishnah itself.

The letter ends with a rich description of the Jewish community in Jerusalem, and especially of its religious activities. As with many such letters—intended in significant part to extol the virtues of the land of Israel and its Jewish inhabitants to readers—the author no doubt indulges in some exaggeration. In doing so, however, he testifies to the great love that Jews in premodern times universally had for the land. He echoes the sentiments of Yehuda Halevi quoted above when he describes the depth of his emotions upon seeing for the first time "the desolate and ruined city [of Jerusalem] from a distance," and how his "spirit overflowed, my heart mourned, and my eyes were filled with tears," upon seeing the Temple mount.

The letter was published for the first time by Adolf Neubauer in *Jahrbuch fuer die Geschichte der Juden und des Judentums,* vol. 3 (Leipzig, 1863), pp. 271–302. The translation is adapted from the English version in Kurt Wilhelm, ed., *Roads to Zion—Four Centuries of Traveler's Reports,* translated by I. M. Lask (New York: Schocken, 1948).

Further Reading

In addition to Kurt Wilhelm's *Road to Zion,* noted above, a significant collection of premodern Jewish travelogues in English translation may be found in E. N. Adler, *Jewish Travellers in the Middle Ages* (1930; reprint New York: Dover, 1987), and Franz Kobler, ed., *A Treasury of Jewish Letters* (Philadelphia: East and West Library/Jewish Publication Society, 1978), vol. 1, pp. 293–319. For studies of this literature, see Salo Baron, *A Social and Religious History of the Jews,* vol. 6 (New York, Columbia University Press, 1958), pp. 219–26, and Joshua Prawer, *The History of the Jews in the Latin Kingdom of Jerusalem* (Oxford: Oxford University Press, 1988), pp. 128–250.

Travel to the Land of Israel by a Disciple of Ovadiah of Bertinoro

O my soul, praise the Almighty for his mercy, by which we have happily finished the journey over the wide sea; we have not been touched by anyone. I must also thank God that he brought us to our destination. May the Almighty favor you so that you, too, may see the Holy Land, and may you live in peace in your land. I am sending you a letter that contains the description of our journey to Jerusalem.

On the fifth of August, 5255 [1495], we departed from Venice with gladness, rejoicing to set out on our way peacefully and directly. On the Sabbath day at the twenty-second hour [4:00 P.M., based on Italian reckoning starting from 6:00 P.M. and continuing for twenty-four hours] we reached Pola, where meat and fish and all delicacies may be found, and all inexpensive. There we spent two days in the magnificent house of Jacob Ashkenazi, may his Rock and Maker guard him, who graciously led us to his house and prepared a feast for his people, as well as "a bed, a chair, and a lamp," and as in the king's house, so here nothing was lacking. There is another Jew here, besides him, to give access to all who would borrow against pledges, and he dwells like a king with his troops. From Venice to Pola is a hundred and fifty miles, a journey of a day and a night, but we were delayed on the way because there was no wind, and we were becalmed.

We set sail from that place with a favorable wind, and reached Corfu on Monday, the seventeenth of August. Corfu is a large city on the shore but not handsome, being mean and dirty, particularly the Jewish quarter. However, the fruits are good, and there we purchased provisions for the way, bread and cheese, and grapes and peaches. The city is six hundred miles away from Pola and we only spent the night there. Therefore, I cannot tell you what the land is like.

We set out from Corfu with a strong and favorable wind, and reached Modone on Friday morning, the twenty-first of the month. This is also a large city, even more beautiful than Corfu. It has many merchants and is a land of olives, oil and wines, figs and pomegranates. However, the countryside is not as beautiful as your region, and those who dwell in it may be compared to cattle. From Corfu to Modone is a distance of five hundred miles.

We set out from Modone and arrived at Rhodes on Friday, the twenty-seventh of the month, and nobody descended from the ships for some time, for fear of the corsairs, the reason being that Rhodes is a city of refuge for pirates because they give the grand master [of the Knights Hospitalers, whose headquarters were at Malta] his share of all the booty they take; therefore the corsairs come to the city for safety. For this reason, the captain wished to be certain that all was safe before any man left his place. Besides, it is necessary to be very careful in Rhodes, and particularly necessary for Jews. Rhodes is a fortified city, large and extremely strong. Most of the houses are of big stone slabs, and men of renown and merchants of every nation and tongue may be found there. There are likewise many Frenchmen in Rhodes because the grand Master is a Frenchman. And the city is five hundred miles distant from Modone.

We departed from Rhodes at noon on the twenty-ninth and reached Famagusta on Thursday, the third of September 1495. There we stayed for three days. It is a fine city full of good things. Never in my life have I seen such plenty of bread and meat and everything else. A man can maintain himself honorably and well there on six ducats a year, and maybe even less. It is true that this is a land that consumes its inhabitants, for the air is very bad and the water too is not good, for which reason the inhabitants are few. In all the places I have mentioned I found large communities, except for Famagusta, where they are scanty. Nor was there any moneylender in the country through which we passed save an Ashkenazi Jew in Famagusta, whose name is Sabbatai and who gives access to those who wish to borrow money. Anybody who desires may borrow against interest, that being fitting and proper in their eyes, and no one will reprimand the lender, that being the custom of the land. But in the other places the Jews are artisans or merchants, and dwell in security with none to disturb them. Famagusta is in the island of Cyprus, and is three hundred miles distant from Rhodes.

The evening of the sixth of September 1495 we departed from Famagusta, and reached the coast of Beirut on Tuesday the eighth. On Wednesday morning we left the ships cheerfully and joyously. To sum up what we have said, from Venice to Beirut took us thirty-four days in all, though we delayed on the way at the places I have mentioned.

Now I want to tell you what I have seen with my own eyes. At all the places we passed, Jews embarked on the ship. Some of them went to Beirut. About one hundred and fifty Jews also arrived with the merchant galley, all of them poor and needy. Thus we were about three hundred altogether. The Arabs behaved very compassionately toward the poor; they distributed money, wheat, bread, and fruit among them. Although they insult the Christians, often shouting behind them, "Dog, son of a dog," they do not offend the Jews. The more I had reason to wonder that no Jews are living there [in Beirut].

We took a house in the company of the exalted and saintly man, our master Rabbi Joseph Saragossi, a Sephardic Jew who is piety itself, and we stayed with his whole household for seven days, before the route by which we would proceed was selected. For we were in doubt whether to proceed by way of Damascus or Sidon, which is only half a day's journey from Beirut but is reckoned as part of the Holy Land. . . .

At Beirut we reached an agreement with a donkey driver to take us to Damascus, all the expenses to be covered by him, including the road taxes and everything else. On the night of Wednesday, the sixteenth of September 1495, we departed from the city to a distance about a bow-shot away and there they gave hay and provender to their asses, and delayed there in order to evade the tax collectors. At midnight we rose and continued on our way all night long without mishap, thank God, and we passed two toll-collecting posts without paying them.

In the morning we reached the third toll-collecting post, where they treated us very well and sold us bread and grapes, so that we ate until we were full; and the donkey drivers paid the toll collectors their due and we passed peacefully on. Thus we continued all day and all night long until we arrived at Damascus. In all that region there are no inns to be found on the road that have rooms, beds, and tables; but at the end of a day's journey a tumbledown roofless caravansary which is called a *khan* may sometimes be found. There they sell bread and fruit and eggs, but there is no place to lodge so that people remain outside in the courtyard together with their asses.

On Friday morning, which was the eve of the New Year, we arrived in Damascus hale and hearty with none of us weary, praise God. We stayed in the house of Rabbi Moses Makran, who took us to his home, where we stayed for five days. In none of the places mentioned are there innkeepers to furnish food as in our lands. When a stranger who does not know their language arrives in Damascus not a man will budge from his place to take any steps on his behalf except our master Moses Makran. May the Name reward him as befits his good deeds.

On Wednesday, the fifth day of October 1495, we departed from Damascus with a donkey driver and reached Safed on Friday morning, and there we took a small room in the house of an extremely poor and needy Jew. In his house we remained for more than a month, and he took one piece of silver a day from the two of us, both for the rent of the room and for his trouble in preparing food and bread for us.

Safed is built on the slope of a mountain and is a great city. The houses are small and inconsiderable, and when the rain falls it is impossible to walk about town on account of the dirt, and also because it is on the hillside. It is also difficult to go out in the markets and the streets even during the summer, for you must always be climbing up and down. However, the land is good and health-giving, and the waters are quite good. And this is the absolute truth. I saw men in Safed who are far older than sixty or seventy years. Among them was an old man aged a hundred and thirty, who was still flourishing, strong and healthy indeed. The holy congregation numbers about three hundred householders, and most of the Jews have shops of spices, cheese and oil, and sundry legumes and fruits. I have heard that a man can make twenty-five ducats out of one of those shops, on which five people can live. The foodstuffs are also cheap in Safed, and our wise and learned master Rabbi Peretz Colombo, may he see children and length of days, Amen, is the head of this city and showed us favor and spoke our praise. Further, he wishes to give us board and lodging in his home and to teach us for twelve ducats a year each if we were prepared to stay there. The congregation pays him what he needs to live on. The amount I do not know, but he also has a shop of foodstuffs to earn his upkeep.

Around Safed there are many caves in which great and pious men have been buried. Most of these are about six miles from the town, and I saw some of them. Therefore, I shall now inform you of what I have heard, and what I have seen with my own eyes.

First of all, near the Jewish quarter in Safed is the burial place of the prophet Hosea ben Beeri of blessed memory. There is no tombstone at the cave mouth; and as soon as I reached Safed I said prayers at this grave. About as far from Safed as one may walk on a Sabbath is the grave of the talmudic master Rabbi Judah bar Ilai; and there is a little village there called Ein Zetim. On the grave is a handsome tomb at which candles are lit, and there I went and prostrated myself and lit candles to his memory.

About six miles from Safed is a certain village called Meron, where very great and pious saints whose names I shall mention are buried. Before I came to the place I saw three graves by the wayside, one being that of Rabbi Judah the

Punished, over whose grave there is only a small heap of stones. A little farther away is the burial place of Rabbi Tarphon of saintly and blessed memory, with a handsome monument above it. A little farther yet is the grave of Rabbi Yose ben Kisma of saintly and blessed memory, without any monument.

After this we reached the village itself and saw the cave of Hillel and his disciples of saintly and blessed memory, who were buried with him there; and they number twenty-four. We entered a certain cave nearby in which twenty-two scholars lie, and they said that these were the disciples of Rabbi Shimon bar Yochai of saintly and blessed memory. And near the spot on the hillside there is an extremely fine monument that can be seen as far as Safed. But together with the disciples were buried their wives, and there is nothing over their graves. The local residents said that monuments had frequently been set over their graves, but they were all destroyed at night. However, I do not know whether it is true.

On Friday, the twelfth day of the month Marheshvan 5256 [October 1495], we left Safed in the company of men from Sicily who had made an agreement with a caravan of donkey drivers, Jews, Christians, and Ishmaelites [i.e. Muslims]. Their pay was one hundred and two pieces of silver per person to bring them to Jerusalem without further expenditure on toll collection or anything else.

On Friday, the eve of Sabbath, we reached the village of Kana, where we stayed until Tuesday. On the way we agreed as to what we had to do, in accordance with the good hand of the Lord upon us. Now you, my lords and masters, must know that from the village of Kana to Jerusalem the holy, the way is exceedingly dangerous because of the robbers and the toll-collection posts, for the collectors may take a man's life and none dare protest.

On Tuesday we left the village and proceeded all night without a word, passing two tax-collection stations without paying them. We passed Dothan, and I saw the pit into which the saintly Joseph, of blessed memory, was flung [Gen. 37:17]. When the morning star arose we stayed in the hills until the stars came out. During the second night we passed Shechem, which lies between Mount Gerizim and Mount Ebal. Mount Gerizim is full of all good things, while Mount Ebal is a desolate wilderness. All this time we journeyed only by night for fear of the toll-collection stations. When night came we rose to go on our way, but the Lord found the transgression of your servants. For the men of the toll-collecting post of Shechem caught us on the road and took us back to a camp half a day's journey from that city, where we remained all night long in fear and dread. On Thursday morning the Jews came to an agreement with them and the donkey drivers to pay fourteen ducats; and as my share I had to pay fourteen silver pieces. On Thursday night we set out from the camp and proceeded all night long in fear and trembling, for we were afraid that the men of Shechem would pursue us, since most of them are men of violence. But the Lord led us in the ways of truth. By the time the morning star arose our feet stood before the gates of Jerusalem the holy city, on Friday morning, the eighteenth day of the month Marheshvan.

When I saw the desolate and ruined city from a distance, and Mount Zion lying waste, a habitation for jackals and a lurking place for young lions that foxes traverse, my spirit overflowed, my heart mourned, and my eyes were filled with tears. I sat down and wept, and rent my garment in two places as required. And I prayed facing our Temple. May the Lord in his loving-kindness bring back the captivity of Jacob speedily and in our days, that we may merit to see the rebuilding of our glorious Temple, so that it be his will. Amen.

After I entered the town we went to the home of that awesome and famous man, that lofty and exalted light of the Exile, first among the shepherds, my master and teacher Rabbi Ovadiah, may his Rock and Maker guard him. To him I made known the thoughts of my heart, and my abject petition, telling how until this day I had been as a wild ass, "as a calf untrained," and that I had come to the land to observe the ways of justice, and how in order to know the Lord I had forsaken my family and the land of my birth to take shelter under his shadow, that he might spare me something of all his goodness, and blow the spirit of life into my nostrils, by teaching me Torah and commandments. Rabbi Ovadiah appeared before me, an old man and full of mercy, and he said: "I shall keep my eyes upon you like a beloved son and treat you well." So I record his praises and the loving-kindness with which he treated me in his great mercy.

He is a great man and the whole land obeys his words. No one will a lift a hand without him, and people inquire often after his opinion from the ends of the earth, and never turn aside from his words. In Egypt, too, and in all the countries in which he [makes] decrees, they are fulfilled. Even the Ishmaelites honor and revere him, as I have heard it said that "by the breath of his lips, he has slain an evil man." Yet, he is extremely humble and modest, and his words are sweet, and he enjoys the company of others, and all people praise him. . . .

In Jerusalem the holy there are about two hundred householders who refrain from any sin or transgression and are heedful in the performance of the commandments. Evening, morning, and noon, they all gather together, rich and poor alike, to pray with full and complete concentration. There are two God-fearing cantors who, when they pray, concentrate on the holy meaning of all that they utter. And twice a day all the congregation stand lovingly to hearken to the words of the Lord in the synagogue. An aged, wise, and understanding man of eighty years named Rabbi Zechariah Sephardi, may he see length of days, Amen, delivers a sermon for [only] about a quarter of an hour, after the morning prayer every day, in order not to burden the congregation, as well as in the evening after the evening prayer. And that is their practice, which they never depart from.

But the great light, Rabbi Ovadiah, speaks only two or three times a year, such as at Passover, the Feast of Weeks, and the Feast of Booths, as well as during the Days of Penitence. And though these are only a few occasions, his voice is pleasant and his words are pure and fine, all of them being words of the living God. And great and small alike listen to him and set their trust in him, so that not even the faintest whisper is heard.

Every day after the prayer and the sermon many people remain in the house of study in order to spend about three hours in the study of the Mishnah and the Talmud. And afterward they "go from strength to strength" visiting the sick and giving gifts to the poor, each one giving what his heart counsels him. The people give much alms although they have little themselves, and there are many poor folk in this city, so that most of the congregation are supported by charity.

There is little to be earned here in Jerusalem the holy from the produce of this area. Any handicraftsmen, such as a goldsmith or blacksmith, or a flax weaver or a tailor, will earn his needs, although scantily. But in Damascus and in Egypt, at Alexandria and at Aleppo, which is Aram Zovah, in all these places handicraftsmen can earn as much as they desire, particularly those who know the Arabic language, according to what I have heard. But here artisans can only earn a meager penny, except possibly goldsmiths. However, food is not so expensive here, and this year bread and wine are cheap, praise the blessed God. I think a man can sustain himself with ten ducats a year. We have made an agreement with Aaron Loasi, who lives in this house, according to which he will provide food and laundry for each of us at the price of forty silver coins a month, but he is not obliged to supply us with wine and oil. He does not pay the rent or provide the bed clothes either. He is obliged only to provide us with meat, fish, or some dairy food every night, and make our breakfast. We have been told, however, that we are paying too high a price; nevertheless, we preferred to make this agreement in order not to be kept away from our studies by having to prepare food. . . .

The houses in Jerusalem the holy are all of stone and do not have many floors one above the other as in your land, nor are there rafters in the houses, nor any wooden buildings. Indeed, wood in this city is extremely expensive and is sold in the shops by weight, which I think is why they do not make upper floors and attics here. But a single courtyard will be surrounded by five or six rooms. Nor does this city have any wells of fresh water. Instead, every courtyard has a single cistern full of rain water, and if there is no rain the water in these pits is used up. And sometimes the Ishmaelites gather together to pour out Jewish wine and smash Jewish vessels, for they say that the rain does not fall on account of the sins of the Jews in drinking wine. Sometimes water reaches the town from a fountain which emerges at Hebron, but there is little water from this, and in the summertime it ceases to flow. In the city the wheat is ground by animals, for there are no water mills at all to do the grinding as in your country.

In the midst of the city near the house of study there is an empty place to which all the congregation go after prayers in order to pray facing the Temple. For from there they can see the holy and awesome place. Near this is the El Aksa Mosque, "the school of King Solomon," may he rest in peace, but only

Ishmaelites enter there. Yet Stella, may she be blessed above all women, Amen, the wife of Moses of Borgo, may his Rock and Maker guard him, saw it from outside with the aid of an Ishmaelite townswoman, an important woman who lives near the school. And I have heard from Stella that the building is made of extremely beautiful stones, radiant and pure as the very heavens, and covered over with pure gold worked by craftsmen. But she did not see the building itself from inside. I have heard tell that it is a magnificent building, and the king of Egypt expended immeasurable wealth on it. The Ishmaelites gather there every Friday at noon and say their prayers. Furthermore, the Ishmaelites refrain from work only during the half hour when they stand in the temple to pray.

Below this school is the valley of Yehoshaphat and the valley of Hinnom, and beyond the valley is the burial place of Zechariah ben Yehoyada the priest, of saintly and blessed memory. Nearby is a building like a tower called the Pillar of Absalom. It is half hidden by stones that have been thrown at it, because there stood the building of Absalom who rebelled against his father. Near this is the Mount of Olives. From the there Moabite mountains and Sodom and Gomorrah and the Dead Sea can be seen.

On the Mount of Olives there is a large cave in which are buried the [biblical] prophets Haggai, Zechariah, and Malachi, of blessed memory. About a half day's journey from Jerusalem the holy is the burial place of the prophet Samuel, of Ramah, of saintly and blessed memory. It is on top of the mountain and there is a fine synagogue there. Every Sabbath eve the congregation sends a lamp there to maintain an eternal light. The [burial place of the] Patriarchs [Abraham, Isaac, and Jacob] in Hebron is also about a day's journey from here, and on that road is the Tomb of [the Matriarch] Rachel, may she rest in peace. But I have not yet been there, as the roads are not safe on account of the Bedouin. Only a few days ago a Jew came here from Hebron with all his household and they took everything he had from him. But I have heard it said that Jews come here from Egypt and Damascus for the Passover festival and go to Hebron quite safely. At that time I shall likewise go with them, if the Lord decrees life for me. . . .

19

Karaite Ritual

Daniel Frank

As Judaism's oldest surviving sect, the Karaites maintain a set of beliefs and practices distinct from those of their Rabbanite brethren. Emerging in the Islamic East during the eighth to tenth centuries C.E., the group adamantly rejected the rabbinic tradition and the authority of those who championed it. In their quest for an authentic, unmediated Judaism, the Karaites turned directly to Scripture, which they sought to interpret rationally. During the tenth and eleventh centuries, Karaite scholars in Iraq and the land of Israel composed an extensive religious literature that encompassed exegesis, law, and theology. Scrutinizing Rabbanite *halakhah* (Jewish law) in light of the biblical text, they consciously rejected one practice after another as unwarranted innovations. They dismissed calendation in favor of direct observation of the moon. They did not extend the prohibition of boiling a kid in its mother's milk (Exod. 23:19, 34:26, Deut. 14:21) to the consumption of fowl with dairy products. They rejected the use of phylacteries (*tefillin*), maintaining that Exodus 13:9, 16, Deuteronomy 6:8 and 11:18 were to be understood metaphorically. Through a reactive process of examination, rejection, and legislation, they promulgated an alternative Judaism that won enough adherents to arouse the Rabbanites' ire. Rabbinic leaders in the East such as Saadya Gaon (882–942) polemicized zealously against Karaite practices; in Spain, where the sect had gained a foothold, such prominent scholars as Judah Halevi (d. 1141) and Abraham ibn Daud (d. c. 1180) launched a vigorous defense of the rabbinic tradition.

Although the sect never won a large following, it struck roots, establishing communities in Syria, Egypt, Asia Minor, the Crimea, Poland, and Lithuania. In time, two main groups would evolve: the "Eastern" Karaites of Islamic lands who spoke and wrote Arabic, and the "Western" or "European" Karaites—including those in Istanbul—who wrote primarily in Hebrew and spoke Greek or Crimean Tatar. Despite their rejection of rabbinic tradition, the Karaites always identified themselves as Jews and never severed their ties with their Rabbanite coreligionists. Through their study of each other's texts, some Karaites and Rabbanites even familiarized themselves thoroughly with the teachings of both groups, which led, at times, to a genuine rapprochement. Only in the nineteenth and twentieth centuries did Karaites living under Russian—and later Soviet—rule seek to disengage themselves completely from Judaism. There are today perhaps 20,000–25,000 Karaites in the world, most of whom are of Egyptian extraction and reside in the state of Israel; smaller communities exist in Europe and the United States.

The development of Karaite ritual was conditioned by the sect's scripturalism, its rationalist tendencies, and the Islamic environment in which it emerged. Early sectarian scholars derided certain Rabbanite practices for their nonbiblical origin, their violation of Scripture's plain meaning, or their superstitious nature. The observances they prescribed were intended to be logical and clearly derived from the Bible. Since they advocated the power of human reason and the independence of the individual exegete, differences of interpretation and practice inevitably arose. Not surprisingly, the history of Karaite *halakhah* offers many instances of internal dissension alongside the ongoing polemics with the Rabbanites.

The following selections illustrate certain central themes in Karaite ritual. The practices themselves—liturgy, ritual slaughter, and Sabbath lights—should all be familiar from Rabbanite usage, but the distinctive Karaite perspective will be immediately apparent. The texts derive from different periods and locations, illustrating a range of sectarian observances.

Liturgy

Reacting to the perceived innovations of Rabbanite prayer, the sectarians sought to recover an authentic biblical liturgy. Karaite prayer books are primarily composed, therefore, of psalms, scriptural passages, and pastiches of verses. Their theoretical treatments of prayer, on the other hand, betray a lively interest in the origins of particular usages, in the mental and physical postures suitable for worship, and in the proper place for prayer. There are discussions of these topics in the codes of Anan b. David (eighth century), Ya'qûb al-Qirqisânî (tenth century), Levi b. Japheth (eleventh century), Judah Hadassi (twelfth century), Aaron b. Elijah (fourteenth century), and Elijah Bashyachi (fifteenth century). Composed in Judeo-Arabic, "The Introduction to the Liturgy of the Damascene Karaites" derives from a late seventeenth-century service book. Although it is obviously grounded in earlier sources, the text eliminates the discussion and dissenting opinions recorded in most of the codes in order to describe the basic requirements and features of Karaite prayer. The opening section of the Introduction—omitted in the excerpt below—discusses the obligation, times, language, and physical orientation of prayer. Our passage commences with the proper place for prayer (the synagogue, Heb. *beit kenesset*), the need for purification, physical and spiritual, and the obligation to don the ritual fringes (Heb. *zizit*). There follows a passage on the prayer leader or cantor (Ar. *al-muṣallî, al-imâm*)—his behavior, posture, mental and spiritual states. Some general remarks on communal prayer are followed by a description of kneeling and prostration. The conclusion—also omitted here—relates to synagogues and their furnishings, Torah scrolls and the Torah service, and the minister or beadle (Ar. *khâdim*). Typically, this text employs a mixed Hebrew and Arabic religious vocabulary. While prooftexts are adduced at every turn to justify specific practices, certain usages (such as ritual washing and prostration) were clearly inspired by Islamic ritual.

Ritual Slaughter

Like the Rabbanites, Karaite Jews require that the slaughter of animals for food (Heb. *shehitah*) follow a prescribed ritual. There are strong similarities between the procedures, which differ, however, in significant details. Neither group accepts meat slaughtered by the other. Unlike the Rabbanites, the Karaites also demand that the slaughterer (Heb. *shohet*) possess a sound theology—specifically, that he understand how a perfectly just God permits the suffering of innocent beasts at the hands of human beings. Karaite preoccupation with the problem of divine justice was inspired by the teachings of the Muslim Mutazilite sect, a rationalist group in Iraq whose doctrines were quite influential during the eighth to eleventh centuries. Like the Mutazilites, the Karaites drew a close connection between theory and practice, religious philosophy and law. But they went beyond the Rabbanite insistence on mental concentration or intention (Heb. *kavvanah*) in the performance of religious obligations, requiring also a theological conceptualization of religious law. Since animal suffering poses a direct challenge to the notion of a wholly righteous God, Karaite theologians and jurists tried hard to resolve the dilemma. They insisted, moreover, that slaughterers learn the solutions proposed and meditate upon them before performing *shehitah*. Not surprisingly, since different approaches to the problem were proposed, a Karaite controversy over ritual slaughter ultimately erupted in the mid-seventeenth century.

Sabbath Lights

Exodus 35:3 states: "You shall kindle no fire (*lo teva 'aru esh*) in all your habitations on the Sabbath day." According to Rabbanite Jews, the verse prohibits the lighting of fires during the Sabbath. Light, on the other hand, has long been recognized as a necessary enhancement of the Sabbath. The second chapter of *Mishnah Shabbat* assumes that lighting lamps is an essential part of the Sabbath preparations. And by the late ninth century—if not earlier—the practice had been consecrated as ritual: Rabbanite Jews have routinely recited the benediction "Blessed be You, O Lord . . . who . . . commanded us to kindle the Sabbath light" on the eve of the Sabbath.

The Karaites, on the other hand, originally believed that the verse prohibited fire on the Sabbath altogether (reading: "You shall not allow fire to burn"). They therefore celebrated the Sabbath day in darkness, an action that the Rabbanites ridiculed. During the fifteenth century, certain Karaites in Istanbul and Adrianople began to adopt the Rabbanite usage in order to brighten their dark dwellings on wintry Friday nights. Interpreting the verse as a prohibition of *kindling* fire, they permitted the lighting of lamps before the commencement of the Sabbath; there was, however, no attempt to consecrate the practice with a blessing. Headed by members of the Bashyachi family, these reformers met stout opposition among the more conservative elements in the sectarian population. The ensuing dispute—which led on at least one occasion to physical violence—continued for centuries, with local communities following either one practice or the other. For those who objected to Sabbath lights, sitting in darkness became a kind of negative ritual—a signal emblem of their Karaism that they flaunted before Gentiles, Rabbanite Jews, and cosectarians alike. Those who permitted light on the Sabbath remained on the defensive. The three selections below illustrate the complex, changing attitude of Karaites toward Sabbath lights.

The Judeo-Arabic text of "The Introduction to the Liturgy of the Damascene Karaites" was published with an English translation by G. Margoliouth, "Introduction to the Liturgy of the Damascene Karaites," *Jewish Quarterly Review* o.s. 18 (April 1906): 505–27. In adapting Margoliouth's translation (pp. 519–24), I have referred to the Arabic original.

Karaite codes all feature treatises on *shehitah*; there are also manuals in question-and-answer format for the would-be *shohet*. The passages below have been excerpted and translated from a Hebrew text of this kind published by Mordechai Vogelmann, "Behinat ha-shohet ha-qara'i," *Hazofeh Quartalis Hebraica* (Budapest) 10 (1925–1926): 231–37. The work is of uncertain date and provenance; it probably derives from Poland/Lithuania or the Crimea and dates from the sixteenth to seventeenth centuries.

The first text relating to Sabbath lights is a Sabbath song entitled "*Yerivay ve-oyevay shime'u le-qoli,*" composed by the Egyptian scholar Israel ben Samuel Dayyan (first decades of the fourteenth century); it reflects the sectarians' staunch opposition to the practice. (By way of contrast, we may note that at least two popular Rabbanite hymns for the Sabbath, "*Mah yedidut*" and "*Yom shabbat qodesh hu,*" make specific reference to Sabbath lights.) The poem was published with a prose translation by Leon J. Weinberger, "Israel Dayyan's Zemer for the Sabbath," *Jewish Quarterly Review* 81 nos. 1–2 (July–October, 1990): 1–11; see also Weinberger, *Rabbanite and Karaite Liturgical Poetry in Southeastern Europe* (Cincinnati: Hebrew Union College Press, 1991), pp. 777–78, no. 481 (Hebrew), 50–52 (English). My translation, in doggerel, aims at the effect of the original; there are also a few lines that I read differently from Weinberger.

Second are excerpts from the treatise on Sabbath in Elijah Bashyachi's code, *Adderet Eliyahu* (1480). It was Elijah who canonized the practice of lighting lamps before the Sabbath. The passages translated, from chapters 17 and 20, describe the different positions on the question and the nature of the Bashyachi reform. I have used the Israeli Karaite print, a facsimile of the Odessa, 1870 edition (N.p.: Ha-moʿetsah ha-artsit shel ʿadat ha-yehudim ha-qaraʾim be-yisraʾel, 1966); the facsimile includes an introductory essay by Zvi Ankori, "The House of Bashyachi and Its Reforms" (Hebrew).

The final passage has been taken from the anti-Rabbanite polemic *Lehem Seʿorim* by the Lithuanian sectarian Solomon b. Aaron (first half of the eighteenth century). The treatise takes the form of a fictitious debate between a Karaite and a Rabbanite who rehearse all of the standard topoi. The Karaite rejects the claim that candle lighting is a religious obligation, dismissing it as the innovation of women. (There is even a snide reference to Beruriah, the wife of the second-century *tanna* Rabbi Meir; on her see *Encyclopaedia Judaica*, vol. 4, p. 701). At the same time, it is clear that some Lithuanian Karaites were not averse to using Sabbath lights—something that would have horrified Israel Dayyan. The translation has been made from two Hebrew manuscripts, St. Petersburg Institute of Oriental Studies, MS A83, fols. 12b–13a, and Oxford Bodleian MS Opp. add. 8°, 25 (N. 2387).

Further Reading

The article "Karaites" in the *Encyclopaedia Judaica*, vol. 10, pp. 761–85 provides sound general orientation. For a survey of recent scholarship, see Daniel Frank, "The Study of Medieval Karaism, 1989–1999," chapter one in *Hebrew Scholarship and the Medieval World*, edited by Nicholas De Lange (Cambridge: Cambridge University Press, 2001). For a fine collection of primary sources in translation, see Leon Nemoy, *Karaite Anthology* (New Haven: Yale University Press, 1952), with chapter on "Karaite Liturgy" (pp. 271–321) that includes the Karaite marriage ritual. Although Zvi Ankori's monograph, *Karaites in Byzantium* (New York: Columbia University Press, 1959) focuses on the transmission of Karaite learning during the eleventh and twelfth centuries, its scope is actually much broader; the copious bibliography also makes this an important reference work. Nathan Schur's *History of the Karaites* and *The Karaite Encyclopedia* (Frankfurt-am-Main: Peter Lang, 1992 and 1995) are accessible works, but must be used with caution. Finally, Jacob Mann's *Texts and Studies in Jewish History and Literature*, vol. 2: *Karaitica* (Philadelphia: Jewish Publication Society of America, 1935) contains a wealth of information and primary sources.

P. S. Goldberg's *Karaite Liturgy and Its Relation to Synagogue Worship* (Manchester: Manchester University Press, 1957) is a brief but useful survey; see also Daniel Frank, "Karaite Prayer and Liturgy," in *Karaite Judaism: An Introduction*, edited by Meira Polliack (Leiden: Brill, forthcoming). On the liturgical use of psalms by tenth-century Karaites, see Daniel Frank, "The *Shoshanim* of Tenth-Century Jerusalem: Karaite Exegesis, Prayer, and Communal Identity," in *The Jews of Medieval Islam: Community, Society, and Identity*, edited by D. Frank (Leiden: E. J. Brill, 1995), pp. 199–245. Two articles that include translations of primary sources are: Leon Nemoy, "Studies in the History of the Early Karaite Liturgy: The Liturgy of al-Qirqisânî," in *Studies in Jewish Bibliography, History, and Literature in Honor of I. Edward Kiev,* edited by C. Berlin (New York: Ktav Publishing House, 1971), 305–32, and Georges Vajda, "La Lex orandi de la communauté karaïte d'après Lévi ben Yefet," *Revue des Études Juives* 134.1–2 (1975): 3–45.

For texts and translations of Karaite *shehitah* manuals, see: M. Lorge, *Die Speisegesetze der Karäer nach einer Berliner Handschrift* (Berlin: Druck von H. Itzkowski, 1907), and Leon Nemoy, "Israel al-Maghribî's Tract on Ritual Slaughtering," *Henoch* 13 (1991): 195–218. On an internal Karaite dispute concerning the slaughterer's beliefs see Daniel Frank, "A Seventeenth-Century Karaite Shehitah Controversy: Causes, Context, and Repercussions," in *Isadore Twersky Memorial Volume,* edited by Jay M. Harris and Bernard Septimus (Cambridge: Harvard University Press, forthcoming). On the intimate connection between Karaite law and religious philosophy, see David Sklare, "Yûsuf al-Basîr: Theological Aspects of His Halakhic Works," in *The Jews of Medieval Islam: Community, Society, and Identity,* edited by D. Frank (Leiden: E. J. Brill, 1995), pp. 249–70.

On the attempt of the Bashyachi clan to sanction the practice of kindling Sabbath lights, see Zvi Ankori, *Karaites in Byzantium* (New York: Columbia University Press, 1959), index, s.v. "Sabbath candles."

The Liturgy of the Damascene Karaites

In the Exile, the best place for prayer is the synagogue, as it is written: "In assemblies bless God the Lord" [Ps. 68:27]. Those who find it difficult to get to the synagogue for one reason or another should pray in a place that is free of unclean matter, as is demanded by both reason and tradition.

No one should pray before having performed essential purification. One should cleanse oneself, then wash the hands thoroughly with something that removes all trace of unclean matter. Next, one should wash the face: the eyes, nose, mouth, and the cavities of the ears. This must be done because the face is exposed to dust, and the eyes to the tears that issue from them, and the cavities of the ears to secreted matter, and the nose to the fluid that issues from it, as is the mouth. Next, one washes the feet up to the ankles, and the hands up to the wrists. This washing is in imitation of our Master Aaron, peace be upon him, and of his children, as it is written: "When they went into the tent of meeting, and when they approached the altar, they washed" [Exod. 40:32]. Next comes the cleansing of one's clothes of unclean matter; it is better still if a man has special garments designated for prayer. Next, the cleansing of the heart and its purification from all pollution, greediness, and evil thoughts, as it is written: "Wash yourselves, make yourselves clean; remove the evil of your doings from before my eyes, cease to do evil" [Isa. 1:16].

If it is true that this is obligatory on everyone at all times, when they are at prayer and when they are not, it is especially binding at prayer. A man should not pray without having made a partition between his heart and the lower part of his body; this is to be done by putting on trousers or a girdle around his middle. Then one takes hold of the *zizit* ("ritual fringes," that is, the prayer shawl) and wraps himself in it, covering his face so as to shut out distracting sights. Then one pronounces the benediction, saying: "Blessed are you, Lord our God, King of the universe, who has sanctified us with his commandments, and enjoined *zizit* upon us." This covering [of the face] is in imitation of the seraphim, as it is written "With two he covered his face" [Isa. 6:2]. It is also in imitation of our master Moses, peace be upon him, as it is written: "And Moses hid his face" [Exod. 34:33].

The leader of the service should not carry anything in his hand, nor should his handkerchief be in his sleeve, nor should there be anything on his shoulder or on his head. He should not point with his hand, or wink, or turn around either to the right or left, and he should not be preoccupied with any story he may have heard. He should not blow his nose or spit at a distance; if necessary, he should spit into the handkerchief he may have at his breast, or at his side on the ground. He should neither be lethargic nor stretch out his hands in agitation. He should not pray while seated on a chest, a chair, or a couch; there should be nothing between him and the ground. He shall then turn toward the *qiblah* [the direction of prayer, facing Jerusalem] in fear and trembling as if he had come into the presence of a mighty ruler, fearing to meet him, trembling for fear of him, and anxious to do him honor, as it is written: "Who shall not fear You, O King of the nations" [Jer. 10:7]. There shall be a space sufficient for prostration between him and the *qiblah*—no smaller, lest he be hemmed in, but no larger, so as to avoid disturbing the person who may lead the service with him.

Before beginning prayers, he should briefly make a devout invocation in order to dispel his [ordinary] thoughts and fix his concentration. Then he should throw himself on the ground, pressing his face upon it and saying: "O God, behold I press the noblest of my members upon the place on which I tread with my feet, the very dust to which I shall return in accordance with what you have told me: 'For dust you are, and to dust shall you return' " [Gen. 3:19]. He should make his soul like the ground on which he has prostrated himself, by confessing to himself that he is composed of dust. The leader of the service must also know the main principles of the Law, and be grounded in all the ordinances. He must be God-fearing and also fear the abyss of transgression and sin, so that he knows and firmly believes that he stands before his Creator in an attitude of obedience, not because he fears punishment or desires reward. When standing, he should place his feet evenly, keeping them apart on account of his toes so that he may be able to steady himself. He should not put one foot upon the other, or fix his hand on his waist, because such a [posture] is not in keeping with [an attitude] of contrition. He should look at the ground, while directing his heart to his Creator. Then he should cross his hands over his heart as a servant does before his lord, well-mannered, confessing the sins that he has committed. For he is a sinner, a transgressor, vile, miserable, unable to guide himself; and there is none to answer or regard him or guide him except God. This should be done with a saddened soul and a broken spirit, as it is written: "The sacrifices of God are a broken spirit" [Ps. 51:19]. Then he shall look for his consolation, and wait for his salvation, and hope for mercy, as it is written: "As the eyes of servants toward the hand of their Master" [Ps. 123:2]. Then he shall stretch out his hands to God, praying for the provision for his needs, while recognizing the multitude of God's gifts to him, as David has said, "I have stretched out my hands toward You" [Ps. 143:6], "I have extended the palm of my hand to You" [Ps. 138:10], "Lift up your hands in holiness and bless the Lord" [Ps. 134:2]. He should focus his inner faculties like the outer ones, as it is written: "We lift up our hearts with the hands to God in heaven" [Lam. 3:41]. Then he should concentrate his attention on prayer.

When reading aloud, he must articulate words, dividing them [properly] with his lips. At the reading of Shema [Deut. 6:4] he should pause between all letters that are alike, so that they do not run together, e.g., *be-khol/levavekha* [with all your heart], *'al/levavkhem* [upon your hearts]. The word *ehad* [one] should be prolonged, as [the worshiper] contemplates the fact that God is the fullness of the heaven and the earth and the four sides of the world. The [word] should be lengthened on the letter D. The leader (Ar. *imâm*) should not lower his voice on account of the congregation who follow him in prayer, and the congregation should not raise their voices above the leader; nor [should they do so] in repeating what he recites. It is stated that a person who, without any mitigating cause, ceases to pray with the congregation and prays in private is worthy of punishment, for this goes against God's words: "In congregations bless the Lord" [Ps. 68:27]. And it is stated that when the imam says: "Magnify the Lord with me" [Ps. 34:4], the congregation shall respond: "Great is the Lord, and highly to be praised" [Ps. 48:2]. And when he says "Lift up your hands in holiness and bless the Lord," they shall lift up their hands and say, "Blessed be the Lord," and other similar responses. The congregation should do what the imam bids them do without raising their voices above his. They must also wait until he has finished before responding as custom requires. For his part, he should not begin [a new section] before the congregants have finished their responses.

The imam must also concentrate, for mental concentration (Heb. *kavvanat ha-lev*) counts above all else. One whose mind is occupied with anything other than prayer is not permitted to pray. The imam shall not be troubled like a drunken or forgetful man, nor shall he be occupied with disturbing thoughts. [He may not lead the services] until he has cleared his mind. He must strive to achieve proper concentration by making every attempt to banish all [distracting] thoughts.

Let us now speak of bowing, kneeling, and prostration. "Bowing" (Heb. *be-rikhah*) is a term applied to the posture of one who rests on his knees with his legs against his thigh. "Kneeling" (Heb. *keriʿah*) is the posture upon the knees without pressing the legs against the thigh, as it is written concerning Solomon, peace be upon him: "He rose up from before the altar of the Lord from bowing upon his knees" [1 Kings 8:54]. If *keriʿah* is joined with the word *appayim* it means bowing down with the forehead, with the breast upon the ground without touching the ground with his face. Prostration (Heb. *hishtahavayah*) means falling down on the face and prostrating the body alone until the vertebrae become loosened. The term also applies to bowing down to the earth with the forehead only, when the word *appayim* is not joined with it. When [*appayim*] is joined to it, [the phrase] signifies bowing down with the forehead together with the breast, as we have said in connection with *keriʿah*.

Let us now speak of the different parts of the service. It is necessary that the imam and the congregation should do alike in the different parts of the service. When he stands they must stand, and when he sits they must sit. If they do the opposite of what he does, this is contrary [to what should be done]. The portions [of the service] during which they should stand include: the giving of praise and exaltation of God; the declaration of divine unity; the reading of the section relating to the sacrifice; the recitation of the Shemaʿ and what follows; the Song [Exod. 15], and the chapters relating to the additional sacrifices (Heb. *musafot*). The portions during which they should sit include: the admission of sins; the recitations of the confessions (Heb. *vidduyot*); the psalm "Be merciful to me" [probably Ps. 57]; and the like.

The verse, "Yet He, being compassionate, forgave their iniquity" [Ps. 78:38] has been designated for the beginning of the service, since prayer is a substitute for sacrifice, by means of which sins are forgiven. Although we can no longer perform sacrifice, God is merciful and forgives, having permitted the words of our lips to take its place. When the leader has begun, the congregation should repeat [after him] with a loud voice.

Prostration takes place on three occasions: first, at the exaltation of God's name; second, at the confession; and third, at the prayer for divine mercy. The congregation, both men and women, should concentrate their attention behind the leader. Both men and women should pray in soberness and purity, for the prayer of the unclean is not accepted—more especially of those who are seriously unclean. Neither men nor women in the congregation should occupy their minds with news or gossip, lest their worship be spoiled, and they be punished by God. They must heed the imam, so that they understand the words he utters. They must not raise their voices above his; when they make responses, their voices should be lower. When the exaltation [of God's name] is uttered, they shall repeat his words, as: "Who is like You among the gods, O Lord?" [Exod. 15:11]; "The Lord shall reign for ever and ever" [Exod. 15:18]; "Holy, holy, holy" [Isa. 6:3] melodiously, gently and sweetly, and with heartfelt longing.

When the imam utters the confessions and admissions of sin, the congregation should evince gentleness, supplication, weeping, penitence, and inward contemplation so that the heart is moved and tears flow. This is the meaning of the verse: "The sacrifices of God are a broken spirit" [Ps. 51:19]. And God will receive and answer those who do so, as He said to Hezekiah: "I have heard your prayer, I have seen your tears" [2 Kings 20:5]. And concerning Hannah it is stated: "And she prayed to the Lord, and kept on weeping" [1 Sam. 1:10]. Prayer in the midst of a congregation is thus better than the prayer of a single person. It is said that the *qedushah* [the prayer exalting God's name] should not be recited by fewer than ten persons, for the exaltation is greater this way. Jews should chant to one another in prayer, as the angels do, for they call one to another, as it is written, "And they called one to another and said" [Isa. 6:3]. Clearly, congregational prayer is superior to the prayer of individuals. May God, exalted be he, accept it. Amen.

Manual for the Would-be *Shohet* (Ritual Slaughterer)

These are the questions which the rabbi puts to a worthy student who applies for certification to perform *shehitah* [ritual slaughter], and these are the answers which the latter is to recite from memory.

Question: Why did the sage Aaron b. Elijah [of Nicomedia; d. 1369] commence his treatise on *shehitah* with the verse "Open my eyes, that I may perceive the wonders of Your teaching" [Ps. 119:18]?
Answer: Because of the word "wonders" (*nifla'ot*), which is to be interpreted in two ways, as the sage himself remarked in connection with the law of the Nazirite. First, because it expresses separation, as in the phrase, "that the Lord makes a distinction between the Egyptians and Israel" [Exod. 11:7], for God chose Israel, desiring them to be holy and wise. Therefore, he separated them and set them apart from the nations by forbidding and permitting them certain foods. In this connection, he issued various strict prohibitions. Second, it indicates something concealed, as in the verse "things too wonderful for me, which I did not know" [Job 42:3]. For the commandments of the Torah are of two kinds, those which are known [solely] via revelation and those which are known rationally; *shehitah* belongs to the former category, which comprises wondrous things that are too obscure for human reason.

Question: When was *shehitah* instituted?
Answer: At the time of Noah, with the verse, "Only you shall not eat flesh with its life, that is, its blood." This is commonly called "a limb from the living animal" (*ever min ha-hay*).

Question: What is the source for our knowledge that *shehitah* requires the severing of the four organs?

Answer: The people's knowledge of *shehitah* derives from tradition (*sevel ha-yerushah;* lit., "the burden of the inheritance"). Israel possesses three [sources of knowledge]: Scripture, analogy, and tradition that has scriptural support.

Question: How many aspects of *shehitah* must we consider?
Answer: Five: First, the carcass of the victim; second, the manner of carrying [out] *shehitah*; third, the qualities of the *shohet*; fourth, the implement by which *shehitah* is performed; and fifth, the function of the victim's carcass, that is, that it be eaten.

. . .

Question: What are the essential qualities of a *shohet*?
Answer: The *shohet* must be pious, humble, constant in his prayers, and completely upright in his dealings. He must not be thieving, violent, lying, arrogant, or irascible. He must be an adult who understands that *shehitah* is accomplished through the severing of the four organs that constitute the blood sources, for in order to lessen the pain of the victim, God commanded us to deprive the animal of its life by these means. [In this way,] He graciously inculcated in us the disposition of mercy so as to preserve the human species. Now in order to uphold God's justice, we are obligated to demonstrate how this action, that is, *shehitah,* does not constitute injustice. In commanding us to slaughter certain animals in order [to promote] the welfare of our bodies, He is "a God of faithfulness and without iniquity" [Deut. 32:4]; for they were expressly created for this purpose. Just as there is no injustice in beasts consuming grass, there is no injustice in animals being slaughtered and consumed for our welfare. We may not slaughter them wantonly, however, but only in order to preserve our lives.

We have said that *shehitah* is the Torah's term [for ritual slaughter]. It may not be performed at various points [on the body], but only at the neck. Therefore, it has been decreed that we must sever the sources of blood in order to [accomplish *shehitah*] in the easiest possible way so as not to cause the animal pain. In [this manner] he guided us toward the moral disposition of mercy, for a number of commandments were decreed in the Torah in order to lead people, by degrees, to the quality of mercy, such as the bird's nest [Deut. 22:6], the prohibition of slaughtering parent and offspring on the same day [Lev. 22:28], the prohibition of plowing with an ox and ass together [Deut. 22:10], and the injunction against muzzling the ox [Deut. 25:4]. For God's mercy extends to all his creatures.

In order to exclude the victim's suffering from the realm of injustice, *shehitah* [must be understood] with reference to four mitigating circumstances, since any suffering to which these circumstances cannot be applied must be accounted evil and wickedness. The four mitigating circumstances are as follows: first, the attainment of future benefit; second, the exaction of an obligation; third, the aversion of greater harm; and fourth, the prevention of injury to oneself. An example of future benefit is the disciplining of children by their parents, who send them to school so that they study Torah. The suffering inflicted upon children in punishing them harshly for this purpose cannot be accounted injustice, since it is intended for their benefit and ultimate advantage; it is devoid, therefore, of injustice. Concerning this, Scripture states: "As a man disciplines his son, the Lord your God disciplines you" [Deut. 8:5]. An example of obligation, would be the lender's demand that the borrower return the loan or property that had been lent. Even though this causes the lender pain and constant suffering until the loan is once again in his possession, this suffering is also devoid of injustice, as it is written in Scripture: "He shall make restitution from the best in his own field and in his own vineyard" [Exod. 22:4]. The aversion of greater harm is exemplified by a person whose hand or foot has been bitten by a viper; consequently, the bite becomes swollen and the poison spreads throughout the limb. The physicians advise amputating the limb that was bitten so that the poison does not spread to the other limbs, thereby leading to the loss of the entire body [i.e., the person's life]. Although the amputation causes enormous pain to the person who was bitten, it is devoid of injustice, since its purpose is the preservation of the rest of the body and the prevention of harm to the other healthy limbs. Concerning this, Scripture states: "But God led the people round by the way of the wilderness toward the Red Sea" [Exod. 13:18]. An instance of the prevention of injury to oneself would be an attempted theft or murder in which the would-be thief or murderer loses a limb; this too would constitute no injustice, as our Sages of blessed memory have stated: "If someone comes to kill you, hasten to kill him [first]" (Babylonian Talmud, *Berakhot* 58a, 62b). Similarly, it is stated in Scripture: "If a thief is found breaking in, and is struck so that he dies, there shall be no bloodguilt for him" [Exod. 22:1].

We have stated: "[The *shohet*] must know how the victim's pain can be excluded from the category of injustice by means of two of these mitigating circumstances, that is, obligation and the aversion of greater harm. The latter, since before Noah's time people used to eat animals while they were still alive by severing one of their limbs. This was an act of cruelty causing the animal terrible pain, since it would suffer for several days [before it died]. So as graciously to inculcate the quality of mercy in us and in order to prevent animals from suffering greatly, God commanded us to slaughter them in the quickest possible manner so that [life] would not remain within their bodies for even an instant. [*Shehitah* may also be justified in terms of] obligation, since God's creation of His creatures was an act of grace and they delight (*mit'addenim*) in His generous goodness, as it is written: "You open your hand, You satisfy the desire of every living thing" [Ps. 145:16]. Since he grants life to his creatures by way of grace, they live as long as he desires. Just as a loan or an object remains in the hand of the borrower, so life is granted to creatures in the form of a loan. Should he take back that life at a particular moment or in a particular manner of his choosing, this pain cannot be called injustice, since that life was granted [in the first instance] as an act of grace. Therefore, in commanding us to slaughter certain animals for our bodies' welfare, God does not commit any injustice, since they were, in any case, created for this purpose.

SABBATH LIGHTS

1. Israel ben Samuel Dayyan, "Yerivay ve-oyevay shime'u le-qoli."

Hear my words, listen my foe:
Think not my fortunes are so low
When you see me in darkness on Sabbath night,
"Though [I sit] in gloom, the Lord is my light" [Mic. 7:8].

The sun of righteousness shines bright
For me and mine each Sabbath night.
My book open, I pray aloud
And at the sound, all heads are bowed.
"Though [I sit] in gloom, etc."

Joyfully my people, sing
Let Sabbath-keepers' voices ring!
For righteous folk in dark there's light
I'll keep the Sabbath e'er aright!
"Though [I sit] in gloom, etc."

Encircled by the Torah's glow,
By precepts' lamp my way I go.
The Law within my temple gleams.
To my foes, I suffer, it seems!
"Though [I sit] in gloom, etc."

O mighty God, my people, see:
Who keep Sabbath by Law's decree.
Favor my foes with wrath and shame,
Then me no longer will they blame!
"Though [I sit] in gloom, etc."

Torah and Prophets both attest
Whose laws are precious, pleasantest.
I'll rouse my soul and sing loudest
For when I sleep, e'ermore I'll rest!
"Though [I sit] in gloom, etc."

2. Elijah Bashyachi, Adderet Eliyahu, 'Inyan Shabbat

Chapter 17.
The sages' debate concerning the interpretation of the verse "You shall kindle no fire in all your habitations on the Sabbath day" [Exod. 35:3]

Jewish scholars are divided into two great factions [over this question]. The Rabbanites maintain that kindling and extinguishing fire constitute one of the thirty-nine major categories of labor [prohibited by rabbinic law on the Sabbath]. According to their interpretation, Exodus 35:3 prohibits the kindling of a wick on the Sabbath day itself. They assert that it is not forbidden for a Jew to light a fire or a lamp on Friday [that is, before the commencement of the Sabbath at sunset] so that it continues to burn on the Sabbath. For [although] lighting a wick is called a "labor," the fire's consumption of the wick or firewood does not constitute an artificial action dependent upon the person who lights the fire; rather, it is a natural process that results automatically. . . . In general, they permitted secondary actions that result automatically without the direct intervention of an initiating [agent], such as the opening of an irrigation ditch on Friday in order to water a garden on the Sabbath, or the arrangement of [water] millstones so that they grind on the Sabbath, or the preparation of olives on Friday so that their [oil] flows on the Sabbath. The Rabbanite scholars call all such activities "secondary actions" which—but for a single initial contact—lack the direct intervention of an agent.

The second faction consists of the Karaite scholars who prohibited all secondary actions on the Sabbath. They claimed that since all secondary actions are extensions [of primary actions], they are included in [the prohibition]: "You shall not do any work" [Exod. 20:10, Deut. 5:14]. In their opinion, the exploitation of every such extension is the same as the actual exploitation [of a primary action]; it is therefore included under the Torah's prohibitions. Since leaving a fire or lamp burning on the Sabbath constitutes a secondary action that—apart from a single initial contact—does not require the direct intervention of an agent, it should be forbidden. They maintained that Exodus 35:3 does not refer to the lighting [of a fire] by an agent, for such actions are included in the prohibition "You shall not do any work." This is, in fact, the Rabbanites' position, that the person who kindles or extinguishes fire [on the Sabbath] is included among those who perform labor [on that day]. [According to the Karaites, however,] Exodus 35:3 does refer to kindling that occurs when the fire burns on its own. . . .

The remainder of chapter 17 and chapters 18–19 are devoted to a close examination of earlier Karaite argumentation and legislation on the subject.

Chapter 20. Author's Apology
"Therefore, hear me, you men of understanding, far be it from God that He should do wickedness, and from the almighty that He should do wrong" [Job 34:10].

In entering this exegetical maze, it has been my aim to render permissible one of the prohibitions relating to the extension [of an action], as will readily be seen from the words of the sages. I have not done so out of an inflated self-opinion, stubbornness, or ignorance, as sometimes occurs with fools who follow their own willful hearts. Rather, it is because I have observed many of the leading authorities of our time these past forty years. First among these were my master and grandfather Rabbi Menahem, my master and father Rabbi Moses his son, Rabbi Michael the Elder and his son Rabbi Joseph, Rabbi Menahem b. Elijah Maruli, and others who, with them and their disciples, championed the Torah in those days. They [all] permitted the kindling of a lamp [before the Sabbath] with their own legal justifications. The practice became widely disseminated in every community, with the exception of a few individuals who came from distant lands where they had neither heard the word of the Lord nor beheld His glory. About thirty years ago, some time after the [aforementioned] sages had died, a few members of our communities came forward. Although they had themselves been disciples of those very sages, they desired to make themselves important within our community by teaching laws so as to acquire the respect of ignorant fools. Several of these men therefore banned the kindling of lamps [before the Sabbath]—an act which they themselves used to perform in the days of [their teachers].

Thus there developed two factions within our community, some who kindle and some who do not. The latter group would revile the former, claiming that they were transgressing the [prohibition of] Exodus 35:3. For they believed that the prohibition against kindling fire derives from this verse. They would say: "The children gather sticks and the fathers set them alight." This situation became extremely difficult for those who do kindle until they approached me and said: " 'Be jealous for the Lord' and inform us if this action is prohibited to us; [if it is,] we will refrain from it so as not to be like willful [transgressors]. But if it is permissible for us why should we desist from it? On what basis did your ancestors permit it [in the first place]? Inform us and we will follow this course. If not, we will say that you [and your ancestors] followed your own willful hearts in acting without possessing an argument to refute the words of those who argue against you." Moreover, when I examined what the scholars of both factions had said and saw how the arguments of the second group refuted all the arguments of the first, I rejoiced greatly, thinking "perhaps in the end there is hope" and we will be permitted to respond to the arguments of [earlier] scholars after we have conducted a true investigation. For the truth is self-evident. . . . [Here, Elijah recalls other instances in which later Karaite authorities overturned certain long-standing decisions of earlier scholars on the basis of reasoned arguments. He also mentions some weaknesses in the arguments of scholars belonging to the second faction and remarks on the misguided, headstrong behavior of those individuals who actually violate the Sabbath in their campaign to promote the kindling of lights.] Therefore, I have investigated and studied the scholars' writings, responding as I have only after lengthy research and reflection, both according to my understanding and what I have learned from my teachers.

The person who kindles a lamp should do so while it is still daytime [on Friday], placing it where no Jew will move it [on the Sabbath]. It may not be kindled by a Gentile on the Sabbath, as is the practice of certain Rabbanites who transgress the words of their teachers. . . . In our opinion, a Jew is forbidden to benefit from the labor of a Gentile on the Sabbath, whether the action was performed for the benefit of the Gentile or the Jew. Therefore, it is forbidden for a Gentile to kindle a lamp in a Jewish home on the Sabbath or for a Jew to make use of it. . . . The Rabbanites have stated that a burning lamp furnishes a portion of the Sabbath's glory and sanctity; this is one interpretation of the verse: "Therefore glorify the Lord with lights" [Isa. 24:15]. It is also stated: "But the wicked shall be put to silence in darkness" [1 Sam. 2:9]. A lamp burned eternally in the Temple on account of its sanctity; it is fitting, therefore, that all Jewish homes have lamps, in honor of the holy books they contain. Can any intelligent person really believe that Moses our teacher or the other prophets and princes used to sit in darkness on Sabbath evenings? No, to a sensible person this is inconceivable!

3. Solomon b. Aaron, Lehem Seʿorim
The Sixth Question

The Rabbanite raised the following objection with the Karaite, asking: "Why is it not the custom among you Karaites to recite the benediction over the Sabbath lights, when they [in fact] constitute a "lamp of commandment" [Prov. 6:23] that burns in honor of the Sabbath?

The Karaite replied: In this objection likewise your words are incorrect and do not accord with what is written in Scripture. You call this a "lamp of commandment," but it is a lamp of transgression! I will put the question to you and you tell me—who issued this commandment and where is this written [in the Torah]? In fact, precisely the opposite is recorded: "You shall kindle no fire throughout your settlements on the Sabbath day" [Exod. 35:3]. Aside from this, the Talmud makes it clear that kindling or extinguishing fire are among the thirty-nine major categories of labor that are forbidden on the Sabbath. Should you argue that it is women who light them and that this is a commandment which devolves upon them [alone], it is likely that this is something they have themselves [invented]. Perhaps it derives from the teachings of "Rabbi Beruriah" [Rabbi Meir's wife], for we have not found any such commandment mentioned in Scripture!

Now if we [Karaites] have the custom—sometimes—of lighting a lamp on the eve of the Sabbath while it is still daytime, this does not belong to the category of commandment but arises out of necessity. For human beings are political by nature and it is impossible for them to manage at night without the light of a lamp, whether for their meals or other needs. Therefore, our sages have not commanded us to recite a benediction over them. For it is obligatory to recite benedictions that state "who sanctified us with His commandments, and commanded us . . ." concerning those matters deriving from a divine commandment. Nowhere, however, is it stated that God commands or obligates human beings to fulfill [the commandment of lighting candles for the Sabbath].

I observe that among your practices are many "commandments" that were instituted by scholars but not by Scripture. Once you became accustomed to them, they became obligatory [in your eyes], though they only came into being after prophecy had ceased. It is, therefore, incorrect to state "who sanctified us with His commandments and commanded us" concerning matters that God did not command.

20

Living Judaism in Confucian Culture: Being Jewish and Being Chinese

Jonathan N. Lipman

By the fifteenth century C.E., Jews had lived in some parts of the Chinese culture area for a very long time. Some scholars believe that Jewish merchants had settled in Chinese trading cities as early as the first century C.E., others that they had arrived only with the rapid expansion of the Muslim world in the seventh to eighth centuries C.E. We do know that the Islamic conquests allowed Jewish merchants, mostly from Persia, to join Arabs, Persians, Turks, and South Asians in the Chinese cities of both Silk Roads—that is, the seaports of China's southeast coast and the great caravan centers of northern China. Certainly foreign in culture, sojourners rather than settlers, these merchants nonetheless adapted to local ways and used local Chinese (as well as the Eurasian lingua franca, Persian) to do business. Like most long-distance merchants, they traveled without their wives and families, and returned home after each journey bearing the valuable silks, porcelains, and other trade goods that China produced in such abundance.

The vast conquests of the Mongols and other Inner Asian peoples in the twelfth to fourteenth centuries C.E. created open routes for merchants all over Eurasia. West and Central Asian Muslims, Christians, and Jews quickly took advantage of changed conditions in China to set up new enterprises, often capitalized or licensed by the Mongol aristocracy. The first evidence for a synagogue in China may be found in the inscription translated here, which claims a date of 1163 C.E. for the earliest construction. The permanent settlements of Jews in China probably date from this period, when Jewish merchants (all male) founded communities in Guangzhou, Ningbo, Ningxia, Xi'an, and Kaifeng (among others), married local women (who presumably became Jews themselves), and began to become ordinary parts of the landscape rather than exotic visitors. Until the Mongols were driven out of China by the rising Ming dynasty in the 1360s, the Jews were counted among the *semuren,* non-Chinese peoples who aided the Mongols in governing the Chinese population and controlling China's markets. (From a European perspective, the Roman Catholic Marco Polo remains the most famous of the semuren.)

Once the Ming forces defeated their Mongol overlords, an event conventionally dated in 1368 C.E., the semuren who chose to remain in China, including Jews, had to adapt to a less flexible, more Sinocentric state and society. This required of them, among other tasks, that they appear civilized—that is, Chinese—in all aspects of public life. Most important, they had to master at least the rules and language, if not the texts, of the dominant state Confucianism, a textual and ritual tradition that had undergone profound changes during the previous centuries but had finally been molded into a rigid orthodoxy under the early Ming emperors (fourteenth to fifteenth centuries C.E.). This period was also characterized by a philosophical orthodoxy among the literati who constituted China's intellectual elite, a vocabulary and way of thinking that brooked no opposition and defined Culture itself. Thus any Jewish community that intended to remain in China had to be able to justify itself, especially any differentness from normative Chinese life, in the lexicon and syntax of Confucianism.

The text translated here represents the first substantial attempt to do that. Inscribed in 1489 C.E. on a vertical stone tablet that stood in the courtyard of Kaifeng's synagogue, this account of Judaism's origins and its presence in China attempts to reconcile the obvious foreignness of Judaism with the tenets and texts of Confucian civilization. Its author, Jin Zhong, was a Jew who had achieved the rank of licentiate (the lowest degree) in the civil service examinations, the Ming empire's ladder to success in the government bureaucracy. (Like all other Chinese names in this introduction and translation, Jin Zhong's is in Chinese order, surname first.) He had therefore mastered the standard curriculum of Confucian classics, the orthodox commentaries of the Song dynasty (tenth to thirteenth centuries C.E.), and the histories, poetry, and prose literature that distinguished the Chinese elite from the common folk. He also knew the chain of transmission of the Jewish law—from Abraham to Moses to Ezra—and the rituals observed in Kaifeng's synagogue, making him an ideal translator of the Jews' exotic creed into terms that would make it seem not only intelligible but moral, in conformity with the strict standards of Confucian culture. That is, Jin Zhong had to make Judaism Chinese, to express its profound ideas in a medium that had no vocabulary for monotheism, no room for sacred texts in any language other than Chinese (the Buddhist scriptures had been translated into Chinese more than a millennium earlier), and little tolerance for values or rituals other than those found in the Chinese classics.

Jin Zhong therefore cited the *Book of Changes* rather than the Torah, the *Analects of Confucius* rather than the Talmud, in his explanation of his ancestral faith. Indeed, even his grammar reveals his debt to his Chinese classical education rather than the Hebrew and Aramaic texts that he would have read (or heard) in the synagogue. Although the Kaifeng community possessed both conventional Jewish texts and leaders knowledgeable in Torah, the inscription contains not a single passage translated from a Jewish text. Rather, Jin Zhong put Chinese prose into the mind of Abraham, Chinese virtues into the character of Moses, Chinese ritual rectitude into the behavior of Ezra. In this he strongly resembled the adherents of other foreign religions that were brought to China and translated into Chinese—Buddhism, Nestorian Christianity, Manichaeism, Islam, Roman Catholicism, and more. Each of these traditions had to be expressed in language that was orthodox, unassailable, and morally compatible with the Confucianism that dominated Chinese public life.

Nevertheless, we do not find here a completely assimilated Judaism, for the Kaifeng Jews had not surrendered utterly to the conventions and values of their Chinese home. Never exceeding a few thousand souls, they did eventually (by the late nineteenth century) assimilate completely into the surrounding society, but they had resisted that process with all their resources, becoming Chinese in material life, language, and patterns of thought while retaining at least a ritual if not also a philosophical difference from their neighbors. They survived as Jews for almost a thousand years with a synagogue, Hebrew texts, and leaders who could read them, and ritual observances at odds with the overwhelmingly large population around them (which included adherents of Islam as well as the various traditions of China). Scholars agree that the small size of the community and its complete isolation from contact with other Jews were the main causes for its gradually reduced capacity to remain Jewish over the centuries.

We must therefore read Jin Zhong's inscription, written at a high point in the community's history, as an attempt to be both Jewish and Chinese, to be civilized in a Confucian context while maintaining the validity of Judaism as a religious tradition. He was not dissembling but translating, not assimilating entirely but combining the laws and practices of Judaism with the obvious truths of Chinese civilization. Euro-American Jews of the nineteenth and twentieth centuries will surely find this effort familiar, as they strive to maintain some core, essence, and practice of their "different" tradition while becoming ordinary, normal, and invisible in their non-Jewish homelands. If a liberal, modernized Judaism makes sense in Euro-American culture, a Confucianized Judaism made sense in Jin Zhong's.

Because we have very few texts from the Chinese Jewish communities—in fact, we have none from any city except Kaifeng—this inscription and the three others that followed it during the next 150 years constitute our most important window into how Chinese-speaking Jews understood their faith. Many scholarly controversies have swirled around them, and we still do not know many things we would like to know about the Kaifeng Jews. Some of the important themes and problems are:

REPRESENTING THE NAME OF GOD

The Chinese language has no name for a monotheistic God; indeed, the very idea would seem nonsensical within Confucian culture. Foreign monotheisms therefore had to resort to coining new words—the Islamic Zhenzhu, "True Master," or the Roman Catholic Tianzhu, "Heavenly Master," are good examples—or to utilizing Chinese ideas that might give the proper impression. Jin Zhong chose the latter course and used four different terms—Tian, "Heaven," Dao, "the Way," Tiandao, "the Way of Heaven," and Huangtian, "August Heaven"—to refer to God. All four terms may be found in orthodox Chinese texts, and none contradicts generally held Chinese notions of ultimate reality; the first Chinese character in "August Heaven" even associates God with the Chinese emperor, Huangdi, "August Ruler." So in this inscription Abraham "meditated upon Heaven," and he achieved a sudden enlightenment into the mysteries of "true Heaven." Moses' devotions on Mount Sinai "touched the mind-heart of Heaven," and he received the orthodox Scriptures. Ezra received "the complete Dao" and "the ancestral Dao" from the patriarchs, and the Jews "have the Temple of Israel to honor August Heaven."

A Chinese non-Jew reading this passage would, of course, never associate the familiar words with a monotheistic Jewish Creator-God (which was unimaginable in Chinese), for Jin Zhong placed even the Creation, a Jewish God's first and most fundamental act, in the Chinese vagueness of "the opening up of the cosmos." (Chinese civilization, according to many scholars, is the only major literate civilization to conceive of the cosmos without any indigenous creation myth, so a Chinese literatus would have no obvious words for that First Act.) We cannot know whether Jin Zhong actually meant what he wrote, or whether he might have been dissembling in order to make Judaism more Chinese than it "actually" could be. But we do know that Jin Zhong studied the Confucian texts all of his life, that he passed at least one level of the imperial civil service exams, and that he therefore had invested himself heavily in being Chinese, while at the same time belonging to and even leading the Jewish community of Kaifeng.

UNDERSTANDING THE PASSAGE OF TIME

Rather than insisting on the Biblical account of humankind's origins, Jin Zhong ingeniously combined Adam, Judaism's first man, with Pangu, a giant sometimes represented as the first man in Chinese myths. (Pangu was probably imported from India along with Buddhism in the first to sixth centuries C.E.) Jin also fixed precise dates for Abraham and Moses according to the Chinese calendar, that is, by the dynasty and reign-name of the Chinese emperor. These dates have no connection to modern calculations of Jewish historical time, which is often based on archeological or epigraphical data, but rather represent Jin Zhong's attempt to place Jewish history in the same chronological framework as the obvious and accepted sequence of Chinese dynasties. Note that the Jewish system of counting time from the Creation has no place in this inscription, for it would be not only foreign but also heterodox, and probably criminal, in Confucian China. "Keeping a private [or sectarian] calendar" constituted a capital offense under the category of lèse majesté in the Ming dynasty law code, for only the legitimate emperor could take charge of the keeping of time and the naming of dates by legitimate reign-names. Chinese-speaking Muslims, too, used the Chinese rather than the Islamic calendar when they wrote in the Chinese language.

PLACING THE JEWS IN CHINESE SOCIETY

The Jewish individuals named in the inscription fall into two categories—either they served as Jewish community leaders or they achieved merit within Chinese society. The inscription lists the seventeen clans of the Kaifeng community, their presence in China justified by command of an unnamed emperor of the Song dynasty: "You have come to my Zhongxia [kingdom]—revere and preserve your ancestral ways. . . ." Naturally, no such edict may be found in the Song dynastic records. Jews such as An Cheng, Gao Nian, Ai Jun, and several members of the author's Jin clan received honorable mention because they held secular office, while others made important contributions to the synagogue's construction, maintenance, and decoration. Apart from the patriarchs, whose Hebrew names are transliterated into Chinese, only two non-Chinese names appear: Andula, which is probably a Chinese version of 'Abd-Allah (Abdullah, the slave of God), a name that a Central Asian Jew or Muslim might hold; and Liewei (Levi), who led the community over three hundred years before Jin Zhong wrote this text. The Jews of Kaifeng had, by 1489 C.E., already lived in China for over three hundred years, twelve generations at least, and had certainly made Chinese their native language by this time. Possession of a proper Chinese surname constituted a crucial element of belonging in Chinese culture, and all but one or two of the seventeen lineage names in the inscription were conventional Chinese surnames. Jin Zhong used words for rabbi (*ustad*) and community leader (*mullah*) that derived from Arabic terms usually associated with Islam, but most of his vocabulary was purely Chinese.

Beyond such public acculturation to Chinese ways, Jin Zhong also advocated that Jews participate in the crucial private ritual of Chinese life, the veneration of ancestors. After describing the worship of Heaven (God) in the synagogue, the inscription insists that homage and offerings to the deceased constitute a crucial part of worship—"To revere Heaven without paying homage to the ancestors is not the proper way to sacrifice to the ancients"—and cites the *Doctrine of the Mean,* one of the core texts of the Confucian canon. Like the Jesuits who arrived in China a century after Jin wrote his inscription, Jin Zhong clearly did not find honoring the ancestors in the Chinese fashion to be polytheistic. Indeed, he included veneration of ancestors in his description of the Jewish seasonal observances, Shabbat, and Yom Kippur, and he paired "venerate the ancestors" with "honor Heaven [God]" in his praise of the community leaders who kept the Jews on the path of virtue.

PLACING THE JEWS IN RELATION TO THE MING STATE

British Jews pray for the queen and the welfare of their country. American Jews ask God to bring peace to their land. Jews in Ming dynasty China also invoked Heaven's aid in protecting and blessing their ruler, the emperor. Like all authorized temples, mosques, and other houses of worship in China, the Kaifeng synagogue had a *wansuipai,* a "long life tablet" dedicated to the reigning monarch, which rested in a small pavilion. According to Bishop William White, the earliest authority on the Chinese Jews, the Kaifeng community came to terms with this potentially polytheistic, or at least non-Jewish, presence in their synagogue by hanging an inscription of the first two lines of the Sh'ma prayer above the wansuipai. Jin Zhong certainly felt obliged to include the emperor in his inscription, assuring the government of the Jews' indebtedness and loyalty to the dynasty. Jin directly thanked the fourteenth-century founder of the Ming dynasty, then compared the emperor to Yu, Tang, Yao, and Shun, sage kings of the Chinese past, and asked Heaven (God) to answer the Jews' sincere prayers for long life to the ruler, blessings on the empire, and universal peace. At least in Jin Zhong's inscription, the Kaifeng Jews belonged in China, partook of the virtues and values of its state and society, and owed loyal devotion to its legitimate rulers. Lacking other evidence, we can only assume that the rest of the community shared his sentiments and included the dynasty in their prayers.

NAMING JUDAISM AND THE JEWS

According to Jin Zhong, Abraham founded the religion of Yicileye (Israel), which he called "the orthodox teaching" or "the Dao of our teaching." He wrote that Judaism came to China from India (Tianzhu), which might indicate a sea route for the initial settlement, except that the Persian origins of the community are clearly marked in the calligraphy of its surviving Hebrew texts. Apart from Yicileye, the only concrete term for Judaism which appears in the inscription is "Pure and True" (Qingzhen), a Chinese word later used to refer exclusively to Islam. Its appearance in this early Jewish inscription has led some scholars to conclude that Chinese Muslims, searching for a Chinese name for their religion, borrowed the term from the Kaifeng Jews. This would certainly conform to the Chinese impression that Islam and Judaism are closely related, even different sects of the same religion. As for the Jews, Jin Zhong calls them only the followers of the teaching, or simply "the people."

COMPREHENDING THE RITUALS OF THE KAIFENG SYNAGOGUE

Many aspects of Jewish ritual may be found in this inscription. Beginning with Abraham's meditation, Moses' abstinence, and Ezra's orthodoxy, the text required Kaifeng's Jews to "undertake ritual and worship" three times daily, then described the synagogue prayer. Chinese ritual life, prescribed in minute detail in numerous texts, always focused more on practice, on performing the actions correctly at the right time and in the right sequences, than on faith (correct belief), which forms part of the core of Jewish religious life. Jin Zhong therefore chose to narrate the motions of Jewish worship—retreating, advancing, turning to left and right—because they could be seen as conforming to Chinese ways in worship. That is, they constituted orthodox practice. Jin Zhong found difficulty in describing only one ritual motion, namely turning to the right during prayers, for that would put the Dao (God) on the worshiper's right, which is a position of inferiority in Chinese social rituals. He solved the problem by saying simply that "[this] is not good" and moving on. Apart from that, none of the ritual behaviors listed here could have been construed as bizarre or heterodox, and that is precisely the impression Jin Zhong wished to give.

As for Shabbat, the idea of a seventh day of rest had never existed in China (indeed, the premodern Chinese "week" was ten days long and contained no regular day of rest), so the inscription cited the *Book of Changes* and connected Shabbat observance to the doing of good deeds and charity, justifying this outlandish practice in familiar terms. So, too, did Jin Zhong rely on the *Book of Changes* to justify Yom Kippur. Nowhere did the text acknowledge that the Kaifeng community conducted its Jewish rituals in Hebrew, which we know that they did, or that the sacred texts that they read were not written in Chinese. The Kaifeng Jews possessed no fewer than thirteen complete scrolls of the Torah (seven of which survive, four in European collections and three in the United States), but the "orthodox Scripture, in fifty-three sections" that Moses received on Mount Sinai could (from this inscription's account) have been in Chinese. Rather, Jin Zhong claimed both orthodoxy and antiquity for Jewish practice and insisted that Jews "observe and preserve the established laws, know how to honor Heaven and venerate the ancestors, and show themselves loyal to their lord." The lord in question was, of course, the Ming emperor. Thus did our text demonstrate the complete compatibility between Judaism and Chinese (that is, Confucian) ways, a compatibility necessary to prove Judaism a moral teaching and Jews civilized people. Lacking other direct evidence from within the Chinese Jewish community, we can only conclude that the other Chinese Jews either concurred with Jin Zhong's description of their place in China or remained silent, confirming the rectitude of living a Jewish life that was also a Chinese life.

I have relied on the transcribed text of the inscription in William Charles White, *Chinese Jews: A Compilation of Matters Relating to the Jews of K'ai-feng Fu* (1942; reprint New York: Paragon, n.d.), vol. 2, pp. 35–39. White includes an ink-rubbing of the original stele (p. 34); a translation (pp. 8–16); and explanatory notes (pp. 19–33). My translation differs from White's in many passages, some of them retranslated or corrected by Donald Leslie and Andrew Plaks (see below).

Further Reading

Our sources on the Kaifeng Jewish community are very limited. White's book, cited above, analyzes virtually all of the Chinese inscriptional material and several other crucial documents, as well as most of the known travelers' and scholars' accounts up to 1942. Donald Leslie, *The Survival of the Chinese Jews: The Jewish Community of Kaifeng* (Leiden: E. J. Brill, 1972), did the most thorough job in seeking out sources other than White's, and he carefully does not go beyond what the sources allow in his historical analysis. Michael Pollak, *Mandarins, Jews, and Missionaries: The Jewish Experience in the Chinese Empire* (Philadelphia: Jewish Publication Society of America, 1980), traces not only the narrative of the Kaifeng Jews but also the efforts by non-Chinese Jews to "save" them. Pollak has also published a technical monograph on the Torah scrolls of Kaifeng—*The Torah Scrolls of the Chinese Jews: The History, Significance, and Present Whereabouts of the Sifrei Torah of the Defunct Jewish Community of Kaifeng* (Dallas: Bridwell Library of Southern Methodist University, 1979)—and a bibliography, *The Jews of Dynastic China: A Critical Bibliography* (Cincinnati: Hebrew Union College, 1993). The work of Chinese scholars on the Kaifeng Jews has been translated, compiled, and edited by Sidney Shapiro, *Jews in Old China: Studies by Chinese Scholars* (New York: Hippocrene, 1984), though many of the articles are inaccurate, and the translations of premodern Chinese sources do not do them justice. A conference on the Jews of China, both the Kaifeng community and the settlement of European, American, and West Asian Jews in China after the mid-nineteenth century, was held at Harvard in 1992. The proceedings of that conference, including important papers on the Kaifeng Jews by Andrew Plaks, Nigel Thomas, and others, will be published under the editorship of Jonathan Goldstein, *Jews in China* (Armonk, N.Y.: M. E. Sharpe, forthcoming). For all other sources on this topic, see Pollak's bibliography.

A Record of the Reconstruction of the Pure and True Temple [Synagogue]

Abraham, the patriarch who founded the religion of Israel, was of the nineteenth generation from Pangu Adam. From the opening up of the cosmos, the patriarchs handed down successively the traditions that they had received. They made no images, flattered no spirits and ghosts, and placed no credence in heterodox practices. At that time, the spirits and ghosts could not aid [them], images afforded [them] no protection, and heterodox practices availed [them] nothing.

So [Abraham] meditated upon Heaven: "[It is] ethereal and pure above, most honorable and beyond compare. The Dao of Heaven 'does not speak, yet the four seasons run their course thereby, and all creatures are born thereby'" [*Analects of Confucius* 17:19]. It is evident that things come to life in the springtime, grow during the summer, are harvested in the autumn, and are stored up in the winter. [Living things] fly, swim, walk, and grow. They luxuriate then decompose, they bloom then fall. Processes of generation go on by themselves; processes of transformation proceed by themselves; things take on shape and form in and of themselves; variety generates variety of its own accord." The patriarch suddenly awoke as if from sleep, enlightened into these profound mysteries. He began truly to seek the orthodox teaching with a view to assisting true Heaven. With all his heart he served [it], and gave himself up wholly to respectful veneration. Then he laid the foundation of the teaching which has been handed down to this day. Examination reveals that this was in the 146th year of the Zhou dynasty [tenth century B.C.E.].

Through transmission, [the teaching] reached Moses, also a patriarch of the orthodox teaching. Examination reveals that he lived in the 613th year of the Zhou [sixth century B.C.E.]. From birth he was gifted with pure and genuine insight. His human-heartedness and righteousness were entirely perfected; his Dao and inherent virtue were complete together. He sought for the Scriptures at the top of Mount Sinai, and [to this end] he fasted forty days and nights. He put away lustful passions and denied [himself] both sleep and food, worshiping with perfect sincerity. His devotion touched the mind-heart of Heaven, and the orthodox Scripture, in fifty-three sections, had its origin from this. Its contents are extremely subtle and mysterious; the good men [recorded there] incite goodness in human hearts, while the evil men [recorded there] repress and warn the unregulated willfulness of humankind.

Thereafter the teaching was transmitted to Ezra, another patriarch of the orthodox teaching. A descendant of the patriarchs, [he received from them] the complete Dao and the continuous lineage. His Way of honoring Heaven and ritual worship revealed the mysteries of the ancestral Dao.

The Dao must be based on purity, truth, ritual, and worship. Purity means it is one, pure, and inimitable; truth signifies rectitude without heterodoxy; ritual denotes reverence itself; and worship is the act of obeisance [bowing]. In the midst of daily occupations, people must not forget Heaven even for a moment, but rather morning, noon, and night, three times a day, should undertake ritual and worship. This is the fundamental principle of the true Dao of Heaven.

What was the common practice of the patriarchal worthies in their cultivation of balanced reverence? First they had to bathe and change their garments; then they purified their Heavenly minds and regulated their Heavenly natural faculties. Then, with great respect they entered before the Scriptures of the Dao. The Dao has no form or figure but is just like the supremacy of the Dao of Heaven.

The simple outline of ritual procedure in the worship of venerating Heaven is as follows: First, the worshiper bends the body to honor the Dao, and the Dao is present in bending the body. Then he stands erect, without leaning, to honor the Dao, and the Dao is present in standing erect. In meditation he preserves [his ability to] nurture [himself]; by silent praise he venerates the Dao, for Heaven should never be forgotten. In movement he examines his conduct, and by vocal praise he honors the Dao, for Heaven knows no substitute. He retreats three paces, and immediately [the Dao is] behind him, so he honors the Dao behind him. He advances five steps and perceives [the Dao] before him, so he honors the Dao before him. Turning to the left he bends his body to venerate the Dao, which is good, for the Dao is on his left. Turning to the right he bends his body to venerate the Dao, which is not good, for the Dao is on his right. He looks upward to venerate the Dao, and the Dao is above

[him]. He looks downward to venerate the Dao, and the Dao is near [him]. In conclusion, he bows to the Dao, and his reverence lies in the bowing.

To revere Heaven without paying homage to the ancestors is not the proper way to sacrifice to the ancients. In the spring and autumn ancestral sacrifices, he should "serve the dead as if serving the living, serve those gone as if serving those present" [*Doctrine of the Mean,* 19:5]. He should offer oxen and sheep, and seasonal food, and should not fail to honor the ancestors because they had already passed on.

In every month there should be four days' observance. [Weekly] observance is the gateway to the Dao, and the foundation upon which good works are stored up. Today a good deed is stored up, tomorrow another good deed, and from this beginning, the doing of good deeds becomes a habit. At the time of observance, no evil is done, but all sorts of good actions are performed. Thus the seven days are brought to a good ending, and a new period commences. As the *Book of Changes* (*I Ching*) says, "The fortunate person, doing good, finds the day insufficient for his intentions." At the four seasons of the year are observances of seven days in consideration of the calamities experienced by the ancestors, and sacrifices are made to the forefathers in order to repay the source [of all good we have received by the ancestors' merit]. Cutting off from all food and drink, there is rigid abstinence for one whole day, reverently calling upon Heaven for repentance of previous faults and for moving toward new good deeds in the present. Is this not the meaning of the forty-second hexagram of the *Book of Changes,* as the sage explains: "The wind and thunder unite, and the Lordly Man sees the good and approaches [it], acknowledges his faults and corrects them"?

Truly, the Dao of our teaching has been passed down, its transmission and reception in order. It came from India, coming according to the command [of Heaven?]. The clans of Li, An, Ai, Gao, Mu, Zhao, Jin, Zhou, Zhang, Shi, Huang, Li, Nieh, Jin, Zhang, Zuo, and Bai, seventy [seventeen?] lineages in all, bore tribute of western cloth to the Song [emperor]. He said, "You have come to my Zhongxia [kingdom]—revere and preserve your ancestral ways; hand them down in Bianliang [Kaifeng]."

In the *guiwei* year, the first year of the Longxing reign period of the Xiaozong emperor of the Song dynasty [1163 C.E.], Levi the ustad [rabbi] was charged with leading the teaching, and Andula ['Abd-Allah?] began to build the synagogue. In the *jimao* year, the sixteenth year of the Zhiyuan reign period of the Yuan dynasty [1279], the ustad rebuilt the ancient synagogue, the Pure and True Temple. It was situated southeast of Earth-Market Street, and each of its four sides was thirty-five *zhang* in length.

When Emperor Gao, [whose temple name was] Taizu, of the great Ming [dynasty], founded the empire, he first calmed the armies and people of the world. To all who responded to his transformation [of the empire], he bestowed land for settlement where they could live peacefully and happily follow their occupations. Truly he possessed a heart that looked upon all with equal benevolence.

Because this temple could not be without leaders, those who were well versed in the orthodox Scriptures and who exhorted others to do good were designated as *Manla* [mullahs, community leaders]—Li Cheng, Li Shi, An Pingdu, Ai Duan, Li Gui, Li Jie, Li Sheng, Li Gang, Ai Jing, Zhou An, Li Rong, Li Liang, Li Zhi, and Zhang Hao. The Dao of their teaching has been transmitted continuously, [so that] to the present, the robes and headdress, the rites and music, all conform to the fixed order of the seasons. The phrases and words, the movements and pauses, all accord with ancient rules. [The fact that] all the [Jewish] people observe and preserve the established laws, know how to honor Heaven and venerate the ancestors, and show themselves loyal to their lord and filial to their parents is entirely due to the work of the Manla.

In the nineteenth year of the Yongle reign period [1421], the physician An Cheng was given a present of incense and permitted to rebuild the synagogue by order of prince Ding of Zhou. A tablet wishing long life to the emperor of the Great Ming was placed in the synagogue. In the twenty-first year of the Yongle reign period [1423], [An Cheng] was granted the surname Zhao and the rank of a commissioner in the Embroidered Uniform Guard by imperial decree, because he made a report to the throne and was adjudged meritorious for it. He was [later?] promoted to be assistant commissioner of the Regional Military Commission in Zhejiang.

In the tenth year of the Zhengtong reign period [1445], Li Rong and Li Liang prepared private funds and rebuilt the front hall [of the temple], three *jian* in size.

In the fifth year of the Tianshun reign period [1461], the river floods swept [the entire synagogue] away, leaving only the foundations. Ai Jing and others petitioned the provincial commissioner, requesting [and receiving] permission to reconstruct the synagogue according to the [model of the] ancient synagogue of the Zhiyuan reign period [i.e., 1279 C.E.], which had been approved by the prefect, the provincial governor, et al. Li Rong again prepared private funds and began the building on a spacious scale—brightly gilt and painted in colors, its splendor was entirely renewed.

During the Chenghua reign period [1465–1488], Gao Jian, Gao Rui, and Gao Hong prepared private funds and constructed an additional rear hall, three *jian* in size, brightly gilt and painted in colors. [They] placed [therein] three copies of the Scriptures. On the exterior [they] constructed a corridor to connect [it] to the front hall. Truly this was a permanent contribution. This then is the complete history of the synagogue.

In the Tianshun reign period [1457–1465], Shi Bin, Li Rong, Gao Jian, and Zhang Xuan went to Ningbo and brought back a copy of our teaching's Scriptures. Zhao Ying of Ningbo brought another copy to Bianliang [Kaifeng] and respectfully presented it to our temple.

Gao Nian, a graduate with the gongshi degree, was appointed magistrate of Ji county, Hui prefecture [Anhui province].

Ai Jun, a provincial graduate (*juren*), was appointed annalist of Prince De's house.

Jin Xuan of Ningxia had an ancestor who had been president of state banquets, while his uncle [Jin] Sheng had been a commander of the Jinwu regiment in the Imperial Escort. [Jin] Xuan bought and placed [in the synagogue] the table of offerings, with its bronze censer, and the pairs of flower vases and candlesticks. His younger brother [Jin] Ying prepared funds in the second year of the Hongzhi reign period [1489] to purchase a portion of the temple's land. Moreover, [Jin] Ying and [Jin] Zhong [who composed this inscription] deputed Zhao Jun to purchase this inscriptional stone. Andula ['Abd-Allah?], who laid the foundation and began the work, Li Rong, and Gao Hong, who completed the construction, all have achieved merit for the temple. All families contributed to the common fund for providing shrines for the Scriptures, a tripartite archway before the Scriptures, and the table for [reading] the Scriptures. Also they provided the [two] racks, the balustrade, the ceremonial tables, the frontal drapes, and all the various articles, utensils, and vessels. Moreover, the painting and decorations beautified the entire compound.

Reflecting on the three teachings [of China—Confucianism, Buddhism, and Daoism], each has its temples in which they honor their Lord. Thus, the Confucians have the Temple of the Great Perfection to honor Confucius; the Buddhists have the Temple of the Holy Countenance to honor Shakyamuni; the Daoists have the Temple of the Jade Emperor to honor the Three Purities. So the Pure and True [the Jews, Ch. Qingzhen] have the Temple of Israel to honor August Heaven.

Although there are some minor discrepancies between their Confucian doctrine and our own, in their main focus of ideas and established practices both are exclusively concerned with honoring the Dao of Heaven, respecting ancestors, valuing the relations of ruler and subject, obedience to parents, harmony within families, correct ordering of social hierarchies, and good fellowship among friends—nothing more than the "five cardinal relationships" of humankind. Alas! People know only that ritual and obeisances in the Pure and True Temple honor the Dao, but they do not know that the great source of the Dao lies in Heaven, and it has been transmitted since antiquity without possibility of falsehood.

Although the followers of our teaching sincerely devote themselves to its practice, could it be only to obtain prosperous fields and profitable business? Since we receive the benevolence of our lord [the emperor] and consume his generous emoluments, we expend our sincerity in rituals and worship and calling upon Heaven, our intention always to repay [the favors of] our empire and [express] loyalty to our lord [the emperor].

We invoke blessings on the emperor of the Great Ming Dynasty, that his virtue may surpass that of Yu and Tang and his sageliness equal that of Yao and Shun. May his intelligence and intuitive wisdom radiate like the descending rays of the sun and moon, and his merciful love and wide benevolence match the vast breadth of Heaven and Earth. For the continuous dignity of the empire we pray that the age of the sovereign may extend to ten thousand years; for the strengthening of the empire, we pray for him a perpetual Heaven and age-long Earth. May the winds be harmonious and the rains favorable, so that together we may enjoy the blessings of universal peace.

We carve this on metal[-hard] stone, so that it may be transmitted through the ages.

Composed by Jin Zhong, Confucian scholar and Zengguang licentiate of Kaifeng city.

Written by Cao Zuo, Confucian scholar and Linshan licentiate of Xiangfu county.

Seal characters by Fu Ru, Confucian scholar and Linshan licentiate of Kaifeng city.

On a fortunate day in the second summer month of the *jiyou* year, the second year of the Hongzhi reign period [1489], jointly raised up by Jin Ying of Ningxia and Jin Li of Xiangfu [in Kaifeng], descendants of the Pure and True [the Jews].

Wu Liang and Wu Hai, stone masons.

Art and Aesthetics

—21—

Defending, Enjoying, and Regulating the Visual

Kalman P. Bland

It is commonly assumed that something qualifies as a religion if it fosters private spirituality, favors transrational belief, and defends ethical idealism. It is commonly assumed that Judaism qualifies as a religion. These two assumptions, combined, distort both religion and Judaism. Religion is more accurately described as a specialized repertory of bodily habits. The habits control our interactions with other people and the natural world. In premodernity, religions were comprehensive systems for regulating the body. In modern societies, religions still govern the body, even if less comprehensively. Premodern Judaism was therefore the set of behaviors that Jewish bodies were taught to perform. The philosophers and mystics defined what Jewish bodies were compelled to learn, know, and understand. The ethicists supervised what Jewish bodies ate, drank, spoke, read, felt, smelled, touched, heard, and saw. The lawyers and judges dictated how and when Jewish bodies were to conduct business, earn a living, wage war, relate to Gentile bodies, spend time and money, build a house, get married, make love, raise children, decorate utensils, cure disease, celebrate holidays, and bury the dead. Since so many premodern Jews were artisans and pawnbrokers, and all the rest invariably encountered artifacts and monuments in their daily lives, it is not surprising that the intellectuals and scholars turned their critical attention to the visual arts. They were obliged to determine what Jewish bodies were allowed to do when it came to the somatics of architecture, sculpture, and painting. The six documents composing this section reveal that premodern Jews acknowledged the legitimacy and power of visual images. To prevent the abhorrent sin of idolatry, premodern Jewish intellectuals defined a Jewish way of making and experiencing art.

That they attended at all to the visual may be unexpected. That they affirmed the legitimacy of art may be even more surprising. Another of the common misunderstandings of Judaism is that it devalues the visual in favor of the auditory. It is generally assumed that Judaism considers the visual arts taboo. Modern conventional wisdom teaches that Jews are a People of the Book but not a People of the Image. It is widely believed that there is "no such thing as Jewish art" and that Jews traditionally lack aptitude for making visual art and interest in beholding it. Because the Ten Commandments prohibit both idolatry and the physical representation of an invisible God, it is widely assumed in Protestant societies that Judaism is visually ascetic. It is frequently said that Judaism is indifferent or hostile to painting and sculpture, and it is often claimed that Judaism is metaphysically aniconic or theologically iconoclastic.

Measured against these popular claims and assumptions, the following documents prove that nothing could be further removed from the historical truth, just as nothing could be further removed from simple logic. If observant Jews are forbidden to eat pork, and they are, it does not follow that they are also forbidden to eat properly slaughtered chicken, beef, and lamb. They are not. If observant Jews are forbidden to worship idols, and they are, it does not follow that they are also forbidden to illuminate manuscripts, engrave burial markers, design jewelry, decorate synagogues with sculptured lions, weave tapestries picturing biblical heroes, hang portraits and paintings on the walls of their homes, or embellish marriage contracts with intricate designs and patterns. Premodern Jews performed all of these visually creative acts. Their creations are preserved in museums and reproduced in photographic collections. Their admiration for the visual arts is succinctly captured in a twelfth-century text that celebrated God's creation of the universe. Its author, Berakhiah Ha-Naqdan, likened God to "someone who sets about to build a palace. He beautifies it and lays it out, and hangs its walls with embroideries, and afterward sweeps the house, and adorns it with tapestries and woodcarvings." Were premodern Jews truly indifferent to architecture and appalled by interior decoration, weaving, and carving, it is unlikely that they would have ascribed these activities to their God. Licensed by their God, the visual arts flourished in premodern Jewish workshops and imaginations. Authorized by their Scripture, the visual arts were generously affirmed in premodern Jewish thought. They were also scrupulously protected and governed by premodern Jewish law.

The selections here are arranged in chronological order, spanning the twelfth to the sixteenth centuries. They represent diverse geographical settings and diverse literary genres: legal codes, talmudic commentaries, religious polemics, biblical grammars, and reports of pilgrimage to sacred sites. Some of the texts quote the others or their authors; they resonate with one another. As an ensemble, the selections disclose overlapping and pervasive continuities in premodern Jewish thought and law. As they discuss visual art, the documents evoke premodern Jewish perceptions of Christianity and Islam. Steeped in the technical formalities of law, science, and theology, the documents reveal how various conflicts involving visual art were defined and resolved.

The first selection was composed by Rabbi Moses ben Maimon (1138–1204). Commonly known in Latin as Maimonides, Rabbi Moses was a native of Andalusia or Islamic Spain. An emigrant, he eventually settled in Islamic Egypt. Philosopher, legal expert, community leader, and physician, Moses Maimonides is perhaps the most famous medieval Jew. He is certainly the most intensely studied and controversial medieval Jew, and he is famous for his philosophic classic, originally composed in Arabic, *The Guide of the Perplexed*. Within Jewish circles, however, the influence of his innovative law code, the *Mishneh Torah,* is unsurpassed. Topically arranged and encyclopedic in scope, it lucidly transformed complex talmudic discussions into clear-cut directives, rendering their Aramaic idioms in elegant rabbinic Hebrew. The excerpts here are taken from the "Book of Knowledge," the first of the fourteen books comprising his code. They classify the regulations governing art under the general rubric of idolatry. Modern readers might expect to find discussions of art in treatises devoted to aesthetics. Prior to the eighteenth century, however, the relationship between art and abstract beauty was less compelling than the question of art's legitimacy. Like all legal documents, the *Mishneh Torah* raises more questions and problems than it answers and resolves.

The second selection was composed by Jacob ben Reuben (1136–118?). He fled his native Spain in 1148 and settled in southern France. Sometime between 1160 and 1170, he composed *The Book of the Wars of the Lord,* one of the first and most widely cited Hebrew treatises directed against Christianity and the New Testament. Composed for a Jewish readership, it is cast in the form of an antagonistic dialogue between a Christian and a Jew. Their arguments are typically scholastic: ancient authorities are ingeniously interpreted in the sharp light of rationality and against the sharper edge of dialectical casuistry. Hoping to persuade the Jew that the Bible obliges him to abandon Judaism and affirm Christian doctrines of salvation and original sin, the Christian finds himself subject to a fierce rebuttal. It takes the form of a nippy lesson in biblical rhetoric, logic, and aesthetics. Jacob ben Reuben seizes the opportunity to declare that Christians egregiously misread Scripture, that Jews are not forbidden to make all forms of art, and that Jews fully appreciate the healing power of legitimate visual images. The ongoing debate with Christianity was one of the factors that helped crystallize the medieval Jewish defense and understanding of the visual arts.

The third selection was composed in the twelfth century by Benjamin of Tudela. The twelfth century was the Age of Crusades. European armies made their way to Palestine, hoping to wrest the Holy Land from Muslim control. The armies succeeded in establishing beleaguered Latin kingdoms in the Middle East. Stimulated by the Crusades, the twelfth century was also the Age of Pilgrims. Saints, relics, and miracles proliferated. Christian shrines and martyria were built to house them; the pious flocked to pay homage and be blessed in return. These developments reinforced the venerable Jewish practice of travel to worship at graves and other sacred sites. Perhaps motivated by a combination of worldly curiosity, hunger for adventure, messianic expectation, and the search for commercial opportunities, Benjamin of Tudela became yet another in a long line of Jewish pilgrims. Benjamin was a traditionally educated, successful merchant in Spain. Among the places he visited were Rome, Constantinople, Jerusalem, Damascus, the Persian Empire, Baghdad, Egypt, and Sicily. Wherever he went, he had an eye for opulent wealth, striking artifacts, feats of architectural genius,

Jewish monuments, and the burial sites of biblical heroes and rabbinic scholars. This excerpt from his travelogue is typical. Benjamin luxuriates in visual detail. He carefully records the material benefits of being near the coffins of Jewish prophets, teachers, and saints. Being a European, he is astonished by the congenial relations between Muslims and Jews. His comments regarding Islam contrast sharply with Jacob ben Reuben's truculent denunciations of Christian theology and practice. In at least one important respect, Benjamin of Tudela nevertheless resembles Jacob ben Reuben of southern France: Neither of them was an iconoclast, neither of them detached Jewish culture from the visual arts.

The fourth selection was composed by Rabbi Meir of Rothenburg (c. 1220–1293). Rabbi Meir was preeminent among the illustrious talmudic scholars of the Rhine Valley. Coping with the troubled thirteenth century, his disciples and contemporaries turned to him often for decisive guidance on all sorts of matters. His authoritative answers were preserved for later generations in volumes of collected responsa and talmudic commentaries or Tosafot (additional glosses). The excerpt from his brief on illuminated prayerbooks appears in both literary forms. It is a beautiful example of typical medieval modes of intense talmudic study. Its supple erudition and keen dialectics display the same scholastic habits of mind revealed in Jacob ben Reuben's argument with his Christian interlocutor.

When readers catalogue the paintings and sculptures Rabbi Meir forbids and permits, they immediately discover that permitted images vastly outnumber the forbidden. And when readers patiently work through his demanding arguments, they stand a chance of experiencing the passionate allure of talmudic study for medieval Jewish intellectuals. Rabbi Meir's arguments are complex, but his main point, the fundamental distinction between two- and three-dimensional images, is crystal clear. It is also philosophically intriguing: Is the difference between art and reality a question of intentional artificiality and theatricality? Rabbi Meir seems to suggest that the more obviously a thing is art the less threatening it is and the less likely it is to be mistaken for what it represents. A flat painting is obviously artificial. A painted sculpture is less so. His other concerns were historical: He was eager to discover the legal principle that justified the abundance of three-dimensional images in King Solomon's palace and Temple in Jerusalem. It may be remembered that Jacob ben Reuben also appealed to the divinely sanctioned, historical precedents established by King Solomon to justify the production of visual artifacts. Finally: Rabbi Meir may be understood as having paid a backhanded compliment to the power of images. He was aware that pictures are liable to distract one's concentration (*kawwanah*) during worship. His awareness of art's distractions, however, was no match for the overwhelming normative endorsement of visual art in Jewish law. Despite his anxieties, he could not forbid the use of illuminated prayerbooks.

The fifth selection was composed by Profiat Duran (c. 1360–1414). The name is Catalan. His Hebrew name was Isaac ben Moses Halevi. Philosopher, polemicist, and Hebrew grammarian, Isaac lived through the terrors of anti-Jewish violence in late medieval Christian Spain. Forcibly converted to Christianity, he eventually reverted to Judaism and dedicated himself to promoting study of the Bible. Unlike Rabbi Meir of Rothenburg, who feared that visual images were liable to interfere with religious devotion, Profiat Duran was convinced that beautiful images and pleasant surroundings were indispensable for achieving success in learning and piety. He understood that the human soul is only efficient when intellect cooperates with its integral partners: the emotions, the "internal" senses of memory and imagination, and the five "external" senses. He used the term "common sense," by which he meant the psychological structure where sight, hearing, taste, smell, and touch are combined and synthesized with memory, thought, and emotion to build our multimedia perception of the world. For him, as for the vast majority of premodern intellectuals, there was no such thing as "art for art's sake." For the vast majority of premodern people, beauty was utilitarian, not considered to be a supreme end in itself. Profiat Duran therefore urged his contemporaries to spend their capital on beautifully decorated and artistically crafted books. As his extended quotation from Moses Maimonides indicates, Profiat Duran was not the only premodern Jew who understood and exploited the intimate and salutary connection between emotions, mental hygiene, and aesthetic experience.

The sixth selection was composed by Rabbi Joseph ben Menahem Caro (1488–1575). He left the Iberian peninsula around the time of the expulsion from Spain in 1492. Rabbi Joseph settled in Turkey, where he remained for many years. In 1536, he migrated to Safed in the Galilee, where he achieved prominence among that remarkable community of saints, scholars, and mystics. Just as Maimonides made Jewish law compatible with secular Aristotelian philosophy, Rabbi Joseph made Jewish law compatible with avid mysticism. He was the leading halakhic (legal) authority of his day, and continues to be so among Orthodox Jews in the late twentieth century. They regularly consult his best-known work, the *Shulhan 'Arukh* (The Prepared Table), a comprehensive legal digest and code of law meant for daily living. Like Rabbi Meir of Rothenburg, Rabbi Joseph's talmudic restrictions against exact imitations of the Temple are poignant. They signal premodern Jewry's historical sadness. They are tokens of mourning for the inimitable glories of an irreplaceable past. Even art has its limits. Like all his predecessors, Rabbi Joseph classified the laws regulating visual art under the rubric of idolatry. Summarizing the premodern Jewish consensus, his formulations of the law are generously permissive. They permit much more visual art than they forbid.

The translations are from the following sources. Text 1 is based on the traditional Hebrew text of *Mishneh Torah*, 5 vols. (reprint New York: 1954; with traditional commentaries): *Sefer Ha-Mad'a: Hilkhoth 'Avodah Zarah*, vol. 1, chapter 3, paras. 6, 9–11. Text 2 is translated from the critical Hebrew edition published by Judah Rosenthal: Jacob ben Reuben, *Sefer Milhamot Ha-Shem* (Jerusalem: Mossad Harav Kook, 1963), pp. 56–59. Text 3 is from the Hebrew edition of Benjamin's travel diary published and translated into an archaic English by A. Ascher: *The Itinerary of Benjamin of Tudela*, 2 vols. (New York: Hakeshet Publishing, 1917), vol. 1, pp. 73–76 (Hebrew). Text 4 is based on the Hebrew text of Rabbi Meir's talmudic gloss published in the traditional editions of the Babylonian Talmud, *Yoma* 54a–b, "Painted Cherubs." See *Talmud Bavli,* 20 vols. (Vilna, 1880–1886; reprint New York: Pardes, 1954). I also consulted the shorter form of the gloss preserved in Rabbi Meir's responsa; see Maharam of Rothenburg, *Sefer She'elot ve-Teshuvot* (Venice, 1515), pp. 14a–15a. For the complete text of the tannaitic document he interpreted, see Jacob Lauterbach, ed. and trans., *Mekilta* (Philadelphia: Jewish Publication Society of America, 1933), pp. 241–43. Text 5 is based on the Hebrew edition of Duran's Hebrew grammar; see J. Friedländer and J. Kohn, ed., *Maase Efod, Einleitung in das Studium der Hebräischen Sprache von Profiat Duran* (Vienna: Holtzwarte, 1865), pp. 13, 19–21. Text 6 is from the traditional Hebrew text of Rabbi Joseph Caro, *Shulhan 'Arukh: Yoreh De'ah; Hilkhot 'Avodah Zarah* (New York: MOP Press, n.d.), Sections 139 and 141.

Further Reading

For the conventional wisdom that defends "no such thing as Jewish art," see Harold Rosenberg, "Is There a Jewish Art?" *Commentary* 42 (July 1966): 57–60. For an indication of the modern provenance of this conventional wisdom, see Kalman P. Bland, "Medieval Jewish Aesthetics: Maimondes, Body, and Scripture in Profiat Duran," *Journal of the History of Ideas* 54, no. 4 (October 1993): 533–37, and Bland, "Anti-Semitism and Aniconism: The Germanophone Requiem for Jewish Visual Art," in Catherine M. Soussloff, ed., *Jewish Identity in Art History: Ethnicity and Discourse* (Berkeley and Los Angeles: University of California Press, 1999), pp. 41–66. For empirical and theoretical refutations of the conventional wisdom, see Richard I. Cohen, *Jewish Icons: Art and Society in Modern Europe* (Berkeley and Los Angeles: University of California Press, 1998), and *The Visual Dimension: Aspects of Jewish Art,* edited by Clare Moore (Boulder, Colo.: Westview Press, 1993). For just two of the many superb photographic collections of premodern Jewish artifacts with accompanying critical essays, see Thérèse and Mendel Metzger, *Jewish Life in the Middle Ages: Illuminated Hebrew Manuscripts of the Thirteenth to the Eighteenth Centuries* (New York: Alpine Fine Arts Collection, 1982), and Gabrielle Sed-Rajna, *Jewish Art,* translated by Sara Friedman and Mira Reich (New York: H. N. Abrams, 1997). For information regarding the lawyers and judges, see *Jewish Law: Introduction to the History and Sources of Jewish Law,* edited by N. S. Hecht et al. (Oxford: Clarendon Press, 1996), and Menahem Elon, *Jewish Law: History, Sources, and Principles,* translated by Bernard Auerbach and Melvin J. Sykes, 4 vols. (Philadelphia: Jewish Publication Society, 1994).

For a critical assessment of Rabbi Moses ben Maimon, together with a generous sampling of his biography and works, see Isadore Twersky, *A Maimonides Reader* (New York: Behrman House, 1972). For detailed insight into his legal activity, see Twersky, *Introduction to the Code of Maimonides (Mishneh Torah)* (New Haven: Yale University Press, 1980). For the concept of idolatry in Jewish thought, see

Moshe Halbertal and Avishai Margalit, *Idolatry*, translated by Naomi Goldblum (Cambridge: Harvard University Press, 1992).

For detailed information regarding Jacob ben Reuben's influential place in the history of the medieval Jewish-Christian argument, see Hanne Trautner-Kromann, *Sword and Shield: Jewish Polemics against Christianity and the Christians in France and Spain from 1100–1500* (Tübingen: J.C.B. Mohr [Paul Siebeck], 1993), and Samuel Krauss and William Horby, *The Jewish-Christian Controversy from the Earliest Times to 1789* (Tübingen: J.C.B. Mohr [Paul Siebeck], 1995). For a portrait of the Jewish community in southern France, see Isadore Twersky, "Aspects of the Social and Cultural History of Provençal Jewry," in *Jewish Society through the Ages*, edited by H. H. Ben-Sasson and S. Ettinger (New York: Schocken, 1971), pp. 185–207. For a comprehensive discussion of modern theories seeking to explain medieval Christian antagonism toward the Jews, see Robert Chazan, *Medieval Stereotypes and Modern Antisemitism* (Berkeley and Los Angeles: University of California Press, 1997).

For textual evidence that places Benjamin of Tudela in the long line of Jewish travelers and pilgrims, see Elkan N. Adler, *Jewish Travellers in the Middle Ages* (1930; reprint New York: Dover, 1987). For the historical context explaining the difference between Benjamin's positive evaluation of Islam and Jacob ben Reuben's derogatory evaluation of Christianity, see Mark R. Cohen, *Under Crescent and Cross: The Jews in the Middle Ages* (Princeton: Princeton University Press, 1994).

For detailed information regarding Rabbi Meir, see Irving A. Agus, *Rabbi Meir of Rothenburg, His Life and Works as a Source for the Religious, Legal, and Social History of the Jews in the Thirteenth Century*, 2 vols. (Philadelphia: Dropsie College, 1947). For the "troubled thirteenth century," see Robert Chazan, *Medieval Jewry in Northern France: A Political and Social History* (Baltimore: Johns Hopkins University Press, 1973), and Chazan, *Daggers of Faith: Thirteenth-Century Christian Missionizing and Jewish Response* (Berkeley and Los Angeles: University of California Press, 1989). For the rabbinic legends related to Solomon's lions and throne, see the summary and bibliographic notes assembled by Louis Ginzberg, *Legends of the Jews*, vols. 4 and 6 (Philadelphia: Jewish Publication Society, 1954–1959). To understand Rabbi Meir against the backdrop of a wider historical canvass, namely, for the cultural difference between two- and three-dimensional forms as a marker separating Byzantine and Latin Christianity, see Hans Belting, *Likeness and Image: A History of the Image before the Era of Art*, translated by E. Jephcott (Chicago: University of Chicago Press, 1994).

For the scant biographical data on Profiat Duran and a detailed description of the anti-Jewish violence that erupted in Spain in 1391, see Isaac Baer, *A History of the Jews in Christian Spain*, translated by Louis Schoffman, vol. 2 (Philadelphia: Jewish Publication Society, 1966), pp. 95–169. For background on Profiat Duran's philosophy, with references to his religious polemics and commentary on *The Guide of the Perplexed*, see Colett Sirat, *A History of Jewish Philosophy in the Middle Ages* (Cambridge: Cambridge University Press, 1985), pp. 352–57. For the complete text of his quotation from Maimondes, see Joshua Gorfinkle, ed. and trans., *The Eight Chapters of Maimonides on Ethics* (New York: Columbia University Press, 1912).

For biographical data and explorations of Rabbi Joseph's rich inner life, see R.J.Z. Werblowsky, *Joseph Karo, Lawyer and Mystic* (London: Oxford University Press, 1962). For portraits of the remarkable sixteenth-century community in Safed, see Joseph Dan, *Jewish Mysticism and Jewish Ethics* (Seattle: University of Washington Press, 1986), and Lawrence Fine, *Safed Spirituality* (Ramsey, N.J., Paulist Press, 1984).

1. Moses Maimonides: Twelfth-Century Laws of Idolatry

CHAPTER THREE, PARAGRAPH 6

Regarding a [Jew] who worships an object associated with idolatry because of love, for example, a [Jewish] person feels desire for some image because its workmanship is particularly beautiful, or worships it because the person fears that it might cause harm, its worshipers imagine that it bestows benefits and harms, if the [Jewish] person considers it a god, the person is guilty and subject to stoning. But if the person worships it in the customary fashion of its cult or with one of the four specific classes of worship [that is, bowing down, making sacrifices, offering libations, and sprinkling blood], merely because of love or fear, [without considering it an actual god], then the person is innocent [of idolatry and is therefore not subject to stoning]. Regarding a [Jew] who embraces an object associated with idolatry, kisses it, honors it by prostration, washes it, clothes it, and places shoes on it, and all similar acts of adoration, the person trespasses against the prohibition, "Do not worship them" [Exod. 20:5], for all these belong to the category of "worship." The person is nevertheless not subject to corporal punishment by lashes, since the performance of any one of these acts is not specifically [defined as idolatry]. If, however, one of these acts was customary in that cult and the person performed it for the purpose of worship, then the person is guilty.

PARAGRAPH 9

If a [Jew] makes an object associated with idolatry for himself, even if the [Jewish] person neither [personally] manufactured it nor worshiped it, the person is subject to lashes, as it is said, "You shall not *make* either a sculpture or any image" [Exod. 20:4]. Similarly, if a [Jew] makes an object associated with idolatry for another person, even if that other person is a [Gentile] idolater, [the maker] is subject to lashes, as it is said, "You shall not *make* molten gods" [Lev. 19: 4]. A [Jew] who makes an object associated with idolatry for and by himself is therefore subject to lashes twice.

PARAGRAPH 10

It is forbidden to make decorative images, even if they are not idolatrous, as it is said, "You shall not make with me . . ." [Exod. 20: 23], namely, ["you shall not make"] images of silver and gold intended only for decoration in order that errant people not mistake them and imagine them to be cultic idols. The prohibition against making decorative images pertains exclusively to the human image only. The human image is therefore not to be fashioned out of wood, plaster, or stone, if that image protrudes, as is the case with images and panel work found in dining and reception rooms, and similar such things. If the person fashions [such an image], [the penalty] is lashes. But if the image was intaglio [incised beneath the surface], or made of pigments like images painted on slates and tablets or images woven into tapestries, these are permitted.

PARAGRAPH 11

Regarding a ring on which there is a seal with the image of a person on it, if the image protrudes, it is forbidden to maintain possession of it, but it is permitted to use it for sealing. And if the image is intaglio, it is permitted to maintain possession of it, but it is forbidden to use it for sealing because the resulting seal becomes a protruding image. Similarly, it is forbidden to make the image of the sun, moon, stars, constellations, and angels. As it is said, "You shall not make with me . . ." [Exod. 20: 23], you shall not make images that resemble my servants, who serve me in the celestial heights, not even [if those images are put] on slates. Regarding the image of cattle and other living creatures, except for the human image, as well as the images of trees, plants, and similar things, it is permitted to make them, even if the image protrudes.

2. Jacob ben Reuben: Religious Polemics

The [Christian] Denier:

I have found in Scripture, "You shall have no other gods before me, you shall not make for yourself either a sculpture or any image" [Exod. 20:3–4]. He therefore forbade even the making of idols. Subsequently, He declared, "Do not bow down to them or worship them" [Exod. 20:5], thereby forbidding ritual worship. Hence, you see that both the making and worshiping [of idols] are forbidden. In this matter and in this fashion, they were forbidden to you at Horeb. Later on in Scripture you see, "God spoke to Moses: 'Make a fiery serpent and place it upon a pole. Whoever is bitten and looks at it, will live'" [Num. 21:8]. In this passage you can see that the Creator commanded Moses to make a sculptured image so that people who were bitten might be cured by looking at it. You are obliged to be astonished by this, for at the giving of

Torah, He forbade making [images] even when no worship is involved, but later He commanded that this sculpture be made in the shape of a serpent in order to cure people who are bitten. If we surmise that Moses himself originated [the cure], the claim would be implausible. And if we assume that the blessed Creator was retracting His first words, the claim would be objectionable. But, perforce, you must conclude that [by means of this rhetorical contradiction] the discerning reader will understand that Scripture is conveying a major and deeply profound secret lesson, something that is not superficially apparent in Scripture.

I will explain the truth to you in its proper entirety. You surely know that the serpent was more clever than all the animals and beasts upon the face of the earth. Scripture attests to it, as it is written, "the serpent was more clever than all the beasts of the field that the Lord God made" [Gen. 3:1]. It became clear to us that all creatures are bitten by the serpent, even the child leaving its mother's womb and entering the world is born with the serpent's bite, namely, death. It is clear to all of us that the serpent caused the death that awaits all creatures. All creatures, therefore, are created together with the serpent's bite. No doctor is able to cure that bite, for it is not like a mere poison within man. As for the serpent being the most clever and the wisest of all creatures, Jesus, our Messiah, resembled it in being greater in wisdom, understanding, and knowledge than all the other creatures in the world. When the Creator commanded Moses, "make a fiery serpent and place it upon a pole," [God] was informing them, by way of an allegorical allusion, that whoever gazes upward sincerely at the One who resembles the shape of the serpent, who in the future will receive the sentence of crucifixion, and resembling [the serpent] is placed on a pole to die, shall live eternally. As Scripture declares, "whoever is bitten and looks upon him shall live" [Num. 21:8]. This means that all creatures, being bitten by the serpent, the bite of death, faithfully seeing him in the time to come, will live. They will not die an eternal death, as did those who died before his coming and who descended to Gehinnom, for no one can be saved from Satan until [Jesus] descended beneath the earth and saved them from the yoke and bitterness. He places his faithful followers and members of his household who believe in him before his gaze in the heavenly realm.

The [Jewish] Champion of Unity:

... My [brief] reply is divided in four parts. First: The question you raised against me involves two scriptural verses. You said that in one verse the Creator forbade us even to make a sculpture or image, and in the other verse the Creator commanded Moses to "make the fiery serpent." Based on the implications of these verses, you claimed that your messiah resembles the serpent. Now, see the many ways in which you raised the question incorrectly. Our blessed Creator never forbade the making of statues and images. He only forbade bowing down and worship. As Scripture states, "You shall not have other gods before me, making for yourself a sculpture or any image" that represents divinity. Similarly, the end of the verse proves the point. It states, "neither bow down to them nor worship them." But Scripture never forbade the making of images or the beautification of an artifact or building. This is precisely what Solomon did when he had numerous images made for the Temple. And this is precisely what Moses, our teacher, himself did when he included the two golden cherubs in the construction of the Tabernacle.

3. Benjamin of Tudela: The Pilgrim's Eye in Persia

The Samorah River is the beginning of Persian lands. About fifteen hundred Jews live there. Here stands the grave of Ezra the Scribe and Priest, who went from Jerusalem to King Artaxerxes and who died there. In front of his grave they built a large synagogue, and on the other side of it the Muslims built a house of prayer because of their great affection for [Ezra]. They love the Jews, for which reason they come there to pray.

From this place it is four miles to Kuzistan, namely, [the biblical land of] Elam, the large province. It is not entirely inhabited. Some of it lies in ruins. The capital city of Shushan, the palace of King Ahasuerus, stands among those ruins. In their midst, there is also an ancient, immense, and beautiful building. In the [city of Shushan], there are seven thousand Jews and fourteen synagogues. The grave of Daniel, blessed be his memory, stands in front of one of those synagogues.

A river divides the city into two parts, and a bridge connects them. On one bank, where the Jews live, are all the markets and commercial centers. All of the wealthy people live there. On the other bank, live all the poor people, for they have in their midst neither markets nor commerce. Nor do they have gardens and orchard parks. Eventually, they became jealous. They said that the others enjoy all that wealth and prestige only because of Daniel the Prophet, peace be upon him, who is buried in their midst. They asked that Daniel be buried with them.

The others did not surrender [Daniel] to them. They did not want to. They warred for a long time. When they could suffer no more, they reached a compromise: the coffin of Daniel would remain on one bank for one year and on the other bank the following year. And so they did, all of them from both sides being reconciled with one another, until one day when Shah Sanegar, the son of a shah, arrived.

He ruled over all the kingdoms of Persia, forty-five of them being under his control. He is the Sultan al-Poras al-Kabir, [the Great Emperor of Persia], in the Arabic language. He ruled from the bridge-gates of the Samorah River to the province of Samarkand, the Gozan River, the cities of Media, the Hafton mountain range, and all the way to the provinces of Tibet in whose forests are the animals that produce musk. His realm measures a trip of four months and four days. Upon his arrival there, this great emperor, Sanegar, king of Persia, saw them carrying Daniel's coffin from one side to the other. [He saw] Jews and Muslims crossing the bridge, and many people accompanied him. He asked what this meant, and they told him the whole story.

He said that it was "improper to deal with Daniel so disgracefully. Measure off from this side and the other an equal distance. Then place Daniel's coffin into another coffin made of glass. Then suspend it with chains of bronze from the exact middle of the bridge. Then, on the same spot, build a house of prayer for all the people of the world. Whomever it pleases shall enter it and pray, whether Jew or Aramean [Gentile]."

To this very day, Daniel's coffin is suspended from the bridge. The king commanded that no one fish in the river a distance of one mile up and a distance of one mile down, in honor of Daniel.

4. Rabbi Meir of Rothenburg: A Talmudic Brief on Illuminated Manuscripts

I was asked concerning the propriety of those who illuminate their holiday prayerbooks with pictures of birds and animals. I replied: It seems to me that they certainly are not behaving properly, for while they gaze upon those pictures they are not directing their hearts exclusively to their Father in heaven. Nevertheless, in this case, there is no trespass against the biblical prohibition, "You shall not make either a sculpture or any image" [Exod. 20:3], as we deduce from the [precedent] recorded in the talmudic chapter, "All the Statues," regarding Rabban Gamaliel [whose models of the moon's phases were considered unproblematic] "because other people produced [the models] for him" [Babylonian Talmud, 'Avodah Zarah 54b]. Furthermore, there are no grounds for even the precautionary suspicion [of idolatry] regarding the pictures, since they are merely patches of pigment lacking sufficient tangible substantiality. We only have precautionary grounds to suspect [idolatry] with respect to a protruding, engraved seal, but not with an intaglio seal, and all the more so in this case where [the image of birds and animals in prayerbooks] is neither protruding nor intaglio. [The image in a prayerbook] is merely [flat] pigment.

Moreover, it seems to me that a Jew is permitted to produce images using all sorts of pigment, without thereby [encroaching] on the prohibition, "You shall not make either a sculpture or any image," since the only forbidden image is the painted sculpture of a complete frontal view. Images made [only] with pigment are permitted. This accords with what is reported in [the talmudic chapter], "A Presumptive Title to Houses": "One who draws an image on the property [that is, on the walls of the house] belonging to a [deceased] proselyte thereby acquires ownership. Rav acquired the garden adjoining his house of study merely by painting a picture" [Babylonian Talmud, *Bava Batra* 54a]. My teacher, Rabbi Samuel, raised a difficulty [by comparing the case of Rav to the case of someone who acquired ownership of a villa belonging to a deceased proselyte by painting a decoration whose minimal size] was "one cubit and whose location was near the doorway" [ibid., 53b]. He resolved the difficulty [by distinguishing between the two cases]. With respect to the second case, the painting did not portray an actual creature. It was merely a design of sorts, representing playful things and floral patterns. By contrast, the shape of an animal or bird is inherently noteworthy, and we therefore do not require that its dimension be one cubit and its location be near the doorway. Rav therefore [must have] drawn the shape of an animal or bird. At any rate, [images that are only made with] different sorts of pigment are permitted.

There is a [tannaitic] tradition [i.e., among rabbis of the Mishnah] recorded in the *Mekhilta:* " 'You shall not make either a sculpture or any image' [Exod. 20:3]. One shall not make something graven, but perhaps one [is allowed] to make something solid? Scripture states, "*any* image," thereby implying that one may not even make something solid, . . . including [figures representing] cattle, birds, fish, locust . . . and even reflected images and the *Surzirim*." It seems to me that this is its meaning: "graven" signifies an image that convexly protrudes; "solid" signifies an image that is concave, intaglio. The biblical phrase, "in the waters beneath the earth," includes a "reflected image," namely, [the artifact that is produced when] someone makes an image and then sculpts a statue of that image's reflection in water. For I might have supposed that [the prohibition] is restricted exclusively to things actually existing in the heavens above and in the earth beneath the sky. [The prohibition therefore] might not include the figure of a shape reflected in water. Scripture however states, "*in* the water," thereby implying [a prohibition against even reflected images]. Some say [that the prohibition] means to include *Surzirim,* which seems to be some sort of water-demon known in Franco-German as *nikhsa*. It is only forbidden to make complete and frontal sculptures of all these things. As I have proved, however, it is not [forbidden] to make painted images [of all these things].

I am nonetheless puzzled by [the golden sculptures associated with] King Solomon's throne. Scripture states, "The king also made a large ivory throne. . . . The throne had six steps . . . and on each side of the seat were arm rests and two lions standing beside the arm rests. Twelve lions stood there, one at each end of a step on the six steps" [1 Kings 10:18–20]. One cannot [justify these sculptures] by saying that they were decreed by God. Scripture states, "Then Solomon sat on the throne *of the Lord* as king in place of David his father" [1 Chron. 29:23], since "prophets [like Solomon] are no longer allowed to introduce [precedents that establish] new regulations [such as the sculptured lions surrounding his throne]." One might suggest that [Solomon's lions] were an exceptional case that establishes no precedent [and therefore pose no problem], just as Elijah's [altar and sacrifices] on Mount Carmel [were an unproblematic, exceptional case that established no precedent; see 1 Kings 18:20–40 and Babylonian Talmud, *Yevamot* 90b]. Perhaps in [Solomon's] case there are grounds for considering the matter exceptional, for when witnesses appeared before him, the lions would roar and growl, as the midrashic legends relate, so that the witnesses would be afraid to offer false testimony. Alternatively, one might [justify Solomon's lions] by saying that other people made them for him. Moreover, there are no grounds to suspect [idolatry] because many people were present [in the throne room], just as there were [many people present] in the case of Rabban Gamaliel [and the lunar models, discussed in Babylonian Talmud, 'Avodah Zarah 43a].

Regarding the engraved images they fixed in all the surrounding walls of the Temple and Holy of Holies, including "the face of a man in the direction of the palm tree on one side, and the face of a young lion in the direction of the palm tree on the other side" [Ezek. 41:18–20; 1 Kings 6:29–30], one ought to say that [they were all made in accordance with God's] "written" decree [1 Chron. 28:19]. One might also say that the prohibition, "You shall not make either a sculpture or any image," only pertains to freestanding objects, but it does not pertain to objects attached to walls, since [wall attachments] are mere decorations, [but not formal idols], their otherwise independent status being canceled with respect to the walls. Even though I can imagine [the validity of this argument], I myself would not offer it as a resolution [to the problem of sculptures attached to the wall of the Temple].

Furthermore, in accordance with the discussion contained in the chapter "All Images" [Babylonian Talmud, 'Avodah Zarah 43a–b], it seems to me proven that one is permitted to make all sorts of images representing faces, including even sculptured faces and protruding seals, except for the human face by itself; the combined image of the four faces comprising the Throne of Glory—man, lion, ox, and eagle; the shape of celestial entities located in the highest and lowest regions of heaven; and sacred furnishings, such as "making a house that replicates exactly the shape of the Temple; a porch in the shape of the Temple porch in accordance with their dimensions, length, and breadth; a courtyard in the shape of the Temple courtyard; a table in the shape of the Temple's table; and a candelabrum in the shape of the Temple's candelabrum." All other [sculptured] objects, however, are permitted.

5. Profiat Duran: Visual Techniques for Studying Torah

THE AUTHOR'S INTRODUCTION

... Of course, [true worship] is contingent upon proper intention and conceptual foundations, for these comprise the true worship owed to God, as it is said, "You shall *love* the Lord your God with all your *heart*" [Deute. 6:5]. But I also say that the mere acts of being busy with, articulating, and reciting [the sacred books] are an integral part of this worship. [These physical activities] are useful in drawing down divine emanation and providence by means of the property attached to [these books], for this too belongs to God's will. Just as some medicinal concoctions work when taken as food or drink, whereas others work when applied topically, some by inhaling, and others by looking—as with eyeglasses used by people with poor vision, so too with respect to this sacred book, [the Bible]. The various effects stemming from [the Bible's] property vary. It too works, in some way, when it is merely looked upon, articulated, and recited.

THE SIXTH METHOD

One should always study from the most beautiful and lovely of books, whose script is attractive and whose pages are glorious both in ornamentation and bindings. One's places of study, I mean the *Batte Ha-Midrash,* ought to be beautifully decorated buildings, for by increasing one's love of learning and the pleasure one takes in it, memory is improved. Moreover, the studious beholding of lovely shapes, beautiful designs and pictures, expands the soul, stimulates it, and strengthens its faculties. Physicians concur with this, and Rabbi [Moses Maimonides] declared that [enjoying beautiful things] is permitted as long as "one's intention is to expand the soul in order that it become pure and clear for mastering the sciences. This [accords with] the dictum uttered by [the talmudic sages]: For the scholar, 'a beautiful dwelling, a beautiful wife, and a made-up bed' [Babylonian Talmud, *Berakhot* 57b]. . . . It is therefore permitted to make designs and pictures on houses, utensils, and garments, for the soul grows weary and thought passes away as a result of constantly looking at ugly things. Just as the body grows weary from undertaking heavy labor unless it relaxes and rests, thereby returning to its natural equilibrium, so too must the soul occupy itself with refreshing the senses by looking at beautiful designs and pictures so that its weariness be removed." . . . this matter, too, is appropriate and obligatory, I mean, decorating God's books and attending to their beauty, gorgeousness, and loveliness. For just as God took delight in adorning his Temple with gold, silver, precious stones, and treasure, so too should it be regarding his sacred books, especially this holy Book [the Bible], which is the temple of God, made by his own hands, so that [the books] be made to resemble the most glorious of all natural bodies, namely, the heavenly body in which he added loveliness and beauty. . . .

THE NINTH METHOD

One should study Scripture and Talmud from books that are written in the Assyrian script . . . which our nation calls the "square script." Because of the loveliness and beauty of this script, its impression persists in the "common sense" and imagination. . . . I have learned from my teachers of blessed memory that this splendid script has the property of improving memory, having learned this themselves from the ancients. I used to think that their [claim] was overstated or an exaggeration. I tried it out in my own studies, however, and discovered that it was true.

THE TENTH METHOD

One ought to study from books whose script inclines toward the thick and heavy rather than the delicate, for thick writing leaves more of an impression on both the "common sense" and imagination than does delicate writing. Furthermore, in old age when sight darkens, one would not be required to shift from one book to another. For this reason, it was customary among all of the ancients to write these books in a thick script.

6. Rabbi Joseph Caro: Sixteenth-Century Laws of Idolatry

SECTION 139, PARAGRAPH 1

It is forbidden to derive any benefit whatsoever from an idol, its utensils, ornaments, and offerings, regardless of whether they belong to an idolater or a Jew. Those belonging to an idolater, however, are forbidden immediately; those belonging to a Jew are not forbidden until after they have been used for actual idolatrous worship.

SECTION 141, PARAGRAPH 4

It is forbidden to make images representing the shape of things in the region of God's presence (*Shekhinah*). [These] include the combined image of the four faces [of the lion, man, ox, and eagle]; the shapes of the [angelic] seraphim, ofanim, and ministering angels; as well as the human image by itself. It is forbidden to make even decorative images of all these. And if an idolater made them on behalf of a Jew, it is forbidden to keep them in one's possession. The qualifying term of this restriction is protrusion. Regarding nonprotruding images, like those woven into garments or painted with pigments on walls, it is permitted to make them. Regarding the image of the sun, moon, and stars, it is forbidden to make them, whether they protrude or not. But if they serve instructional, judicial, or forensic purposes, it is permitted [to make images of the sun, moon, and stars], even if they protrude.

PARAGRAPH 5

Regarding a ring on which there is a seal with the image of a person on it, if the image protrudes, it is forbidden to maintain possession of it, but it is permitted to use it for sealing. And if the image is intaglio, it is permitted to maintain possession of it, but it is forbidden to use it for sealing because the resulting seal becomes a protruding image.

PARAGRAPH 6

Regarding images of cattle, animals, birds, and fish, as well as images of trees, plants, and similar things, it is permitted to make them, even if the image protrudes.

PARAGRAPH 7

One authority states that they specifically forbade images of the human being and the Dragon [only] if those images are complete in representing all of the bodily organs. A [bust], the image of a head, and a torso, [the image of] a body without a head, have nothing forbidden about them, whether they be found or manufactured.

PARAGRAPH 8

One should not build a house that replicates exactly the Temple, imitating the dimensions of its height, length, and width; a porch in the shape of the Temple porch; a courtyard in the shape of the Temple courtyard, a table in the shape of the Temple's table, and a candelabrum in the shape of the Temple's candelabrum. One may, however, make [a candelabrum] with five, six, or eight shafts. One may not make one with seven shafts, even if it is made of different metals, even if it lacks cups, knobs, and floral designs, and even if it is not eighteen hand-breadths high.

22

Illustrating History and Illuminating Identity in the Art of the Passover Haggadah

Marc Michael Epstein

When one examines illuminated manuscripts of the Haggadah (pl. Haggadot, the liturgical text read at the Passover *Seder*) dating from the thirteenth through the eighteenth centuries, and the sixteenth- through eighteenth-century printed haggadot that both emulated and departed from the illuminated models, it is easy to regard the illustrations in these books as straightforward depictions of narrative or ritual—what Pooh Bah, in the *Mikado,* rather uneconomically termed "merely corroborative detail intended to give artistic verisimilitude to an otherwise bald and unconvincing narrative." But to yield to this temptation is to miss a great deal of richness. It is true that these illuminations appear at first glance to be simple illustrations of the texts they accompany, mirrors of sacred history or of the progress of the ritual meal that takes place in the world outside the window of the page. But they also have a life of their own as separate, yet interdependent "texts" that, like the others in this volume, may be fraught with issues of Jewish identity and self-image, with polemics and politics. These visual sources are a crucial component of "Judaism in practice." They form a contextual progression and engage in a dialectic between themselves and with the user of the manuscript during the *Seder*. Can one, after all conceive of a moment of "Judaism in practice" more central to the Jewish experience as a whole than the *Seder* experience? Can one conceive of the *Seder* without the Haggadah? And—although they tend to be taken for granted—can one conceive of the Haggadah without the illustrations that accompany it?

The tradition of illustration of the Haggadah goes back almost as far as the oldest known manuscript Haggadot, and it must always be kept in mind that the audience of the Haggadah was never simply an audience of readers but also an audience of actors, one that viewed the book not only as a text but as a script for the ritual reenactment of the Exodus, a drama for which the illustrations set the scene, and to which they added color and detail, filling in various narrative and conceptual lacunae. The Haggadah text explicitly advertises itself as a certain kind of "mirror," in which "in each and every generation, one must envision oneself as if one had come forth from Egypt." Through the Haggadah, in other words, one is to attempt to experience the *Seder* as if one had been involved personally and actually in the miracle of the redemption of Exodus. Such a connection is facilitated by the illustrations, which depict the scriptural and rabbinic narratives cited by the text. Yet those illustrations do more than merely re-present narrative. The Haggadah is a book whose actual text is less important than what is said about it—how it is interpreted. Its very title, "the telling," reminds us that although it serves as a guide, an instruction manual, a script, and an outline, in performance at the *Seder* it is not a mere text but a hybrid of the words on the page with the polyphony of voices weaving in and out of those words. The received text is conservative and familiar—it was so already in the Middle Ages. But this actual and prescribed text provides the "background drone" that is enlivened and vivified by the commentary and discussion by the participants in the *Seder*, which provide creative and innovative interpretation. In a parallel fashion, the illustrations of the Haggadah serve both as countertext and commentary. If the letter of the law concerning the eve of the *Seder* is that "you shall tell your child [of the Exodus]," and the spirit of the commandment is "everyone who expands upon the telling of the Exodus from Egypt, is indeed praiseworthy," it is, in fact, the illustrations as commentary that facilitate the fulfillment of both letter and spirit of the commandment of what is called *sippur yeziat mizrayim*—the telling of the Exodus from Egypt. Small wonder that the colophon of an illuminated Haggadah created by Avraham of Ihringen of Germany in 1732 paraphrases the Haggadah's mandate, asserting that "everyone who expands upon the scribal illumination and the illustration of the Exodus from Egypt is indeed both praiseworthy and superb!"

Sources and Types of Illustrations

There are four basic types of illustration present in illuminated and printed illustrated Passover Haggadot. One finds illustrations of narratives or ideas found in the Haggadah text itself (we will call this genre "haggadic illustration"); illustrations of biblical or midrashic texts not actually referred to in the text of the Haggadah ("extrahaggadic illustration"); illustrations of *Seder* rituals; and (generally toward the end of the book or manuscript) eschatological illustration. Of these categories, two—illustrations of ritual and haggadic illustration—depict the contents of the actual Haggadah text. The other two categories, those of extrahaggadic and eschatological illustration, take up and expand upon themes of the larger story of the Exodus, or upon ideas that, although perhaps hinted at by the actual Haggadah text are not explicit in it. But it would be a mistake to assume that haggadic or ritual illustration is literal or straightforward and that only extrahaggadic or eschatological illustration can serve to polemicize, to define, or to affirm a specific vision of Jewish identity. All of these types of images can, in fact, tell us a great deal about the attitudes and self-understanding of the patrons or audience of the works in which they appear.

It is important to distinguish between haggadic and extrahaggadic illustration and to describe how they work together. Extrahaggadic illustration is nowhere more evident than in medieval illuminated Haggadot of the Sefardic realms, in which the text, with its haggadic illustrations (*mazzah,* unleavened bread, and *maror,* bitter herbs, depicted on the pages that contain the blessings over those ritual foods, for instance) is often prefaced by a series of extrahaggadic depictions of selected events and incidents from the creation of the world until the Exodus. The Exodus (in accordance with midrashic tradition) arose in God's mind even earlier than its mention to Abraham at the Covenant of the Pieces (Gen. 15:7–21); it was a part of the sacred destiny of the people who would become the Children of Israel even from the moment of the creation of the world. This iconographic strategy of centralizing the Exodus in the Jewish sacred story and emphasizing its foreordainment and ineluctability, mirrors the poetic strategy of the Avodah, a type of liturgical poetry for Yom Kippur, the Day of Atonement, which, like the Haggadah text, comprises a "reenactment," in this case, a meticulous description of the Yom Kippur ritual in the Holy Temple while it yet stood. The poem's climax is the recounting of the high priest's pronouncement of the Name of God from before the Holy of Holies. But this awesome and paramount moment is prefaced by a long recitation and description of events in the history of the world since the creation that lead up to that juncture in increasing crescendos of inevitability, just as the illustrated "historical preface" to Spanish Haggadot leads up to the central event of the Exodus.

Narrative illustration in Ashkenazic Haggadot is less panoramic, more selective. In the Middle Ages, illustrations remain fairly limited and they tend to be haggadic, with such depictions as the rabbis in Bnai Brak, the four sons, the labors of the Israelites, the plagues, and the drowning of the Egyptians—all referred to explicitly in the text of the Haggadah. Yet by the eighteenth century, Ashkenazic illuminated Haggadot, under the influence of a number of famous printed Haggadot, most notably those of Venice (1609) and of Amsterdam (1695), are replete with extrahaggadic illustrations. Ashkenazic artists developed a series of narrative illustrations that strategically condensed the story of the Exodus and linked it with the ultimate redemption in a way (and occasionally with polemic intents) absent from or only hinted at in the text itself. This series is interspersed with illustrations of the Haggadah text itself, and so one typically encounters a series that includes, in the following order, the rabbis of Bnai Brak, the four sons, Abraham destroying the idols, Abraham and the three angels, Moses striking the Egyptian, Pharaoh's daughter finding Moses, the transformation of Moses' rod before Pharaoh, the plague of frogs, the drowning of Egyptians in the Red Sea, the Israelite travels in the desert from Raamses to Sukkot, the giving of the Torah, the Passover in Egypt, King David praying/composing the Hallel, and the rebuilt Temple.

There are other illustrations that appear in some Haggadot, such as the Israelites laboring, or Abraham crossing the river, or Pharaoh killing the firstborn males. The order of the illustrations is linked to the various Haggadah texts that evoke them. Thus, for instance, the depiction of a grown-up Moses striking the Egyptian tends to precede that of the discovery of baby Moses by Pharaoh's daughter, despite the fact that, historically, it should have followed it. The rearrangement occurs because the scene of Moses striking the Egyptian contains as its backdrop the building of Pharaoh's store cities, and the text which that illustrates ("and they built store cities for Pharaoh") precedes in the Haggadah the text illustrated by the finding of Moses ("every child which is born . . . cast into the Nile"). Some later Haggadot (for instance, one printed in Trieste in 1864) have different, and often more logical arrangements that follow "historical" sequence more closely, largely ignoring the actual text of the Haggadah.

What is clear despite the variations is that these illustrations are intended to be a shorthand narration of the events of the Exodus that fills major lacunae in the text. Strangely enough, in spite of the fact that the Haggadah develops from the commandment to narrate the Exodus, the received text ultimately does no such thing—certainly not in the way in which one might expect, with excerpts from the actual story in Exodus. It is well known, for instance, that the name of Moses is mentioned only once in the Haggadah, in a peripheral context, in conformity with the theological necessity of affirming that God accomplished the redemption, "not by the hand of a messenger." The omission of Moses is but one of a number of glaring gaps in the received text. Instead of a simple, cohesive, and flowing narrative, the core of the Haggadah consists of an exegesis of the "wandering Aramean" passage from Deuteronomy (26:5–9), which promotes collective memory but leaves out much of the story. The apparent lack of narrative in the text of a ritual whose purported purpose is to narrate the Exodus tends to irk, and it has been redressed in various strata of Haggadah reform that have reinserted Moses and incorporated passages from Exodus in order to tell the story in a more straightforward way. Even before these reforming insertions of narrative, however, there were insertions of iconography of the sort we will shortly consider. These textual and extratextual illustrations work together to make it clear that there is a cohesive narrative, that "saying the Haggadah" constitutes the "telling the story of the Exodus from Egypt." In the following pages, we will examine some examples of characteristic illustrations from each of the categories noted above. This is by no means intended to be an exhaustive survey, but merely a selection of a pertinent example of each of these categories, beginning with illustrations of the Haggadah text itself.

Further Reading

At one time, facsimiles of medieval Haggadot were very expensive and hard to come by, but happily in the past few years more and more popular-priced editions have become readily available.

Two notable examples are the *Joel Ben Simeon Haggadah,* edited by David Goldstein (New York: Abrams, 1985) a Haggadah of the Ashkenazic tradition with Italianate influences in its illumination, and a selection of illuminations from the *Golden Haggadah,* a classic example of Sefardic illumination, in a new popular paperback edition edited by Bezalel Narkiss (London: British Library, 1997).

The classic catalogue of Haggadot is Avraham Ya'ari, *Bibliography shel Haggadot Ha Pessah* (Jerusalem: Wahrman, 1969), which has recently been surpassed by Yizhak Yudlov's *Ozar Ha Haggadot* (Jerusalem: Magnes, 1997). These volumes leave practically no bibliographic stone unturned when it comes to describing every known printed edition of the Haggadah.

Standard surveys on Jewish illumination include Bezalel Narkiss's *Hebrew Illuminated Manuscripts* (Jerusalem: Keter, 1969), and Josef Guttman's *Hebrew Manuscript Illumination* (New York: Braziller, 1978)—each work exhibiting only one characteristic folio or bifolium from each manuscript in question. Yosef Hayim Yerushalmi's *Haggadah and History* (Philadelphia: Jewish Publication Society, 1974) presents printed Haggadot in a similar survey format: one or two interesting pages from each volume are reproduced opposite a discussion the volume and the particular pages. Mendel Metzger has published *La Haggada enluminée: Étude inconographique et stylistique des manuscrits enluminés et décorés de la Haggadadu XIIIe au XVIe siècle* (Leiden: E. J. Brill, 1973), which groups, describes, and interprets illuminations of the medieval Haggadot by topic. Also helpful for contextualizing medieval Jewish art in the setting of its sociology and material culture is Therese and Mendel Metzger's Jewish *Life in the Middle Ages* (New York: Alpine, 1982). An important work is *Illustrated Haggadot of the Eighteenth Century* by Haviva Peled-Carmeli (Jerusalem: Israel Museum, 1983), the catalogue of a 1983 exhibition at the Israel Museum that surveyed an important but neglected stratum in the history of the Haggadah—illuminated Haggadot produced as luxury items after the advent of printing.

Taken as a whole, all these works, if short on analysis, provide a basis for collecting data on what exists in the realm of Haggadot. The reader interested in serious study of the Haggadot themselves would do well to consult the individual Haggadot to which these works lead, because only when one sees all the illustrations spread out can one get a feeling for the totality of their sequential and contextual dimensions.

Narrative Illustrations

"We were slaves . . . / And the Egyptians oppressed us": Haggadic Illustration

The famous beginning of the Haggadah "narrative" (or non-narrative, as we have discussed), "We were slaves to Pharaoh in Egypt," is accompanied in the Barcelona Haggadah of the fourteenth century by an illustration of the Jews laboring in Egypt (Figure 22.1). The labors of the Israelites are depicted under the watchful

ART OF THE PASSOVER HAGGADAH

Figure 22.1. "We were slaves to Pharaoh in Egypt." Haggadah, Barcelona, mid-fourteenth century. British Library, London, MS Add. 14761, fol. 30v. Photo: British Library. Reproduced with permission.

eyes of their Egyptian taskmasters. We see Israelites making bricks and raising them into position on buildings. Both Egyptians and the Israelites, it must be noted, are depicted in contemporary dress. This is not merely the result of the lack of knowledge of ancient Egyptian fashions on the part of the medieval artists. Artists of this period and place, if not familiar with specifically Egyptian modes of dress, knew how to archaize costume, and did so when it suited them. This depiction of Egyptians and Israelites as urban Aragonese Christians and Jews of the late fourteenth century is a deliberate attempt to bring the historical suffering of Egyptian bondage into the realm of contemporary experience, enabling the patron and audience of this manuscript to empathize with his or her ancestors. Thus, the illustration accomplishes at least two things in terms of the halakhic mandates of the *Seder*: it elaborates on the narrative such that details are supplied—what, for instance, does it mean to labor "in mortar and with bricks"? And it promotes an empathy with the narrative by literally dressing it in contemporary clothing, casting the narrative not only in an historical but also in a reflexive light—"In each and every generation, one must envision oneself as if one had come forth from Egypt."

But the illustration does something further: it comments on the eschatological dimension of suffering and a theodicy—an explanation of evil—which, if it cannot justify the pain of slavery, certainly exercises the muscle of hope. In the top margin, we have the depiction of a hare being served a drink by a dog. This illustration at first seems out of place—perhaps the unimaginative artist had exhausted his supply of iconography depicting forced labor and filled the space with what art historians tend to identify as a "drollery," or a humorous image. This image certainly seems to be a typical example of the iconography of the *mondus inversus*—a "world turned upside down"—in which, instead of pursuing the hare as dogs are wont to do, this one serves a hare. But there may be a deeper meaning. Scholars of Jewish art have noted that the hare can stand as a symbol for the Jewish people. A second illumination (Figure 22.2), this one from the Sarajevo Haggadah, another Aragonese manuscript of the fourteenth century, serves to illustrate the phrase, "And [the Egyptians] oppressed us: . . . [we] built Pithom and Raamses, store cities for Pharaoh." Here, over two buildings that schematically represent the cities built by Jewish slave labor, a dog pursues a hare as an allegory for the Egyptian oppression of the Jews. Read in the context of the Sarajevo illumination, the implication of the dog serving the hare in the Barcelona Haggadah becomes clear. Although the historical reality is represented by the central illumination of the page, the eschatological hope is for a world turned upside down, a reversal of fortunes: "We were slaves, but one day the Egyptian dogs will serve us!" Thus, a single illustration, linked closely with the text itself, serves on several levels: halakhic, narratological, self-referential, polemical, and eschatological.

Moses Striking the Egyptian: Extra-Haggadic Illustration

What did Ashkenazic illuminators do with the same text? An interesting example of the addition of an extra-haggadic illustration is that of Moses beating the Egyp-

Figure 22.2. "And [the Egyptians] oppressed us: . . . [we] built Pithom and Raamses, store cities for Pharaoh." Haggadah, Aragon, mid-fourteenth century. Sarajevo, National Library, Heb. MS 1, fol. 47r. Reproduced with permission.

tian (Figure 22.3). In the Amsterdam Haggadah of 1695 and in the illuminated Haggadot that imitate it, it comes to subsume the place of the illustration of the labors of the Israelites. The depiction of the building of Pithom and Raamses is relegated to the background of the scene, and a depiction of events from Exodus 2:10–12, which is not discussed in the actual Haggadah text, takes the foreground. It is a particularly turbulent scene, both in terms of its content and its implications about identity: Moses, hitherto having been raised as an Egyptian prince in the house of Pharaoh, went out one day "among his kinsfolk and witnessed their labors." It is unclear whether Moses knows that these slaves are his kinsfolk in the way that the omniscient narrator and his audience do. But the ambiguity surrounding Moses' understanding of his own identity is addressed as the biblical text (Exod. 2:11–15) continues:

> He saw an Egyptian beating a Hebrew, one of his kinsfolk. He turned this way and that, and seeing no one about, he struck down the Egyptian and hid him in the sand. When he went out the next day, he found two Hebrews fighting; so he said to the

Figure 22.3. Moses slaying the Egyptian taskmaster. Copperplate by Avraham bar Ya'akov. *Seder Haggadah Shel Pessah* (Amsterdam: Weisel, 1695), fol. 7v. Courtesy of the Library of the Jewish Theological Seminary of America. Photo: Suzanne Kaufman.

offender, "Why do you strike your fellow?" He retorted, "Who made you chief and ruler over us? Do you mean to kill me as you killed the Egyptian?" Moses was frightened and thought: Then the matter is known! When Pharaoh learned of the matter, he sought to kill Moses; but Moses fled from Pharaoh. He arrived in the land of Midian, and sat down beside a well.

At first glance this account appears completely peripheral to the narrative direction of the Haggadah, nothing more than a colorful depiction of an incident in Moses' coming of age. But it is, in fact, a turning point in the story. Moses learns who he is here. If he doesn't know that these Israelites are his kin in verse 11, that fact is certainly obvious to the Hebrew in verse 13, who resents the fact that Moses describes the man he has been beating as "your fellow," not seeming to understand that he is Moses' fellow as well. Moses fails to "pass" in this incident. He is identified as a fellow Hebrew—regardless of the fact that he appears (as we shall see) and views himself as an Egyptian. As such, he has no particular right to lord it over his fellows. Moses certainly gets the message: "The matter is known!" But to which matter does he refer? His murder of the taskmaster would not have merited the death penalty from Pharaoh—after all, if he had been a bona fide Egyptian prince and he had killed an underling, he would have, at most, been subject to a fine but certainly not sentenced to death. No, the "matter" which is known is the fact that Moses is a Hebrew. Pharaoh had, perhaps, known it all along, but he was banking on the fact that Moses would not learn of it. Now that Moses has found out, he has, in effect, become a Hebrew, and is subject to Pharaoh's original decree against male children, "if it is a boy, kill him."

But how Hebrew has Moses become? True, he goes to Midian to sit beside a well, like his ancestors Isaac and Jacob. The biblical employment of the well as a metaphor for seeking one's past is pervasive; it parallels the way we speak of "seeking our roots" today. But if he is imitating the odysseys of his ancestors, he does it with little consciousness, certainly not with the God-consciousness we might expect of the future leader par excellence of the Jewish people. Moses does not encounter the "God of the Hebrews . . . the God of your father" for the first time until the third chapter of Exodus. In this second chapter, Moses remains very much an Egyptian. When he comes to Midian, he is well-nigh indistinguishable from the Egyptians among whom he was raised. His speech, his appearance, his manner, his carriage, manage to deceive Jethro's daughters: Having been aided by this mysterious strange in their struggle against on-the-job harassment by some pesky shepherds, they report to their father, who is incredulous at their early arrival home in the evening, that "an Egyptian man saved us." Yet we, the readers of the biblical text, know the whole story—we know that this is "our" Moses. He senses it, as well—his consciousness has been raised by the moment of revelation that enabled him to see the Jew who was being beaten by the Egyptian as "one of his kinsmen"—but he is not sure to what it has been raised until his fateful encounter with "the God of your father," for which the incident of the recognition of his kinship with that father, those ancestors, that people, has been a preparation.

The medieval Spanish illuminations illustrating the verse "the Egyptians oppressed us" respond to that ancient oppression, as well as the contemporary oppression it evoked, even for Jews well-off enough to commission these manuscripts. They do so by allegorizing the pathos of oppression (the hare pursued by the dog) or symbolizing the hope for an eschatological redress of the oppression (the hare being served a drink by the dog). In the Amsterdam Haggadah of 1690, and in eighteenth-century Ashkenazic illumination, the complex identity politics that grow out of the image of Moses beating the Egyptian are very much the point of its depiction. This is why it becomes necessary to push the illustration of the verse from the Haggadah text itself literally into the background, and to "bring to the fore" the extratextual biblical narrative of Moses striking the Egyptian. Although this feeds the fantasy of Jewish power, it also presents the patrons of the manuscript with an opportunity to make a statement about their own identity and affiliation. These patrons are the elites, the communal leadership of the day. In Spain, they are the courtier class, in Amsterdam, the more monied merchant class, in Ashkenaz of the eighteenth century, they are the court Jews and their circles. In the material culture they left behind, the documents in which they figure, the letters they wrote, the literature in whose creation they participated or whose diffusion they sponsored, they appear as modern Moses figures. Like Moses, they are princes of the wider culture, but like Moses, they show concern for their fellow Jews and perceive themselves as the leaders of the generation, viewing themselves and being viewed by common Jews as the saviors from oppression when it rears its ugly head by virtue of their proximity to circles of power and influence. These men and women appear, in all the externals of their breeding, taste, and material culture, to be "Egyptian," that is, to be part of the broader culture in which they participate. But the illumination of this particular scene emphasizes that the patrons see themselves as coming down squarely on "the Jewish side" of their identity despite their participation in the material culture of their surroundings. The depiction of Moses (symbolic of the contemporary Moses—the patron of the manuscript) striking down the Egyptian (symbolic of the contemporary Egyptians—Christian oppressors) is quite a risky and a politically edgy image to use, but by its very riskiness it serves as an internal statement of solidarity on the part of the wealthier, materially more assimilated class with the community of their "kinsmen." By the choice of this scene, they proclaim themselves willing to defend their fellow Jews and prepared to fight external oppression. This seemingly inconsequential extra-haggadic illustration is, in fact, of central importance in serving to define and bolster the identity of the patrons who commissioned it.

Ritual Illustrations

THE ORDER OF THE SEDER AND ITS RITUALS:
A WORLD AS IT WAS OR AS IT WAS WISHED TO BE?

Ritual illustration serves to bolster identity, as well, but in an even more internal way that assuages the insecurities of the privileged class about their privilege and their fears of losing it at any moment. Narrative illustrations call upon the reader to insert herself or himself into the biblical or rabbinic story order to enhance the experiential component of the *Seder* as mandated by the idea of "in every generation"—to see himself or herself in "historical costume." Ritual illustrations, by contrast, directly address the reader in his or her own context; reflecting exclusively the contemporary audience, the householder-owner of the book is represented in contemporary garb. Here is one such illustration from a Haggadah written and illustrated by Meshullam Zimel Sofer of Polna in Vienna, 1719 (Figure 22.4). The audience, the well-heeled and well-connected Oppenheim family, is clearly meant to identify with the figures in the illustrations. Yet can we assume that these figures are "straightforward depictions" of the ways in which the Oppenheims "typically" dressed and lived? There is lavishness, ostentation, and "fancy-dress" drama to these illustrations—the interiors, costumes, and furniture change in each panel—and though one could argue compellingly that they depict the world of the wealthy patrons "as it was," it is more likely that they depict that world in which the patrons wished to represent themselves as residing.

There is a parallel here with another aspect of "Judaism in practice," the custom of displaying one's most lavish and precious housewares in the home during the seder—"vessels of silver and gold"—not because this was the way in which one always entertained, but specifically because this was unusual. Passover was a time to show another face—the face of free people—in stark contradistinction to the

Figure 22.4. Family at the Seder. Haggadah written and illustrated by Meshullam Zimel Sofer of Polna, Moravia. Vienna, 1719. Jewish National and University Library, Heb. MS 8 5573, fol. 4r. Photo courtesy of the Jewish National and University Library, Jerusalem. Reproduced with permission.

life of slavery. Although such illustrations of ritual in contemporary garb, if they have been considered at all, have by and large been mined in the past as concrete evidence of social mores or material culture, we ought to resist the temptation to do so, understanding that they may depict an ideal rather than a real world. The nineteenth-century east European rebbe Menahem Mendel of Kotzk was once rumored to have asked his students which was the most difficult Jewish holiday to observe. They answered that it was Sukkot, the Feast of Tabernacles, because it required the erstwhile householder to leave the warm comforts of home to dwell in a fragile and permeable hut for eight days in the first blush (and it was never a shy one) of the long Polish winter. The Kotzker, for whom the greatest pain was caused not by physical discomfort but by the psychological pain of self-deception, replied that it was not Sukkot but Passover which was the most difficult holiday to observe. His students were amazed. "But Rebbe," they argued, "on Passover, one sits in the comfort of home, in one's best clothes, surrounded by the most magnificent of vessels, amid one's family, and eats a beautiful and lavish meal, all the while recounting the glories of the Exodus from Egypt." "True," replied Menahem Mendel, "but it is all a falsehood, don't you see? One recites from the Haggadah, 'we were slaves to Pharaoh in Egypt.' We *were* slaves? That is self-deception, for we are *still* slaves, perhaps not to the same Pharaoh, but slaves nonetheless. To deny this is a lie that all the lavish accouterments of the *Seder* cannot cover up." The householders and families depicted so lavishly in the haggadot are an outcry against the inescapable realities of servitude and subjugation that existed on one level or another even for the very wealthy patrons of such books in the often dark times in which these manuscripts were produced.

One notes a distinct contrast between the approaches of the medieval Ashkenazic and the Sefardic worlds. In Ashkenazic-influenced manuscripts during the Middle Ages, one tends to see the depictions of the head of the household alone performing the ritual actions. This has the effect of isolating and focusing on the head of the household, who is likely to be the person using the book. The Haggadah thus becomes a personal mirror. Sefardic illuminations reflect more of the communal aspects of the *Seder*: women and children are seated at table, servants are depicted (Figure 22.5). The Sefardic trend is continued in the famous Venice Haggadah of 1609, which depicts the entire household (Figure 22.6). This configuration influenced subsequent printed haggadot, even Ashkenazic ones. But the original and fundamental difference in depiction reflects halakhic differences between Sefardic and Ashkenazic practice—instructions in Ashkenazic Haggadot often indicate that the head of the household or the men at the table perform a given ritual, washing before the eating of the *karpas* greens (vegetable such as parsley), for example, or reclining. Sefardic halakhah for the seder tends to be more egalitarian, and to assign specific roles and responsibilities to women and children. Women recline (if they are "women of consequence"), and children enact the Exodus with the basket of *mazzot* (unleavened bread) on their heads. These differing halakhic tendencies and sociological shadings are reflected in the illuminations.

Figure 22.5. "This is the bread of poverty." Haggadah, Barcelona, mid-fourteenth century. British Library, London, MS Add. 14761, fol. 28v. Photo: British Library. Reproduced with permission.

Figure 22.6. The Order of the Seder. Woodcut from *Seder Haggadah Shel Pessah* (Venice: Di Gara, 1609), fol. 2r. Courtesy of the Library of the Jewish Theological Seminary of America. Photo: Suzanne Kaufman.

MAROR ZEH, "THIS BITTER HERB": POLEMIC

Of particular interest is the limited use of misogynistic iconography in the illumination of the phrase Maror *zeh,* "this bitter herb"—an instance in which polemic iconography intrudes upon or blends with ritual iconography. The polemic manifests itself primarily in Italian and italianate manuscript Haggadot of the fifteenth and sixteenth centuries. It is directed from the husband to the wife—he points at her, rather than at the actual bitter herb, as he identifies the source of bitterness (Figure 22.7). This is an unlovely and unloving statement under any circumstances, but it is particularly disturbing since historically the wife would undoubtedly have done much of the preparation for the holiday, making the entire *Seder* possible. The very fact that husbands could recite the narrative of the Exodus "at the hour when *mazzah* and *maror* (bitter herb) are placed before you" was, in most cases, due to the ministrations of their wives; this misogynistic joke thus seems particularly disrespectful and ill-placed.

There have not, as yet, been any satisfactory explanations of this image beyond tacit admissions of its misogyny. Is what is at issue here a domesticized, chauvinistic rereading of the idea of servitude—has the husband been called upon to do more around the household in the pre-Passover season than he is accustomed to doing? Might he feel hemmed in by his added responsibilities, enslaved in a "narrow place" (*Mizrayim,* "a narrow place" = Egypt), and therefore accuse his wife, in a tongue-in-cheek manner, of embittering his life with "slavery"? Is this part of the attempt by male Jews to understand and define their own personal *mizrayim,* in this case providing a male safety valve for the psychological tensions of marriage in a culture of few conveniences? Do the positive depictions of women as salvific in the haggadah (Pharaoh's daughter, Jewish wives and mothers who went against Pharaoh's death decree in order to convince their husbands to have children with them) balance out this negative image? And is this ultimately a negative image of woman, or of the man who thus denounces and characterizes her? Is it a parody of the husband and does the usage carry with it an element of carnival? Is it something no Jewish husband would ever actually do, and therefore, something to be found humorous? Such a mysterious and disturbing image only serves to remind us that there is much explication that still remains to be assayed in parsing Jewish art as text. Both this specific example and the more general questions we have raised about "realism" in ritual illustrations show that such illustrations can by no means be characterized as merely descriptive of material culture or customs.

Eschatological Illustration: Elijah the Prophet

Finally, let us turn our attention to an example of eschatological illustration. Many Haggadah illustrations—like the Barcelona "We were slaves"—have some element of eschatology in them. But eschatology becomes explicit in depictions such as that of Elijah the Prophet. It is common custom that at the *Seder,* following

Figure 22.7. "This bitter herb." Rotschild Miscellany, Ferarra, 1470–80. Israel Museum, Jerusalem, MS 180/51, fol. 131r. Photo courtesy of the Israel Museum, Jerusalem.

the meal, Jews open the door "for Elijah the prophet." Yet this custom is not made explicit in the instructions of the Haggadah, nor is it part of the text. According to the rabbinic tradition, which bases itself on a statement by the prophet Malachi (3:23–24), Elijah is the herald of Messiah. Although his "appearance" has become an occasion that is primarily a delight for children, the moment when he is evoked is actually an occasion of high tension and great drama at the *Seder,* the moment at which a passage cursing the oppressors of Israel is read at the open door. In the Ashkenazic tradition, the passage is succinct, though in places where Jews had experienced extraordinary persecution, one finds versions of these curses that go on for an entire page in manuscript. The text in the printed Haggadah is "Pour out Your wrath upon the nations which do not know You, and upon the kingdoms which do not invoke Your Name [some texts: For they have devoured Jacob and laid waste to his dwelling]. Pour out Your indignation upon them and cause Your fierce anger to overtake them. Pursue them in wrath and destroy them from under the heavens of the Lord." Thus Elijah is evoked not as a harbinger of a more peaceful world, as it has become the custom to think of the messianic denouement in more recent times, but as the initiator of just revenge against Israel's oppressors. The Messiah heralded by Elijah is the successor of the Davidic line—the true world emperor as opposed to the pope or the sultan—and with his restoration will come revenge against those who have tormented Israel. Thus, appearances of Elijah in the Haggadah may speak explicitly or implicitly to themes of revenge, aligning this eschatological image with other vengeful images such as that of Moses striking the Egyptian, the plagues on Egypt, and the drowning of Pharaoh and his host. This is made explicit in the Prague Haggadah, in which Elijah appears between images of Samson and Judith, two heroes who avenged the Jews in times of persecution, and Adam and Eve, whose misdeed was judged by God—emphasizing that no matter how much Jews may want to take revenge into their own hands, it is God's wrath and not human wrath that is to be poured upon the nations (Figure 22.8).

The theme of judgment and vengeance is a continuation from the other page in the Prague Haggadah that contains a text to be recited at an open door, "This is the bread of poverty." That page is illustrated with images of David and Goliath and the Judgment of Solomon. The Prague Haggadah, the first printed Haggadah with extensive illustration, was the model for later printed Haggadot, and it is clear from its context in this first illustrated printed Haggadah that the illustration of the prophet Elijah, tame and folksy as it often seems, is a shorthand for Jewish dreams of vengeance against oppression.

On several other holidays during the Jewish year that celebrate miraculous salvation, Jews thank God for "performing miracles for their ancestors in those days at this season." This sentiment is not expressed in those words at any time during Passover, since it is a holiday whose redemption is not merely remembered but also reenacted; it is explicitly, rather than implicitly, linked with hopes for a speedy and present redemption. Thus, "Pour out Your wrath" is the Haggadah's answer to "in those days at this season." It may be viewed, in fact, as the climax

Figure 22.8. "Pour out your wrath." Woodcut from *Seder Haggadah Shel Pessah* (Prague: Sons of Shlomo HaKohen, 1526), fol. 25r. Courtesy of the Library of the Jewish Theological Seminary of America. Photo: Suzanne Kaufman.

of the Haggadah, the moment that most explicitly invokes God's miraculous intervention in the present situation, in the same way that God intervened in history to redeem the Israelites from Egypt. Elijah's appearance signals the moment of the interpenetration of the miraculous into the quotidian; a historical figure reappears to usher in the age to be born, just as the redemption of the Exodus foreshadows the redemption to come. In this sense, Elijah as manifestation of history "repeating itself" is both a symbol of the Exodus and a bridge to the ultimate redemption. Such a transition is certainly worthy of being signaled by an eschatological illustration to highlight the fact that the passage being read is not merely a curse. It serves to cue the viewer that the text is doing something much more profound than its literal words might suggest. It is invoking God to enter history.

The centrality of these illustrations, their relationship with the Haggadah text and the drama of the *Seder,* can only be hinted at by these examples. The illustrations of the Haggadah could call upon God to enter history. They could also invite their patrons and their original audience to gaze into the mirror of history and see themselves, allowing them to critique the society in which they dwelled and to express their dreams regarding the transformation of that society. Finally, these illustrations, "read" carefully, provide the latter-day viewer with the precious opportunity to glimpse the self-revealing self-perceptions of those original patrons and audiences, over their shoulders in history's mirror, by the grace of art.

23

The Arts of Calligraphy and Composition, and the Love of Books

Lawrence Fine

Sacred books have been an integral part of Jewish culture as far back as the period of ancient Israel. The earliest books in the ancient world were in the form of scrolls or rolls, and the most sacred ritual object in all of Judaism has always been the scroll of the Torah (*Sefer Torah*), containing the entirety of the Five Books of Moses. A scroll of the Torah was typically rolled from both ends toward the middle, each end being attached to a cylindrical handle known as an *ammud* (pillar), or *ets hayyim* (tree of life). Sometimes Torah scrolls had a handle only on the right end, while on the left side sufficient parchment was left blank so that it could be wrapped around the whole scroll. From evidence found in Talmudic literature, it is clear that there were also scrolls that contained both single and multiple books of the Bible, but it is the scroll containing the Five Books of Moses that occupies a central place in the synagogue ritual of reading the Torah in a performative manner.

Great care must be taken with respect to the preparation and writing of the Torah on a scroll, and the process is governed by elaborate rules. A scroll of the Torah is written only by a professional scribe (*sofer*), an individual trained in the intricate art of such writing. The tools and materials used by the scribe include the parchment upon which the words are written—quill, ink, stylus, and ruler—as well as a *tikkun* (guide), a book containing the exact wording of the text of the Torah so that he can replicate it with absolute precision. A scroll can be used for ritual purposes only if it is perfectly accurate, containing not even the slightest mistake.

The *Sefer Torah* is used for public recitation in the synagogue on various occasions, on Sabbaths and festivals, as well as Mondays and Thursdays. At the appropriate moment in the service, it is taken out of the ark (or closet) in which it is traditionally kept. This constitutes a dramatic, ceremonial ritual, in which the Torah itself is celebrated through liturgy and song as it is about to be read before the congregation. The sanctity of the Torah scroll is such that it has to be treated with great respect and reverence. Thus, custom requires that people stand in the synagogue in the presence of a Torah scroll, as it is removed from the ark and carried around the synagogue so that people can reverently kiss it as it passes by. The parchment itself is not supposed to be directly touched with one's hands, on account of which a *yad* or "pointer" is used while the Torah is being ceremonially read. Individuals called up to the Torah to recite a blessing over it kiss the Torah (by touching the edge of a prayer shawl to the Torah and then kissing the shawl) before and after a section of it is read. If a scroll of the Torah accidentally falls to the ground, the entire congregation is required to fast for that day. It is permitted, even required, to violate the Sabbath so as to save a *Sefer Torah* from harm. When a scroll is moved to a permanent site, it is customary to do so in a ceremonial way, carrying it through the streets under a canopy, accompanied by singing and dancing. These and other customs reflect the awe in which the *Sefer Torah* is held, and the love with which it is regarded.

Although a Torah scroll is, from the perspective of Jewish ritual practice, the most important handwritten book in Hebrew, there are thousands of other sacred Hebrew books in the form of manuscripts that have survived, primarily from the tenth century forward. These encompass a wide range of subjects: prayer, philosophy, mysticism, ethics, biblical interpretation, law, talmudic commentary, Haggadot (for the celebration of Passover), and so on. By the early Middle Ages, Hebrew books produced as scrolls or rolls had begun to be replaced by the codex, the form of the book much as we know it today, sheets of paper or parchment folded into quires and stitched together at the center so that it could be opened and read in a convenient manner. Hebrew manuscripts were produced using a wide variety of technological, scribal, and aesthetic traditions that reflected the different cultural influences upon Jewish bookmakers. Manuscripts from the Near East, Persia, Spain, Ashkenaz, Italy, and the Byzantine region can be identified by the varying techniques and types of Hebrew script that were used in these places.

The production of handwritten books started to wane, however, with the advent of the printing press in the fifteenth century. Hebrew incunabula (books printed before the end of the fifteenth century) were produced in Italy, Spain, Portugal, and Turkey. Students of Hebrew printing generally agree that a group of eight or nine books known as the Rome Incunabula were the first books printed in Hebrew type. Although they bear no date of publication, it appears that six of these books were printed between 1469/1470 and 1472. Soon after this, Hebrew printing spread rapidly throughout Italy. The first Hebrew book printed in Spain was apparently in 1476, and a Hebrew book appears to have been printed in Constantinople in 1493.

Although there was some initial resistance to the revolutionary technology of the printing press, Jewish communities enthusiastically embraced printed books within a couple of decades of their appearance. (In Yemen books continued to be copied by hand until the nineteenth century, mostly because of the country's geographical isolation, and certain kabbalistic books were not printed due to their especially esoteric nature.) Printing was called the "crown of all science," and the practice of this craft, like that of the writing of sacred books by hand, "the work of heaven" or a "divine craft" (*melekhet shamayim*). Some tied it to the prophet Isaiah's prediction that "the earth shall be full of the knowledge of the Lord" (Isa. 11:9). An interesting attestation concerning the wonder felt about printed books is found in a colophon (information provided about a book at its end) to the French scholar Rashi's commentary on the Torah, which was printed in Zamora, Spain, probably in 1487. The printer included a poem that he had composed: "With the power of the Lord we have finished, to spread the Torah among his people. Behold, it was written without fingers, its form is square, without a ruler, in an absolutely straight line. The paper was placed on the ink, unlike the way [the pen is usually placed on the paper], and the sheet upon the reed."

Before long, Hebrew printing presses could be found just about wherever Jews lived, thus radically increasing the availability of books for prayer and study. Although even printed books were not necessarily cheap, they were certainly less expensive and more accessible than handwritten books. These factors had incalculable influence on the ability of individuals to fulfill the religious obligation (and desire) to study sacred texts. The order and division of the books of the Hebrew Bible, and especially the division into chapters, as we have them today, are a consequence of printing. The printing of such aids as dictionaries and grammars made it easier to comprehend the Bible and other works.

Immeasurably important for Jewish culture was the first complete printing of the Babylonian Talmud by the Christian printer Daniel Bomberg at Venice between 1520 and 1523. Most of the early printers of Hebrew books were Christians, as Jews were not generally permitted to run printing houses. Jewish scholars and artisans, however, were integrally involved in the task of preparing works for press. Bomberg's edition of the Talmud established its printed format for all time, including standardized pagination, the inclusion of Rashi's commentary at the inner margin of the Talmud page, and the commentary known as Tosafot at the outer margin. The primary text, the Talmud itself, was placed between these two commentaries, and arranged so that each section of Mishnah was immediately followed by the relevant Gemara text. The structuring of the page of the Talmud in this way, and the inclusion of these elucidating commentaries, have helped facilitate study of these foundational texts to this very day.

As for prayer books, their printing empowered congregants in synagogues by making them less dependent on cantors and prayer leaders. Special prayer books for festivals, *mahzorim,* came into existence, primarily as a result of printing, as did prayer books for special ritual occasions of various types. Printing also contributed to the development and crystallization of different liturgical traditions on the basis of regional variation and other factors. In general, the printing of books provided great incentive to further scholarship in all areas of Jewish literature and thought, and thus contributed in the most significant way to Judaism's development.

As was the case with the *Sefer Torah,* both manuscripts and printed books were to be treated as sacred objects, although for a while there was debate around the question of whether printed books possessed the same level of sanctity as handwritten ones. Books are not to be thrown or left upside down, but are to be kept protected in cases so that they do not become damaged. One must not use a book except for the purpose for which it was intended. Books that have become tattered and worn out are to be stored properly in a synagogue, or buried in the ground in a dignified manner. Books that were especially well made were admired and prized. There was much discussion about the importance of sharing one's books with others by lending them out. This obligation was taken especially seriously by the German Pietists of the twelfth and thirteenth centuries, who discouraged the concept of private ownership of books in favor of the idea that the the "owner" merely held the book in trust. The book "belonged" to whoever was studying from it at a particular time.

The texts presented here are selections from an ethical will composed by Judah ibn Tibbon (c. 1120–c. 1190) for his son Samuel (c. 1160–c. 1230). Judah was born in Granada, Spain, but he emigrated to Lunel, in southern France, where he practiced medicine. He is best known, however, as the "father of translators" on account of the numerous translations of Jewish books from Arabic into Hebrew for which he was responsible. He translated many of the seminal works of medieval Jewish philosophy, which had originally been written in Arabic under the influence of Islamic culture, including Bahya ibn Paquda's *Hovot ha-Levavot,* Judah Halevi's *Kuzari,* Saadia Gaon's *Emunot ve-De'ot,* and Solomon ibn Gabirol's *Tikkun Middot ha-Nefesh.*

Judah's ethical will to his son Samuel is a document of unusual interest, in part because it so richly reflects the aesthetic values of Islamic culture during this period. These include the importance of cultivating the art of calligraphy and fine composition style in both Hebrew and Arabic, especially for the writing of letters and poetry. He seeks to teach his son that high achievement in these pursuits will serve him well personally and professionally. In the will, Judah severely admonishes Samuel for not living up to the high standards that Judah has set for him. He rebukes him for not being sufficiently ambitious, and for not cultivating the natural talents that he possesses. We are especially interested in Judah's remarks about the importance of caring for one's books and one's library in the proper way. Judah was clearly a lover of books, and he was intensely concerned that Samuel take good care of the extensive library that he had provided for him. Judah's devotion to his son was such that he even composed certain books specifically for Samuel's edification.

Samuel ultimately took his father's advice to heart. He left Lunel to live in Arles, Beziers, and Marseilles, where he developed the skills with which his father was so concerned. Samuel emulated his father by becoming an extraordinarily important translator in his own right. He is most famous for his translation into Hebrew of Moses Maimonides' great philosophical work, *The Guide of the Perplexed.* This immense achievement brought him considerable public honor, and it established the style of philosophic Hebrew that was employed for centuries to come.

The translation is adapted from Israel Abraham's *Hebrew Ethical Wills* (Philadelphia: Jewish Publication Society of America, 1926).

Further Reading

For studies of the history of Jewish printing, see Leonard Singer Gold, ed., *A Sign and a Witness—2,000 Years of Hebrew Books and Illuminated Manuscripts* (New York and Oxford: New York Public Library and Oxford University Press, 1988); Raphael Posner and Israel Ta-Shema, eds., *The Hebrew Book—An Historical Survey* (Jerusalem: Keter, 1975); and Abraham J. Karp, *From the Ends of the Earth—Judaic Treasures of the Library of Congress* (New York: Rizzoli, 1991). See as well Cecil Roth, "The People and the Book," in Roth, *Personalities and Events in Jewish History* (Philadelphia: Jewish Publication Society of America, 1953), pp. 172–81.

From the Ethical Will of Judah ibn Tibbon

I have honored you by providing an extensive library for your use, and have thus relieved you of the necessity to borrow books. Most students must bustle about to seek books, often without finding them. But you, praise God, lend and do not borrow. Of many books, indeed, you own two or three copies. I have, in addition, prepared for you books on all scholarly subjects, hoping that your hand might "find them all as a nest" [Isa. 10:14]. Seeing that your Creator had graced you with a wise and understanding heart, I journeyed to the ends of the earth, and fetched for you a teacher in secular subjects. I minded neither the expense nor the danger of the ways. Untold evil might have befallen me and you on those travels, had not the Lord been with us.

But you, my son, deceived my hopes. You did not choose to utilize your abilities, hiding yourself from all your books, not caring to know them or even their titles. Had you seen your own books in the hand of others, you would not have recognized them; had you needed one of them, you would have not known whether it was in your possession or not, without asking me. You did not even consult the catalogue of your library. . . .

Seven years and more have passed since you began to study Arabic writing [that is, calligraphy] but, despite my entreaties, you have refused to obey. Yet you are well aware how our foremost men achieved high distinction only through their proficiency in Arabic writing. . . . Nor have you acquired sufficient skill in Hebrew writing, though I paid, as you must remember, thirty golden pieces annually to your master, the clever Rabbi Jacob son of the generous Rabbi Ovadiah. And when I persuaded him to teach you to write the letters, he answered: "It will be enough for him to learn one letter a year." If you had paid attention to this remark of his, you would have striven to become a better scribe than he or his sons. . . .

My son, make your books your companions, let your bookcases and shelves be your pleasure grounds and gardens. Bask in their paradise, gather their fruit, pluck their roses, take their spices and their myrrh. If your soul be satiated and weary, change from garden to garden, from furrow to furrow, from prospect to prospect. Then your desire will renew itself, and your soul will be filled with delight. . . .

My son, if you compose anything, read it through a second time, for no person can avoid mistakes. Do not let any consideration of hurry prevent you from revising a short letter. Be punctilious as to grammatical accuracy, in conjugations and genders, for the constant use of the vernacular sometimes leads to error in this regard. A man's mistakes in composition bring him into disrepute. . . . Be careful in the use of conjunctions and adverbs, and how you apply them, and how they harmonize with the verbs. I have already begun to compose for you a book on the subject, to be called *Principles of Style*, may God permit me to complete it. And if you are in doubt about anything and have no book to refer to, abstain from expressing it. Seek to cultivate conciseness and elegance; do not attempt to write verse unless you can do it perfectly. Avoid heaviness, which spoils a composition, making it disagreeable to reader and listeners.

The same applies to poetry. The lines must not drag, verbose style must be eschewed. The words must be harmonious to the ear and light on the tongue. . . . See to it that your penmanship and handwriting is as beautiful as your style. Keep your pen in fine working order; use ink of good color. Make your script as perfect as possible, unless forced to write without proper materials, or in a pressing emergency. The beauty of a composition depends on the writing, and the beauty of the writing on pen, paper, and ink. And the beauty of the writing reflects upon the worthiness of the writer. Seek to improve your writing in accord with your ability. . . .

Examine your Hebrew books at every new moon, the Arabic volumes once every two months, and the bound codices once every quarter year. Arrange your library properly, so as to avoid tiring yourself out in searching for the book you need. Always know the case and chest where the book should be. A good plan would be to set in each compartment a written list of the books that it contains. If, then, you are looking for a book, you can see from the list the exact shelf it occupies without rearranging all the books in the search for a certain one. Examine the loose leaves in the volumes and bundles, and preserve them. These fragments contain very important matters that I collected and copied out. Do not destroy any writing or letter of all that I have left. And look over the catalogue frequently in order to remember what books are in your library. . . .

Never refuse to lend books to anyone who does not have the means to purchase them for himself, but act this way only with respect to those who can be trusted to return the volumes.... Cover the bookcases with rugs of fine quality. Protect them from water from above and from mice, and from any kind of damage, for they are your good treasure. If you lend a volume, make a note of it before it leaves your house, and when it is returned, draw your pen over the entry. And at each Passover and Sukkot call for all the books you have loaned out to be returned to you.

24

Jewish Preaching in Fifteenth-Century Spain

Marc Saperstein

The extant texts of medieval and early modern Jewish sermons, whether in manuscript or in print, look like hundreds of other texts of Jewish philosophy or ethical literature, and might therefore appear to pertain primarily to the intellectual realm. But if we think of these texts as records of an event—a unique act of oral communication between a preacher and a congregation of listeners—then the sermon is quite different from the ordinary medieval or early modern Jewish book, even when its content is similar.

The context for the delivery of the sermon grounded it in the religious practice of the Jewish people. It was most commonly presented in the course of the Sabbath morning service, either immediately before or soon after the prescribed scriptural reading, and it was invariably linked with the verses from Scripture. Something of the aura of the Torah scroll and of the customary acts that exhibited the Jew's reverence for the Torah was naturally associated with the discourse that homiletically unraveled its meaning. The physical setting elevated the speaker above the listeners in the synagogue, surrounding him with many of the sancta of public Jewish religious life. Although the sermon was not a formal requirement of public worship—the Jew fulfilled the religious obligation of prayer even if no sermon was heard—and Jewish law provided little guidance on the details of sermon construction or delivery, preaching was recognized as an ancient tradition, and in many communities it was understood to be an important component of the rabbi's responsibilities toward his people.

Moreover, the sermon recorded in the extant texts was not just something written; it was spoken, a text enacted. All of the elements associated with the word "delivery" were significant: the appearance of the preacher, the sound of his voice, his gestures, the level of his animation, his pace and pitch, his emphases and silences. In the best preachers, the quality of the sermon was dependent not merely upon the power of an intellect or the quality of writing but also on a highly sophisticated performance art.

The sermon was delivered in the presence of an audience, usually representing an entire community of Jews, which brought its own agenda to the event. For many in the audience, the sermon was the primary vehicle through which the tradition was communicated and mediated, the classical texts interpreted and applied to the needs of the present hour. This produced a special dynamic in the relationship between preacher and congregation. The listeners could emerge from the sermon educated and informed, shamed or inspired, bored, offended, or enraged. On occasion, they might react to the preacher as he was speaking: by getting up and walking out in protest, or by verbally challenging the preacher's presentation as it was being said. Reports of such incidents provide dramatic examples of the unexpected intrusion into the orderliness of ritualized behavior.

For the guidance of preachers, medieval Christians produced a large number of treatises, many under the title *ars praedicandi,* the art of preaching. For reasons not entirely clear, contemporary Jewish literature has preserved little of this genre. The ideals and conventions of the medieval Jewish preacher are most readily deduced from the extant texts of sermons, and from occasional descriptions of Jewish preaching in various works of Jewish literature. The following texts provide the only two known examples of prescriptive guidance from the Middle Ages. Neither had been published until the last few years. There is also a dramatic description of actual Jewish preaching in fifteenth-century Spain and the reaction of some congregants to a mode of philosophical homiletics they did not like.

The first brief, anonymous text is from a newly discovered manuscript that contains a miscellany of philosophical sermons and other texts, most of them written in Spain in the first half of the fifteenth century. Many of these works emanated from a circle influenced by Rabbi Hasdai Crescas, a leading rabbinic scholar, communal leader, and one of the most profound philosophical thinkers of the late Middle Ages, though he was a critic of Aristotelian philosophy. The author claims to have been urged to write the text because of the chaotic state of contemporary Jewish homiletics, but this may be no more than a literary convention or topos. It appears to be the earliest known Jewish *ars praedicandi,* and provides ten principles of effective preaching as guidance for the practitioner.

Some of these principles are commonplaces in Christian homiletical works of the time: the caution against prolixity, the insistence that the preacher be of irreproachable moral character, the warning against raising intellectual problems about a revered text without providing a satisfactory solution to them. Other principles reflect internal Jewish issues pertaining to exegesis of biblical verses or rabbinic dicta. Particularly interesting is the advice about preparation of the sermon (first writing the text, and then memorizing it so that the delivery will be totally fluent) and the manner and technique of its delivery. The content of the text is not especially original or innovative; its importance lies in the fact that it reflects the tastes and traditions of practitioners of the art, and perhaps of the much more numerous members of the community that listened to them.

The second text, which dates from about a generation later, was written by Joseph ibn Shem Tov, scion of an illustrious family of fifteenth-century Spanish

Jewish intellectuals. The author, who held positions at the cabinet level under two kings of Castile, also wrote works of technical philosophy, a biblical commentary, an anti-Christian polemical tract, and a discursive work comparing the Aristotelian and Jewish conceptions of the ultimate good. Texts of a number of his sermons have survived in manuscript. His treatise "Ein ha-Qore" (Judg. 15:19: "The Wellspring for the One who Proclaims," that is, the preacher) is largely devoted to material on the homiletical art, both prescriptive and critical of the actual behavior of contemporary preachers.

This discussion is organized by pegs in the biblical verse, "Cry with full throat, without restraint; Raise your voice like a ram's horn! Proclaim to My people their transgression; To the House of Jacob their sin" (Isa. 58:1). In its biblical context, the verse applies to the role of the prophet, but traditional Jewish preachers often invoked it as a model for their own vocation. It is not that they claimed the actual mantle of prophecy, as it was rare for a medieval Jew to claim to be directly inspired by God or that he was uttering "God's word." Rather, there was a suggestion that the preacher, particularly when rebuking the congregation for shortcomings in their religious and ethical behavior, played a role in their own age analogous to that of the prophet in biblical times.

Drawing from the simile in the verse, Ibn Shem Tov uses the image of the ram's horn, associated with the observance of the Jewish New Year (Rosh Hashanah), to illustrate various aspects of the preacher's task. Some of the points are theoretical: of the five Aristotelian arts of reasoning, not logical demonstration, sophistry, dialectic, or poetry, but only rhetoric is appropriate for the preacher. Others focus directly on the relationship between the preacher and his listeners. The preacher must be able to determine the nature of the audience and to pitch his message accordingly: not so long as to make them grow weary, neither on a level above their comprehension nor overly simplistic and obvious. When he has to criticize the people—an integral component of his role—he must do so without fear of the wealthy or powerful.

Interspersed with these prescriptive statements are critical references to the practice of contemporary preachers. They often do not devote their sermons to the theme of the day (the prescribed scriptural reading, or the central motif of the holiday). They speak for too long, thereby becoming a burden to the congregation. They incorporate modes of discourse inappropriate for the sermon, including material incomprehensible to the audience (and, according to a sarcastic barb, even to the preacher himself). Unlike their Christian counterparts, they refrain from speaking honestly to powerful, wealthy Jews, on whom they may depend for their livelihood, giving instead an obsequious message that ignores the true problems of the time. To guard against this danger, the author counsels that preachers should be economically as well as temperamentally independent.

The third text is of an entirely different genre, a letter to the author's son, and it reveals a rather negative "view from the pew." It was triggered by the report of a preacher who cited an enigmatic messianic statement from the Talmud without explaining it and defusing its apparently heretical meaning: that no Messiah will come to the Jews in the future. But before discussing the actual statement, the author surveys the contemporary scene of Spanish Jewish preaching, giving several examples of behavior that appears to him as outrageous. The underlying issue is the excessive influence of philosophy in the pulpit. This is dramatized by a childhood memory of a preacher who set out to prove the unity of God philosophically through a reductio ad absurdum of the antithesis—a standard technique of scholastic argumentation: "If God is *not* one, then such and such must necessarily follow," leading to an impossible conclusion. The problem was not in the doctrine taught by the preacher but in the suggestion that the unity of God should not remain a matter of faith but required philosophical argumentation to demonstrate; it is this that impelled a pious listener to stand up, protest, and lead a walk-out from the presence of the undoubtedly baffled preacher.

The list of abuses is illuminating: the preacher who interpreted the laws of the Holiness Code (Lev. 19) in a figurative or allegorical manner, the use of allegorical interpretations for narratives of the Torah, the use of problematic rabbinic statements "not intended for public discussion" and, in general, the excessive preoccupation with Greek philosophers to the neglect of traditional Jewish texts. We see in this text the reaction of a cultural conservative to the incorporation of what he considered to be improper "external influences" into the worship service—what some would view as lamentable acculturation, and others as evidence of the dynamic capacity of Judaism to accommodate and integrate elements from the broader civilization in which Jews lived.

The first text is found in Moscow Günzberg MS 926, fols. 45v–46v. The English translation is taken from my *"Your Voice Like a Ram's Horn": Themes and Texts in Traditional Jewish Preaching* (Cincinnati: Hebrew Union College Press, 1996), pp. 166–74, where extensive annotation provides many comparable statements in medieval Christian texts and exemplification in actual Jewish sermons of the thirteenth to fifteenth centuries. The Hebrew text is on pp. 175–78. The second passage is found in several manuscripts, including Oxford Bodleian MS Moch. 350 (Neubauer 2052), fols. 113r–117v. The translation is taken from my *Jewish Preaching 1200–1800* (New Haven: Yale University Press, 1989), pp. 387–93, which also contains a translation of a dramatic sermon by the author delivered in Segovia following an attack upon the Jews during Holy Week. The third passage was first published by David Kaufmann in *Beit ha-Talmud* 2 (1882): 110–25 (the passage cited is on pp. 117–18), reprinted in *Sefer Magen ve-Romah ve-Iggeret li-Veno* (Jerusalem: Hebrew University, 1970). The translation is taken from *Jewish Preaching 1200–1800*, pp. 384–87.

Further Reading

For more on medieval and early modern Jewish preaching, consult my two books cited in the above paragraph, which provide an introductory survey, thematic studies, and many primary texts illustrating Jewish preaching practice between 1200 and 1800 C.E. Of the essays included in *Preachers of the Italian Ghetto* (Berkeley and Los Angeles: University of California Press, 1992), edited by David Ruderman, the one most closely linked with the practice of religion is Elliott Horowitz's discussion of the eulogy, several examples of which can be found in my two books. For a full, though somewhat later, Jewish *Ars praedicandi,* dating from the seventeenth century, see Henry Sosland's edition of *A Guide for Preachers on Composing and Delivering Sermons: The "Or ha-Darshanim" of Jacob Zahalon* (New York: Jewish Theological Seminary of America, 1987). One area in which the sermon impinges directly upon religion in practice is in the preaching of rebuke for religious shortcomings. See my article, "The Preaching of Repentance and the Reforms in Toledo of 1281," and Carmi Horowitz, "Rhetoric, Reality and Aspirations to Holiness in 14th Century Jewish Preaching," both in *Models of Holiness in Medieval Sermons* (Louvain-la-Neuve: Fédération Internationale des Instituts d'Études Médiévales, pp. 157–92.)

Treatise for the Guidance of Preachers

One of my colleagues asked me to compose a short summary to teach the path of excellence in a sermon. For many have followed an unpaved path; they have spoiled the sermon's order, its splendor, dimmed its radiant luster. I decided to heed him and fulfill his request, to prepare and pave the road that leads ever upward. I have divided it into ten requirements [for good preaching], that it may be easily accessible to those who seek it out. And as all greatness belongs to God, the source of whatever praiseworthy we may utter, I will raise a prayer that words be placed in my mouth, as the Psalmist said, "Let my lips send forth praise" [Ps. 119:171].

First: the biblical verse or statement on which the preacher is to construct his sermon must be suitable to serve as the foundation of the structure. You know that a building depends upon the dimensions of its foundation. Therefore the preacher should select a passage or statement that encompasses most of the topics of the Torah lesson, or the specific topic he intends to preach upon, and then arrange accordingly the rabbinic midrash, if he finds one. Be careful to read the verse without any error, and explain where it is taken from and whether it is connected with what precedes it, in which case they should be presented in coherent order. A reminder of this: "The mind of a wise person makes his speech intelligent" [Prov. 16:23].

Second: begin by explaining the simple meaning of the verse following the gist of its words. If there is more than one meaning for one of the words, this should be explained. If it is a verse that has both an exoteric and an esoteric meaning, first explain the exoteric meaning, that is, the figurative text (*mashal*) and then the esoteric meaning, its underlying significance (*nimshal*). Connect the Torah lesson or the specific topic you intend to preach upon with these levels of meaning. For example, if the intended topic for the sermon pertains to the exoteric meaning, after explaining the verse, use it to support this topic, making the connection clear, and afterward explain the esoteric meaning. If the topic pertains to the esoteric meaning, explain exoteric and esoteric together, and use the esoteric meaning as support for this topic. A reminder of this: "Apples of gold in ornaments of silver" [Prov. 25:11].

Third: avoid aggadic statements expressed in a hyperbolic or enigmatic manner incompatible with reason, unless you know an explanation or interpretation that renders them rational. Do not preach about matters that are too weighty or wondrous for you, or about a subject that is perplexing or raises doubts without being able to resolve such problems in your talk; otherwise, the difficulty will remain unresolved, and this is a treacherous path. A reminder of this: "My words bespeak the uprightness of my heart" [Job 33:3].

Fourth: be wary of preaching about matters that are accepted, popular beliefs among the people. Rather, the goal should be to guide the people in beliefs that are true and based on the tradition of our ancestors, and in the high ethical qualities that are desired. Be extremely careful about using all that can be found neatly organized in books. . . . Rather, select from them straightforward matters that are quite beneficial to the audience and will cause it no harm. Many things that can be found in books are indeed correct in the way of truth, but most people cannot understand them. They should be addressed in a sermon only by an expert speaking to other experts. A reminder of this: "Put crooked speech away from you; keep devious talk far from you" [Prov. 4:24].

Fifth: do not jump from one topic to another that is apparently unrelated unless some connection can be shown. It is one of the great rules of this art: a preacher must know how to structure material aesthetically, making one topic lead to another that is related to it. If the sermon is intended to address a particular subject, do not begin with it at the outset. Rather, begin with another topic that fits the biblical passage, and then derive the main subject of the sermon out of the discourse, or come to it later. This is a fine technique. If you have to deliver a rebuke, do so in the context of the topic being discussed, for this will provide an opening. For example, if preaching about the benevolence of the patriarch Abraham—how he gave bread and water to his guests, running to bow down before them—after doing justice to this, you may say, "But we are guilty, for there is no one who acts with compassion," and so forth. This benefits greatly those who understand; it is the right way. They will cover their mouths with their hands, so stinging to them will be the rebuke. A reminder of this: "A ready response is a joy to a person" [Prov. 15:23].

Sixth: do not speak too long. If you intend to explain a particular topic, do not use excessive verbiage. For the topic intended is like a grain of wheat, and the accompanying verbiage is like the chaff. What use is there in filling a sack full of chaff for the sake of the grain of wheat it contains? Rather, be long on content and short on words. Bring only those proofs and that interpretation which turn out to be true. Do not dwell at length on different interpretations, or on proofs that are subject to disagreement, of the type, "Rabbi So-and-so said this, Rabbi So-and-so said that." Even in topics of disputation, do not be excessively long-winded. A reminder of this: "Where there is much talking, there is no lack of transgressing" [Prov. 10:19].

Seventh: try to say something new in the sermon, whether concerning the simple meaning of the verse, or the interpretation of an aggadic statement, or in organizing the discussion of the central topic, for this is a great achievement for a preacher. Do not speak about things that are already commonplace for the people, the learned and even the unlearned. Avoid speaking about matters that will be a source of embarrassment to those who hear the sermon, such as the techniques of sexual intercourse or the woman in her menstrual period and the like, unless you speak of such things in general terms, euphemistically, in order to remove obstacles from the path of the people. A reminder of this: "Find favor and good sense" [Prov. 3:4].

Eighth: be a decent person, following the statement of the sages, "Preach well and act well." How reprehensible it is when one rebukes others for something about which he does not rebuke himself or control his own desires. If the audience senses that he does not uphold high standards of ethical or religious behavior, they will pay no heed to his words, which will make no more impression upon their hearts than a drop of water falling upon flintstone. Sometimes a preacher will have to suppress his lofty statements, when he remembers that he himself does the opposite. But if his behavior is consistent with his words and his rhetoric, then he may speak with assurance; his audience will acclaim his message and believe in it. A reminder of this: "One who obeys shall speak unchallenged" [Prov. 21:28].

Ninth: write your sermon down on paper. If it is too much work to write it in its entirety, then write down its main points, and divide it into sections, and associate images with them in your mind so that you will be able to speak fluently. Go over again and again the material that you will preach, so that you may bring it to life. Do not rely on your expertise; you may forget part of the structure, or stumble on your words, and you will feel humiliated when your shame is displayed for all to see. When you speak in public—and all the more so at an assembly of scholars—be careful to polish and refine your words seven times over. Whatever you say that is susceptible to ambiguity must be explained and interpreted, lest the audience reproach you by attributing to you some harmful doctrine that the words might seem to imply. A reminder of this: "Then he saw, and gauged it, he measured it and probed it. And *then* he said to the man" [Job 28:27–28].

Tenth: speak calmly and quietly—a calm manner that brings about repentance—not with anger or contentiousness. If what you see and hear require you to rebuke, consider well who is before you. Do not take pride in your wisdom and understanding. Ask permission from the congregation and from the scholars in your presence, even if you are more learned than they, and all the more if they are more learned than you. Let this be concise; do not bring lengthy proofs or other matters, as most of the preachers are accustomed to do. Do not use the ready-made texts of "asking permission" that can be found in books; this is a waste of time. Conclude the sermon with the verse that began it; return in order to connect the end with the beginning. Conclude with a positive sentiment, thereby bringing good at the end from the [verse at] the beginning. A reminder of this: "The end of a matter is made good from its beginning" [Eccles. 7:8].

The types of sermons are three. The first is compound, such as a sermon the divisions of which are based on the divisions in the opening verse. The second is simple, such as one who takes a single theme, and brings many proofs from verses and aggadot and other rabbinic statements to explore the topic. The third is neither simple nor compound, but composed of questions and answers, simple interpretations of verses and [discussion of] topics.

Joseph ibn Shem Tov, from "Ein ha-Qore"

The fourth part explains the meaning of the simile "like a shofar raise your voice" [Isa. 58:1]. Do not think that this refers to projecting the voice loudly; that is already implied in the first part of the verse, "Cry aloud," so that such a meaning here would be redundant and superfluous. I think, rather, that there are three aspects of this comparison: first, the purpose of the sound of the shofar; second, its time; and third, the different kinds of sounds. A sermon is related to all three.

First, the purpose in the sounding of the shofar is to make the hearts of sinners quake. The prophet said, "When a shofar is sounded in the town, do the people not take alarm?" [Amos 3:6], showing clearly that its effect is to instill fear. In tractate *Rosh Hashanah* [16b], the rabbis said, "Why do they blow when the people are sitting, and then blow again while they are standing? In order to confuse the prosecutor." So the sermon should be such that it instills fear and awakens the hearts of sinners, so that they will return to God and be forgiven.

Second, the sounding of the shofar is appropriate at one particular time: on the New Year's Day and on the Day of Atonement. Similarly, the sermon must conform with the occasion and its theme. In this way it will be appropriate, and its benefit will be received. The sages said, "On a holiday, one should preach about the theme of the holiday"—similarly in tractate *Megillah* [4a]—and we choose a prophetic reading related to the theme of the Torah lesson.

Most of the preachers of our generation err in this respect, for I have not seen them preach sermons related either to the theme of the day or to the audience. In my judgment, it is proper that on every Sabbath throughout the year the sermon be related to the theme of the Torah and prophetic reading, and on the festivals it should be about the theme of the festival. On the ten days between the New Year's Day and the Day of Atonement, sermons should always relate to the nature of this period, namely, sin and the healing of souls. I praise this approach, unless there is a reason against it, such as a newly arising matter that requires a novel sermon outside the framework of the biblical chapters. . . .

One of the most desirable qualities in a preacher is the ability to observe the kind of audience before him and to speak for a length of time that will not cause them to grow weary of the sermon, for if they do, the desired benefit will not accrue. We are indeed guilty in this matter. The sentences issuing from our mouths are sweet to our palate, and we are therefore not conscious of whether the sermon is long or short, or if the air is cold or hot, nor are we hungry or thirsty. We think that the same is true for those in the congregation who hear us! We therefore become a burden upon the community, and we are led to other errors as well. This often happens to preachers of this generation. It should be corrected in our sermons. For we do not preach to ourselves but to others, and we should therefore always think of the purpose of the sermon insofar as possible.

Third, there are two primary sounds of the shofar: a simple, straightforward sound, and one that is very wavering and staccato. The first is called *teqiah,* the second *teruah;* these terms are derived from biblical language. Then there is another intermediate sound, a composite of the other two, called by the talmudic sages *shever.* . . . Similarly, the preacher should look up and see who is in the congregation, and bearing these three sounds in mind, begin to speak and arrange his sermon intelligently.

The congregation may consist of wise and learned people, or it may consist of ordinary people, or possibly even of a mixture of both categories. Now the preacher must speak in such a way that his message will be understood, gearing the content to his audience. If the congregation consists of ordinary Jews, he should speak about simple matters, so that the audience will understand and the desired benefit will be obtained. This is similar to the *teqiah,* a simple sound. If there are learned and knowledgeable people present, he should speak of profound and original matters, not straightforward truths that are known to all. This is like the teruah, a complex sound.

If both categories are present together, his speech should be composed of both kinds of material, like the shever, intermediate between *teqiah* and *teruah.* He may divide his sermon into separate parts appropriate for each group, or he may give one sermon appropriate for all. But if he divides it into parts, while he is delivering the section intended for the learned, the masses will be there to no avail, and while he delivers the part intended for the masses, there will be no purpose in the presence of the wise. The ideal is to have the entire speech encompass both groups, so that the wise will find something new, and the masses will understand. If this is indeed possible, it is preferable to the other way.

Now it has been explained elsewhere that there are five categories of speech, which are the same as the five well-known arts of reasoning: logical demonstration, sophistry, dialectic, rhetoric, and poetry. It is worth investigating which of these arts is the most appropriate for use in preaching.

We say that the art of logical demonstration is difficult to use for two reasons. First, the subjects of most homiletical statements, whether affirmative or negative, are not known through logical demonstration, for we have few logical axioms that apply to such matters. For the most part, they are investigations of Torah problems, the truth of which cannot be established by demonstration.

The second reason is that the art of logical demonstration is extremely exalted. There are few preachers who can use this mode of argumentation having fully mastered all its subtleties, and it is extremely unusual or even impossible to find an appropriate audience. This is apparent to any expert in logic. Obviously this category of speech cannot encompass an audience containing both the learned and the masses.

The art of sophistry should be repudiated by every preacher, for the purpose of the sophist is to expound upon something untrue. Not only does this fail to remove the sickness from the souls of the listeners; it actually exacerbates that sickness.

As for the art of dialectic, the purpose of the debater is to convince the people of his view—whether it be true or not. His sole concern is that his argument be compelling. But the purpose of the preacher is to convince the people only of what is true. He should therefore repudiate this art as well, insofar as possible, using it only when it is necessary to resort to the distinctive premises of its syllogisms: namely, premises that are generally accepted opinions. In such circumstances it may be permissible for the homiletical art. The difference between these three disciplines—logical demonstration, sophistical reasoning, and dialectic—has been explained in the third book of the *Metaphysics*. You may look there.

The art of poetry is inappropriate for preaching because it is remote from the nature of the masses. The ancients also condemned those who spoke of theoretical matters in this way, as Aristotle said, condemning Plato in the *Poetics*. It is abundantly clear that whoever indulges in this art is dealing with something totally alien to the nature of homiletics.

This leaves only the art of rhetoric, which attempts to beautify even the most profound ideas and to express them through vivid analogies, so that the masses can attain an accurate image of them and the intellectuals can see them in a new light. This is especially true for the content of Torah investigations, the material suitable for the homiletical art, for the expression of esoteric matter through analogy, parable, or allegory attracts the attention of people, so that they will listen, and accept or spurn as appropriate.

Thus the best of the arts for preaching is the art of rhetoric. The more the preacher masters this art, and the more at home he is in the techniques of speech and argumentation that will persuade the listeners to accept what he says, the greater will be his stature in homiletics. Indeed, the art of preaching is included in the category of rhetoric. The ancients actually called the art of rhetoric "homiletics", and they called its modes of argumentation "homiletical argument." . . .

Most of the preachers in our time fail in this regard. Some preach about midrashim and rabbinic statements according to their simple meaning in a manner that benefits neither the masses nor the wise. Some speak about false doctrines in the fashion of debaters or sophists, using these two arts—dialectics and sophistical arguments; or they somehow use the art of poetry, citing the profound words of the sages and ascribing deep meanings to the aggadot; or they speak confusingly with syllogistic arguments, benefiting no one. They think that they excel in syllogistic proofs, but for the most part they preach about things that neither they nor their listeners understand, hoping that they will be esteemed as intellectuals because they preach about the mysteries of creation and of the Torah.

I once heard people tell of a man who thought much of his own intellectual abilities. He began a sermon delivered to the leaders of the community by saying that his sermon would be divided into three parts: the first part would be comprehensible to him and to them, the second part comprehensible to him but not to them, and the third part neither to him nor to them. Indeed, I would think that many sermons of our time are of this third category.

What has happened to the art of preaching is the same as what happened to medicine, which wise men have described as a courtyard without gates, meaning that so many people have access to it. Whoever wants to take a fee and kill people for their money may come and take a fee, and the expert cannot be distinguished from the nonexpert. . . . This is especially true for the Jewish people, for we all think of ourselves as wise and understanding. This matter should be corrected. . . .

The fifth part explains the meaning of the phrase, "Declare to my people their transgression" [Isa. 58:1]. This teaches about the purpose of the sermon: to recall the sins, offenses, and transgressions committed by the elders and leaders of the people. It teaches that the preacher must be neither ashamed nor afraid of them, for God will be with him in his conflict. This is the meaning of "My people." He said "their transgression" because the sin is essentially related to the sinner himself and the one for whom the sin is committed. I have already explained this in my sermons, where it is made clear that the greater the status of the sinner, the greater will be considered the sin. . . .

From this it becomes clear that the master of this art must be strong in God's sight, not a meek and self-effacing personality. He must have the heart of a lion and be prepared to reproach kings and nobles for their sins, so that they will emerge truly chastened. . . . Most of the preachers of our generation are too obsequious, especially to the powerful. They tell such men that they are righteous because they depend upon those men for their livelihood.

The harm that comes from such sycophancy is readily discernible; indeed, this was the reason for the destruction of Solomon's Temple. You can see in the Book of Kings that the false prophets, those of evil counsel, were always telling the kings, "You are a good man, you are doing what God wants." The true prophets vigorously protested. "If a ruler listens to falsehood, all who serve him are evil" [Prov. 29:12]; the sages understood this verse to apply to what I have said. They also stated that from the day when sycophancy prevailed, the decree was sealed against us, for our sins [cf. *Sotah* 41b].

This frequently occurs with our nation, more so than with others, from what I have observed of these matters. A Gentile may preach against kings and nobles, proclaiming their sins for all to hear. But in our own nation no one will raise his tongue against any Jew whatsoever, and certainly not if the man is wealthy or a potential benefactor. Now since the cause of this harmful situation is the fact that the preachers of rebuke are poor and destitute, it is desirable that such men, who stand before the God of Israel, should not be devoid of material wealth. Solomon noted long ago that "the poor man's wisdom is despised, and his words are unheard" [Eccles. 9:16].

Therefore, the qualities either necessary or desirable in the preacher include wisdom ..., admirable ethical traits ..., inner courage ..., and the wealth necessary to provide for his sustenance. Note that I said "necessary"; superfluous wealth is an obstacle to his success, as the philosopher noted in the tenth book of his *Ethics*.... The most important of these qualities is strength of character, not of body. For even if the king or the noble should wax angry at his sermons, it is on God's behalf that he preaches.... This is why R. Aqiba was killed: because he had the people gather in congregations and he preached publicly, despite the wrath of the evil king....

Hayyim ibn Musa, from Letter to His Son

Our complaint is against the preachers—may God sustain those who are inwardly upright and good. But as for those who turn onto crooked paths, who consider themselves wise and clever, but are evil speakers of perversion, philosophizers who have long led Israel astray—may God lead them into the power of the inimical angels of Samael.

Once in my youth I heard a preacher speak, using the technique of philosophical investigation, about the unity of God. Several times he said, "If God is not one, then such and such must necessarily follow [leading to a reductio ad absurdum]. Finally one of the leaders of the synagogue, a deeply religious man, rose and said, "They seized all of my property in the massacres of Seville [in 1391]; they beat me and covered me with wounds until they left me for dead. All this I endured through my faith in "Hear, O Israel, the Lord our God, the Lord is One" [Deut. 6:4]. Now you come upon the tradition of our ancestors with your philosophical investigation, saying, 'If God is not One, such and such must follow!' I believe more in the tradition of our ancestors, and I have no desire to hear this sermon." With that, he walked out of the synagogue, and most of the congregation followed. Even though Maimonides engaged in this kind of analysis, his purpose was to argue against the Gentiles, not to preach it to the congregation.

I have also seen one of the preachers—renowned as one of the most learned in the realm—who homiletically interpreted the entire lesson beginning "You shall be holy" [Lev. 19:2] in a figurative manner. In the middle of his sermon he said, "*Et shabbetotai tishmoru* [lit., "You shall keep my Sabbaths"] [Lev. 19:3] means 'My insignificant things,' *las mis cosas baldías*," heaven help us! I had some words with him, and I criticized all that he said, especially this interpretation. He replied that Rashi had said the same thing on the first verse of the lesson Eqeb [Deut. 7:12]: "the lesser commandments that people trample underfoot." I said, "There is no comparison. That homiletical interpretation is appropriate there, but it is heretical here." We argued at great length.

I have also seen students disputing each other in their sermons, speaking about matters alien to our tradition. This occurred in the presence of the esteemed rabbi Don Abraham Benveniste, may he be remembered for life in the world to come. Two young talmudic scholars preached this way, using figurative interpretations so provocative that the rabbi arose and castigated their dispute, quoting, "I am peace, but when I speak they are for war" [Ps. 120:7]. He then said to the congregation, "My brothers, children of Abraham, believe that when the Bible says 'In the beginning God created' [Gen 1:1] or 'Jacob left Beersheba' [Gen. 26:10], it is to be understood in its simple meaning. Believe also in all that is written in the Torah, and what the rabbis explained in accordance with their tradition. Do not believe those who provocatively speak of alien matters."

Truly, my son, even worse sinners than these are the ones who preach about aggadot that were not intended for public discussion, whether the hyperboles, such as the account of Og, who uprooted a mountain three parasangs high [Babylonian Talmud, *Berakhot* 54b], or the tales of Rabbah bar bar Hana [Babylonian Talmud, *Baba Batra* 73a–74b], or statements of esoteric truth. They quote such statements according to their simple meaning, thereby engendering contempt for the sages among the idlers.

Now there is a new type of preacher. They rise to the lectern to preach before the reading of the Torah, and most of their sermons consist of syllogistic arguments and quotations from the philosophers. They mention by name Aristotle, Alexander, Themistius, Plato, Averroes, and Ptolemy, while Abbaye and Raba are concealed in their mouths. The Torah waits upon the reading stand like a dejected woman who had prepared herself properly by ritual immersion and awaited her husband; then, returning from the house of his mistress, he glanced at her and left without paying her further heed.

We should say the mourner's prayer over this entire situation.... Happy is the one who shuts his eyes and does not see them, who stops up his ears and does not hear their evil words. It should be enough for them to begin with a biblical verse or a rabbinic dictum, to incorporate the obvious meaning of biblical verses and rabbinic statements into words of ethical import, and to speak of the laws relating to the Sabbath and the festivals. If they proudly bring appropriate principles from the sciences, provided they are not harmful and do not corrupt faith or divert the heart of a single member of the congregation into thinking improper thoughts, this is all right.

Magic and Mysticism

25

The Book of the Great Name

Michael D. Swartz

Magic has had a long and rich history in Judaism. Ancient Jews enjoyed a reputation as masters of magical lore in the Greco-Roman world. Archaeologists have found Hebrew and Aramaic amulets written on silver lead dating from talmudic Palestine; and while the Babylonian Talmud was being completed, Jews in the Babylonian town of Nippur wrote hundreds of magical incantations on clay bowls, which were buried under the doorways of houses. Collections of medieval manuscripts, such as the Cairo Genizah, abound in amulets, magical handbooks, and mystical texts with magical elements. One can go to New York or Jerusalem today and buy magical books and amulets that are nearly identical to the ancient ones. Jewish magical texts have been used for healing and exorcism, to win favor and love from other people, to cause pain or expel an enemy, and even to increase one's capacity to learn Torah.

Magic is notoriously difficult to define. Historians of religion know that magic is not a separate phenomenon from religion but part of it. We can also see that magic varies from culture to culture. In Judaism, magic usually includes these three elements: first, the process of adjuration of intermediaries, such as angels or demons; second, the use of powerful and arcane names of God as the source of the magician's authority; and third, the use of these techniques for the personal needs of an individual. Magical texts have their own traditions, such as specific, complex combinations of letters that are said to be secret names of God, lists of angels appointed by divine authority over elements of the universe, and heroes from the Bible who are said to have possessed esoteric knowledge. At the same time, Jewish magicians adopt traditions and values of their own Judaic culture. Thus we can find texts that purport to give the secrets of improving one's memory automatically, thus transforming the practitioner into a great scholar. We also find that visionary texts for ascending to heaven in order to gain a mystical vision use magical names and techniques. Yet at the same time, not all Jewish authorities approved of these practices.

One such collection, the visionary literature of late antiquity and the early Middle Ages known as Hekhalot, contains a cryptic text for reciting a powerful magical name of God. Many of the texts in this literature describe the ascent to heaven undertaken by a great rabbi of the past, who undergoes ordeals on his journey through the seven "palaces" (*hekhalot*) leading up to the divine throne (the *merkavah*), and who eventually participates with the angels in the heavenly praise of God. Among those are also texts for more "practical" purposes, such as increasing memory or power. The text presented here is one example of this.

This text does not have a title, but we will call it the Book of the Great Name. It is particularly interesting because it contains several motifs common to Jewish magical texts in one unit: extravagant claims for the power of the magic, instructions for a complex ritual of preparation and purity to be performed before the recitation, fragments of poetic hymns praising God and His name, and attestations to the origins of the magical name in Israel's mythic history. Of particular interest is the text's emphasis on the power of the magical book, complete with dire warnings of what will happen if the book is sold or its contents revealed.

The text is appended in the manuscripts to *Hekhalot Rabbati,* one of the most important of the early Jewish mystical texts. It is written in Babylonian Aramaic, and presents some difficulties in translation and interpretation. It was evidently compiled from several sources, not all of them understood by the editor. It was probably written sometime after the compilation of the Talmud, perhaps between the sixth and ninth centuries C.E. It is likely that many of the traditions that influenced this text—such as the preparatory rituals and hymns of praise—had developed well before the author's time.

The passage begins with an introduction, which consists of a blessing or invocation that stresses God's creation of the world by means of His esoteric wisdom and testifies that these secrets were not given to human beings except through the agency of the angels. It is important to magical texts that they contain introductions attesting to the supernatural origins of the practices they contain. These introductions reassure the reader that although the text they are reading is not in the canon of holy books to which they are accustomed, it has nevertheless divine authority.

The text proceeds with instructions for performing the ritual of the Great Name. These consist of a preparatory regimen lasting eighty days that involves unusual abstentions and proscriptions; and a ritual for the last day to be performed at a river, in which the book is to be opened and its contents recited. This ritual is an excellent illustration of the way magical practices are accompanied by ritual purification. Ritual purity, which is not the same as good hygiene or spiritual virtue, was considered in ancient Judaism to be required of anyone who wanted to approach the presence of God in the Temple. In the world view of the writer, it was believed that in order to be with divine beings such as angels, it was necessary to attain a state of ritual purity beyond anything required by Jewish law. For example, whereas rabbinic law requires men to avoid their wives when they are in menstruation, this text requires the (male) practitioner to avoid even bread baked by a woman, who might contaminate it with an infinitesimal degree of impurity.

He must also stay away from foods that might cause odors, such as vegetables, garlic, and onions; Jewish legends describe how angels can smell humans in their midst. In instructing the avoidance of physically exceptional persons, such as lepers and twins, the author may be echoing the biblical requirement (Lev. 21:16–23) that no priest with a physical deformity must enter the sanctuary.

After his purification, the practitioner is to go to the river with the magical book and recite the powerful divine names in it. The river was considered not only to be where ritual ablution can be performed but also a place of mysterious encounters with divine beings, like Jacob's at Jabbok (Gen. 32:23–33) and Ezekiel's vision at the River Chebar (Ezek. 1). At the end of the text it is stated that at the river he will see a "man," perhaps like that of the Jacob story. According to another manuscript, he will encounter the divine presence, the Shekhinah, although he may not see the face of that presence and live (cf. Exod. 33:20).

After this ritual is described, the passage continues with a warning and testimony regarding the book itself: Dire consequences will result if the book is sold at any price. On the other hand, the text promises extravagant rewards for those who preserve its secrets and recite them in holiness. This passage reflects the notion that the active power of the text is located in the physical book that the reader holds, and in particular the magical names it contains.

A long series of magical names, interlaced with brief, cryptic instruction and statements about the origin of the name at Mount Sinai and the burning bush, follows. There is also a brief Aramaic hymn praising God, who by his name enables human beings to walk on water. The passage concludes with a reiteration of the instructions and a testimony to the protective power of the book.

This text was published in Peter Schäfer, *Synopse zur Hekhalot-Literatur* (Tübingen: Mohr, 1981), §§489–95, from four major manuscripts. This translation, however, is based on an unpublished manuscript, MS Florence Biblioteca-Medico-Laurenziana Plut. 44/13, fols. 125a-124a, supplemented by MSS Oxford 1531 Bodleian Library, Michael 9 (Neubauer 1531) and New York Jewish Theological Society of America 8128 from the *Synopse*. In the following translation, additions or variants from those manuscripts are placed in braces ({ }). Portions of the text are translated in Ithamar Gruenwald, *From Apocalypticism to Gnosticism* (Frankfort: Peter Lang, 1988), pp. 267–70. A full German translation appears in Peter Schäfer, *Übersetzung der Hekhalot-Literatur*, vol. 3 (Tübingen: Mohr, 1989), pp. 188–209; Schäfer also includes MS Florence in his translation. Words or phrases in parentheses (( )) were added by this translator for clarification. Brackets ([ ]) enclose translations that are especially tentative. Paragraph numbers (such as §489) refer to Schäfer's edition.

Further Reading

The best general introduction to Jewish magic is still Joshua Trachtenberg, *Jewish Magic and Superstition: A Study in Folk Religion* (New York: Behrman House, 1939;

repr. New York: Atheneum, 1970). For a characterization of Jewish incantations in light of the problem of the definition of magic, see Michael D. Swartz, "Scribal Magic and Its Rhetoric: Formal Patterns in Hebrew and Aramaic Incantation Texts from the Cairo Genizah," *Harvard Theological Review* 83, no. 2 (1990): 163–80. For editions of ancient and medieval magical texts, see Joseph Naveh and Shaul Shaked, *Amulets and Magic Bowls* (Jerusalem: Magnes, 1987), and *Magic Spells and Formulae* (Jerusalem: Magnes, 1993); Peter Schäfer and Shaul Shaked, *Magische Texte aus der Kairoer Geniza* (Tübingen: Mohr, 1994); and Lawrence H. Schiffman and Michael D. Swartz, *Hebrew and Aramaic Incantation Texts from the Cairo Genizah: Selected Texts from Taylor-Schechter Box K1* (Sheffield: Sheffield Academic Press, 1992). The major themes presented in this text, particularly the magical book and preparatory rituals, are discussed in Michael D. Swartz, *Scholastic Magic: Ritual and Revelation in Early Jewish Mysticism* (Princeton: Princeton University Press, 1996), especially chapters 6 and 7). On *hekhalot* literature see Gershom Scholem, *Major Trends in Jewish Mysticism* (New York: Schocken, 1954), chapter 2; Peter Schäfer, *The Hidden and Manifest God: Some Major Themes in Early Jewish Mysticism* (Albany: State University of New York Press, 1992), and David J. Halperin, *Faces of the Chariot: Early Jewish Responses to Ezekiel's Vision* (Tübingen: Mohr, 1988).

The Book of the Great Name

(§489) Blessed be the great Name of the One who, in the beginning of his wisdom, created heaven and earth, and who did not reveal his wisdom to human beings, but gave it to the ministering angels, and the ministering angels revealed the secret to human beings. Anyone who finds this book and discovers all that is written in it must not lie on his bed for forty upon forty days. He must not see the face of a male or female twin, or the face of a male or female leper, {or a man or a woman who has a flux; nor may he see a woman in menstrual impurity}. He must not eat bread (baked by) a woman or water (drawn by) a woman, but must knead with his own hands and mill it with his own hands, and bake one loaf a day and eat it. He shall not eat meat, nor may he eat any kind of fish, nor drink wine or intoxicating drink; nor may he eat onion and garlic, or garden vegetables. If a seminal emission occurs, even on the last day, all the previous days are rendered invalid, and he must return to the beginning. He shall wear white garments and immerse in a river every day for those eighty days, in the evening and the morning, and be clean.

On the last day he shall take this book in his hands and go down to the river in a place that is hidden from human beings, and open it and read from it. And when he finds two incantations [that appear together], he shall say, "Powerful {YH}" and strike his heart. {And if he raises his eyes to heaven and sees the face of the *Shekhinah* he will die.} And if he lowers his eyes to the ground he will live. And when it is revealed to him, he shall hurry twenty paces back. And when {he says his blessings}, he shall study it.

He must not exchange it for gold or silver, nor for precious stones, nor for a gleaming pearl. Anyone who does exchange it will not live out his life in his (allotted) days. He will beg for his death and not die; he will beg for his life and not live. He will eat his own flesh in his hunger; his days will turn to nights and his nights will become like days to him. Then he will die in an earthquake and his body will not be buried, an evil spirit will strangle him, and a lion will eat him. (§490) But anyone who does not reveal this great Name will be blessed before his Master. It will be well for him in his death and well for him in his life. Kings will praise him and [chiefs will exult] and give honor to him. He will be saved from all trouble. They will place a powerful crown on him and he will seem to them like an angel of God. They will scatter at his feet and all the words that come out of his mouth will be proper. Satan will have no power to harm him. No man will be able to rise against him in anger and he shall succeed in everything he puts his hand to.

Now, obey all that I command you: Love God every day; act honestly and justly with human beings, and feed the hungry and clothe the naked, and gather the exiles and homeless to your house. And honor the great name by uttering it in holiness. Anyone who knows this great Name will (be able to) take a lion by the ears and a serpent by the skull of its head. If he rages at the sea it will dry, and if he rages at a fire it will be extinguished. If he wants to kill, he can kill, and if he wants to revive, he can revive with it.

Before Him the earth quakes, and mountains and heights tremble. Before Him the earth and the (angelic) creatures raise up song and melody, and say: Holy, holy, holy {is the Lord of hosts; the whole earth is full of his glory} (Isa. 6:3). And they honor his great Name in each and every dwelling. Whoever wants to be wise should read this book every day, but should not pronounce the Name every day and bless his Name. He should not be afraid. 300 chariots (*merkavot*) of his glory, his 72 Names, 1,200 appellations, 66 letters, 96 characters, 24 sanctifications of his glory, 42 (rays of) splendor of his dignity. He spoke and the world came to being, and his Name endures forever and ever. [Nothing precedes him in goodness and nothing follows him in evil] (that is, nothing is better and nothing lacks evil more than he), to the end of all generations.

(§491) {And this is the great, mighty, awesome, and powerful Name:} (YH YH YH YH YH YH YH YH YH YH YH YH YH YH YH YH YH YH YH YH YH YH YH YH YH YH YH YH YH YH YH YH YH YH YH YH YH, 37 (times). Holy God, Holy God, Holy God, Holy God, Holy God, Holy God, Holy God, 7 (times). YH (28 times). You are he who has compassion on human beings and on the spirits that go forth from the earth: 'YṬPS HYH, the Name, YH (16 times). 'BL MTHBT RB QRB K'PP KNGPZ 'NMT YZB TSYMK QMBG L'QWS HYH. You are one in heaven and you are one on earth. You are 'BRWMSN; You are 'GRSMY; You are 'BRH HM HW YH YHW 'HYH 'H 'W HH 'H HWH WH HW ḤYDYH and YH (25 times). Holy God, (6 times). YH (15 times). (§492) This is his Name, which he uttered to Moses at Mount Sinai: QYYM HW' 'W BZZ

ZMZZ SQS ZTT'L MMS ZZ NZ. YH. These are the words that a man says when he walks along with his adversary; he should call out: [given to him, by this, his great Name], which is enduring: YWY, which was revealed to Moses at the (burning) bush. "This is my Name forever:" (Exod. 3:15): SBWR HSNWR SM QM QWPQS, which endures until the end of all generations.

(§493) YHW HW HW HW HY HYH YH; it is enduring. YH (51 times). 'LBT 'BTWN YGTWN GNZ YH (10 times). Holy God (7 times) YH (25 times). LWQTM YHS'L YHS'L TRBNPY'L YHNYK WSHRYSYYH KDM MTWS YH BYTT BWTTW 'ZT YH BR HMHQ BHM 'YNH ZL'' MMK WB'ZW TWS BRKW BYH HMRWZ LH MDRWN ''RM' Z'DZDM' WGNH, which is written by itself: BTR KS'Y 'WHRN. He shall walk with him at night, and if he begs for his mercy, he will be saved.

> El Shaddai, WYW, El Shaddai, the preeminent God,
> who was the exalted Master since Creation.
> ZWR ZR, master of every living thing,
> who {possesses} everything,
> and gave all trouble and burden to those kneaded from the dust;
> who gave life to the spirit of all flesh,
> and a soul to those kneaded from the dust.
> He spoke and all came to be,
> and he called to the world and it was created,
> he placed paths in the mighty waters,
> and in the depths of the sea he paved his way
> by his great and awesome Name.
> And by his wondrous power,
> the righteous {walk} on water and do not drown,
> (for the water is) subdued by the power of the great Name.

Seven angels rule over fire: TRMWM, 'Uriel, and 'Afiel, and Gabriel, Nuriel, Panael, Serafiel, you, Nuriel, you, MZMY KTLT HZY HZYT' MN GZRW, hail, ŠLPT' QWR KMY' 'ŜBR WPSR, like snow, W'L LBS [he shall not wear it and will not be burned] Nuriel BWSRY and BSRY L' YLBŠ. [I have protected myself and sealed myself] with the ring of the great and awesome Name before which heaven and earth tremble.

(§494) (YH 40 times) [Heart of the King, Heart of the King.] MŠQRB ZL 'BRTWM 'BRYNWS 'NTWS ZLWL ZLMWN 'N'L, Ezekiel, that was engraved on the tablets of stone, and the warriors of the great name, Michael and Raphael and Zivael. (The rest of this paragraph consists entirely of magical names and obscure phrases).

(§495) Any man who reads this book must go by himself to the river to a place that is concealed from human beings and from the spirits that go out into the world. There he will see a man, and he will survive by his mercy, and by his prayer he will be saved.... [The name is:] 'KLMT SKTRB QRB B'H' 'PẒ GPẒ TMNT' YẒB TSYMK QMBR GL'KWM. No fire will occur in a house in which this book is placed, nor will destruction befall it.

26

Visionary Experiences among Spanish Crypto-Jewish Women

Renée Levine Melammed

In 1500, an unexpected turn of events created a new set of challenges for the Spanish Inquisition—instituted by the Catholic Church in order to combat what it regarded as heresy—and the Castilian *converso* community (of those who converted from Judaism). A number of visionaries of Jewish ancestry appeared on the scene; all claimed to be prophets bearing a message of salvation that was specifically directed at the *conversos*. Needless to say, this group of converts and their descendants provided fertile ground for such claims. Three different sets of messianic tidings were proclaimed at the turn of the sixteenth century; all emanated from the region of Extremadura. These reports of halcyon days were extremely appealing to the *converso* community, and many *conversas* (female *conversos*) in Castile jumped on the messianic bandwagon. Two of the messengers themselves were *conversas;* the most eminent and charismatic was a twelve-year-old girl, Inés of Herrera, although Mari Gómez of Chillón also had a significant following. At the same time, a butcher named Luís Alonso made promises of better days and imminent redemption, and even approached some of the same conversos who would also be influenced by Inés; the earliest accounts of contact with these individuals dates to 1495.

The Inquisition realized that a movement of this nature was extremely dangerous as well as disruptive; it had the potential to spread quickly throughout Spain and to awaken dormant Jewish proclivities in *conversos* who had never previously judaized, that is, continued to practice Judaism in a concealed manner. Clearly, it needed to be nipped in the bud; expedient and drastic measures had to be taken to round up all of its followers as quickly as possible. As mentioned, such tidings had wide appeal and followers ranged from extremely young *conversa* girls to older women who had previously confessed to judaizing and usually, after receiving light penance, had been readmitted to the Church in the 1480s.

VISIONARY EXPERIENCES

The examples below, all based on confessions made to the Inquisitorial court, refer to *conversas* influenced by Inés. Unfortunately, the trial proceedings of Inés herself are not extant but, as will be seen, there are numerous confessions and accusations that reveal a great deal about her visionary experiences. Angels appeared to her along with the prophet Elijah; the prophetess gave instructions as to how to prepare for the coming of the Messiah and how to celebrate the fact that the *conversos* would soon be transported to the Promised Land. Some were dancing and singing; others were fasting, and observing the Sabbath and Passover and other holidays. Many were anxious to be wearing their best clothes in preparation for the journey. Two of the accounts included here are from relatives of the maiden from Herrera, namely, her stepmother and a cousin.

The original documents of the texts translated here are located in the Archivo Histórico Nacional in Madrid, Spain, classified by name under *judaizantes* (judaizers) who resided in the Archbishropic of Toledo. Each proceeding is registered by file (*legajo*) and a subordinate number (*número*).

Further Reading

Haim Beinart has written a series of articles in various languages on the messianic movement. Available in English is "Inés of Herrera del Duque: The Prophetess of Extramadura," in *Women in the Inquisition: Spain and the New World*, edited by Mary Giles (Baltimore: Johns Hopkins University Press, 1998), pp. 42–52. Readers of Hebrew and Spanish should refer to Yael Beinart Kaplan, "A Bibliography of the Writings of Haim Beinart," in *Exile and Diaspora* (Hebrew) (Jerusalem: Ben Zvi Institute, 1988), pp. 583–98. An entire chapter of my book, *Heretics or Daughters of Israel?: The Crypto-Jewish Women of Castile* (New York: Oxford University Press, 1999), is devoted to this messianic movement among groups of *conversas*, differentiating between those women who were relapsed judaizers, namely, women who had already confessed to the Holy Tribunal in the 1480s (and had been reconciled to the Church), and those who were judaizing for the first time in the 1500s because of this movement.

Confession by Isabel Rodríguez of Agudo
Leg. 178, no. 15 (1501)

I admit my guilt . . . in that I was told of a maiden who was [there] the daughter of Juan Estevan who had ascended to heaven and was approached there by an angel, and how she had told of the many marvelous things she had seen there and how Elijah was due to come and prophesy and the Messiah would come to take the *conversos* to the Promised Land. And having heard all this, I decided to go the maiden and to speak to her and I went to her house and there were other people there ... [and she spoke of] going to those sacred lands and that we should not fear the Inquisition or anything else in any way because it is God's will and no one was opposing [her]; and convinced by her false words and deceitful reasons, the devil, our adversary, turned my will in this way and deceived me so that I would believe all I heard of the said maiden, and I believed that the Law of Moses would save me and did those things that she said in the said way, to fast Jewishly, not eating or drinking the whole day until the stars emerged at night, sometimes on Mondays and on Thursdays. Likewise I admit my guilt that willingly I wanted to observe the Sabbath, and sometimes I observed for a little while, and at others I refrained from housework, and likewise I lit the Friday night candles in honor of the said Sabbath and observed those nights sometimes.

Likewise I admit my guilt that I removed the fat from meat sometimes and avoided eating pork and pork products and meats of dead animals and drowned birds and rabbit and hare and fish without scales.

Likewise I admit my guilt that in the false hope of going to those Holy Lands I made a blouse for the journey.

Likewise sometimes I looked at the sky in order to see those signals that they said would be perceived, and thus I existed in the false belief and hope until I learned that the said maiden was a prisoner and Your Reverences had ordered her to be seized there in Herrera.

Confession of Beatriz Ramírez, wife of Juan Estevan, and stepmother of Inés
Leg. 176, no. 1 (1500–1501)

I admit my guilt in that Christmas past, my said husband Juan Estevan told me how his daughter Inés had ascended to the sky and saw there the deceased and the living; and how the *conversos* were very well prepared [for the Messiah], and many other wonderful things that would have taken too long to recount. In effect, he told me that our salvation was in believing and serving the Law of Moses and its rites and ceremonies. And convinced of the aforesaid, which had been repeated to me numerous times, I began to observe the Sabbath, more by will [intention] than by deed, excusing myself from engaging in work sometimes when I could on the said Sabbaths, wearing clean blouses whenever possible, and lit candles Friday afternoon in honor of the said Sabbath and decorated my home, and likewise I occasionally prepared the Sabbath meals on Fridays, ... and likewise I once gave my husband a clean shirt for the Sabbath.

In addition, Reverend Sirs, my husband told me to fast the fast of the Jews, not eating or drinking the entire day until the stars emerged at nightfall [on] some Mondays and Thursdays and I did so, believing that it would be advantageous for the salvation of my soul as I was told by the said Inés, his daughter.

And also I refrained from eating pork, and all of these things were done believing in the Law of Moses and the coming of Elijah and the Messiah, hoping to go with the other *conversos* to the Promised Land as the aforementioned had told me. I am taken to be a sinner for having offended our Savior and Redeemer Jesus Christ and our Holy Catholic faith.

Confession of Beatriz of Herrera
Leg. 137, no. 7 (1500–1501)

I admit my guilt that about a year ago I was in the home of Juan Estevan when his daughter Inés said to me: "Come here, cousin, would you like to see your mother who is long deceased? and to save your soul? and to go to the Holy Lands? There you will find many young men, and you and your sisters will have good luck and good fortune there. I ascended to the sky and the angel carried me there with him and I saw there such thrones of gold and the deceased as well as the living as they were in their glory! You will see your mother and will go to those sacred Promised Lands. Fast, for all these things can be attained through the Jewish fasts, not eating or drinking the whole day until nightfall when the stars appear." And I told her that I could not do this and she told me, "Do it when you are alone in your house, especially on Thursdays. Say that you have eaten and do not eat until nightfall." And I, convinced by this and of many other things I was told, and for the sake of seeing my mother alive, who had passed away when I was a very young child, declare that I was enchanted by her lies and falsehoods and I fasted on those Mondays and Thursdays when I could.

Charge in the accusation in trial of Elvira González of Agudo, the wife of Gonzalo Palomino
Leg. 153, no. 18 (1502–1503)

That in honor and in the belief of the said dead law of Moses, she awaited the Messiah, believing that he would come to carry her and the other *conversos* to the Holy Lands of Promise. For this purpose, she dressed up, attired in her best clothes and blouses and clean headdresses, celebrating for many days, believing that she would be carried away by the Messiah whom she awaited, wearing the very clothes in which she would be found. . . .

In addition, it was charged that the defendant had fraternized with other heretics and discussed the things said by the maiden from Herrera who was taken to be a prophetess, and how she had ascended to heaven and seen the angels and the deceased as well as those burned at the stake by the Inquisition, all seated in thrones of gold; and [had seen] Elijah prophesying and that he was going to arrive in a cloud to predict on earth to the *conversos*, and that they were believing in the Law of Moses, observing the Sabbath and fasting Jewish fasts such as those on Mondays and Thursdays, not eating all day until sunset and the stars emerged, and abstaining from eating bacon and other foods forbidden to the Jews, and that those who had no faith would be abandoned at a gate. And she believed this and observed and took pleasure in conversing about these issues with other heretics. Because she was convinced by this, she instructed and induced other persons to believe . . . meeting with those who observed, and letting them understand that Jewish law was superior to that of the Christians. And maintaining this and believing for certain in the coming of the Messiah, she met with other relatives to communicate and discuss this. And she had clothes and new blouses [ready] for this departure.

Confession of Isabel González of Almadèn
Leg. 158, no. 8 (1502–1503)

Isabel, the daughter of Fernando González, the cobbler, resident of the village of Almadèn, absent, stated that when my father went to see the maiden of Herrera, the daughter of Juan Estevan, and [ever] since he returned, he told us, myself and my stepmother, and . . . [others]: "Believe as you believe in God, that there is a maiden in Herrera who ascended to Heaven, and the angel came to Elijah and said that we must go to the Promised Lands, and said that we would see our deceased and that they were alive and that one must marry in the Promised Land and that all the *conversos* must go there and that there food was abundant and that those who did not believe would remain behind." . . . And my father and my [step]mother told me not to believe in Jesus Christ, but rather in Moses and they told me to fast on Yom Kippur as this would be perceived as good in the eyes of the Lord and I would see my mother, and if I did not, I would remain there as a lost soul. And I was told to clean the candles on Friday nights and to light them in honor of the Law of Moses. And likewise I saw that my stepmother did not spin on the Sabbath and was told that it was a sin to spin on days like the Sabbath and on Friday nights. . . . I was told, "Fast girl and believe it all and you will not be lost like your mother and do not believe in Jesus Christ."

I confess my guilt in that I withdrew from Our Holy Catholic Faith and fasted three or four days, not eating until nightfall, and at night, ate eggs and sometimes fish and this I fasted with my sister. And I lit clean oil lamps on Friday nights and threw dirt on them so that they would not appear [to be clean], and I believed that we would be going to those Promised Lands and that we would find my mother there along with everyone that I was told, and many things to eat, and that there we would not have to do anything except celebrate and I believed all this and observed and I repent of it all.

27

Mystical Eating and Food Practices in the *Zohar*

Joel Hecker

The *Zohar,* the Book of Splendor, was composed in thirteenth-century Spain among the theosophic kabbalists of Castile. Claimed by Rabbi Moshe de Leon, who authored the bulk of the work, to be the authentic teachings of the renowned second-century talmudic figure Rabbi Shimon bar Yochai, the *Zohar* quickly attained prestige and authority not only because of its supposed authorship but also because of its magnificent literary creativity. Synthesizing rabbinic law, homiletical exegesis of the Hebrew Bible, legend, innovative custom, and polemic into a comprehensive mystical system, the *Zohar* soon became the central and canonical book of Jewish mysticism.

Much of the *Zohar* proceeds with a narrative of rabbis from the ancient period who wandered through the Galilee exchanging mystical homilies, sharing esoterica ranging from the most abstruse elements of kabbalistic theosophy to practical measures. The reader of the *Zohar* was supposed to engage the biblical text and to perform its commandments with mystical intent in order to gain mystical visions, to attain communion with the masculine and feminine aspects of the Divine, and to effect unification between them and the other *sefirot* (dimensions of divine being).

The texts that we will be examining here train their focus upon certain rites and their effects in both supernal and terrestrial realms.

Because of the *Zohar*'s interest in the mystical meanings and effects of performance of the commandments, many of which are performed bodily, the role of the body takes on special significance. In fact, the *Zohar,* and the Kabbalah in general, makes use of the embodied symbol as a primary vehicle for their mystical and esoteric enterprises. Embodied symbols are not wholly ephemeral matters; rather, they are transparent signs such that mundane realities have an immediate effect upon and relationship to the divine realms. Ultimately, the mundane serves as an entryway or portal to these supernal reaches. For the kabbalist, to be embodied acts as a primary element that forms his horizon as he envisions the world; he is irreducibly embodied and his mystical reading of Scripture, with all of its concrete symbols, is viscerally informed. Simply put, in using the term "embodied symbol" I intend that the body is the means of understanding, imagining, seeing, and feeling a range of mystical experiences.

Although sexuality is the primary cache of embodied symbolism for the kabbalists, the act of eating with its attendant ritual observances serves as a valuable lens through which to see the ways in which the kabbalists experienced their bodies. What we will see in the passages to come is that contemplating texts concerned with eating or foods, or contemplating food in response to considering texts, lead the mystics to profound experiences. Because eating is a physical event that one undertakes daily, the *Zohar*'s treatment of it presents an imaginative activity strongly rooted in the physical. Moreover, there is a daily engagement with food that serves to distinguish eating from the more abstract or ethereal nature of philosophical contemplation.

The kabbalists exemplify the imaginative capacity to place themselves in the very scene of a text they are reading, a type of reading that can be called experiential or pneumatic hermeneutics. In other words, contemplating texts regarding food, or contemplating food in response to reading texts, leads them to mystical experiences that are framed by their experiences of their bodies, which are in turn shaped by their readings of the texts themselves. This kind of praxis—emerging from reading—yields a heightened multisensory experience in which the meaning of the practice is neither explicitly told nor shown, but rather experienced. Indeed, this approach to reading texts and practice enables the kabbalists to manifest the construction of reality born of the hybrid mix of Kabbalah, *halakhah* (Jewish law), and the embodied symbol. Finally, emerging from the use of experiential hermeneutics and embodied symbolism employed by these kabbalists in their discussion of practices surrounding the consumption of food (but applicable to other aspects of embodiment, as well) is a spatio-temporal continuity of the body, that enables communion between the kabbalistic devotee and his table, his food, and his fellow.

A number of texts are included here that deal with different aspects of the meal, all of which have had a continued history up to this day in the lives of those for whom these mystical passages inform their religious consciousness and practice. Text 1 treats the Sabbath meals. In the pattern of the classical midrash, the *Zohar* begins its homily by responding to an exegetical problem in the Bible. If no manna fell on the Sabbath day, how could the Bible, in the first chapter of Genesis, assert that God blessed it? The *Zohar* suggests that since blessing comes from the seventh day, it is a result of the dining on the Sabbath, symbolically the supernal Sabbath, namely, the feminine *sefirah* (pl. *Sefirot;* aspect of divinity), *Shekhinah,* (the Divine presence), that, indeed, blessing does reign the rest of the week. In fact, for blessing to rest upon that table so that it can then serve to nourish the other "days" of the week, that is the middle six *sefirot,* one must set the table, preparing its food for, the *Zohar* says, "blessing does not rest upon an empty place." Following the legal prescription, three meals must be eaten in order to derive the desired benefits. Moreover, those three meals correspond to three manifestations of Divinity: *Atiqa Qadisha* (the Holy Ancient One), *Ze'ir Anpin* (the Impatient One), and the Field of Holy Apples. Although much of zoharic Kabbalah delineates the Godhead in terms of ten *sefirot,* some of its sections configure Divinity differently, with these three manifestations. *Atiqa Qadisha* corresponds to the uppermost *sefirah, Keter,* where mercy resides; *Ze'ir Anpin* designates the next eight sefirot; and the Field of Holy Apples represents the *Shekhinah.* Further, it is not merely eating that is emphasized but the delight that one takes in the process which serves to perfect "faith" in the upper and lower worlds.

The meals that the mystic eats are sacred meals, and his very being is transformed as he acquires a new soul, pleasuring in the pleasure of the Consort, the *Shekhinah.* Omitting a meal, however, causes a defect to appear in the (sefirotic) world above while, below, he creates a fissure in the social group, demonstrating that he does not belong. Kabbalistic ritual is thus performative insofar as there are values attached to the performance which, depending upon the act, deem the person worthy or not.

Texts 2 and 3 are variants of lists that enumerate ten essential components for a meal that will be eaten in purity, ten meanings said to be derived from the heavenly academy. In the first of these lists, the second through fourth components treat the hand washing that precedes a bread-based meal and that has been part of prescribed Jewish practice since talmudic times. The aim of this sanctified behavior while eating is expressed as an act of self-angelification. Scriptural verses that enjoin purity practices upon Israel with regard to the cultic table in the Temple are reinterpreted through experiential and kabbalistic reading to refer to the individual's domestic table with the ideal aim of becoming actually angelic. Hand washing is a double-edged ritual—one can mythically join either the realm of the holy or demonic through one's observance or neglect of this ritual.

The hands and the ritual washing of them become symbols here that provide vehicles for thinking, imagining, and communicating. One of the fundamental dynamics in kabbalistic literature entails the containment of the "left side" in the "right side," the demonic in the holy, and the feminine in the masculine. The moment of final perfection within the Godhead or within the human occurs when these polarities are reconciled, with one being subsumed within the other. That dynamic is given expression here by enjoining the diner to wash the right hand with the left hand. Though hand purification requires washing both hands, the laving of the right hand receives priority.

The transparent nature of kabbalistic symbolism is exemplified in the passage that correlates the numbers of joints in one's hands with the various names of the Divine. It is through these fleshy channels that blessing flows bilaterally. The body is revealed to be a linguistic construct, with its various components corresponding to the individual units of the Hebrew language, its letters, and in this case, the most holy combinations of those letters. In Text 3, the *Zohar* provides a more complex model to which one should conform in order to summon the divine efflux—bread on the table and cup of wine in the right hand. In this configuration the bread, corresponding to the *sefirah Yesod,* the phallic member of the Godhead, is deemed to be connected to the wine, representing the *sefirah Gevurah* (the attribute of Judgment), which is in turn grasped in the right hand, symbolizing the *sefirah* of *Hesed* (the attribute of Love). This series of connections and containments results in the lower being contained in the upper and the left contained in the right, so that all of the *sefirot* are united as one entity that results in an overflow onto the table, blessing the bread. Through the adoption of this physical gesture and domestic layout, the mystic and his table become a veritable replica of the *sefirot,* affirming, demonstrating, and effecting the unity of the Divine. In this instance, and others, a presumed audience enables the performance to serve double duty: as theurgy above and as demonstrations below.

In Texts 3 and 4 we find instances of talismanic theurgy, in which some component of the meal serves to draw divine blessing downward to the table. In the first, the *Zohar* says that one must have bread present upon the table when reciting the concluding blessing. In the next passage, reciting words of Torah while seated at the table serves the talismanic aim. The magical goal of inducing a flow of blessing from above into the table is elicited by the strategic placing of bread upon the table or recitation of sacred words, a holy speech act.

As there was dualistic liminality of hand washing, so too are there two avenues, or specifically two tables, with regard to reciting words of Torah. When one engages in holy discourse, one's table is compared to that of the Temple; if not, it is the table (or altar) referred to by Isaiah as one covered with vomit and filth. The determinant of identity is the religious intention that one brings to the table and the religious activities performed there. This is already indicated in the rabbinic teaching that plays upon Isaiah 28:8. When Scripture says, "no place is left" (*beli maqom*), the rabbis understand this to be a lack of awareness of God, drawing upon the rabbinic cognomen for God of *maqom,* meaning place. In the zoharic rendering, the table is infused with words of Torah and is thus inducted into the realm of holiness; the lack of words of Torah effects an induction into the inverse realm. Thus, returning to the rabbinic statement that introduced the homily— that blessing will not reside in an empty place—the *Zohar* explains how one maintains the "fullness" of a table: through investing the table with one's own "blessing" that mirrors the divine blessing being invoked.

The words uttered become part of the meal that is set before the Divinity, eaten upon a supernal replica of the individual's table in the world below. This completes a cycle in which God creates food, and the food is consumed by the mystic who produces blessings and holy utterances that nourish God—a kind of spiritual ecosystem. In this manner, the food chain is complete: the person invests the table with wisdom, which in turn draws food-wisdom from above so that the table remains continually full. Such a table is properly configured, as the letters of the words of Torah have been contained within it. In this way it has been prevented from becoming, according to the rabbinic warning, a table full of filth and vomit. These two visions, vivid tables acting as visualized imaginative models (a table composed of the letters of the Torah and a table full of filth and vomit) compete for the kabbalist's intention in his performance of the commandments.

Ultimately the formalization of the meal with its requirements for blessings, words of Torah, proper hand washing, and so on, blurs the boundaries among the physical, social, and mystical.

Text 5 comes from the opening section of the *Zohar*, which enumerates a listing of commandments and, significantly, maintains that feeding the poor is the ninth commandment. In this passage the *Zohar*'s conception of gender creates the matrix for understanding the relationship between rich and poor. We find a notion that feeding the poor will theurgically unite the masculine and feminine aspects of the Divinity. The use of female gender imagery to render male-male relationships is a common way for kabbalistic literature to explain the stratification of society with the powerful, wealthy, or wise in the position of the masculine, and the weak, impoverished, or ignorant in the position of the feminine. Offering nourishment to the indigent corresponds to the sexual dynamic of male "giving" to the female and thus becomes an expression of potency and love; however, as a result, this correspondence helps color the meaning of the *Zohar*'s understanding of sexuality, as well. It renders the *Zohar*'s ubiquitous use of the term "support" in the context of the divine romance in a more literal way, thus nuancing the nature of the relationship and vitiating its erotic charge.

The translation of "The Sabbath Meals," *Zohar* 2:88a–88b, comes from Isaiah Tishby, *Wisdom of the Zohar*, translated by David Goldstein (New York: Oxford University Press, 1989), pp. 1,286–90. Reprinted by permission of the Littman Library of Jewish Civilization. All other translations are my own on the basis of *Sefer ha-Zohar*, 3 vols., edited by Reuven Margaliot (Jerusalem: Mossad ha-Rav Kook, 1984). "Hand Washing before a Meal" is from *Zohar Hadash* 86d–87b (*Midrash Ruth*); "Reciting Grace over Bread" is from *Zohar* 1:240a; "The Table of the Holy One and the Table of Vomit and Filth" is from *Zohar* 2:153b–154a; "Feeding the Poor" is from *Zohar* 1:13b.

Further Reading

Elliot Ginsburg's *The Sabbath in the Classical Kabbalah* (New York: State University of New York Press, 1989) examines Sabbath practices described in kabbalistic texts through the beginning of the fourteenth century. Joel Hecker's doctoral dissertation (New York University, 1996), "Each Man Ate an Angel's Meal: Eating and Embodiment in the Zohar," supplies a thorough treatment of mystical eating practices and techniques as represented in the *Zohar* and late thirteenth-century Spanish Kabbalah. In his *Through a Speculum That Shines: Visionary Experience and Imagination in Jewish Mysticism* (Princeton: Princeton University Press, 1994), Elliot Wolfson offers a recasting of the kabbalah, arguing that visionary experience is the foremost modality of the Jewish mystical enterprise from the ancient period through the time of the composition of the *Zohar*. Isaiah Tishby's *The Wisdom of the Zohar,* 3 vols. (Oxford: Oxford University Press, 1989), is the most comprehensive scholarly analysis of the *Zohar,* comprising topically arranged, annotated translations of zoharic texts and systematic introductions to the topical sections, including discussions of the *sefirot,* Torah, Sabbath and festivals, and the Ten Commandments.

1. The Sabbath Meals

"Remember the Sabbath day to hallow it" [Exod. 20:8]. Rabbi Isaac said, "It is written 'And God blessed the seventh day' [Gen. 2:3]. But of the manna it is written 'Six days shall you gather it, but on the seventh day is the Sabbath; there shall be none on it' [Exod. 16:26]. How can there be blessing on the Sabbath if there is no food there? But it has been taught: All blessings both above and below depend on the seventh day. And it has been taught: Why did manna not appear on the seventh day? Because from that day all the six supernal days receive blessing, and each one of them provides its sustenance to the world below, each one on its particular day, from that same blessing with which they are blessed on the seventh day. Therefore, whoever is at the level of faith should arrange a table and prepare a meal for the eve of the Sabbath, so that his table may be blessed throughout the six weekdays; for it is at that time that the blessing is ready with which each of the six days of the week is blessed. But there is no blessing at an empty table. Consequently, on the eve of the Sabbath one should prepare one's table with food and nourishment."

Rabbi Isaac said, "The same is true of the Sabbath day also."

Rabbi Judah said, "One should take delight in this day and eat three meals on the Sabbath, in order to bring satisfaction and delight to the world on this day."

Rabbi Abba said, "It is in order to bring blessing to the days of the upper world. On this day the head of *Ze'ir Anpin* becomes full of the dew that descends from *Atiqa Qadisha,* the most recondite of all, and he drops the dew three times on the Field of Sacred Apples, once the Sabbath has begun, so that they may all be blessed together. Therefore a man must experience delight on these three occasions for celestial faith depends on *Atiqa Qadisha, Ze'ir Anpin,* and the Field of Apples, and one should take delight and rejoice in them. Whoever subtracts a single meal damages the world above, and great will be his punishment. Therefore, everyone should prepare a table three times from the inception of the Sabbath; the table should not be left empty. Then blessing will rest upon him during the remaining days of the week. It is through this that faith appears in the world above and upon this it depends."

Rabbi Shimon said, "If a man completes these three meals on the Sabbath, a voice issues forth and makes a proclamation about him, saying 'You shall take delight in the Lord'—this is one meal, which represents *Atiqa Qadisha,* the most holy of the holy ones; 'and I will make you ride upon the high places of the earth'—this is a second meal that represents the Field of Sacred Apples: 'and I will feed you with the heritage of Jacob your father' [Isa. 58:14]—this is the perfection that is completed in Ze'ir Anpin. One should perfect each meal in relation to these, and take delight in the meals and rejoice in each one of them, because this is perfect faith. This is why the Sabbath is more to be honored than all the other festivals and holy days, for everything is to be found in it; and such is not the case with any other festival or holy day."

Rabbi Hiyya said, "It is because everything is to be found in it that it is mentioned three times, as it is written, 'On the seventh day God finished' [Gen. 2:2]; 'He rested on the seventh day' [ibid.]; 'God blessed the seventh day' [Gen 2:3]."

When Rav Hamnuna Sava was seated at a Sabbath meal he would rejoice in each one, and he would say, "This is a holy meal of *Atiqa Qadisha,* the most recondite of all." And at another meal he would say, "This is a meal of the Holy One, blessed be he." And so with every meal. And he would rejoice in each one of them. And when he had finished the meals he would say, "The meals of faith have been completed."

Rabbi Shimon would say when he came to the table, "Prepare the meal of supernal faith, prepare the meal of the King." And then he would sit and rejoice. And when he had finished the third meal a proclamation would be made about him: "You shall take delight in the Lord; and I will make you ride upon the high places of the earth; and I will feed you with the heritage of Jacob your father."

Rabbi Eleazar said to his father, "What order do these meals follow?"

He said to him, "Concerning the Sabbath eve it is written, 'I will make you ride upon the high places of the earth.' On this night the Consort with the whole Field of Apples is blessed, the man's table is blessed and an additional soul is given to him. This night is the Consort's joy and one should rejoice and eat the meal of the consort. Concerning the Sabbath day, the second meal, it is written 'You shall take delight in (*'al*) the Lord'—specifically 'above (*'al*) the Lord,' for at that moment *Atiqa Qadisha* is revealed and all the worlds rejoice and are made whole. We prepare the joy of *Atiqa,* and it is without a doubt his meal. Concerning the third Sabbath meal it is written, 'I will feed you with the heritage of Jacob your father'—this is the meal of Ze'ir Anpin, who is complete, and the six days of that completion are all blessed. One should rejoice in his meal, and complete the meals, because these meals are the perfect faith of the holy seed of Israel, for this supernal faith is theirs and belongs to no other people. Hence it is written '[It (i.e., the Sabbath) is a sign] between me and the children of Israel' " [Ex. 31:17].

Come and see. It is through these meals that Israel are recognized as sons of the King, as belonging to the royal palace, and as the sons of faith. If a man impairs just one meal he causes a defect to appear in the world above, and shows that he does not belong among the sons of the supernal King, among the sons of the royal palace, or to the holy seed of Israel, and he becomes subject to the three tribulations: the judgment of Gehinnom, and the like.

Come and see. On all the other festivals and holy days a man should rejoice and also cause the poor to rejoice, because if he rejoices on his own without giving to the poor, his punishment will be severe, since he keeps his joy to himself and does not give joy to the poor. Concerning him it is written, "I will spread dung upon your faces, the dung of your festivals" [Mal. 2:3]. But if he rejoices on the Sabbath, even if he does not give [joy] to others, he is not liable to punishment as on the other festivals and holy days, for it is written, "the dung of your festivals"—"the dung of your festivals" not "the dung of your Sabbath." And it is also written "Your new moons and your appointed seasons my soul hates" [Isa. 1:14]; it does not mention the Sabbath. That is why it is written "[It is a sign] between me and the children of Israel [forever]."

Since the whole of faith exists in the Sabbath, a man is given an additional soul, a celestial soul, a soul that contains all perfections, on the model of the world to come, and that is why it is called "Sabbath" (as a foretaste of the rest in the world to come). What is the Sabbath? It is the name of the Holy One, blessed be He, the name that is perfect on all sides.

Rabbi Jose said, "This is indeed so. Woe to the man who does not complete the joy of the holy King. What is that joy? These three meals of faith, the meals in which Abraham, Isaac, and Jacob are comprised, all of them being one joy above another, faith perfect on all sides."

2. Hand Washing before a Meal

The second [element that is necessary for a proper meal] is washing one's hands before a meal. What is the reason? Eating requires cleanness like that of the ministering angels above. This is what Rav Hamnuna Saba said, "What is the meaning of the verse, 'Each man ate an angel's meal' [Ps. 78:25]? It refers to the bread that the ministering angels eat." What is the practical implication? As the ministering angels eat in holiness, purity, and cleanness, so must Israel eat in holiness and purity. As it is written, "you shall sanctify yourselves" [Lev. 11:44]—this refers to the first waters; "and you shall be holy"—this refers to the after-waters. "For holy am"—this is good oil; "I"—this is the grace after meals. And when Scripture says, "you shall sanctify yourselves" it intends that anyone who eats in holiness, purity, and cleanness is likened to the ministering angels, for they are holy. And as it is written, "for holy am I" teaches that one must have [proper] intention when reciting the grace after meals. Anyone who eats without washing his hands causes his eating to be impure.

And what does the *Shekhinah* say? "Do not eat of a stingy man's food ['Bread of the Evil Eye']; do not crave for his dainties" [Prov. 23:6]. What does this mean? There is an attribute of affliction in the world whose name is "Evil Eye" and whoever eats without washing his hands, that attribute of affliction rests upon him and all of that food is called "Bread of the Evil Eye." For Rav Hamnuna said as follows, "Two attributes attend a person's table: one is the attribute of goodness and one is the attribute of evil. When a person sanctifies his hands and recites a blessing, the attribute of goodness proclaims, "This is the table of the Holy One, blessed be He," and rests his hands upon the person's head and says to him, "You are my servant, you are the servant of the Omnipresent," as it is said, "And He said to me, "You are my servant, Israel in whom I glory" [Isa. 49:3]. And when a person does not sanctify his hands and proceeds to eat, the attribute of evil says, "He is mine," immediately resting his hands upon him, rendering him impure and his food is called "Bread of the Evil Eye."

There was a story in Babylon of a man who invited a poor person to his home to eat. The indigent saw that [his host] did not wash his hands and had proceeded to eat. The indigent rose from the table and left. The other called to him saying, "Stay and eat!" He responded, "God forbid that I should eat with you for of you it is written, 'Do not eat of a stingy man's food ["Bread of the Evil Eye"]'; moreover, your food is impure, as well." And it is written, "You are not to make yourselves impure through them, becoming impure through them" [Lev. 11:43].... For anyone upon whom the "Spirit of the Evil Eye" rests receives a sealed impurity for which there is no release. The matter came before the rabbis and they gave the indigent man one hundred *zuz*. Rabbi Haggai cried and said, "Happy are you, O Israel, happy are you who are occupied with the Torah and the commandments." And what of the indigent who constrained himself and restrained his belly, and guarded himself, concerning himself only for the glory of his Master? What wonderful reward is prepared for the one who learns Torah!

The third element is to wash one's right hand with the left hand because the right has greater stature than the left in all matters and it is required that the left wash the right and serve it. For a person's right hand, as is the case above, should have greater stature than the left.

The Torah was given with the right as it is written, "from His right hand, a fiery stream for them" [Deut. 33:2], and it is written, "The right hand of YHWH is exalted! The right hand of YHWH is triumphant!" [Ps. 118:16]. This relates to Moshe's raising his hand and Israel becoming triumphant. In order to sanctify one's hands the left must sanctify the right.

When a *kohen* [priest] ascends to the stage [to utter the blessing of the *kohanim*], who washes his hands? One would say that it is the person who comes from the left side, for he serves the *kohen* who ascends the stage. Thus, the right is established as it should be and is sanctified by the left.

Here too [in the case of hand washing before a meal], the right can only be sanctified from the left. Further, one must wash all the joints of the hand. There are fourteen joints that are called *yad* ("hand," with the numerical value fourteen). This is the esoteric meaning of "Hand on Yah's throne" [Exod. 17:16], as was established by Rav Hamnuna Sava....

The fourth element is that one must raise one's hands when one utters the blessing after washing, sanctifying his hands, as it is written, "Lift your hands toward the sanctuary and bless the Lord." What is the meaning [of this practice]? The letters bear the supernal image: there are four fingers that are joined as one, each one with three joints—this is the mystery of the image of the supernal chariot for the holy chariot has four [faces] and twelve joints. Similarly, the ineffable name of four letters bears twelve letters. Thus the letters of the ineffable name have twelve joints, each and every one called a letter. The extra finger [the thumb] that is beyond the others has two joints. These two joints are the two hidden letters in the two supernal, hidden levels, the most exalted of them all. This is the key to everything above regarding the Hidden One who is unrevealed. All of these joints are extended toward that Hidden One after they have been sanctified because everything is blessed from it. Once the fingers have been sanctified one must extend them upward to arouse those supernal, holy joints. Thus there are five fingers and their fourteen joints, yielding nineteen and, with the two supernal joints, give a total of twenty-one in the right arm, corresponding to [the name] EHYEH, whose numerical value is twenty-one. Similarly, on the left hand there are twenty-one corresponding to EHYEH, whose numerical value is twenty-one. This is EHYEH ASHER EHYEH [I am that I am (Exod. 3:15)]. . . .

3. Reciting Grace over Bread

Come and see. One who is reciting the Grace over bread should not utter the blessing in front of an empty table and there must be bread upon the table and a cup of wine in his right hand. Why? In order to connect the left to the right. Also, so that the bread, from which one is blessed, should be connected to them, so that all of it should be connected together as one to bless the holy Name as is proper. For bread is connected to wine and wine to the right side and then blessing rests upon the world and the table is perfected as is proper. Rabbi Isaac said, "If the opportunity to have this guest occurred just so that we might hear these words it would have been sufficient for us."

4. The Table of the Holy One and the Table of Vomit and Filth

It is written about a table over which words of Torah are not recited that "Yea, all tables are covered with vomit and filth, so that no space is left" [Isa. 28:8], and it is prohibited to recite a blessing over such a table. Why is this so? Because there is one kind of table and another kind of table. There is a table that is prepared before the Holy One, blessed be He, above and it is always prepared to have words of Torah recited upon it and to comprise the letters of the words of Torah within it. He gathers them toward himself comprising them within

Himself, and they are perfected and rejoice in Him and He [also] rejoices. It is said about this table, "This is the table that stands before YHWH" [Ezek. 41:22]. There is another table that does not have a portion in the Torah and does not have a portion in the holiness of the Torah, and that table is called "vomit and filth"; this is the one that has no place inasmuch as it has no portion in the side of holiness. Consequently, a table over which words of Torah are not recited is a table of vomit and filth. It is the table of another idol. That table will have no portion in the mystery of the supernal God. With a table that has had words of Torah uttered upon it, the Holy One, blessed be He, takes it and places it as part of His own portion. Moreover, the archangel Suria takes all of those words [of Torah] and places an image of that table before the Holy One, blessed be He. All of those words of Torah that were uttered upon it rise upon that table [above] and it is crowned [by them] before the Holy King. The table of a person is established to purify him of all his sins. Meritorious is the one who has established both of these things at his table: words of Torah and a portion for the poor from that table.

5. Feeding the Poor

The ninth commandment: To be generous to the poor and to give them food, as it is written, "Let us make man in our image after our likeness" [Gen. 1:26]. "Let us make man"—from a combination of masculine and feminine. "In our image"—the rich; "after our likeness"—the poor. For the rich are from the masculine side and the poor are from the feminine side. As they are in one combination, and one is concerned about the other, and one gives to the other, and bestowing goodness one upon the other, this is the way that people should be below: the rich and the poor should be in one unity, giving one to the other and bestowing goodness one upon the other. "They shall rule the fish of the sea...." We see this mystery in a book of King Solomon: whoever concerns himself with the poor with the intention of his heart, his image never changes from the image of Adam. Once the image of Adam is inscribed upon him he can rule over all creatures of the world with that image. This is as is written, "The fear and the dread of you shall be upon all the beasts of the earth...." [Gen. 9:2]. All tremble and fear before that image that is inscribed upon him because that is a supernal commandment that elevates human beings with this image of Adam beyond all other commandments. From where do we learn this? From Nebuchadnezzar. Even though he dreamed that dream [in Daniel 4:7–14, in which he is transformed into a beast], as long as he was generous toward the poor his dream did not rule over him. Once he looked askance at giving to the poor, what was written? "The words were still on the king's lips [when a voice fell from heaven, ... You are being driven away from men, and your habitation is to be with the beasts of the field. You are to be fed grass like cattle]" [Dan. 4:28–29]. Immediately his appearance was altered and he was banished from other people.

28

Devotional Rites in a Sufi Mode

Paul B. Fenton

The century that witnessed the rise of the Maimonidean dynasty in thirteenth-century Egypt was one of great social and spiritual turmoil for Oriental Jewry. Persecution and messianic delusion in the Yemen, Crusader wars in the East, and Almohad persecution in the Muslim West had brought waves of Jewish refugees to their former land of bondage. These social upheavals fostered religious mutations, for there emerged among the Jews a pietistic trend, which, dissatisfied with the excessive rationalism of the Aristotelian school, turned their minds to mystical speculations. At this time, Egypt had become the scene of an unprecedented flourishing of Islamic mysticism, institutionalized in the form of important brotherhoods gathered around great charismatic masters in the urban centres. No doubt their increasing religious impact had repercussions on the local Jewish populations, for whom they represented an immediate spiritual model. Perhaps in reaction to the ritual formalism resulting from the legal codification enacted throughout the geonic period, the doors of the synagogue were opened to the revitalizing influence of Muslim mysticism. The resultant movement embodies one of the most profound influences of Islam on Jewish spirituality. Its followers called themselves Hasidim, Pietists; and named their discipline *derekh ha-hasidut,* "the Pietist way," or *derekh la-shem,* the "path to God," both of which expressions recall the Arabic *tariq,* the term with which the Sufis designate their spiritual path.

The Pietist movement was not a marginal sect, for it enjoyed widespread popularity under the leadership of the greatest political and religious figure of the time, Abraham Maimuni (1186–1237), who was none other than the only son of Moses Maimonides. Indeed, much information concerning the movement can be culled from his magnum opus, the *Kifayat al-'abidin,* "Compendium for the Servants of God." In addition, the treasure-trove of the Genizah has recently enriched our knowledge of the practices and doctrines of the Jewish Sufi movement. The latter produced a rich and varied literary output, which patently displays the influence of Sufi concepts and terminology. Their writings are not just judaized adaptations of Muslim texts, however, but original compositions, ingeniously transposed into the biblical and rabbinic texture. Their revisionist spirit led them to develop their own specific theories and an original exegesis, by which they read into scripture the various practices that they had, in fact, borrowed from Islamic models.

One of the disciplines that received special attention, as could be expected was that of daily worship. Thus the Pietists composed theoretical manuals on the purpose and import of prayer, which demonstrated significant borrowing of Sufi elements. Among the better-known manuals of this type is the section on prayer included in the *Kifaya*, which mentions certain practical "reforms" introduced by Maimuni's spiritual companion, Rabbi Abraham he-Hasid (d. 1223). These include a number of devotional rituals, clearly inspired by Muslim models, whose purpose was to enhance the decorum of the synagogue and to intensify the spiritual dimension of worship. Preliminary preparation for prayer was introduced, as well as the ritual ablution of both the hands and feet, though this was not strictly required by Jewish law. Conversely, the meritoriousness of this latter rite, obligatory in Muslim law, was emphasized in Sufi sources. Worshipers were arranged in rows, as in mosques, continuously facing Jerusalem throughout the synagogue service. Different postures, such as standing, kneeling, bowing, and the spreading of hands, were prescribed for certain parts of the liturgy.

In addition to canonical prayers, nightly vigils and daily fasts were recommended, as well as the typically Sufi practice of contemplation (*muraqaba*) in a solitary retreat (*khalwa*), during which *dhikr*, ritual repetition of the divine Names, might also be carried out. It is also known that, because of their protracted devotions, the Egyptian Hasidim established special prayer halls, such as Abraham Maimuni's own private synagogue, where the Pietist rituals were observed. In an effort to assert their authenticity and gain credence within the Jewish fold, the Pietists often presented their novel rituals as a restoration of practices previously prevalent among the ancient prophets of Israel, as Abraham Maimuni puts it in the *Kifaya* (II, 320): "Do not regard as unseemly our comparison of [the ways of the ancient prophets] to the conduct of the Sufis, for the latter imitate the prophets [of Israel] and walk in their footsteps, not the prophets in theirs." Though hardly compatible with the traditional Jewish principle of collective prayer, even the practice of solitary meditation, together with the Sufi notions of the repetition of the divine Name and reliance on God (*tawakkul*), were considered by Rabbi Abraham as being of Jewish origin:

> Also do the Sufis of Islam practice solitude in dark places and isolate themselves in them until the sensitive part of the soul becomes atrophied so that it is not even able to see the light. This however requires strong inner illumination wherewith the soul will be preoccupied so as not to be pained over the external darkness. Now Rabbi Abraham he-Hasid used to be of the opinion that solitude in darkness was the thing alluded to in the statement of Isaiah: "Who is among you that feareth the Lord, and heeds the voice of His servant? Though he walketh in darkness and hath no light, let him 'trust in the name of the Lord, and rely upon his God' " [Isa. 50:10].
>
> *Kifaya* II, 418

Though difficult to estimate the extent and duration of the influence of the Jewish Sufi tendency, it is not unlikely that some of their practices survived in certain circles and were absorbed by later mystical movements such as the Eastern Qabbalists.

The following text on prayer has been extracted from a Pietist treatise discovered in the Cairo Genizah. Like most of the texts from this source, it reflects more popular aspects of religious life. Again, like many Genizah writings, it has come down to us in a fragmentary form, and the name and time of its author are unknown. However, given the Sufi coloring of its content, it almost certainly belongs to the Pietist movement of thirteenth-century Egypt. According to the text, the purpose of prayer as well as the performance of the religious precepts is to arrive at a constant awareness and "presence with God," in an effort to activate the spiritual correlation (*munasaba*) that binds man to Him, leading in turn to the soteriological knowledge of God. The Sufi doctrine of *munasaba* was particularly developed by al-Ghazzali (d. 1111) and Ibn Arabi (d. 1240). Other Sufi terms are also present, such as the contemplative disciplines of "turning upward" (*tawajjuh*), meditation (*muraqaba*), and solitary devotion (*khalwa*), as well as the spiritual stations of "proximity," "intimacy," and "presence," which string the mystic path. Of singular interest is the reference to the practice of *dhikr* or "recollection of the divine Name," which is perhaps the most characteristic of Sufi rituals. The present text testifies to this devotional form in Jewish circles, including the appropriate biblical proof texts, though no practical details are furnished.

This extract, which appears here in English for the first time, was originally written in Judaeo-Arabic. It is translated from the Arabic, published by P. Fenton, "A Mystical Treatise on Prayer and the Spiritual Quest from the Pietist Circle," *Jerusalem Studies in Arabic and Islam* 16 (1993): 137–75.

Further Reading

A general historical account of the relations between Jewish and Islamic mysticism can be found in P. Fenton, "Judaism and Sufism," *Routledge History of World Philosophies,* vol. 1, *History of Islamic Philosophy,* edited by S. H. Nasr and O. Leaman (London: Routledge, 1996), pp. 755–68; and in his *The Treatise of the Pool, al-Maqala al-Hawdiyya by Obadyah Maimonides,* 2nd ed. (London: Octagon, 1995). The writer has also published and translated a number of Pietist texts, the most important of which is *Deux traités de mystique juive* (Lagrasse: Verdier, 1987); which also contains an extensive bibliography. A more detailed discussion of specific authors or concepts are to be found in the following articles of his: "Some Judaeo-Arabic Fragments by Rabbi Abraham he-Hasid, the Jewish Sufi," *Journal of Semitic Studies* 26 (1981): 47–72; "A Judaeo-Arabic Commentary on the Haftarot by Rabbi Hanan'el b. Shemu'el ha-Dayan, Abraham Maimonides Father-in-Law," *Maimonidean Studies* 1, edited by Arthur Hyman (New York: Yeshiva University Press, 1990): 27–56; "La tête entre les genoux, contribution à l'étude d'une posture méditative dans la mystique juive et islamique," *Revue d'Histoire et de Philosophie Religieuses* 72 (October–December 1992): 413–26; "A Mystical Treatise on Perfection, Providence and Prophecy from the Jewish Sufi Circle," in D. Frank, ed., *The Jews in Medieval Islam* (Leiden: E. J. Brill, 1995), pp. 301–34; "Solitary Meditation in Jewish and Islamic Mysticism," *Medieval Encounters* 1, no. 2 (October 1995): 271–96. Abraham Maimonides' *Kifaya* was partially edited and translated by S. Rosenblatt, *The High Ways to Perfection of Abraham Maimonides*, 2 vols. (New York and Baltimore: Johns Hopkins University Press, 1927–1938).

On the Purpose of Prayer

CHAPTER

Know that by virtue of the spiritual correlation (*munasaba*) [between the human and divine] enshrined within the human frame, to which God alluded in the verse: "Let us make man in Our image, after Our likeness" [Gen. 1:26], it behoves the wise to press his soul to turn toward its Beloved, besides Whom he must love none else, as it is said: "and thou shalt love the Lord thy God with all thy heart, with all thy soul and with all thy might" [Deut. 6:5]. Thereupon the soul will be fit for the continuous contemplation (*muraqaba*) of its Beloved and the attachment to the supernal abode through which its obtains life, deliverance, and salvation, as David prophesied: "Because he is devoted to Me, I will deliver him" [Ps. 91:14]. This is the ultimate goal beyond which there lies no other.

Thereafter, the soul must continuously be aware of this state, not forsaking it for an instant by inattention, lest it be led astray and distract its master, even carrying him off to the depths of death. For the soul would thereby have become estranged from the supernal world on account of its heedlessness and rejection of it, through its clinging to matter and its pursuit of material desires and ends.

It is precisely to this "turning upward" [*tawajjuh*] that God has called attention in the first and second paragraphs of the monotheistic confession, saying: "And these words which I command thee . . . thou shalt speak of them when residing in thy house, and when thou walkest by the wayside" [Deut. 6:6]. Now the whole of time is included in this verse so that your heart should never be empty of Him, not even for an instant. Not only is this an expression of honor for you on the part of God but it is also an ennoblement of your person, as it is written: "when thou liest down and when thou risest up" insofar as it is God's will that He occupy your labor, and your conversation with your soul, the thought of your heart, the reflection of your mind, and the speech of your tongue, the vision of your eyes, and the hearing of your ears, the movement of your limbs, the pace of your feet. All your gestures and acts will be conditioned by His generosity and ennobled by His remembrance (*dhikr*), so that His bounty may envelop you, His providence encompass you, His success accompany you, His lights serve you, His angels bear you, and His creatures, great and small, obey you.

This "turning upward" and contemplation have been described by David, the sincere seeker, faithful lover, pure gnostic, endowed with modesty, meekness, and contrition, when he said after having attained and reached them: "I have placed the Lord continually before me; He is at my right hand; I shall never be shaken" [Ps. 16:8]. This then should be the manner of orientation and contemplation.

Now since God is aware that man is forgetful, that the soul's resolve is feeble at the outset of its quest on account of its being immersed in the world of sensual objects, lacking experience in the delights of divine meditation and the contemplation of his attributes, acts, and virtues, He enjoined that physical symbols be placed upon the body bearing His name and some of His noble attributes, and containing a testimonial and a reminder of spiritual notions and the metaphysical realm, saying: "And thou shalt bind them for a sign upon thine hand and they shall serve as a symbol between thine eyes . . ." [Deut. 6:8]. However, this can only be effective after purification of one's exterior and sanctification of one's interior from the treachery, wiles, and weaknesses of the [lower] soul.

As for external purification, it is no secret for him who pursues this noble quest, as Solomon has said: "At all times thy garments shall be white" [Eccles. 9:8]. The expression "all times" alludes to the moments of spiritual preparedness, be it total or partial, whereas "white garments" refer to the purity of one's ritual acts, which are the garments of the soul. External cleanliness, the ablution of clothes, the body, and the hands and feet are a necessary prerequisite at times of spiritual preparation, already referred to by [Moses] the prophet in the verse: "And thou shalt make a laver of copper and a stand of copper for it, for ablutions" [Exod. 30:18]. Indeed, the laver served its purpose during their external preparation for worship, since purity is a standing requirement for all who seek to draw near to God.

Next the individual should be mindful to eliminate waste and should delay [prayer] until such time as the gradual discharge of waste be completed. This is an obligation to which one must be extremely attentive so as not to commit an impious and reprehensible act.

As for internal sanctification, it entails first the purification of one's ritual acts, which endow the individual with human qualities. Thereafter one will ascend to divine qualities, which will necessarily lead to the obtaining of the spiritual correlation, in order to draw nigh unto him. Since the explanation of this [mystery] would prove very lengthy, I can mention only a part thereof as an indication of its extent. This includes:

1. the training of the soul to oppose its desires and abandon the pleasures of the [lower] soul, such as [excessive] talk, and to be taciturn even about truthful matters, let alone futile ones;
2. the opposition to all the whims and desires of the [lower] soul;
3. the cleansing and education of the [soul] by the observance of good deeds, that is, the avoidance of prohibited things and
4. the improvement of the character by the practice of the positive commandments.

These are obvious to any disciple of this noble pursuit, such as: "Thou shalt not take vengeance or bear any grudge" [Lev. 19:18], and: "Thou shalt love thy neighbor as thyself" [ibid.]. For vengeance and grudges are most blameworthy characteristics equal to hate, rancor, and the harboring of vindictive thoughts. It is necessary to purify the soul of these and similar traits in order to ascend the ladder of proximity and attain the station of the pietists by fulfilling the utmost purpose of both the positive and negative precepts.

Indeed, the precepts possess both a beginning and an end; the beginning is determination and the end transcendence. For instance, the beginning of the precept of "loving one's neighbor as oneself" implies the equation of one's will with that of one's neighbor, whereas the end implies the preferring of one's neighbor to oneself, which is the level characteristic of the Pietists. Likewise, the practice of the precepts progresses in a similar manner, until the seeker eventually attains the utmost aim by realizing the loftiest goals of the precepts. If he performs the commandments in this manner he will attain the spiritual correlation between his soul and the Creator.

Upon obtaining this spiritual correlation, all veils will be lifted between them, he will attain divine knowledge. At that instant, the individual will be transported into a state of "absence," having fulfilled his purpose and attained his goal without any intermediary. He will be uplifted from the state of humanity to that of gnosis, in accordance with the description given by David of that sublime, noble and exalted state in the words of God: "I will protect him for he knoweth My name, when he calleth Me, I will answer him" [Ps. 91:14]. This state will come to pass through the "lifting of the veils," which refer to the physical attributes, for the divine can only truly be realized through the effacing of the human, and this can only be accomplished through the observance of the commandments. For instance, it is obvious concerning the prohibition: "thou shalt not curse the deaf" [Lev. 19:14] that a deaf person will suffer no hurt by being insulted, but it is the soul of him who utters the curse, which, without his being aware, is sullied, profaned, defiled, and reduced to cinders.

If this be the case with certain secondary precepts, how much more so with what concerns the primary precepts such as the belief in God and his unity, the denial of polytheism and agnosticism, or faith in the Torah and its prophet. For one whose belief is unstable cannot properly practice, and were he to perform the commandments, these would prove fruitless, for belief is the foundation of practice. Thus when David recommended to his son Solomon to lay firmly the foundations that bear goodly fruit, which is the divine-given Torah, he exclaimed: "And thou Solomon, my son, know thou the God of thy father and serve him" [1 Chron. 28:9].

CHAPTER

Know that the purpose of prayer is sevenfold, though God knows better. First, acknowledgment of the primary Being, which implies the affirmation of God's existence.

Second, the realization of God's existence and unity by not turning to other deities and placing in them one's confidence in absolute dependency and gratitude.

Third, God's proximity to the individual who seeks Him with sincerity of tongue and heart.

Fourth, to tarry exclusively at His gate.

Fifth, the soul's attachment to Him so that it be not abandoned to the desires of his [lower] soul, thereby condemning his fate to perdition. Such was the case of our nation according to the verse: "A wild ass used to the wilderness in her heat sniffing the wind" [Jer. 2:24]. "Be not like a horse or a mule without understanding" [Ps. 32:9], since they were unrestrained by any limit. For though he performs good deeds, he who observes not the commandments must surely turn aside, and likewise he who avoids not prohibitions must certainly go astray.

Sixth, the soul's ardent desire to return to its holy abode.

The seventh virtue accruing from the advantages of prayer is the soul's obtaining of bliss through worship of its Maker and Creator, its Sustainer and Nourisher, its Aid and Guide, its Bearer and Provider, its Molder and Tutor, who will return it to its supernal world, as it is written: "And the dust returneth to the earth as it was, and the spirit returneth to God who gave it" [Eccl. 12:7]. Now, the latter is the worship of the gnostics who know, love, and serve him, obtaining thereby the sweetness of proximity (*qurb*), the perfume of intimacy (*'uns*) both at times of absence and presence (*hudur*). By "absence" we mean external life and mundane existence, which is absence in regard to the world of the intellects and souls, and an exile within the world of generation and corruption. As for "presence," it signifies the internal and everlasting life within his nearness and presence. This is the awakening after slumber, soberness after drunkenness and drunkenness after soberness, relief after adversity, liberty after captivity, freedom after servitude, life after death, and presence after absence, reuniting after separation. This beatitude can only be attained through a sincere search and a perpetual and faithful quest throughout the period of terrestrial life in this netherworld, as the saint David proclaimed, after having realized this state: "As for me, I shall behold Thy Face in righteousness, then when I awake, I shall be satisfied with beholding Thy form" [Ps. 17:15].

CHAPTER

As for the first purpose, which is the very axis of prayer, know that the advantages of prayer are not an end in themselves but are intended to enhance the divine soul and arouse its faculties. Indeed, on account of man's preoccupation with and his immersion in this world, intercourse with its inhabitants, seeing them and listening to their conversation, and dealing with their transactions, the soul's faculties that assist her in obtaining her perfection are necessarily dimmed and weakened. One of the advantages of prayer is the removal of the harmful ideas that cling to the mind, and the cleansing of the imagination of those pernicious fancies that prevent the acquisition of salubrious and upright thoughts. On account of that very reason, it is stated that the ancient pietists would tarry for an hour in preparation for prayer [*Mishnah Berakhot* 5:1]. How considerable are the advantages that accrue from this preliminary hour in terms of the clearance of the mind and imagination and the eviction of harmful and vile elements, heard and seen, as a result of preoccupation with the world and dealing with its inhabitants and their doings.

Thereafter one should utilize this refined thought in reflecting on the manner in which the individual will stand before the Truth in order to praise Him and ask of Him his needs, to thank Him for His immense bounty toward man in enabling him, an insignificant earthly creature, to stand before the Sovereign of the universe and present his petition. For the divine dignity is mighty and awful, before Whom one cannot present oneself in a casual fashion but one must wholly prepare oneself both externally to meet His presence and internally to formulate one's request, as we have been cautioned by the prophet: "Prepare to meet thy God, O Israel" [Amos 4:12].

Then he will reflect on how man can stand before Almighty God, with what terms he may extol Him, how he may address His majestic rank, how to tender his request, how to accept His gift with graciousness, how to recognize those demands of which he is undeserving, and how to decline them, too, with graciousness. How, too, to express his gratitude, and whether the latter should be proportionate to his personal possibilities, or in accordance with the received benefit, or in accordance with the majesty of the Benefactor and Bestower. And finally, how he may withdraw from His divine and noble Presence.

Were the individual to meditate on these awesome notions as a preliminary to appearing before God at the appointed prayer time, he would be overcome by vigilance and respect in his presentation, praise, acceptance, gratitude, and withdrawal, conscious from Whom he is receiving and of his own worthlessness. These then are the manifold advantages of this preliminary hour before worship, after which he will perform his prayers in humility, contrition, reverence, and preparedness before the divine Presence. Know then that what is granted at that moment is in accordance with the individual's spiritual state and the elevation of his intent.

[The ancient Pietists] would then tarry for an hour following worship. This is to permit man's return to himself, to reflect on his foregoing standing before

God, his praise, his thankfulness, his audacity in requesting his wants and needs in view of God's exaltedness and grandeur, and man's own insignificance and his forwardness in making demands of the awesome, divine, and noble Presence. [He will meditate, too] on the manner in which he praised His noble and sublime rank, how he confronted Him, the extent of his gratitude, the position of his feet as he stood, that of his hands as he begged, the manner of his speech as he spoke, the look in his eyes as he watched, the posture of his head as he bowed. In short, what worth is man or his tribute, or his esteem, or his petition, especially if his request be an earthly one unrelated to obedience to God and his pleasing Him on account of what He has granted. Indeed, earthly demands are base and are not requested by him who is endowed with an elevated intent. Furthermore, material necessities are allotted to each being at every moment according to its need, as David has said: "Thou providest them their food in due season" [Ps. 145:15]. Thus worldly needs do not come by request but by obedience and homage. Were one to consider properly his form of praise and thanksgiving, he would be ashamed of himself to present them to God. Have you not observed that when [Moses] the prophet praised God with those sublime and mighty attributes, that is, the "thirteen attributes of mercy," he only [dared] extol Him because of the necessity to intercede [on behalf of the Israelites] [Exod. 34:6–9]. Consider the great humility and dread that took hold of him then, despite his own prestige, as it is written: "And Moses made haste, and bowed his head toward the earth, and prostrated himself" [Exod. 34:8]. After having regained his senses, he entreated: "Let the Lord, I pray Thee, go in the midst of us; for they are a stiff-necked people; and pardon our iniquity" [Exod. 34:9]. This then is the state of one whom God has described as possessing knowledge of Him [Deut. 34:10].

Now, various reasons motivate people to pray at length. First, God Himself has commanded us not to seek assistance from another deity, He alone being capable of satisfying our needs. The second reason is that God is hidden and concealed from our view. These reasons have led people to the excessive recital of prayers and audacious praises, which in turn have led them to fallaciousness and discussions, while the Truth has remained beyond all of that.

Since man is deeply engaged in worldly affairs and pressed for time, while life is short and the demands on man are immense, and his purpose precious, perhaps he can obtain these mentioned commodities by repeated and continuous worship, I mean the polishing of his soul and the cleansing of its tarnish. For prayer has been instituted at specific times—in the early morning shortly after sleep, which is an unconsciousness similar to death, in order to awaken the soul so that it become known to him who misprizes this treasure insofar as he has little esteem for its position, as David has related of its state: "To declare Thy loving-kindness in the morning, and Thy faithfulness in the night" [Ps. 92:3]. Early-morning prayer has yet another advantage of great benefit for him who stops to consider—it precedes one's mundane occupations. There is the possibility that during early prayer the soul will induce God's providence and that the latter will protect him from overhearing wicked rumors, perceiving loathsome sights, and from hearing destructive gossip, as the prophet said: "death and life are in the hands of the tongue" [Prov. 18:21], and furthermore, the individual will not be overcome by the imaginings and ramblings that stem from such dealings.

The evening prayer was instituted before retiring, following one's daily dealings, in order to eliminate from the mind what remains therein of the vestiges of those imaginings, so that the individual can sleep soundly and encounter in his slumber what is appropriate. The afternoon prayer was instituted in the latter part of the day for various reasons. First, man is engaged in physical pursuits only during the daytime. Therefore this prayer was introduced close to evening worship, so that through this sequence of prayer the soul might be cleansed of what it has accumulated during the day. Thus when the senses are at rest, visions may be revealed to it that arouse its longing for its celestial abode, or it may be shown a form guiding it to deeds that will draw it near to its Creator, or notions stimulating and invigorating its resolve be disclosed to it.

The afternoon prayer has yet another aspect which, in regard to the soul, is like the relationship of watering and sowing. Since the sun governs the act of sowing during the daytime and not at night, so also must irrigation take place during the day and not at night. Similarly, since the soul is attached to sensual objects only during the daytime, it is in need of prayer to refresh it, time and again, in order for it to remain in its state of purity, ready to receive the gifts of the influx, the lights of its Master. Indeed, it is impossible for the intellect to apprehend aught of its Creator unless it polishes the mirror, which is the soul. Thereafter, through the shining of the soul, the revelation of its soundness, the effulgence of light upon it, the intellect will perceive all that it is capable of beholding, as David said: "In thy light shall we see light" [Ps. 36:10].

Know, brother, that it is necessary to preserve these moments so that no instant of them is lost devoid of humility, contrition, and restraint. God has moments when He examines the hearts of his servants. . . . [T]hese are perhaps prayertimes at moments when people are poring over the affairs of this world or are absorbed in its pursuit, that is, at the commencement of the day and the opening of the market, at dusk when one seeks the last earnings, and at midday. David has called attention thereunto in the verse: "[I will call upon God] . . . evening, morning, and at noonday" [Ps. 55:18], explaining that these are times when the entreaties of the needy pious ones are answered: "I will pray and pine and he will hearken to my voice" [ibid.] It is related that certain seekers were only answered on account of the afternoon prayer as a grace [Babylonian Talmud, *Berakhot,* 6b].

Reflect, O brother, how this grace can come about and be fitting to those who come forward. How wonderful that the afternoon prayer is called "offering" (*minhah*), to be sure, it is a "great gift" whose hour is from noonday onward, which is a special moment indeed, superior [*zahar,* a play on *zuhr,* "midday"] to all other times. It is possible that in the story of Adam and Eve, the verse: "And they heard the voice of the Lord God walking in the garden in the breeze of the day" [Gen. 3:8], refers to this moment. To be sure, one commentator has explained "breeze" as the "heat of the day"; now, the heat of the day commences at the seventh hour, which is the time of the afternoon prayer. As for the spiritual force that the soul particularly perceives at this moment, as well as the illumination and brilliance that the trained soul will especially experience in its essence at this time, it is impossible to qualify in words or to describe in any expression. Of such things David has said: "Taste and see that the Lord is good" [Ps. 34:9].

Reflect, O brother, on the greatness of these precious moments, and how wonderful their mystery. Beware then of neglect, apathy, or lack of initiative before the gates, as it is said: "Happy is the man who hearkeneth to Me, watching daily at My gates, waiting at the posts of My doors" [Prov. 8:34]. Know that your drawing near unto Him depends on your obedience to Him, and obedience signifies hearkening to His voice, and executing His command. How can you hear Him if you be afar? Only he who frequents His Presence and stands before Him can hear His speech and have knowledge of His will. Solomon said, speaking in lieu of God and using the language of love, " 'Happy is the man who hearkeneth to Me, watching daily at My gates, waiting at the posts of My doors' " [ibid.]. And in this verse, for him who understands, there is sufficient guidance.

29

Pietistic Customs from Safed

Lawrence Fine

One of the salient characteristics of the great kabbalistic renaissance that took place in the Galilean village of Safed in the sixteenth century was the development of an exceedingly wide array of new ritual practices. Many of these practices are known to us through a genre of ethical or pietistic literature known by the term *hanhagot,* referring to rules of behavior or conduct. Whereas other types of ethical works explore broad general problems in a systematic fashion, the *hanhagot* literature focuses on the most specific, practical details of religious life. In place of speculative, theoretical, or analytical concerns, the *hanhagot* generally comprise lists that, in a terse format, enumerate practical behavioral standards and expectations. In tone they are conspicuously directive and didactic, traits that they share with medieval Hebrew ethical wills, letters containing ethical and spiritual counsel written by a father to his children in anticipation of his death.

What is the relationship between these special practices and the traditional corpus of religious commandments (*mitsvot*) to which virtually all premodern Jews felt themselves bound? Some of them represent an attempt merely to accentuate the importance of certain traditional legal precepts. At the same time, they often add a new twist to such normative obligations, by a call for greater stringency of observance, by stressing some particular aspect of a precept, or by attaching new features to it altogether. On the other hand, a large number of these *hanhagot* go beyond the usual realm of the *mitsvot* altogether by adding novel obligations whose purpose is to enrich the life of piety. In this way, they serve to differentiate such piety from conventional patterns of observance. For example, the frequently mentioned practice of a midnight vigil to mourn the exile of the Jewish people from their ancient homeland, the unusually intensive preoccupation with studying the text of the Mishnah, and the participation in prolonged regimens of fasting are practices that set off the Safed kabbalists from their brethren in other places whose piety was restricted to more typical rabbinic behavior. Although rites such as these technically fall into the category of *minhag* (custom) as contrasted with what is strictly obligatory according to the requirements of Jewish law, it is clear that for the Safed community many of these new "customs" acquired the status of obligation.

A great many of these and other devotional rites from Safed found a prominent place in the religious life of subsequent generations, both among Near Eastern and European Jewries, especially from the seventeenth century forward. For example, *Kabbalat Shabbat* (Welcoming the Sabbath), the special liturgy that ushers in the Sabbath on Friday evenings, became a highly popular and enduring feature of Jewish ritual. Likewise, the practice of reciting the biblical Song of Songs on Sabbath eve, as well as Proverbs 31:10–31 at the festive table, originated in Safed. Even today these Sabbath customs are exceedingly popular, although in many communities their kabbalistic origins have faded into the background.

The custom of holding a midnight vigil for the exile of the *Shekhinah,* the feminine dimension of divinity in the kabbalistic schema, was especially common in eastern Europe until relatively recent times. Similarly, the custom of assembling for study throughout the night on the Feast of Weeks (Sukkot), Hoshanah Rabbah, and the seventh night of Passover, became widespread. In fact, the dusk-to-dawn study session for the Feast of Weeks has experienced renewed popularity in our own time. An entire literature developed that served as a vehicle through which these practices found their way into homes and synagogues in Jewish communities all over the world. It includes manuals called *Tiqqunim,* which contain detailed instructions and texts related to a specific rite, such as *Tiqqun Leil Shavuot* for the Feast of Weeks. It includes, as well, more general anthologies of kabbalistic customs, among the most important of which are *Seder ha-Yom* by Moses ibn Makhir, Jacob Semah's *Shulhan Arukh ha-Ari* and *Naggid u-Metsaveh,* and *Shaarei Tsiyon,* composed by Nathan Hannover.

The first of the two sets of *hanhagot* presented here was authored by Abraham Galante (second half of the sixteenth century). Galante was one of the leading disciples of Moses Cordovero (1522–1570), the latter being one of the two most important kabbalists of Safed, along with Isaac Luria (1534–1572). Galante wrote a kabbalistic commentary on the *Zohar* entitled *Yareach Yaqar* (*The Precious Moon*), a book that reflects Cordovero's influence. In addition, he wrote esoteric commentaries on the Book of Lamentations and the rabbinical treatise *Pirqei Avot* (Chapters of the Fathers). Galante was influenced, as well, to some degree by Isaac Luria, although it does not appear as if he was ever among Luria's formal disciples. In his several compositions he occasionally mentions Lurianic interpretations, relates anecdotes about him, and in more than one instance indicates that he personally heard a teaching from Luria.

Whereas a similar set of customs authored by Cordovero appears to have been written expressly for his circle of students and colleagues, Galante's list of *hanhagot* contains rules clearly pertaining to the Safed community as a whole. This is evidenced by the primarily descriptive style in which these customs are stated, in contrast to Cordovero's prescriptive format. It is apparent from these rules and customs that the community at large was expected to participate in the life of disciplined piety and special spiritual exercises. We find here one of the very earliest descriptions of the dramatic ritual surrounding the day preceding the New Moon, which became known as *Yom Kippur Qatan* (Minor Day of Atonement). Galante also provides us with valuable information concerning an array of special rites associated with several festivals. Thus, for example, we learn of the practice of assembling at midday on the day before Passover for the purpose of study, as well as that of spending the entire seventh night of this holiday in the same way. Of particular interest is the report that on Passover there were some "who fulfill the precepts of Gleanings, the Forgotten Sheaf, *Pe'ah*, Heave-Offerings, Tithes, and *Chalah*." These include obligations an individual had with respect to the ancient Temple in Jerusalem while it still stood. The fact that there were some who practiced these in the sixteenth century suggests the air of expectation that prevailed in Safed for the time when these rituals might once again be relevant for one and all.

Even in a community such as sixteenth-century Safed with its array of striking personalities, the figure of Abraham Berukhim (c. 1515–c. 1593), stands out. Berukhim was born in Morocco and immigrated to Palestine, probably prior to 1565. In Safed he associated himself with the kabbalistic circle of Moses Cordovero and Solomon Alkabets. Berukhim eventually became one of the primary disciples of Isaac Luria. In addition to the set of *hanhagot* below, Berukhim wrote a short but highly influential tract entitled *Tiqqunei Shabbat* (Rules for the Sabbath). He was also responsible for having gathered zoharic manuscripts that had been circulating in Safed and had not been included in the first printed editions of the *Zohar*. These were subsequently published under the title *Zohar Hadash* (New Zohar).

Although we do not know much in the way of specific details about Berukhim's life, there is a good deal of evidence concerning the particular character and style of his piety, and the distinctive place he held in the Safed community. We know that he was among the few who were personally instructed by Luria regarding how to prepare for and practice the most esoteric forms of contemplation that Luria taught. Luria's leading disciple, Hayyim Vital (1543–1620), reported that Berukhim told him that he was advised by Luria to avoid all idle conversation, to rise at midnight and weep on account of his generation's lack of esoteric knowledge, and to study long sections of *Zohar,* all for the purpose of readying himself for mystical experience. Berukhim also received detailed instructions for the practice of meditative exercises known as yihudim ("unifications" of the divine Name).

Accounts of some of Berukhim's own pietistic activities are preserved in the semi-legendary letters of Solomon of Dresnitz, composed in Safed at the beginning of the seventeenth century. He informs us that Berukhim was in the habit of exhorting others to rise at midnight for purposes of study and lamentation. The profound sense of urgency to repent and of communal obligation that characterized the Safed community is vividly exemplified in Berukhim's zeal as described in Solomon of Dresnitz's letters, as follows:

> There was a certain individual here in Safed, may it be rebuilt and reestablished speedily in our day, whose name was the honored Abraham ha-Levi [Berukhim], may

the memory of the righteous be for a blessing. . . . Every midnight he would rise and make the round of all the streets, raising his voice and crying out bitterly: "Rise in order to honor God's name, for the *Shekhinah* [Divine presence] is in exile, and our holy Sanctuary has been consumed by fire, and Israel is in great distress!" Many things of this nature would he proclaim; and he would summon each of the scholars by name and would not move away from the window until he saw that he had already arisen from his bed. And by the hour of one in the morning the entire city would be filled with the voices of those studying Mishnah, *Zohar,* exegetical interpretations of our sages of blessed memory, as well as Psalms, the Prophets, hymns, and supplicatory prayers.

Berukhim's urgent appeals were not limited to the midnight vigil; he was apparently as vigorously concerned about the proper observance of the Sabbath. Known as the "great patron of the Sabbath," he is reported to have run about town on Friday mornings to the homes, markets, and streets to urge the homemakers and householders to hurry with their Sabbath preparations. He would enjoin businessmen to close their shops in sufficient time to welcome the Sabbath Bride in the proper manner. Berukhim also stands out among his peers on account of his extreme ascetic behavior. The following account by Solomon of Dresnitz— despite its somewhat exaggerated quality—attests to this behavior.

This pious one used to practice another custom. He would go out into the markets and the streets, calling for repentance. He would gather groups of penitents, lead them to the Ashkenazi synagogue, and say to them: "Do as you see me do." Then he would crawl into a sack, ordering them to drag him the entire length of the synagogue in order to mortify his flesh and humiliate his spirit. After this he enjoined them to throw stones at him, each weighing a pound and a half, which they would do. Following this, he would come out of the sack. A bed, covered with nettles that burn the flesh like fire, would be prepared for him, and he would remove his clothing, throw himself naked upon the thorns and roll around until his body was covered with blisters. In a similar way, he would simulate the four kinds of punishments meted out [in ancient times] by the rabbinic court. Then he would say to those assembled: "My brethren, whosoever desires to save his soul from the netherworld must do as I have done." And immediately they all rushed at once and submitted themselves to all of the same torments, crying out in bitterness of soul and confessing their sins. They would not leave there until they had accomplished compete and permanent repentance.

As for Berukhim's *hanhagot,* they tend to accentuate some of the more stringent and ascetic practices of the community, reflecting his own penchant for this type of piety. Of special interest in this connection is the description of a brotherhood of penitents whose members fasted regularly and observed rites of mourning and self-affliction on an established basis. It is not unlikely that this group was constituted of *conversos* (Jews converted under duress) from Spain, whose goal was to atone to the fullest extent possible for the sins they had unwillingly committed.

On the other hand, the severe picture he draws is tempered by references to the joyous celebration of the Sabbath, the existence of a fellowship dedicated to gladdening the hearts of bridegroom and bride at the conclusion of the Sabbath, and the joyful celebration of the New Moon. His account also provides us with some interesting information about social realities. Thus we note his mention of the very young age at which some parents saw to the marriage of their children, the daily collection of charity in the synagogues, the instruction of women and children by traveling teachers, and the practice of raising orphans.

The two texts translated below are found in a manuscript in the library of the Jewish Theological Seminary of America. They were published for the first time in Hebrew by Solomon Schechter as Appendix A in his *Studies in Judaism,* second series, (Philadelphia: Jewish Publication Society of America, 1908), pp. 294–99. They were translated into English in Lawrence Fine, *Safed Spirituality* (New York: Paulist Press, 1984), 42–46, 50–53.

Further Reading

For general introductions to sixteenth-century Safed, see Solomon Schechter's essay "Safed in the Sixteenth Century," in his *Studies in Judaism,* second series (Philadelphia: Jewish Publication Society of America, 1908), as well as Lawrence Fine's *Safed Spirituality,* noted above. See also Gershom Scholem, *Major Trends in Jewish Mysticism* (New York: Schocken, 1946), pp. 244–86, as well as his *On the Kabbalah and Its Symbolism* (New York: Schocken, 1965), pp. 118–57.

The Pious Customs of Abraham Galante

Holy and worthy customs practiced in the land of Israel that were copied from a manuscript written by the perfect and righteous sage, our honored rabbi and teacher, Abraham Galante, a resident of Safed, may it be rebuilt and reestablished speedily in our day.

These are the rules "which if a man practices, he shall live by them . . ." [Lev. 18:5].

1. On the eve of the New Moon all the people fast, including men, women, and students. And there is a place where they assemble on that day and remain the entire time, reciting penitential prayers, petitionary devotions, confession of sins, and practicing flagellation. And some among them place a large stone on their stomach in order to simulate the punishment of stoning. There are some individuals who "strangle" themselves with their hands and perform other things of a like nature. There are some persons who place themselves into a sack while others drag them around the synagogue.

2. On the night of the New Moon there are men of action who rise at midnight and recite psalms.

3. There are some individuals who wear a prayer shawl and don phylacteries at every afternoon prayer service, just as is customarily done at the morning service; this practice is widespread among the people.

4. On the eve of Passover, at midday, there are those who assemble in the synagogues and house of study in order to study the laws of the paschal sacrifice as found in the RaMBaM [Moses ben Maimon or Maimonides]. They pray the "great" afternoon service and depart to prepare the "guarded unleavened bread" (*matsah shemurah*). There are those who are in the habit of cutting the wheat for the unleavened bread with their own hands, and who fulfill the precepts of Gleanings, the Forgotten Sheaf, *Pe'ah*, Heave-Offering, Tithes, and *Challah*. They recite the blessings over the eating of the unleavened bread with that which has been subjected to ten ritual precepts.

5. On the intermediate days of the festival of Passover, at midday, they assemble in the synagogues and recite the Song of Songs, translating it and commenting upon it each day.

6. On the seventh night of Passover, they rise at midnight and read until the "Song at the Sea" in *Midrash Vayosha;* they sing songs of Torah until the dawn. They then recite petitionary prayers, at the conclusion of which they rise to their feet and sing the psalm "When Israel went out of Egypt" [Ps. 114] in a sweet voice.

7. Every night during the period of the Omer [the seven weeks between the second day of Passover and the beginning of the Feast of Weeks], they concentrate upon a different word of the psalm "The Lord will forgive us [Ps. 67], which is composed of forty-nine words, as well as upon one letter from the verse: "Let the nations be glad and sing for joy . . ." [Ps. 67:5]. Each night on which they recite this psalm following the counting of the Omer, they raise their voices when they come to the particular letter designated for that night. There is a tradition among them that an individual who contemplates in this fashion will never spend a single night in prison, even if he should commit some capital offense.

8. On the eve of the Feast of Weeks there are those who sleep one or two hours after completely preparing for the festival. This is because, at night, following the [festive] meal, every congregation assembles in its own synagogue and those present do not sleep the whole night long. They read selected portions from the Torah, Prophets, and Hagiographa, the Mishnah, *Zohar,* and rabbinic homilies until the break of down. And then all the people ritually immerse themselves [immediately] prior to the morning service, as it indicates in portion Emor of the *Zohar* [3: 97a–98b]. This is in addition to the immersion that they practice on the eve of the Feast of Weeks.

9. Every Sabbath eve they go out into the field or to the courtyard of the synagogue and welcome the Sabbath. Everyone dresses in his Sabbath garments. They recite the psalm, "Give to the Lord, O heavenly beings" [Ps. 29] and the Sabbath hymn, followed by the "Psalm for the Sabbath day" [Ps. 92].

10. On the seventeenth day of [the Hebrew month of] Tammuz, at noon, they assemble in the synagogues, weeping, lamenting, and recounting that on that very day, at that very moment, the destruction of the Temple took place, on account of which we are dispersed throughout the lands of the nations.

11. On the eve of the [Hebrew month of] Av an individual takes a pitcher of water and seats himself between the baking oven and the cooking stove, resembling one whose dead were lying before him.

12. On the eve of the Ninth of Av they do not leave the synagogue whatsoever; there they study *Sefer Ben Gurion* and *Shevet Yehudah*. Also, they avoid eating meat on the evening of the Ninth of Av.

13. On the night of the Day of Atonement they do not sleep at all, thus following the example set by the nobility of Jerusalem who stayed awake throughout the night; they spend it studying the laws of the Day of Atonement and its prohibitions, as well as by singing songs, praises of God, and liturgical hymns.

14. On the eve of the New Moon men, women, and students fast.

15. Throughout the night of Hoshanah Rabbah they recite psalms as well as penitential prayers, alternating between one and the other.

16. On the eve of the three pilgrimage festivals [Passover, Feast of Weeks, Sukkot] there are men of good deeds who purchase a lamb and divide it among the poor.

17. There are men of good deeds who prepare three measures of fine flour and bake "guarded unleavened bread," giving three pieces to each and every needy person.

18. The pious are careful to pray with the congregation [that is, in a *minyan*] in the evening, morning, and afternoon.

19. One ought to be among the first ten persons at the synagogue for worship in the morning as well as in the evening.

20. It is proper to avoid conversation during the entire prayer service, as well as while the Torah scroll is open. This prohibition even includes conversation having to do with matters of Torah.

21. It is proper to establish regular times for the study of Torah, during the daytime as well as at night, and to refrain from sleeping before periods of study.

22. There are men of action who recite the psalm "By the waters of Babylon" [Ps. 137] at the table.

23. An individual ought to forgive transgressions and to pardon anyone who injures him, whether through speech or deed. It is all the more important never to take such a person to a [Gentile] court, where they employ idolatrous practices.

24. A person should wash his hands when he rises from bed before touching anything whatsoever and before treading upon the ground. This is in order to drive away impure spirits.

25. When an individual leaves his house, it is fitting for him to place his hand upon the *mezuzah* [on the doorpost] so as to remind himself of God's unity and of His commandments.

26. An individual ought to be careful with respect to taking false vows and oaths, for through the sin associated with doing so a man's children are stricken, as it says: "In vain have I smitten your children . . ." [Jer. 2:30]. Furthermore, it is written: "Thou shalt not take the name of the Lord thy God in vain; for the Lord will not hold him guiltless that taketh His name in vain" [Exod. 20:7]. These are the rules of the covenant that God established with Israel "which, if a man practices, he shall live by them . . . " [Lev. 18:5]. They constitute a "fence around the Torah" and correspond numerically to the sacred name YHVH. And the God of Jacob will support those who fulfill these obligations.

27. There are certain especially pious individuals who fulfill the tithe obligation [to the poor] by doubling it, that is, with one-fifth of all their earnings. They set aside their money in a chest so that they have it available to them and can give generously in fulfillment of their pledge. Even among the poor themselves there are those who follow this custom.

28. There are some who practice the custom of welcoming the Sabbath following the afternoon service dressed in Sabbath garments. They recite the Song of Songs followed by the hymn for the *Kabbalat Shabbat* [Welcoming the Sabbath], "Come, my Beloved." And on the night of the Sabbath they recite eight chapters of Mishnah *Shabbat,* eight more in the morning and eight in the afternoon. It is for this reason that our holy teacher [Judah the Prince, editor of the Mishnah] included twenty-four chapters in Mishnah *Shabbat,* corresponding to the twenty-four ornaments for the Sabbath Bride. "And now, I pray thee, let the power of the Lord be great" [Num. 14:17] to enable us to serve our Creator, blessed be He, as in the injunction to "depart from evil and do good . . . " [Ps. 34:15]. Amen, may it be so.

The Pious Customs of Abraham Berukhim

These are additional pious customs practiced in Safed, may it be rebuilt and reestablished speedily in our day. Some of these were recorded above as well.

PIETISTIC CUSTOMS FROM SAFED

These rules are those of the exalted saint, the honored teacher, Abraham ha-Levi, resident of Safed, may it be rebuilt and reestablished speedily in our day. May God protect and preserve him.

1. It is a practice among most of the scholars of Torah, those who revere God, to pray the afternoon service while wearing a prayer shawl and phylacteries. Some individuals wear them throughout the day, even while walking along the way.

2. The majority of congregations, including nearly one thousand women, fast on the eve of the New Moon.

3. There is a Fellowship of Penitents whose members fast regularly and who pray the afternoon service each day in weeping and in tears. They practice flagellation and wear sackcloth and ashes. Among them there are some who fast two days and nights every week. Some do so for three days and nights.

4. Most of the scholars of Torah, when they rise in the middle of the night in order to study, sit upon the ground, wrap themselves in black, mourn and weep on account of the destruction of the Temple. Such also is the custom of the Fellowship of Penitents at the afternoon service of the eve of the New Moon.

5. Most of the scholars of Torah learn Mishnah by heart; there are some among them who have memorized two orders [of the six orders or divisions of the Mishnah], others three, and so on.

6. Some Torah scholars, those who revere God, practice ritual immersion in order to cleanse themselves of nocturnal pollution. Further, on Sabbath eve, they ritually immerse themselves so as to establish a distinction between the sacred and the profane. And they wear white clothes throughout the Sabbath.

7. A number of groups go out on the eve of the Sabbath [into an open field] while it is yet day, dressed in white clothes, and welcome the Sabbath. They recite the psalm "Give to the Lord, O heavenly beings" [Ps. 29] and the hymn "Come, my Beloved," as well as the "Psalm for the Sabbath day" [Ps. 92]. Then they say: "Come, O Bride."

8. During each of the three Sabbath meals they sing and rejoice. They do likewise on the day of the New Moon and on festivals. Furthermore, they study eight chapters of the tractate *Shabbat* at each of the three Sabbath meals.

9. The majority of townsfolk leave side-curls measuring one finger wide from above the ear. And there are some who leave a width of two fingers.

10. There are certain individuals whose practice it is to go from courtyard to courtyard, and to all the stores, in order to warn people concerning the approach of the Sabbath and to welcome it while it is still daytime.

11. There are some individuals who eat "secular" food while in a state of ritual purity on two occasions: on the Sabbath preceding Passover and during the

Ten Days of Penitence [from the beginning of the New Year through the Day of Atonement].

12. There are some who see that their sons and daughters are married at the age of thirteen or fourteen, in contrast to those who do not do so until the age of twenty-five or older because of financial considerations; by such an age they will have committed a number of transgressions for which capital punishment is deserved.

13. There exists a certain fellowship that goes out at the conclusion of every Sabbath to sing, dance, and gladden the Bridegroom and the Bride.

14. Most of the scholars of Torah eat "guarded" unleavened bread on the night of Passover. Certain individuals do so on all seven nights and adhere to a number of rituals more strictly than do others.

15. All of the Torah scholars study throughout the night of the Feast of Weeks until the break of dawn, as well as through the night of Hoshanah Rabbah. Likewise, a great many people rise on the night of Hoshanah Rabbah for penitential prayers.

16. In every synagogue, charity is collected prior to the main service, during the [recitation of the] "Song of the Sea."

17. There are teachers who travel throughout the region for the purpose of instructing women and young children in the prayers and blessings.

18. Certain Torah scholars spend the entire Sabbath night engaged in study.

19. There are certain especially pious scholars of Torah who neither eat meat nor drink wine during the entire week, because they mourn the destruction of the Temple and because of their own transgressions.

20. There are some people who celebrate the New Moon much as they do the Sabbath, by eating, drinking, and dressing well. So, too, as at the conclusion of the Sabbath, they have a lamp burning and a prepared table.

21. There are individuals who avoid swearing oaths altogether, even with respect to the truth; and they are careful always to speak the truth.

22. Some pietists fast for three days and nights, four times each year, during each of the four seasons.

23. There are those who raise orphans in their own homes, and attend to their marriages at the appropriate time.

24. On the New Moon of the month of Nisan the scholars assemble and occupy themselves with the laws having to do with the [ancient] Sanctuary.

25. On the New Moon of the month of Nisan a number of groups assemble and study all the laws connected with the vessels of the Sanctuary. And they

recite the portion: "And it came to pass on the eighth day" until the verse "And when all the people saw it . . ." [Lev. 9]. Likewise, the passage: "And it came to pass on the day that Moses had made an end of setting up the tabernacle . . ." until the verse "This was the offering of Nahshon . . ." [Num. 7:1–17]. And each day they recite the portion describing the offerings of the princes [Num. 7].

30

Jewish Exorcism: Early Modern Traditions and Transformations

J. H. Chajes

The notion that a spirit distinct from one's soul can penetrate one's body, fill it, and invest it with new powers and prophecies, beneficent or detrimental, is first attested to in Jewish culture in the Book of Genesis. Pharaoh remarks to his attendants about Joseph: "Is there anyone like this in whom dwells the Spirit of *Elohim*?" (41:38) Addressing Moses in Exodus 31:3, the Lord announces that he "will fill [Bezalel] with the Spirit of *Elohim*" to enable him to create the Tabernacle with the necessary in-spiration [lit. taking in of the spirit] (cf. Num. 14:24, 24:2, and 27:18). Perhaps the best Hebrew biblical illustration of the spirit that possesses, bringing transformation and prophetic illumination, is to be found in Samuel's instructions to Saul after having anointed him with oil: "You shall come to the hill of God, where the garrisons of the Philistines are, and it shall come to pass, when you have come there to the city, that you shall meet a band of prophets coming down from the high place with a lute, and a timbrel, and a pipe, and a lyre, before them; and they shall prophesy. And the spirit of YhVh will come upon you, and you shall prophesy with them, and shall be turned into another man" (1 Sam. 10:5–6). Alas, by chapter 16, we find that an evil spirit has taken the place of the spirit of YhVh; a kind of musical exorcism is suggested to Saul by his servants: "The spirit of YhVh departed from Saul and an evil spirit from YhVh tormented him. And Saul's servants said to him, 'Behold now, an evil spirit from *Elohim* is tormenting you. Let our lord now command your servants, who are before you, to seek out a man, who knows how to play on the lyre, and it shall come to pass when the evil spirit from *Elohim* is upon you, that he will play with his hand and you shall be well'" (1 Sam. 16:14–16).

The New Testament features scores of explicit references to demonic possession. Jesus' mission on earth was summarized by Peter in Acts as "doing good and healing all that were oppressed by the devil" (Acts 10:38), and the Gospel of Mark concludes with a description of the signs that enable one to identify a true

Christian: "These are the signs that will be associated with believers: in my name they will cast out devils; they will have the gift of tongues; they will pick up snakes in their hands and be unharmed should they drink deadly poison; they will lay their hands on the sick, who will recover" (Mark 16:17–18). Exorcism, along with other abilities to resist malevolence and to offer benevolence, are the marks of the Christian, according to this source.

Rabbinic literature also contains stories that refer to or describe exorcisms. A well-known example of the former is the case of a Gentile who asked R. Yohanan ben Zakkai for an explanation of the customs associated with the Red Heifer (see Num. 19), which appeared to him to be magical. The rabbi responded that the process of slaughtering the animal, burning it, collecting its ash, and using the ash to purify, was analogous to the Gentile's own customs for exorcising evil spirits (*Pesikta de-Rav Kahana*). Another example is the talmudic story in the Babylonian Talmud, *Me'ilah* 17a–b, in which Shimon ben Yochai's successful exorcism of the emperor's daughter leads to the rescinding of anti-Jewish legislation.

In his *Antiquitates Judaicae,* Josephus describes the exorcism of a demoniac by a Jew named Eleazar before Vespasian and his court. As Josephus tells it,

> Eleazar applied to the nostrils of the demon-possessed man his own ring, which had under its seal-stone one of the roots whose properties King Solomon had taught, and so drew the demon out through the sufferer's nose. The man immediately fell to the ground, and Eleazar then adjured the demon never to return, calling the name of Solomon and reciting the charms that he had composed.
>
> *Antiquitates Judaicae* vol. 8, pp. 42–49

Indeed, the Christian Origen, writing in the third century, testified to the broad recognition in the ancient world that Jews and Jewish formulae were particularly powerful agents against demons.

> Not only do those belonging to the nation employ in their prayers to God, and in the exorcising of demons, the words, "God of Abraham, and God of Isaac, and God of Jacob," but so also do almost all those who occupy themselves with incantations and magical rites. For there is found in treatises on magic in many countries such an invocation of God, and assumption of the divine name, as implies a familiar use of it by these men in their dealings with demons.
>
> *Against Celsus,* vol. 4, p. 33

Origen is mindful of the fact that the Jews remain the authorities on these matters, "for we learn the history of the names and their interpretation from those Hebrews, who in their national literature and national tongue dwell with pride upon these things, and explain their meaning" (*Against Celsus,* vol. 4, p. 34). A broad consensus in the ancient world to this effect is indirectly revealed in the many Jewish elements that found their way into both pagan and Christian exorcism rituals. Indeed, R. Kotansky, among others, has suggested that "the concept of an unfamiliar spirit possessing a human being by somehow infiltrating the body and securing control over the faculties is Semitic; it is largely foreign to Greek thought in classical and Hellenistic times."

Magical manuscripts dating from the late medieval period such as *Shushan Yesod ha-'Olam* (London, Sassoon MS 290) preserve Jewish exorcism techniques that bear striking similarities to those of antiquity. There is quite a variation in the techniques suggested in these manuscripts, though the ingredients that go into most of them would certainly be found in every good magician's cabinets. The procedures almost universally call for the adjuration of angels, some of them demonic, in the classic form "I adjure you angel so-and-so to come and to do such-and-such." (The word "exorcism" derives from the Greek *horkos*, meaning oath or adjuration; the Hebrew equivalent—in both the legal and magical sense—is *hashba'ah*.) The exorcist must adjure the appropriate angel for the job, recognizing that each day has its own angel, who must be enlisted in the task for the operation to be a success. The procedures share much in common with the magical bowls of antiquity, the Greek Magical Papyri, and magical fragments from the Cairo Geniza. Bowls are still very much in use—they are written upon, erased, and filled with living waters made murky by the erasure. This potion is in turn given to the possessed to drink. Other passages suggest the use of deer skin in lieu of a bowl; others still recommend that the magical names be written directly upon the forehead and arms of the possessed herself. Psalms, among them the famous anti-demonic Psalm 91, also have their uses here, again suggesting parallels going back to Qumran, on the one hand, and forward to the Catholic Roman Ritual, on the other. Most of the techniques suggested for treating demonic possession have other uses, as well—they are truly broad-spectrum remedies. Thus we find the same technique prescribed for protection from injury, evil impulses, bad dreams, to succeed in business, to overcome fear, to stop a crying child, to assist a woman in childbirth, for protection while traveling, and against demons of various sorts (Sassoon MS 290, §265).

When the kabbalists of sixteenth-century Safed, then an important town in the Galilee, were faced with cases of demonic possession in their midst, techniques such as this one constituted their paradigms for conducting exorcisms. Our transition to the kabbalists of Safed is not an arbitrary one, for among the first narratives relating possession cases among Jews since antiquity (as opposed to liturgical techniques preserved in manuscripts), fully half a dozen relate to cases in Safed between 1545 and 1572. It is worth noting that this apparent upsurge in spirit possession in Jewish culture occurred precisely during the period referred to by many historians as "the golden age of the demoniac" in Europe (see, for example, E. W. Monter in his *Witchcraft in France and Switzerland*, p. 60). Although we cannot enter here into the problem of the historical background of this resurgence (see "Further Reading"), it is clear that by the mid-sixteenth century, the construction of spirit possession in Jewish culture had undergone a transformation that would also redefine the magical practices of exorcism.

This reconstruction of possession was due to the increasing preoccupation with the doctrine of *gilgul*, or transmigration, among Jewish mystics in this period. As a result, whereas ancient and medieval Jewish formulae for conducting exorcisms assumed the invading spirit to be a devilish spirit, from the sixteenth century onward, the "default" spirit is taken to be the disembodied soul of a human being. Such a soul was understood to have sinned to such an extent that he was no longer qualified to enter even *Gehinnom,* Jewish purgatory, where ordinary souls were considered to spend up to a year undergoing purgation and purification before ascending to Paradise. Without *Gehinnom,* a disembodied soul remained in a hopeless state of limbo subject to endless tortures. According to the kabbalists, such a soul might seek refuge and temporary respite from these tortures in the body of a living human. The penetration of this evil soul into a living person's body was understood as a type of reincarnation known as *'ibbur,* or impregnation, and indeed the most common scenario (by a ratio of about 2:1) was for a male soul to penetrate the body of a female victim.

Anthropological, sociological, and historical literature are replete with analyses of the prominence of women in possession cults. The most common explanations offered are of a functionalist nature, that is, that women "use" the idiom of possession as an "oblique aggressive strategy" to overcome the limitations inherent in their position in society, which "does not allow for reasonable self-assertion" (see, for example, I. M. Lewis, *Ecstatic Religion*). Along these lines, psychodynamic readings often emphasize sexual deprivation as underlying the prominence of women in this phenomenon. I would like to point out for the sake of perspective that it is not insignificant that half of those possessed by evil spirits were men, and that nearly all those possessed by benevolent divine spirits were men, as well. Moreover, it is possible to view spirit possession as a type of religious behavior that is "normal" in particular religious environments. Functionalist or pathological explanations deprive the participants in such environments of a legitimate mode of religious expression, albeit one that today's society deems abnormal and in need of "scientific" explanation.

One consequence of the sixteenth-century kabbalistic reconstruction of demonic possession was that it provided for the possibility that the exorcist-kabbalist could simultaneously free the victim of her unwelcome intruder and offer the disembodied soul the "fixing" (*tikkun*) necessary for him to merit a place in *Gehinnom*. Thus, unlike earlier Jewish exorcism techniques (or Catholic procedures as codified in the Roman Ritual, for example), the early modern Jewish techniques evince concern for the welfare of both souls involved in the tragedy.

R. Isaac Luria (1534–1572), the preeminent kabbalist of the sixteenth century, began teaching in Safed in 1570, some twenty-five years after R. Judah Hallewa witnessed R. Joseph Karo's involvement in a Safedian possession case involving a disembodied soul. Although R. Luria was not responsible for the reconstruction of the phenomenon, he does seem to have been the first kabbalist to suggest innovative exorcism techniques that reflected the new twofold objective of the ceremony. He was also adverse to the use of various forms of magic, including adjurations and other techniques that formed a central part of prior Jewish exorcism practice. He thus provided instruction to his disciple R. Hayyim Vital

(1542–1620) in a new exorcism technique built upon the principles of his complex metaphysical system. Rather than supplanting the old techniques entirely, the new approach took its place among other practices that served Jewish exorcists in diverse cultural settings well into the twentieth century.

I have translated four primary sources on Jewish exorcism, chosen on the basis of their importance and intrinsic interest. The first is the account of R. Joseph Karo's encounter with a possessed boy in 1545, shortly after his arrival in Safed. Although R. Karo was able to save the boy, he does not seem to have had the expertise or techniques at his disposal to allow him to save the poor possessing spirit. The Karo account is from Judah Hallewa, *Zafnat Pa'aneah* MS Dublin, Trinity College, B. 5. 27, fols. 144a–145a. Cited in Moshe Idel, "*'Iyunim be-Shitat Ba'al 'Sefer ha-Meshiv'* [Investigations in the Methodology of the Author of '*Sefer ha-Meshiv*']," *Sefunot* 2. 17 (1983): 224. The translation is based upon a corrected transcription of the unique MS, which was copied in 1628 (see p. 245a).

Following the Karo exorcism, I have presented an abridged translation of the Lurianic procedure as presented by R. Hayyim Vital: H. Vital: *Sha'ar Ruah ha-Kodesh,* edited by Yehuda Zvi Brandwein (Jerusalem: n.p., 1988), pp. 88b–90b. I have shorn the translation of most passages that would be unintelligible to the reader unversed in Lurianic theosophy. The same technique, with some interesting liturgical elaboration and diagnostic discussion, may also be found in the translations of the seventeenth-century cases involving R. Samuel Vital (Hayyim's youngest son, 1598–c. 1678) and R. Moses Zacuto (c. 1620–1697). As a postscript, I have translated a passage from a Hasidic account that shows how complex magical-theurgic practices could be avoided if there was some good cake around. S. Vital: *Sha'ar ha-Gilgulim* (Jerusalem: n.p., 1863), pp. 77b–78a. Zacuto: *Iggerot ha-Remez* (Livorno, 1780), pp. 2a–b. Hasidic account cited in G. Nigal, *Sippurei Dibbuk be-Sifrut Yisrael* (Dibbuk Stories in Jewish Literature), 2nd ed. (Jerusalem: Reuven Mass, 1994), p. 258.

The reference above to *Pesikta de-Rav Kahana* is from the volume edited by D. Mandelbeim (New York: Jewish Theological Society of America, 1962), vol. 1, p. 74. The quotation from R. Kotansky is from "Greek Exorcistic Amulets," in *Ancient Magic and Ritual Power,* edited by M. Meyer and P. Mirecki (Leiden, New York, and Köln: E. J. Brill, 1995), 246. E. W. Monter's book was published in Ithaca and London: Cornell University Press, 1976. I. M. Lewis, *Ecstatic Religion: A Study in Shamanism and Spirit Possession,* 2nd ed. (London and New York: Routledge, 1989).

Further Reading

On Talmudic-era rabbinic exorcism, see M. Bar-Ilan, "*Gerush Shedim 'al-yedai Rabbanim: Mashehu 'al 'Issukam shel Hokhmei ha-Talmud be-Kheshafim* (Exorcism of Demons by Rabbis: On the Involvement of Talmudic Sages in Magic),"

Da'at 34 (1994): 17–31. Y. Bilu has offered penetrating psychological insight into dibbuk possession in a number of articles. See his "The Taming of the Deviants and Beyond: An Analysis of *Dibbuk* Possession and Exorcism in Judaism," in *The Psychoanalytic Study of Society,* edited by L. B. Boyer and S. A. Grolnick (Hillsdale, N.J. and London: Analytic Press, 1985), 1–32. D. B. Ruderman's works on R. Abraham Yagel examine relevant issues of demonology, disease, and purgatory. See his *Kabbalah, Magic, and Science: The Cultural Universe of a Sixteenth-Century Jewish Physician* (Cambridge: Harvard University Press, 1988). In a recent article, I attempted to understand the proliferation of demonic possession among Jews from a comparative historical perspective, and analyzed the techniques of R. Hayyim Vital and R. Moses Zacuto translated here: "Judgements Sweetened: Possession and Exorcism in Early Modern Jewish Culture," *Journal of Early Modern History* 1.2 (1997): 124–69. Most of the surviving narratives were published by G. Nigal in *Sippurei Dibbuk.* See also my review in *Kabbalah: Journal for the Study of Jewish Mystical Texts* 1 (1996): 288–93. More techniques are in M. Benayahu, *Toledot ha-Ari* (Jerusalem: Ben-Zvi Institute of the Hebrew University, 1967), pp. 290 ff. On transmigration in Judaism, see G. Scholem, "Gilgul: The Transmigration of Souls," in *On the Mystical Shape of the Godhead,* edited by J. Chipman (New York: Schocken, 1991), pp. 197–250. On Jewish magic, see the still unsurpassed J. Trachtenberg, *Jewish Magic and Superstition: A Study in Folk Religion* (New York: Behrman's Jewish Book House, 1939), and the recent contributions of M. Idel, including "Jewish Magic from the Renaissance Period to Early Hasidism," in *Religion, Science, and Magic, in Concert and in Conflict,* edited by J. Neusner, E. S. Frerichs, and P. V. McCracken Flesher (New York, Oxford: Oxford University Press, 1989), pp. 82–117.

Joseph Karo, Exorcist

I further testify that in that year, the year 5305 from the creation (1545 C.E.), here in the upper Galilee, a spirit entered a small boy, who, while fallen, would say amazing things. Finally, they sent for and assembled many great sages, along with men of deeds—myself among them.

The sage R. Joseph Karo, may peace be upon him, came and spoke with that very spirit. [The spirit] did not respond until [R. Karo] decreed upon him the punishment of *Niddui* [like *Herem,* a form of excommunication] if he did not speak; he then began to reply.

The sage said to him, "What is your name?" He said, "I do not know my name." "Who are you?" "I am a dog." "And before that what were you?" "A Black Gentile." "And before that what were you?" "An Edomite [Christian] Gentile." "And before that what were you?" "From those people who know the Holy Tongue."

He said to him, "What were your first actions?" He said, "I do not remember." "Did you know Torah or Talmud?" "I used to read the Torah but I knew no

Talmud." "Did you pray?" "I did not pray except on the Sabbath and festivals." "Did you don phylacteries?" "Never did I don phylacteries." He said to him, "There is no fixing you." He said, "They already decreed on me . . ."—that he cannot be fixed.

He said that it had been two years since he departed from the body of the dog, and that since the father of the boy killed a dog at that same time, he said to the father of the boy, "Just as you distressed me when you killed the dog that I was within, so I will kill your one and only son."

At that moment the sage R. Joseph Karo called out upon him "It is incumbent upon us to praise . . ." seven times, forward and backward, and he decreed upon him a niddui to depart from anywhere in the Galilee. And so it was that the young man was healed. This is what I saw with my own eyes at that Holy Convocation.

The Lurianic Yihud for Removing an Evil Spirit

A *yihud* [magical-theurgic "unification"] that my teacher, of blessed memory, taught me to remove an evil spirit: [For] sometimes the soul of an evil person is yet unable to get into *Gehinnom* because of his numerous transgressions. He wanders continuously, and sometimes enters the body of a man or a woman and subdues them, [which] is called the falling sickness. By means of this *yihud*, his soul is somewhat fixed, and he leaves the person's body.

Now this is how it works, as I myself have done it and tried it. I would take the arm of that [possessed] person and place my hand on his pulse, on his left or right forearm, for there is the garment of the soul, and there it is clothed. I then focus my mind upon the soul that is clothed in that pulse, intending [here and throughout, forms of "intend" are used for forms of the Hebrew idiom *kavvanah*, or "contemplative intention"] that it depart from there through the power of the *yihud*. While still holding his hand on his pulse, I then say the following verse [Ps. 109:6] forward and backward. I focus my mind on the names that emerge from it: the numerical values of each word, the first letters of the words and the last letters of the words, as you know. By this means I intend that he depart. He then speaks from inside the body, everything you ask of him, and you command him to depart. Sometimes it is necessary to blast the *shofar* [ram's horn] near his ear and to intend the name KR''A ST''N vocalized throughout with *Sh'va*, also its permutation through A''T B''Sh, vocalized throughout with *Sh'va*, the name being DGZBNT [all permutations of the second sextet of the forty-two-letter divine Name, associated with divine judgment].

Know that this spirit does not come alone, for a *satan* [demonic spirit] holds him and drags him here and there, to complete the punishment for his transgressions. [The spirit] is unable to do anything without [the satan's] permission, for God has made him a watchman over him, as it is written in the *Zohar* [2.41b]: 'The evil one—the evil inclination is his judge.' [Babylonian Talmud *Berakhot* 61a]. King David, of blessed memory, in the verse "Appoint over him a wicked man, and may Satan stand at his right" [Ps. 109:6], was cursing the wicked [to wit] that the Blessed Holy One should appoint a wicked soul over him, to penetrate and harm him, and that a *satan* should come along to stand at the right of this soul, to assist him to remain there. Now, sometimes the soul departs and the *satan* stays alone guarding its place. Thus the transmigrated soul is not there at all times. When he departs and travels at known hours for them to punish him, he must depart from there to receive his punishments. Either way, that *satan* who is assigned to him dwells there, to keep his place. One does not recuperate from that sickness until both of them depart. And you know that the Blessed Holy One sweetens bitter with bitter [Midrash *Tanhuma, Be-shallah* §24/Buber ed. §18] and although this verse seems to be a command to appoint over him this wicked soul, it in fact alludes here to its fixing, through the intentions that we will write.

[Here there is a lengthy series of mystical names and intentions.] You must intend that the spirit depart by the power of these names. If it does not depart, return to the aforementioned verse, and intend all the names again. At the conclusion of each round, say strongly, 'Depart, depart, quickly!' You should know that everything depends on your shoring up and strengthening your heart like a warrior, without any fear. Let your heart not soften, for he will become stronger and not heed your words. You must also decree upon him that he leave from no place other than the space between the nail of the big toe and the flesh, in such a manner that he not damage the body in which he resides. Also decree upon him with the power of the aforementioned names that you intended, and by the power of Herem and Niddui, that he neither harm nor enter any Jew's body ever again.

Know that he will strongly resist [your command] to speak, so as to avoid embarrassment before the listeners. Know that when he speaks, the body of the person remains like a dead rock, and the voice of the spirit goes out of his mouth, without movement of the lips, in a fine voice, like the voice of a small child. Also when it rises from the body to the mouth to speak, it will rise in the shape of a round vertebra arising by way of the neck through the skin of the neck. So too when it descends to the nail of the toe of the foot to depart.

Know, too, that when you ask him who he is and what is his name, he will lie to you and say someone else's name, or insult you, all in order to avoid the decree that you will decree upon him to depart [which is only effective if you know his name]. Thus you must decree upon him with Herem and Niddui, and with the power of the aforementioned names that you intend, so that he not lie, and so that he tell you who he is and his name with utter truthfulness.

Moreover, this matter must be done with purity, immersion, holiness, and extreme concentration.

The Spirits in Esther Weiser

Said the youth Samuel Vital: Today I will utter riddles concerning that which happened to me in Egypt [Cairo], may God protect it. This happened to Esther, blessed among women, daughter of R. Yehuda Weiser, may the Lord protect him and grant him life; she was stricken and remained in her stricken state with heart pain for more than two months following her marriage.

One day thereafter, they compelled me to go and visit her. I went to visit her, and found her in the manner of the stricken, and I was in doubt as to whether it was a *mazzik* [afflicting being], or a demon, or an evil spirit of an Israelite.

I advised them to bring a cleric from the Gentiles to visit her, and thus they did. In the middle of the matter, the *mazzik* which was within her spoke in a loud voice and said that he was a Gentile, and that he had entered her out of his lust for her. Among other things, he said that he had, with a small blow, struck me in my thigh—for that reason I have had pain in my thigh—so that I would be unable to go to heal her.

Afterwards, the Gentile cleric toiled over her, and said that he had already conquered the *mazzik* with a small flask, and buried it in the earth, which is how he deals with them.

Then, all of the sudden, a voice cried from the mouth of the maiden, and spoke and said, "I have been left by myself, alone in the body of this maiden, and I am the spirit of a Jew! Therefore hurry, and call to me the Sage R. Samuel Vital, may the Lord protect him and grant him life, in order that he heal me, and remove me from this."

Immediately they called me, and I was obliged to go to her out of the honor of those who came. At the time I approached her, I was still uncertain as to whether it was a Jewish spirit, or a demon, or a *mazzik,* and I sat by his side. She was lying like a silent stone, covered in a white sheet. Out of uncertainty I said, "Shalom upon Israel." Immediately, the lips of the maiden moved and she responded to me, "Blessed is he who comes, Shalom upon you, blessing and goodness." I said to him, "You are a Jew?" He responded, "Yes." I said to him, "If you are a Jew, say *Shema Yisrael.* [Deut. 6]" He then said '*Shema Yisrael,*' etc. . . .

I then began to speak with him, and he responded to me appropriately, all that I asked of him, until I had asked him who he was, and who his father was, and what land he came from, and when he died, and how was he buried, and how many years he lived, and what his punishment was, and what his sin was, and who the transmigrant here was, whether the soul [*nefesh*] or the spirit (*ruah*), and who was appointed over him, and whether he sits alone here, or if he has a watchman over him. To everything he responded properly and rightly, with nothing perverted or twisted to his words, and without my having had to decree upon him a decree like the rest of the spirits, their ways being known to all those cognizant of science.

Afterward I asked him, "Now what do you want?" He responded, that I fix him and remove him from this body with my great wisdom, for he recognized me from that which they decreed upon me in heaven. I said, "If so, how did you praise yourself, and say, 'I struck the sage Samuel in his hip, so that he would not come to me again.'?" He responded that it was not him, God forbid, but "that Gentile *mazzik* who was with me." It was he who said that he struck me, and he lied and deceived; in order to glorify himself he said this. But he does not have the ability, God forbid, to touch me. I said to him, "If so, why did you come to me in a dream of the night on Monday night, the seventeenth of Tammuz, and afflict me?" He responded, "True, I was the one who came, but the one who afflicted you was that Gentile *mazzik*; I did not sin against you at all."

I said, "And you, why did you come with him?" He responded, "To request of you that you fix me, finally." I said, "Now, what do you want?" He responded, "It is my will that you fix my soul and my spirit, and that you remove me from this body." I said, "Thus will I do tomorrow." He answered back, and said, "Why delay, with two suffering spirits like this, my spirit, and the spirit of this maiden? It is within your power to do so." He petitioned me greatly. Finally, I adjured him with a severe adjuration not to deceive and depart, only to return and (re)enter her; and also that in his departure he not injure the maiden herself, nor her family, nor those standing there at the time of his departure from the body, nor anyone of Israel; and also that he not remain any longer here in Egypt, but rather that he go immediately on his way to *Gehinnom* to be healed there. Aside from this, I decreed upon him all of the above with *Herem* and *Niddui,* etc. . . . . Afterward, I said to him that he give us a true sign in his departure and that he say "*shalom aleikhem*" [peace be upon you] during his departure. And thus he did, and thus he spoke, three times.

Afterward, I summoned ten scholars to be present, and I started to feel his right pulse, and I intended the verse "Appoint over him a wicked man, and may Satan stand at his right" [Ps. 109, 6] as it is written by me at length, and also other intentions known to me to fix his soul and his spirit. His lips then fluttered, and he said aloud with us first the psalm "The Lord answer thee in the day of trouble" [Ps. 20] in its entirety. And the psalm "Let the graciousness of the Lord our God be upon us" [Ps. 90] "O thou that dwellest in the covert of the Most High" [Ps. 91], [and] *Ana Be-koah* [the prayer of R. Nehuniah ben HaKana, the acrostic of which forms the forty-two-letter divine Name], in its entirety. And I intended the name KR''A ST''N. And afterward "Answer me when I call, O God of my righteousness, [thou who didst set me free when I was in distress] . . . " [Ps. 4].

And afterward this prayer: "In the name of the unique God, you are great, and great is your Name in strength; please Lord, the honored and awesome, the majestic and beautiful and sanctified, the exalted and blessed, the examiner and inquirer, the straightened and the lofty, the hidden and concealed, the mighty in seventy-two names, the one unique, clear and pure, the hearer of cries, the receiver of prayers, who answers in times of suffering, incline your ear to my prayer, to my supplication, and to my plea that I pray before you and ask of you. And you will hear from heaven, the place of your dwelling, and receive with mercy and good will this spirit who remains before us, transmigrated in this maiden, who is called so-and-so daughter of so-and-so, who is called so-and-so, and receive our prayers that we pray for him to fix his soul and his spirit, and to remove him from this transmigration, and to bring about his admission to the judgment of *Gehinnom*, and to allow his soul and his spirit to escape from the catapult of the *mazzikim* and from the suffering in which he wallows. May this transmigration and this humiliation be considered an atonement for all of his transgressions, his sins and his crimes. May these words of ours be words of advocacy before you for this soul and this spirit, and may your mercy prevail over your attributes [of judgment] upon him, in our recalling before you the thirteen ATTRIBUTES OF MERCY: God King sitting on the Throne of Mercy, etc.; And he passed over," etc. . . . And while saying the thirteen attributes, "Lord, Lord, God merciful and forgiving" [Exod. 34:6–7], blow the *shofar* [ram's horn] as is the custom of all the penitential prayers (*slihot*) and afterward say the thirteen attributes of Micha the prophet: "Who is God like You," etc. . . . [Mic. 7:18].

Afterward say "The tale of iniquities is too heavy for me; as for our transgressions, thou wilt pardon them" [Ps. 65:4], and the verse "Happy is the man whom thou choosest, and bringest near, that he may dwell in thy courts; may we be satisfied with the goodness of thy house, the holy place of thy temple!" [Ps. 65:5], and the verse "And all these thy servants shall come down unto me, and bow down unto me, saying: 'Get thee out, and all the people that follow thee; and after that I will go out.' And he went out from Pharaoh in hot anger." [Exod. 11:8], and say this verse three times. Afterward say "Depart! Depart! Depart!" and intend the intentions that are in this verse, as written by me.

And immediately as I was finishing the word "Depart!" three times, he lifted the left foot of the maiden up before all the people, and left from the little toe of her foot and shouted in a loud voice, and said, "Unto you, peace!" three times and I responded to him "Go in peace! Go in peace!" three times. Immediately the maiden sat and opened her eyes and looked at me, and she was embarrassed. And she said, "What are these people doing?" For she did not know a trace of what we had done. She then kissed my hand, and ate and drank.

This I accomplished on Thursday, 26 Tammuz 5426 from Creation, here in Egypt. I have written all of this as a memorial to those who come after us, so that they might know that there is a God in Israel. The youth Samuel Vital.

R. Moses Zacuto's "Order" for a Woman Possessed by an Evil Spirit

To the eminent sage, his honor our rabbi, Rabbi Samson Bacchi from Casale, may the Compassionate One keep and preserve him. . . .

Now regarding that evil spirit in the woman in Turin, of whose case you have informed me. You have already performed for her the Order [exorcism] of the Rav [R. Isaac Luria], may his memory live on in the World to Come, which did not help, providing only temporary results.

I was surprised by the matter, for the strength of this intention is very mighty to subjugate that spirit to the strong judgments, particularly given his being from *Sitra Ahra* [demonic "Other Side"], as your lord has inferred from his name. You did not, however, inform me of the signs that indicate that it is to be diagnosed as a spirit and not as madness, for the outstanding sign that a spirit is present is when his voice is heard through a part of the body other than the mouth, and also when its location is seen in the swelling of some place like the throat, or the breasts of a woman and the like; some of them also say something regarding the future.

However, in any case, you may afflict it through the burning of wicks of sulfur, and if, when the smoke reaches the nostrils, it becomes angry and enraged, add more of the like, and say the verse, "He will rain down upon the wicked blazing coals [and sulfur; a scorching wind shall be the portion of their cup."] [Ps. 11:6]. If he has not been subdued into declaring himself, have ten scholars and God-fearers assemble; the greatest of them should ritually bathe first, and they should all don phylacteries on their heads. When they come to them [sic] they should begin [saying] "May the pleasantness" [Ps. 90:17] quietly, and when they say "only with your eyes will you behold" [Ps. 91:8] they should intend the name KhH''T [part of the seventy-two-letter Name of God; used by Moses, according to magical sources, to kill the Egyptian [Exod. 2:12] and to split the Red Sea (Exod. 14)] according to the words of the Rav [Luria], may his memory live on in the World to Come. Afterward, they should all say "It is incumbent upon us to praise . . ." with the known intentions, and also "And therefore we hope to you. . . ." When they reach "But we bow down . . . ," one of them should blast a great blast [from a *shofar*]. After this, they should all say the verse "Appoint over him a wicked man, [and may a *satan* stand at his right]" [Ps. 109:6] and intend the intentions of the judgments alluded within it. They should all look in his face when saying this verse forward and backward. If he is not subdued, the greatest should powerfully fortify himself, with great concentrated intention, and say in his ear the verse "Appoint" with its vocalizations, forward and backward, with the intention of all the names.

Everything must be prepared before him in writing, lest there be anything whatsoever missing of the names or the intentions, in the first letters, or the last letters, or the middle letters. If any change or sign of submission is seen in him, add twice or thrice the order of the verse, its intention, and similar material like the amulet I gave to the friend of God R. Benjamin Kohen of Reggio, according to the Rav, of blessed memory. You should write it in purity upon clean parchment and hang it upon her so that it help her.

If none of this proves remedial, please let me know if there are any of the signs I have mentioned, and if she tears her clothing, if her form changes, if her eyes are bloodshot, and so forth—all the details that you can specify. Then I will know what to do for her.

A Hasidic Exorcism

Once, a *dibbuk* came to the holy R. Elazar of Koznitz [rebbe from 1849 to 1862], may the memory of the righteous and holy be a blessing. Now, the *dibbuk* was in the body of a woman. . . . After a few days, the holy Rabbi R. Elazar said that [his son, the holy rabbi of Moglinza, and he] should go to their homes with her. Thus they did, and they went with her. It happened that on the way, the woman fainted and the *dibbuk* left her, and she recovered.

The holy rabbi wanted to play down the matter, and said that it was because she had eaten some cake at his holy sister Raizele's, that the *dibbuk* left her.

—31—

Rabbi Menahem Nahum of Chernobyl: Personal Practices of a Hasidic Master

Arthur Green

Hasidism is a mystical revival movement that began among east European Jews in the mid-eighteenth century. It started in Podolia, the southeastern corner of the old Polish kingdom, in what is today the Ukraine. Within the course of less than a hundred years it had spiritually "conquered" most of Polish Jewry and become a major force on the historical scene, transforming the formerly obscure and elitist Jewish mystical tradition into the basis for a broad-based popular religious movement. Until the present day, and despite many changes in its inner character, Hasidism has continued to play an important role in the religious and social life of the Jewish people.

From the outset, the Hasidic revival operated on two levels. On the one hand, it represents the fullest development of popular pietism among Ashkenazic Jews. It glorified the simple devotee over the learned rabbi; it offered access to the most profound sorts of religious experience to those who approached only with a humble heart and a passionate desire to do God's will. It took long-venerated terms and categories (especially the *sefirot,* the ten aspects of the Divinity), which for earlier mystics had referred to secrets of the inner life of God, and used them in the most casual way to refer to emotional experiences accessible to nearly anyone. On the other hand, Hasidism set out to create a new elite model of the *zaddik* (lit., "righteous one" or holy man; pl. *zaddikim*) who would serve as standard-bearer of the Hasidic message, model of the pious life, and actual channel for the flow of divine blessing into the lives of his adherents. These *zaddikim,* sometimes also called *rebbes* or teachers, and their descendants (dynastic leadership was copied from the pattern of eastern European nobility) came to serve as leaders of the various Hasidic communities, as they do to this day. Each rebbe bears the name of the town where his dynasty originated, carrying it with him even as the dynasty moves to another country or continent.

Hasidism was a movement originally disseminated mostly through oral teaching. Each week the rebbe would speak at his Sabbath table about the Torah portion read in the synagogue that week; these homilies were often memorized and were much discussed by his disciples. Only later were collections of such teachings committed to writing, published either by the master himself or posthumously by sons or followers. These collections of teachings became the "classic" writings of the Hasidic tradition. The oral homilies were accompanied by tales, stories about the rebbes themselves, parables for moral edification, or wondrous accounts of the deeds and rewards of simple pious souls. The tales remained an oral genre, growing and gaining embellishments as they passed from one generation to the next. Only much later (toward the turn of the twentieth century) were most of them committed to writing.

The text presented here belongs to a third (and much smaller) genre of Hasidic literature, called *hanhagot* or Regimens of Conduct. It became customary for religious figures to record for their disciples brief lists of personal practices to which they gave special attention. The list served as a sort of ethical testament, studied and followed carefully by family members and followers after the master's death. The custom of recording *hanhagot* is not limited to Hasidism. Its roots go back to the Middle Ages and the Pietistic communes of early Ashkenazic Jewry. In the great mystical revival of the late sixteenth century, centered around the Pietists of Safed, the custom became widespread among both Ashkenazic and Sephardic figures.

This text is published in Hebrew under the title *Hanhagot Yesharot* (*Upright Practices*) by Rabbi Menahem Nahum of Chernobyl (c. 1730–1798). The preacher of Chernobyl was one of the leading disciples of R. Dov Baer of Mezrich (Pol. Miedzyrzec), who turned the teachings of his own master, R. Israel Ba'al Shem Tov (1700–1760) into a religious movement to be spread throughout the Jewish world. The Ba'al Shem Tov was the charismatic spiritual figure in whose image Hasidism was created. Throughout the movement's history, each *hasid* (devotee) has traced his own relationship back, through a chain of masters and disciples, to the Ba'al Shem Tov. R. Dov Baer, the *maggid* (preacher) of Mezrich, was the mystical ideologue and driving force behind the movement's spread. After his death in 1772, each of the followers led in his own way, and Hasidism began to take on distinctive dynastic and regional variations.

R. Menahem Nahum, a traveling preacher, made his home in Chernobyl, a mostly Jewish townlet near Kiev. He was succeeded by his son, R. Mordecai of Chernobyl (1770–1837), one of the most popular and powerful Hasidic leaders of his day. During this period the family took on the surname Twersky. R. Mordecai was father to eight sons, each of whom, and many of whose further sons and grandsons, became rebbes in various Ukrainian towns, mostly in the areas south and west of Kiev. The *hanhagot* of R. Menahem Nahum, along with his collected homilies *Me'or 'Eynayim* (The Light of the Eyes), are seen as foundational documents to the various dynasties that spring from this family tree, including those of Tolne, Skvira, Rakhmastrivka, Hornistopl, Trisk, and, through marriage, the various dynasties of the Ruzhin-Sadegora line. Several of these dynasties continue to exist, their centers now located either in Israel or the United States.

Lists of *hanhagot* were among the tools used to give each Hasidic group its particular coloring. Bear in mind that these lists were issued to communities that were already committed to living wholly within the strict regimen of *halakhah* or the "path" of Jewish law. Careful observance of the Sabbath, thrice-daily prayers, and countless other traditional practices could be taken for granted. The *hanhagot* of the rebbe lay atop this universally accepted grid of halakhic praxis. Its point (as our author quotes in the third paragraph below), is to "sanctify yourself within the realm of that which is permitted." Even the full halakhic life with all its restrictions and obligations does not automatically make for holiness. The Hasidic revival comes about because Jews who observe the Law in all its detail can still do so without sufficient *kavvanah,* inner spiritual direction. It is this lack that Hasidism comes to fulfill. True, every deed is to be filled with *kavvanah,* for there is no deed, place, or moment where God is not to be found. "God needs to be served in every way," as the Hasidic sources have it. That message, well conveyed in our text, is of the essence of Hasidism. Nevertheless, the rebbe took special care in *these* matters and you, as his disciple, are to give them extra attention as well.

Hasidism, like the Kabbalah that precedes it, is a mystical tradition overlaid on a revelation-based normative tradition of great antiquity. Although some of the roots that shape later mystic expression may be as old as the tradition itself, the mystical language and theology are fairly late. Thus Hasidism constantly struggles, for example, to find elements of its own semi-pantheistic God concept in the highly personified theology of the biblical and early rabbinic sources. Hasidism's well-known emphasis on joy and a sense of well-being as required for God's service sometimes seem to fly in the face of the rabbis' denigration of this world as the place of tears and scene of our bitter exile. The Hasidic faith that God is everywhere and that all things can be vessels of God's service sometimes seems belied by the very strong distinctions made in the normative tradition between holy and profane, permitted and forbidden, pure and defiled. Although the *Hasidim* lived wholly within the norms of halakhic praxis, in theory they were constantly seeking to stretch its limits.

The texts translated here are partly from the original edition of 1817 and partly from those additional *hanhagot* of R. Menahem Nahum first printed in *Razin de-Orayta* (Secrets of the Torah) of Ze'ev Sevi of Zbarash (Warsaw, n. p., 1903).

Further Reading

The full text of the *Hanhagot Yesharot* has been translated by the author of this chapter as *Upright Practices,* published together with *The Light of the Eyes* in the

Classics of Western Spirituality series (New York: Paulist Press, 1982). Although there is no current history of Hasidism that can be recommended, Gershon Hundert's *Essential Papers on Hasidism* (New York: New York University Press, 1990) contains some important materials. More recent scholarly studies are found in *Hasidism Reappraised,* edited by Ada Rapoport-Albert (London: Littman Library, 1996). A beginner's guide to understanding Hasidic texts is the author's "Teachings of the Hasidic Masters" in Barry W. Holtz, *Back to the Sources* (New York: Summit Books, 1984). Topically arranged selections from Hasidic sources are to be found in Louis Jacobs's *Hasidic Thought* (New York: Behrman House, 1984), and in Norman Lamm's *The Religious Thought of Hasidism* (New York: Yeshiva University Press, 1999). The only scholarly treatment of the *hanhagot* themselves is Ze'ev Gries's *Sifrut ha-Hanhagot* (in Hebrew) (Jerusalem: Bialik Institute, 1989).

TEXT 1

1. "The beginning of wisdom is the fear of the Lord" [Ps. 1:10]; keep this ever before you. Believe with full faith that the Creator, blessed be He, the King of Kings whose glory fills all the earth, stands before you in each moment and sees all your deeds, both those that are public and those hidden in the depths of your heart. This should lead you to a constant sense of shame, of which Scripture says: "So that His fear be on your faces and you will not sin" [Exod. 20:20]. On this verse the sages asked: "How is the fear of God present on a person's face? And they answered: "In shame."

2. Purify your mind and thought from thinking too many different thoughts. You have only to think about one thing: serving God in joy. The word BeSiMHaH [In Joy] has the same letters as MaHaShaBaH [thought]; all thoughts that come to you should be included in this single one. [Serving God in joy is one of the essential pillars of Hasidism.] Of this Scripture speaks in "Many are the thoughts in a person's mind, but it is the counsel of the Lord that will stand" [Prov. 19:21]. Understand this.

3. Our rabbis say: "Sanctify yourself within the realm of that which is permitted." In the moment of sexual union turn your thought to the sake of heaven. Recite the prayer of the RaMBaN [Rabbi Moses ben Nahman] as it is printed in *The Gates of Zion.* [Before the sex act] say: "For the sake of the union of the Holy One, blessed be he, with His *Shekhinah.* . . ." [The physical union of man and wife is taken as an earthly replica of the union of "male" and "female" forces within divinity.] See further what is written in the *Shulhan 'Arukh, Orah Hayyim* [R. Joseph Caro's Code of Jewish Law], section two hundred forty, concerning holiness before the act of union. Remember how careful the sages sought to be concerning this holiness.

4. Give as much in alms as you are able, as Scripture says "You establish me in righteousness" [= almsgiving; Isa. 54:14]. How good and pleasant it is to

have a box for alms and to place three coins in it (or at least one) before each prayer. Before eating too you should set aside a coin.

5. Fast one day in each week. Be alone with your Maker on that day and confess explicitly all your sins against Him, even those of your youth. Be ashamed and ask forgiveness; cry, for "all the gates are locked except that of tears." Then turn back to rejoicing over the fact that you have attained full repentance.

6. Keep away from depression to the utmost degree. Thus you will be saved from several sins, especially those of anger and pride. Be intelligent and judicious in the matter of worry over your sins. Depart from them with a whole heart, ask God for forgiveness, and then serve Him wholeheartedly. Have complete faith [in the effectiveness of your repentance], following the rabbis' teaching: "If a man betrothes a woman on the condition that he be a righteous person, that woman is considered betrothed, even if he had been [well-known to be] completely wicked. He might have had a thought of repentance."

7. Fulfill the teaching of the *Sayings of the Fathers* that teaches: "Be of very, very humble spirit before every person." When you see a wicked person, say in your heart "Even he is greater than I." "The more the knowledge, the greater the pain" [Eccles. 1:18].

8. Pray and study with fear and love. [Love and fear of God, the key emotions of the religious life, must be held in proper balance.] Know that the letters [of the text before you] are called heaven and earth, and that all the worlds and all creatures great and small are given life by His word. "This is the whole of man" [Eccles. 12:13]. Understand this.

9. Keep yourself from being cross toward your household in any matter. Let your speech be pleasant, for "the words of the wise are heard when pleasant" [Eccles. 9:17].

10. Cleave to the wise and to their disciples; learn always from their deeds. Keep away from people who do not have good qualities of character. This is the main thing: good qualities.

11. Study books of moral teaching each day, something on the order of *The Beginning of Wisdom* [by R. Elijah De Vidas, first published in Venice, 1579]. That work is filled to overflowing with wisdom, fear of God, and praiseworthy qualities.

12. Keep away from having your head turned; accept not a drop of human praise. Praise that you receive from people is to be considered a great liability. Those who speak ill of you are in fact doing you a great favor. Your intent should be only for the sake of His great Name, to do that which is pleasing to Him.

13. Accept whatever portion the Lord gives you in love, whether it be for good or for illness and suffering. Thus did our rabbis teach on "with all your might"

[Deut. 6:5]—thank God for every portion that He gives you, whether good or ill. "Evil does not come from the mouth of the most high" [Lam. 3:38], but only good. Compare this to those bitter medicines that are needed to heal the body. The same are needed for healing the soul.

14. If you find yourself unable to study or pray with fear and love, continue in any case to engage in study and to recite your prayers to God with complete faith. This is what the rabbis have taught: "A person should ever involve himself with Torah and the commandments, even if not for their own sake." "Not for their own sake" means that even if he has no fear or love, he should keep doing them for the sake of heaven. They also said: "From doing them [even if] not for their own sake, he will reach the stage of doing for their own sake," that is, he will attain to fear and love. Of this the prophet speaks when he says, "'Are not my words like fire?' says the Lord" [Jer. 23:29]. [The words of study and prayer are so powerful that they will ignite the proper religious emotions.]

15. Perform many acts of loving-kindness: dowering poor brides, visiting the sick, and all the other things of which the sages spoke. This is one of three things that stand at the very pinnacle of the world order. Praise no one and speak ill of no one. The Baʿal Shem Tov has already said it: "If you want to praise anyone, praise God; if you want to speak ill of anyone, speak ill of yourself" and know your lowly state. If you possess some good quality, it belongs not to you but to God. Thus Scripture says: "Let not the wise man praise himself for his wisdom, nor the rich man for his wealth" [Jer. 9:22]. All this was given to you by God. Your bad qualities—those are indeed your own.

16. Remember God always: "I place YHVH ever before me" [Ps. 16:8]. If you fail to do so even for a moment it is considered a sin. Thus the Baʿal Shem Tov taught on "Blessed is the man for whom God does not think of a sin" [Ps. 32:2]. ["What does the verse mean?"] he asked. "Does the Lord give up on sins?" Rather interpret it this way: When a person does not think of God—when God is out of his thoughts—that is sin. Consider this to be a very grave matter. Thus you will take care and not forget Him. Such a person [one whose thoughts never depart from God] is indeed blessed.

17. Each day study from the Torah, Prophets, and Writings, from the Mishnah and the Gemara [Talmud], each in accord with your own abilities. Do it all for the sake of God's great name, and for no other purpose. "Then you will walk surely on your way."

18. Take care, insofar as possible, not to speak before [the morning] prayer. Do so only for very great need. Consider your deeds before you pray, and repent of them. Humble your heart by considering your own smallness and lowliness. Thus will you prepare all the rungs of your soul to receive some bit of the fear of heaven as you stand before Him. Of this Scripture says: "Prepare to meet your God, O Israel" [Amos 4:12].

TEXT 2

Know first that God exists. He was first, and He created all things, both above and below. His creations are without end!

All began with a single point—the point of supernal wisdom, *hokhmah*. The power of the Creator is present in all of His creations; the wisdom of God fills and takes on the garb of every thing that is. Of this Scripture speaks in saying: "Wisdom gives life to those who possess it" [Eccles. 7:12].

Believe with a whole and strong faith that the Creator is one, single, and united. He is the first of all causes and origins, utterly endless, blessed is He and blessed is His name. He created many worlds, higher and lower, without limit and without end. Of these Scripture says: "Worlds without number" [Song of Songs 6:8; a word play of *'alamot* and *'olamot*].

Believe with a whole and strong faith that He both fills all the worlds and surrounds them, that He is both within and beyond them all. He created the lower world for the sake of the Torah and Israel, that His blessed divine Self might be revealed. There is no King without His people Israel.

Believe with a whole and strong faith that "the whole earth is full of His glory" [Isa. 6:3] and that "there is no place devoid of Him." His blessed glory inhabits all that is. This glory serves as a garment, as the sages taught: "Rabbi Yohanan called his garment 'glory.'" His divine Self wears all things as one wears a cloak, as Scripture teaches: "You give life to them all" [Neh. 9:6]. This applies even to the forces of evil, in accord with the secret of "His kingdom rules over all" [Ps. 103:19]. All life is sustained by the flow that issues forth from Him. Were the life flow to cease even for a moment, all that is sustained by it would become but an empty breath, as though it had never been.

Believe with a whole faith that the slightest motion of your little finger can move great spiritual worlds above, as the Ba'al Shem Tov has taught.

Believe with whole faith that man contains all the worlds within him, as the ARI [R. Isaac Luria, famous kabbalist of the sixteenth century], the holy *Zohar* [the great book of kabbalistic teachings], and various midrashim have taught. This being the case, God must be proclaimed King through every single deed we do, through study and prayer as well as fulfilling the commandments [for thus is His kingdom proclaimed] over all our limbs. Even ordinary conversation must be made holy.

God's sight should be brought into our daily words and thoughts. With every word and with each thought we must cleave again to their root in God, since it is only by His power that we think or speak. When you have full faith in this, You will come to realize that all the events of your life have come about through God. Whether or not they have turned out as you wanted, you will consider them all to be for the good, since "evil does not come from the mouth of the most high" [Lam. 3:38], but only good. Of this I have spoken earlier. Within every bad thing there dwells His power of goodness, that which gives it life. This can be seen only by one whose eyes are properly directed; otherwise the veils of sin tend to intervene and blind the human eye. To purify your sight, do not look beyond your own four ells; these will be the four letters of the name YHWH, that which calls all being to be. [Here the "four ells" or the narrow boundaries of *halakhah* are interpreted mystically, to stand for the four letters of the divine Name.]

Mend all your bad qualities by means of goodness; subsume the left within the right, as the holy *Zohar* has taught. [Cultivate] all those qualities of which the pious authors speak. Then the good will gain in strength and lift itself out of the evil in which it had been enshrouded. Once evil is left on its own it will vanish altogether, and then our righteous Messiah will arrive—speedily and in our day! Amen. Selah.

Believe all of the above with a whole faith, and at every single moment be prepared to give your life for it . . . .

. . . By holding fast to the praise of God, by singing the hymns of Israel's sweet singer [the psalms of David] you will be able to destroy the accusing and evil forces. Indeed King David prayed that his songs would be sung in the synagogues and houses of study. By them we can restore the crown to its former place, and the lily [*Shekhinah* or the divine presence, "asleep" in exile] will awaken.

Be among those who take stock of themselves each night before they lie down. Give an account of your sins and repent of them. Even a thought of repentance will suffice. Since *teshuvah* [repentance, return to God] was one of the seven things that preceded the world into existence, time does not apply to it, and thus a thought alone will do to "sweeten" all. In this way you can send forth your soul (all three of its levels) to rise upward to the place of contemplation.

Rise up from sleep at midnight, for that is a time when God's desire is especially to be found. Serve him in the midst of night and perform the midnight vigil [prayers instituted by the kabbalists to mourn the exile and increase Israel's longing for redemption]. As that vigil is joined to your morning prayer, you will be unified and will attach yourself to that which is above; then you will be able to bring forth whatever it is that you seek from God. Midnight prayer and service is a great thing; it is this that brings about peace above. If not for this, God forbid, those who are joined together [the transcendent God and his indwelling presence] would be separated.

Take special care when reciting the *Shemaʿ* to pronounce each word. See that you are not distracted, at least not during the *Shemaʿ* (the twice-daily proclamation of God's unity), but recite it in fear and love. Each letter you recite in this way will help to bring life to your limbs.

See too that you honor the Sabbath as fully as you are able within your means. Do so with food and drink and in other ways as well. The letters of SHaBbaT are those of TaSHeB [return], to indicate that "he who keeps the

Sabbath, even if he is as idolatrous as was the generation of Enosh, will be forgiven."

Here is a basic principle: The root of all things is in almsgiving. By this deed you uplift the sparks from their broken state, and in this way you uplift your own self as well. The letters of ZeDaQaH [almsgiving] contain the letters of ZeDeQ [righteousness]. In acting as a ZaDDiQ you are a holy spark of the cosmic ZaDDIQ, [by your righteous act you partake in the Zaddiq's uplifting of *zedeq-shekhinah*], from poverty and exile. Enough said. [The ways in which the commandments allow humans to partake of divinity are among the secrets of the Kabbalah, not to be discussed publicly.]

Here is the rule: By any holy deed or by any life-sustaining alms that you offer to the poor, you uplift a holy spark that lay amid the evil forces, and thus you come to holiness. No "act of holiness" can take place, however, in the presence of fewer than ten [a *minyan* or quorum of ten Jews, required for public ritual], and those ten are in turn a hundred. In this way is ZeDaQaH formed, and thus is a soul uplifted from its broken state.

This too is a basic principle: See that you bring your own negative qualities to submission. Hold fast to good qualities. In this way too you will cause sparks to rise from their broken state. This is why a person must recite a hundred blessings each day. The meaning of this is as follows: "Blessings" refer to the pond above [BeRaKHaH, "blessing" = BeReKHaH, "pond"] and the streams that flow forth from it. You have to bring about the flow of these hundred blessings upon you, these hundred that also represent the ten good qualities. Overcome your own bad qualities and cleave to Him, bless His name, and in every way bring down the flow of His bounty upon you.

When you stand up to pray, decide first that you will attach yourself only to pure and virtuous thoughts, rejecting this lowly world down to the very last degree. Thus you may bring yourself to the most sublime joy of spirit, becoming joined to Him in a wondrous way. In this you attain to *malkhut,* the "I" of God. Thence you may bind yourself further and enter into a state of union, until you reach the Nothing, the World of Contemplation, that which is referred to as "Who?" Of this the sages say, "Know before *Whom* you stand," meaning that: You stand before the "Who" [the mysterious, unknowable Godhead]. Unification means that you not separate mind from words, especially during the 'amidah [prayers], when the true union and coupling takes place. In this way that union may come to be revealed in the lower world as well. Amen. May this be His will.

When you awake at midnight, as we have suggested above, be sure that your very first thought is that of attachment to God. How great is the Creator! He has just restored your soul to you! As you glorify God, ask yourself for what purpose He has sent that soul back to you. Realize that it is for the sake of His service, that you serve Him with soul through Torah, worship, and commandments. As you begin to pray, accept the fact that you worship Him even though your soul may pass out of you in prayer. Keep your thought fastened on your blessed Creator throughout the day.

Do the same with your emotions: [Here begins a list of the seven lower *sefirot*, (aspects of divinity) understood by Hasidic authors as the divine roots of human emotions. The seven are described here as love, fear, glory, victory, praiseworthiness, attachment, and kingship.] Should something like improper love of this-worldly pleasure be aroused in you, know that it stems from a spark of divine *hesed* [love]. You have caused that spark to fall into the hands of evil; it alone gives life to those evil forces. It is within your power to uplift those holy sparks, to separate the proper food from that which is to be cast aside, to find the hidden good. The Creator has so made it that we might have a choice: "See that I place before you life and death, good and evil. Choose life . . ." [Deut. 30:19].

Treat all other emotions and human qualities in the same manner: improper desire for glory, for praise, improper attachments and loyalties.

Fear no one but God. Scripture's words "The fear of the Lord is His treasure" [Isa. 33:6] are to be understood thus: [Our] awe before His greatness is God's own treasure. There are various types of fear, to be sure, but [the true treasure is] that sense of awe before His greatness, fear of the Lord because He is Master and Ruler, indeed the very source of all the worlds. Such awe will lead you to serve Him with all your strength and intensity. No longer will you be pulled away by the attractions of this lowly and despicable world. Day by day you will grow in the strength of His service. You will do this not for fear of death, of punishment, or of hell: all of these are nought in the face of your true fear of the Creator.

Further: Do not *glorify* yourself, however great your learning or your good deeds, your wealth or your fine qualities. Glory belongs only to God.

So too all the rest. Do not *triumph* over any person. Grant triumph only to Him, His alone is the only true victory. Yours is rather to triumph over your evil urge, that which leads you away from the good and into the path of evil.

Further: If people should come to *praise* you, do not let it lead you to self-importance. Rather give praise constantly to God, to Him who created you out of nothing and brought you into being. It is He who sustains you from your mother's womb unto the very day of your death. Were the Creator's concern to depart from you for but a moment, you would not survive that moment in the world.

Further: with regard to *attachment*. Attach your thought always to the Creator; do not turn it away even for a moment to think of the vanities of this world. As soon as you turn your thought elsewhere you are considered as an idolator, as Scripture says: "You will turn aside and worship other gods" [Deut. 11:16]. [As soon as you turn away from the Lord, you are inevitably worshiping other gods.]

Further: with regard to *kingship*. Proclaim God King over all your limbs; "Let there be in you no other god" [Ps. 81:10]. On this verse the sages ask:

"Who is the "other god" that dwells inside the human heart?" Their answer: "The evil urge and his retinue are called by this name."

God has made everything in parallel form: As there are seven holy qualities, so are there seven evil ones parallel to them. It was so made in order to "grant reward to the righteous who sustain a world that was created by ten utterances," who triumph over the seven wicked qualities and cleave to God through their own goodness, breaking down the evil urge and those that support it. So too in order to "take leave of the wicked who destroy a world that was created through ten utterances," who spend all their days in pursuit of their own desires, seeking out the pleasures of this lowly and despicable world. In doing so they deny the One, Single, and Unified God. In the end they will have to give account to the King of Kings, the Holy One, blessed be He, for every single one of their deeds.

Should someone whisper to you, however, that he is so thoroughly defiled by the stain of sin that there is no repentance for him—God forbid that this be the case! There is nothing that stands in the way of repentance, for repentance was one of those seven things that preceded the Creation itself. No force of judgment has a place there, and just a thought—a thought of complete repentance and resolve never to return to that folly—will suffice to gain forgiveness for all one's sins. From that day forward, of course, one must cleave firmly to God and break down all one's bad qualities. Of this the rabbis said: "Whoever sacrifices his own [evil] qualities has all his sins forgiven. Subjugate your evil qualities and rise above them. Join your mind to your body [for the upper three *sefirot*, representing the mind, are like the seven lower ones, the bodily emotions], and rise above all these measured qualities to that place where there is no judgment at all.

Raise everything to the level of *binah* and there it will all be "sweetened," as the *Zohar* says: Even though *binah* is the source of judgment-forces [*binah* is the mother of the seven lower *sefirot*, including *din*, the force of judgment], it is only in their root that they can be transformed. Then are all your sins forgiven. Everything you have done up to that day, however, you will still have to weigh, all in accord with the pleasure you took in this world and its delights. The same will apply to all the other qualities. You must bring yourself to sorrow over this, fasting regularly on Mondays and Thursdays, either those following Passover or those following Sukkot, during the weeks referred to as *shovevim tat* [an acronym for the first eight Torah portions from the Book of Exodus]. So too every eve of the new moon, considered to be a small Day of Atonement. Fasting on that day has to do with the waning of the moon. We have mentioned its meaning above: The *Shekhinah* is in exile, as Scripture says: "I am with him in sorrow" [Ps. 91:15]. You have to participate in the *Shekhinah*'s suffering.

Remarkable Lives

32

The Life of Moses ben Maimon

Joel L. Kraemer

Moses son of Maimon (also known as Maimonides) was born in Cordoba, Spain, in about 1138. The conventional date of his birth, 1135, still widely accepted, is erroneous. The 1135 date is based upon information given in a problematic text by Moses ben Maimon's grandson David (Text 3), whereas the correct date, accepted by scholars like S. D. Goitein, Joseph Kafah, S. Z. Havlin, and M. A. Friedman, is based upon what Moses ben Maimon himself says at the end of his *Commentary on the Mishnah* (Text 1). The actual birth date of about 1138 is accepted by the *Hebrew Encyclopaedia* and appears on the Israeli thousand-shekel note issued in 1984. As Moses ben Maimon was born in about 1138, he was around ten, and not thirteen, when he and his family were forced to leave Cordoba in the wake of the Almohad invasion in 1148.

Abu 'Imran Musa b Maymun al-Qurtubi (al-Isra'ili al-Andalusi), as he appears in Arabic sources, was an Andalusian to the core of his being. He places himself squarely in a Spanish tradition of learning. At the beginning of the *Letter to Yemen*, he parries his correspondents' flattery by modestly proclaiming his inferiority to his countrymen, saying: "I am one of the least of the sages of Spain whose adornment has been stripped in *Exile*." He looked to the sages of Sefarad as his authorities in legal matters. Foremost among his Andalusian masters in jurisprudence, along with his father, were the esteemed R. Isaac Alfasi and his great Lucenan heir R. Joseph ibn Megas, whom Moses ben Maimon reverently called "my teacher."

A popular tradition relates that Moses ben Maimon was a descendant of R. Judah ha-Nasi, the redactor of the Mishnah, and thus traced his genealogy back to King David. Moses ben Maimon makes no mention of this in his writings, however, and we may dismiss it as legendary. He was the son of a scholar, R. Maimon, and the scion of an illustrious succession of sages that he traces back seven generations (Text 1).

After leaving Cordoba, Moses ben Maimon and his family spent a number of years wandering throughout Spain, settling for a while in Almeria, before finally emigrating in 1159 or 1160 to Fez, Morocco. The Almohads (al-Muwahhidun, or Unitarians), a radical Muslim religio-political movement that held sway in Spain and North Africa, gave non-Muslims the option of conversion to Islam, exile, or death. It was under these circumstances that Moses ben Maimon wrote his *Epistle on Apostasy* (*Iggeret ha-Shemad*) (Text 2), a sequel to the *Epistle of Consolation* (*Iggeret ha-Nehamah*), by his father, R. Maimon, which had been written to reassure the ailing community that there was divine solicitude and future redemption. In Moses ben Maimon's *Epistle on Apostasy,* sent out to Jewish communities in Morocco, the young scholar permitted Jews to feign Islam while practicing Judaism secretly. He strongly recommended, however, that they leave the country and find a safer place where they could practice Judaism openly.

Arabic sources report that during this period Moses ben Maimon practiced Islam under duress. The main informant for this account is Jamal al-Din Ibn al-Qifti in his *Ta'rikh al-Hukama'* (*History of the Sages*) (Text 4). Ibn al-Qifti was a contemporary of Moses ben Maimon, who probably knew him in Cairo, where Ibn al-Qifti lived until 1187. Later in Aleppo, Ibn al-Qifti befriended Joseph, son of Judah, originally from Ceuta in Morocco. Joseph was Moses ben Maimon's pupil and the addressee of the *Guide of the Perplexed.* Ibn al-Qifti relates that when the Christians and Jews of Morocco were forced to convert to Islam, Joseph concealed his true religion and practiced Islam publicly, an account similar to the one about Moses ben Maimon. Although Ibn al-Qifti's book has come down to us in a later recension, and contains some errors, we have no reason to doubt the information on Moses ben Maimon and Joseph, son of Judah. That they simulated the practice of Islam is explicable under the circumstances.

Moses ben Maimon and his family eventually left Morocco in April 1165, embarking from the port of Ceuta, and traveled east to the land of Israel. He describes his voyage and sojourn in the land of Israel in a record of dates to be commemorated (Text 3). During the voyage, the sea became stormy and the ship almost went under. Moses ben Maimon, his household, and descendants commemorated this deliverance from a near-death experience with an annual fast. Eventually, the family disembarked safely in Acre. "And thus," says Moses, "I was saved from apostasy." About four months later, the family traveled from Acre to Jerusalem, "at a time of danger." This was, after all, the Crusader period, and the Christians were then in Jerusalem. After praying at the site of the temple, the group visited the tombs of the Patriarchs in Hebron. Moses speaks elsewhere about visiting the holy place. In his letter to Japheth, son of Elijah (Text 5), he recalls this visit: "For I, he [David] and my father, my teacher, may the memory of the righteous be a blessing, and you, all four of us, walked together in God's house in fear and trepidation. I shall not forget our wandering together in wastelands and forests after the Lord." And in the Epistle to Yemen, he speaks of departing from the West, "to gaze upon the graciousness of the Lord, to frequent His holy place" (see Ps. 27:4).

Finding no means of livelihood and threatened by the perils of warfare, the family left the land of Israel, most likely by sea, and made their way to Egypt. In

1166, they arrived in Alexandria, where they stayed for some time before finally settling in Fustat (Old Cairo).

In Fustat, Moses ben Maimon first traded in precious stones, and also taught science and philosophy (Text 4). This was toward the end of the Fatimid dynasty, some time between 1166 and 1171. According to Ibn al-Qifti in this text, members of the ruling dynasty wanted to send Moses ben Maimon to serve as physician to the king of the Franks in Ascalon, but he declined. An account in popular biographies (for instance, Yellin and Abrahams; see Further Reading) relates that Moses b. Maimon was summoned to Ascalon to serve as physician to Richard I the Lionhearted (Coeur-de-Lion) (reigned 1189–1199), but refused the invitation because he preferred Cairo to the prospect of London. Ibn al-Qifti merely says that the Franks requested a physician from Cairo to attend to their king in Ascalon, that the Egyptians chose Moses ben Maimon, and that he refused. As the incident apparently occurred between 1166 and 1171, the Frankish king was probably Amalric I and not King Richard I, as has been shown by Bernard Lewis (see Further Reading).

Early in his stay in Egypt, Moses ben Maimon completed his *Commentary on the Mishnah* (1168), a work written in Arabic, begun when he was twenty-three, during the years of wandering (Text 1). In the course of these early years, he also wrote his *Treatise on Logic,* a work on the calendar, and his *Hilkhot ha-Yerushalmi,* summaries of laws from the Jerusalem Talmud.

In 1172, he wrote a letter to the Jews of Yemen (*Iggeret Teman*), who were suffering from forced apostasy, as had the Jews in Spain and North Africa. He writes to lift the spirits of Yemenite Jews who were enduring the torment of forced conversion, pinning illusionary hopes on a messianic figure. Moses ben Maimon places their anguish within a divine plan, assuring them that it will end, that a real messianic advent awaits them in the near future. He writes as a physician, a healer who sends a pharmacopoeia, a medicine of the soul, a restorative that relieves pain and distress: "Our hearts languish and our minds are confused, our strength falters because of the great troubles that have come upon us, the forced apostasy at the two ends of the world, east and west." It was a time of wavering faith and despondency. Like many before him, Moses ben Maimon perceived catastrophe, wars, revolutions, and apostasy as presentiments of the footsteps of the Messiah. He says that many of his contemporaries, their confidence shaken, depressed by the infirmity of the Jewish people and by the exultation of its adversaries, went astray, abandoning the faith, although others never strayed into doubt or betrayed their belief. Like Abraham bar Hiyya and others, Moses ben Maimon evidently viewed the Crusades as the ultimate dramatic showdown between the two world powers, Christendom and Islam, and as a prelude to the final Redemption of Israel. He sees these events as messianic travails, a harbinger of the restoration of prophecy and a messianic advent in the near future. A powerful motive of Moses ben Maimon in compiling his legal compendium, the *Mishneh Torah,* and a driving force in his composition of the *Guide* was the aim of reconstituting the Jewish people as an excellent community, as wise and understanding, to prepare it for the advent of the anticipated messianic age.

In the years 1168 to 1178, Moses ben Maimon wrote his monumental compendium of Jewish law, the *Mishneh Torah*. Prior to this, he had written the *Book of Commandments* as a kind of prelude to the *Mishneh Torah;* in it he listed the 613 commandments and posited principles for identifying and enumerating them. The *Mishneh Torah* established his reputation worldwide and for all times as the authority par excellence on legal matters. Moses ben Maimon's authoritative rank is shown by the fact that even Joseph Caro, famous author of the *Shulhan ʿArukh* law code, takes the *Mishneh Torah* as a foundation for his formulations and legal determinations.

Moses ben Maimon explains in a letter to his pupil Joseph both his motives for composing the *Mishneh Torah* and the disappointing reception it had (Text 6). He expresses similar thoughts in a letter to a judge, R. Phineas. The judge had expressed the anxiety of many that Moses ben Maimon's failure to note in his legal compendium the names of rabbinic authorities, the Tannaim and Amoraim, would cause the sages to be totally forgotten, and that people would cease studying the Talmud, as the *Mishneh Torah* would replace it.

At the beginning of the Ayyubid dynasty (after 1171), al-Qadi al-Fadil—Saladin's advisor, chancellor, and chief administrator—took Moses ben Maimon under his wing and gave him a stipend (Text 4). Al-Fadil was the most prominent man of the age after Saladin, and was, along with members of the royal family, the sultan's surrogate when he was away from Cairo. He was also an intellectual, a bibliophile, and great epistolary stylist and litterateur. One could not climb in the political and social hierarchy without the protection of a powerful patron, and Moses ben Maimon's career followed the meteoric ascent of his benefactor.

Al-Fadil had good reasons for extending his patronage to his Jewish colleague. Moses ben Maimon was already a leader of the Jewish community, having directed campaigns to ransom Crusader captives imprisoned at Bilbays in Egypt, in 1168, and in the Nile delta region. He was erudite, and he was a physician. Furthermore, I suggest, al-Fadil and Moses ben Maimon had mutual commercial interests. Al-Fadil had accumulated great wealth through the India and Maghreb (Northwest Africa) trade. Moses ben Maimon also engaged in commerce, certainly the India trade and presumably also the Maghreb trade. From al-Fadil's point of view, Moses ben Maimon could be a loyal ally who would assure unswerving support by the Jewish community of the new Ayyubid dynasty and assistance in the struggle against the Crusaders. From Moses ben Maimon's vantage point, the eminent al-Fadil could represent the interests of the Jewish community in the corridors of power. It was a friendship based upon mutual benefit but also mutual respect, common intellectual concerns, and personal affection. When a Muslim jurist, a man from Ceuta, accused Moses ben Maimon of having converted to Islam and then reverting to Judaism, a crime punishable by death according to Islamic law, al-Qadi al-Fadil saved his friend's life by arguing that forced conversion was invalid (Text 4).

Moses ben Maimon assumed the position of Ra'is al-Yahud (Head of the Jews) around the time when Salah al-Din (Saladin) ascended to the throne of the sultanate (September 1171). His rise to power thus coincided with the ascension of the Ayyubids and was most likely due to his friendship with al-Qadi al-Fadil, who was instrumental in the Ayyubid victory.

As Moses ben Maimon emerged to communal prominence, he also began to serve as physician to the royal court as a protégé of al-Fadil. The court physician also acted as an advisor to the sovereign. The two roles, head of the Jewish community and court Jew, traditionally went hand in hand in Egypt.

Moses ben Maimon lived in Egypt for nearly forty years, and was totally immersed in the cultural life of his Arab-Islamic milieu. He moved in the highest intellectual and political circles in Cairo. He writes to his pupil Joseph, son of Judah (*Epistulae,* ed. Baneth, p. 69): "I tell you that I have already acquired a very great reputation in medicine among the distinguished men [of the kingdom], such as the supreme judge [Sadr al-Din ibn Durbas], the amirs [army officers], the court of al-Fadil, and other leaders of the country, from whom one does not receive a thing." Whether Moses ben Maimon served as physician to Saladin is uncertain. He did administer to members of the sultan's family, including his son al-Malik al-Afdal and his nephew Taqi al-Din 'Umar. He also befriended, perhaps through al-Qadi al-Fadil, members of Cairo's intellectual elite, including the well-known poet Ibn Sana' al-Mulk, whose flattering lines of verse on Moses ben Maimon are often quoted (Text 9).

During the early part of his residence in Egypt, Moses ben Maimon's father, R. Maimon, died, and his younger brother David was drowned during a voyage to India. When Moses was about forty-one, he wrote a letter to Japheth, son of Elijah of Acre, whom he had befriended during his brief stay in the Holy Land in 1165 (Text 5). In this letter, written eight years after the event (in 1491 Seleucid Era [as I read the colophon of Vatican MS Neofiti 11/16, 104b] = 1179 C.E.), Moses ben Maimon mentions calamities in his early years in Egypt, including sickness, financial disaster, and conspiracies of informers to have him killed. But the greatest misfortune that befell him in his lifetime, he says, was the drowning of his brother David in the Indian Sea. Moses reacted severely to news of David's death. He describes a terrible condition, a paralyzing melancholy lasting for a year, from which he almost died. "All joy," he says, "is gone." Moses ben Maimon's symptoms point to a clinical depression, which may occur when a person sensitized by stressful life events, especially loss and separation, confronts a situation of extreme adversity such as the demise of a loved one. Moses ben Maimon had invested in David's business ventures. As a result of this tragedy, Moses was compelled to take up medicine as a profession, not merely as an avocation and course of study. He maintained an interest in commercial trade, however, as can be deduced from his later correspondence.

As the head of the Jews in Egypt, Moses ben Maimon had broad communal responsibilities. Despite his onerous schedule, he supervised the most minute details of communal activity. In a letter preserved in the Cairo Genizah (Text 7), he writes to a community official instructing him about the removal of earth from some communal property, and advises him concerning a cow that was kept on the property and a tenant farmer, a Muslim named ʿAli al-Sharawi. We find this attention to details of public life in the conduct of Muslim rulers in their exercise of justice within their societies. In Moses ben Maimon's case it was also an act of imitatio dei, of following in God's ways as governor of the universe and bestower of providential care, mercy, loving-kindness, and justice. While deeply mired in quotidian affairs and communal issues, Moses ben Maimon constantly sought solitude, and his life was a struggle to attain the quietude he needed for contemplation and the intellectual love of God for which he yearned with such passion (see *Guide of the Perplexed,* III. 51).

Moses ben Maimon married into a prominent family, another factor in his star's rise in Egypt. He married the daughter of Abu al-Mahasin Mishaʾel al-Shaykh al-Thiqa, sister of a prominent scribe, Abu al-Maʿali, who married Moses ben Maimon's sister. In June 1186 (when Moses ben Maimon was about forty-eight years old), his son Abraham was born; Abraham was to follow in his father's footsteps as physician, philosopher, and communal leader. In a document written when Abraham had reached adolescence, (c. 1200), Moses ben Maimon writes in praise of his son, saying that "When I consider the condition of this world, I find consolation only in two things: in contemplating and studying and in my son Abraham" (Text 8). He had written previously in his letter to Japheth (Text 5), "And were it not for the Torah, which is my delight, and for scientific matters, which let me forget my sorrow, 'I would have perished in my affliction' " (Psa. 119:92). These were hard times for Moses ben Maimon, a period that also witnessed a horrific epidemic, one of the worst plagues in the history of Egypt (1201–1202).

Moses ben Maimon wrote his celebrated *Guide of the Perplexed* in about 1185–1190. In 1191, a Muslim philosopher named ʿAbd al-Latif al-Baghdadi visited Cairo (Text 10). He desired to meet three intellectuals, one of them being Moses ben Maimon. His testimony is precious, as it is written by a man who acutally met him, was a Muslim, and whose encounter was close to the time of the *Guide*'s composition. Of Moses ben Maimon he writes that "He was of superior merit but was overcome by the desire to have first rank and to serve powerful people." We learn from al-Baghdadi that Moses ben Maimon was opposed to its being read or studied by Gentiles. ʿAbd al-Latif describes the *Guide* as a book written for the Jews. He finds the treatise damaging to religion—not only to the Jewish religion but also to religious laws and beliefs in general. Unfortunately, he gives no explanation for why he believed so.

In this period (1190–1191), Moses ben Maimon wrote his *Epistle on Resurrection*. This was in response to a letter by the Babylonian gaon Samuel ben Eli to Yemen that accused Moses ben Maimon of not believing in the resurrection of the dead. The latter argues that the resurrection is generally accepted among the religious community, and that it should not be interpreted symbolically. This was, we should remember, in response to a dangerous allegation that might easily have embroiled him with the state authorities. Saladin conducted himself as a pious Muslim and opposed philosophers and those who denied fundamental beliefs like resurrection.

In the last decade of the century (1190–1200), Moses ben Maimon was occupied with his medical practice and with serving in the royal entourage. In the meantime, a young scholar in Lunel, Samuel ben Judah ibn Tibbon (c. 1160–1230), prepared a Hebrew translation of the *Guide* at the prompting of several Lunel luminaries such as Jonathan ha-Kohen. Samuel corresponded with Moses ben Maimon, raising questions about the *Guide* and presenting problems of translation. Moses ben Maimon replied to him in a letter of 1199 with detailed corrections of Samuel ibn Tibbon's translation (Text 11). In addition, he responded to a request by Samuel to be allowed to come and visit him. Moses ben Maimon discouraged the visit, and in the course of doing so gave a summary of his arduous daily schedule. This was toward the end of his life, when he was burdened with serving the royal court. His daily routine was very taxing and involved, aside from the court, a clinical practice in his home. We must be mindful that this was after he had written his great works.

According to the document of his grandson David, Moses ben Maimon died in 1204 (Text 4). Since that document is not reliable for the date of birth, it is possible that this date also is not well founded. However, given Moses ben Maimon's age and maladies and the terrible conditions in Egypt at the time, it is plausible that he died at around this time. Moreover, there are independent witnesses that he died in 1204. According to Ibn al-Qifti, Moses ben Maimon requested that his descendants have him buried in Tiberias, and this was apparently done (Text 4). A tombstone marks the gravesite where he is believed to have been interred.

The selections below are from the following sources: Text 1. Moses b. Maimon, *Commentary on the Mishnah, Tohorot,* edited by Y. Kafah (Jerusalem: Mosad ha-Rav Kuk, 1963), p. 456. Text 2. From Moses b. Maimon's *Epistle on Forced Apostasy (Iggeret ha-Shemad)* in I. Shailat, *Letters and Essays of Moses b. Maimon* (Jerusalem: Maʿaliyot, 5,747–48 [1985/6–1988/9]), pp. 53–55. Text 3. *Commentary on Rosh ha-Shanah,* ascribed to Moses b. Maimon, in I. Shailat, *Letters,* pp. 224–25. Text 4. Ibn al-Qifti, *Taʾrikh al-Hukamaʾ,* edited by J. Lippert (Leipzig: Dietrich, 1903), pp. 317–19; see also Bernard Lewis, "Jews and Judaism in Arab Sources (Moses b. Maimon)," in *Metsudah* 3–4 (1945): 171–80 (in Hebrew); and Lewis, *Islam,* vol. 2: *Religion and Society* (New York: Oxford University Press, 1987), pp. 189–92. Text 5. Letter to Japheth, son of Elijah, in Shailat, *Letters,* pp. 228–30. Text 6. From a letter to Joseph, son of Judah, in Mose ben Maimon, *Epistulae,* edited by D. H. Baneth, 2nd ed. (Jerusalem: Magnes, 1985), pp. 50–54. Text 7. Autograph letter to a communal official, Genizah manuscript, Taylor-Schechter 10 J 20, f. 5v, in Shailat, *Letters,* pp. 242–45. Text 8. "In Praise of Abraham," in *Epistles,* ed. Baneth, p. 96. Text 9. Verses on Musa b. Maymun by Ibn Sanaʾ al-

Mulk, translated by F. Rosenthal, "Moses b. Maimon and a Discussion of Muslim Speculative Theology," in *Jewish Tradition in the Diaspora: Studies in Memory of Professor Walter J. Fischel,* edited by M. Maswari Caspi (Berkeley: Judah L. Magnes Memorial Museum, 1981), p. 110. Text 10. ʿAbd al-Latif al-Baghdadi's description of a meeting with Musa ben Maymun, in Ibn abi Usaybiʿa, *ʿUyun al-anbaʾ fi Tabaqat al-Atibbaʾ,* edited by A. Müller (Cairo-Königsberg: al-Matbaʿa al-Wahbiyya, 1882–1884), vol. 2, pp. 202ff: see also see also Lewis, "Jews and Judaism," pp. 175–76. Text 11. From Moses ben Maimon's letter to Samuel ibn Tibbon, in Shailat, *Letters,* pp. 550–51.

Further Reading

M. Ben-Sasson, "Maimonides in Egypt: The First Stage," in *Maimonidean Studies,* edited by A. Hyman. vol. 2 (New York: Yeshivah University Press, 1991), pp. 3–30; J. Blau, ed. *Teshuvot ha-Rambam (Responsa),* 2nd ed., 4 vols. (Jerusalem: Mekitse Nirdamim, R. Mas, 1986); M. Cohen, "Maimonides' Egypt," in *Moses Maimonides and His Time,* edited by E. Ormsby (Washington, D.C.: Catholic University of America Press, 1989), pp. 21–33; P. Fenton, "A Meeting with Maimonides," *Bulletin of the School of Oriental and African Studies* 45.1 (1982): 1–4; S. D. Goitein, "The Life of Maimonides in the Light of New Finds from the Cairo Geniza," *Peraqim* (New York) 4 (1966), pp. 29–42 (Hebrew); Goitein, "Moses Maimonides, Man of Action: A Revision of the Master's Biography in Light of the Geniza Documents," in *Hommage à Georges Vajda,* edited by G. Nahon and Ch. Touati (Louvain: Peeters, 1980), pp. 155–67; Goitein, "The Moses Maimonides-Ibn Sanāʾ al-Mulk Circle," in *Studies in Islamic History and Civilization in Honour of Professor David Ayalon,* edited by M. Sharon (Jerusalem-Leiden: Cana and E. J. Brill, 1986); A. H. Freimann, "The Genealogy of Maimonides' Family," *Alumma* 1 (1935): 8–32. A. S. Halkin and D. Hartman. *Crisis and Leadership: Epistles of Maimonides* (Philadelphia: Jewish Publication Society, 1985); S. Z. Havlin, "Le-Toldot ha-Rambam," *Daat* 15 (1985): 67–79; A. J. Heschel, *Maimonides: A Biography,* translated by J. Neugroschel (New York: Farrar, Straus, Giroux, 1982); J. L. Kraemer, "Six Unpublished Maimonides Letters from the Cairo Genizah," in *Maimonidean Studies,* vol. 2, edited by A. Hyman (New York: Yeshivah University Press, 1991), pp. 61–94; B. Lewis, "Maimonides, Lionheart, and Saladin," in *L. A. Mayer Memorial Volume* (= Eretz-Israel, vol. 7) (Jerusalem: Israel Exploration Society, 1964), pp. 70–75; Lewis, "The Sultan, the King, and the Jewish Doctor," in *Islam in History: Ideas, People, and Events in The Middle East,* new edition (Chicago: Open Court, 1993), pp. 175–85; S. Pines, "Maimonides," in *Dictionary of Scientific Biography,* vol. 9 (New York: Scribner, 1974), p. 29; I. Twersky, *A Maimonides Reader* (New York: Behrman House, 1972); Twersky, *Introduction to the Code of Maimonides* (New Haven: Yale University Press, 1980); D. Yellin and I. Abrahams, *Maimonides,* 3rd rev. ed. (New York: Hermon, 1972).

1. The Colophon to the Commentary on the Mishnah

I am Moses, son of R. Maimon the judge, son of R. Joseph the sage, son of R. Isaac the judge, son of R. Joseph the judge, son of R. Obadiah the judge, son of R. Solomon the master (*rav*), son of R. Obadiah the judge, may the memory of the holy ones be a blessing. I began to compose this commentary when I was twenty-three years old, and I completed it in Egypt when I was thirty years old, in the year [14]79 of the Seleucid era [= 4928 A.M. = 1168 C.E.].

2. From Moses Ben Maimon's *Epistle on Apostasy* (*Iggeret Ha-Shemad*)

Therefore, whoever is martyred so as not to acknowledge the prophetic mission of that person [Muhammad] shall definitely be considered someone who has performed a commandment and who has a great reward with God, the exalted, for he has sacrificed his life for the sanctification of the Name.

But if someone should come to inquire of us if he should be martyred or confess [the Muslim declaration of faith], one says to him to confess and not suffer martyrdom. However, he should not remain in the kingdom of that ruler but rather stay at home until he leaves that kingdom. And if he needs to carry on his livelihood, then let him practice [Judaism] in secret. . . .

The advice I give to all my friends and to those who seek advice from me is to leave these places and to go to a place where he can practice his religion and keep his Torah without coercion. He should not fear but leave his house and his children and all that he owns. For the religion of God, which he has bequeathed us, is great and its obligation takes precedence over all those accidental things that are despicable in the eyes of the enlightened. For they do not last, but the testament of God is what endures. . . .

3. Appended to the *Commentary on Rosh Ha-Shanah,* Ascribed to Moses Ben Maimon

The book was copied in Acre by the esteemed R. Samuel, son of Abraham Skeil, from the autograph copy of our master Moses, Light of the Exile, of blessed memory. He also found the following at the end of the book in the hand of the master:

On the eve of Sunday, 4 Iyyar [18 April], I set sail [from Morocco]. And on the Sabbath, 10 Iyyar [24 April], in the year 4925 A.M. [1165 C.E.] a great wave almost inundated us, the sea being very stormy. I took a vow that I would fast for these two days [every year] and observe them as a regular public fast, I and all my family and household. I shall command my descendants to do so until their last generation and to give charity according to their means. I vowed that I would remain in solitude on 10 Iyyar [every year] without seeing anyone, but rather worshipping and studying all day in privacy. Just as I found at sea that day only [the presence of] the Holy One, blessed be he, so I shall not see any person or sit with anyone [on that day] unless I am compelled to do so.

On the eve of Sunday, 3 Sivan [16 May], I disembarked safely in Acre, and thus I was saved from apostasy. And so we arrived in the land of Israel. I took an oath that this day would be one of rejoicing and celebration and of giving gifts to the poor, I and my family, until the last generation.

On Tuesday, 4 Marḥeshvan [12 October] [49]26 A.M. [1166 C.E.], we left Acre to go up to Jerusalem at a time of danger. I entered the [ruins of] the great and holy temple and prayed there on Thursday, 6 Marḥeshvan [14 October]. On Sunday, 9 Marḥeshvan [17 October], I left Jerusalem for Hebron to kiss the tombs of my ancestors in the Cave [of Machpelah]. On that day I stood in the cave and prayed, praise be to God, [in gratitude] for everything. I took an oath that these two days, namely, 6 and 9 Marḥeshvan, would be a holiday for me, a day of prayer and rejoicing in God, [a day] for festivities and eating and drinking. May God assist me in everything, and help me realize "my vows to the Lord I shall fulfill." Amen. Just as I had the merit to pray in [Jerusalem] in its desolation, so shall I and all [the people of] Israel witness its consolation speedily. Amen.

On the eve of Thursday . . . and on Tuesday, 12 Sivan [14 May 1166?], the Lord saw my misery, and my brother arrived safely. I dedicated this day to charity and fasting.

Until here [R. Samuel b. Skeil] copied from the autograph by the hand of the man of God, our masterMoses, of blessed memory.

And [R. Samuel] also copied from the autograph of our master, the Nagid, our master David, the grandson of Rabbenu Moses, of blessed memory, as follows:

Our Moses was born to his father, our master Maimon, of blessed memory, on 14 Nisan [30 March], 1446 Seleucid Era, which is 4893 A.M. [rather 4895 = 1135], in Cordova. And he retired from this world and gained the world to come in 1516 Seleucid Era [1204 C.E.] on Monday eve, 20 Teveth [13 December]. My father, my teacher [Abraham], was born to his father in the month of Sivan and died on Monday night, 18 Kislev, which was a Shemitta [Sabbatical] year.

4. Ibn Al-Qifti's Entry on Moses Ben Maimon Al-Isra'ili Al-Andalusi

This man was an Andalusian, a Jew by religion. He studied the sciences of the ancients in Andalus. He was proficient in mathematics and mastered logic. He studied medicine there and had expert knowledge of it but did not venture to practice [medicine].

'Abd al-Mu'min b. 'Ali al-Kumi, the Berber [the Almohad leader, 1133–1163], who gained control in the Maghreb, proclaimed in the lands where he ruled that Jews and Christians should be expelled, fixing a time limit for their [departure]. ['Abd al-Mu'min] stipulated that whoever of them converted to Islam could remain in his place and continue to pursue his livelihood on condition that he accept what is incumbent upon Muslims. But whoever was steadfast in the views of his coreligionists must leave before the set time. If he remained after the time he would forfeit life and property by jurisdiction of the ruler. When the order came into force, those with little property left, while those with much property remained, being chary of family and wealth, professing Islam openly while harboring unbelief. Moses ben Maimon was one of those who did this, remaining in his country. When, at that time, he feigned the distinguishing marks of Islam, he also adhered to its specific [rituals], including the study of Qur'an and prayer.

He kept this up until he had the chance to travel. After assembling his property when this was feasible, he then abandoned Andalus [here = North Africa?] for Egypt, along with his family. [Moses ben Maimon] settled in the town of Fustat among its Jews. He could then follow his religion openly. He dwelled in the Masisa [Mamsusa] Quarter, and engaged in commerce in precious stones and the like. People studied the ancient sciences with him. This was at the end of the 'Alid [Fatimid] dynasty.

They [members of the ruling dynasty] wanted to employ him along with other physicians and to send him to the king of the Franks in Ascalon. For [the king] had requested that [the Egyptians] send him a physician. They chose [Moses ben Maimon]. But he adamantly refused this service or to go along with this business.

When al-Ghuzz [the Turks] ruled in Egypt, after the dissolution of the 'Alid dynasty, al-Qadi al-Fadil 'Abd al-Rahim b. 'Ali al-Baysani brought [Moses ben Maimon] under his patronage, took care of him and gave him a stipend. He participated with the [court] physicians. [Moses ben Maimon] did not have an independent [medical] opinion because he lacked experience in the practice [of medicine], nor was he qualified for treatment and management [of health issues].

He married in Cairo the sister of a Jewish scribe named Abu al-Ma'ali, the secretary of the mother of Nur al-Din 'Ali, called al-Afdal, son of Salah al-Din [Saladin] Yusuf ibn Ayyub. She gave birth to a son [Abraham], who is now a physician in Cairo, following after his father. Abu al-Ma'ali married a sister of Moses [ibn Maymun]. She give birth to several children, among them Abu al-Rida the physician, a quiet and intelligent doctor in the service of Qilij Arslan in the Land of the Rum [Seljuq Anatolia]. Moses ben Maimon died in Cairo in the course of the year 605 [A.H. = 1208–1209 C.E.]. He requested that his descendants take him, after temporary burial, to the Sea of Tiberias and to inter him there, as he wished to be among the graves of Israelites and their prominent jurists, and it was done. [There follows a list of his writings.]

Toward the end of his life he was harassed by a man from Andalus, a jurist named Abu al-'Arab ibn Mu'isha [al-Kinani al-Sabti], who came to Fustat, met [Moses ben Maimon], and accused him of having converted to Islam in Andalus, defaming him [with apostasy], intending to cause him harm [by having him executed]. 'Abd al-Rahim b. 'Ali al-Fadil prevented this, claiming that when a man is forcibly converted to Islam, the conversion is not legitimate.

5. Letter of Moses Ben Maimon to Japheth Ben Elijah of Acre

To the esteemed, great, and revered master and teacher, Japheth, the wise and astute sage and discerning judge, may God preserve him, son of the esteemed, great, and revered master and teacher, Elijah, the pious judge, may the memory of the righteous be a blessing. From his friend who yearns for him in his absence and prays for the increase of his honor, Moses son of R. Maimon, the teacher (*rav*), may the memory of the righteous be a blessing.

Your letter, precious unto me, has arrived, and I was astonished by its contents. For you complain that I did not take the initiative and inquire about your well-being from the day we left the beautiful land [of Israel], and that I have not sent a letter to you. The matter you brought up was certainly meant to admonish [me], but it is rather you who should be admonished. "You are a betrayer and have not been betrayed" [Isa. 33:1].

Moreover, a few months after we departed, my father and master died, may the memory of the righteous be a blessing. Letters of condolence arrived from the furthest West and from the land of Edom [Europe], a distance of several months, but you disregarded this.

Furthermore, I met with many well-known calamities in Egypt [cf. Deut. 31:17 and Ps. 71:20], including sicknesses, financial loss and the attempt by informers to have me killed. The worst disaster that struck me of late, worse than anything [cf. 2 Sam. 19:8] I had ever experienced from the time I was born until this day, was the demise of that upright man [David ben Maimon], may the memory of the righteous be a blessing, who drowned in the Indian Sea while in possession of much money belonging to me, to him, and to others, leaving a young daughter and his widow in my care.

For about a year from the day the evil tidings reached me I remained dangerously ill [lit., prostrate in bed] with a severe inflammation, fever, and numbness of heart [cf. Deut. 28:22, 28, 35; Job 2:7], and well-nigh perished. From then until this day, that is, about eight years, I have been in a state of inconsolate mourning. How can I be consoled? For he was my son; he grew up upon my knees; he was my brother, my pupil. It was he who did business in the market place, earning a livelihood while I dwelled in security.

He had a quick grasp of Talmud and a superb mastery of grammar. My only joy was to see him. "The sun has set on all joy" [Isa. 24:11]. For he has gone on to eternal life, leaving me dismayed in a foreign land [cf. the first Moses in Exod. 2:22, 18:3]. Whenever I see his handwriting or one of his books, my heart is churned inside me and my sorrow is rekindled. In short, "I will go down mourning to my son in Sheol" [Gen. 37:35]. And were it not for the Torah, which is my delight, and for scientific matters, which let me forget my sorrow, "I would have perished in my affliction" [Ps. 119:92].

In spite of this, I complain not of any sage, disciple, friend or acquaintance. I should complain about you above all others. For I, [my brother,] my father and master, may the memory of the righteous be a blessing, and you—all four of us—"walked together in God's house with the throng" [Psa. 55:15]. But you did not seek or inquire [concerning my welfare]. I would be justified in not answering your letter that has now arrived pertaining to power of attorney. But "my affection is drawn up in full and secured" [cf. 2 Sam. 23:5]. I shall not forget our wandering together in wastelands and forests after the Lord, and thus do not ascribe to you sin and transgression. "But love covers up all faults" [Prov. 10:12].

God knows how much I am distressed by the hard times you mention. The whole matter "grieved me deeply unto death" [Jon. 4:9]. If you were here with me, I would care for you properly, and I would honor and delight you according to my capacity.

I rejoice greatly over this son that God has given you—R. Elijah, the astute pupil. I heard that he studies Torah, and that he is a clever fellow, and treads the right path. "Your sons will succeed your ancestors; you will appoint them princes throughout the land" [Ps. 45:17]. May this be God's will. Shevat 1491 S[eleucid] E[ra] [December 1179–January 1180 C.E.].

6. From a Letter to Joseph Ben Judah on the *Mishneh Torah*

Know that I have not composed this compendium [the *Mishneh Torah*] to gain authority among the Jews or to achieve fame, so that I should be distressed by opposition to the aim for which I composed it. I have only composed it in the first place, God knows, for myself, to be released from study and searching for what is needed, as well as for the time of old age and for the sake of God, may he be exalted. For, by God, "I am moved by zeal for the Lord, God of Israel" [cf. 1 Kings 19:10, 14], as I have witnessed a community lacking a true [legal] collection and without correct, precisely formulated opinions. I accordingly carried out what I did for the sake of God alone. This is the first point.

The second point. I knew and clearly ascertained when I composed [the *Mishneh Torah*] that it would surely fall into the hands of some evil and envious person who would denigrate its virtues, and act as if it were dispensable or faulty, as well as some foolish ignoramus who would not appreciate the value of what was accomplished, and consider it useless. [And it would reach] some raving, befuddled novice who would struggle with some of its passages owing to fundamental ignorance of them or intellectual ineptitude to grasp precisely what I have formulated precisely. Furthermore, it would reach some rigid, dull religionist who would attack the foundations of belief it contains. These are the majority. Yet it would surely reach "the survivors whom the Lord calls" [Joel 3:5], people of justice, fairness, and good sense; and they would appreciate the value of what I have achieved, you being the first among them.

If you were the only one I have in my generation, it would be sufficient. All the more so, as I have received letters from the sages of France and from others, along with their names, who admire what has been accomplished and request that the rest be sent. And it has already reached the ends of the inhabited world. All that I have described for you concerning those who do not receive it as it deserves relates only to my time. But in the time to come, when envy and ambition disappear, all Israelites will be satisfied with it alone, everything else lying fallow, except for those who seek something to busy themselves with throughout their lives without attaining any objective. This is the second point, which implies that nothing befell me that I had not anticipated.

The third point. This composition is not comparable to the *Torah*, God forbid, which is the true guidance for mankind, nor does it approach the words of the prophets. Yet only some people have followed them, while others have turned away. Ignorance of the value of this composition is not graver than ignorance of what is unknown of metaphysical matters, not to mention other things. If someone were to yield to anger or misery on account of everyone who is ignorant of some truth, or resists something certain, or obstinately follows some caprice, then surely "All his days his thoughts are grief and heartache" [Eccles. 2:23]. This is not what should be done.

The fourth point. Let me recount for his honor some of my moral qualities, although you have personally experienced all of them. Know that there are with me in the city people who have neither fame, nor status, nor competence. But their arrogance and envy are such that they will not study this great composition and have never even set eyes upon it, in order to avoid it being said that this one is confined to having to learn from the words of so-and-so and is accordingly beneath him in knowledge. Thus they merely sustain the opinion of the common people in this, and are always "as the blind grope in darkness" [Deut. 28:29].

7. Autograph Letter to a Community Official

I rejoice at the health of his honor the Sheikh al-Watiq, may God protect him. I have sent him forty dirhams along with the bearer of this letter. Use some [of the amount] for removal of earth, and take for yourself two dirhams per diem for the past days when repairs were done.

Furthermore, do not continue to hire out the cow. One cup in morning and evening is sufficient for you if you take it constantly. It will satisfy [you]. Do not depart in any way from the advice of al-Hajj 'Ali al-Sharawi concerning all that he suggests. And do not let any other lessee enter the place. There is no other activity which should be done in the garden until we make another agreement with the lessee, and I shall take care of it myself.

If you wish to visit after Saturday, please do so. And may your welfare increase.

8. In Praise of His Son Abraham

When I consider the condition of this world, I find consolation only in two things: in contemplating and studying and in my son Abraham, for God, may he be blessed, has given him grace and blessing from the blessing of his namesake who believed in God and in his promise. May he give him long life, for he is most humble and has fine moral qualities, and he has a subtle mind and fine nature. And with the help of God he shall no doubt have a name among the great [cf. 1 Chron. 17:8]. I entreat God, may he be blessed, to protect him and to shower upon him his mercy to the utmost.

9. Praise by Ibn Sana' Al-Mulk

> Were [Moses ben Maimon] to treat the [present] time with his knowledge,
> He would cure it through knowledge from the disease of ignorance.
> Were the full moon to ask him for treatment,
> It would indeed obtain the perfection it claims.
> On the day of the full moon, he would give it medication against its brownish freckles,
> And cure it of disease on the last day of the month.

10. Description of 'Abd Al-Latif Al-Baghdadi

Moses [ben Maimun] came to see me. He was of superior merit but was overcome by the desire to have first rank and to serve powerful people. [Moses ben Maimon] wrote a book for the Jews and called it the *Book of Guidance* [*Guide of the Perplexed*] and cursed whoever would write it in a non-Hebrew script. I read it and found it to be a bad book which destroys the foundations of religious laws and beliefs, whereas he thought that he was restoring them.

11. From Moses Ben Maimon's Letter to Samuel Ibn Tibbon (1199)

I dwell in Fustat while the king resides in Cairo, and between the two places there are two Sabbath limits [4,000 cubits = slightly more than one mile]. I have a very difficult assignment with the king. I must see him daily at the beginning of the day. When he is weak, or when one of his sons or concubines is ill, I do not leave Cairo, and most of my day I spend in the king's palace. And I must attend to the king's officers every day. One or two officials is invariably ill, and I must undertake their medical treatment.

In sum, every day I go up to Cairo early in the morning, and if there is no mishap or incident, I return to Fustat after midday in any case. As soon as I arrive, in a state of hunger, I find all the vestibules [of my home] filled with Gentiles, noble and common, judges and magistrates, a mixed multitude, who know the time of my return. I dismount from my riding animal, wash my hands, and go out to them to appease them to wait for me while I have a light repast, which I do from time to time. I then go out to heal them and write [prescriptions] for them. They come in and out sometimes until night, and at times, by faith in the Torah, until the end of two hours into the night [around 8:00 P.M.]. I speak with them while lying down because of great fatigue. When night falls I am so utterly exhausted that I cannot speak.

The upshot is that no Israelite can speak with me or meet with me except on the Sabbath. Then they all come after the [morning] prayer, and I direct the community concerning what they should do all week. They study light things until noon, and then go on their way. Some of them return and study again until the evening prayer.

This is my daily schedule, and I have only told some of what you would see, with the help of God, may He be exalted.

33

Dolce of Worms: The Lives and Deaths of an Exemplary Medieval Jewish Woman and Her Daughters

Judith R. Baskin

The small Jewish communities of medieval France and Germany, an area Jews called Ashkenaz, lived in an atmosphere of religious suspicion and legal disability. By the beginning of the thirteenth century, Christian rulers and Church ordinances had barred Jews from virtually any source of livelihood but moneylending. They were often compelled to wear distinctive clothing and badges to distinguish them from Christians; toward the end of the Middle Ages, Jews were either expelled from areas where they had long lived (including England in 1290 and Spain in 1492) or forced to live in crowded ghettos. Despite their political insecurity, medieval Jews enjoyed a high standard of living and were significantly acculturated. Women's status was higher than among Jews in the Islamic milieu, as indicated by the larger dowries they brought into marriage and their freedom of movement. The eleventh-century rabbinic ruling forbidding polygyny for Jews in Ashkenaz, attributed to Rabbi Gershom ben Judah, who also ruled that no woman could be divorced against her will, are further evidence of women's positive situation. In this milieu, Jewish women were active participants in the economic survival of their families; independent businesswomen, including widows who controlled significant resources, traveled alone on business, possessed property, and appeared in court on their own behalf, despite talmudic regulations to the contrary.

Dolce of Worms, the remarkable woman on whom our documents center, came from the elite, leadership class of medieval German Jewry; she was the daughter of a prominent family and the wife of a major rabbinic figure, Rabbi Eleazar ben Judah of Worms (1165–1230), also known as the *Roqeah* (the Perfumer), after the title of one of his most famous works. Dolce and her husband were also members of a small circle of Jews distinguished for their piety, the *Hasidei Ash-*

kenaz, the German-Jewish Pietists. The introspective and penitential religious outlook of the *Hasidei Ashkenaz* had a significant impact on the Jews of Germany and France in the unsettled atmosphere following the First Crusade of 1096, during which a number of Rhineland Jewish communities had been ravaged by Christian Crusaders. The main documents of this movement, written in the twelfth and thirteenth centuries, include many mystical works, as well as a volume reflecting their ethical concerns, *Sefer Hasidim* (The Book of the Pious), an important historical source for everyday Jewish life in medieval Germany. This volume is attributed to R. Judah the Pious (1140–1217), although some parts were probably written by Judah's father, R. Samuel b. Kalonymous he-Hasid. R. Eleazar, who was Judah's most prominent disciple, may also have written some of the passages in *Sefer Hasidim,* and could have been its editor.

Eleazar ben Judah left a number of writings, both esoteric and personal, and these latter documents include two accounts, one in prose and one in poetry, describing the lives and the deaths of his wife Dolce and their daughters, Bellette and Hannah, who were murdered in November 1196. According to these texts, two armed men, who had apparently gained entry to the household, set upon the family circle of the *Roqeah,* which comprised his wife, two daughters, at least one son, a number of students, and a junior teacher. Although earlier generations of scholars have assumed that the murderers were marauding Crusaders, there were no massed Crusader forces in Germany at this time. If the two attackers were Crusaders, they were not part of any crusading host passing through Worms but were acting as individuals, out of hope of monetary gain. The *Roqeah*'s home was almost certainly selected on account of the activities of Dolce, a major banker and moneylender who supported her household financially. It was likely that the miscreants believed they would find money or other precious objects in her home. Nor did these attacks go unpunished. The Christian authorities, following the German emperor's mandate of protecting the Jews of his realm, quickly captured and executed at least one of the men.

Although the prose account concentrates on the events of the attack and its devastating aftermath, the poetic eulogy recounts the range of endeavors of "the saintly Mistress Dolce" and her daughters. Based in part on Proverbs 31, the biblical description of the "woman of valor," this document, which records numerous and poignant details of its subjects' daily lives, constitutes an important source for the activities of medieval Jewish women in general, as well as a moving tribute to Dolce and her daughters. The epithets Eleazar uses in describing his wife, "pious" or "saintly" (*hasidah*), three times in the prose account and again at the very outset of the poetic eulogy, as well as "righteous" (*tzadeket*), tell us a great deal about the qualities for which women in her culture were most esteemed. The *Roqeah* also uses the Hebrew *ne'imah,* "Pleasant," three times in the elegy— a play on the meaning of Dolce's name. The name Dolce, also transliterated Dulcia, Dulzia, or Dulcie, is of Latinate origin, based on the adjective *dulcis*, "agreeable, pleasant, charming, kind, or dear." Medieval Jewish women often had vernacular rather than Hebrew names. Of Dolce's two daughters, one had a vernacular name, Bellette, the other a Hebrew name, Hannah.

The *Hasidei Ashkenaz,* convinced of God's justice, believed that the catastrophes that had befallen the Jews of France and Germany must be understood as divine punishments. A major theme of their pietistic literature, including the texts presented here, was the need for individual and group atonement for the sins, both real and imagined, that they maintained had brought deserved divine chastisements on their community. R. Eleazar's lamenting elegies for his murdered wife and children have a quality of self-abasement and unquestioning submission to the divine will that is profoundly disturbing to a contemporary reader. This penitentional tone is not unusual, however, in medieval Jewish literature, and is a major component of how medieval Jews understood their relationship with God.

In both his prose and poetic laments, Eleazar describes Dolce's economic activities. Financial matters were not the only focus of Dolce's life, however. Her husband describes her as managing an extensive household; in addition to caring for the needs of her husband and three or more children, her ménage also included her husband's students and at least one junior teacher. She provided food and clothing for all of these individuals. Dolce also paid for hiring additional teachers and for the purchase of parchment from her earnings. She sewed books together from thread she had herself spun, and repaired torn books, as well. Moreover, Dolce's needlework skills were also of use in the communal domain of the synagogue. She is credited with preparing gut thread and sewing together the quite extraordinary number of forty Torah scrolls (the handwritten scroll containing the first five books of the Hebrew Bible that is used in synagogue worship and is symbolic of the revelation of the divine word to the people of Israel); she is also have said to have spun thread for other religious objects, and to have prepared candles for religious use. History shows that Jewish women have always made contributions to enhance the synagogue and its sacred objects. Whereas prosperous women donated Torah scrolls for the service, oil and books for study, and left legacies for the upkeep of the synagogue, poorer women gave their needlework in the form of Torah binders and covers, and as curtains for the ark containing the Torah scrolls. These actions can be seen as female strategies for imprinting their existences on a realm of activity in which they were otherwise secondary. As the wife of the rabbi, Dolce undoubtedly felt a special responsibility to provide for the synagogue's needs.

Nor were Dolce's contributions to the synagogue the fruits of her physical labors alone. The daughter of a prosperous family, Dolce was unusually well educated. Certainly, all Jewish women acquired domestic skills in childhood. These included not only the rudiments of cooking, needlework, and household management but also the rules of rabbinic Judaism applicable to home and marriage. Basic religious training was considered essential so that a woman would know how to observe dietary laws, domestic regulations pertaining to the Sabbath and festivals, and the other commandments relevant to her family life. But higher educational achievements, such as literacy in Hebrew—which was standard for

Jewish boys—only rarely applied to girls, and then only to those from select families. Dolce is among several medieval Jewish women who are described as women's prayer leaders. Another such woman, from the thirteenth century, is Urania of Worms, whose headstone epitaph commemorates her as "the daughter of the chief of the synagogue singers. His prayer for his people rose up to glory. And as to her, she, too, with sweet tunefulness officiated before the women to whom she sang the hymnal portions." Medieval Worms, which had a separate room for women attached to the synagogue, may have had special traditions associated with women and worship.

Dolce also took on other communal responsibilities relating to women, again in her prominent role as the rabbi's wife. She is described as adorning brides and bringing them to their wedding in honor. These activities may also have been a source of additional income; certainly among medieval Jews of the Muslim world the "bridecomber," who made wedding arrangments for a bride and her family, was a recognized female occupation. Beyond preparing and escorting the bride, Dolce, as a respected investment broker, may also have been involved in arranging matches and negotiating the financial arrangements that accompanied them. Similarly, Dolce is said to have bathed the dead and to have sewed their shrouds. These acts are considered particularly meritorious in Jewish tradition, and generally Jews had burial societies that took on these responsibilities, men caring for men, and women caring for women. Dolce, clearly, figured prominently in such essential activities connected with the pious women of her community.

R. Eleazar stresses Dolce's piety (*hasidut*) in both the prose and poetic texts, stating that all of her actions were inspired by a desire to fulfill the divine will, the pietist's highest goal. Dolce is described as knowing what was permitted and what was forbidden according to Jewish law, and as always eager to learn from her husband's teachings. She was able to go far beyond the ordinary woman in the extent and content of her religious devotions due to her unusual knowledge of the traditional Hebrew liturgy, and she may have been atypical, too, in the extent of her synagogue attendance. It would appear that Dolce was training her daughters to follow in her footsteps, since their father relates not only their needlework skills but also their knowledge of Hebrew prayers and their melodies. In everything, as the *Roqeah* puts it in the poetic lament, Dolce was concerned to "fulfill her Creator's commandments."

Yet it is significant that R. Eleazar's final words of praise for Dolce in his poetic eulogy are that she rejoiced to perform her husband's will and never angered him. Here, R. Eleazar is expressing the standard rabbinic view, also shared by the thirteenth-century R. Moses of Coucy, who taught in his *Sefer Mitzvot Gadol* (positive commandment 12), that although "a woman is exempt from both the commandment to learn Torah and to teach her son, even so, if she aids her son and husband in their efforts to learn, she shares their reward for the fulfillment of that commandment." Dolce, more than anything, is revered for having facilitated in every way the spiritual activities of the men of her household, and this is why her husband has not the slightest doubt of her overwhelming merit. The reward that R. Eleazar invokes for his beloved wife in the final phrase of the poetic lament, to be wrapped in the eternal life of Paradise, is a recognition of her deeds, upon which so many were utterly dependent. As Proverbs 31:31, on which his elegy is based, concludes, "Extol the fruit of her hand, / And let her works praise her in the gates."

Both the prose passage and the poetic elegy survive, with some variations, in two manuscripts in the Bodleian Library in Oxford: Heb. MS Michael 448, fol. 30, and Heb. MS Oppenheim 757, fols. 25–27; they are listed in Adolf Neubauer, ed., *Catalogue of the Hebrew Manuscripts in the Bodleian Library and in the College Libraries of Oxford* (Oxford: Oxford University Press, 1886–1906), 762, 798. The Hebrew texts are reproduced in Israel Kamelhar, *Rabbenu Eleazar mi-Germaiza, ha-Roqeah* (Rzeazow: Reitan, 1930), pp. 17–19; and in Abraham Meir Habermann, ed., *Sefer Gezeirot Ashkenaz ve-Zarfat* (Jerusalem: Tarshish, 1945) pp. 164–67. My translations are based on the printed text in Haberman, *Sefer Gezeirot,* pp. 164–67, with reference to Kamelhar and to photocopies of both manuscripts. Various parts of the poetic elegies have been previously translated into English several times. My version of the poem in memory of Dolce is informed by the translation of Ivan Marcus in his article cited below; I have also consulted the translations of the poems in memory of Bellette and Hannah that appear in T. Carmi, *The Penguin Book of Hebrew Verse* (New York: Penguin, 1981), pp. 387–88.

Further Reading

Discussions of Dolce, and of Jewish women in medieval Europe in general, include Judith R. Baskin, "Women Saints in Judaism: Dolce of Worms," in *Women Saints in World Religions,* edited by Arvind Sharma (Albany: State University of New York Press, 2000), pp. 39–70; Baskin, "Jewish Women in the Middle Ages," in *Jewish Women in Historical Perspective,* edited by Baskin (Detroit: Wayne State University Press, 1991; 2nd ed. 1998); pp. 101–2 and Ivan G. Marcus, "Mothers, Martyrs, and Moneymakers: Some Jewish Women in Medieval Europe," Conservative Judaism 38.3 (Spring 1986): 34–45. Emily Taitz, "Kol Ishah—The Voice of Woman: Where Was It Heard in Medieval Europe?" *Conservative Judaism* 38.3 (Spring 1986): 46–61; and Taitz, "Women's Voices, Women's Prayers: Women in the European Synagogues of the Middle Ages," in *Daughters of the King: Women and the Synagogue,* edited by Susan Grossman and Rivka Haut (Philadelphia: Jewish Publication Society, 1992), pp. 59–71, addresses medieval Jewish women's religious roles and activities. On the *Hasidei Ashkenaz,* see Ivan G. Marcus, *Piety and Society: The Jewish Pietists of Medieval Germany* (Leiden: E.J. Brill, 1981).

1. Eleazar ben Judah of Worms, the *Roqeah*

In 4957, on the twenty-second of Kislev [15 November 1196], after I, Eleazar the small and the lowly, had expounded Parashat *V'yashev Ya'akov* [the weekly scriptural reading, "And Jacob settled," Gen. 37–40] in safety, and I was sitting at my table, two marked men came to us, and they drew their swords and struck my pious wife, mistress Dolce. They broke the head of my elder daughter Bellette, and they struck my younger daughter Hannah in the head, and they both died. And they wounded my son Jacob from the crown of his head to half his cheek to his chin. And they wounded my head and my hand, on my left side, and they wounded my students and my schoolmaster. Immediately the pious woman jumped up and ran out of the winter quarters and cried out that they were killing us. The despicable ones went out and cleaved her in the head from the windpipe to the shoulder, and from the shoulder to the waist, across the width of the back and her front, and the righteous woman fell dead. And I secured the door, and we cried out, until help should come to us from heaven. And I cried out over this pious woman, praying for revenge. And thus it happened. For after a week they caught the murderer who killed her, and who killed my two daughters, and wounded my son, and they killed him. I was left in want of everything and in great affliction and overwhelming suffering.

Before her murder, she purchased parchment for the writing of books. She supported me and my son and my daughters by [lending] other people's money. Because of my great sins she was killed, and my daughters. As God is my witness, she was put to much trouble so that I and my son might study. And woe is me concerning them! How much blood was spilled, and she was dying before my eyes! May the Holy One show us their revenge and take pity on their souls, and may he have compassion for the survivor who remains, and on my son, and on all of his people Israel. Amen.

2. Eleazar ben Judah of Worms: Poetic Elegy 1

The poetic form of this elegy, written in two line couplets and based on the biblical passage Proverbs 31:10–31, possesses a complexity that is impossible to transmit in English translation. The first word of each verse of Proverbs 31:10–31, which describes an exemplary wife, often known as the "woman of valor," begins with a successive letter of the Hebrew alphabet. The equivalent, in English, would be a poem whose successive two-line couplets begin with a word starting with the letter A and proceed through the alphabet to a final couplet beginning with a word starting with Z. In Eleazar's elegy, many of the first lines of his poetic couplets begin with the first few words of the corresponding verse in Proverbs; and even when they do not, the first letter of the first word of each couplet begins with the appropriate letter of the alphabet; thus his poem retains the alphabetic pattern of the original, in addition to elaborating on its contents. Eleazar also introduces an additional acrostic: the first letter of the first word of the second line of each couplet spells out Eleazar, Ha-Qatan, HeAluv, veHaEvyon, "Eleazar the small, the lowly, and the bereft," the author's epithet for himself. The present translation makes no attempt to represent these structural patterns. Quotations from Proverbs 31, sometimes somewhat altered, appear throughout the elegy for Dolce, not only at the beginning of couplets. They are represented here in italics, followed by the appropriate citations, based on the translation of the Jewish Publication Society, 1978.

> *What a rare find is a capable wife* [31:10]: Such a one was my saintly wife, Mistress Dolce.
> *A capable wife* [31:10]: the crown of her husband, the daughter of community benefactors. A woman who feared God, she was renowned for her good deeds.
> *Her husband put his confidence in her* [31:11]: She fed him and dressed him in honor to sit with *the elders of the land* [31:23] and involve himself in Torah study and good deeds.
> *She was good to him, never bad, all the days of* [31:12] his life with her. She made him books from her labor; her name [signifies] "Pleasant."
> *She looked for* white *wool* for fringes; *and set her hand to them with a will* [31:13]. *She set her mind* [31:16] to fulfill divine commandments and all who observed her praised her.
> *She was like a merchant fleet [bringing her food from afar]* [31:14] to feed her husband so that he might immerse himself in Torah. Her daughters saw her and *declared her happy* [31:29] *for her merchandise was excellent* [31:18].
> *She supplied provisions for her household* [31:15] and bread to the boys.
> How *her hands worked the distaff* [31:19] to spin thread for books. Vigorous in everything, she spun threads for phylacteries, and [prepared] sinews [to bind together] scrolls and books; she was as swift as a deer to cook for the young men and to fulfill the needs of the students.
> *She girded herself with strength* [31:17] and stitched together some forty Torah scrolls. She prepared meat for special feasts and set her table for all of the community.
> *Judging wisely* [31:18], she adorned brides and brought them [to the wedding] in appropriate [garments]. "Pleasant" bathed the dead and sewed their shrouds.
> *Her hands* [31:19] stitched the students' garments and torn books. From her toil she often contributed to Torah scholars.
> *She gave generously to the poor* [31:20] and fed her sons and daughters and her husband. She enthusiastically fulfilled the will of her Creator day and night.

Her lamp never went out at night [31:18]: she prepared wicks for the synagogue and the study rooms and she said psalms.

She sang hymns and prayers and recited supplications. Every day she extended her hands to say the prayers beginning *nishmat kol hai*, and *ve-khol ma'aminim*.

She invoked *pittum ha-qetoret* and the Ten Commandments. In all the cities she taught women, enabling their "Pleasant" intoning of songs.

She knew the order of morning and evening prayer; she came early to the synagogue and stayed late.

She stood throughout the Day of Atonement and chanted; she prepared the candles. She honored the Sabbaths and festivals for those who devoted themselves to the study of Torah.

Her mouth was full of wisdom [31:26]: she knew what was forbidden and what was permitted. On the Sabbath she sat and listened to her husband's preaching.

Outstanding in her modesty, she was wise and well-spoken. Whoever was close to her was blessed. She was eager, pious, and amiable in fulfilling all the commandments.

She purchased milk for the students and hired teachers from her exertions. Knowledgeable and wise, she served her Creator in joy.

Her legs ran to visit the sick and to fulfill her Creator's commandments. She fed her sons and urged them to study, and she served the Holy One in reverence.

She was happy to do the will of her husband and never angered him. Her actions were "Pleasant." May the Eternal Rock remember her.

May her soul be enveloped in the wrappings of eternal life. *Extol her for the fruit of her hands* [31:31] in Paradise.

3. Eleazar ben Judah of Worms: Poetic Elegy 2

The second elegy, also written in two-line couplets, immediately follows the first in both manuscripts. It does not incorporate any alphabetic acrostics. The final paragraph of the second poem, beginning "Over and over," in which the *Roqeah* mourns the deaths of all of his children, appears only in manuscript Oppenheim 757; it was almost certainly written at a later date.

Let me relate the life of my older daughter Bellette. She was thirteen years old and as modest as a bride.

She had learned all the prayers and songs from her mother, who was modest and pious, "Pleasant," and wise.

The maiden followed the example of her beautiful mother; she prepared my bed and pulled off my shoes each evening.

Bellette was busy about the house and spoke only truth; she served her Creator and spun, sewed, and embroidered.

She was imbued with reverence and with love for her Creator; she was without any flaw. Her efforts were directed to Heaven, and she sat to listen to Torah from my mouth.

And she was killed with her mother and with her sister on the evening of the twenty-second of Kislev, when I was sitting peacefully at my table.

Two despicable ones came and killed them before my eyes and wounded me and my students and also my son.

Let me tell about the life of my younger daughter [Hannah]. She recited the first part of the Sh'ma prayer every day.

She was six years old and spun and sewed and embroidered. She entertained me and she sang.

Woe is me for my wife and for my daughters! I cry out in lamentation. How much have my sins found me out!

Woe is me for my disaster! I am stricken by sufferings and by wretchedness; my posterity and my equilibrium have fled from me.

Woe is me! What shall I answer to my Creator? For my sins they were killed; His judgments are true; how they roar out.

Their blood shall be clarified before Him and He will avenge them; where no eye can see, their souls will be wrapped in eternal life.

And may He look down and show compassion for my sons, the surviving remnant, and allow them to live in reverence and to fulfill the commandments of the Torah.

The One who is great in counsel compensates the man according to his deeds; Rock of perfection, faithful God, who is blessed in His great deeds.

May He be blessed to eternity for his faithfulness is true; blessed is the Lord forever, Amen and Amen.

Over and over my sins have found me out. All my sons and daughters are dead.

Woe is me for my amiable wife; woe is me for my sons and daughters! I [continue to] grieve.

The Judge who judges me is faithful to me; He has crushed me on account of my transgressions and my crimes.

To You, O Lord, is the justice, and to me the shame; to God is the justice and to me the sins and the wickedness.

I will bless You with every punishment and I will dedicate song; I will kneel and bow down before You.

34

The Earliest Hebrew First-Crusade Narrative

Robert Chazan

At the end of November 1095, Pope Urban II called for an armed pilgrimage to recapture the sacred sites of Christianity in the Holy Land from the Muslims, thereby inaugurating the Crusades. This new movement eventuated almost four years later in the stunning conquest of Jerusalem by the Western warriors. Along the way, the First Crusade took a series of unexpected turns, including savage attacks perpetrated during the spring months of 1096 by unruly German bands upon a number of major Jewish communities in the Rhineland and Jewish heroism in resisting these assaults.

The so-called *Mainz Anonymous,* the oldest surviving Hebrew account of Jewish fate during the tumultuous attacks of 1096, is a preeminent achievement in medieval Hebrew narrative. The anonymous author made no effort to describe the totality of Jewish suffering and heroism in 1096; he was focused, rather, on a particular set of Rhineland settlements, the Jewish communities of Speyer, Worms, and Mainz. In order to achieve maximum understanding of what befell these communities, this early narrator felt it necessary to sketch the broad background of the crusade—its origins, its objectives, its participants, and its potential for provoking anti-Jewish animosity. Only against this broad backdrop could the fate of the three Rhineland Jewish settlements be properly portrayed and understood.

The *Mainz Anonymous* provides detailed data about Christian and Jewish behaviors and thinking. This detailed information was intended to guide Jews in the face of possible recurrence of crusading violence, to exonerate the Jews of 1096 from accusations of shortsightedness in their response to rapidly escalating dangers, to exculpate Jews who converted, and to obviate criticism of Jews who performed the most radical kind of martyrdom by taking the lives of family members, especially children. All these objectives were achieved through the combination of detailed and accurate information and dramatic and moving storytelling.

Alongside these immediate objectives, the *Mainz Anonymous* also wrestled with timeless concerns. Although every human tragedy evokes soul searching, the 1096 catastrophe was accompanied by disheartening and dangerous Christian interpretation. The *Mainz Anonymous* and two other Hebrew narratives all tell of Christians, some hostile and some friendly, attempting to convince Jews that the slaughter must serve as decisive evidence of God's abandonment of the Jewish people. In the light of this evidence of divine rejection, no sensible course remained for Jews other than conversion. This Christian interpretation posed a serious challenge for the survivors of 1096; Jewish leaders and authors had to provide an alternative reading of the events of 1096, and they did.

For the *Mainz Anonymous,* the atrocities by no means proved divine rejection of the Jews; they constituted a divine decree, with all the mystery associated with such edicts. Whatever the precise basis for this divine decree, the Jews of 1096, through their heroic rejection of Christianity and their reaffirmation at all costs of Jewish faith, transformed tragedy into triumph. According to the *Mainz Anonymous,* the great heroes of the 1090s were not the Christian warriors who conquered Jerusalem; the great heroes were the Jewish martyrs. The extraordinary devotion exhibited by the Jewish victims of crusader aggression would inevitably win divine favor and reward. The juxtaposition of immediate and timeless objectives makes the *Mainz Anonymous* an innovative, effective, and illuminating milestone in Jewish history writing.

In this brilliantly organized narrative, we see random evidence of normal patterns of Jewish existence. Rhineland Jews lived in tightly knit communities, by and large segregated from their Christian neighbors and led by a respected elite of wealth and learning. Jewish leadership negotiated with the local authorities and, on occasion, even with the crusaders themselves. Both the leaders and their followers were committed to punctilious observance of Jewish law. The symbols of Jewish tradition permeated Jewish culture in the Rhineland. The Jewish minority and the Christian majority coexisted in a normally stable but inherently volatile tension. This information on normal patterns of Jewish existence is corroborated by the sources that have survived from the established authorities, such as rabbinic responsa, biblical commentaries, and commentaries on the talmudic corpus.

In addition, the *Mainz Anonymous,* by virtue of its focus on the unusual events of 1096, serves to illuminate a set of realities that the more sedate sources generally ignore. The Jewish communities of the Rhineland were somewhat more heterogeneous than we might have expected. Note, for example, the martyr Jacob ben Sullam, whose mother was not Jewish. Jacob, in his moment of martyrdom, reveals some of the fractures within the tightly knit Jewish community: "All the days of my life till now, you have despised me. Now I shall slaughter myself." The act of self-slaughter would win Jacob the respect denied him during his lifetime.

Especially striking is the role of women in the Jewish martyrdom of 1096. Although women appear only tangentially in the more normative sources from the period, in the *Mainz Anonymous* and the other two Hebrew First-Crusade narratives, they play a central role. Women goad their men into action; they often, in fact, take the lead themselves. Although the *Mainz Anonymous* and its companion narratives are replete with moving tales, the lengthiest and most stunning single episode involves Rachel of Mainz. Rachel is a thoroughly human figure, a remarkable combination of commitment and doubt, of devotion and anguish. She is determined to kill her children, lest they fall into the hands of the crusaders and be baptized. Despite the depth of her commitment, she wails upon taking hold of the knife with which she will do her deed. Her greatness lies not in the absence of human feeling but rather in her capacity to overcome human emotion in the name of her faith.

The Hebrew 1096 narratives also reveal to us the depth and intensity of the Christian-Jewish religious struggle. The parallels between Christian and Jewish commitment to martyrdom in 1096, between the Christian and Jewish projection of self-sacrifice as the highest religious value, between Christian and Jewish focus on Jerusalem, between Christian and Jewish certainty of the rewards of afterlife—all reveal to us the extent to which the Rhineland Jews were embedded in their Christian environment and had absorbed many of its values. It is of course precisely this embeddedness and this closeness that makes it all the more important for the *Mainz Anonymous* to establish distance and difference, to emphasize the gap between Jewish truth and Christian error, between Jewish virtue and Christian shortcoming.

In addressing both the immediate and timeless issues that beset him, the Jewish author of the *Mainz Anonymous* ultimately chose to make his points by telling the tale. By reading carefully the narrative itself, the author and the reality he sought to portray can best be appreciated.

The *Mainz Anonymous* has survived in one manuscript copy only, a fourteenth-century Italian manuscript that is preserved in Darmstadt, Germany. The text, along with the other two 1096 narratives, was edited by Adolph Neubauer and Moritz Stern, *Hebräische Berichte über die Judenverfolgungen während die Kreuzzüge* (Berlin: Verlag von Leonhard Stein, 1892); a translation of all three narratives was provided by Shlomo Eidelberg, *The Jews and the Crusaders* (Madison: University of Wisconsin, 1977). The present translation is taken, with minor changes, from Robert Chazan, *European Jewry and the First Crusade* (Berkeley and Los Angeles: University of California Press, 1987).

Further Reading

Fullest analysis of the events of 1096 can be found in Robert Chazan, *European Jewry and the First Crusade*. A more popularly oriented study is Chazan, *In the Year 1096...; The First Crusade and the Jews* (Philadelphia: Jewish Publication Society, 1996). For a survey of prior research on the three Hebrew narratives, see Anna Sapir Abulafia, "The Interrelationship between the Hebrew Chronicles on the First Crusade," *Journal of Semitic Studies* 27 (1982): 221–39. For a full investigation of the three Hebrew narratives, see Robert Chazan, *God, Humanity, and History: The Hebrew First-Crusade Narratives* (Berkeley: University of California Press, 2000).

The Mainz Anonymous

I shall begin the account of the former persecution. May the Lord protect us and all Israel from persecution.

It came to pass in the year one thousand twenty-eight after the destruction of the Temple that this evil befell Israel. There first arose the princes and nobles and common folk in France, who took counsel and set plans to ascend and to rise up like eagles and to do battle and to clear a way for journeying to Jerusalem, the Holy City, and for reaching the sepulcher of the Crucified, a trampled corpse who cannot profit and cannot save for he is worthless. They said to one another: "Behold we travel to a distant land to do battle with the kings of that land. We take our lives in our hands in order to kill and to subjugate all those kingdoms that do not believe in the Crucified. How much more so [should we kill and subjugate] the Jews, who killed and crucified him." They taunted us from every direction. They took counsel, ordering that either we turn to their abominable faith or they would destroy us from infant to suckling. They—both princes and common folk—placed an evil sign upon their garments, a cross, and helmets upon their heads.

When the [Jewish] communities in France heard, they were seized by consternation, fear, and trembling.... They wrote letters and sent emissaries to all the [Jewish] communities along the Rhine River, [asking that they] fast and deprive themselves and seek mercy from [God who] dwells on high, so that he deliver them [the Jews] from [the crusaders'] hands. When the letters reached the saintly ones who were in that land, they—those men of God, the pillars of the universe, who were in Mainz—wrote in reply to France. Thus was it written in them [their letters]: "All the [Jewish] communities have decreed a fast. We have done our part. May God save us and save you from all distress and hardship. We are greatly fearful for you. We, however, have less reason to fear [for ourselves], for we have heard not even a rumor [of such developments]." Indeed we did not hear that a decree had been issued and that a sword was to afflict us mortally.

When the crusaders began to reach this land, they sought funds with which to purchase bread. We gave them, considering ourselves to be fulfilling the verse: "Serve the king of Babylon, and live." All this, however, was of no avail, for our sins brought it about that the burghers in every city to which the crusaders came were hostile to us, for their [the burghers'] hands were also with them [the crusaders] to destroy vine and stock all along the way to Jerusalem.

It came to pass that, when the crusaders came, battalion after battalion, like the army of Sennacherib, some of the princes in the empire said: "Why do we sit thus? Let us also go with them. For every man who sets forth on this journey and undertakes to ascend to the impure sepulcher dedicated to the Crucified will be assured paradise." Then the crusaders along with them [the princes] gathered from all the provinces until they became as numerous as the sands of the sea, including both princes and common folk.

They circulated a report . . . : "Anyone who kills a single Jew will have all his sins absolved." Indeed there was a certain nobleman, Ditmar by name, who announced that he would not depart from this empire until he would kill one Jew—then he would depart. Now when the holy community in Mainz heard this, they decreed a fast. They cried out mightily to the Lord and they passed night and day in fasting. Likewise they recited dirges both morning and evening, both small and great. Nonetheless our God did not turn away from his awesome wrath against us. For the crusaders with their insignia came, with their standards before our houses. When they saw one of us, they ran after him and pierced him with a spear, to the point that we were afraid even to cross our thresholds.

It came to pass on the eighth of the month of Iyyar, on the Sabbath, the measure of justice began to manifest itself against us. The crusaders and burghers arose first against the saintly ones, the pious of the Almighty in Speyer. They took counsel against them, [planning] to seize them together in the synagogue. But it was revealed to them and they arose [early] on the Sabbath morning and prayed rapidly and left the synagogue. When they [the crusaders and burghers] saw that their plan for seizing them together was foiled, they rose against them [the Jews] and killed eleven of them. From there the decree began, to fulfill that which is said: "Begin at my sanctuary." When Bishop John heard, he came with a large force and helped the [Jewish] community wholeheartedly and brought them indoors and saved them from their [the crusaders' and burghers'] hands. He seized some of the burghers and cut off their hands. He was a pious one among the nations. Indeed God brought about well-being and salvation through him. R. Moses ben Yekutiel the *parnas* [warden] stood in the breach and extended himself on their behalf. Through him all those forcibly converted who remained here and there in the empire of Henry returned [to Judaism]. Through the emperor, Bishop John removed the remnant of the community of Speyer to his fortified towns, and the Lord turned to them, for the sake of his great Name. The bishop hid them until the enemies of the Lord passed. They [the Jews] remained there, fasting and weeping and mourning. They despaired deeply, for every day the crusaders and the Gentiles and Emicho—may his bones be ground up—and the common folk gathered against them, to seize them and to destroy them. Through R. Moses the *parnas*, Bishop John saved them, for the Lord inclined his heart to save them without bribery. This was from the Lord, in order to give us there a remnant and a residue through him.

It came to pass that, when the sad report that some of the community of Speyer had been killed reached Worms, they [the Jews of Worms] cried out to the Lord and wept loudly and bitterly, for they saw that a decree had been issued from heaven and that there was no place to flee, neither forward nor backward. Then the community divided itself into two groups. Some of them fled to the bishop in his towers; some of them remained in their homes, for the burghers promised them vainly and cunningly. They are splintered reeds, for evil and not for good, for their hand was with the crusaders in order to destroy our name and remnant. They gave us vain and meaningless encouragement, [saying]: "Do not fear them, for anyone who kills one of you—his life will be forfeit for yours." They [the burghers] did not give them [the Jews] anywhere to flee, for [the members of] the community deposited all their money in their [the burghers'] hands. Therefore they surrendered them.

It came to pass on the tenth of Iyyar, on Sunday, they plotted craftily against them. They took a trampled corpse of theirs, that had been buried thirty days previously and carried it through the city, saying: "Behold what the Jews have done to our comrade. They took a Gentile and boiled him in water. They then poured the water into our wells in order to kill us." When the crusaders and burghers heard this, they cried out and gathered—all who bore and unsheathed [a sword], from great to small—saying: "Behold the time has come to avenge him who was crucified, whom their ancestors slew. Now let not a remnant or a residue escape, even an infant or suckling in the cradle." They then came and struck those who had remained in their houses—comely young men and comely and lovely young women along with elders. All of them stretched forth their necks. Even manumitted servingmen and servingwomen were killed along with them for the sanctification of the Name which is awesome and sublime, . . . who rules above and below, who was and will be. Indeed the Lord of Hosts is his Name. He is crowned with the splendor of seventy-two names; he created the Torah nine hundred and seventy-four generations prior to the creation of the world. There were twenty-six generations from the creation of the world to Moses, the father of the prophets, through whom [God] gave the holy Torah. Moses came and wrote in it: "The Lord has affirmed this day that you are, as he promised you, his treasured people which shall observe all his commandments." For him and his Torah they were killed like oxen and were dragged through the market places and streets like sheep to the slaughter and lay naked, for they [the attackers] stripped them and left them naked.

It came to pass that, when those who remained saw their brethren naked and the modest daughters of Israel they then acceded to them [the attackers] under great duress, for the crusaders intended to leave not a remnant or a residue. There were those of them who said: "Let us do their will for the time being, and let us go and bury our brethren and save our children from them." For they had seized the children that remained, a small number, saying that perhaps they would remain in their pseudo faith. They [the Jews who converted] did not desert their Creator, nor did their hearts incline after the Crucified. Rather they cleaved to the God on high. Moreover, the rest of the community, those who remained in the chambers of the bishop, sent garments with which to clothe those who had been killed through those who had been saved. For they were charitable. Indeed the heads of the community remained there [in the bishop's chambers] and most of the community was saved during the first incident. They sent to those forcibly converted messages of consolation: "Fear not and do not take to heart that which you have done. For if the Holy One, blessed be he, saves us from the hands of our enemies, then we shall be with you for both death and life. However do not desert the Lord."

It came to pass on the twenty-fifth of Iyyar that the crusaders and the burghers said: "Behold those who remain in the courtyard of the bishop and in his chambers. Let us take vengeance on them as well." They gathered from all the villages in the vicinity, along with the crusaders and the burghers; they besieged them [the Jews]; and they did battle against them. There took place a very great battle, one side against the other, until they seized the chambers in which the children of the sacred covenant were. When they saw the battle raging to and fro, the decree of the King of Kings, then they accepted divine judgment and expressed faith in their Creator and offered up true sacrifices. They took their children and slaughtered them unreservedly for the unity of the revered and awesome Name. There were killed the notables of the community.

There was a certain young man, named R. Meshullam ben R. Isaac. He called out loudly to all those standing there and to Zipporah, his helpmate: "Listen to me both great and small. This son God gave me. My wife Zipporah bore him in her old age and his name is Isaac. Now I shall offer him up as did our ancestor Abraham with his son Isaac." Zipporah replied: "My lord, my lord. Wait a bit. Do not stretch forth your hand against the lad whom I have raised and brought up and whom I bore in my old age. Slaughter me first, so that I not witness the death of the child." He then replied: "I shall not delay even a moment. He who gave him to us will take him as his portion. He will place him in the bosom of Abraham our ancestor." He then bound Isaac his son and took in his hand the knife with which to slaughter his son and made the benediction for slaughtering. The lad answered amen. He then slaughtered the lad. He took his screaming wife. The two of them departed together from the chamber and the crusaders killed them. "At such things will you restrain yourself, O Lord?" Nevertheless, he did not turn away from his great wrath against us.

There was a certain young man, named Isaac ben Daniel. They asked him, saying: "Do you wish to exchange your God for a wretched idol?" He said: "Heaven forfend that I deny him; in him shall I trust. Thus shall I commend to him my soul." They put a rope around his neck and dragged him throughout the entire city, through the mud of the streets, up to the place of their idolatry. His soul was still bound up in his body. They said to him: "You may still be saved. Do you wish to convert?" He signaled with his finger—for he was unable to utter a word with his mouth, for he had been strangled—saying: "Cut off my head!" and they severed his neck.

There was still another young man, named R. Simhah the *cohen* [priest] son of our teacher R. Isaac the *cohen*. They sought to sully him with their fetid waters. They said to him: "Behold, all of them have already been killed and they lie naked." Then the young man answered them cleverly: "I shall fulfill all your desires, but take me with you to the bishop." They took him and led him to the chamber of the bishop. The nephew of the bishop was there with them. They began designating him with the name of the loathsome offshoot, leaving him in the chamber of the bishop. Then the young man took out his knife and gnashed his teeth in anger against the prince, the relative of the bishop, as does the lion over its prey, and sank the knife in his belly, and he fell and died. He turned and stabbed two more until the knife broke in his hand. They all fled to and fro. But when they saw that the knife had broken, they assaulted him and killed him. There was killed the young man who sanctified the [Divine] Name and who did what the rest of the community did not do, for he killed three of the uncircumcised with his knife. The rest had devoted themselves and had fasted daily. Previously they had wept, each for his family and friends, to the point where their strength dissipated. They were unable to do battle against them [the enemy); rather they said: "It is the decree of the King. Let us fall into the hands of the Lord. Then we shall come and see the great light." There they all fell for the unity of the [divine] Name.

There was also a respected woman there, named Minna, hidden in a house underground, outside the city. All the men of the city gathered and said to her: "Behold you are a remarkable woman. Know and see that God does not wish to save you, for they [the Jews of Worms] lie naked at the corner of every street, unburied. Sully yourself [with the waters of baptism]." They fell before her to the ground, for they did not wish to kill her. Her reputation was known widely, for all the notables of the city and the princes of the land were found in her circle. She responded and said: "Heaven forfend that I deny the God on high. For him and his holy Torah kill me and do not tarry any longer." There the woman whose praises were sung at the gates was killed.

All of them were killed and sanctified the divine Name unreservedly and willingly. All of them slaughtered one another together—young men and young women, old men and old women, even infants slaughtered themselves for the sanctification of the [divine] Name. Those who have been designated by name did so; the rest who have not been designated by name did so all the more. They behaved in a way never seen by the human eye. With regard to them and those like them it is said: "[Rescue me from the wicked with your sword,] from men, O Lord, by your hand, from men whose share in life is fleeting. [But as to your treasured ones, fill their bellies. Their sons too shall be satisfied, and have something left over for their young.]" "[Such things have never been heard or noted.] No eye has seen [them], O God, but you, who act for those who trust in you." They all fell by the hand of the Lord and returned to their rest, to the great light in paradise. Behold their souls are bound up in the bond of life, with the God who created them, to the end of days.

It came to pass that, when the saintly ones, the pious of the Almighty, the holy community in Mainz, heard that some of the community of Speyer had been killed and the community of Worms [had been attacked] twice, then their spirit collapsed and their hearts melted and turned to water. They cried out to the Lord and said: "Ah! Lord God of Israel! Are you wiping out the remnant of Israel? Where are all your wondrous deeds about which our ancestors told us, saying: 'Truly the Lord brought you up from Egypt.' But now you have abandoned us, delivering us into the hands of the Gentiles for destruction." Then all the leaders of Israel gathered from the community and came to the archbishop and his ministers and servants and said to them: "What are we to do with regard to the report which we have heard concerning our brethren in Speyer and Worms who have been killed?" They said to them: "Heed our advice and bring all your moneys into our treasury and into the treasury of the archbishop. Then you and your wives and your children and all your retinue bring into the courtyard of the archbishop. Thus will you be able to be saved from the crusaders." They contrived and gave this counsel in order to surrender us and to gather us up and to seize us like fish enmeshed in a fatal net. To be sure, the archbishop gathered his ministers and servants—exalted ministers, nobles and grandees—in order to assist us and to save us from the crusaders. For at the outset it was his desire to save us, but ultimately he failed.

It came to pass on a certain day that a Gentile woman came and brought with her a goose that she had raised since it was a gosling. This goose went everywhere that the Gentile woman went. She said to all passersby: "Behold this goose understands that I intend to go on the crusade and wishes to go with me." Then the crusaders and burghers gathered against us, saying to us: "Where is your source of trust? How will you be saved? Behold the wonders that the Crucified does for us!" Then all of them came with swords and spears to destroy us. Some of the burghers came and would not allow them [to do so]. At that time they stood . . . and killed along the Rhine River, until they killed one of the crusaders. Then they said: "All these things the Jews have caused." Then they almost gathered [against us]. When the saintly ones saw all these things, their hearts melted. They [the Christians] spoke harshly with them, [threatening] to assault and attack us. When they [the Jews] heard their words, they said—from great to small: "If only we might die by the hand of the Lord, rather than die at the hands of the enemies of the Lord. For he is a merciful God, the only King in his universe."

They left their houses empty and came to the synagogue only on the Sabbath, that last Sabbath prior to our disaster, when a few entered to pray. R. Judah ben R. Isaac entered there to pray on that Sabbath. They wept copiously, to the point of exhaustion, for they saw that this was the decree of the King of Kings. There was a venerable scholar, R. Baruch ben R. Isaac, and he said to us: "Know that a decree has truly and surely been enacted against us, and we will not be able to be saved. For tonight we—I and my son-in-law Judah— heard the souls praying here loudly, [with a sound] like weeping. When we heard the sound, we thought that perhaps they [those praying] came from the courtyard of the archbishop and that some of the community had returned to pray in the synagogue at midnight out of pain and anguish. We ran to the door of the synagogue, but it was closed. We heard the sound, but we comprehended nothing. We returned home shaken, for our house was close to the synagogue." When we heard these words, we fell on our faces and said: "Ah! Lord God! Are you wiping out the remnant of Israel?" They went and recounted these incidents to their brethren in the courtyard of the burgrave and in the courtyard of the archbishop. They likewise wept copiously.

It came to pass on the new moon of Sivan that the wicked Emicho—may his bones be ground up on iron millstones—came with a large army outside the city, with crusaders and common folk. For he also said: "It is my desire to go on the crusade." He was our chief persecutor. He had no mercy on the elderly, on young men and young women, on infants and sucklings, nor on the ill. He turned the people of the Lord into dust to be trampled. The young men he put to the sword and their pregnant women he ripped open.

They camped outside the city for two days. Then the heads of the [Jewish] community said: "Let us send him money, along with our letters, so that the [Jewish] communities along the way will honor him. Perhaps the Lord will treat us with his great loving-kindness." For previously they had liberally spent their moneys, giving the archbishop and the burgrave and their ministers and their servants and the burghers approximately four hundred marks, so that they might aid them. It availed them nothing. We were unlike Sodom and Gomorrah, for in their case ten [righteous] were sought in order to save them. For us neither twenty nor ten were sought.

It came to pass on the third of the month of Sivan, on that very day when Moses said: "Be ready for the third day." On that very day, the crown of Israel fell. Then the students of Torah fell and the scholars disappeared. The honor of the Torah fell. He threw down from heaven to earth the glory of Israel. Fear of sin and humility came to an end. Men of deeds, the luster of wisdom and purity, those who turn back evil decrees and the anger of their Creator disappeared. The givers of charity in secret diminished. Truth was eclipsed; the preachers disappeared; the revered fell and the arrogant multiplied. Woe for all these! From the day that the second Temple was destroyed, there have been none like them; after them there will be no more. For they sanctified the [divine] Name with all their hearts and with all their souls and with all their might. They are blessed.

It came to pass at midday that the wicked Emicho—may his bones be ground up—he and all his army came, and the burghers opened up the gates for him. Then the enemies of the Lord said one to another: "Behold the gates have been opened by themselves. All this the Crucified has done for us, so that we might avenge his blood on the Jews." They came with their standards to the archbishop's gate, where the children of the sacred covenant were—an army as numerous as the sands on the seashore. When the saintly and God-fearing saw the huge multitude, they trusted in and cleaved to their Creator. They donned armor and strapped on weapons—great and small—with R. Kalonymous ben Meshullam at their head.

There was a pious one, one of the great men of the generation, Rabbi Menahem ben Rabbi David the *levi*. He said: "All the congregation, sanctify the revered and awesome Name unreservedly." They all replied: . . . [He said]: "All of you must do as did the sons of our ancestor Jacob when he sought to reveal to them the time of redemption, at which point the divine presence left him. [Jacob said]: 'Perhaps I too am sullied as was my grandfather Abraham [from whom proceeded Ishmael] or like my father Isaac [from whom proceeded Esau]. [His sons said to him: 'Hear O Israel! The Lord is our God; the Lord is One'.] [Do] as did our ancestors when they answered and said, as they received the Torah at this very time on Mount Sinai: 'We shall do and hear.' " They then called out loudly: "Hear O Israel! The Lord is our God, the Lord is One." They all then drew near to the gate to do battle with the crusaders and with the burghers. They did battle one with another around the gate. Our sins brought it about that the enemy overcame them and captured the gate. The men of the archbishop, who had promised to assist, fled immediately, in order to turn them over to the enemy, for they are splintered reeds.

Then the enemy came into the courtyard and found R. Isaac ben R. Moses [and others and struck them] a mortal sword blow. Not so for the fifty-three souls who fled with R. Kalonymous through the chambers of the archbishop, exiting into a long room called . . . and remaining there.

The enemy entered the courtyard on the third of Sivan, on the third day of the week, a day of darkness and gloom, a day of densest clouds. May darkness and day gloom reclaim it. May God above have no concern for it; may light never shine upon it. O sun and moon! Why did you not hide your light? And you stars, to whom Israel has been compared, and you twelve constellations, like the number of the tribes of Israel, the sons of Jacob, how was it that your light not cease to provide illumination to the enemy who intended to blot out the name of Israel? Ask and see—was there ever so numerous a set of sacrifices from the days of Adam?

When the children of the sacred covenant saw that decree had been issued and that the enemy had overcome them, they all cried out—young men and old men, young women and children, menservants and maidservants—and wept for themselves and their lives. They said: "We shall suffer the yoke of awe of the sacred. For the moment the enemy will kill us with the easiest of the four deaths—by the sword. But we shall remain alive; our souls [will repose] in paradise, in the radiance of the great light, forever." They all said acceptingly and willingly: "Ultimately one must not question the ways of the Holy One blessed be he and blessed be his Name, who gave us his Torah and commanded us to put to death and to kill ourselves for the unity of his holy Name. Blessed are we if we do his will and blessed are all those who are killed and slaughtered and who die for the unity of his Name. Not only are they privileged to enter the world to come and sit in the circle of the saintly, the pillars of the universe. What is more, they exchange a world of darkness for a world of light, a world of pain for a world of happiness, a transitory world for a world that is eternal and everlasting." They all cried out loudly and in unison: "Ultimately we must not tarry. For the enemy has come upon us suddenly. Let us offer ourselves up before our Father in heaven. Anyone who has a knife should come and slaughter us for the sanctification of the unique Name [of God] who lives forever. Subsequently let him pierce himself with his sword either in his throat or in his belly or let him slaughter himself." They all stood—men and slaughtered one another.

The young women and the brides and bridegrooms looked through the windows and cried out loudly and said: "Look and see, God, what we do for the sanctification of your great Name, rather than abandon your divinity for a crucified one, a trampled and wretched and abominable offshoot . . . , a bastard and a child of menstruation and lust."

They were all slaughtered. The blood of this slaughter flowed through the chambers in which the children of the sacred covenant were. They lay in slaughtered rows—the infant with the elderly . . . [making sounds] like those made by slaughtered sheep. "At such things will you restrain yourself, O Lord; will you stand idly by and let us suffer so heavily? Avenge the blood of your servants that has been spilled."

Behold, has such a thing ever happened before? For they jostled one another, saying: "I shall sanctify first the Name of the King of Kings." The pious women threw money outside, in order to deter them [the enemy] a bit, until they might slaughter their children, in order to fulfill the will of the Creator. . . .

It came to pass that, when the enemy came to the chambers and broke down the doors and found them convulsing, still writhing in their blood, they took their money and stripped them naked. They struck those remaining and left not a remnant or a residue.

Thus they did in all the chambers where there were children of Israel, [children of] the sacred covenant, with the exception of one chamber which was too strong. The enemy did battle against it till evening. When the saintly ones [in that chamber] saw that the enemy was mightier than they were, the men and the women rose up and slaughtered the children. Subsequently, they slaughtered one another. Some fell on their swords or knives. The saintly women threw rocks through the windows. The enemy in turn struck them with rocks. They [the Jewish women] endured all these rocks, until their flesh and faces became shredded. They cursed and blasphemed the crusaders in the name of the Crucified, the profane and despised, the son of lust: "Upon whom do you rely? Upon a trampled corpse!" Then the crusaders advanced to break down the door.

There was a notable lady, Rachel the daughter of R. Isaac ben R. Asher. She said to her companions: "I have four children. On them as well have no mercy, lest these uncircumcised come and seize them and they remain in their pseudo faith. With them as well you must sanctify the holy Name." One of her companions came and took the knife. When she saw the knife, she cried loudly and bitterly. She beat her face, crying and saying: "Where is your steadfast love, O Lord?" She took Isaac her small son—indeed he was very lovely—and slaughtered him. She . . . said to her companions: "Wait! Do not slaughter Isaac before Aaron." But the lad Aaron, when he saw that his brother had been slaughtered, cried out: "Mother, Mother, do not slaughter me!" He then went and hid himself under a bureau. She took her two daughters, Bella and Matrona, and sacrificed them to the Lord God of Hosts, who commanded us not to abandon pure awe of him and to remain loyal to him. When the saintly one finished sacrificing her three children before our Creator, she then lifted her voice and called out to her son: "Aaron, Aaron, where are you? I shall not have pity or mercy on you either." She pulled him by the leg from under the bureau, where he had hidden, and sacrificed him before the sublime and exalted God. She then put them under her two sleeves, two on one side and two on the other, near her heart. They convulsed near her, until the crusaders seized the chamber. They found her sitting and mourning them. They said to her: "Show us the money which you have under your sleeves." When they saw the slaughtered children, they smote her and killed her. With regard to them and to her it is said: "Mother and babes were dashed to death together." She died with them, as did the [earlier] saintly one with her seven sons. With regard to her it is said: "The mother of the child is happy."

The crusaders killed all those in the chamber and stripped them naked. They were still writhing and convulsing in their blood, as they stripped them. "See, O Lord, and behold how abject I have become." Subsequently, they threw them from the chambers through the windows naked, heap upon heap and mound upon mound, until they formed a high heap. Many of the children of the sacred covenant, as they were thrown, still had life and would signal with their fingers: "Give us water that we might drink." When the crusaders saw this, they would ask them: "Do you wish to sully yourselves with the waters [of the baptism]?" They would shake their heads and would look at their Father in heaven as a means of saying no and would point with their fingers to the Holy One blessed be he. The crusaders then killed them.

All these things were done by those whom we have designated by name. The rest of the community all the more proclaimed the unity of the sacred Name, and all fell into the hands of the Lord.

Then the crusaders began to exult in the name of the Crucified. They lifted their standards and came to the remnant of the community, to the courtyard of the burgrave. They besieged them as well and did battle against them and seized the entranceway to the courtyard and smote them also.

There was a certain man, named Moses ben Helbo. He called to his sons and said to them: "My sons Simon and Helbo, at this moment hell and paradise are open [before you]. Into which do you wish to enter?" They answered him and said: "Bring us into paradise." They stretched forth their necks. The enemy smote them, the father along with the sons.

There was a Torah scroll there in the chamber. The crusaders came into the chamber, found it, and tore it to shreds. When the saintly and pure daughters of royalty [the Jewish women] saw that the Torah had been torn, they called out loudly to their husbands: "Behold, behold the holy Torah. The enemy is tearing it." Then they all, the men and the women, said together: "Woe for the holy Torah, perfect in beauty, the delight of our eyes. We used to bow before it in the synagogue; we used to kiss it; we used to honor it. How has it now fallen into the hands of the unclean and uncircumcised!" When the men heard the words of the saintly women, they became exceedingly zealous for the Lord our God and for the holy and beloved Torah. There was there a young man named R. David ben Rabbi Menahem. He said to them: "My brethren, rend your garments over the honor of the Torah." They rent their garments as our teacher commanded. They then found a crusader in a chamber, and they all—both men and women—rose up and stoned him. He fell and died. Now when the burghers and crusaders saw that he had died, they did battle against them. They went up on the roof over the place where the children of the covenant were, broke the roof, shot at them with arrows, and pierced them with spears.

There was a certain man named Jacob ben Sullam. He was not from a family of notables. Indeed, his mother was not Jewish. He called out loudly to all standing near him: "All the days of my life till now, you have despised me. Now I shall slaughter myself." He slaughtered himself for the Name which is most sublime, which is the Name of the Lord of Hosts.

There was, in addition, a certain man named Samuel the elder ben R. Mordechai. He also sanctified the [divine] Name. He took his knife and plunged it into his belly, spilling his innards upon the ground. He called to all standing near him and said to them: "Behold my brethren what I do for the sanctification of the Eternal." There the elder fell for the unity of the [divine] Name and sanctified his awesome God.

The crusaders and burghers turned from there and came to the center of the city, to a certain courtyard. There was hidden David the *gabbai* [synagogue assistant] ben R. Nathaniel—he, his wife, his children, and all the members of his household—in the courtyard of a certain priest. The priest said to him: "Behold there remains in the courtyard of the archbishop and in the courtyard of the burgrave neither a remnant nor a residue. They have all been killed, cast out, and trampled in the streets, with the exception of a few whom they baptized. Do likewise and you will be able to be saved—you and your wealth and all the members of your household—from the hands of the crusaders." The God-fearing man replied: "Indeed go to the crusaders and to the burghers and tell them to come to me." When the priest heard the words of David the *gabbai*, he was very happy over his words, for he thought: "This distinguished Jew has agreed to heed us." He ran to meet them and told them the words of the saintly one. They likewise were very happy. They gathered around the house by the thousands and the ten thousands. When the saintly one saw them, he trusted in his Creator and called to them, saying: "Lo! You are the children of lust. You believe in one who was born of lust. But I believe in the God who lives forever, who dwells in the highest heaven. In him have I trusted to this day, to the point of death. If you kill me, my soul will repose in paradise, in the light of life. But you will descend to the nethermost pit, to everlasting abhorrence, to hell, where you will be judged with your deity, who was a child of lust and was crucified." When they heard the pious one, they were enraged. They raised their standards and camped about the house and began to call and shout in the name of the Crucified. They assaulted him and killed him and his saintly wife and his children and his son-in-law and all the members of his household and his maidservant. All were killed there for the sanctification of the [divine] Name. There fell the saintly one and the members of his household.

They turned and came to the house of R. Samuel ben R. Naaman. He likewise sanctified the [divine] Name. They gathered around his house, for he alone of all the community had remained in his house. They asked him and sought to baptise him with fetid and impure waters. He put his trust in his Creator—he and all those with him. They [the Jews] did not heed them [the crusaders and burghers]. They killed all of them and threw them all from the windows.

All these things were done by those whom we have singled out by name. The rest of the community and the notables of the congregation—what they did for the unity of the Name of the King of Kings, the Holy One blessed be He and blessed be His Name, like R. Akiba and his associates. . . .

35

Leon Modena's Autobiography

Mark R. Cohen

Leon Modena (1571–1648) was one of the most enigmatic and captivating figures of the Venetian ghetto in the Age of the Baroque. Rabbi, preacher, translator, and teacher, seller of amulets, matchmaker, musician, printers' proofreader, commercial broker, and gambler—he broke the mold for Jews in that period. He was the friend of Christian intellectuals and public figures, and the author of an extraordinary range of books from rabbinic opinions to a dialogue both praising and condemning gambling.

Modena descended from French Ashkenazic Jews, probably victims of one of the expulsions from France in the fourteenth century. As moneylenders, they had settled in northern Italy, whose city-states were then just opening up their doors to Jewish creditors. Leon (his Hebrew name, Judah Aryeh, corresponds to the Italian, for Aryeh means "lion" and the lion is the symbol of the tribe of Judah) was born in 1571. He was a precocious child and student (at least, to hear him tell it in his autobiography). Like others of his breed, he studied both Jewish and secular subjects, the latter including poetry, voice, dancing, and Latin.

Though initially prosperous, his family experienced much financial hardship when Leon was growing up. In his own adult life, Leon also suffered from lack of financial success. He yearned to become a professional rabbi, even though in Venice at that time rabbis were not salaried. Rather, they were paid per rabbinic service, mainly responsa (legal opinions based on Jewish law). But even his rabbinical ordination did not come until he was nearly forty. Before then, and even after, and despite his many intellectual gifts, he often had to resort to tutoring children, something he did not enjoy. He earned also from other jobs outside the rabbinate, for instance, singing as a cantor, composing flowery Hebrew letters for people, drawing up contracts, serving as secretary for Jewish confraternities, and more. Stricken with anxieties, financial and other, he often gambled away what he accumulated.

He recorded the stresses of his personal and family life and also some of his personal triumphs in a Hebrew manuscript that he entitled *Hayye yehudah* (The

Life of Judah). This is one of the first Jewish autobiographies, discounting Josephus's *Life*, which that ancient author wrote in Greek and for a Roman audience. *Hayye yehudah* was meant to be kept in the family, and also for his students to read—not, unlike most of his writings, to be published. The text bears similarities to but also telling differences from contemporary Christian autobiography, as Natalie Zemon Davis has shown in an important comparative essay (see suggestions for Further Reading). It paints a vivid picture of a family, including its women, embedded in the bustling Jewish (and Italian) society of the seventeenth century.

Hayye yehudah reveals much about the religious atmosphere in Modena's still premodern Jewish society. Everywhere in the book the presence of God is to be felt. He is thanked and praised. His blessings are invoked. His mercy is sought. And when the writer suffers, he states, "I do not know why God continues to treat me so roughly."

By Modena's time, the Kabbalah, Jewish mysticism, esoteric in earlier centuries, had permeated Italian-Jewish religiosity. Modena knew many kabbalists and had studied its doctrines. Ultimately, he came to oppose it, and he wrote a treatise against it, appropriately titled *Ari nohem* (The Roaring Lion), a pun on his name. A staunch defender of Judaism against Christianity, he also composed a book against that religion, *Magen va-herev* (Shield and Sword). Like the autobiography, neither of these polemical works was published during the author's lifetime.

Nor was his defense of Judaism against a vituperous treatise challenging the validity of the Oral Law (the Talmud) and of rabbinic Judaism, in general. He claimed to have come across it in 1622 and to have copied it in order to refute it. Modena's defense was called (punning again on his name) *Sha'agat aryeh* (The Roar of the Lion), and the attack on the rabbis, *Kol sakhal* (Voice of a Fool). A recent book attempts to settle an old debate by attempting to prove that Modena was a closet critic of rabbinic Judaism and himself the author of *Kol sakhal*.

Rabbinic responsa, commentaries, and polemical works reflect the ambiance of the religious elite. But the "Autobiography" is special in that it depicts religious life "on the ground." The Jewish life cycle of births, marriages, and above all confessions, elegies, burials, and mourning—the religious rites surrounding death—play a prominent role in the narrative. When, on the eve of their wedding, Modena's intended wife Esther is about to die, tragically for him, she summons a sage (*hakham*) to her bedside to make confession—a pious practice introduced to Ashkenazic Jewry in the Middle Ages.

Life in the synagogue dominated Jewish existence in the ghetto. There were several synagogues in Modena's Venice, and some of them can still be visited by tourists today. Leon was an outstanding preacher. As was customary, he preached in Italian (when he published his sermons, however, he used Hebrew). Thus, non-Jews could attend and understand, and his renown as an orator attracted Christians to the ghetto to hear him. His reputation among Christian intellectuals abroad was based, in part, on his rhetorical skill on the synagogue pulpit. Among Jews, Leon was also a much-sought-after teacher for what we would call adult education, which, like services and sermons, formed part of the robust synagogue life of the ghetto.

In the seventeenth century, much organized religious life took place outside the synagogue, especially in Jewish confraternities (Heb. *hevrot*), which imitated the Christian model. Modena supplemented his income by preaching and teaching for the Ashkenazic Torah Study Society. He even compiled a confessional for the burial confraternity known as the Gemilut Hasadim Society (Society for Good Deeds). And he contributed a poem to a book for the Shomerim la-Boker Society, a confraternity influenced by Kabbalah whose members arose early in the morning to hold penitential vigils.

Alongside synagogue, confraternity, and expressions of faith in the supreme being, the autobiography provides a healthy dose of what we call "popular religion." Modena's life, like that of many of his Jewish contemporaries, attests to the characteristic modus vivendi in Judaism between certain types of popular magic or superstition and "official" rabbinic religion, the law-oriented religion of the Talmud and of the divinely ordained duties. Bibliomancy—seeking an omen by asking a child what biblical verse he had learned that day in school—figures as a favored device when trouble looms. The same Rabbi Leon Modena who preaches, teaches, and issues responsa also writes, teaches, and traffics in amulets and engages in dream divination. Astrology is a commonplace for him, as when he expresses the conviction that the heavens are battling against him and his family.

In one of the segments from the autobiography excerpted below, Modena has his horoscope foretold "by four astrologers, two Jews and two Christians." When he learns that the stars predict his death in just two years time (and this is confirmed by a palm reading), Modena regrets having requested the horoscope. As if to cancel it after the fact, he dons his cap as rabbi and exponent of "official" Judaism and acknowledges that engaging in the very act runs counter to the belief in God's omnipotence. "So here I am today, pained on account of the past and anxious about the future. But God will do as He pleases."

The autobiography also presents the author (and others) engaged (often along with Christians) in the popular pastime of alchemy. Modena's uncle was attracted to alchemy. Leon himself (in one of the episodes selected) pursued the magical art. And his son Mordecai set up an alchemy laboratory in the ghetto, only to fall ill and die from exposure to the chemical fumes. This tragedy in Modena's life— the loss of his firstborn son—repeated itself later on when another son, named Zebulun, was murdered by a gang of Jews to which he belonged, practically before Modena's eyes.

The autobiography provides glimpses of living under sufferance in Christian society, with its double-edged sword. Modena basked in the attention proffered upon him by Christians. Though locked at night, the ghetto was far from isolated from Christian society. Modena, like his fellow Jews, mingled with Christians during the day in other parts of Venice, and we have already noted that Christians were to be found mingling with Jews in the ghetto. Yet Jewish life was tenuous.

Anti-Semitism did not dissolve in Jewish-Christian interfaith sociability. When individual Jews were suspected of wrongdoing, often the entire community was held responsible. In a long episode from the years 1636 to 1637, not excerpted here, two Jews received stolen goods and hid them in the ghetto. During the investigation, arrest, and trial, a threat of general expulsion hung over the heads of all the Venetian Jews. The terror subsided only after the sentence was handed down, in which banishment was extended—unprecedentedly—to relatives of the guilty parties. One of Modena's sons-in-law was among those so punished.

Perhaps it is a precursor of a new age to come that Modena could hope to change Christian attitudes toward the Jews and thereby foster their integration into general society. He was fully aware of the centuries-old Christian belief in the inferiority of Judaism and misanthropy of the Jews. So he wrote a small book in Italian, but only in manuscript, describing Jewish rites and beliefs, the first such book ever written by a Jew primarily for non-Jewish readers. It was an apologetic treatise in which Modena countered Christian stereotypes, depicted rabbinic Judaism as rational (he denied that Kabbalah was central in Jewish life), and portrayed Jews as nonsuperstitious and ethical. But, typical of the ghetto mentality with which he lived, Modena panicked (the episode is excerpted below) when he learned that a Catholic friend had published the manuscript in Paris (in 1637). The author immediately pulled out an old copy and rushed it to the Venetian inquisitorial office, hoping to preempt penalizaton. After receiving the Paris edition, he published a revised one in Venice (in 1638), expurgating passages he believed Catholics would find objectionable. In similar vein, Jews during the emancipation era two centuries later would defend Judaism and the Jewish people against Christian revulsion in an attempt to win civil and social equality.

The texts presented here are drawn from *Hayye yehudah* (The Life of Judah), the autobiography of Leon Modena, translated by Mark R. Cohen (see Further Reading).

Note on the Translation

The Hebrew of the autobiography is generously peppered with biblical allusions, often fragments of verses applied in a fresh and linguistically catchy manner in a new context. Only those verses that are actual quotations are indicated below. More examples of this stylistic feature are noted in the full translation.

Further Reading

The Autobiography of a Seventeenth-Century Venetian Rabbi: Leon Modena's "Life of Judah", translated and edited by Mark R. Cohen (Princeton: Princeton University Press, 1987), with three introductory essays, "The Significance of Leon Modena's Autobiography for Early Modern Jewish and General European History," by the translator and Theodore K. Rabb; "Leon Modena: The Autobiography and the Man," by Howard E. Adelman; and "Fame and Secrecy: Leon Modena's *Life* as an Early Modern Autobiography," by Natalie Zemon Davis; and Historical Notes by Howard E. Adelman and Benjamin C. I. Ravid. Mark R. Cohen, "Leone da Modena's *Riti*: A Seventeenth-Century Plea for Social Toleration of Jews," *Jewish Social Studies* 34 (1972): 287–321; reprinted in *Essential Papers on Jewish Culture in Renaissance and Baroque Italy*, edited by David B. Ruderman (New York and London: New York University Press, 1992), pp. 429–73. Howard E. Adelman, "Success and Failure in Seventeenth Century Venice: The Life and Thought of Leon Modena, 1571–1648," Ph.D. dissertation, Brandeis University, 1985. Talya Fishman, *Shaking the Pillars of Exile. "Voice of a Fool," an Early Modern Critique of Rabbinic Culture* (Stanford: Stanford University Press, 1997).

The Introduction

With God's help may we do this successfully.

This is the life story of Judah Aryeh, son of the noble and trustworthy Isaac of blessed memory, son of the gaon and physician, Rabbi Mordecai of blessed memory, son of the venerable Isaac of blessed memory, son of the wealthy Moses of blessed memory, Modena:

"Few and evil have been the days of the years of my life" [Gen. 47:9] in this world.

Inasmuch as the King's [God's] word has power to remove man from this world on the day of his death—after which all is forgotten—for more than twenty-four years I have desired in the depths of my soul to set down in writing all the incidents that happened to me from my beginnings until the end of my life, so that I shall not die, but live. I thought that it would be of value to my sons, the fruit of my loins, and to their descendants, and to my students, who are called sons, just as it is a great pleasure to me to be able to know the lives of my ancestors, forebears, teachers, and all other important and beloved people.

In particular, I longed to bequeath it as a gift to my firstborn son, the apple of my eye, the root of my heart, whose bright countenance was similar to mine, a man of wisdom, Mordecai of blessed memory, who was known as Angelo. All my thoughts were of him. I was proud of him, and he was the source of all my joy. But for those twenty-four years up to the present I did not succeed in writing this down as a memoir in a book. Now that God has taken away my joy—it being two months since God took him away, leaving me desolate and faint all day long—my soul has refused to be comforted, for I will go to my grave mourning for my son, waiting for death as for a solemnly appointed time.

And so, at the age of forty-seven, an old man, full of disquietude, I resolved, in the month of Tevet 5378 [December 29, 1617–January 26, 1618] to begin and to finish, God willing, giving an account of all the essential as well as of the incidental happenings in my life. Should my children or children's children or students or others who know me look at it, they will see the woes that befell me. From the moment I entered the world I had neither tranquillity nor quiet nor rest, and then disquietude came upon me, namely, disquietude over my son Mordecai of blessed memory. I await death, which does not come.

Subsequently, from year to year, at six-month intervals, I shall add to this account what new happens to me. After that will come my will concerning my body, soul, and literary remains—and God will do what is proper in his eyes. . . .

PRECOCIOUS CHILD. FATHER ESTABLISHES A SYNAGOGUE. FINANCIAL BAD LUCK.

There in Cologna (c. 1576) took place the wedding of my [half-]brother Samuel to Giuditta, the daughter of Angelo da Lipiani of Pesaro, with a banquet and celebration. At the table I recited words of Torah that my teacher had taught me, and those who heard it marveled. My teacher then was Rabbi Malachi Gallico of blessed memory, a rabbi, physician, and kabbalist.

Around that time a certain Christian named Priamo was severely beaten and injured. A discussion about whether he would die took place in the presence of my revered father and my teacher and some people and guests in our house, and I jumped up and said, "He will surely die, for there is an explicit scriptural reference to this—'Their fruit (*piryamo*) shalt Thou destroy from the earth'" [Ps. 21:11]. At that, they all had a good laugh and said of me, "The young pumpkin is known by its young shoot" [Babylonian Talmud *Berakhot* 48a].

In the month of Elul, at the end of the year [5]338 [August-September 1578], we left Cologna and moved to Montagnana, a village five miles away. My revered father set up a synagogue there in his house in order to pray to God, and it exists to this day, in the house of Zerah Halevi, may God his Rock protect him and grant him long life. [He did so] because for many years the local men had not prayed in a prayer quorum (*minyan*) on account of quarrels among them. But we put everything back in order.

In the year 5339 [1578/1579] the constellations began to war against us with a strong hand and an outstretched arm. In the month of Nisan [March-April 1579], at the request of Cardinal Alvise d'Este, my revered father of blessed memory was thrown into prison because of a debt of fifteen hundred scudi that had already been repaid. He sat there for about six months, and even after his release they distrained all our money for three years at the request of Alvise Mocenigo, who was supposed to have collected it from the aforementioned cardinal. The expenditure for claims and counterclaims was great, and no one gained, but rather everyone lost and squandered money. My mother of blessed memory girded her loins like a man and rode to Ferrara and to Venice in order to speak with noblemen and judges of the land. From that time on we became impoverished, for in three years that false accusation caused us damage amounting to more than eight thousand ducats, as well as much anxiety. . . .

UNHAPPY TUTOR. A MARITAL MATCH AND DREAM DIVINATION. TRAGEDY THWARTS A MARRIAGE OF LOVE.

At the beginning of the month of Tammuz 5349 [began June 15, 1589] in order not to remain idle, I began to give lessons in Torah to the son of Manasseh Levi of blessed memory and to Joseph the son of Zerah Halevi, may God his Rock protect him and grant him long life. I continued in this profession until 5372 [1611/1612] in spite of myself, because it did not seem fitting to me.

After this my mother spoke to me each day, saying, "If you would heed my command and comfort me in my troubles you would take as your wife my niece, namely, Esther—the daughter of my mother's sister Gioja, the wife of Isaac Simhah, may God his Rock protect him and grant him long life—for she seems fitting to me. I will thereby create a marital tie within my family and peace will reign in our house." And so she requested of my revered father of blessed memory in every conversation. She wrote to her sister about it, and she gave her answer. And so the matter stood.

Anyhow, I had engaged in dream divination, using prayer without conjuration, in order to see the woman intended as my mate. In my dream, an old man held my hand and led me to a certain wall upon which was drawn a portrait covered with a curtain. When he drew aside the veil I saw a portrait of my cousin, Esther, as well as the color of her garment. While I was still gazing at the image, it changed, and another one, which I could not clearly make out, replaced it. In the morning I reported the dream to my revered father of blessed memory and to my mother, but they did not believe it.

Then, in the month of Elul 5349 [August-September 1589] my mother of blessed memory and I arrived in Venice on our way to Ancona to retrieve property and goods that had been in the hands of my [half-]brother of blessed memory, because his wife had seized them and we had not seen even a shoelace of it. Afterward we changed our mind about going on and lingered in Venice; and while there, my mother and her sister and the relatives again discussed the match. We completed the marriage agreement, shook hands, and made the symbolic acquisition with great rejoicing. I pointed out to my mother that she [Esther] was wearing clothes of the same color and ornamentation that I had described more than a year previously when I had seen her in my dream. She was truly a beautiful woman, and wise, too. I said that "finds" and not "found" applied to me [allusion to Prov. 18:12, as per a midrash in Babylonian Talmud, *Berakhot* 8a].

When the wedding date, which was the 13th of Sivan 5350 [June 15, 1590], approached, I wrote to my revered father, who was then in Bologna, so that he would come. I also invited my friends and relatives, and we all traveled to Venice immediately after Shavuot, rejoicing and lighthearted. When we arrived there, we found the bride confined to her bed, and everyone said that nothing was wrong except for a little diarrhea and that she would soon recover. Her illness grew worse from day to day, however, until she lay near death. Yet her heart was like that of a lion, and she was not afraid.

On the day she died, she summoned me and embraced and kissed me. She said, "I know that this is bold behavior, but God knows that during the one year of our engagement we did not touch each other even with our little fingers. Now, at the time of death, the rights of the dying are mine. I was not allowed to become your wife, but what can I do, for thus it is decreed in heaven. May God's will be done."

Then she requested that a sage be summoned so that she could make confession. When he arrived she recited the confessional prayer and asked for the blessing of her parents and my mother. On the night of the Holy Sabbath, the 21st of Sivan 5350 [June 22, 1590]—almost on the night that my [half-] brother of blessed memory had died—at the hour of the entry of the Sabbath Bride, my own bride departed from this life of vanity for eternal life and passed away. The weeping on the part of all who knew her, both within and outside her family, was great. May she rest in peace. . . .

POVERTY. GAMBLING. TUTORING THE YOUNG, PREACHING, AND TEACHING ADULTS IN FERRARA. DEPRESSION AND YEARNING FOR VENICE.

During the entire year 5364 [1603/1604] I lived in poverty and distress, and did not turn away from the evil of playing games of chance. Finally, at the end of the year, at the end of Elul [ended September 24, 1604], I went to Ferrara. There I contracted to stay and teach the sons and grandsons of the wealthy Joseph Zalman of blessed memory in his house. After a month I brought my wife and children to live there. Only Zebulun remained in Venice, for my in-laws and my brother-in-law Moses of blessed memory would not let him go.

There I was received with great affection and was honored and welcome in that household like a lord benefactor. Unbelievable as it is to tell, that entire holy community, great and humble alike, loves me dearly to this day. They appointed me their regular Sabbath preacher in the Great Synagogue and loved and praised my words. Some young men organized an academy and [study] society, and to fill my pockets, I would teach them each weekday, and on the Sabbath [give them] words of Torah and a sermon. In this way I accumulated more than 260 scudi a year. I boarded at the table of the aforementioned Zalman, but despite this, I was overcome by depression and did not live there willingly, due to my great longing and love for Venice, the city of my birth. . . .

STILL GAMBLING. ALCHEMY.

In Kislev 5374 [November-December 1613], I resumed doing evil by playing games of chance, and from then on only evil surrounded me.

On the 10th of Tishrei 5375 [September 13, 1614], my son Mordecai of blessed memory went away as a result of the vexations of a certain wicked and sinful man, and gave up teaching the students of the society. Upon his return in the month of Kislev [November-December 1614] he began to engage in the craft of alchemy with the priest Joseph Grillo, a very learned man. He worked at it assiduously and became so adept that all the venerable practitioners marveled at what such a lad knew. Finally, in the month of Iyyar [April-May 1615], he arranged a place in the Ghetto Vecchio and with his own hands made all the preparations needed for the craft. There he repeated an experiment that he had learned to do in the house of the priest, which was to make ten ounces of pure silver from nine ounces of lead and one of silver. This I saw done by him twice and examined it and sold the silver myself for six and a half lire per ounce. It stood the test of the coppella [a vessel for distinguishing gold and silver from other metals], and I knew that it was real. Even though the process required great work and labor and took two and one-half months each time, in the end it could have yielded a profit of about a thousand ducats a year. And this is not vanity, for I also wasted my life trying to understand things such as these, and I would not have deluded myself had not sin caused me.

On the holiday of Sukkot 5376 [October 15–23, 1615], much blood from Mordecai's head suddenly started flowing out of his mouth, and from then on he ceased to engage in that craft because he was told that possibly the vapors and smoke from the arsenic and salts that go into it had done harm to his head. He remained like this for two years until his death, limiting himself to some light activities. . . .

A HOROSCOPE PREDICTS THE TIME OF HIS DEATH. DEATH OF HIS SON. SORROW DRIVES HIM BACK TO GAMBLING.

I will not refrain from telling you here that from my youth I had had a passionate desire to learn from the astrologers, on the basis of my birth date, what would happen to me during the days of my life and how many they would be. I had seen the horoscope that a certain man named Alessandro Bivago had compiled for my revered father of blessed memory in Bologna when he was seventeen. He told him everything that would happen to him year by year, and not one word failed to come true. He said that he would live seventy-two and one-half years, and it turned out to be seventy-two and two months. From that time on, I yearned for something like it. A horoscope was compiled for me by four astrologers, two Jews and two Christians, and to this day, on account of my sins, what they wrote has proved accurate. The time of my death is predicted for the age of fifty-two, approximately, and I am fifty now. Palmistry also indicates that it will occur about the age of fifty.

I now regret having undertaken that endeavor, for man's only proper way is to be pure before God, and he should not make such inquiries. So here I am today, pained on account of the past and anxious about the future. But God will do as he pleases. My only prayer to him is that he should not take me away before I repent of my sins. Ever since I was born I have had no joy, that I should worry about lacking it; neither have I seen any good in this world, that I should have difficulty leaving it. These, my final days, are burdensome.

May the Creator be praised for everything forever. If the time or any other that has been decreed for me according to the aforementioned persons should pass, I will write of that fact further on. But if their words prove to be true, one of the readers should write it here below.

My bowels, my bowels. I writhe in pain. The chambers of my heart moan within me as I come to tell with twofold brokenheartedness about the death of my son Mordecai of blessed memory. After the holiday of Sukkot 5376 [ended October 16, 1615], when he first began to bleed from his mouth, it recurred, at first once a month, after that once a week, and then from Passover [5]377 [began April 30, 1617] on, every day. I tried frantically to cure him, but could not find a remedy. I saw no sign of benefit in any of the many medicines that I gave him. Finally, in the month of Elul [September 1617], his illness grew worse. I had eleven doctors, Jewish and Christian, consulting about his malady, some during personal visits and others through correspondence. He wished very much for the remedies of the aforementioned priest Grillo, having seen an example of his treatment of others. But, as it differed from the ways of all the other doctors, I was afraid to treat him accordingly. Only close to his death, to satisfy his wishes, did I allow him to take them.

About that time I dreamed that he said to me, "I have taken a house for myself outside the ghetto." I responded, "Show me where, so that I may come and find you." He answered, "I do not want to tell you, for I do not want you to come to find me." Meanwhile, bedridden, he continued to wane.

On the Sabbath of Repentance [5]378 [October 7, 1617], he got up from his bed to come hear two of my sermons. That evening he returned to his bed and began to run a fever, the likes of which he had never previously known. Finally, on the night of the arrival of Tuesday the 9th of Heshvan 5378 [November 7, 1617], his appointed time drew near, and he confessed his sins and recited many psalms and confessional prayers. He lay dying for about three hours, and then, about the ninth hour [3:00 A.M.], his soul returned to the Lord who had given it to him.

Truthfully, were it not for the maxim of the talmudic sages of blessed memory, "Just as the Holy One, blessed be He, gives the righteous the strength to accept their reward, so He gives strength to the wicked to accept their punishment" [*Sanhedrin* 100b], I could not possibly live with the pain and sorrow that have seized me from then until now. Not a day passes that this death is not fresh to me, as if his corpse were lying before me. The saying, "It is decreed that the dead should be forgotten by the heart" [*Pesahim* 54b] does not apply to me, for it is today three years since his death, and wherever I turn he is there before me.

He was an average-looking man, slender and not fat, with a hairy body. His face was not pale, but he had a small, rounded beard. He pleased all who saw him and was wise in all worldly matters, as well as in the advice he gave when anyone asked him about matters divine. He preached well in public, delivering sermons in Florence, Mantua, Ferrara, and Venice. He was neither a happy nor a sad person, and got along well with people. None surpassed him in respect for parents. We were like two brothers, for he was twenty-six years and two months old [at his death] and I was forty-six and a half. Alas for me, I lost him, and I do not even know how to count his praises.

Later on it was reported to me in Ferrara, as he had related it, that one year before his death he told a certain woman how he had asked in a dream to be shown the woman decreed to become his wife and was shown a coffin covered in black.

I thought that my son Zebulun, may God his Rock protect him and grant him long life, would bring me consolation, but to this day his ways have not been straight, and he adds trouble and sorrow to my pain. May God guide him in the path of his commandments, so that he may console me before I die.

Following the death of the apple of my eye and root of my heart, I returned out of great anxiety to the enemy that always drove me out of the world—namely, playing games of chance—from which I had abstained for two years in order to please my aforementioned son. Until Passover 5380 [began April 9, 1620], I compounded the evil day after day....

PREACHER RENOWNED AMONG JEWS AND CHRISTIANS.

When the Torah portions Tazria and Metzora were read in 5389 [April 28, 1629], I preached in the synagogue of the Sephardim, may God their Rock protect them and grant them long life. In attendance were the brother of the king of France [perhaps Gaston, duc d'Orléans, 1608–1660, brother of Louis XIII and son of Maria de Medici], who was accompanied by some French noblemen and by five of the most important Christian preachers who gave sermons that Pentecost. God put such learned words into my mouth that all were very pleased, including many other Christians who were present. All the congregations gave great praise and thanks. There had never been anything like it during my thirty-seven continuous years in this work of God. People wrote to distant places all over Italy about how unique it was. Both before and afterward, noblemen and other great men came to hear my sermons, notably Duke Candale and Duke Rohan [Henri, duc de Rohan, c. 1572–1638, the Huguenot leader living in exile in Venice, and his associate, Henri de Hogoret d'Epernon, duc de Candale], among others. May God be praised by all for imparting the grace to his servant to hallow his name in public before Gentiles. May it not become [a source of] pride and haughtiness for me....

COUNTERREFORMATION PERILS OF PRINTING HEBREW BOOKS.

Previously I mentioned the start of the printing of my book *Beit yehudah*, a supplement to the sayings contained in the book '*E[in] y[israel]* [an anthology of midrashim in the Talmud]. Never in my entire life had I so desired anything as to see it printed and distributed and disseminated among the dispersion of Israel, for I was certain that from it I would earn merit and honor and an everlasting reputation, which would never be lost. I began to have it printed in Adar 5394 [February 1634], as mentioned before. Many impediments intertwined concerning it, however, and the matter dragged on until Heshvan 5395 [October-November 1634]. Before that, in Elul [5]394 [August-September 1634], some scoundrels from among our own people had informed the Cattaver [the Ufficiali al Cattaver, who regulated relations between Christians and Jews in Venice] about the printing, and it closed down the print shop. It remained tightly sealed off for about six months. Then it was reopened, and they [the printers] returned to their work and to printing my aforementioned book, which was almost entirely done by my grandson Isaac min Haleviim, may God his Rock protect him and grant him long life. I had introduced him to that craft about two years earlier so that he would learn to derive benefit from working with his hands in a clean and easy craft and, at the same time, not desist from his studies.

On Wednesday the 28th of Iyyar 5395 [May 16, 1635], police suddenly entered the print shop and arrested my grandson Isaac along with two of his young friends; they put them in prison, in darkness [in a poorly lighted cell, used for more serious crimes], and sealed off the print shop once again. I was very distressed when, despite great efforts at intercession, I was unable to conclude the matter and set him free. With difficulty, after fifteen days, they allowed him to leave the darkness for light, though still in prison, and he remained there for a total of sixty-six days. I went back and forth every day, with labor and effort and great expense, until God in his great kindness had mercy, and by decree of the Quarantia Criminal [the chief criminal court in Venice], he was released without fine on Friday the 28th of Tammuz 5395 [July 13, 1635]. . . .

A BOOK FOR GENTILES ABOUT JUDAISM AND THE JEWS, THE HISTORIA DE RITI HEBRAICI.

[1637] While my heart was still full of sorrow because of the separation from my son-in-law and daughter, there came an enormous anxiety, fear, and heartache the likes of which I had never before experienced among the very great multitude of troubles and sorrows that had mounted upon me every day since I was born. About two years earlier I had given a certain Frenchman who knew the holy tongue [Hebrew], M. Giacomo [Jacques] Gaffarel [French Catholic orientalist, Hebraist, mystic, and bibliophile, 1601–1681], a certain book to read. I had written it more than twenty years earlier at the request of an English nobleman, who intended to give it to the king of England [James I, ruled 1603–1625]. In it I relate all the laws, doctrines, and customs of the Jews at the present time in their dispersion. When I wrote it I was not careful about not writing things contrary to the Inquisition, because it was only in manuscript and was meant to be read by people who were not of the pope's sect [that is, Protestants].

After reading it, that Frenchman asked me to leave it with him and he would print it in France. I agreed, but did not think of editing out the things that the Inquisition in Italy might find unacceptable in a printed book. Two years later, after I had given up hope that the Frenchman might print it, on the second day of Passover 5397 [April 10, 1637], someone brought me a letter from him, in which he told me that he had printed the book in Paris. He did not divulge to whom he had made the dedication or whether he had changed anything in the book, or the like.

My heart immediately began pounding, and I went to look at a copy of it that I still had from the time I had written it. I saw four or five things of importance of which it is forbidden to speak, much less to write, and needless to say to print, against the will of the Inquisition. Heartbroken, I shouted and tore at my beard until I almost lost my breath. I said to myself, "When this book is seen in Rome, it will become a stumbling block for all the Jews and for me, in particular. They will say, 'How insolent are they to print in the vernacular, informing the Christians not only of their laws, but also of some matters contrary to our religion and beliefs.' " As for me, where could I go? I could not escape to Ferrara or to any other place in Italy.

But, I was imagining the danger so much greater than it actually was—for in the end the items turned out not to be so forbidden—that my sighs were many and my heart faint, and I almost went out of my mind, and none of my friends could comfort me. Then God, the kind and merciful, put into my mind the idea to seek the advice of the inquisitor, may he be blessed and praised, for he had always acted like one of the righteous Gentiles in his dealings with me. So I made a voluntary declaration to the Inquisition [a record of this, as well as the submitted manuscript of the *Riti*, is found in the archives of the Venetian Holy Office], which protected me on every count and on which I relied. Thus, after about a month of indescribable pain and sorrow, I relaxed.

Not long afterward the aforementioned Frenchman arrived in Rome, and from there he sent me a copy of the book that had been printed in Paris. I saw that he had been clever and considerate enough to delete the four or five items over which I had worried. He had also addressed a letter to me in the introduction, enthusiastically praising and glorifying me and my work [Modena suppressed that fact that Gaffarel criticized him for omitting certain mystical and occult practices and even tried to convince the author to convert to Catholicism]. He dedicated the book to a nobleman, the ambassador of the king of France, who had just come here to take up residence near the government of Venice, may its glory be exalted. This ambassador wrote me a letter in his own hand praising me on his own behalf and on behalf of the king. Thus, I was greatly relieved of my fear and apprehension.

Despite this, because many errors in correct spelling had occurred during that printing, and there still remained a few things that I feared might not seem proper to the Catholics, I decided to print it a second time here in Venice, deleting and adding items as I wished for that purpose [the second edition, Venice 1638]. It is sold today by their booksellers, and so far, about six months having passed, nothing but praise for it has been heard. I dedicated the second edition, like the first, to that ambassador, and he gave me a gift of thirty-four ducats, which defrayed the costs of printing. . . .

A GREAT-GRANDDAUGHTER IS BORN. MARITAL STRIFE. ILLNESS AND FEAR OF IMMINENT DEATH. GAMBLING AGAIN.

On the 5th of Tevet 5401 [December 18, 1640], at midnight, a daughter was born to my grandson Isaac, may God his Rock protect him and grant him long life. He named her Sarah, may she be blessed above all women of the house, after his father's mother. May God cause her to be worthy of marriage and good deeds. Amen.

In [5]401 close to Hanukkah [began December 9, 1640], my wife took seriously ill for about a month, and from then on, throughout the winter, she was sad and distressed for no reason. The following Passover [began March 26, 1641], she became sick again, and her illness lasted a long time, until Sivan [May-June 1641], when my daughter Diana came from Padua and stayed here for about a month and a half and then left. About two months later she came again and stayed here until Rosh Hashanah [5]402 [September 5, 1641], because all that summer either both of us or my wife alone were sick and depressed.

That Sivan [began May 10, 1641], my wife assumed a strange mood, and she began to quarrel with me and make me angry. This has been and will be the destruction, ruin, and desolation of my money, body, honor, and soul until this day. If I were to live another hundred years I would not recover from any of those four things. God is the one who knows whether she fought with me for no reason, when I had committed no wrong and there had been no evil deeds or transgressions on my part. I cannot write about how foolish she was, or of how from day to day I was led astray by her wheedling from failure to failure and from evil to evil. I can only give an outline.

We quarreled all day long from the month of Sivan [May–June 1641] until after Sukkot [ended September 27, 1641]. I would grow angry and shout and act foolishly. My blood would boil, my heart would flutter, and my insides would churn up. From time to time she would vow to keep still and to cease being boisterous, but a few days later she would resume her foolish behavior. We carried on this way during the entire summer of 5401 [1641] and during the whole month of Tishre 5402 [September-October 1641]. On the 4th of Heshvan 5402 [October 8, 1641], I took her with me to Padua on condition that there be peace between us. We stayed there with my daughter Diana, may she be blessed above all women of the house, for five days. Immediately upon our return, however, my wife resumed her old provoking, so that I could no longer bear it.

Meanwhile, I developed an abscess, pus, and a pulmonary infection. And about the middle of the month of Kislev [November 1641], I became bedridden with fever, pains, and [other] severe symptoms, in particular the shortness of breath called asthma. Finally, at the beginning of the month of Tevet [began December 4, 1641], the doctors diagnosed me as dying. I recited the deathbed confessional prayer, while in the synagogues prayers were offered up for me as I was dying. But God did not wish to kill me. Nonetheless, my illness kept dragging on, and the shortness of breath and pains grew worse and worse, until I got sick and tired of staying in bed and began to get up in the month of Shevat [January 1642]. But I still suffered from insomnia every time I got back into bed, and it lasted for about seven months. It was so difficult for me to speak, pray, or preach that I despaired, saying, "I will no longer be able to serve the public as I have for the past forty-nine years, or even to associate with other living beings."

Because I had spent about 130 ducats in cash on my illness by the beginning of the month of Shevat [began January 2, 1642], and because my wife did not stop causing me grief day and night, I became angry at myself, lost control, and returned to the "sin of Judah" [of which I have] written several times, namely, playing games of chance, which utterly consumed me and schemed against me. I did so much more evil than on previous occasions that I lost six hundred ducats in the course of a full year. I am still burdened with debts from this amounting to more than three hundred, and I have nothing let to buy food for my household. . . .

HIS EMPLOYMENT HISTORY.

I wish to write here as a record the many endeavors I have tried in order to earn my living, trying without success.

Jewish pupils
Gentile pupils
Teaching writing
Preaching
Sermons for others
Cantorial work
Secretary for societies
Rabbinate
Decisions [of Jewish law]
Judging
Yeshiva
[Conferring] diplomas of "rabbi" and "haver"
Letters for abroad
Music
Poems for weddings and gravestones
Italian sonnets
Writing comedies
Directing them
Drawing up contracts
Translating
Printing my writings
Proofreading for print
Teaching arcane remedies (*segullot*) and amulets if necessary
Selling books of arcane remedies
Commercial brokerage
Matchmaking

HIS WILL OF 1634

With God's Help
Will

For many years I have had in mind making a will and arranging things for the time of my punishment [i.e., death] regarding what should be done with my body, writings, books, and compositions, because I have no wealth or riches for disposal. And now, on this Tuesday the 3rd of Sivan 5394 [May 30, 1634], my head and limbs being heavy, and feeling weak, I took my pen in hand lest time and chance befall me this very minute. This is my word and my wish. First of all regarding burial, eulogy, and gravestone:

Many years ago I had a dream that I was asked about the manner in which my burial should be conducted, and I responded, "In such a manner." I now decree and order that so it should really be done.

The coffin should be rectangular, instead of with a sloped top. Upon it let them place only books I have written, both printed ones and ones in manuscript. But let them take care with those in manuscript lest someone lay hands on them. Therefore, let them lay out only the large and well-bound ones.

The cantors shall not chant behind my coffin Tokhahot [confessional poetry] for others but rather either the Ma'alot Psalm [that begins] "I will lift my eyes unto the mountains" [Ps. 121]; or [the text that begins] "For unto thee, O Lord, do I lift up my soul" [Ps. 86:4] and ends "His soul shall abide in prosperity and his seed shall inherit the land" [Ps. 25:13]; or [the text] composed by my grandson I[saac] m[in] H[aleviim], may God his Rock protect him and grant him long life, [that begins] "O thou that dwellest in the covert of the Most High" [Ps. 91:1].

Regarding the eulogy, both at the cemetery and afterward during the first month, I had already decided to demand that there be no eulogy at all when I began to compose a eulogy of my own to be recited by my son-in-law Rabbi Jacob min Haleviim of blessed memory. [Written in the margin: (and after) his death, my grandson, the son of Rabbi J(acob) mentioned above.] But God took him away before taking me. Without me I do not want people to listen to my voice, but rather to do as they wish. I would only adjure them in the name of God, and if I could I would so decree, that they not dwell at length on my praise but only say that I was not a hypocrite; that my beliefs were consistent with my actions; that I was a God-fearing man; that I turned from evil more in private than in public; that I showed no more favoritism to admirers or relatives or myself for my benefit than seemed to me to be proper; that I was well liked by people, both great and humble; and let them make the effort to quote in my name original verses or sayings.

Let them bury me near the entrance to the cemetery that leads out to the field, next to my mother, sons, grandfather, and uncle. Let them march around my grave according to the custom of the Levantines.

Let my son Isaac, may God his Rock protect him and grant him long life, come to the Italian synagogue all the [first] year to recite Kaddish.

Before three months have passed let them erect a durable gravestone that will last as long as possible, inscribed exactly as the following words are.

The words of the deceased:

> From above they have transferred to the possession of Judah Aryeh,
> Modena [punning, he separated the word *mi-modena*, "from/of
>   Modena," into two smaller words, *mi-mo dina*, "from whom (namely,
>   God), judgement"], now acquainted with him and at peace,
> Four cubits of ground in this compound
> By making the acquisition binding, and eternal.
> Died, on the day . . .

If, however, one of my poetically minded students sees fit, they may put the second stich before the first and substitute for "now acquainted with him and at peace" the line "Herewith hidden and concealed"—as appears best to them. And this latter way seems right to me.

36

The Early Messianic Career of Shabbatai Zvi

Matt Goldish

In 1665–1666, the Jewish world experienced its largest messianic outbreak since the rise of Christianity. This outbreak was centered around the person of Shabbatai Zvi (1626–1676), a rabbi and mystic from Izmir (Smyrna) in Turkey. Shabbatai, who appears to have had grave doubts about his own messianic qualifications and mission at first, was endorsed and encouraged in this role by the brilliant young visionary, Nathan of Gaza. Nathan's fame as a scholar and seer ensured that the eccentric Shabbatai would be taken seriously.

Shabbatai studied Talmud and Kabbalah under great masters in Izmir, and he soon developed a very intense spiritual life of scholarship and asceticism. His personality was magnetic, though mercurial, and many were attracted to him. However, he was troubled from a young age not only by thoughts of messiahship but also by uncontrollable urges to commit "strange deeds," offenses against Torah law that brought him into conflict both with his own religiosity and with the leadership of the Jewish community.

This was the cause of Shabbatai's expulsion from Izmir in the early 1650s, which began a period of wandering and soul-searching that would last most of his life. After spending time in various Turkish and Greek communities, and suffering an expulsion from Salonika for "marrying" a Torah scroll, Shabbatai settled in Palestine, where he was more pitied than persecuted. In 1663 he was sent to Egypt to collect money for the impoverished Jerusalem Jews, and there he found favor with Raphael Joseph Chelebi, leader of Egyptian Jewry. In 1664 he married Sarah, an Ashkenazi girl with an unfortunate reputation, who apparently bore him a son. Still troubled by illusions of grandeur and bizarre urges, he traveled to Gaza in the spring of 1665 to meet with Nathan, the famous kabbalist who might give him a *tikkun*, a spiritual repair regimen for his troubled soul.

The world of both men changed forever as a result of this fateful meeting, because Nathan recognized in Shabbatai the object of his recent visions about the Messiah. It is unknown whether the two had been familiar with each other in Jerusalem, where both had studied in 1663, but there is an almost bizarre quality to the dynamic between these two rabbis in their 1665 encounter. Shabbatai, who wanted nothing more than freedom from what he recognized as delusions, was instead convinced by Nathan that he was indeed the Messiah. With this began Shabbatai's career as post-Talmudic Judaism's greatest messianic pretender, and Nathan's career as his prophet. Further visions confirmed the truth of Shabbatai's mission for Nathan, and the fame of the new "redeemer" spread among Jews, Christians, and Muslims.

The movement did not go unopposed. The failure of key rabbis near its wellsprings to voice clear objections, however, left critics bereft of ammunition. Meanwhile, the enormous penitential movement that accompanied messianic ecstasy around the Jewish world caused many leaders to adopt a laissez-faire attitude. Lay prophets and wildly embellished epistles circulating in Europe and the Ottoman Empire raised expectations to a feverish pitch, which continued until the Turkish Great Vizier, alarmed by potential economic damage from the abandon of Jewish businessmen, called Shabbatai before him in early 1666. The astounding outcome of this interview was not Shabbatai's execution, as one might expect, but his imprisonment in a sort of luxury facility with easily bribed guards. This situation only did more to enhance Shabbatai's reputation, and visitors poured in from around the world to be with him. Eventually this too ended, and in his second interview before the diwan Shabbatai fared less well. Rather than forfeit his life when conversion to Islam was demanded of him, he chose to convert, in which condition he lived out his life. The movement did not die with Shabbatai's conversion but went underground.

The document before us is a fanciful biography by one believer whose faith remained steadfast. Baruch ben Gershon of Arezzo (a town in Tuscany) wrote this account of Shabbatai and his movement in the early 1680s, when Sabbateanism had been largely abandoned and recalcitrant Sabbateans were actively persecuted by embarrassed Jewish communities. In this atmosphere, his own perception of this project is most odd and deserves attention. He opens the work by stating that many Jewish sages have written histories of their people, and he mentions some of the well known figures. He continues:

> Similarly did the great and sage rabbis of Venice follow in their footsteps in 428 [1668] in the matter of Nathan of Gaza and what he said about Shabbatai Zvi, as can be seen in that work *A Remembrance for the Children of Israel* which they published and sent to all the dispersion of Judah and Israel. But since I saw that from it a person cannot know the events fully as they occurred, because he [Nathan] speaks only a small amount, I therefore came my humble self to help the many and extend the discourse.

The rabbis of Venice, in composing the original *Remembrance for the Children of Israel,* had in mind a goal quite the opposite of Baruch's—the defamation and ruin of Sabbateanism. Yet Baruch cast his own work in terms of an expansion on the original *Remembrance,* a circumstance that remains deeply puzzling.

It seems that Baruch was writing for an audience of his fellow believers, but only a few manuscripts of *Remembrance* are extant, and its impact is very difficult to gauge. The work is a hagiographical biography that contains numerous points of interest both for the history of the movement and for historiography of the period. Upon comparing Baruch's narrative with those of other eyewitnesses to the Sabbatean outbreak, one immediately notices vast lacunae, particularly in matters that might reflect poorly on Shabbatai. Rather than attempt a linear account of events, Baruch puts forth his story in detailed episodes that expand on areas of the author's interest. The skillful literary style of the work serves to imbue Shabbatai's life with the glowing hues of sainthood, obscuring all that which was strange or ugly in the halcyon days of 1665–1666, and easing the messiah's image from the historical to the mythical plane. Nevertheless, there is much genuine history to be gleaned from the *Remembrance*.

In the section translated below, Baruch begins with Shabbatai's background, then skips to the background of his bride Sarah, bringing the strands back together as the two meet and marry. He then invests a long section on the prophet Nathan of Gaza and his visions concerning Shabbatai's messianism. Again Baruch rejoins the strands in his account of the meeting between messiah and prophet, and then continues with a more or less chronological account of their doings. He interrupts at several points with long excurses on prophetic outbreaks and events in specific communities.

Prophecy is indeed the most prevalent theme in Baruch's account. Everyone involved in the movement—Shabbatai, Nathan, Sarah, and numerous believers—is a prophet. In the middle of the seventeenth century, often described as a period of widespread "crisis" at many levels, prophecy became an important hedge against the skepticism and lack of controlled boundaries felt by Europeans in particular. The people involved in the early stages of the movement were almost all of European background, as one may quickly ascertain, for example, by looking at the Spanish and Portuguese names of the popular prophets in Izmir and Aleppo. On the other hand, the spirit possession and ecstatic trance states of Nathan bear distinct resemblance to patterns widely found among the Muslim Sufi mystics of the Middle East. Prophecy was pivotal in the acceptance and spread of this movement, as it was for so many contemporary millenarian outbreaks in Europe and the Mediterranean.

The centrality of women in prophetic roles is especially noteworthy. Shabbatai's wife finds her way to him through the miraculous prophecies she experiences on the eve of her wedding, and her destiny as wife of the messiah is confirmed by her ability to prophesy accurately in Livorno. One of the most crucial events confirming faith in Shabbatai was the eruption of popular prophets in various Mediterranean cities. Central among these were women, and every account of these strange occurrences stresses their role. This may again be compared with widespread contemporary phenomena in the Christian world, including the prophetic *beatas* of Spain, the prophetesses of early Quakerism and other English Civil-War era sects, and the women among the French prophets of the Huguenot exile, to mention only a few. Women, who were marginalized in the public practice of Judaism as well as Christianity, found an influential voice in the prophetic calling.

Knowledge concerning both internal and external dynamics of Jewish communities can be inferred from Baruch's account. Jews under Islam and Christianity generally had to maintain a fairly low profile, avoiding conflict with the magistrates of their respective towns. In order to maintain stability, it was sometimes deemed appropriate to denounce uncontrollable Jewish heretics or radicals before city officials in order to dissociate the local Jews from their activities. Though one must be careful about drawing simplistic parallels, one may be reminded of the first-century Jerusalemite Jews' decision to "betray" Jesus to the Romans. Shabbatai was indeed denounced in various places. We must not rely solely on Baruch for information on the outcome of these denunciations, but his testimony appears correct: the failure of unbelievers to halt the progress of the movement suggests their lack of success in this strategy.

Conflicts between believers and unbelievers were most severe within Jewish communities early in the movement, because a short time later any unbelievers who were left feared to identify themselves as such. Supplementing Baruch's account with information from the Dutch preacher Thomas Coenen, the Venetian Rabbi Isaac Min ha-Levi'im, and many other witnesses allows for a fascinating window into Jewish communal politics, particularly those involving the rabbinic leadership, at the time when Sabbateanism exploded onto the scene.

The biography of Shabbatai Zvi presented by Baruch of Arezzo, then, proves a rich source about Jewish life in the seventeenth century, both in its general state and under the impact of the radical Sabbatean enthusiasm.

The translation is based upon A. Freimann, *Injane Sabbatai Zewi* (Berlin: Mekize Nirdamim, 1912), pp. 45–51.

Further Reading

Moshe Idel, *Messianic Mystics* (New Haven: Yale University Press, 1998). Harris Lenowitz, *The Jewish Messiahs* (Oxford: Oxford University Press, 1998). Yehuda Liebes, *Studies in Jewish Myth and Jewish Messianism* (Albany: State University of New York Press, 1993). Gershom Scholem, *Sabbatai Sevi: The Mystical Messiah* (Princeton: Princeton University Press, 1973). Stephen Sharot, *Messianism, Mysticism, and Magic: A Sociological Analysis of Jewish Religious Movements* (Chapel Hill: University of North Carolina Press, 1982).

Baruch ben Gershon of Arezzo, *A Remembrance for the Children of Israel*

On the ninth day of the month of Av 386 [Summer 1626] a son was born to Mordecai Zvi, and his name in Israel was called Shabbatai. A previous son had been born whose name was Elijah, and after him was born another son named Y[eh]osef. The child Shabbatai grew, was weaned, and was brought to school where he began to study. He had a great passion for the Torah of God, and in the company of people he behaved with abstinence, righteousness, and great holiness.

One day he was studying Torah with the sages, among whom was the humble and virtuous Rabbi Moses Pinheiro (long may he live!), who resides at present in Livorno, when he began to weep bitterly. The sages asked, "What troubles you that you cry so?" He replied, "I know about myself that I am the messiah, and against my own will I do strange things against God and His Torah. This is the occasion for my weeping." Those present expressed their amazement to each other.

After this he traveled from Izmir where he was born and went to his own land, Eretz Zvi [Palestine], where he continued to study Torah day and night. When the rabbis saw his righteousness and trustworthiness, they sent him to Egypt as a funds collector for the Palestinian communities, after which he returned to Jerusalem.

In the land of Ashkenaz [Germany/Poland] lived a Jewish man to whom was born a woman child. While she was still small the Gentiles came, took her by force and converted her. They gave her over to a certain very wealthy Gentile woman who had but one son. When this son and the [adopted] daughter grew up she wished to marry them to each other and give them all her money, property, and belongings.

It happened one night, on the eve of the day they were to go to their house of worship for the wedding before the city magistrate, as is their wont, that the father of the girl, who had died about two years previously, came to her in a dream. He said to her, "Woe to you and woe to your soul! What have you done?" Upon hearing her father's voice, the girl broke out in cries and weeping, saying "Father! Father! What can I do if I am in their power and they do not permit me to go where I wish?" Replied the father, "Listen to me now. Wear this leather cloak which I am giving you and go to the graveyard this night. Sit there and the Lord will be your confidence; he will not let your foot be caught." And this is what she did. Early in the morning the people of the city came to bury a certain Jew there, and the community saw the girl in the same cloak. Upon it was written in clear script, "This will be the wife of the Messiah."

They immediately took the girl and sent her from one place to the next and from one city to another, through Venice, until she was brought to Livorno. She remained there a long time until a ship came through headed for Egypt. While she was there she prophesied about the future and all her statements came true. It came to pass that when the great sage Rabbi Isaac ha-Levi Valle (long may he live!) heard these things, he too went to speak with her. He asked her to reveal to him the [spiritual] roots of his soul and other things which may not be written, and she answered him according to what he wished to know. He knew for certain that her answers were correct and true. Now the woman who owned the house said to the above-mentioned sage, in the presence of the girl, "I am aware of the claim made by this girl that she will be the wife of the Messiah." The girl said nothing.

Now the people of Livorno sent her to Egypt, to the hand of the great and exalted noble Rabbi Raphael Joseph, the *chelebi* in Egypt, treasurer to the king. He received her with great honor and told her that he wished to marry her to a friend of his, and he would give her much money. She declined, saying that she must go to Jerusalem where her proper and appropriate mate was to be found. Therewith he sent her to Jerusalem with a straight and reliable Jew. When they reached the city she saw our master (may he be raised up!), upon which she said to the Jew who was with her, "Do you see that sage there among the sages? He is the one destined for me."

Our master lifted his eyes and saw the girl. He said to the sages who were with him, "That girl coming toward us is my proper spouse. . . ." The wedding was made, but he did not consummate it until after he placed the pure turban [of Islam] on his head. She bore him a son and a daughter, as will be told, God willing.

In the year 425 [1665] in the city of Gaza (may it be rebuilt speedily!) lived the sage Rabbi Abraham Nathan, son of Rabbi Elisha Ashkenazi (long may he live!), who was then about twenty-two years of age, possessed of a wife and children. One day close to Purim time he experienced a great spiritual enlightenment, and thereafter he knew the consciences of men and their transgressions. He would call them in one by one and tell them, "I know that you transgressed such-and-such a law in such-and-such a place at such-and-such a time." Each one would admit that he was correct, and he would then give them penances for the repair of their souls. For this reason his name spread in those regions until many people began arriving at Gaza to speak with him and get a penance for their souls.

Many sages even arrived from Jerusalem, including the sage Rabbi Israel Benjamin, great-grandson of the wise and godly kabbalist Rabbi Israel Benjamin the Elder. He [Nathan] told him, "Go please to the graveyard, where you will find an old man with a pitcher of water in his hand and a kerchief over his shoulder. Take the pitcher from him and pour water on his hands, then read him the passage [Deut. 21:8] 'Forgive thy people Israel.'" He [R. Israel] went there and found nothing. He returned to R. Nathan and said to him, "I went there and found no man." He replied to him, "Return there a second time," which [R. Israel] did. There he found an old man with a pitcher of water in his hand. He took the pitcher from the man's hand, and the man allowed him to wash his hands. He then recited to the man the passage "Forgive thy people Israel," and the elder replied "'. . . and the blood shall be forgiven them.'" [Deut. 21:8]. [R. Israel] returned to R. Nathan and reported, "I have done all which you commanded me." Rabbi Nathan informed him that the old man was

Zacharias the prophet, that R. Israel Benjamin had the soul of his murderer, and that he had now performed the appropriate penance, so that this great transgression of Zacharias's murder was now remitted for all the Jews.

Following this, the sage R. Nathan said to the sages of Gaza that for the sake of God they should greatly honor the sage Shabbatai Zvi when he returned to Gaza, because he is a very awesome man of God. To this end the sage R. Jacob Najara prepared a room for him with a bed, table, chair, and lamp [2 Kings 4:10], and with the ornaments of kingship. When [Shabbatai] arrived they all went out to meet him. They received him with great honor and accompanied him to the aforementioned house, where they held a great feast and celebration. Upon completion of the meal, they gave the sacramental cup of blessing to R. Nathan. When he came to the passage [in the grace after meals] of "The Compassionate One . . . ," he said "May the Compassionate One bless our master, our king messiah Shabbatai Zvi." At this [Shabbatai] screamed and told him "Silence!"

When the holiday of Shavu'ot arrived, Rabbi Nathan called to the scholars of Gaza to study Torah with him the entire night. And it occurred that in the middle of the night a great sleep fell upon R. Nathan. He stood on his feet and walked back and forth in the room reciting the entire [Talmud] tractate *Ketubot* by heart. He next told one of the scholars to sing a certain hymn, then he asked another of the scholars [to sing.] Meanwhile, all those scholars heard [sic] a wonderful and very fragrant smell, as the smell of a field which the Lord has blessed [Gen. 27:27]. They therefore investigated the neighboring streets and houses to find out whence this fragrant odor came, but could discover nothing. Meanwhile, he [Nathan] leaped and danced [2 Sam. 6:16] in the room, shedding one piece of clothing after another until his underclothes alone remained. He then took a great leap and fell flat on the ground. When the rabbis saw this they wished to help him and to stand him up, but they found that he was like a dead man. There was present the scholar Rabbi Meir HaRofe, who felt his hand in the manner of the doctors and pronounced that he had no life at all. They therefore placed a cloth over his face, as is done to the deceased, far be it from us.

Presently a very low voice was heard, and they removed the cloth from his face; and behold, a voice emitted from his mouth, but his lips did not move. And he said, "Take care concerning my beloved son, my messiah Shabbatai Zvi"; and it said further, "Take care concerning my beloved son, Nathan the prophet." In this way it became known to those sages that the source of that wonderful odor they had smelled was in the holy spiritual spark which came into R. Nathan and spoke all these things.

Afterward he rested a great rest and began to move himself. His colleagues helped him to stand up on his feet, and asked him how it had happened and what he had spoken; he replied that he did not know anything. The sages told him everything that had happened, at which he was very amazed.

The next night they gathered with Rabbi Nathan to learn the whole night, he sitting in one room and the sages in another. He told them, "Do not eat anything." When their learning commenced he came out of his room and said "One of you has eaten!" One of the sages admitted that he had unthinkingly partaken of a raisin he had in his bag. [Nathan] was away for another hour when he returned and said to them "One of you has had a nocturnal emission!" And so it was. These events and truths caused all of them together to greatly honor Rabbi Nathan so that even the Turks heard of him, but they could say nothing, as if struck dumb.

Afterward Rabbi Nathan was told in a dream vision at night that he should carry out a *hafsaqah* [an arduous fast] since he was destined to see a great vision; and so he did. On Sunday, the 25th day of the month of Elul 425 [Fall 1665] he isolated himself in a room, and the sages were in an adjoining room. On Monday, following the morning service, a great vision came to him. He beheld the light that God created on the six days of Creation; he viewed from one end of the universe to the other; and he saw a scene [the Chariot] like that which Ezekiel the prophet saw. And he saw the following engraved in supernal lights: "Thus saith the Lord: Behold your savior is coming, Shabbatai Zvi," etc. And he was dressed in it like an angel, and he forced him to say these words. He heard a decree in the heavenly academy being decreed and saying: "In one year and a few months you will reveal and you will see the kingdom of the House of David." He [Nathan] swore on the life of the world [i.e., God] that what he said was true, and that he really had this vision. He furthermore adjured that he had read an ancient book in which it was written that in the year 387 [1626/7] a son would be born to Mordecai Zvi who would subdue the great dragon, etc.

Now from many places people made their way to Gaza to beg a *tikkun* [mystical penance] for their souls, and letters were written from distant lands for this purpose. In order to test him to determine whether [Nathan's] words were accurate, people would write long lists of names of those seeking a *tikkun,* and among them they would include one person who had died or a small baby still at its mother's breast. He would state a penance for each person, but when he got to a person who was already dead he would write next to it "His death was his penance"; and by the name of a baby, "free of transgressions." In this way they knew that his words were true and trustworthy.

Our master now traveled from Gaza toward Izmir, the city of his birth. When he passed Jerusalem, where lived the sage Hayyim [another MS reads Hagiz] who did not believe in him, agents were sent to the qadi, the [Muslim] judge of the city, and they maligned him by claiming they had sent him to raise money in Egypt and now wanted his accounts of what he had collected. The qadi sent one of his servants to bring [Shabbatai], and our master went. When the qadi saw him he was seized by a fit of trembling, and he greatly honored [Shabbatai], inviting him to sit in a chair raised above his own. They spoke together for about a half hour, after which [Shabbatai] asked permission to ride a horse in the city, which was immediately granted. He mounted the horse and circled around Jerusalem from outside seven times. He then returned to the city, and nobody understood his intent.

He left Jerusalem and went to Aleppo (that is, Aram Tzovah), where the Jews received him with great honor. Now, despite the fact that his fame had spread throughout the world as the messiah, and that the Jews said it quite openly, neither the Turks nor the pasha who was mayor said a thing. It was as if they had been struck dumb and were unable to speak a word because they were taken by a great shuddering.

In Kislev 426 [Fall 1665] he arrived in Izmir, and there too they received him with great honor. He went to the home of his brothers, R. Elijah and R. Joseph. And even though here too it was known to the pasha and qadi and all the Turks that the Jews believed in him as their messiah, not one of them opened his mouth to make a noise.

Now the king [Shabbatai] sat in his palace and many Jews came to kiss his hand, as is the custom to do to important persons. Many who were not of our nation came as well to do him honor and support him, so that constantly, day and night, his gates never closed from the entry of hosts of Gentiles come to serve him and do his bidding.

When this was observed by his brother, the sage R. Elijah, who did not believe that he was the Messiah, he [Elijah] feared that, God forbid, because of him [Shabbatai] a disaster would befall their community and all the [Jewish] communities under the rule of the Turkish king. He said to himself, "Better that he alone [Shabbatai] die than that God forbid the communities all be destroyed." One day when he found him alone in a room, he approached him with a drawn sword in hand wishing to strike him, God forbid. But our master laid eyes upon him and he [Elijah] was struck with a great trembling, at which he fell before him like one who is dead, so that he was unable to do him any harm.

After this [Shabbatai] began to do things which appeared strange. He would pronounce the divine Name [Tetragrammaton] according to its spelling, eat forbidden meats, and do other things against God and his Torah. He likewise encouraged others to imitate his evil deeds. On the morning of Thursday, which was the third day of Hanukkah, he went to the Algazi synagogue dressed in royal finery and began to recite the hymns with such pleasantness that the congregation was astounded to hear his beauty and songs. On Friday the sage [Rabbi] Galante arrived there and pronounced concerning [Shabbatai] that in truth he was definitely the Messiah.

On the holy Sabbath he prayed at great length. He then betook himself to the Portuguese synagogue, but since many of them did not believe in him they locked the doors of the synagogue. In great anger he sent for an axe and he struck the door on the Sabbath until they opened them, upon which he entered the synagogue. At this point they were saying the Nishmat prayer. He commanded them to stand, and he began to sing prayers until the allotted time for [the Amidah] prayer had passed. Therewith he announced, "Today you are exempted from [the Amidah] prayer. Read only the Shema' prayer, without its accompanying blessings."

He next removed a book of the Pentateuch from his bag and declared that he was holier than a Torah scroll. He began to read the Torah, and he called up his older brother Rabbi Elijah as *kohen* ["priest," the honor given only to descendants of Aaron the high priest to read first in the Torah]. He then appointed him king of Turkey, and his second brother he appointed Caesar of the Romans. And he called upon many men [another MS adds "and women"] upon whom he conferred monarchy, also demanding that each pronounce [the name of] God as it is spelled.

The following day those who did not believe in him denounced him to the qadi, who is the [Muslim] judge of the city, concerning all these evil things. He sent for [Shabbatai], but when he came before him a great trembling seized [the qadi] and he did [Shabbatai] great honors. He then sent to have those men who had slandered [Shabbatai] come, but they feared for their lives and made an undercover escape.

Despite his performance of strange acts like these, his fame spread in the world as the holy Messiah and that of Rabbi Nathan as a true prophet. Almost all the Jewish people believed in them without any sign or wonder-working. Their fame spread also among the uncircumcised [Christians] and among the Turks, among whom there was not one who dared speak or make a noise because a trembling from God was upon them.

This was the cause for a great awakening of repentance among the Jews in all their habitations. From the land of Israel an order of *tikkun* was sent to be recited day and night, which was then printed in Mantua and in Amsterdam, a great city of sages and scribes. Many people would observe several fasts extending from one Sabbath to the next. Men, women, and children would stand in synagogue day and night reciting prayers, penitential hymns, and supplications, adding many ritual ablutions and almsgiving. It is certain that no general movement of repentance like this ever occurred, even in the days of Mordecai and Esther. They would close their stores and do none but the most minimal amount of business. Edom [the Christians] and Ishmael [the Muslims] saw all and yet said nothing evil about the Jews, instead standing together with them with love and great affection.

In the month of Shevat [Spring 1666] our master dressed in royal attire of beaded gold, holding a book of the Pentateuch in one hand and in the other a golden scepter of the sort carried by the great Caesars. He left his house followed by about 500 Jews, traversing the main street of the town and the thoroughfares of the city of Izmir, [the Jews] calling loudly "Long live the king our master! Long live our master the king!" The Turks saw this and heard their words but they said nothing. Rather, they bent their knees and bowed to the ground before him. And although these things were known to the pasha and the qadi as well as the city officials, none opened his mouth nor damaged the Jews physically or economically in any way.

After this, prophecy came upon many men, women and children in Izmir, Constantinople, Aleppo, and elsewhere. The same message came from all of them. They would bear witness and declare "Shabbatai Zvi is the Messiah of the God of Jacob!" Now this is the manner of the prophecy which came during those days. A deep sleep would come upon [the prophets] and they would fall upon the ground like dead people with no breath remaining in them. About a half hour later breath would come from their mouths though their lips would not move, and they would recite passages of song and passages of comfort. They would all declare, "Shabbatai Zvi is the Messiah of the God of Jacob." Afterward they would rise back to their feet knowing not what they had said or done.

In the city of Izmir over 150 prophets prophesied, among whom were these who blasphemed [pronounced divine Names]: the wife of our master, the wife of Jacob Peña, the wife of Vana, the wife of Jacob Serrano, the wife of Jacob Benveniste, the wife of Jacob Capua, the sage Daniel Finti [Pinto?], Joseph ha-Levi, Solomon the son of Rabbi Daniel Valencin, Joshua Morletto, Samuel Bomuano [Bon Homme], Moses Shefami, Elijah Bonseneor, and a certain orphan. And these are the names of the prophets of Aleppo: R. Isaiah ha-Kohen, Moses Galante, Daniel Pinto, the wife of Yomtov Laniado, the wife of Rabbi Nissim Mizrahi, the daughter of Rabbi Abraham Tammon, and others to the number of twenty prophets and prophetesses.

Herewith is a transcription of the prophecy uttered by Abraham the son of Rabbi Jacob Jeshurun from Izmir, 4 Shevat [early spring] 1666:

> God, I have heard your speech. The Lord rules, the Lord ruled, the Lord will rule for ever and ever. Hear, Israel, the Lord is our God, the Lord is One. Blessed be the Name of his glorious kingdom forever and ever. Our king Shabbatai Zvi has already been crowned with the crown. A great ban has been placed in heaven on those who do not believe. The Lord, guardian of Israel, our prayers have already been heard. A song of ascents: From the depths have I called you, O Lord. There is great joy; blessed are all those who are alive. They have already brought the crown of our Lord the King. Woe to he who believes not, because he is under the ban. Joyous is he who merits to live in this time. A song of ascents: Happy is every one who fears God. A great joy will be made. Hear, O Lord, and pity me. The crown has already been given him. His kingdom is a kingdom over all the worlds. The king, the sage Shabbatai Zvi, already sits on his throne of kingship. Hear, Israel! The Jews are precious in the eyes of God. Let the righteous ones rejoice in God. Give thanks to the Lord, for he is good. God is true, Moses is true and his Torah is true, Shabbatai Zvi is true. A great joy. Open your hands. The Lord, he is God! The king Shabbatai Zvi already sits on his throne. Hear, Israel. A song of ascents, when God returns the exile of Zion. Great joy to the Jews. The Lord is God. Happy is the man who fears God. How great are his signs and how mighty his wonders. When God returns

the exile of Zion. Great joy. Give thanks to the Lord, for he is good. Give thanks to the God of the heavens. The Lord rules, the Lord ruled. Woe to him who believes not. Our lord the king already rules. To you, God, is righteousness. Great joy. A song of ascents, when God returns the exile of Zion. They have already fallen before the Jews. The star of our king has already risen. Give thanks to the Lord, for he is good, his mercy endures forever. Have pity on me, Lord, and lift me up. From distress I called upon the Lord. Blessed is he who comes in the name of the Lord. The Lord will answer you in the day of trouble. Give thanks to the Lord, for he is good [thrice]. God is powerful and valiant forever, the King who sits on his throne of mercy. The Lord of Hosts sits on his throne of kingship. God will do battle for you. God is the glorious King, selah. God is powerful and mighty—may his kingship be raised high! True, true, true. Save me, O Lord, according to your mercy. Joy to the Jews. Save me according to your mercy [thrice]. Give thanks to the Lord, for he is good. Blessed be the Name of his glorious kingdom forever and ever. Hear, Israel, for you will light my candle [twice]. Great is the Lord, and much to be praised. There is no evil inclination. Lord, hear my prayer! Give thanks to the Lord, etc.

Each of these things he repeated four or five times.

When our master traveled from Izmir to Constantinople, to the Grand Turk, he went on a ship by sea with four sages. He declared that the soul of one of them was that of Jehosephat and another of Zedekiah, from the kings of Israel. This ship traveled in the company of another ship. It occurred that a great storm rose over the ocean so that they thought the ships would be smashed. When our master saw this he placed one foot on the mast of the ship, upon which there appeared there the image of a pillar of fire. In almost one instant they found themselves standing in Constantinople, but the ship that accompanied them sank in the deep waters; its whereabouts is unknown to this day.

Before he arrived at the city of Constantinople, representatives of the [Jews of the] city went to the great vizier, the viceregent, and said to him as follows. "Our lord should be aware that a certain man of our nation is approaching here who claims to be the Messiah, but we do not believe in him. Now tell us what we should do." When the vizier heard this he sent for our master and placed him in a prison where the king's prisoners are incarcerated. He sat there for two days and one night. While he was there a great enlightenment came over him so that his face shone like the light of a torch, and night was bright as day wherever he was.

Afterwards the vizier sent to have him brought before himself and the mufti, who is a great minister who is in charge of their religion. When he arrived before them, one sage who accompanied him said to our master, "Bend over and bow down before these ministers, for that is the custom." Our master replied to him, "Silence! I know what to do, and I do not wish to bow before them," and indeed he did not rise nor move in front of them. He said to the vizier, "State in what language you wish me to address you, for I am prepared in all of them." With this [the vizier] began to speak in four or five languages, ending with Arabic, and he [Shabbatai] answered him in all of them. [The vizier] enjoyed him so much that even though [Shabbatai] deserved to die, he did not wish to execute him, and instead commanded that he be taken to a certain apartment in the king's palace, where he sat in peace and fairness.

When all this was heard in the land of Italy, especially in the city of Venice, and the vast majority became believers (for God remembered his nation to give them bread, the bread of salvation!), her sages and leaders gathered and agreed to do a great repentance, the likes of which was certainly never seen in the history of that city. Afterward they sent a messenger to Constantinople to inquire of those sages and tell them [*Sic*] whether the tidings of our redemption and the unfettering of our souls were true. Similarly, if it was all simply castles in the air they should also tell them the truth, and if the matter was still in doubt they should inform them in which direction their understanding of it fell. They replied to them that the sage Shabbatai Zvi is the true redeemer, and that anyone who doubts him is like one who doubts the Lord his strength.

37

The Life of Glikl of Hameln

Paula E. Hyman

The Yiddish memoir of Glikl bas Yehuda Leib, commonly referred to today as Glückel of Hameln, offers us an unparalleled view of the daily lives of Ashkenazi Jews in the late seventeenth and early eighteenth centuries. Glikl began to write her autobiography when she was forty-three, to assuage her grief at the untimely death of her husband after thirty years of marriage and to provide her children with a sense of their family heritage as well as with an extended ethical will. In doing so, she revealed her own understanding of God's role in history and in an individual's life as well as many of the customs of her community.

Glikl was not the typical Jewish woman of her time, nor was her milieu an ordinary one. Born in Hamburg, she was the daughter of Beila and Yehuda Leib, a wealthy merchant and *parnas* (syndic) of the community. Her first husband, Haim the son of Joseph ben Baruch Daniel Halevi of Hameln, was also a prosperous merchant, who settled in Hamburg. After his death, Glikl continued the trade in pearls and gems and the moneylending that had sustained the family. Her second husband, Hirsch (or Cerf) Levy of Metz, whom she married after a decade of widowhood, was a rich financier and communal leader; his bankruptcy after their marriage embittered Glikl's last years. The wealth of her family of birth enabled Glikl to receive a general and Jewish education that she put to good use in her commercial dealings as well as in writing her memoirs.

Glikl and her family stood at the periphery of the circles of court Jews, the international traders who served the economic needs of central and western European princes, and they arranged strategic marriages within their ranks. Most notably, one daughter married into the Gompertz family, who were agents of the Elector of Brandenburg, and a son married into the powerful Wertheimer family of Vienna. Glikl and Haim's social, economic, and cultural contacts ranged from Amsterdam and Metz to the west and to Hamburg and Prague, Leipzig, and Poland to the east. Because both Glikl and her husband traveled to fairs to conduct business and made matches for their children throughout western and central

Europe, the world that Glikl comments on is the geographically vast one of Ashkenazi Jewry.

Glikl was born in late 1646 or early 1647 and died in 1724. This was a period in which the socioeconomic role of Jews reached a high point in Europe, in large part through the activity of urban commercial families such as Glikl's and Haim's that were part of a network of traders. Prosperity based on commerce, however, was contingent on factors beyond the merchants' control, and consequently financial insecurity was a common feature of mercantile families. This was also a period of political instability in which warfare was almost constant and every traveler might encounter violence on his journey. Glikl was born at the very end of the Thirty Years War, heard family stories of the Chmielnicki pogroms of 1648–1649, witnessed the messianic hopes that accompanied reports of the movement of Shabbatai Zevi in the 1660s, and worried about the safety of her large family. As a Jew, she felt particularly vulnerable to the whims of rulers and thugs alike; Jews recognized their subordinate status in a Christian-controlled world. Her relations with the non-Jews in whose midst Jews lived were mixed; they were always instrumental and mostly, but not entirely, fraught with suspicion and maltreatment.

What made life particularly insecure for all Europeans of the time, however, was neither war nor street violence but the possibility of death at any time. Recurrent plagues decimated entire communities. Although Glikl raised twelve of her fourteen children to adulthood, at a time when one-third to one-half of all children died before the age of ten, every illness and every pregnancy brought fear. Several of her grown children predeceased her. The constant presence of death compelled ordinary persons, and not just theologians, to wonder about the vagaries of fortune and the question of God's justice. In her memoirs Glikl reflects a great deal on the connections between personal and communal behavior and personal and communal reward or punishment.

Glikl's is the only memoir written by a Jewish woman in the early modern period—at least, the only one to have survived. As such, it offers a rare opportunity to hear a woman's voice and to see how a Jewish woman of her class understood her life. Living in a time when the domestic and the commercial spheres had not yet been separated, Glikl perceived herself as her husband's partner not only in rearing a family but also in conducting a business. Moreover, commerce itself was a family enterprise, and concluding advantageous marriages for their offspring was a way for husband and wife to solidify the family's fortunes. Consequently, Glikl interlaces her narrative with comments about her marriage, her responsibilities as a mother, and her economic activities. She situates her story within a tight-knit, self-governing Jewish community that was rich in institutions and sometimes beset by internal disputes. Its members were conscious of mutual obligations and defined Gentiles, or the "uncircumcised," as Glikl called them, as the Other. For Glikl there is no secular space; every aspect of life is governed by Jewish legal norms and ethical values.

THE LIFE OF GLIKL OF HAMELN 485

Where did Glikl learn those norms and values? She mentions that her father had his daughters as well as his sons taught both religious and secular matters. She clearly read and wrote Yiddish, but is most unlikely to have read Hebrew. The Hebrew material she cites from the Bible and the Talmud was probably presented to her orally, in sermons, or in Yiddish books. There is a scholarly debate as to whether she read German, which would have been highly unusual for a Jewish woman of her time, but she doubtless had access to some German versions of particular stories she recounts. Her major source of Jewish learning was the voluminous ethical literature and collections of stories published in Yiddish for a female readership. She also drew on *tkhines*, Yiddish petitionary prayers written for and occasionally by women and published widely in her time, and especially on the *Tsene-rene,* the collection of biblical, midrashic, and medieval interpretations, all organized around the Torah portion of the week.

Glikl expresses her spirituality in her struggle with her own sense of sinfulness—which she sees manifest in her lack of patience and excessive grieving over her losses—and in her lifelong attempt to accept God's will. She displays the traditional Jewish understanding of exile as a collective divine punishment of the Jewish people as well as the traditional hopes for messianic redemption. Her memoir reflects her admiration of the men in her family who engaged in the forms of piety prescribed by Jewish tradition, which she describes. She mentions that she sent two of her sons, the most intellectually talented, to learn in *yeshivot* (schools of advanced Talmud study). The artfully crafted stories that Glikl inserts in her autobiographical narrative are central to an understanding of her spiritual values; they represent her means to teach a moral lesson but also to engage in the traditional Jewish custom of arguing with God.

Glikl divided her autobiography into "seven little books"; the first four and the beginning of the fifth were written shortly after Haim's death in 1689, the rest of the fifth in the 1690s and edited later, the sixth in 1702 in the aftermath of her second husband's bankruptcy, and the last in 1715, with a final paragraph dated 1719. The only extant manuscript is not in Glikl's hand; it was copied from Glikl's original by one of her sons, Moses, rabbi of Baiersdorf. It remained in manuscript form for almost two centuries, until the German scholar David Kaufmann published a transcription of the original Yiddish in German script in 1896.

The passages of Glikl's memoirs presented here are drawn, with small changes, from Beth-Zion Abrahams' slightly abbreviated English translation of Kaufmann's transcription. Entitled The *Life of Glückel of Hameln, 1646–1724. Written by Herself,* it was published in 1962 (London: Horovitz), pp. 2, 3, 7; 8, 9, 10 (Book One); 17, 18, 19; 32, 33, 37, 38 (Book Two); 45–46, 47; 71, 73 (Book Three); 96, 97 (Book Four), 104, 106, 107, 108, 109, 114 (Book Five); 178, 179, 180, 182 (Book Seven).

Further Reading

For the English-language reader interested in Glikl and her times, there are a number of useful resources. Jonathan Israel's *European Jewry in the Age of Mercantilism, 1550–1750* (New York: Oxford University Press, 1985) provides a fine overview and original analysis of the economic and political status of the Jews of Europe, from England to Poland. *From Court Jews to the Rothschilds: Art, Patronage, and Power, 1600–1800,* edited by Richard I. Cohen and Vivian Mann (Munich and New York: Prestel Verlag, 1996) offers a lavishly illustrated introduction to court Jewish society, as well as an essay on Glikl's attitudes toward the court Jews. Robert Seltzer's *Jewish People, Jewish Thought: The Jewish Experience in History* (New York: Macmillan, 1980) integrates the sociopolitical and intellectual history of the Jews throughout history, although it pays little attention to gender or popular culture.

In her study of three seventeenth-century European women who left autobiographical writing, *Women on the Margins* (Cambridge: Harvard University Press, 1995), Natalie Zemon Davis offers the best and most comprehensive account of Glikl's life in English as well as an insightful interpretation of her memoir. Chava Weissler has demonstrated the importance of tkhines for the understanding of Jewish women's spirituality in early modern Europe. Her pathbreaking essays include "The Traditional Piety of Ashkenazic Women," in Arthur Green, ed., *Jewish Spirituality from the Sixteenth-Century Revival to the Present,* vol. 2 (New York: Crossroad, 1987), pp. 245–75; " 'For Women and for Men Who Are Like Women': The Construction of Gender in Yiddish Devotional Literature," *Journal of Feminist Studies in Religion* 5 (Fall 1989): 7–24; and "Prayers in Yiddish and the Religious World of Ashkenazic Women," in Judith Baskin, ed., *Jewish Women in Historical Perspective* (Detroit: Wayne State University Press, 1991), pp. 159–81. Weissler's book, *Voices of the Matriarchs: Listening to the Prayers of Early Modern Jewish Women* (Boston: Beacon, 1998) provides the best analysis of Jewish women's spirituality in the early modern period.

The Life of Glikl of Hameln

BOOK ONE

I begin writing this, with the help of heaven, after the death of your pious father, to stifle and banish the melancholy thoughts that came to me during many sleepless nights. We are strayed sheep that have lost our faithful shepherd. I have spent many sleepless nights and for fear of falling into melancholia, I arose in the wakeful hours and spent the time writing this.

I do not intend to write a book of morals, for I am not able to do so. Our wise men have written such books: and we have the holy Torah from which we may learn what is useful and what will lead us from this to the future world.

We must hold fast to the Torah. As an example: a ship full of passengers sailed the seas. A passenger on deck leaning toward the waves fell overboard and began to sink. Seeing this, the captain threw a rope and called to him to hold it tight and he would not drown. We in this world of sin are as if we swim in the sea, not knowing at which moment we may drown. But almighty God who created us without sin—through the sins of Adam the Evil Spirit overpowers us—also created hosts of angels without any evil inclinations to do his work. They do good only. Besides these, God created beast and fowl who know nothing of good; and then man in his own image, with sense like the angels, but also with will to commit—God forbid—evil, or do good. But gracious God threw us a rope for our guidance, to which to hold fast and so save ourselves. This is our holy Torah. Hold tight to it and you will not drown. . . .

So, one should follow this path: as soon as he has committed a great or a minor sin, repent immediately and do penance, as our teachers of morals have written; so that the sin may be blotted out of his book of records, and a merit be marked in its place. When the sinner lives on, doing naught but evil, and dies in sin, woe! For how will it fare with him in the world-to-come when his book of records is full of sins, and the opposite pages where the balance of repentance and good deeds should be, are blank! Therefore, you sinner, you are in debt. How will you repay your Creator who in very truth warned you?

Why then should I write of the tortures and sorrows that a sinful person must suffer, with what anxiety, bitter tears and suffering as long as he has to pay his debts because of his great sins? Because God is merciful and takes from the sinner his debts in this world if he pays them off singly. If, for instance, he does penance, prays, gives charity and does good deeds singly; thus he can pay off his debts in this world. . . .

Dear children, I must not go into further depths, for then another ten books would not be enough for me. Read the German [i.e., Yiddish] *Brandspiegel* and the *Leib Tov*. In the books of morals you will find everything.

This I beg of my dear children: Have patience. If God sends you an affliction, accept it meekly and do not cease to pray. Perhaps he will have mercy. Who knows what is best for us sinful folk? Who knows if it is good to live in great riches and have much pleasure, enjoying all that the heart desires in this transient world; or if it is better, if the heavenly Father holds much from us in this sinful world so that we can have our eyes always fixed on heaven. Our gracious Father: call on him with hot and sincere tears every moment. I am sure that the true and good Lord will show mercy and redeem us from this long sorrowful exile. Great is his mercy. He is full of graciousness. What he has promised us, that will come to pass. Only, let us be patient!

Almighty God did all this in his infinite mercy that parents should love their children and help them to do right. And then the children, seeing this from their parents, do the same to their children.

For example: There dwelt on the seashores a bird that had three fledgelings. Once, seeing that a storm was coming and that the sea waves rose over the shore, the old bird said to the young ones, "If we cannot get to the other side at once we shall be lost." But the birdlings could not yet fly. So the bird took one little one in his claws and flew it over the sea. When halfway across, the parent bird said to his young one, "What troubles I have to stand from you, and now I risk my life for you. When I am old, will you also do good to me and support me?" On which the fledgeling replied: "My dear beloved father, just take me across the sea. I will do for you in your old age all that you demand from me."

On this the old bird threw the birdling into the sea so that he was drowned and said, "So should be done with such a liar as you." He flew back and returned with the second one. When they reached halfway across, he spoke to this one as he had to the first. The little bird promised to do all the good in the world. But the old bird took this one too and threw him into the sea, saying, "You also are a liar."

He flew again to the shore and brought the third birdling. When he came midway, he said to him, "My child, see what hardships I undergo and how I risk my life for your sake. When I am old and cannot move any more, will you be good to me and support me in my old age, as I do you in your youth?" To which the little bird answered his parent, "My dear father, all that you say is true, that you take great care of me and my need. I am in duty bound to repay you, if it is possible; but I cannot promise for certain. But this I can promise: when one day I have a birdling of my own, I will do for my young as you have done for me." On this the father said, "You speak well and are also clever. I will let you live and take you across the water."

From this we can see that God gave the unreasoning bird sense to bring up his young; and the difference: how parents toil for their children while they, if they had the trouble with their parents as their parents with them, would soon tire. . . .

That parents love their children is no surprise. We find the same among unreasoning creatures who have young and look after them until they are grown and can fend for themselves. And they are left to themselves. We humans are in this sense better. We seek to support our children till they are grown; not only when they are small but as long as we live. . . .

Rachel mourning for her children—"I am the one who has seen affliction" [Lam. 3:1]—it is indeed a very great affliction to be childless. To my understanding it would have been much easier for Abraham had the Lord asked him to slay himself than that he should slay his only son Isaac. For who can witness the doing-away of his own offspring? Still, Abraham would do this out of his great love for God. . . .

BOOK TWO

A plague—God preserve us—broke out, and my grandfather and several children died of it. My grandmother was left bare and destitute with two unmarried daughters. They fled from the house, just as they were, taking nothing with them. Often did she tell me of the terrible hardships she underwent. . . . So my poor grandmother and her daughters underwent severe trials and had to go from house to house until the plague had passed. When she returned to disinfect her house, she found all her best things gone and little left. The very floorboards had been pulled up by the neighbors and the rooms were bare. What could they do? My grandmother still possessed some [loan] pledges and with these managed to bring up all her remaining children, my aunt Ulka and my mother Beila—may she live long!. . . .

To return to my grandmother Mattie. When she settled Ulka she found herself with nothing left to support her eleven-year-old orphan, my mother. They went to live with her daughter, Glück, the wife of Jacob Ree. Though he was not a man of riches, Reb Jacob Ree was very honest. He gave his children dowries of from 400 to 500 reichstaler and made fine matches for them with young men of good families. After a time differences arose because the orphan grandchildren visited her often, so that my grandmother left this daughter and went to live with Ulka. She and my mother, who knew how to make pointed gold and silver lace, supported themselves. My mother found favor in the eyes of the Hamburg dealers; they gave her gold and silver to work and for the first transaction Jacob Ree stood as surety. When the dealers saw that she was honest and prompt in her work, they trusted her, so that in time she was able to take in girls and teach them the trade. She and her mother lived from this, and clothed themselves neatly and cleanly. But besides this they had little, and at times no more than a crust of bread all day. Still they did not complain but trusted God not to forsake them—and my mother has the same trust today. I wish I had such a nature; God does not bestow the same gifts on everyone. . . .

Before I was twelve years old I was betrothed and the betrothal lasted two years. My wedding was celebrated in Hameln. . . . Everyone knows the difference between Hameln and Hamburg. I, a young child brought up in luxury, was taken from parents, friends, and everyone I knew, from a town like Hamburg to a village where only two Jewish families lived. And Hameln is a dull, shabby place. But this did not make me unhappy because of my joy in my father-in-law's piety. Every morning he rose at three and wrapped in *talith* [prayer shawl], he sat in the room next to my chamber studying and chanting Talmud in the usual sing-song. Then I forgot Hamburg. . . .

At the end of the first year of married life, my husband would not stay any longer in Hameln. . . . So . . . he moved to Hamburg. . . . When we reached Hamburg my father, of blessed memory, undertook to give us *kest* [room and board] for two years. My husband, being a stranger to the city, looked about, to see what he could do. At that time the jewelery trade was not so well developed as now. The citizens and Gentile bridegrooms wore little or no jewelery and it was the fashion to wear chains of pure gold and only give presents made of gold. There was less profit to be made out of gold than out of precious stones. My husband's first business was trading in gold. He ran about all day from house to house buying up gold, which he sold either to the smelters or to the merchants who sold it again to the betrothed young men. This brought good profit, and though he was busy running about on business all day, he never once missed learning the appointed Talmud lesson for the day. And until he went on long journeys he fasted every Monday and Thursday. . . . There is much to write of him; he was such a loving and faithful husband and father. His like will not be found. All his days he refused any prominent position in the community, laughing at people when he saw what store they set by these things. In short: he was a pattern of a pious Jew, as were also his father and brothers. I know that even great rabbis do not pray with such devotion as he did. When he, peace on him, was in his room praying, and anyone came to sell him something, even the greatest bargain, neither I nor anyone of the household dared disturb him to tell him of it. Because of this he once neglected a deal and lost a profit of several hundreds. But he did not mind this, for he served his God with zeal, and He rewarded him doubly and trebly, as it is said, "Trust in the Lord and the Lord will be your trust." . . .

BOOK THREE

During this time I was brought to bed with my daughter Mattie; she was a beautiful child. And also, about this time, people began to talk of Shabbatai Zevi, but "woe unto us, for we have sinned," for we did not live to see that which we had heard and hoped to see. When I remember the penance done by young and old—it is indescribable, though it is well enough known to the whole world. O Lord of the universe, at that time we hoped that you, O merciful God, would have mercy on your people Israel and redeem us from our exile. We were like a woman in travail, a woman on the labor-stool who, after great labor and sore pains, expects to rejoice in the birth of a child, but finds it is nothing but wind. This, my great God and King, happened to us. All your servants and children did much penance, recited many prayers, gave away much in charity, throughout the world. For two or three years your people Israel sat on the labor-stool—but nothing came save wind. We did not merit to see the longed-for child, but because of our sins, we were left neither here nor there—but in the middle. Your people hope daily, that you in your infinite mercy will redeem them yet and that the Messiah will come—if it be your divine will to redeem your people Israel.

The joy, when letters arrived, is not to be described. Most of the letters were received by the Portuguese [Sephardim]. They took them to their synagogue and read them aloud there. The Germans [Ashkenazim], young and old, went into the Portuguese synagogue to hear them. The young Portuguese on these occasions all wore their best clothes and each tied a broad green silk ribbon round his waist—this was Shabbatai Zevi's color. So all, "with kettle-drums and round dance" went with joy "like the festival of the house, of the pouring of the water," to hear the letters read. Many people sold home, hearth, and everything they possessed, awaiting redemption.

My father-in-law, peace unto him, who lived in Hameln, moved from there, leaving things standing in the house, just as they were, and went to Hildesheim. He sent us here, to Hamburg, two big barrels of linenware, in them were all kinds of food—peas, smoked meat, all sorts of dried fruits—that could keep without going bad. The good man thought they would leave from Hamburg for the Holy Land. These barrels were more than a year in my house. At last, fearing that the meat and other things would get spoilt, he wrote that we should open the barrels and take out all the food, so that the linen underneath should not spoil. They remained here for three more years, my father-in-law always expecting to need them at a moment's notice for his journey.

But this did not suit the Almighty. We knew well that he had promised us that if we were devout and pious from the bottom of our hearts, he would have mercy on us, if only we obeyed his word: "Love your neighbor as yourself." But the jealousy, the needless hate, that is among us! No good can come of it. That which you have promised, dear Lord, will be graciously fulfilled. If it is delayed because of our sins, when the right time comes we shall surely have it. For this we pray and hope, great God, that we will rejoice in a perfect redemption. . . .

There are many troubles of which I cannot tell, particularly now, for to whom can I tell them? We have no one in whom to confide save God, our father in heaven; may he be our help, and to his people Israel, and make us rejoice even as he has afflicted us. When my husband was alive trouble did not miss us, bringing up our children and other worries. Some things may be told, but others must not be mentioned. My beloved companion would allay all my worries and comfort me, so that somehow they passed easily. But now, who is my comforter? and who listens to my heavy thoughts now, and lightens my sad heart as kindly and easily as he? . . .

My daughter Mattie, peace be unto her, was in her third year, and a more beautiful and clever child was nowhere to be seen. Not only did we love her, but everyone who saw her and heard her speak, was delighted with her. But the dear Lord loved her more. When she entered her third year, her hands and feet suddenly swelled. Although we had many doctors and much medicine, it suited him to take her to himself after four weeks of great suffering, and left as our portion heartache and suffering. My husband and I mourned indescribably and I feared greatly that I had sinned against the Almighty by mourning too much. . . .

I was pregnant with my daughter Hannah and soon after was brought to bed. Because of my great sorrow over my child of blessed memory, about whom I would not be comforted, I was dangerously ill, and the physicians doubted my recovery and wished to resort to the last, most desperate of remedies. Not thinking I could understand what they were saying, they discussed it with my family. I told my husband and mother that I would not take the medicine that had been mentioned. This they told the physicians, and though the latter tried their best to persuade me to take it, it was of no use, and I said to them, "You may say what you like; I take nothing more. If God will help me, He can do so without the medicine. If it is another decision of the great Lord, what can the medicine help?" I begged my husband to dismiss the physicians and pay them off; this he did. And the blessed Name gave me the strength, and five weeks after my confinement I went to the synagogue, although still somewhat weak. Daily I improved, and at length dismissed my nurse and wet-nurse and myself saw to all that was necessary for my household. And at last I had to submit and forget my beloved child, as is the decree of God, "I am forgotten as a dead one to the heart" [Ps. 31:13]. . . .

Therefore, my heart's children, though I know well that some are pressed by the loss of money and even the loss of children, what does sorrow and lamenting help? We ruin our health, shorten our life, and cannot serve the Almighty with a heavy heart, for the Shekinah [the feminine dimension of divinity] cannot dwell in a sad body. When the prophets wished the Shekinah to inspire them, they had all kinds of musical instruments played to them so that the body should be glad—as may be read in our books. When your father lived, I, your mother, lost a child of three to whom none could be compared, as I have already written. I was not so understanding as King David. When his first child by Bathsheba was ill, he recited many prayers—and gave away much in charity—and did all he could for it. When the child died, the servants were fearful of breaking the news to him because of his great grief over the child's illness. The king understood from their silence that the child had died, and asked them. As no one answered him he knew for certain that his child was dead. He rose from his ashes and asked for water and ordered food and drink. The servants wondered at this and said, "While the child lived you did not rest by day or night, but sat on ashes; but now that the child is dead, you have accepted the decree and said, 'Blessed be the true judge. The Lord has given and the Lord has taken away—blessed be the name of the Lord for ever and ever.' And now you order food and drink!"

And the king answered his servants, "While the soul was still in the child's body, I did all I could for his recovery—called aloud, wept, did penance, prayed, gave charity, and thought that perhaps God would show mercy. But nothing helped, and the Holy One, blessed be he, took away his pledge. Of what use is weeping now? My son cannot return to us; but we shall go to him."

See, therefore, how the saintly David acted. From this we may learn and take as an example.

We were sinful in sorrowing so much. After this, as long as my husband and I suffered any loss or misfortune, trembling and fearing that we had lost everything, God always assisted us most graciously.

BOOK FOUR

Meanwhile my husband and Leib Goslar fell seriously ill, and in the middle of the fair were taken to Halberstadt. . . . On the eve of the festival all the merchants arrived home, save only my husband, and each, before he went to his own home, came and comforted me that everything was for the best. They did all in their power to appease and allay my fears. But how could this help? Our festival may easily be left to the imagination; indeed, because of it I could do nothing. But immediately after Yom Tov . . . I prayed and fasted all day, arranged for people to learn Talmud, did much charity and everything else in my power. God—blessed be he—had mercy and helped my husband so that he recovered a little and was able to hire a wagon. . . . Thus, weak and ill, my husband arrived home. But we praised God fervently that "He had given him to us and not to earth." The Lord prolonged his life six years and allowed him to marry off two more children. . . .

But I have forgotten to write of the death of my saintly father-in-law. . . . It is impossible to tell of my husband's grief and tears. Immediately after the seven days of mourning, he hired ten rabbis and set aside a room in our house in which nothing was done by day and night other than Talmud learning by the *minyan* [quorum of ten]. My husband during the whole year did not journey from home, so that he night not miss *Kaddish*. . . .

BOOK FIVE

My heart-beloved children, the history of your father, Reb Chaim Hameln Segal, of blessed memory, is before you. Good and pleasant would it have been if the Holy One had left him to us so that together we had led all our children under the marriage canopy. But what shall I say and how shall I speak? My sins caused this; I a sinner did not merit anything else. . . .

On entering the house, I saw my husband standing near the oven, groaning. I was alarmed and asked what ailed him. He answered, "I fell down and fear it is something serious." . . . I saw my sad plight before me and begged him for heaven's sake to let me send for a doctor and call in some people. He said, "I would sooner die than reveal this rupture to people." I stood before him weeping aloud and asked, "What are you saying? Why should people not know? You have not had it from any sin or disgrace." But my words had no effect: he had persuaded himself that this would harm his children in some way and that people would say it was hereditary: he loved his children so deeply. . . . When it was day, I said to him, "Praise be to God that it is day! I will send for a doctor and a surgeon." He would not allow this but asked instead that we should send for Abraham Lopez, who was a Sephardi, a barber-surgeon as well as a physician.... This was early Wednesday morning.... In great pain and with much fear Thursday, day and night also passed. On Friday Lopez brought a physician from Berlin, who had been the medical adviser of the Elector for several years. He gave my husband something to swallow and applied a plaster: they were of no help....

My husband, of blessed memory, said he would be content with all that God did. But to me he did not reveal half the seriousness of his illness. My son Leib, of blessed memory, was a youth of sixteen years at the time, and he remained with him. When I went out of the room, he called to him and exhorted the youth so that he wept. But as soon as my husband saw me enter the room, he said to him, "Be quiet, for God's sweet mercy. Mother is coming in; do not let her see you crying." He was already in his death throes, yet he still thought of me.

On Sabbath, after dinner, my mother went to him, and fell on him kissing him, and crying with tears: "My son, will you leave us thus? Have you nothing that you desire to ask of us?" And he answered: "My dearest mother-in-law, you know I have loved you as though you were my own mother. I have nothing to ask of you; only comfort my Glückelchen." These were his last words to my mother. After this more physicians and surgeons came, but it was all in vain. At the close of Sabbath there was no one but I [sic] and Abraham Lopez; he wanted no one else. At midnight the surgeon was again sent for; Lopez thought that the wound was now ready for cutting. But when the surgeon came he saw immediately that there was no hope, and went away again. Then I said to him: "My heart, may I make you more comfortable?" (for it meant touching him, and I was then unclean [a menstruant]). He answered: "God forbid, my child; it won't be so long now before you will have bathed." But he did not live till then.

I stood there a while longer talking with Abraham Lopez. He advised me to send for Feibusch Levi, who was able with sick people. I called up the children's teacher also. It was two o'clock, Sunday morning. Feibusch went straight to my husband and asked: "Reb Chaim, have you anything to ask?" He answered: "I have nothing to will; my wife knows about everything; let her do as she has done up to now." He then asked Feibusch to hand him the learned Rabbi Isaiah Horowitz's work. This he studied for half an hour, then said to the children's teacher and Feibusch, handing back the book, "Do you not see my condition? Take my wife and children out; it is high time." We were forcibly pushed out; our parting may be imagined. After this Reb Feibusch wished to talk to him, but he answered him no more and spoke to himself; only his lips moving. This lasted about half and hour, and then Reb Feibusch said to Abraham Lopez: "Lay your ear close to Reb Chaim's mouth, to try to hear what he says." Lopez did so, and heard after a little while: "Shema Yisroel Adonai Elohenu Adonai Echod" [Hear, O Israel, the Lord our God, the Lord is One]. Then his breath

THE LIFE OF GLIKL OF HAMELN

was hushed, and his soul escaped in holiness and purity. From this end it was clear what sort of a man he was.

What shall I write, my dear children, of our great loss? To lose such a husband! I who had been held so precious by him, was left with eight orphaned children, of whom my daughter Esther was a bride. May God have mercy and be father to my orphans, for he is the only father of the fatherless. But though I silence my weeping and lamentation, I shall have to mourn my friend all the days of my life. He died on Sunday, Tebeth 24, 5499 [January 16, 1689], and was buried the same day. The whole community mourned and lamented him: the unexpected blow had fallen so suddenly. Surrounded by my children, I sat the seven days of mourning, a pitiful sight, I and my twelve children thus seated. I immediately ordered men for prayers and Talmud study for the whole year, to study day and night in the house. My children recited *Kaddish* untiringly. All our friends and acquaintances, men and women, came every day of the week to console us. My children, brothers, sisters, and friends comforted me as well as they could. But each one went home with a loved one, while I remained in my house in sorrow with my orphans. . . .

You have seen how your father died in holiness and purity and I have written how I made up my accounts, then went to my brother-in-law Reb Joseph that he should go over everything to see whether I had priced the things too cheaply or too dearly. He examined them and said to me: "You have priced everything too low. If I sold my goods so cheaply, I should—God forbid—be bankrupt." I replied, "I think it is better for me to price them low and sell them dear, than that I should price them high and have to sell cheaply. I have made my accounts so that even if I sell at the cheap prices, there will be a handsome capital for my orphans."

So I made full arrangements for the auction and got handsome prices. Everything sold well. If the creditors had not pressed me but had given me six months' grace, I would have obtained even better prices. Still, everything went off well, and God be praised, I suffered no losses. As soon as the money came in, I paid out what was owing, and within a year all the debts were paid off. Further, the rest of the ready money I loaned out at interest.

BOOK SEVEN

I cannot refrain from mentioning what happened on the Sabbath of the Feast of Weeks in the year 5475 [1715], when we were in synagogue. The reader and cantor, Rabbi Jokel of Rzeszow in Poland, had begun to intone the morning prayer "O Lord, Creator of lights," in his sweet voice. Before he had reached the blessing, many people heard the sound as of something breaking. The women in the upper balcony thought the arch of the roof would fall in on them. The rumbling sound grew louder, just as though stones were falling. The alarm was very great; the women in the upper gallery rushed to get out, each wanting to be the first to save her life. . . .

The terror of what happened cannot be described. The women who were saved came out of the crush with heads uncovered and clothes torn from their bodies.... More than fifty women lay on the stairs, wedged together as though stuck with pitch; living and dead lying under one another.

The men came running up together, each to save his own; but only with great labor, and slowly, were the women taken off one another. The men rendered great help; there were many citizens, Gentiles came into the Judengasse with ladders and hooks to bring the women down from the top gallery, for no one knew what was happening there....

You can imagine the lament that went up when the six dead women were dragged out from under the living. An hour before they had been hale and well. May the Lord be merciful and turn his wrath from us and all Israel....

Later, people went up to the top gallery to see whether any part of the arch or the building had fallen in. Nothing was out of order and we do not know whence the evil fortune came. We can only put it down to our sins! Woe to us that such should have come to pass in our day, and that we should hear and be burdened with such heaviness of heart. The verse "I will bring fear into your hearts" was confirmed. "Therefore is our heart faint, for these things our eyes are dim," because of this desecration of the Sabbath and holy days and the disturbance of prayer. As the Prophet says, "Who hath required this at your hand to trample my courts?" This holy day, when our Holy Law was given to us, and God chose us from among all peoples and tongues, if we had merited it, we would have rejoiced in the Giving of the Torah and the Holy Commandments. But now, "we are a reproach to our neighbors, a mockery to those around us," just as if the Temple was destroyed in our own days....

A number of devout women together hired ten Talmud scholars to go to synagogue every morning at nine to recite psalms and study Talmud for the sake of the orphans who had to say Kaddish. May the souls of those killed be received with grace and may their lives, so sadly lost, be an atonement for all their sins, and their souls be bound in life and the Garden of Eden. May they forgive those who, by trampling on them, were partly guilty of their deaths.

I would not have written of this in my book, only it was an occurrence that had never happened before, and, I hope, never will again. I would that everyone, man, woman, youth, and girl might take this to heart and pray to God that such a punishments should not again be visited on any Jewish child. May he redeem us from this long exile. Amen! and Amen!

I cannot, unfortunately, put it down to anything else but the disgraceful happenings on the Rejoicing of the Law festival in 5475 [1714]. As usual, all the Scrolls of the Law had been taken from the Holy Ark and seven placed on the desk when a brawl began among the women. In the fray they tore one another's head-coverings from their heads so that they stood bare-headed in the synagogue! Then the men began to quarrel and fight one another. Though the great Rabbi Abraham Broda in a loud voice threatened them with excommunication, to make them keep their peace and not desecrate the festival, it was of no use. The rabbi and the *parnas* [syndic] left the synagogue quickly to arrange what each one's fine should be.

In Nissan 5479 [March 1719] a woman was on the bank of the Moselle, scouring dishes. About ten o'clock at night it began to grow light as day and she looked into the sky which was open like a [indecipherable] and sparks leaped from it and afterwards the heavens came together again as though a curtain had been drawn across and it was again dark. May God grant that this is a sign for good. Amen!

38

Israel ben Eliezer, the Baal Shem Tov

Dan Ben-Amos

Tales of rainmaking, healing, and the magical supply of provisions are part of the biblical narrative tradition. Elijah the Prophet, and later his disciple Elisha, end drought (1 Kings 18; 2 Kings 3:14–21), offer hope and cure to barren women, revive their children when they die (1 Kings 17:17–24; 2 Kings 4:8–37), and magically provide for the needy (1 Kings 17:8–16; 2 Kings 4:1–7). Elisha, whose reputation as a healer spread beyond the boundaries of Israel, cures a leper and transfers his disease to another, morally inferior, person (2 Kings 5). Trafficking with demons and ghosts in the Bible is restricted to non-Israelite mediators of the supernatural, and is forbidden to the Israelites (Exod. 22:17; 1 Sam. 28:7). The Book of Tobit (one of the books of the Apocrypha) provides accounts of magical cures and demonic exorcisms, yet it does not glorify any individuals as healers.

Talmudic and midrashic literature contains stories about pious men and miracle workers. For example, Honi the Circle Drawer and Nakdimon bin Gorion (Babylonian Talmud, *Ta'anit* 19b–20a, 23a) make rain, and Hanina ben Dosa's piety immunizes him against snakebites (Babylonian Talmud, *Berakhot* 33a) and enables him to bring provisions down to earth directly from Paradise (Babylonian Talmud, *Ta'anit* 25a). None of these saintly individuals occupied positions of religious or social leadership. Though admired for their piety and healing abilities, they are rather marginal in the rabbinic world of learning and politics. At that time, in spite of the biblical restriction, some rabbis and healers were known to exorcise demons, and they occasionally engaged in such activity on behalf of the Jewish community at large rather than for a particular individual (Babylonian Talmud, *Me'ilah* 17b).

With the spread of Islam to North Africa and Spain, and with the dispersion of Jewish communities throughout the Mediterranean basin and Europe, miracle tales and stories of demons and spirit possession became an integral part of Jewish oral tradition, though only a few were committed to writing and subsequently published. The eleventh-century Jewish-Italian family history *Megilat Ahima'atz* includes stories of demonic possession, and the twelfth-century *Sefer Hasidim*, composed in Germany, contains numerous narratives concerning demons and their harm to human beings. A few leading medieval Jewish figures became the subject of cycles of miracle stories, including, ironically, Moses Maimonides (1138–1204), the famous Jewish physician and rationalist philosopher.

It was not until the rise of the Hasidic movement in the southeast of Poland-Lithuania in the second half of the eighteenth century, and its spread to other east European countries during the nineteenth century, that these themes gained wide popularity and acquired renewed religious significance. Influenced by saint veneration in certain Jewish communities of the Mediterranean, Hasidism served as fertile ground for the resurgence of the miracle tale in east European Jewish culture. It offered the requisite ideological and social conditions in which this genre could flourish. At least three reasons might account for such a development: the social composition of the Hasidic movement; the rise of the *zaddik* (pl. *zaddikim*) as a charismatic communal leader; and the development of social occasions for the oral performance of such tales.

Hasidism was a popular movement that attracted the lower socioeconomic segments of east European Jewish society. For the petty traders and shopkeepers, the craftsmen, poor villagers, and tavern keepers, Hasidism offered sanction for religious life without the need for sophisticated learning. It provided venues for religious devotion in which rabbinic education was insignificant. As an ecstatic movement, Hasidism emphasized spiritual engagement with the divine through song and dance, for example, rather than through the intellectualized study of the Talmud, an activity more characteristic of traditional rabbinic culture. Hasidism bestowed dignity upon the wretched among the Jews and gave religious purpose and hope to the depressed and the desperate. For such individuals, stories constituted a prominent form of teaching, enabling the exploration of religious meaning through parables and tales rather than through the intellect.

The primary function of these narratives was to validate the charismatic leadership of the *zaddik*, the religious individual at the head of any particular Hasidic community. Thus, the tales extol his superior moral behavior and spiritual abilities over other types of religious leaders, his healing capabilities over professional physicians, and his magical powers over the most wicked sorcerers among the Gentiles. Transforming the *zaddik* into a social leader (rather than an isolated ascetic), the stories celebrate his magical ability to heal, to assure offspring to barren women and infertile couples, to combat evil witches and demons, and to defeat the enemies of the community. In addition, the tales recount the unique ability of the *zaddik*, as the pillar of his people, to engage in devotional prayers that enable his appeals for mercy on behalf of his community to ascend to the throne of God.

The glorification of these zaddikim through such tales acquired the status of a meritorious act in and of itself. In Hasidic society it was a *mitzvah*, a religious act, to extol the zaddik as a holy man. The Hasidism engaged in conversations about their zaddikim while waiting for an audience with them, in the synagogues, and during the third meal of the Sabbath around the *zaddik*'s table. The Hasidic rebbes themselves told stories, as diviners in other cultures often do, in response to their supplicants' plight. In turn, these tales, in and of themselves, became the subject of stories about the *zaddikim* who told them.

Rabbi Israel Baal Shem Tov (1700–1760)—known as well by the acronym Besht—is regarded by Hasidic tradition itself as the movement's founder. The Besht was himself a storyteller and was said to have elevated the art of storytelling from entertainment and ethical instruction to a level of mystical experience. The Besht himself became the subject of the most important collection of Hasidic tales. In oral tradition the Hasidim called their tales *sippurei zaddikim* (tales of saints), and described the act of narration with the adverbial phrase *le-saper be-shevah* (lit., "to tell in praise of . . ."). This phrase may have been the basis for the adoption of the title *Shivḥei ha-Besht*, the collection of tales about the Baal Shem Tov, although it was also clearly modeled after the title of an earlier book about the Safed kabbalist Isaac Luria (1534–1572), which had been published in 1629 as *Shivḥei ha-Ari* (In Praise of the Ari).

As a generic term for tales of healing and other miracles, the noun, *shevah* (praise) is a printer's innovation. Yet, Israel Yoffe, the printer of *Shivḥei ha-Besht,* who published the first Hebrew edition of the book in Kopys in 1814, contributed more than just a title. He helped to remold the popular image of the Besht after the pattern of traditional Jewish cultural heroes by adding to his biography themes and motifs that appear in the life stories of earlier figures.

Prior to reaching the printing press, the tales had circulated orally among the growing Hasidic communities during the second half of the eighteenth century, probably during the Besht's lifetime and certainly following his death. Then, probably toward the end of the century, Rabbi Dov Baer ben Samuel, the son-in-law of a scribe, Rabbi Alexander the Shoḥet, who wrote amulets and who accompanied the Baal Shem Tov for eight years, wrote down a large number of tales that he himself heard from people he considered reliable. In most cases he was careful to note down his sources, and only in a few instances do the tales begin with the narrative formula *pa'am aḥat* (one time), indicating indefiniteness. The manuscript was copied numerous times and circulated widely. Earlier variations among the Hebrew and Yiddish printed editions had suggested the existence of such manuscripts, but the discovery of an eighteenth-century manuscript copy of the book confirmed this to be the case.

Israel Yoffe's printed edition opens with a tale about the Besht's parents, who were childless well into their mature years, calling to mind Abraham and Sarah and other prominent biblical figures. Rabbi Eliezer, the Besht's father, is taken as a war prisoner to serve in the court of a foreign king, where he advances to the position of a military advisor. Like the depiction of Moses in the medieval *Chronicle of Moses,* his military advice helps his king defeat his enemies. As a reward, again as with Moses in the *Chronicle,* under compulsion he marries a princess, but winds up revealing to her his Jewish identity and marital status. She releases him from this forced marriage and sends him home to his own wife. On the way he encounters Elijah, who promises him a son as reward for his virtuous behavior.

The circumstances of the Baal Shem Tov's birth also resonate with legendary motifs associated with the birth of Rashi (1040–1105), the great medieval French interpreter of Jewish tradition.

The printer thus transformed the collection of mostly hagiographic episodes into a narrative that follows a common biographical pattern that leading Jewish figures share, modified in the light of Hasidic traditions. The story begins with parental childlessness, and continues with birth as a reward for meritorious action, unpromising childhood, and the public assumption of leadership. The main corpus of the tales consists of a series of supernatural and mystical narratives extolling the Besht as a healer, exorcist, ecstatic, and revealer of events occurring in distant places and in the future. Toward the end of the collection we find a deathbed story describing the last hours of the Besht as he is surrounded by his disciples.

For many years *Shivḥei ha-Besht*, together with selected writings of his disciples that appeared after his death, were the only sources upon which it was possible to construct the biography of the founder of Hasidism. Well aware of the precarious nature of oral tradition as an historical source, scholars of Hasidism have tried to read between the lines for the purpose of establishing biographical information about the Besht. Evidence from Polish archival documents recently studied by Moshe Rosman, which attest to the residence of the Baal Shem Tov in the town of Miedzyboz, has added significantly to our historical picture of this figure. Instead of a religious revolutionary at odds with the communal establishment, as some historical studies attempted to portray him, he appears to have been accepted by the established community hierarchy in Miedzyboz, and even was supported financially. The Besht appears to have been a charismatic itinerant healer, a *baal shem* (master of names), who knew how to manipulate and combine holy names for magical purposes and who, according to his followers, exhibited ecstatic inclinations. Others like him traveled through the Jewish villages of Poland-Lithuania and other regions.

Hasidic-type groups existed even before the Baal Shem Tov, as attested in *Shivḥei ha-Besht* itself. As such, the Besht was not Hasidism's founder in a strict sense, although the movement's identity is bound up with him. By the second half of the eighteenth century, the Hasidic movement had gained considerable momentum by drawing a significant number of adherents. By the time the tales were published, Hasidism had become a widespread movement geographically, and was characterized by a certain degree of internal conflict and tension. The oral tales that found their way into the manuscript collection already contain information, for example, about the rivalry between Rabbi Dov Baer of Mezhirech, "The Great Maggid" (1704–1772), who became the Baal Shem Tov's successor following the latter's death in 1760, and another prominent disciple of the Besht, R. Jacob Joseph of Polnoyye (d. 1782). For a movement that had experienced such tensions, the figure of the Besht as portrayed in the tales may have served as a unifying force.

The following texts are a selection from *In Praise of the Baal Shem Tov [Shivḥei ha-Besht]: The Earliest Collection of Legends about the Founder of Hasidism*, translated by Dan Ben-Amos and Jerome R. Mintz (Bloomington: Indiana University Press, 1970; reprint editions: New York: Schocken Books, 1984; Northvale, N. J.: Jason Aronson, 1993), pp. 22–23, 28–31, 35–36, 37, 61–62, 81–84, 129–31, 192, 224–25, 241–42, 253.

Further Reading

The original Hebrew edition of *Shivḥei ha-Besht,* first published in 1814, appeared in numerous reprints and several editions, the latest of which, based on a newly discovered manuscript, is Yehoshua Mondshine, ed., *Shivḥei ha-Besht: A Facsimile of a Unique Manuscript* (Jerusalem, 1982), and an annotated edition by Avraham Rubenstein, ed., *In Praise of the Baal Shem Tov* [Hebrew] (Jerusalem: Rubin Mass, 1991). Moshe Rosman casts new light, supported by eighteenth-century documents, about the historical personality of the Besht in his study *Founder of Hasidism: A Quest for the Historical Baal Shem Tov* (Berkeley and Los Angeles: University of California Press, 1996). More generally, the study of Hasidic thought and literature has generated voluminous scholarship. An article that surveys the major trends and issues of this research is Zeev Gries, "Hasidism: the Present State of Research and Some Desirable Priorities," *Numen* 34 (1987): 97–108, 179–213. Important studies are found in Gershon David Hundert, ed., *Essential Papers on Hasidism* (New York: New York University Press, 1991). Studies that focus on the magical dimensions of Hasidic belief and practice include Moshe Idel, *Hasidism: Between Ecstasy and Magic* (Albany: State University of New York Press, 1995), and Gedalyah Nigal, *Magic, Mysticism and Hasidism: The Supernatural in Jewish Thought* (Northvale, N.J.: Jason Aronson, 1994). Among the studies of Hasidism and the Hasidim in the New World are Janet S. Belcove-Shalin, ed., *New World Hasidim: Ethnographic Studies of Hasidic Jews in America* (Albany: State University of New York Press, 1995); Jerome R. Mintz, *Legends of the Hasidim: An Introduction to Hasidic Culture and Oral Tradition in the New World* (Chicago: University of Chicago Press, 1968), and Mintz, *Hasidic People: A Place in the New World* (Cambridge: Harvard University Press, 1992).

Shivḥei ha-Besht

THE BESHT AND ROBBERS

The mountains were immense. Between them a deep ravine, and the sides of the cliffs were steep. Once the Besht was walking deep in meditation. There were robbers standing on the other mountain. When from afar they saw him walk to the edge of the mountain engrossed in his meditations, they said, "He will probably fall to the bottom and break his bones, God forbid." When he came near the edge, the other mountain moved toward him and the ground became level. He continued to walk and the two mountains were divided behind him as they were previously. On his return, when he came to the edge, one mountain moved toward the other and it became flat. And so it happened several times during his walking back and forth. The robbers saw that he was a holy man and that God was with him, and they made peace with him. They came to him and told him what they had seen, and they said: "With our own eyes we saw that you are a holy man. We appeal to you to pray for us that God will make us successful in our chosen path of endeavor, for which we are sacrificing our lives."

The Besht told them: "If you swear to that you will not hurt nor rob a Jew, then I will do as you ask." They swore to him. From that day on if there was any quarrel or disagreement among them, they came to him and he arranged a compromise.

THE BESHT'S JOURNEY TO THE HOLY LAND

Once the robber came to him and said, "Sir, we know a short way to the land of Israel through caves and underground passages. If you wish, come with us and we'll show you the way." He agreed to go with them. While they were on their way they came to a wide ditch full of water mud, and mire. They crossed it on a board that was extended from one bank to the other. While crossing it they leaned on a pole that they stuck into the mud. The robbers went first. When the Besht wanted to step on the board he saw there the flaming sword that turned every way [Gen. 3:24], and he turned back, since there would have been great danger for him if he had crossed. And the Besht said in his heart: "There is surely a reason why I have come to this place."

THE BESHT REVEALS HIMSELF TO THE SECT OF THE GREAT HASIDIM

When the time for him to reveal himself approached, it happened that one of the students of our master and rabbi, Rabbi Gershon, went to him. On Tuesday he stayed with the Besht, who received him with great honor, and after dinner the guest said: "Israel, prepare the horses for me so that I can leave immediately." The Besht harnessed the horses to the wagon.

Afterwards, the Besht said: "What would happen if you, sir, stayed here over the Sabbath?" The visitor laughed at him. But he had gone only half a verst [about two-thirds of a mile] when one wheel broke. He returned and replaced it with another wheel and started off again. The second time something else broke, and he had to stay over on Wednesday and Thursday, as well. On Friday other things happened to him, and he finally had to remain at the village for the Sabbath. He was very unhappy about it and wondered what he would do there with the peasant. In the meanwhile he was surprised to see the Besht's wife prepare twelve loaves of *hallah,* and he said to her, "What need have you for twelve loaves of *hallah*?"

She answered him: "What does it matter if my husband is a simple man; he is still observant. Since I saw my brother saying the *kiddush* blessing over the twelve loaves of *hallah*, I prepare them in the same manner for my husband."

He asked her if they had a bathhouse, and she answered, "Yes, we have, and we have a *mikveh* [ritual bath] also."

He said: "What need do you have for a *mikveh*?"

She answered: "My husband is an observant man and he goes daily to the *mikveh*."

Nevertheless, the guest was sad because of his delay there. Soon it came time to pray the *Minḥah* [prayer] and he said, "Where is your husband?"

"He is in the field with the sheep and the cows," she said. He prayed *Minḥah* and the Reception of the Sabbath and the *Maʿariv* [all prayers] by himself.

The Besht did not return home for a time, as he was praying in his house of seclusion. When he came home he changed his manners and dress and speech, and he said: "Good Sabbath!" He said to his guest: "see, I said that you would remain here for the Sabbath and here you are."

The Besht stood at the wall to make it appear as if he were praying. After that the Besht said to himself that if he were to make the *kiddush* himself with his customary special devotion, the guest would realize the truth. Therefore, he honored his guest by asking him to make the *kiddush*. They sat down at the table to eat, and in the way of peasants his wife sat next to him. They ate the evening meal with joy and good feeling, but the guest could not remove his sadness from his heart. The Besht said to him: "Rabbi, let us hear some Torah from you." On that Sabbath the reading of the Torah was the portion of Exodus, and so in a simple way the guest related to him the story of the Egyptian exile under the rule of Pharaoh. Then they made the bed for their guest near the table, and the Besht slept next to his wife.

At midnight the guest awoke and saw a large fire burning on the oven. He ran to the oven because he thought that the wood on the oven was burning. He saw that it was a great light—then he was hurled backward and he fainted. The revived him and the Besht said: "You should not have looked at what is not permitted you." The guest marveled at what had happened.

In the morning the Besht went to praying house of seclusion as usual, and afterward he returned home joyfully with his head held high. Inside the house he walked back and forth singing *Asader le-Seʿudata* and he made *Kiddusha Rabbah* in his customary way with wonderful devotion. In the course of the meal he asked the guest to say Torah but the guest was perplexed and did not know what to say. He cited a phrase and interpreted it. The Besht responded: "I heard another interpretation of this phrase." After the meal he went to his house of seclusion, and after *Minḥah* he returned and revealed himself. He said Torah and revealed such secrets of the Torah that no one had ever heard before. They prayed *Maʿariv* and he made the *Havdalah* in his usual fashion. Afterwards, he commanded his guest to go to our master and rabbi, Rabbi Gershon, but he was not to reveal anything. He was to go instead to the Sect of the Great

Hasidim in the town, and also to the rabbi of the community, and say these words: "There is a great light living near your community, and it will be worthwhile for you to seek him out and bring him to town."

When all the Hasidim and the rabbi heard these things, they decided that it must refer to the Besht. They recalled their questions about him, which now seemed clear. All of them went to his village to invite him to come to town. The Besht had foreseen what would happen, and he went toward the town as they were going out to see him. When they encountered each other they all went to a place in the forest where they made a chair out of the branches of trees. They placed him on the chair and they accepted him as their rabbi. And the Besht said torah to them.

Up to this point I heard the unfolding of these events in the name of Admor, may his soul rest in heaven. The other events and miracles that occurred I shall print according to the manuscript that I obtained.

THE BESHT'S PRAYER PRODUCES RAIN

There was a time when there was no rain. The Gentiles took out their idols and carried them around the village according to their custom, but it still did not rain. Once the Besht said to the *arrendator:* "Send for the Jewish [people in] the surrounding area to come here for a *minyan* [quorum of ten]." And he proclaimed a fast. The Besht himself prayed before the ark, and the Jews prolonged the prayer.

One Gentile asked: "Why did you remain at prayer so long today? And why was there a great cry among you?" The *arrendator* told him the truth—that they prayed for rain—and the Gentile mocked him sharply, saying, "We went around with our idols and it did not help. What help will you bring with your prayers?"

The *arrendator* told the words of the Gentile to the Besht, who said to him: "Tell the Gentile that it will rain today." And so it did.

THE BESHT EXORCISES DEMONS FROM A HOUSE

Once an arrendator from a small town came to the Besht. The *arrendator* was bewitched. Anything left inside his house, in a utensil, or even money in his pocket, was reduced to half overnight. He went to the Besht, and the Besht ordered his scribe to write protective amulets for all his rooms. And he returned with the *arrendator* to his home. When they arrived at the house, the Besht collected all the amulets on the table and then he went to the market. The members of the household saw the spirit whirling like a whirlwind from the corner until it quit the house. There was a big fenced yard around the house that had a small gate. When the Besht went to his inn, it seemed to him that there was a huge Cossack at the gate. The closer he came to the yard, the smaller the demon became, and when he came very near the demon disappeared. The Besht placed protective amulets there. The people of the house told him how the spirit had whirled around and then left the house. He searched in the bed, in the rooms, and between the barrels that were there, because this was his way of driving the demon from his hiding places. Then he returned home.

Immediately, a Gentile woman, the miller's wife, came to the *arrendator* in tears, and she said to the *arrendator* in Russian: "I am smart, but you are smarter." It was because the spirit had gone to her house sullen and angry. "I was not at home and he killed two snakes."

RABBI JACOB JOSEPH RECOGNIZES THE GREATNESS OF THE BESHT

I heard this from the famous Hasid, the wise rabbi of the holy community of Polonnoye, who was the head of the court in the community of Shargorod. When he had heard that the Besht had come to the holy community of Mohilev, since then he was not yet a *Hasid*, he had said to himself: "I will go there also."

He traveled so that he would come to the Besht before the morning prayers on Friday. When he arrived, he saw that the Besht was smoking a pipe. This seemed strange.

"Afterward, during the prayer, I wept as never before in my life, and I realized that it was not my weeping.

"Later, when the Besht traveled to the land of Israel, I was left desolate until he returned. Then I began to travel to him and remained for some time with him. The Besht used to say that it was necessary to elevate me. After I had been with him for about five weeks, I asked, 'When, sir, will you elevate me?' "

THE GREAT MAGGID AND THE BESHT

I heard from the rabbi of the holy community of Derazne, who formerly was the head of the court in the holy community of Pavlysh, the story of how the rabbi, the Great Maggid, was attracted to the Besht. The Great Maggid fasted from one Sabbath to another seven or eight times successively, and he became seriously ill. Once, Rabbi Mendle of the holy community of Bar came to the community of Torchin, where he stayed with an elder of the community. The Maggid lived in a small house, which was attached to that of the elder. Rabbi Mendel entered the passageway of his host and he heard the Maggid studying with a pupil. The Maggid's explanations appealed to him. He entered the room and saw that the Maggid was very sick. He said to him: "Have you not heard that there is a Besht in the world? You, sir, should go to him and he will cure you."

The Great Maggid answered: "It is better to seek God's protection than to put one's trust in a human being."

When Rabbi Mendel came to the Besht, he praised the Maggid and said: "I have been to the community of Torchin and I saw there a holy vessel."

The Besht said: "I have known of him for several years and I long for him to come to me."

There are several versions of how the Maggid came to the Besht. But I heard that his relatives pressed him to go to the Besht. When he came to the Besht, he found him sitting on his bed studying, and he shook his hand. The Maggid asked the Besht to cure him.

The Besht scolded him and said: "My horses do not eat *matzoth* [unleavened bread]."

The Maggid began to perspire from weakness. He went outside and sat on the step in front of the house in order to rest. He saw a very young man, and he called him over and said to him: "Please go to the Besht and tell him: 'Why do not you follow the phrase: "Love ye therefore the stranger"?'"

The young man was Rabbi Jacob of Annopol. He felt pity for the Maggid and so he went to the Besht. He was afraid to talk with him, and so he wisely managed to go to the end of the house and then immediately turned back to leave. On his way out he said: "There is an unhappy man sitting in front of the house and he asked me to ask you, sir, why you have not fulfilled the phrase 'Love ye therefore the stranger'?" And he left the house.

The Besht immediately gathered ten men and went to the Maggid to appease him. He wanted to cure him with words. I heard from Rabbi Gershon of the community of Pavlysh that the Besht visited him daily for about two weeks and sat opposite him and recited psalms. After that the Besht said to him: "I wanted to cure you with words alone since this is an enduring remedy, but now I have to cure you with medication." The Besht gave him an apartment and for each Sabbath he gave him twelve golden coins for his expenses.

Rabbi Jacob of Annopol and Rabbi Elijah visited him often. Sometime they argued about problems in the Gemara and in the Tosaphoth.

The Maggid could not go to the Besht because he was so weak. After a little while he began to recover, and he used to go to the Besht to sit at his table. Once he fainted, and they tried for half a day to revive him. The Besht went three times to the *mikveh,* and he sent for a certain man who lived three versts away in order to buy from him a precious stone, a diamond, for thirty red coins, and they ground the stone and gave it to the Maggid to drink.

After that, Rabbi Jacob and his friend came to visit him and they asked him why he had fainted, but he did not answer them at all. They asked the people of the household whether he had left the house during the night. They said, "He went outside and stayed there, and when he returned home, he began to feel faint. They asked him where he had been."

He said, "The Besht sent his *gabbai* [synagogue assistant] to me at midnight. I found the Besht sitting with a small candle on his head. He was dressed in a coat of wolf fur turned inside out, and he asked me whether I has studied Kabbalah. I answered that I had. A book was lying in front of him on the table and he instructed me to read aloud from the book. The book was written in short paragraphs, each of which began: "Rabbi Ishmael said: 'Metatron, the Prince of Presence, told me.'" I recited a page or half a page to him.

"The Besht said to me: It is not correct. I will read it to you.' He began to read, and while he read he trembled. He rose and said: 'We are dealing with *Ma'aseh Merkavah* and I am sitting down.' He stood up and continued to read.

"As he was talking, he lay me down in the shape of a circle on the bed. I was not able to see him any more. I only heard voices and saw frightening flashes and torches. This continued for about two hours. I was extremely afraid and that fear caused me to feel faint."

And let me, the writer, say that it seems to me that that was the way his torah [personal understanding of Torah] was revealed to him. I heard from the Hasid, the rabbi of the holy community of Polonnoye that he received his soul's torah from the Besht amidst thunder and lightening. Moreover, he said that this revelation was accompanied by musical instruments, as it is said in the holy *Zohar*. But I have not seen in the *Zohar* any mention of musical instruments accompanying the giving of Torah." I did hear from the rabbi this explanation: "As all the Israelites received the Torah as one people in the same way the Besht received it as an individual."

Once, after the Besht's followers asked him the meaning of a sentence in the *Zohar* and he explained it to them, they asked the Maggid, God bless his memory, the same question, and his explanation amplified the answer of the Besht. They told this to the Besht and he said: "Do you think that he learned the Torah by himself?"

When the Maggid, God bless his memory, was ready to leave the Besht, the Besht blessed him. Afterward, the Besht bent his head for the Maggid to bless him, but the Maggid refused. So the Besht took the Maggid's hand and put it on his head, and the Maggid blessed him.

This is as far as it goes.

THE BESHT RESUSCITATES A CHILD

I heard from Rabbi Pesaḥ, the son of Rabbi Jacob of Kamenka, that while the Besht was traveling he came to a city, and a herald told him that he should stay as a guest in a certain house. He came to that house, and they refused to receive him as a guest because the son of the householder was seriously ill. The Besht sent his scribe to the house, and the woman said, "How is it possible for you to stay here overnight? Don't you see that the boy is sick and I am in great sorrow?" And she cursed the Besht.

The householder did not dare interfere. He went out to appease the Besht and told him that it was impossible to stay there. The Besht promised that if he remained with him as a guest the boy would live, and so he was received in the home.

The Besht went immediately to the *mikveh* and he perceived that the boy's condition was poor. He ordered that no one remain in the house. Everybody went to another house. He ordered his scribe to leave the house, as well. He would call him to ask for wine for the *kiddush* [blessing] since this took place on the eve of the holy Sabbath.

The Besht remained alone with the boy. He prayed Minḥah near him. He remained awake long into the night.

The scribe was afraid that the Besht would endanger himself, God forbid, by his great efforts in praying for the sick boy, since it was a dangerous situation. The scribe went to the door and slowly opened it, and he heard the Besht saying to the boy's soul: "Enter this body. You must enter it because I cannot swear a false oath."

The scribe did not know whether the boy was dead or still alive. The boy had a little bit of life in him. The scribe went away from the door, and after a short while he returned and entered. He found the Besht lying on the floor with his arms and legs stretched out.

The Besht stood up and said: "I told you, didn't I, to enter the boy's body?" And he shouted: "Hirsh, bring me wine for the *kiddush*." He ate with the scribe, and he did not sleep the entire night. In the morning he gave the scribe instructions and medicines, and then he went to pray in the *beth-hamidrash* [study house].

The boy's mother gathered that the child had recovered, and she began to sob. The scribe heard her and asked: "Why are you crying?"

She said to him: "How can I not cry after I cursed such a pious man?"

He answered her: "Do not cry. My rabbi is a good man and he will forgive you."

When the Besht returned from prayer he also heard her crying. He asked the scribe about it and learned the reason. He sent the scribe to her and told him: "Tell her not to cry. She should prepare a good dinner for the third meal. I promise her that the boy will sit with us at the table."

The reason why the Besht lay on the floor with his hands and legs extended was his agreement to accept "fiery lashes" for his oath to cure the boy. The soul was compelled to reenter the boy's body. His action ensured that the boy would live more than sixty years and that he would have sons, and he would earn a good living all his life. From this we see that the time for the boy's death had come, and therefore the Besht had to pray for the number of years he would live, for his livelihood, and for his having children.

RABBI GERSHON IN THE HOLY LAND

I heard from the rabbi mentioned above [the rabbi of our community] that once the Besht said: "I am puzzled. On Sabbath eve during prayer I looked for Rabbi Gershon, and I did not find him in the land of Israel. On Sabbath morning during prayer I saw him in the land of Israel, and I do not know what happened, unless he went outside the border." Several years later Rabbi Gershon came to him, and the Besht asked him about this matter, and Rabbi Gershon did not know either. Later he recalled that they had honored him with the *mitzvah* [precept] of the *berith* [circumcision] in Acre, and he had kept the Sabbath there. In Acre there are two synagogues, one in the land of Israel and one outside. "On Sabbath Eve I went to pray in the synagogue outside, but later it hurt my heart that I had not prayed in the land of Israel, and so the following day I prayed in the synagogue in the land of Israel."

STORYTELLING AND MA'ASEH MERKAVAH

When there was a *berith* at the house of the head of the court of the holy community of Horodnya, I heard from the rabbi of the holy community of Polonnoye, and then from the rabbi of our community that the Besht said: "When one tells stories in praise of the *tsaddikim* [hasidic masters], it is as though he were engaged in *Ma'aseh Merkavah* [Account of the "Chariot"]."

"THE HOUR HAS COME BUT NOT THE MAN"

In the holy community of Old Konstantynow there was a man who did not have children. He visited the Besht several times. Once the Besht promised him that his wife would give birth to a baby boy, and he told him to let him know when she had delivered.

And so it was that his wife gave birth to a baby boy, and he went to the Besht with great joy to tell him of his wife's delivery. But when he came to the Besht and broke this news to him, the Besht restrained himself for a long while, and then he began to weep uncontrollably and his hands hung limply at his side.

The man asked him: "Why are you crying, sir?"

He said: "Because I see that on the day that the boy will be *bar-mitzvah* he will be drawn into the river, God forbid." And the Besht said: "You will probably forget completely about it, but here is a sign for you to remember. On that day the boy will put two stockings on one foot and he will search for the second. You must guard him very carefully the entire day and prevent him from seeing water. 'If the verdict is postponed overnight it comes to naught.' But if you do not watch him then he certainly will be drawn into the river, God forbid."

In the course of the time the whole matter was completely forgotten.

On the day that the boy became *bar-mitzvah* the man went to pray in the synagogue while the boy was still asleep. When he returned from the synagogue the boy was searching in every corner of the house. His father asked him: "What are you looking for?"

He said to him: "I lost a stocking."

His father saw that he was wearing two stockings on one foot. When he saw this he recalled the warning, and he was careful to watch the boy that day.

During the day the sun was very hot and all the people of the town ran to swim in the river. The boy sneaked out as well, and ran to the river. They immediately ran after him and brought him back home. When his father realized that the boy fought to swim in the river, and it was impossible to keep him from it, he put him in a room and locked the door. All day long the boy cried bitterly: "Let me out! Where is the compassion a father should have for his children? I am hot from the sun."

But they did not pay any attention to him, and they did not give him even a drop of water to drink.

After the Minḥah, when all the people of the town were near the river, a creature with a head and two hands came out of the water, slapped his hands on the water and said: "The one who is mine is not here." Then it sank and disappeared.

At once the fever subsided, and the boy slept. And with the help of God he grew up well, and he had a long life, as the Besht, God bless his memory, had said.

THE BESHT PREVENTS A BLOOD LIBEL

Once the disciples of the Besht came to his house on the afternoon of Passover eve to fulfill the *mitzvah* of baking *matzoth*. It was their custom to bake as a group while singing the Hallel. The Besht was walking back and forth in the yard of the synagogue absorbed in deep thought. As the disciples had to wait for a few hours, they became very upset. Meanwhile, they saw that the Besht had recognized the priest from afar and had approached him. He began to talk with him and they strolled together for a long time. Afterward, the Besht invited him home, he offered him a seat, he treated him with Passover mead, and he continued to talk with him. Then the priest left and the Besht saw him out. Afterward, the Besht said: "Now we will soon begin to bake the *matzoth*. The day has begun to wane."

The disciples asked him: "Why did you have to talk with the priest for so long?"

He said that the priest had planned to throw a murdered bastard into the synagogue street on Passover night and then blame all the people of the town. By talking with him so long and by treating him well, he had erased the plot from the priest's mind.

THE DOCTOR

Once a well-known, great doctor came to the duchess of the town. The duchess praised the Besht highly, saying that he was a great man and knowledgeable in medicine.

The doctor said: "Tell him to come here."

She said: "Since he is a great man, it would be in keeping with his honor if we send a carriage for him as one does for governors." She sent for him and he appeared before them.

The doctor asked the rabbi whether it was true that he was knowledgeable about medicine.

He answered him: "It is true."

He said: "Where did you study and with what expert?"

He said: "God, blessed be he, taught me."

The doctor laughed at him.

The rabbi immediately asked him whether he could diagnose an illness from one's pulse. The rabbi said: "I have a deficiency. You try to diagnose my pulse. I will take your pulse and diagnose your condition."

The doctor took the rabbi's pulse. He could tell that there was something wrong, but he did not know what it was, because he was lovesick for God, blessed be He, and this was beyond the grasp of the doctor.

The rabbi took the doctor's pulse, and he returned his face to the duchess and asked her: "Were such and such precious objects stolen from you?"

She said: "Yes. It has been several years since they were stolen from me, and I do not know where they are."

The rabbi said: "Send someone to his inn and open his trunk. There you will find all of these objects."

She immediately sent someone and the objects were found there according to his holy words. The doctor left there in disgrace and contempt.

39

The Scholarly Life of the Gaon of Vilna

Allan Nadler

Among the hundreds of great rabbis and Talmudic authorities whose scholarship graced the eight-century history of east European Judaism, none quite matched the renown of the Lithuanian sage Rabbi Elijah ben Solomon of Vilna (1729–1797), the legendary *Vilner Gaon* (genius of Vilna). Although he never held an official rabbinical position and spent most of his years in a singularly intense and private pursuit of Talmudic erudition, the Gaon left a remarkable legacy that has shaped traditional Lithuanian Judaism to this day. He typified the intensely single-minded devotion to rabbinical studies that, largely as the result of his own towering influence, became the hallmark of Lithuanian Jewish piety.

The Gaon's life coincided precisely with the advent and rapid rise of Hasidism across eastern Europe. Hasidism's emphasis upon popular piety as opposed to ecclesiastical scholarship and its astonishingly fast spread to the Jewish masses of Poland and Russia were perceived as serious challenges to the established Judaism of the day and as threatening the authority of the rabbis charged with the latter's propagation and protection. Due to his unparalleled scholarly stature, it was the Gaon of Vilna who became the standardbearer and titular founder of the movement that rose against Hasidism in order to protect traditional rabbinic Judaism, and whose followers ultimately became known as the *Mitnagdim* (opponents).

The *Mitnagdim* not only polemicised against Hasidic doctrine; they waged an uncompromising war against its practitioners, placing them under the rabbinic ban of excommunication and, when possible, denouncing their *zaddikim* (Hasidic religious leaders; lit., righteous men) as subversives to the Czarist authorities. Among the most prominent Hasidic *zaddikim* active during the Gaon's lifetime was Rabbi Shneur Zalman of Lyadi (1745–1813), the founder of the Habad school (today best known as Lubavitch), who was jailed several times in St. Petersburg as a consequence of the *Mitnagdim*'s denunciations. According to Habad traditions, when R. Shneur Zalman traveled to Vilna in order to initiate a theological dialogue with the Gaon in hopes of calming his opposition to Hasidism, he stood disgraced at the Gaon's doorstep, shut out of the hermetically sealed home in which the great rabbi was immersed in his studies, adamantly refusing to receive him.

The key difference between the *Mitnagdim* and the *Hasidim* during the formative years of this great theological dispute centered on the respective roles of sober Talmudic scholarship and mystical rapture in Jewish religious life. For the Gaon and his followers, the sober study of Torah was the sole avenue for authentic religious experience. They argued that it is only through the unflagging devotion to comprehend fully the will of God as it is inscribed in the Torah that man could come to know his Creator. The *Mitnagdim* accordingly placed the pursuit of *Torah lishmah*—that is, pure Torah scholarship, engaged in with no ulterior motives and pursued as an autonomous religious good—at the pinnacle of the hierarchy of Jewish spiritual values. The *Hasidim,* on the other hand, taught that such exclusive emphasis on learning deprived the untutored Jewish masses of religious experience and resulted in an elitist, arid, unemotional, and spiritually vacuous Judaism. The extreme intellectualism of the rabbis, the *Hasidim* further argued, had created a tragic rift between them and the vast majority of the Jewish people whose spiritual mentors they were supposed to be. To invigorate the regnant, scholarly, and effete Judaism of their day and to heal the deep divide between the rabbinical elite and the Jewish masses, *Hasidism* simplified and popularized the formerly esoteric kabbalistic teachings that emphasized the immanence of God in the created Universe, His closeness to all people, both the educated and the ignorant, and the need for joy and spiritual euphoria in order to commune with the divine presence.

The long-term effects on Lithuanian Jewry of the Gaon of Vilna's singular and passionate emphasis upon scholarship as the only authentic form of spirituality, and his determined battle with Hasidism, were significant. Among his elite cadre of personal disciples, Rabbi Hayyim b. Isaac (1749–1821) founded a *yeshiva* (rabbinical academy) in his Belorussian town of Volozhin, where the supremacy and dignity of rabbinical scholarship, as taught by the Gaon, served as the guiding principle. The Volozhin *yeshiva* spawned a network of similar rabbinical seminaries across Lithuania, Belorussia, and eastern Poland, which have remained the religious institutional foundation of Mitnagdic Judaism until today. The Gaon's legacy of scholarship even shaped the popular image of the Lithuanian Jew in folklore and literature as profoundly learned, skeptical, emotionally reticent, lacking in overt religious enthusiasm, and prone to intellectual snobbery. The age-old Hasidic Yiddish epithet for Lithuanian Jews, *kalter tseylem kop* (cold-hearted and intractable), captured this image of an emotionally distant, stubborn scholar inaugurated by the Gaon.

Ironically, just as the *zaddikim* who founded the Hasidic movement were the subjects of wildly exaggerated hagiographies that recounted their spiritual greatness and miraculous exploits, the Gaon's towering legacy resulted in a parallel tradition of fantastic legends about his brilliant and erudite scholarship. In the decades immediately following his death, the disciples of the Gaon set themselves to the task of immortalizing his scholarship and his memory. They did this primarily by publishing dozens of terse scholarly commentaries to the traditional rabbinic canon that the Gaon left, either in manuscript or as oral traditions received from him by his students. Along with this posthumous explosion of the Gaon's publications there also appeared a large number of books, pamphlets, and articles fabulously extolling his wisdom and scholarship, often in superhuman terms. R. Hayyim of Volozhin, who published some of the Gaon's most important legal and mystical commentaries, often prefaced these publications with lengthy tracts in effusive praise of his master. In the most remarkable of these prefaces, to the Gaon's commentary on the kabbalistic text *Sifra De-Zeniuta,* R. Hayyim describes at great length the Gaon's struggle against mystical revelations that he felt interfered with his cognitive, scholarly pursuit of the truth. In sharp contrast to the Hasidic rebbes, whose very authority derived in large part from their claims to mystical knowledge and clairvoyance, the Gaon repudiated the nocturnal angels who approached him with fantastic revelations, and stubbornly insisted on basing his religious knowledge solely upon the findings of sober scholarship.

The document presented here, R. Israel b. Samuel of Shklov's preface to *Pe'at ha-Shulkhan,* is among the finest example of such hagiographies of the Gaon. R. Israel of Shklov (d. 1839) was a close and devoted disciple of the Gaon, who ministered to his master on his deathbed and later collaborated in the publication of some of his commentaries to the codes of Jewish law. Like the Gaon, R. Israel was keen on clarifying sections of the Talmud that had been neglected by earlier authorities and had a particular interest in the emendation of corrupt rabbinical texts.

R. Israel was one of a large number of rabbis from the Belorussian town of Shklov who were devoted disciples of the Gaon. The town of Shklov, in fact, enjoyed a unique relationship with the Gaon, particularly in connection with his battle against Hasidism. In 1772, Shklov became the first Jewish community to issue an official ban against the Hasidim, reputedly at the behest of the Gaon. The rabbis of Shklov, often referred to in subsequent rabbinic sources collectively as Hakhmei Shklov (the sages of Shklov), were also among the most enlightened Jewish leaders of their day, and tended to be receptive to the new currents of culture and modern critical scholarship that were beginning to arrive in Russia from western Europe at the beginning of the nineteenth century. So, for example, one of the leading rabbinic scholars of Shklov, R. Barukh Schick, translated Euclid into Hebrew, claiming in his introduction that he did so at the behest of the Gaon in partial fulfillment of the latter's' program of enhancing knowledge of the Torah by spreading scientific wisdom among the Jews.

In this remarkable text, we may observe some of the salient features of the Gaon's posthumous image. The most prominent of these characteristics is the astonishing scope of the Gaon's knowledge, his unrivaled erudition in the entire canon of traditional Jewish texts. Although the major focus of R. Israel of Shklov's testimony is clearly on his master's incredible personal discipline, asceticism, and scholarly erudition in every branch of classical Judaic wisdom, he touches upon some other themes that form an important part the Gaon's historical legacy.

Along with this total mastery of traditional Jewish learning, the Gaon is also extolled for knowledge of less conventional disciplines, particularly the secular sciences. Of singular interest in our text is the surprising reference to the Gaon's interest in the religious significance of music. This may in part be directed against the Hasidim, who were widely criticized by the *Mitnagdim* for abusing music through their practice of undisciplined ecstatic singing and wild rapturous dancing. Although it is clear that the Gaon himself viewed his pursuit of such non-rabbinic disciplines as trigonometry and medicine as only ancillary to his Torah studies, and directed solely to complement and complete his comprehension of God's revealed wisdom, many of the earliest proponents of the *haskala* (Jewish enlightenment) in eastern Europe viewed the Gaon as a harbinger of their own campaign for the educational and cultural modernization of Europe's Jews. Thus, for example, Shai Ish Hurwitz, a leading nineteenth-century propagandist for the Russian *haskala*, very clearly enlisted the Gaon's authority in order to legitimize the educational reforms that were at the center of its program for Jewish enlightenment:

> It was the Gaon who first created an opening, like the eye of a needle, for the critical textual study of the Talmud, which finally resulted in today's critical, literary scholarship.... The Gaon was a trailblazer in the field of Jewish education. He eliminated Rabbinic casuistry (*pilpul*), and was the first to establish a logical pedagogical order of study whereby Jewish children would begin with Bible and Hebrew grammar, followed by Mishnah, and only then begin the study of Talmud—a program that was later championed by all of the *maskilim*, [participants in the modern Jewish "Enlightenment"] in particularly Isaac Baer Levinsohn (the father of the Russian *haskala*). Who knows if all of the latter's' [i.e., the *maskilim*'s] efforts for the improvement of Jewish education would have taken root had it not been for the pioneering work of the Gaon? Moreover, the Gaon was a scientific scholar the likes of whom had not been seen in Israel since the days of the great geonim of Babylonia and North Africa. At his behest, Joshua Zeitlin established his center for Jewish scientific scholarship [in Shklov] ... and at his command, Barukh of Shklov decided to translate Euclid into Hebrew.... And in all of this he was a shining example for his many disciples. The Gaon's students came into close contact with the biblical scholars and pioneers of the enlightenment who were assembled in those days in Berlin under the direction of Moses Mendelsohn, in a joint effort to find ways in which to improve the spiritual condition and education of the Jewish people.
>
> Shai Ish Hurwitz, "Ha-Hasiduth ve-ha-Haskala," *He-Atid* 2 (1909): 31–32.

Among the unconventional disciplines pioneered by the Gaon, referred to by both Hurwitz and R. Israel of Shklov, was the textual criticism of Judaism's sacred texts. Unlike the vast majority of traditional, or Orthodox, rabbis to this very day, the Gaon was unafraid of correcting and emending texts that, based on his independent analytical speculation, he considered to be flawed. A trailblazer in the critico-analytical interpretation of Talmudic texts, the Gaon also tended to disregard the age-old tradition of uncritical veneration for the views of the rabbinical authorities of earlier generations, and displayed uncommon boldness in criticizing, and often simply ignoring, the juridical opinions of his rabbinic forbears. R. Israel of Shklov alludes to this brave willingness to overturn established precedents in Jewish law at the very beginning of our text, when he refers to the Gaon as being like one of the generation of the *rishonim* (earlier sages), a reference to the rabbis who lived before the close of the *Shulkhan Arukh,* the authoritative sixteenth-century code of Jewish law whose decisions were widely regarded as sacrosanct by all subsequent rabbinic legislators who became known as the *aharonim* (later sages)

In his introduction to *Pe'at ha-Shulkhan,* a discursive code of the Jewish ritual and agricultural laws whose observance is limited to residents of the land of Israel, R. Israel of Shklov asserts that he had relied very heavily upon precisely these trailblazing legal and textual interpretations of the Gaon, whom he regards as his primary teacher. The extensive praise of the Vilner Gaon contained in this text is presented as justification of R. Israel of Shklov's juridical methodology, particularly when relying on the Gaon's opinions that defy legal precedent or that are based on critical emendations of sacrosanct rabbinical texts.

My translation is based upon Israel b. Samuel of Shklov, *Sefer Pe'at ha- Shulkhan* (Säfed, 1834), pp. 5a–6b.

Further Reading

Although there is no full English biography of the Vilner Gaon, a fairly good account of his theological differences with and battle against Hasidism can be found in E. J. Schochet, *The Hasidic Movement and the Gaon of Vilna* (Northvale, N.J.: Jason Aronson, 1994). The fullest treatment of the theology of the Mitnagdim is Allan Nadler, *The Faith of the Mithnagdim: Rabbinic Responses to Hasidic Rapture* (Baltimore: Johns Hopkins University Press, 1997). A thorough treatment of the rabbis of the town of Shklov in the early nineteenth century is David Fishman, *Russia's First Modern Jews: The Jews of Shklov* (New York: New York University Press, 1995). Very few of the Gaon's original writings or those of his disciples are available in English. Two notable exceptions are the Gaon's remarkable ethical testament, published in Israel Abrahams, *Hebrew Ethical Wills,* vol. 2 (Philadelphia: Jewish Publication Society of America, 1948), and an excerpted English version of R. Hayyim of Volozhin's aforementioned introduction to the Gaon's commentary to *Sifra De-Zeniuta,* in Louis Jacobs, ed., *Jewish Mystical Testimonies* (New York: Schocken, 1977).

The Scholarly Life of the Gaon of Vilna

Behold how our holy and pious rabbi, of blessed memory, was an untarnished pearl, like one of the generation of the *rishonim,* as the sacred teachings contained in his writings demonstrate. For he authored more than seventy works, in which all of his words, though very concise, were fiery, like unto the heavenly stars. And among [his writings] are numerous, very brief and esoteric books . . . regarding the secrets of the Torah, which require many extensive commentaries.

He completed all of his written works before he reached his fortieth year, after which he did not write anything. Whatever was [subsequently] published [in his name] was actually written by his disciples. For he was a mighty fountain whose teachings could not fully be captured in print by any one individual. I heard from his eldest son, of blessed memory, who heard directly from him, that he developed one hundred and fifty interpretations of a single verse from the [biblical] Song of Songs, but no scribe was found sufficiently swift to record all these views, and he himself did not want to spend the time necessary to record them all. . . . It is further related that when he finished his commentary to the Song of Songs, he lifted his eyes to the heavens and, in an intense mystical state, he blessed and praised God for having enabled him to apprehend the full light of the entire Torah, both its exoteric and esoteric parts.

He declared: "All of the sciences are necessary for [the comprehension of] our Torah and are included within it." And he knew them all fully, and enumerated them: algebra, trigonometry, geometry, and the wisdom of music. He particularly praised the latter [i.e., music]. For he used to say that the secrets behind most of the Bible's cantillations and the songs of the Levites and the commentaries to the *Zohar*, are unfathomable without it. And through the beauty of [music] men can attain a mystical death, and its secrets that are enshrined in the Torah can empower men to revive the dead. He also said that Moses himself brought down from Mount Sinai numerous tunes and notes, out of which all other songs are composed; and he [the Gaon] knew them all.

As for the medical sciences, he knew surgery and its attendant procedures. Although he wanted to master pharmacology and planned to study it with the physicians of his day, his righteous father forbade him from studying this. For he feared that its mastery would lead him to neglect his Torah studies each time he would be called upon [for prescriptions] to save lives. And his father similarly warned him against studying witchcraft. . . . As for philosophy, he claimed to have mastered it in its entirety and to have learned only two things from it . . . and all the rest of it must be discarded.

As a consequence of all this, he declared that, thank God, he had totally mastered the entire Torah that was given at Mount Sinai, as well as all of the prophetic and other biblical writings. Also [he apprehended] the entire oral Torah . . . so that by his later years, there did not remain a single doubt regarding any *halakha* [Jewish law] or Talmudic passage . . . to the point where he understood the entire corpus of the oral Torah and the halakhic codes, including every commentary written to the *Shulkhan Arukh* [the authoritative sixteenth-century code of Jewish law]. He clarified them all, and exposed all obscurities to the light of day and corrected all the flawed texts.

As for the esoteric teachings [in the kabbalistic texts of] *Zohar, Tikkunei Zohar, Sefer Yezirah,* and the writings of Rabbi Isaac Luria, of blessed memory, he completed them all and corrected many textual errors, thus editing these books of all scribal mistakes. In fact, there were only two very difficult matters in the entire esoteric lore that remained unresolved by him ... of which he said that if he only knew who had their solutions, he would walk until he reached him and wait for the answers until the coming of the Messiah.

Who can recount his righteousness and piety, that he never engaged in mundane conversation, and he never accepted any communal or rabbinical responsibilities, nor anything else that might divert him [from Torah study]. He despised all financial rewards, and would just study in isolation, in the woods, or alone in his house.

When he departed for the land of Israel, some of the communal leaders gave him money to cover his expenses. And when, for reasons known only to him, he turned away and came back home, he returned all of the money. When he would travel into *golah* [a self-imposed exile from his home], he would become renowned for his many wondrous deeds, wherever he went. . . . And when he returned home, he would only study Torah in a state of self-denial. He would close all the shutters of his house [even] during the day and study by candlelight so as not to be disturbed by the eyes of passers-by. Such was the nature of his study in the days of his youth that he would always review the entire text of the Babylonian Talmud each month.

For all of these reasons, it is appropriate to call our rabbi the "Saint" and "Holy One." It is impossible [adequately] to describe the intensity of his study of the holy Torah. He would review each chapter and tractate [of the Talmud] hundreds and thousands of times. Then again, on account of his abundant affection for the holy Torah, he might spend an entire, long midwinter night reviewing [over and again] just a single *mishna* from the order of *Toharot*. In his younger years, he would spend the frigid winter days studying in his unheated room, where he would keep a bucket of ice water in which to immerse his feet, so as not to doze off. . . .

A great rabbi from this region . . . recounted that one year, just before the festival of Sukkot, he [the Gaon] rebuked the [congregation] assembled before him and proclaimed that there is an obligation upon every student of Torah to commit at least one tractate of the Talmud to memory. He would thereby never have to neglect the commandment constantly to be studying the Torah at all, even while traveling or when in an unlit place. Upon hearing this directive from the Gaon's very holy mouth, this particular rabbi immediately and with intensive effort studied the Talmudic tractate of *Sukkah* [dealing with laws of the biblical festival of Sukkot, or Tabernacles], reviewing it over and over again until he had committed it to memory. He then examined himself in it and also had his erudition tested before others, in order to be sure that he had properly committed it to memory.

Subsequently, during the intermediate days of the festival [of Sukkot], while a group of great talmudic scholars were gathered before the Gaon, this rabbi entered and proclaimed before the assembled: "I have completed studying tractate *Sukkah* and I have committed it to memory." And the Gaon responded: "So, would you like me to test your knowledge by asking you a few questions?" And he answered him: "Yes, for I know it by heart." So the Gaon asked him a question that he could not answer, regarding the exact number of dissenting opinions between each of the various groups of rabbis [cited] in this tractate. Subsequently, the Gaon opened his mouth and enumerated, like someone counting precious gems, each and every [talmudic dispute], and he dissected and analyzed the minute details of every aspect of each such case. . . . [B]ehold how amazing was his erudition in every tractate of both the Babylonian and Palestinian Talmuds, and in the entire Torah.

He knew each and every textual variant and scribal error in the Talmud. . . . He even knew the names and the personal affairs of every human being in the world, and he could tell you where all of these are alluded to in the Torah.

How great, lofty and amazing was his comprehension of the [Torah's] secrets and many wonders! Aside from his holy published [commentaries on the kabbalistic texts] *Sifra de-Zeniuta, Sefer Yetsira,* and on parts of the *Zohar,* we still have many of his manuscripts in our possession. There I saw a secret doctrine that was revealed to him by the [biblical patriarch] Jacob, our forefather, regarding a matter in the writings of Rabbi Isaac Luria, with which he was having some difficulty.

He tended often to reject the commentaries of the earlier rabbinical authorities, in order to develop his novel exegetical approach to the true understanding [of the text]. Indeed, in many places it is clear and evident that he merited a revelation of the truth as a consequence of his exceedingly diligent scholarship, and with heavenly help that he received [as a reward] for his studies that were pure and without ulterior motives.

He was indeed a mighty fountain! And so let us follow his light with respect to all of his holy teachings.

APPENDIX

The Jewish Festivals

Passover (Pesach), springtime festival that celebrates the Exodus of the Israelites from bondage in Egypt. A week-long celebration during which unleavened bread (*matsah*) is eaten, and the story of the liberation from Egypt is retold at a festive meal, the *seder*. One of the three "pilgrimage festivals" (*shalosh regalim*), during which, in Temple times, people came to worship and offer sacrifices in Jerusalem.

Feast of Weeks (Shavuot), in ancient times a celebration of the early harvest in the land of Israel, although it eventually became as well a celebration of the revelation of the Torah by God at Mount Sinai. Begins seven weeks from the second day of Passover. One of the *shalosh regalim*. Associated with the reading of the book of Ruth.

Ninth of Av (Tishah be-Av), day of fasting and mourning that commemorates the destruction of the First and Second Temples in Jerusalem, late summer. Associated with the reading of the book of Lamentations.

New Year (Rosh Hashanah), the New Year festival in late summer or early fall. Begins a ten-day period of repentance and introspection that culminates with Yom Kippur.

Day of Atonement (Yom Kippur), day of fasting, centered around prayer, repentance, and introspection in the synagogue. Most important day of fasting in the Jewish calendar.

Feast of Booths or Tabernacles (Sukkot), beginning five days after Yom Kippur, a week-long commemoration of the dwelling in temporary shelters by the Israelites as they journeyed through the wilderness following the Exodus from Egypt. It also celebrates the final harvest of the year, and is one of the *shalosh regalim*. For Sukkot individuals and families build and decorate a *sukkah* in which they have their meals for the week. Sukkot is followed by an additional two festive days, Shemini Atseret (Eighth Day of Assembly), and Simchat Torah (Rejoicing in the Torah). In Israel, Simchat Torah coincides with the one-day celebration of Shemini Atseret.

Hanukkah, historically, a relatively minor winter festival that celebrates the triumph of the Jewish Maccabees over the Greek-Syrians, and the rededication and repurifying of the ancient Temple in Jerusalem. Lasts for eight days, on each of which candles are lit at night in a *menorah* or candleholder.

Fifteenth of Shvat (Tu be-Shvat), New Year for Trees, historically a relatively minor festival of thanksgiving for the fruits of the trees. Falls in late winter.

Feast of Lots (Purim), festival celebrating the victory of Persia's Jews over their enemy Haman, as accounted in the book of Esther, which is chanted in the synagogue. Falls in late winter, early spring.

Sabbath (Shabbat), the seventh day of the week, celebrating the completion of the process of creation by God. Begins at sundown on Friday and ends with nightfall on Saturday, during which time no activity considered by rabbinic tradition as labor is performed. Characterized by communal prayer in the synagogue, three festive meals, study of Torah, and joyful companionship with family and friends.

INDEX

Aaron ben Elijah, 249
Aaron ben Jacob ha-Kohen, 121
Abrahams, Israel, 415, 420, 517
Abrahmovitch, Sholom Jacob. *See* Seforim, Mendele Mokher
Abravanel, Benvenida, 203
Abulafia, Abraham, 18
Abulafia, Anna Sapir, 440
Abyss of Despair (Hannover), 215–16, 220–26 (text). *See also* "six pillars of the world"
Adderet Eliyahu (Bashyachi), 251
Adelman, Howard, 56, 189, 457
Adler, E. N., 240, 287
Against Celsus (Origen), 387
aggadah, 5
Agnon, Shmuel Yosef, 66
Agus, Irving A., 287
aharonim, 517
Ahavat Shalom (The Love of Peace), 33–34, 211–12; pact of, 212–14 (text)
Ahl al-Kitab (People of the Book), 230
Ai Jun, 269
al-Baghdadi, 418: on Maimonides, 427 (text)
al-Fadil, 416–17
al-Harizi, 238
al-Isfahani, 230–31
al-Junayd, 187
al-Kurani, 186–87
al-Mulk, 417: on Maimonides, 427 (text)
al-Nahawendi, Benjamin, 22
al-Qifti, 414, 415, 419: on Maimonides, 422–24 (text)
al-Qirqisani, 229–30, 233, 249
al-Qumisi, Daniel, 22
al-Qushayri, 186
al-Sharani, 186, 187
alchemy, 32, 455
Alexander the Shochet, 500
Alfandari, Hayyim, 210
Alfasi, Isaac, 11, 218, 413
Algasi, Israel, 210
Algasi, Yom Tov, 210

Alkabez, Solomon, 75–76, 377
Almohads, 11, 414
Almoravids, 11
Alonso, Luís, 348
"Alternative Prayer Canon for Women, An" (Kay), 65, 205
Amalric I, 415
Amittai ben Shefatia, 44: *seliha* of, 51 (text)
amoraim, 4
Amram, 104
Amulets and Magic Bowls (Naveh and Shaked), 344
An Cheng, 269
Analects of Confucius, 266
Anan ben David, 21–22, 230, 249
'Ananiyya, 230
Andula, 269
Ankori, Zvi, 252, 253
"Anti-Semitism and Aniconism" (Bland), 286
Antiochus Epiphanes, 24
Antiquitates Judaicae (Josephus), 387
Ari nohem (The Roaring Lion) (Modena), 454
ars moriendi, 158
ars praedicandi, 326
Ashkenazic Jewry, 13, 15, 105, 399, 429–30, 431, 483–84; and the Crusades, 13. *See also* Hasidism; Pietism, German
Ashkenazic Torah Study Society, 455
"Aspects of the Social and Cultural History of Provençal Jewry" (Twersky), 287
Assaf, Simcha, 194
astrology, 32, 455
Autobiography of a Seventeenth-Century Venetian Rabbi, The (Cohen, ed. and trans.), 456–57
Av, 41
Avraham of Ihringen, 299
Azikri, Eleazar, 33
Azulai, Hayyim Yosef David, 211

Baal Shem Tov (Master of the Good Name), 20, 400, 500–501
Baer, Dov, 400, 500, 501

Baer, Isaac, 145, 287
Balaban, Majer, 217
Bar-Ilan, M., 390–91
Bar-Levav, Avriel, 159
Baraita de-Niddah, 134
Baron, Salo, 192, 194, 220, 238, 240
Baruch of Arezzo, 471–73: biography of Shabbatai Zvi, 473–82 (text)
Bashyachi, Elijah, 249, 251: on Sabbath lights, 261–63 (text)
Basir, the bell maker, 187–88: wife's petition concerning, 189–90 (text)
Baskin, Judith, 27–28, 137–38, 189, 433
Basola, Moses, 238
Beginning of Wisdom, The (de Vidas), 33
"Behinat ha-shohet ha-qara'i" (Vogelmann), 251
Beinart, Haim, 146, 349
Belcove-Shalin, Janet S., 502
"Beliefs, Rites and Customs of the Jews Connected with Death" (Bender), 159
Belting, Hans, 287
Ben-Sasson, M., 420
Benayahu, Meir, 159, 212, 391
Bender, Alfred Philip, 159
benedictions, 40, 42–44: the Amida, 40; "Creator," 40, 42, 46 (text); "Love," 40, 46 (text); "Redeemer," 40, 46 (text); Sanctification, 42–43. *See also* poetry, liturgical
Benjamin of Tudela, 24, 192, 238, 283–84: as pilgrim in Persia, 291–92 (text)
berakhot. *See* benedictions
Berechia, Aaron, 155
Berger, David, 194
Berukhim, Abraham, 33, 377–79: as "great patron of the Sabbath," 378; list of *hanhagot*, 382–85 (text)
Besht. *See* Baal Shem Tov
Bet El. *See* "Pietist's Study House of Bet El"
Beta Israel. *See* Falashas
Between Muslim and Jew (Wasserstrom), 232
"Bible Interpretation as Exhibited in the First Book of Maimonides' Code" (Greenberg), 175
"Bibliography of the Writings of Haim Beinart, A" (Kaplan), 349
Bibliography shel Hagadot Ha Pessah (Ya'ari), 302
Bilu, Y., 391
Birkat ha-Shem (Blessing of the Lord) (Naphtali), 156
Birnbaum, Philip, 45
Black Jews, 24–25. *See also* Falashas

Bland, Kalman, 34–35, 286
Blau, J., 420
Bogaty, Jacob, 219
Bomberg, Daniel, 320
Book of Changes, 266, 271
Book of Commandments (Maimonides), 416
Book of the Devout (Azikri), 33
Book of Doctrines and Beliefs (Gaon), 33
Book of Jewish Women's Prayers, A (Tarnor, ed. and trans.), 65
Book of Jubilees, 25
Book of Travels (Benjamin of Tudela), 238
Book of the Wars of the Lord, The (Jacob ben Reuben), 283
book production, Hebrew: codex, 319; incunabula, 319; manuscripts, 319; printing, 319–20
books, treatment of, 35, 321
Brisk, 216, 218
brit milah. *See* circumcision
Brody, 210, 215
Buddhism, 267: monastic tradition in, 212
burial societies. *See hevra qadisha*
Burning Lights (Chagall), 65–66

Cairo Genizah, 188, 229, 341, 364, 366: magical fragments in, 388; on prayer, 366, 367–74 (text)
calligraphy, 35
Canonization of the Synagogue Service, The (Hoffman), 45
Cardin, Nina Beth, 205
Caro, Joseph. *See* Karo, Joseph
Chajes, J. H., 391
Charlemagne, 13
Chattel or Person (Wegner), 107
Chazan, Robert, 31, 287, 440, 441
Chelebi, Raphael Joseph, 470
childbirth, 204–5, 208–9 (texts): *hadas* ritual, 144, 146–47 (texts)
China: Jewish community in, 23, 265–67; and the *semuren*, 265–66. *See also* Confucianism; Jin Zhong; Kaifeng
Chinese Jews (White), 271
Chisea, Bruno, 233
Chmielnicki, Bogdan, 215
Christianity, 230: Nestorian, 267
Chronicle of Moses, 500
circumcision, 102: the *ba'alat brit* and, 106; the *mohel* and, 102; order of, 109–10 (text); the *sandek* and, 113–14 (texts); women's role in, 103–4, 104, 105, 106–7, 112–13 (text), 113 (text), 114 (text)

INDEX

Coenen, Thomas, 473
Cohen, Mark R., 287, 420, 456–57
Cohen, Richard, 286, 486
Cohen, Shaye J. D., 134
Cologne, 13, 132
Commentary on the Mishneh (Maimonides), 413, 415: colophon to, 421 (text)
Commentary on Rosh Ha-Shanah, 421–22 (text)
Compilation of Matters Relating to the Jews of K'ai-feng Fu, A (White), 271
"Concept of Death in Sefer-ha-Hayyim by Rabbi Shimon Frankfurt, The" (Bar-Levav), 159
"conduct" literature. See *hanhagot*
Conduct Literature (Gries), 159
confraternities, Jewish, 455
Confucianism, 266
Conservative Judaism, 16, 21
conversas, 30, 143–44: and childbirth and purity rites, 144, 146–48 (text); confessions to the Inquisitorial court of, 349, 349–52 (texts); and death and mourning rites, 144–45, 148–54 (text)
conversos, 378
Conversos on Trial by the Inquisition (Beinart), 146
Cordovero, Moses, 19, 33, 77, 376, 377
Corinaldi, Michael, 25–26
Cossacks, 215
Council of the Four Lands, 156, 219–20
Covenant of Blood (Hoffman), 107
Cracow, 216–17, 218
Crescas, Hasdai, 326: treatise for the guidance of preachers, 329–32 (text)
Crisis and Leadership (Halkin and Hartman), 420
Crossing the Jabbok (Goldberg), 66, 159
Crusades, the, 283, 429–30, 438: Maimonides' view of, 415. See also Christianity; *Mainz Anonymous*
crypto-Jews. See *conversas*; *conversos*
"Custom, Law, and Gender" (Adelman), 56

Daggers of Faith (Chazan), 287
Daily Prayer Book (Birnbaum), 45
Dan, Joseph, 194, 288
d'Arpino, Anna, 54
David ben Joseph Abudraham, 53
David ben Shmu'el Halevi, 217–18
Davis, Natalie Zemon, 454, 486
Day of Atonement. See Yom Kippur
Days of Awe, 63. See also Rosh Hashanah; Yom Kippur
Days of Awe (Agnon), 66

525

de Leon, Moses, 19, 74–75, 353
de Vidas, Elijah, 33
Dead Sea Sect, 21
death: medieval preoccupation with, 484; rituals, 144–45, 148–54 (texts), 155–58
Delmedigo, Joseph Solomon, 218
demon possession. See exorcism
Deux traités de mystique juive (Fenton, trans.), 366
Di Rossi, David, 238
"Die Krakauer Judegemeinde-Ordnung von 1595 . . ." (Balaban), 217
Die Speisegesetze der Karäer nach einer Berliner Handschrift (Lorge), 253
Diena, Azriel, 55
dietary laws, 4; women's responsibility for, 28
divorce, 101, 107–8 (texts)
"Doctrine of Abu 'Isa al-Isfahani and Its Sources, The" (Erder), 233
Doctrine of the Means, 269
Dolce of Worms, 34, 429–33
Duran, Profiat, 284–85: on visual techniques for studying Torah, 294–96 (text)
Duties of the Heart (Ibn Pakuda), 33

"Each Man Ate an Angel's Meal" (Hecker), 357
Ecstatic Religion (Lewis), 389
education, medieval, 118: community involvement in, 218–20; elementary school curriculum, 216–17; and the Jewish school initiation rite, 115–19, 122–30 (texts). See also *perushim*; *Sefer Huqqei ha-Torah*; *yeshivot*
"Educational and Literary Activities of Jewish Women in Italy during the Renaissance and the Counter-Reformation, The" (Adelman), 56
Egypt, 186: Pietism in, 364–66. See also Maimonides, Moses; Sufism
Eight Chapters (Maimonides), 33
Eight Chapters of Maimonides on Ethics (Gorfinkle, ed.), 288
"Ein ha-Qore" (Ibn Shem Tov), 326, 332–36 (text)
Ein Sof (the Infinite), 18–19
Elbogen, Ismar, 45
Eleazar ben Judah of Worms, 17, 119, 134, 135, 192, 429–33: writings of, 434–37 (texts)
Eleazar of Mainz, 29, 135: ethical will of, 140–42 (text)
"Elementary and Secondary Education in the Middle Ages" (Thorndike), 195
Elijah ben Solomon of Vilna. See Gaon of Vilna
Elijah of Ferrara, 238

Elijah of Pesaro, 238
Elon, Ari, 88
Elon, Menahem, 6–7, 286
Elon, Tidhar, 88
embodied symbolism, 353–55
Emden, Jacob, 82
Emunot ve-De'ot (Saadia Gaon), 321
Encyclopedia Judaica, 212, 252
Ephraim of Leczyca, 220
Epistle of Consolation (Maimon), 414
Epistle on Apostasy (Maimonides), 414, 421 (text)
Epistle on Resurrection (Maimonides), 418–19
Erder, Yoram, 233
Essential Kabbalah, The (Matt), 79
Essential Papers on Hasidism (Hundert, ed.), 402, 502
ethical wills, 156–58
European Jewry and the First Crusade (Chazan), 440
European Jewry in the Age of Mercantilism, 1550–1750 (Israel), 486
Exodus: importance in Judaism of, 300; reenactment of, 298–99: and *sippur yeziat mizrayim*, 299. *See also* illuminated manuscripts
exorcism, 32: and the "golden age of the demoniac," 388; Jewish exorcism techniques, 387–88; kabbalistic reconstruction of, 388–90; in the New Testament, 386–87; in the Old Testament, 386; primary sources on, 391–98 (texts); Roman Ritual, 389
experiential hermeneutics, 354

Faces of the Chariot (Halperin), 344
fairs, 220
Faith of the Mithnagdim, The (Nadler), 517
Falashas, 25–26
Falk, Joshua, 217
"Family and Gender in Jewish Venice" (Adelman), 56
Farisol, Abraham, 54
fasting, 43: and women, 203, 206 (text)
Feast of Weeks. *See* Shavuot
Fenton, P., 366–67, 420
festivals: annual procession of, 41; and pilgrimages, 237. *See also* specific festivals
"Finding Women's Voice in Italian Jewish Literature" (Adelman), 56
Fine, Lawrence, 78, 288, 379
fingernail paring, 144, 148 (texts)
Fishbane, Michael, 159
Fishman, David, 517

Fishman, Talya, 457
Fleischer, Ezra, 45
Flynn, J. C., 232
folk rituals, 31–32
" 'For the Human Soul Is the Lamp of the Lord' " (Weissler), 65
" 'For Women and for Men Who Are Like Women' " (Weissler), 486
Founder of Hasidism (Rosman), 502
"Four Kinds of Death Penalty" ritual, 158
Fram, Edward, 220
France, 18
Frank, Daniel, 252, 253
Frankfurt, Simeon, 64
Freimann, A. H., 420
Friedman, M. A., 413
From Court Jews to the Rothschilds (Cohen and Mann, eds.), 486
From the Ends of the Earth (Karp), 322
"From Separation to Displacement" (Baskin), 137–38
fuqara, 187

Galante, Abraham, 33, 76, 376–77: list of *hanhagot*, 379–82 (text)
"Games of Death in Jewish Books for the Sick and the Dying" (Bar-Levav), 159
Gao Nian, 269
Gaon of Vilna, the, 513–17
Gaon, Saadia, 33, 229, 248, 321
Gate of Unification Concerning the Aeons, The (Sarah bas Tovim), 62, 63, 66–68 (text)
Gates of Repentance, The (Gerondi), 33
Gazelle, The (Scheindlin), 45
Gehinnom, 389
Geller, Beverly, 122
Gemara, 4, 5; Babylonian, 4; Palestinian, 4
gematria, 87, 157
Gemilut Hasadim Society, 455
"Genealogy of Maimonides' Family, The" (Freimann), 420
Genesis Rabbah, 133
"Genizah Specimens" (Schechter), 44
geonim, 6, 191, 229: and canonization of the prayer book, 39
Gerondi, Jonah, 33
Gershom ben Judah, 429
Gershom, Rabbenu, 15
"Gerush Shedim 'al-yedai Rabbanim" (Bar-Ilan), 390–91
Geschichte des Erziehungswesens (Guedemann), 194
gezerot tah vetat, 215

INDEX

"Gilgul" (Scholem), 391
gilgul. See transmigration of souls
Ginsberg, Elliot, 357
Ginzberg, Louis, 287
Glikl of Hameln, 29, 34, 483–85: memoirs of, 486–97 (text)
Glückel of Hameln. See Glikl of Hameln
God, Humanity, and History (Chazan), 441
Goitein, S. D., 188, 189, 413, 420
Golb, Norman, 192, 194
Gold, Leonard Singer, 322
Goldberg, P. S., 252
Goldberg, Sylvie-Anne, 66, 159
Golden Haggadah (Narkiss, ed.), 302
Goldstein, David, 78, 302
Goldstein, Jonathan, 272
Gombiner, Abraham, 74
Gorfinkle, Joshua, 288
Greece, 15
Greek Magical Papyri, 388
Green, Arthur, 401–2, 402
Greenberg, Moshe, 175
Gries, Zeev, 155, 159, 402, 502
Guedemann, Moritz, 191, 194
Guide for Preachers on Composing and Delivering Sermons, A (Sosland), 329
Guide of the Perplexed (Maimonides), 171, 283, 321, 414, 418
Guttman, Josef, 302

ha-Kohen, Jonathan, 419
ha-Levi'im, Isaac Min, 473
ha-Nagid, Joseph, 11
ha-Naqdan, Berakhhiah, 282
ha-Nasi, Judah, 3, 171, 413
ha-Parhi, Estori, 238
Hadassi, Judah, 249
hadith, 232
haftarah, 75
Haggadah, 35, 298–99. See also illuminated manuscripts
Haggadah and History (Yerushalmi), 302
Hai Gaon, 105, 107: on the order of the Redemption of the Firstborn, 110–11 (text)
haircutting rite, 118–19
halakah, 4, 5, 131, 216, 248, 354, 401: books of halakhot, 6; books of pesakim, 6; on immersion, 133
Halbertal, Moshe, 287
Halevi, David, 217–18
Halevi, Judah, 42, 237, 248, 321: piyyutim of, 48–49 (texts); and "songs of Zion," 237
Halevi, Moses. See Duran, Profiat

527

Halkin, A. S., 420
Hallamish, Moshe, 78
Halperin, David J., 344
Hamburg Miscellany, 135
Hananel ben Hushiel, 8
hanhagot, 33–34, 155, 375–76, 400, 401
Hanhagot Yesharot (Upright Practices) (Nahum), 400
Hannover, Nathan, 215, 376
Hanukkah, 41
Hareuveni, David, 203
Hartman, D., 420
Harvey, Warren, 175
hasid, 17
Hasidei Ashkenaz. See Pietism, German
Hasidic Movement and the Gaon of Vilna, The (Schochet), 517
Hasidic People (Mintz), 502
Hasidic Thought (Jacob), 402
hasidim, 18, 74
Hasidism, 20–21, 119, 399–400, 401, 499–500, 513–14: "classic" writings of, 400; and the derekh ha-hasidut, 364; and the derekh la-shem, 364. See also Baal Shem Tov; zaddiqim
"Hasidism" (Gries), 502
Hasidism (Idel), 502
Hasidism Reappraised (Rapoport-Albert, ed.), 402
Hasidut Ashkenaz. See Pietism, German
haskala, 516
havdalah, 35
Havlin, S. Z., 413, 420
Hayon, Gedaliah, 210
Hayye yehudah (Modena), 453–56
Hayyim ben Isaac, 514
Hayyim of Volozhin, 515
"He Said, She Said" (Melammed), 175
he-Hasid, Abraham, 365
he-Hasid, Samuel, 134, 430
Hebrew and Aramaic Incantation Texts from the Cairo Genizah (Schiffman and Swartz), 344
Hebrew Book, The (Posner and Ta-Shema, eds.), 322
Hebrew Encyclopaedia, 413
Hebrew Ethical Wills (Abrahams, ed.), 517
Hebrew Illuminated Manuscripts (Narkiss), 302
Hebrew Manuscript Illumination (Guttman), 302
Hecht, N. S., 286
Hecker, Joel, 357
Heinemann, Joseph, 45

hekhalot, 17, 342
Hekhalot Rabbati, 342: Book of the Great Name, 17, 342–43, 344–47 (text)
Hellenizers, 117
Hemdat Yamim, 81, 82, 87
Her Share of the Blessings (Kraemer), 107
heresiographers, 230
Heretics or Daughters of Israel? (Melammed), 349
Heschel, A. J., 420
hevra qadisha, 64, 144, 155–56
hevrot. See confraternities, Jewish; *hevra qadisha*
Hidden and Manifest God, The (Schäfer), 344
hiddur mitzvah, 35
High Holiday Prayer Book (Birnbaum), 45
High Ways to Perfection of Abraham Maimonides, The (Rosenblatt, ed. and trans.), 367
Hilkhot ha-Yerushalmi (Maimonides), 415
hilkot niddah. See women, and ritual immersion
Hinduism, 24, 230
History of Jewish Literature, A (Zinberg), 220
History of Jewish Philosophy in the Middle Ages, A (Sirat), 287
History of the Jews in Christian Spain, A (Baer), 145, 287
History of the Jews in the Latin Kingdom of Jerusalem (Prawer), 240
History of the Karaites (Schur), 252
History of the Sages (al-Qifti), 414
Hoffman, Lawrence A., 45, 107
Hokhmei ha-Sephardim be-Erets Yisrael (Weiss), 212
Horby, William, 287
Horowitz, Carmi, 329
Horowitz, Elliott, 159, 329
Horowitz, Isaiah, 33, 75, 77
Hosea ben Beeri, 239
Hovot ha-Levavot (Ibn Paquda), 321
Hundert, Gershon, 402, 502
Hurwitz, Shai Ish, 516

Ibn Daud, Abraham, 248
Ibn Gabirol, Solomon, 44, 321: *reshut* of, 51 (text)
Ibn Makhir, Moses, 376
Ibn Megas, Joseph, 413
Ibn Musa, Hayyim, 327–28: on contemporary preaching, 336–38 (text)
Ibn Paquda, Bahya, 33, 321
Ibn Shahun, Nissim, 8
Ibn Shem Tov, Joseph, 326–27: on contemporary preaching, 332–36 (text)

Ibn Tibbon, Judah, 321: ethical will of, 321–22, 322–24 (text); as "father of translators," 321
Ibn Tibbon, Samuel, 321, 419
Ideals Face Reality (Fram), 220
Idel, Moshe, 155, 391, 473, 502
Idolatry (Halbertal and Margalit), 287
Iggeret Teman (Maimonides), 415–16
illuminated manuscripts, 35, 298–99: Amsterdam Haggadah, 300, 306–8; Barcelona Haggadah, 302–4; and Elijah the Prophet, 313, 315; eschatological illustrations in, 313–17; and the Exodus, 299–301; extrahaggadic illustration, 300–301; haggadic illustration, 300–301; and the *modus inversus*, 304; narrative illustrations in, 302–8; Prague Haggadah, 315–17; ritual illustrations in, 308–13; Sarajevo Haggadah, 304, 305; sources and types of illustrations for, 299–301; and theodicy, 304; Venice Haggadah, 300, 310, 312
Illustrated Haggadot of the Eighteenth Century (Peled-Carmeli), 302
"Images of Women in Italian Jewish Literature in the Late Middle Ages" (Adelman), 56
In the Year 1096 . . . (Chazan), 440
India: and the Bene Israel (Children of Israel), 23–24; and Cochin Jewry, 24–35
Inés of Herrera, 348
"Inés of Herrera del Duque" (Beinart), 349
initiation ritual, 115–16, 117–19, 122–30 (texts)
Inquisition, the, 143–44, 348–49. *See also conversas*, confessions to the Inquisitorial court of
"Interrelationship between the Hebrew Chronicles on the First Crusade, The" (Abulafia), 440
Introduction to the Code of Maimonides (Twersky), 174–75, 286, 420
"Introduction to the Liturgy of the Damascene Karaites, The," 249–50, 251
"Is There Jewish Art?" (Rosenberg), 286
Isaac ben Immanuel mi-Lattes, 205
'Isawiyya, 230–31
" 'Isawiyya Revisited, The" (Wasserstrom), 232
Islam, 2, 186, 267: and emergence of Jewish sectarianism, 229; and forced conversions, 414; as the "Pure and True," 270; Shi'ism, 231. *See also* Sufism
Israel: ancestors of, 63; travel in, 237–40
"Israel al-Maghribi's Tract on Ritual Slaughtering" (Nemoy), 253

INDEX

Israel ben Eliezer. *See* Baal Shem Tov
Israel ben Samuel Dayyan, on Sabbath lights, 251, 260 (text)
Israel of Shklov, biography of the Gaon of Vilna, 515–17 (text)
Israel, Jonathan, 486
Isserles, Moses, 106–7, 143: on elimination of women from the circumcision ritual, 114 (text)
"Italian Jewish Women" (Adelman), 56
Italy, 15. *See also* Modena; Verona

Jacob ben Asher, 53, 218
Jacob ben Reuben, 283: on religious polemics, 289–91 (text)
Jacob ben Sullam, 439
Jacob Joseph of Polnoyye, 501
Jacobs, Louis, 402, 517
Jerusalem, 239–40: importance to Judaism of, 237
Jewish Art (Sed-Rajna), 286
Jewish culture: and inward acculturation, 116–17; and outward acculturation, 117
Jewish Culture in Eastern Europe (Shulvass), 220
Jewish Education and Society in the High Middle Ages (Kanarfogel), 194
Jewish Icons (Cohen), 286
Jewish law: kabbalist view of, 85; medieval, 3–7; and *minhag*, 15–16; negative precepts, 99; positive precepts, 99. See also *halakha*; Mishnah; Talmuds; Torah
Jewish Law (Elon), 286
Jewish Law (Hecht, ed.), 286
Jewish Life in the Middle Ages (Metzger and Metzger), 286, 302
Jewish Liturgy (Elbogen), 45
Jewish Magic and Superstition (Trachtenberg), 343, 391
"Jewish Magic from the Renaissance Period to Early Hasidism" (Idel), 391
Jewish Messiahs, The (Lenowitz), 473
Jewish Mystical Testimonies (Jacobs, ed.), 517
Jewish Mysticism and Jewish Ethics (Dan), 288
Jewish People, Jewish Thought (Seltzer), 486
Jewish Publication Society of America, 45
Jewish Travellers in the Middle Ages (Adler), 240, 287
Jewish Views of the Afterlife (Raphael), 159
Jewish Women in Historical Perspective (Baskin, ed.), 189
"Jewish Women in the Middle Ages" (Baskin), 138, 433

529

Jewish-Christian Controversy from the Earliest Times to 1789, The (Krauss and Horby), 287
Jewish-Christian Debate in the High Middle Ages, The (Berger), 194
Jewish-Christians, 21
Jewry and the First Crusade (Chazan), 440
Jews in China (Goldstein), 272
Jews in Old China, The (Shapiro), 272
Jews of Dynastic China, The (Pollak), 272
"Jews of Europe and the Moment of Death in Medieval and Modern Times, The" (Horowitz), 159
Jews of Islam, The (Lewis), 189
Jin Zhong, 23, 266–67, 268, 272–77 (text): on the rituals of the Kaifeng synagoge, 270–71; on Judaism and the Jews, 270; on the Jews in Chinese society, 269; on the Jews in relation to the Ming dynasty, 269–70; on the name of God, 267–68; on the passage of time, 268
Jochnowitz, George, 54
Joel Ben Simeon Haggadah (Goldstein, ed.), 302
Joseph, son of Judah, 414
Joseph Karo (Werblowsky), 78–79, 288
Josephus, 387: autobiography of, 454
"Judaeo-Arabic Commentary of the Haftarot by Rabbi Hanan'el b. Shemu'el Dayan . . ." (Fenton), 366
Judah of Worms. *See* Eleazar ben Judah of Worms
Judah the Pietist, 17, 119, 134, 430
Judah the Prince. *See* ha-Nasi, Judah
Judaism: and aesthetics, 34–35; in Asia and northeast Africa, 10 (map); complexity of, 1; early modern, 2, 52; and ethical practice, 33–34; geonic period, 6–7; Hellenistic period, 21; in the lives of ordinary people, 31–33, 455; local and regional variation, 8, 11, 13, 15–16; medieval, 1–2; in the Middle East and North Africa, 9 (map); modern, 2–3; in northern and eastern Europe, 14 (map); premodern, 281; rabbinic, 2, 3, 5, 21, 131; and religious study, 28; sectarian, 21–23; in southern Europe, 12 (map); talmudic period, 229; and visual images, 281–82; and women, 26–31
Judaism and Hebrew Prayer (Reif), 45
"Judaism and Sufism" (Fenton), 366
"Judaism in practice," 298
judaizers. See *conversas*; *conversos*
Judeo-Arabic Commentary of the Haftarot . . ." (Fenton), 366–67
"Judgements Sweetened" (Chajes), 391

Kabbalah, 18–19, 82, 353–54, 454: classical, 19; and the configuration of divinity, 355; "ecstatic," 18; and *gematria*, 87; in Poland, 210–12; "prophetic," 18; rites of, 19–20; view of nature, 82–86. See also *Peri 'Ez hadar*; "Pietist's Study House of Bet El"; Safed; *Zohar*
Kabbalah (Scholem), 212
Kabbalah in Liturgy, Halakhaha and Customs (Hallamish), 78
Kabbalah, Magic, and Science (Ruderman), 205, 391
Kabbalat Shabbat (Welcoming the Sabbath), 20
Kafah, Joseph, 413
Kaidanover, Zvi Hirsch, 33
Kaifeng, 23, 266–67
Kaplan, Yael Beinart, 349
Karaism, 21–22, 229, 248–49; "Eastern," 248; "European," 248; liturgy of, 249–50, 253–57 (text); practice of prayer in, 28–29; and ritual slaughter, 250, 257–60 (text); and Sabbath lights, 250–51, 260–64 (text); treatises on *shehitah*, 251; "Western," 248
Karaite Anthology (Nemoy), 252
Karaite Encyclopedia, The (Schur), 252
Karaite Liturgy and Its Relation to Synagogue (Goldberg), 252
"Karaite Prayer and Liturgy" (Frank), 252
Karaites in Byzantium (Ankori), 252, 253
Karnarfogel, Ephraim, 194
Karo, Joseph, 6, 75–76, 285, 416: as exorcist, 391–92 (text); on sixteenth-century laws of idolatry, 296–97 (text)
Karp, Abraham J., 322
kashrut. See dietary laws
Katz, Naphtali ha-Kohen, 156: ethical will of, 156–58, 159–67 (text)
Kaufmann, David, 194, 485
kavvanot, 19, 85, 86, 211, 250, 284, 401
Kay, Devra, 65, 205
Kazi, A. K., 232
Khawarij, 229
Khotsh, Tsevi Hirsh, 64
Kiss of God, The (Fishbane), 159
Kifayat al-'abidin (Compendium for the Servants of God) (Maimuni), 364
Kitab al-Anwar w'al-Maraqib (Book of Lights and Watchtowers) (al-Qirqisani), 229–30, 233
Kitab al-Milal wa 'l-Nihal (Book of Religions and Sects) (Shahrastani), 230–32, 233–36 (text): on the 'Ananiyya, 230; on the 'Isawiyya, 230–31; on the Maghariyya, 231–32; and People of the Book, 230
Klirs, Tracy Guren, 65
kneytlakh legn. See laying wicks ritual
Kobler, Franz, 240
kohanim, 102, 192
Kol Bo, 53, 121
"Kol Ishah" (Taitz), 433
Kol sakhal (Voice of a Fool) (Modena), 454
Kotansky, R., 387–88
Kraemer, J. L., 420
Kraemer, Ross Shepard, 107
Krauss, Samuel, 287
Krzywonos, Maxim, 215
Kuzari (Halevi), 321
kvorim mesn. See measuring graves ritual

La Haggada enluminée (Metzger), 302
"La Lex orandi . . ." (Vajda), 253
"La tête entre les genoux . . ." (Fenton), 367
Lag Ba-Omer, 118
Lamm, Norman, 402
"Law of Israel," 101: on women, 107–8 (texts)
"Law of the Jews." See "Law of Israel"
"Law of Moses," 101: on women, 107–8 (text)
laying wicks ritual, 61: prayer for, 69–72 (text)
"Le-Toldot ha-Rambam" (Havlin), 420
Legends of the Hasidim (Mintz), 502
Legends of the Jews (Ginzberg), 287
Lehem Se'orim (Solomon ben Aaron), 252
Leipzig Mahzor, 116, 117
Lekhah Dodi (Alkabez), 75
Lenowitz, Harris, 473
"Leone da Modena's Ritta" (Cohen), 457
Les Dissidences de l'Islam (Vadet, trans.), 232
Leslie, Donald, 271
Levi ben Japheth, 249
Levine, Reneé C., 146
Levites, 102
leviyyim, 192
Lewin, Benjamin Manasseh, 105
Lewis, Bernard, 189, 415, 420
Lewis, I. M., 389
Liebes, Yehuda, 74, 78, 473
Liewei, 269
"Life Cycle Liturgy as Status Transformation" (Hoffman), 107
"Life of Maimonides in the Light of New Finds from the Cairo Geniza, The" (Goitein), 420
Likeness and Image (Belting), 287
Lipman, Jonathan, 23
"Literacy of Jewish Women in Early Modern Italy, The" (Adelman), 56

Literature of the Synagogue (Heinemann and Petuchowski), 45
Livre des religions et des sects, 232
Lockwood, Wilfrid, 233
Loeb, Isadore, 192, 194
Lorge, M., 253
Lublin, 216, 218
Luria, Isaac, 19, 82, 84, 86, 118, 211, 376, 377, 389, 500
L'viv, 216, 217, 218

Ma'amadot u-Moshavot (Benayahu), 159
ma'aseh, 7
Ma'avar Yabbok (Berechia), 155
Madonna and Child, Jewish adaptation of, 116
Magen Avraham (Gombiner), 74
Magen va-herev (Shield and Sword) (Modena), 454
maggid, 75
Maggid Meisharim (Karo), 75
Maghariyya, 231–32
magic, 32, 341: and bowls of antiquity, 388. See also *Hekhalot Rabbati*
Magic and Superstition (Trachtenberg), 343
Magic, Mysticism and Hasidism (Nigal), 502
Magic Spells and Formulae (Naveh and Shaked), 344
Magische Texte aus der Kairoer Geniza (Schäfer and Shaked), 344
Maharam. See Meir of Rothenberg
Maharil. See Moellin, Jacob
Mahzor Leipzig, 121
Mahzor Vitry, 119, 120: on the initiation ritual, 124–28 (text)
mahzorim. See poetry, liturgical
Maimon, Rabbi, 413, 414, 417
Maimonides, David, 417
Maimonides, David, II, 186, 413, 419
Maimonides, Moses, 6, 33, 84, 171–74, 282–83, 285, 499; curriculum of, 173; on his son, 427 (text); on laws of idolatry, 288–89 (texts); letters of, 424–27 (texts), 428 (text); life of, 413–20; on women, 173–74
Maimonides (Heschel), 420
"Maimonides" (Pines), 420
Maimonides (Yellin and Abrahams), 415
"Maimonides in Egypt" (Ben-Sasson), 420
Maimonides Reader, A (Twersky), 286, 420
"Maimonides, Lionheart, and Saladin" (Lewis), 420
"Maimonides' Egypt" (Cohen), 420
Maimuni, Abraham, 18, 364, 418
Mainz, 13, 438

Mainz Anonymous, 31, 438–40, 441–52 (text)
Major Trends in Jewish Mysticism (Scholem), 210, 212, 344
Mandarins, Jews, and Missionaries (Pollak), 271–72
Mandelbaum, David Abraham, 88
Manichaeism, 230, 267
Mann, Jacob, 252
Mann, Vivian, 486
Marcus, Ivan, 32, 121–22, 194, 433
Margoliouth, G., 251
Margolit, Avishai, 287
Mari Gómez of Chillón, 348
marriage, 101–2
martyrdom, during the Crusades, 31, 439–40. See also Mainz Anonymous
Mas'at Binyamin (Benjamin of Tudela), 192
maskilim, 516
"Match, The" (Peretz), 62
Matt, Daniel C., 79
measuring graves ritual, 61: prayer for, 72–73 (text)
"Medieval Jewish Aesthetics" (Bland), 286
Medieval Jewry in Northern France (Chazan), 287
Medieval Stereotypes and Modern Antisemitism (Chazan), 287
Mediterranean Society, A (Goitein), 188, 189
"Meeting with Maimonides, A" (Fenton), 420
Megilat Ahima'atz, 498
Meir of Brod, 218
Meir of Rothenberg, 7, 105–6, 135, 284: on illuminated manuscripts, 292–94 (text); responsa of, 142 (texts)
mekhavvenim, 211
Melammed, Renée Levine, 146, 175, 189, 349
Mendel, Menahem, 310
menstruation. See women, and ritual immersion
Me'or 'Eynayim (The Light of the Eyes) (Nahum), 400
Meqorot le-Toledot ha-Hinnukh be-Yisra'el (Assaf), 194
Merit of Our Mothers, The (Klirs, ed.), 65
merkavah, 17, 342
Meshullam of Volterra, 238
Messianic Mystics (Idel), 473
Messianism, Mysticism, and Magic (Sharot), 473
Metzger, Mendel, 286, 302
Metzger, Thérèse, 286, 302
Michal, and prayer, 3, 56–57 (texts)
midrash, 8, 41–42: pattern of, 354
midrash aggadah, 8

midrash ha-gadol, 192
Midrash Hasidim Bet El. *See* "Pietist's Study House of Bet El"
mikveh, 76, 132. *See also* women, and ritual immersion
minhag, 15–16, 375
Mintz, Jerome R., 502
minyan, 27, 158
miracle stories, 498–500
Mishnah, 3, 4, 5, 101, 107, 131, 171: standard commentary on, 239; studying *al derekh ha-emet*, 75
Mishneh Torah (Maimonides), 6, 171–74, 283, 416: *Book of Knowledge*, 172; *Laws of the Study of Torah*, 172–74, 175–85 (text)
Mitnagdim, 513–14
mitsvot, 4, 375
Modena, 55
Modena, Aaron Berekhiah, 53, 54
Modena, Leon, 453–56: autobiography of, 457–67 (text); will of, 467–69 (text)
Modena, Mordecai, 455
Modena, Zebulun, 455
Moellin, Jacob, 106: on the *sandek*, 113–14 (text)
Mondshine, Yehoshua, 502
Monter, E. W., 388
Mordecai of Chernobyl, 400
Moses ben Maimon. *See* Maimonides, Moses
Moses ben Nachman, 238
Moses of Coucy, 218, 432
"Moses Maimonides, Man of Action" (Goitein), 420
"Moses Maimonides-Ibn Sana al-Mulk Circle, The" (Goitein), 420
"Mothers, Martyrs, and Moneymakers" (Marcus), 433
Muqqatam mountain, 187
Muslim Sects and Divisions (Kazi and Flynn, trans.), 232
Muslims. *See* Islam
Musta'rabim, 11, 13
Mutazilites, 250
"Mystical Treatise on Perfection, Providence and Prophecy from the Jewish Sufi Circle, A" (Fenton), 367
mysticism: Heklahot, 16–17, 116, 342; Merkavah, 16–17, 42, 74, 116. *See also Hekhalot Rabbati*

Nadler, Allan, 517
Naggid u-Metsaveh (Hannover), 376
Nahum, Menahem, 400–401: list of *hanhagot*, 402–9 (text)
Nakhalas Tsevi (Inheritance of Tsevi) (Khotsh), 64
Narkiss, Bezalel, 302
Nathan of Gaza, 82, 470–71
Naveh, Joseph, 344
Nazirites, 186
Nehar Shalom (River of Peace), 211
Nemoy, Leon, 252, 253
Neoplatonism, 44
New World Hasidism (Belcove-Shalin, ed.), 502
New Year's Day for Trees. *See* Tu bi-Shevat
niddah, 131–32: as deserved female chastisement, 133–34. *See also* women, and ritual immersion
Nigal, Gedalyah, 391, 502
North Africa, 8, 11
"Notes on Maimonides' Book of Knowledge" (Strauss), 175

"Obligation of Talmud on Women According to Maimonides, The" (Harvey), 175
Of Bygone Days (Seforim), 65
Orhot Hayyim (Paths of Life), 121: on the initiation ritual, 128–30 (text)
Origen, 387
Ostrih, 215, 217–18
Out of the Depths I Call to You (Cardin), 205
Ovadiah of Bertinoro, 238, 239: letter to, 240–47 (text)
Ozar Ha Haggadot (Yudlov), 302

Palm Tree of Deborah (Cordovero), 33
Pangu, 268
Passover, 35
Pe'at ha-Shulkhan, 517: on the Gaon of Vilna, 515–17, 517–20 (text)
Peled-Carmeli, Haviva, 302
"People and the Book, The" (Roth), 322
Peretz, I. L., 62
Peri 'Ez Hadar, 81–83, 86–87. *See also* Tu bi-Shevat
perushim, 191, 193–94. *See also* education, medieval; *yeshivot*
Pesah, 41
Petahiah of Regensburg, 238
Petuchowski, Jakob J., 45
Pharisees, 21
philosophy, and Torah, 173
Phineas, Rabbi, 416
phylacteries, 29, 52–53: women's wearing of, 56–67 (texts)

INDEX

pidyon ha-ben. See Redemption of the Firstborn
"Pietist's Study House of Bet El," 210–11: pact of, 212–14 (text)
Pietism, German, 15, 17–18, 119, 134, 192–93, 429–30: and education, 192–93; and ownership of books, 321; themes of, 17, 431
Piety and Society (Marcus), 433
pilgrims, 237, 283
pilpul, 516
Pines, S., 420
Pirqei Avot (Chapters of the Fathers) (Galante), 376
piyyutim. See poetry, liturgical
poetry, liturgical, 41–44, 229: Avodah, 300; for the benedictions of the Shema, 47–51 (texts); Golden Age, 44; *mahzorim,* 41; *selihot,* 43–44. *See also* benedictions; prayer, communal
Poland, 216: communal government, 219; fairs in, 220; and Hasidism, 399; and Jewish love of learning, 215–20; religious toleration in, 216; *yeshivot* in, 216
Pollak, Michael, 271–72
Polo, Marco, 266
"popular religion," 31, 455
Portugal, 11: and mass conversion of Jews, 19
Posner, Raphael, 322
possession cults, 389. *See also* exorcism
POTAH incantation, 115, 120
Poznan, 216, 218
Prawer, Joshua, 240
prayer: communal, 39–41; prayer books, 320; private, 100; public, 100; and *tephillin,* 52–53. *See also* poetry, liturgical
Prayer in the Talmud (Heinemann), 45
"Prayers in Yiddish and the Religious World of Ashkenazic Women" (Weissler), 486
Preachers of the Italian Ghetto (Ruderman, ed.), 329
preaching, fifteenth-century Spanish, 35, 325–28: guidelines for, 329–38 (texts)
"Preaching of Repentance and the Reforms in Toledo of 1281, The" (Saperstein), 329
prophecy, seventeenth-century, 472: women's role in, 472–73
Prophets, reading of, 39
Provençal, 192
Purim, 41
purity, ritual, 131, 135, 137, 342–43: Falasha practice of, 25–26; and men, 132; sources of pollution and, 131

Qalonimos family, 17
Qarafa al-sughra, 186–87

Rabad of Posquieres (Twersky), 194
Rabban, Yosef, 24
Rabbanites, 232, 248–29
"Rabbi Aaron Berechia of Modena and Rabbi Naphtali Ha-Kohen Katz . . ." (Bar-Levav), 159
Rabbi Hayyim Yosef David Azulai (Benayahu), 212
Rabbi Meir of Rothenburg (Agus), 287
"Rabbis and Reality" (Adelman), 56
Rachel of Mainz, 440
Rahabi, David, 25
Rahabi, Ezekial David, 24
Raphael, Simcha Paul, 159
Rapoport-Albert, Ada, 402
Rashi, 15, 53, 501: in the Cracow curriculum, 217; on Sabbath lights, 263–64 (text)
Rav Amram Gaon, 30–31
rebbes. See zaddiqim
Red Heifer ritual, 387
Redemption of the Firstborn, 102–3: geonim innovations and, 111–12 (text); order of, 110–11 (text); women's role in, 103–4, 105, 106–7
Reform Judaism, 15, 21
Regimens of Conduct. *See hanhagot*
Reif, Stefan, 45
religion, definition of, 281
Religious Thought of Hasidism, The (Lamm), 402
Remembrance for the Children of Israel (Baruch of Arezzo), 471–73, 473–82 (text)
responsa literature, 6–7, 135, 229, 453
"Rhetoric, Reality, and Aspirations to Holiness in 14th Century Jewish Preaching" (Horowitz), 329
Richard I the Lionhearted, 415
rishonim, 517
ritual objects, design of, 35
ritual slaughter, 204, 250: women and, 206–8 (texts)
"Ritualization of Life," 155
Rituals of Childhood (Marcus), 121–22, 194
Road to Zion (Wilhelm), 240
Roman Catholicism, 267: monastic tradition in, 212. *See also conversas; conversos;* Inquisition, the
Rome, 54
Rome Incunabula, 319

Roqeah (the Perfumer). *See* Eleazar ben Judah of Worms
Rosenberg, Harold, 286
Rosenblatt, S., 367
Rosh Hashanah, 41, 43, 63, 327
Rosman, Moshe, 501, 502
Roth, Cecil, 322
Rubenstein, Avraham, 502
Ruderman, David, 205, 329, 391
Rudolph I, 105
Russia's First Modern Jews (Fishman), 517

Sabbath in the Classical Kabbalah, The (Ginsberg), 357
Sabbath laws, 4
Sabbatai Sevi (Scholem), 473
Sabbatianism, 20, 30, 471. *See also* Shabbatai Zvi
Sacred Poetry in Hebrew in the Middle Ages (Fleischer), 45
Sadducees, 21
Safed, 19–20, 30, 76, 211, 239: and exorcism, 388; and *hanhagot*, 33; Pietistic customs from, 375–79; and the Tu bi-Shevat seder, 81. *See also* Cordovero, Moses; Luria, Isaac
"Safed in the Sixteenth Century" (Schechter), 379
Safed Spirituality (Fine), 78, 288, 379
Saladin, 416, 417, 419
Salaman, Nina, 45
Samaritans, 232
Samson ben Tzadok. *See* Tashbetz
Samuel ben Eli, 418
Samuel, son of Qalonimos, 17
Sanctification ritual, 42–43
Saperstein, Marc, 328
Sarah bas Tovim, 62–64
Schäfer, Peter, 343, 344
Schechter, Solomon, 44, 379
Scheindlin, Raymond P., 45
Schick, Barukh, 515
Schiffman, Lawrence H., 344
Schochet, E. J., 517
Scholastic Magic (Swartz), 344
Scholem, Gershom, 78, 192, 210, 212, 344, 391, 473
Schur, Nathan, 252
"Scribal Magic and Its Rhetoric" (Swartz), 344
scrolls, 319–19: women's care of, 431. *See also Sefer Torah*
Sed-Rajna, Gabrielle, 286
Seder ha-Yom (Ibn Makhir), 376

Seder Rav Amram Gaon, 104, 107: on the order of the circumcision ritual, 109–10 (text)
Sefardim, 11, 13
Sefer Bahir, 18–19
Sefer ha-Asufot (Book of Collections), 119–20: on the initiation ritual, 123–24 (text)
Sefer ha-Hayyim (Book of Life) (Frankfurt), 64, 72–73 (text)
Sefer ha-Mitsvot (Book of Commandments), 22
Sefer ha-Roqeah (Book of the Perfumer), 119: on the initiation ritual, 122–23 (text), 135; on women, 140 (text)
Sefer ha-Zohar, 82
Sefer Hamelammed, 53
Sefer Hasidim (Book of the Pietists), 17, 135, 192–93, 430, 498–99: promotion of education for girls in, 28, 118; on women, 138–40 (texts)
Sefer Huqqei ha-Torah (Book of the Statutes of the Torah), 191–94: on education, 198–202 (text); influence of Christian monasticism on, 193–94; twelve statutes of, 195–98 (text)
"Sefer Hukkei ha-Torah" (Dan), 194
Sefer me'irat einayim (Falk), 217
Sefer Mitzvot Gadol (Moses of Coucy), 432
Sefer Torah, 318–19
sefirot, 18, 83–85, 353, 355, 356, 399
Seforim, Mendele Mokher, 65
Selected Liturgical Poetry of Solomon Ibn Gabirol (Zangwill, trans.), 45
Selected Poems by Judah Halevi (Salaman, trans.), 45
Selected Poems of Moses Ibn Ezra (Solis-Cohen, trans.), 45
selihot. See poetry, liturgical
Seltzer, Robert, 486
Semah, Jacob, 376
Sephardim. *See* Sefardim
"Servants and Sexuality" (Adelman), 56
sevarah, 7
"Seventeenth-Century Karaite Shehitah Controversy, The" (Frank), 253
Sforno, Ovadia, 52
Sha'agat aryeh (The Roar of the Lion) (Modena), 454
Sha'ar Ha-Hakhana (Gate of Preparation) (Naphtali), 156
Sha'arei Tsiyon (Hannover), 215, 376
Shabbatai Zvi, 20: biography of, 473–83 (text); early messianic career of, 470–73. *See also Remembrance for the Children of Israel*; Sabbateanism

Shahrastani, Muhammad, 230–32
"Shahrastani on the Maghariyya" (Wasserstrom), 232–33
Shaked, Shaul, 344
Shaking the Pillars of Exile (Fishman), 457
shaliah tzibbur, 54
Shapiro, Sidney, 272
Sharabi, Shalom Mizrachi, 210–11
Sharot, Stephen, 473
Shavuot, 32, 41, 74, 120: and the *haftarah,* 75; and the *tikkun* ritual, 74–78, 79–80 (text), 376
she 'elot u-teshuvot. See responsa literature
Sheelot uteshuvot (Isaac ben Immanuel mi-Lattes), 205
Shekinah, 75–76, 77, 78, 343, 354
shelo asani ishah blessing, 53, 57 (texts)
Shema, 39–40; benedictions framework of, 40; recitation of, 42
Shenei Luhot ha-Berit (Horowitz), 75
Shimon bar Yohai, 19, 118, 239, 353; and the adorning of the "bride," 77–78, 79–80 (text)
Shivhei ha-Ari (In Praise of the Ari), 500
Shivhei ha-Besht, 500–501, 502–12 (text): Mondshine edition, 502; Rubenstein edition, 502
Shklov, 515: and the Hakhmei Shklov, 515
Shomerim la-Boker Society, 455
"*Shoshanim* of Tenth-Century Jerusalem, The" (Frank), 252
Shovavim, 87
Shulhan Arukh ha-Ari (Semah), 376
Shulkhan Arukh (The Prepared Table) (Karo), 6, 285, 517
Shulvass, Moses, 220
Shushan Yesod ha-'Olam, 388
Siddur Kavvanot Ez Hadar (Elon), 88
"Sidrei Tikkunim" (Wilhelm), 78
Sifra, 171
Sifra De-Zeniuta (Hayyim of Volozhin), 515
Sifrei, 171
Sifrut ha-Hanhagot (Gries), 402
Sign and a Witness, A (Gold, ed.), 322
Simeon ben Israel Judah Frankfurt, *tkhine* of, 72–73 (text)
Simha of Vitry, 120
sippur yeziat mizrayim, 299
Sippurei Dibbuk (Nigal), 391
sippurei zaddikim, 500
Sirat, Colett, 287
"six pillars of the world," 216: Charity, 216, 224–25 (text); Divine Service, 216, 224 (text); Justice, 216, 225–26 (text); Peace, 216, 226 (text); Torah, 216, 221–24 (text); Truth, 216, 226 (text)
"Six Unpublished Maimonides Letters from the Cairo Genizah" (Kraemer), 420
Sklare, David, 253
Social and Religious History of the Jews, A (Baron), 194, 220, 240
Sod Hag ha-Shavu'ot (de Leon), 74–75
Solis-Cohen, Solomon, 45
"Solitary Meditation in Jewish and Islamic Mysticism" (Fenton), 367
Solomon ben Isaac. *See* Rashi
Solomon of Dresnitz, 377–78
"Some Death and Mourning Customs of Castilian Conversas" (Melammed), 146
"Some Judaeo-Arabic Fragments by Rabi Abraham he-Hasid . . ." (Fenton), 366
"Some Non-Halakhic Aspects of the *Mishneh Torah*" (Twersky), 175
"Some Parallels in the Education of Medieval Jewish and Christian Women" (Baskin), 138
Sosland, Henry, 329
Spain, 8, 11: and the *converso* phenomenon, 143; and the Expulsion, 11, 19, 285; and the Golden Age, 11, 42; and Kabbalah, 19; under Muslim rule, 11. *See also conversas; conversos;* Inquisition, the
Speyer, 13, 132, 438
spirit possession. *See* exorcism
Straight Path, The (Kaidanover), 33
Strauss, Leo, 175
"Studies in the History of Early Karaite Liturgy" (Nemoy), 253
Studies in Jewish Myth and Jewish Messianism (Liebes), 473
Studies in the Zohar (Liebes), 74, 78
"Study of Medieval Karaism, The" (Frank), 252
"Success and Failure in Seventeenth Century Venice" (Adelman), 457
Sufism, 18, 186–88: devotional rites in, 364–66; doctrine of *munasaba,* 366; practice of *dhikr,* 366; wife's petition concerning, 189–90 (text)
Sukkot. *See* Shavuot
Suliteanu, Gisela, 66
"Sultan, the King, and the Jewish Doctor, The" (Lewis), 420
Survival of the Chinese Jews, The (Leslie), 271
Swartz, Michael D., 344
Sword and Shield (Trautner-Kromann), 287
synagogue: and the aliyah, 27; daily public services in, 39; in the Jewish ghetto, 454–55;

public protest practices and, 55, 59–60 (text); and restrictions on women, 27; Scripture reading in, 39; seating in, 54–55, 57–59 (text); and the *shaliah tzibbur*, 54. *See also* prayer; women, in the synagogue
synagogue hymns. *See* poetry, liturgical

Ta-Shema, Israel, 322
ta 'wil, 232
Taitz, Emily, 433
takkanah, 15
talit, 115
Talmuds, 2, 5, 53; Babylonian, 4–5, 131, 171; and conflicting religious practices, 16; content of, 5; Jerusalem, 4, 171; miracle stories in, 498; *Niddah* tractate, 131–32; Palestinian, 4–5; printing of, 320
"Taming of the Deviants and Beyond, The" (Bilu), 391
Tammuz, 41
tannaim, 3
Ta'rikh al-Hukama (History of the Sages) (al-Qifti), 414
Tarnor, Norman, 65
Tashbetz, 106, 107: on removing women from the synagogue, 112–13 (text)
taslik, 186
"Teachings of the Hasidic Masters" (Green), 402
Techinas (Zakutinsky), 65
Tehillah Le-David (Mandelbaum), 88
tekhinnes. *See tkhines*
Temple: artistry of, 34; destruction of, 21; importance to Judaism of, 237
Ten Days of Penitence, 63
tephillin. *See* phylacteries
Teshuvot ha-Rambam (Blau, ed.), 420
tevilah. *See* women, and ritual immersion
Texts and Studies in Jewish History and Literature (Mann), 252
Theology and Poetry (Petuchowski), 45
Thorndike, Lynn, 195
Three Gates, The (Sarah bas Tovim), 62, 63, 68–72 (text)
Through a Speculum That Shines (Wolfson), 357
tikkun, 86, 87, 157, 389, 470
Tikkun leil Shavuot. *See* Shavuot, and the *tikkun* ritual
tikkun ritual. *See* Shavuot
Tikkun Middot ha-Nefesh (Ibn Gabirol), 321
Tiqqunei Shabbat (Rules for the Sabbath) (Berukhim), 377
Tiqqunim, 376
Tishby, Isaiah, 78, 357–58

tkhines, 29, 61–64, 133–34, 485: eastern European publication of, 64–65. *See also Gate of Unification Concerning the Aeons, The; Three Gates, The*
Toledot ha-Ari (Benayahu), 391
Toledot ha-Yehudim be-Ir Rouen (Golb), 194
Torah, 3: annual cycle of readings, 41; ethical instruction in, 33; foods symbolic of, 116; giving of, 74; kabbalist view of, 83–84; and philosophy, 173; reading of, 39; recitation of, 356–57; scroll of, 318–19; study of, 27–28, 172, 192; "textless," 173; Torah *lishmah*, 514. *See also Sefer Torah*
Torah Scrolls of the Chinese Jews, The (Pollak), 272
Tosafot, 284, 320
Tosefta, 53, 101, 107, 171
tovim, 62
Trachtenberg, Joshua, 343, 391
"Tradition and New Creation in the Ritual of the Kabbalists" (Scholem), 78
"Traditional Piety of Ashkenazic Women, The" (Weissler), 486
"Traditional System of Melopeic Prose of the Funeral Songs . . ." (Suliteanu), 66
transmigration of souls, 86, 388–89
Trautner-Kromann, Hanne, 287
Treasury of Jewish Letters, A (Kobler, ed.), 240
Treatise of the Pool, The (Fenton), 366
Treatise on Logic (Maimonides), 415
tsaddiqim. *See zaddiqim*
Tsene-rene, 485
Tu Be 'Shvat Anthology (Waskow and Elon, eds.), 88
Tu bi-Shevat, 81–88, 88–95 (text): tree symbolism in, 87. *See also Peri 'Ez Hadar*
Turei zahav (David ben Shmu'el Halevi), 217–18
Turkey, 211
Twersky, Isadore, 174–75, 192, 194, 286, 287, 420
Two Tablets of the Covenant (Horowitz), 33

Ultra-Orthodox Judaism, 118, 119
uncleanness. *See* purity, ritual
Under Crescent and Cross (Cohen), 287
Upright Practices (Green), 401–2
Upsheerin, The (Geller), 122
Urania of Worms, 432
Urban II, 438

Vadet, J. C., 232
Vajda, Georges, 253

INDEX 537

Valley of Vision, A (Ruderman), 205
Vayiqra Rabbah, 77–78
Verona, 54–55
Visual Dimension, The (Cohen), 286
Vital, Hayyim, 76–77, 377, 389–90: on exorcism, 392–93 (text)
Vital, Samuel, on exorcism, 394–96 (text)
Vogelmann, Mordechai, 251
Voices of the Matriarchs (Weissler), 65, 486
Volozhin, 514

Wahl, Saul, 218
Waskow, Arthur, 88
Wasserfall, Rahel, 138
Wasserstrom, Steven M., 232–33
"Weeping, Death, and Spiritual Ascent in Sixteenth Century Jewish Mysticism" (Wolfson), 159
Wegner, Judith Romney, 107, 132
Weiss, Shraga, 212
Weissler, Chava, 65, 133–34, 189, 205, 486
Werblowsky, R. J. Zwi, 78–79, 288
White, William Charles, 270, 271
". . . Who Made Me a Woman" (Jochnowitz), 54
"Wife-Beating among Early Modern Italian Jews, 1400–1700" (Adelman), 56
Wilhelm, Kurt, 240
Wilhelm, Y. D., 78
Wisdom of the Zohar, The (Goldstein, trans.), 78
Wisdom of the Zohar, The (Tishby), 357–58
Witchcraft in France and Switzerland, 388
Wolfson, Elliot, 159, 357
women: and the "axiom of limited obligation for women," 99, 100; during the Crusades, 31, 439–40; and cursing in the synagogue, 55; and pietistic practices, 29–30; and possession cults, 389; and prayer, 52–54; rabbinic law and, 26–27, 99, 107–8 (text); and ritual immersion, 28, 131–37, 138–42 (texts), 144; as prophetesses, 472–73; and rituals, 28–29, 30–31; and study of sacred texts, 27–28; in the synagogue, 54–55, 56–60 (text), 112–13 (text); as ritual slaughterers, 204, 206–8 (texts); status in the Islamic milieu, 429; and "women's misvot," 28. *See also conversas*
Women and Water (Wasserfall, ed.), 138
"Women in Spanish Crypto-Judaism 1492–1520" (Levine), 146

Women on the Margins (Davis), 486
"Women Saints in Judaism" (Baskin), 433
"Women's Voices, Women's Prayers" (Taitz), 433
Worms, 13, 132, 432, 438

Ya'qub al-Qirqisani on Jewish Sects and Christianity (Chiesa and Lockwood), 233
Ya'ari, Avraham, 302
Yagel, Abraham, 203
Yareach Yaqar (The Precious Moon) (Galante), 376–77
Yehudai the Pious, 104, 192
Yellin, D., 415, 420
Yemen, 415
"Yerivay veoyevay shime'u le-qoli" (Israel ben Samuel Dayyan), 251
Yerushalmi, Yosef Hayim, 302
yeshivot, 192, 514: in Poland, 215–18
Yiddish, 61, 62, 64
yihudim, 377
Yoffe, Israel, 500–501
Yom Kippur, 41, 42, 43–44, 63: and the Avodah, 300
Yom Kippur Qatan, 377
Yudghan, 232
Yudlov, Yizhak, 302
"Yusuf al-Basir" (Skalre), 253

Zacuto, Moses, on exorcism, 396–98 (text)
zaddiqim, 20, 34, 399, 499–501, 513
Zakutinsky, Rivka, 65
Zalman, Shneur, 513–14
Zangwill, Israel, 45
zawiya, 186
Zealots, 21
zeman mattan torateinu. *See* Shavuot
Zinberg, Israel, 220
Zionist movement, 2, 24
Zohar (Book of Splendor), 19, 64, 81, 353–54: on feeding the poor, 357, 363 (text); on hand washing before meals, 355, 360–62 (text); on reciting grace over bread, 355–56, 362 (text); on Sabbath meals, 354–55, 358–60 (text); on the table of the Holy One, 356–57, 362–63 (text); on the *tikkun* ritual, 74, 77–78, 79–80 (text)
Zohar Hadash (New Zohar), 377
Zoroastrianism, 230